Praise for *The Movement and the Sixties*

"Anderson has done the nearly impossible, giving us historical and intellectual synthesis."

The Seattle Times

"Well-written, accessible history....A valuable counterpoint to the reductionist and revisionist views now prevalent."

Christian Science Monitor

"[Anderson's] sweeping study is a valuable, refreshingly unbiased reassessment of the '60s legacy."

Publishers Weekly

"[Anderson] chronicles the most troubled decade of his country's modern history and seeks to analyze its causes. It is a disturbing tale, well told....It is the merit of Terry Anderson's book that it captures the tone, as well as the events, of a decade in which America finally emerged from cold-war simplicities and began the painful discovery of itself."

The Economist

"Anderson brings order to the period's chaos in his rigorous account of the intellectual origins of modern dissent....His passionate remembrance galvanizes the book....A highly accessible survey that should be the standard for years to come."

Kirkus Reviews

"...a concise, thorough and thoughtful history of the social and political movements that began with the end of World War II and concluded with our nation's withdrawal from Vietnam....Anderson offers a refreshing answer to the question of how the counterculture can be evaluated."

Houston Chronicle

"[Anderson] leaves no lunch counter unturned. It is all there, from Rosa Parks and the Summer of Love to bra burnings and the March on the Pentagon....Mr. Anderson is right about the continuing influence of the counterculture on America."

Wall Street Journal

"...a testament to the fervor and spirit of a time that we still use as a yardstick of our national personality."

Orlando Sentinel

The Movement

and

The Sixties

Terry H. Anderson

New York

OXFORD UNIVERSITY PRESS

Oxford

Oxford University Press

Oxford   New York
Athens   Auckland   Bangkok   Bombay
Calcutta   Cape Town   Dar es Salaam   Delhi
Florence   Hong Kong   Istanbul   Karachi
Kuala Lumpur   Madras   Madrid   Melbourne
Mexico City   Nairobi   Paris   Singapore
Taipei   Tokyo   Toronto

and associated companies in
Berlin   Ibadan

Copyright © 1995 by Terry H. Anderson

First published in 1995 by Oxford University Press, Inc.,
198 Madison Avenue, New York, New York 10016

First issued as an Oxford University Press paperback, 1996

Oxford is a registered trademark of Oxford University Press

Library of Congress Cataloging-in-Publication Data
Anderson, Terry H., 1946–
The movement and the sixties / Terry H. Anderson.
p.   cm.   Includes bibliographical references and index.
ISBN 0-19-507409-2
ISBN 0-19-510457-9 (Pbk.)
1. Radicalism—United States—History.
2. Protest movements—United States—History.
3. United States—Social conditions—1960–1980.
I. Title.   HN90.R3A6764   1995
303.48'4'0973—dc20   94-16344

6 7 8 9 10

Printed in the United States of America
on acid-free paper

For

Rose

Acknowledgments

The Movement and The Sixties took eight years to research and write. Any author who spends that much time on one project accumulates many debts, and I would like to thank those who supplied their knowledge, scholarship, and friendship.

Many people submitted to interviews, exchanged ideas, corresponded, or gave me their notes, papers, manuscripts, permissions, or other information: Richard Braungart, Terry DuBose, Allen Ginsberg, Kendall Goh, Alexis Greene, Madelyn Hochstein, Timothy Leary, Julian McMurrey, Jerry Rubin, Gilbert Shelton, Charles Sherrod, David Singer, Mel Small, Geoffrey Smith, Amy Swerdlow, Steve Vaughn, the late Abbie Hoffman, and many others who read chapters.

David Hoffman of Varied Directions in Camden, Maine, invited me to serve as senior adviser to the six-hour documentary, *Making Sense of the Sixties*, and he opened his vast archives of taped interviews. Ricki Green and the staff of WETA brought me to Washington, D.C., where I participated in the "Sixties School" for that program, and where I met many other scholars and participated in additional interviews and discussions. The program was aired nationally in 1991 on PBS.

At Texas A&M University, many of my colleagues shared information or gave advice—Dale Baum, Roger Beaumont, Jim Bradford, Robert Calvert, David Chapman, Joseph Dawson, John Impson, Arnold Krammer, Cozette McGaugh, and Betty Miller Unterberger. One feels fortunate to have such fine colleagues, and friends, and that includes Mary Johnson and her staff, who were helpful and even politely laughed at my jokes. Hundreds of my students challenged my assumptions, questioned my interpretations, and stimulated new ideas. Some also introduced me to articles or books, and many conducted interviews as part of my free-for-all class on recent American history. While too numerous to mention by name, I am very grateful to them. Three undergraduates were so outstanding that I hired them as my research assistants. Heidi Knippa, Christine L. Palmer, and Ryan Melton tracked down sources and surprised me with their discoveries. A one-semester faculty development leave was generously funded by the Texas A&M Association of Former Students.

Acknowledgments

Many scholars and some former activists read chapters or my articles that have been incorporated into this manuscript. Julia Kirk Blackwelder, Robert Divine, James Gilbert, Maurice Isserman, John Lenihan, and Douglas Miller critiqued my views on the cold war era. Albert Broussard analyzed my writings on the civil rights struggle and its legacies. Kenneth Heineman and Steve Maizlish examined the chapter on student activism, while Michael Rossman commented extensively on campus events and especially on the Free Speech Movement. Staughton Lynd read parts concerning antiwar activity at mid-decade, and corrected me on his participation. David Farber thoughtfully examined my chapter on 1968 and challenged my assumptions on hippie capitalism. Elsie Kersten and Chester Dunning questioned my chapter on the counterculture, and shared many of their experiences. George Herring read many drafts concerning America and Vietnam, and he directed me to additional sources. Sara Alpern and Mary King read my writings on the changing status of women from the 1950s to liberation, and they both prompted modifications of nuance and of substance. Maria-Cristina Garcia also read about women's liberation, and she proved invaluable concerning the Chicano movement. Most of these generous people also read my preface and Legacies chapter, prompting countless revisions. While I take responsibility for any mistakes and for the interpretation, I am very grateful to these scholars and friends: They made this a better book.

Many others helped in their own way. At Oxford, Sheldon Meyer listened to the ideas of a relatively young historian in the mid-1980s, and for a number of years gave his support and eventually an encouraging contract; Stephanie Sakson performed thoughtful copy-editing; and Karen Wolny and Andrew Albanese produced a handsome book. Richard S. Kirkendall read most of the manuscript, offering valuable advice and encouragement. He, along with Robert H. Ferrell and David Pletcher at Indiana University, trained an eager student to become a historian. Merle Curti and the late Chuck DeBenedetti discussed ideas, exchanged information, and provided inspiration and friendship. David Ogden accomplished the incredible feat of being my pal since 1980. He also was foolish enough to play tennis with me, where I instructed him in the fine art of racquet tossing; he taught me punmanship, and how to swap lies while drinking beer.

My brothers, Steve and Jeff, shared their views of the era and their good cheer. JD also recalled many memories and then carefully read the entire manuscript, as did my mother Emily, who along with my father Howard, reminded me of the older generation's convictions. My companion, Nancy Rose Eder, read every sentence, discussed every idea, and critiqued every chapter. For this misery, she demanded that I name all her relatives, her home town, and the Labradors; I agreed, then tricked her. Last report, she still has a sense of humor.

Contents

THE MOVEMENT AND THE SIXTIES

It would be difficult to think of a more depressing piece of news, but
there you have it: The 1960s are back.
Jonathan Yardley, *Washington Post*, 1987

We were young, we were reckless, arrogant, silly, headstrong—and
we were right. I regret nothing!
Abbie Hoffman's last speech, 1989

Ever since those turbulent times, Americans have been debating the era
that began in 1960 at Greensboro and that ended in the early 1970s when
Congress passed the Equal Rights Amendment and the U.S. Army came
home from the Vietnam War. The long decade was an endless pageant
of political and cultural protests, from sit-ins at lunch counters to gunfire
at Wounded Knee. The irrepressible issues, the shocking events, forced
citizens to consider disturbing questions—was America racist, imperialist,
sexist? And the relentless demonstrations, the fires in the streets, forced
neighbors to take a stand and decide publicly about policies concerning a
legion of new topics—from civil rights to women's liberation. America
was opened to scrutiny. Nothing was sacred, everything was challenged,
and the result was an era we simply call "The Sixties."

This book is about the sixties, and for most people who lived then, the
decade did not end in the early 1970s. The scars ran deep. In the 1980s
a Houston citizen blamed the "high crime rate on what happened during
the '60s," and another added that because of that era, "Drugs are rampant, and venereal disease and teen-age pregnancy rates are among the
highest in history." The decade's defenders have been just as emotional.
"I get a little tired of my generation being blamed for all the problems of
the past 20 years," a Dallas man wrote in 1989. "There are lots of us who
held jobs, went to college, joined the Peace Corps, marched for our civil

rights and yes, even died in service to our country." Another agreed, and remembered the "energy, the community and the joy in a shared mission with shared values . . . and we miss it."

Intellectuals also have feuded over the sixties. During those impassioned days, Seymour Martin Lipset, Nathan Glazer, Daniel Bell, Irving Howe, Sidney Hook, and others characterized student protesters as irrational, irresponsible, anti-intellectual extremists. William O'Neill wrote a critical history of the era, *Coming Apart*, and historian Richard Hofstadter labeled the era "The Age of Rubbish." Other academics were more positive. Historian Howard Zinn spent time with civil rights volunteers in the South and wrote of their "unquenchable spirit." Sociologist Helen Swick Perry experienced the counterculture in San Francisco and was attracted to hippie philosophy, while Theodore Roszak added that the "young, miserably educated as they are, bring with them almost nothing but healthy instincts."[1]

The battle continued throughout the next generation. In the 1970s former activists such as Wini Breines, Sara Evans, and George Vickers completed graduate school and produced important monographs which challenged negative views, and in the neo-conservative 1980s a potpourri of books appeared. Some authors aimed at attracting aging baby boomers who once manned the barricades and supposedly desired to relive their past; that dynamic and unforgettable year, 1968, was the topic of five books. Others, such as former college administrator William McGill, condemned the excesses of radicals, while activists such as Tom Hayden, Todd Gitlin, and Mary King published "participant histories" which generally described the era in terms of positive social change. To add chaos to confusion, a few former radicals, including Peter Collier and David Horowitz, recanted their past and claimed that theirs was a "destructive generation" which led the nation to crime, poverty, even AIDS.

The discord over the sixties will last for some time. The activists of the era exposed issues and created demonstrations that provoked deep emotions. This book also is about their behavior, the social activism commonly called "The Movement."

Generally speaking, academics have investigated the movement from four perspectives. Social scientists have developed what could be called the leadership approach by examining the type of persons who became movers and shakers, the vanguard of the movement. Historians have examined the rise and fall of organizations, especially Students for a Democratic Society, Student Nonviolent Coordinating Committee, Southern Christian Leadership Conference, and Clergy and Laymen Concerned about Vietnam. Scholars have emphasized the importance of new left ideology, while others have focused on one important arena of activism and have produced studies about Mississippi in 1964, Chicago in 1968, and Berkeley and Madison.[2]

Those approaches are important, but this book is different. First, this is not a memoir or participant history. While I experienced the decade with fascination, I was not a leader or member of any movement organization. Nevertheless, and like many students then and some readers now, I felt part of the "movement" and of the "sixties generation." Second, this book is a national study. While people in certain areas of the country obviously demonstrated more often, and more vigorously than in other locales, social activism became almost a national phenomenon that eventually involved all types and ages of Americans. Those who demonstrated in Iowa City, Atlanta, New Orleans, Reno, Seattle, or Austin felt just as much part of the movement as those in Berkeley, New York City, or Washington, D.C. This book, therefore, is not a history of a small circle of friends, a few outspoken radicals who resided along the East Coast or in the Bay Area.

Consequently, and unlike previous authors, I will not define the movement by organizations, leaders, or ideology, but in broader terms. Defining, tracing, and explaining the movement and the sixties is the topic of this book, but first I must make some caveats and prefatory remarks.

There are two possible approaches to this topic. An author could trace one form of social activism from 1960 to the early 1970s, and then start over on another aspect of the movement. While that would be efficient, it would be out of context. This book, therefore, develops activism as it unfolded, chronologically, each event building upon another, as the movement became a kaleidoscope of activity and as the sixties expanded in complexity and swelled in emotion. Second, "activist" is a term free of race and gender. People of all races and sexual orientations marched, and the gender or race of those demonstrators is mentioned only when it is significant. The focus here is not on one race or gender, but on activism during the decade. "Citizen" is the term used here to denote mainstream society, the vast majority of the population who generally did not protest and who eventually were labeled the silent majority. Also, some readers today might feel terms used here connoting race or ethnic background are inappropriate, but I am using terminology that was appropriate in the 1960s.

Finally, *movement* in this book connotes all activists who demonstrated for social change. Anyone could participate: There were no membership cards. Activists usually appeared at the protest because they held similar positions on an issue. Sara Evans, a civil rights volunteer, later wrote, "Above all the term 'movement' was self-descriptive. There was no way to join; you simply announced or felt yourself to be part of the movement—

usually through some act like joining a protest march. Almost a mystical term, 'the movement' implied an experience, a sense of community and common purpose."

Activists defined and redefined their movement throughout the era. In the early years demonstrators referred to the "struggle" for civil rights while others later felt part of "student power" or the "peace movement," and if they rejected the draft, the "resistance." During and especially after 1968 alienation soared, the ranks of protesters swelled, and the counterculture bloomed. Political activists then described themselves as the "conspiracy," the "underground," while long-haired hippies talked about "the people." The movement lost focus, and by 1971 a participant defined it as "a grand geodesic dome fitted together from pieces of Marx, Freud, Zen, Artaud, Kesey, Lenin, Leary, Ginsberg, Che, Gandhi, Marcuse, Laing, Fidel and Lao Tzu . . . with a 40-watt rock amplifier strapped to the top—a gaudy, mindblowing spectacle and an impossible intellectual synthesis."

Movement, then, was an amorphous term that changed throughout the decade, but nevertheless there were some common aspects about it and its participants. Activists questioned the status quo, usually feeling that it was unjust, and then they responded. Todd Gitlin of Students for a Democratic Society stated, "The movement didn't simply demand, it *did*." Some activists did by action: Put your body on the line! Protest! Others did by the "great refusal," repudiating the values and morals of the older generation. Some shifted back and forth, but generally speaking those in the movement rejected what they considered was a flawed establishment.

The movement was a loose coalition, and alliances often defined it. Students, clergy, intellectuals often marched first, and later they were joined by many others, from ecologists to hippies to women's liberationists. The National Mobilization to End the War in Vietnam included numerous organizations, and when cultural activists in Ann Arbor, Michigan, met to discuss drugs in the city representatives appeared from the White Panthers, Black Berets, God's Children Motorcycle Club, the Sunnygoode Street Commune, and Congolian Maulers, a "commune of art, music, and general freaks."[3]

Social activism swelled during the sixties, and by the end of the decade the movement was attacking almost every institution—from the armed forces to religion, from business to government. It became a "mass movement," the behavior of a sizable portion of citizens, but like all such movements throughout American history, only a minority ever participated. Numbers are not precise, but it appears that between 1965 and 1968 only 2 or 3 percent of students considered themselves activists while only 20 percent had participated in at least one demonstration. The event that provoked the largest college protest, the Kent State tragedy of 1970, resulted in demonstrations from about two million students when four times that attended universities, and the largest demonstration, Earth Day, resulted in about 20 million participants at a time when there were 200 million Americans.

The movement always was a minority, and it also had a certain time and place, a geography of activism. It began in the South, from Greensboro to Selma, and spread up the east and west coasts to elite universities where students often formed or joined new left organizations. Before 1965 most midwesterners considered the movement "something down south about civil rights," but as men went off to war, activism spread to the liberal cities with large universities in the heartland—Ann Arbor, Bloomington, Chicago, Columbus, East Lansing, Lawrence, Madison, Milwaukee, Minneapolis. Midwestern activism naturally reflected the character of the people. It was not as aggressive as on the coasts, or "less ideological and more laid back," a Brown University student noticed when he visited the University of Minnesota. As activists shifted focus from civil rights to other issues, the movement had the least appeal in the mountain states and South, areas that prided themselves on so-called traditional values. While there were exceptions—islands such as Boulder, Austin, New Orleans, and Atlanta—a *Life* correspondent reported that southerners regarded antiwar protesters as "disloyal, disruptive, disrespectful, damned near criminal." In 1968 two movies were popular: *The Graduate* was a hit in large liberal cities, while *The Green Berets* played to crowds in small-town America. Few southern universities witnessed demonstrations on issues other than civil rights; church-affiliated ones like Brigham Young or Baylor did not experience much activism at all; and liberal ones such as Emory and Rice did not see protesters until the late 1960s. When a former civil rights activist and professor from Princeton arrived to teach at Rice in 1966, he was "struck by the quiet."[4]

Examining the movement is complicated by another characteristic—participants continually changed. Although generalizations are difficult, there are some themes. The first wave of activists were children of the fifties. Most were born in the late 1930s and early 1940s, attended high school in the fifties and college in the early sixties. They usually were intellectual, idealistic, and ideological. They wrote platforms, organized, and discussed ideas with various elder statesmen of the "old left" of the 1930s. Some of them assumed that they were part of a vanguard, providing leadership for a new America. They put their careers, even their lives, on the line, and they provoked America out of the 1950s. The legacy of the older activists was that they exposed the issues, formed the organizations, began mobilizing, confronted the status quo—and cracked the cold war consensus. They began the movement.

The first wave surged forward, crested, and brought America to the rip tide of 1968.

During and after that tumultuous year there was a gradual transition to a second wave of activists that lasted into the early 1970s. Children of the sixties, they were postwar baby boomers molded as teenagers watching their older siblings demonstrating on television. They began attending college in mid-decade and graduated after 1968. They agreed with older siblings that the nation was racist, sexist, and imperialist. Since they opposed those ills, there was little need to debate them. They addressed new issues, and the movement became so broad that these activists felt part of it without joining any organization, and without even marching against the war. Alienation soared during the presidency of Richard Nixon. After years of what these activists considered blundering national politicians, they opposed almost all forms of leadership. Confronting authorities became almost "normal" behavior, as was adopting the demeanor and attitudes of the counterculture. The second wave flowed along two currents—empowerment and liberation. Activists realized that they would have little influence on a conservative president, and so many addressed local issues, empowering themselves in their communities, while others tossed off mainstream traditions and liberated themselves, plunging into a sea of counterculture, attempting to bring about a New America.

Naturally, in any mass movement there are exceptions that do not conform to the first and second wave model. Some activists dropped in and out of the movement, or they made their one stand and then continued earlier pursuits. Others were stuck in time and never could leave Ann Arbor, Boulder, Madison, or many other Berkeleys. As the movement spread in the late 1960s, activists uncovered new issues, resulting in new organizations, networks, and manifestos. And certain areas of the nation experienced various phases at different times or had pressing local issues that did not concern activists nationally.

Nevertheless, the second wave crested in the early 1970s. It came crashing down on the bedrock of the nation's white male establishment, and the result was a sea change, a different America.

Accepting this broader, more fluid definition of the movement means that this book will challenge the previous interpretations emphasizing leaders, organizations, and ideology. Social scientists have postulated that certain personality types were attracted to social activism, and they offered a number of answers to why one would become involved. Some leaders were driven by deep feelings of elitism and populism which compelled them to reject authority. Others were committed youth who found solidarity and feelings of worth in demonstrating for a cause, and still others had been educated by liberal parents who raised their kids to question and reason.

All these ideas are interesting, and they probably explain the personality traits and incentives of a few leaders in a group such as Students for a Democratic Society. None of these theories, however, explains why America experienced a mass movement during the late 1960s. Is one to believe that because intelligent parents raised a few thousand bright students the nation witnessed its largest demonstrations in history? One could argue that all social movements throughout history have been led by such people. Fine students always are attending the best universities, but why did they not revolt in other decades, why did they in the 1960s? And why did a few million others participate?

Not because of a few charismatic leaders. This book will not adopt the leadership approach, and a basic theme is that the movement was generally leaderless. True, during the early phase of the movement, when the organizations were small, there were some leaders of national stature. Who knows what would have happened if Martin Luther King, Jr., kept quiet, and not inspired so many by declaring "I Have a Dream." Leaders were important in the early 1960s when the movement focused on a single issue, but they lost influence as social activism expanded. Furthermore, activism continued after the tragic assassinations of national figures in 1968. During antiwar protests in Austin, Texas, in 1971, officials demanded that activist Terry DuBose disperse the crowd. "I can't do that," DuBose responded, "we don't have leaders. . . . We all agree on what we're doing. Every individual is responsible for themselves. If I tell them to disperse . . . they're going to laugh at me." DuBose and thousands of others were "coordinators." They organized the demonstrations, set the dates, formed networks, and if they were provocative, the media put them on the evening news. "We're not leaders," declared Abbie Hoffman, "we're cheerleaders."

Nor is this book an organizational history. While I have consulted documents published by hundreds of groups, the focus here is not to trace the rise and demise of influential organizations of the decade. Without a doubt, these groups were important, for they brought people together to discuss issues, exchange ideas, and make contacts. When they formed might explain something about a collective response to a national problem, but how they developed, why they disbanded, does not reveal much about social activism, especially during the second wave. The movement was relatively organized in the early 1960s, especially when it concerned only civil rights, but as issues broadened, as activists flooded the streets, the movement became so vast, so widespread, that no one could organize it. By 1968 the first wave tired of organizational activities, endless meetings, discussions, and reports. "Organizing is just another name for going slow," said college rebel Mark Rudd, and others opposed the idea of organizing because it was not free, too bureaucratic, too much like the establishment. "The Crazies have a rule," remarked Paul Krassner, "that in order to become a member one must first destroy his membership card." Significant organizations of the first wave, SDS and the Student Nonviolent Coordinating Committee, fell apart, but second-wave activists formed new groups that concerned new issues, and they assembled thousands of ad hoc committees and local coalitions. By 1969, a mailing list contained addresses of 1700 local and national movement organizations. Most of these were grassroots groups, and most had a short lifespan, lasting until the resolution of a local problem. The demise of groups is not a measure of the success or failure of social activism: Organizations did not define the movement.

Nor did ideology. Scholars often look for intellectual threads that tie loose ends together, especially in a social phenomenon as vast and nebulous as the movement. Consequently they have written about the rise of new left thought in the early 1960s. Many view the role of ideas espoused in the writings of Paul Goodman or Herbert Marcuse or William Appleman Williams as fundamental in developing a coherent ideology which inspired and motivated activists. This might be more relevant during the early sixties at some elite universities where students actually read contemporary books and discussed ideas; when they formed organizations such as SDS they revealed their intellectual heritage in documents such as the *Port Huron Statement*. Yet as the movement expanded, new left ideology was diluted and its influence declined. A 1969 survey found that over 80 percent of college students identified with "my generation," but just 13 percent did with the new left, and that latter figure dropped to 3 percent for those not attending college. True, activists held similar ideas about America, most of them agreeing about racism or imperialism, some about sexism. But only a tiny number had read the ponderous writings of Marcuse, or the *Port Huron Statement*, and when a few radicals shouted "revolution" their rhetoric failed to sway the generation because it had little support from the average demonstrator. As an underground journalist wrote about a friend, "He hadn't read Zinn, Lacouture, Fall, Robert Scheer, Tom Hayden, or Staughton Lynd but he decided that the war in Vietnam was 'bullshit' and he would have no part of it." In fact, if there was an ideology of the movement then it probably could be described more accurately as the traditional American philosophy—pragmatism. It was a grubby, shouting pragmatism that most activists adopted in the street to confront the establishment and address the issues of the sixties.

This book, therefore, is not a history of new left ideology, of colorful leaders, or of various organizations. While these approaches are necessary and informative, they only examine one part of the movement, and in doing so they fail to explain the motive: Why did millions of citizens become activists, take to the streets, and participate in the movement? As will be developed throughout this book, activists felt that problems existing in the nation were inconsistent with the American ideal, with ideas expressed in the Declaration of Independence and U.S. Constitution. All men were not created equal, nor were women in America. For reasons that will be explained, social activism developed as a response to numerous problems that had been festering in the nation for many years, and protesters revolted in their own way to reform what they considered was a corrupt system. Regardless of the rhetoric shouted in the heat of the moment, activists of the sixties were similar to those who rebelled during the nation's other major reform eras—the Revolution, Jacksonian democracy, the populist and progressive eras, and the 1930s. While all those eras concerned different issues, they all challenged the establishment and tried to change the Republic. And so it was in the sixties. As activist Mickey Kaus stated, "We wanted to remake America, not destroy it."[5]

I have arrived at these and other ideas because I have used some of the same but many different sources than most commentators and historians who have written about the sixties.

In the early 1970s a veteran activist wrote that he was quite disturbed. George Vickers had just read many popular books and articles on the movement and he complained that "the vast majority were highly critical of the New Left and generally tried to explain it as a tiny minority of psychologically defective individuals." Vickers was troubled and offended by these analyses, for they did not ring true.

To redress that situation, Vickers decided to write his own study, which is similar to why I decided to write this book. Attending undergraduate and graduate school in the late 1960s and most of the 1970s, I read a few popular histories on the sixties, and realized then that the authors had misunderstood or distorted the movement. These commentators were older, and perhaps their interpretation was a natural result of the passion of the decade, but also it was a consequence of the sources they employed. Invariably, they relied on the mainstream press, which would be appropriate for many topics, but not for all forms of social activism in the sixties. The movement was a revolt against the establishment, and major newspapers were a pillar of the foundation. Editors often published slanted reports, and that was especially true of articles about antiwar demonstrators and campus activists at mid-decade and later about the counterculture, black power, and women's liberation. During the Berkeley Free Speech Movement, for example, the *San Francisco Examiner* and *Oakland Tribune* wrote that the student activists were communist-inspired fanatics. Later, when 800 uniformed servicemen and activists protested the war by marching on streets outside of Fort Hood, Texas, the *Austin*

American-Statesmen reported that patriotic local residents confronted demonstrators and prevented them from completing their parade, which activists noted was not true, another example of "media lies."[6] Because activists did not trust the press, they formed their own, establishing over 600 underground newspapers which by 1970 had a circulation of about five million; and they established at least three national wire services while printing up libraries of posters, leaflets, and newsletters. Naturally, one can not dismiss major national newspapers. Generally, their reporting was fine on issues they supported, such as the civil rights struggle, and later in the decade their articles became more critical toward the government and more tolerant toward activism. These establishment sources have been used. Yet one cannot neglect the underground sources, as almost all authors have done so far, for that is tantamount to writing a history of the American Revolution by examining only British documents—and not those of the rebels.

Using both sources, along with many valuable memoirs, participant histories, and monographs, results in a book that examines the rise and fall of a flowing movement. Naturally, this single volume does not try to be comprehensive, and most likely the reader would tire from a longer book because social activism tends to be repetitious. But this study does attempt to describe the most significant events and examine why they happened and how they shaped the movement and the sixties.

I set the stage by investigating the postwar era, the spawning bed for future activism, and then examine two responses to cold war culture—the civil rights struggle and rise of the student new left, both of which merged during the early 1960s. The focus then shifts to mid-decade when a new generation appeared on campus, activists who continued picketing for civil rights and began striking for student power and marching against the war in Vietnam. Eventually, two compelling issues—race and war—provoked more Americans to become involved, and an increasing number of youth became alienated from the values of the establishment. The first wave surged forward, and in 1968 the decade underwent a rip tide, a movement and a nation torn apart, left or right, us versus them. The result was the emergence of the second wave that flooded into the early 1970s, and the concluding chapters discuss the most important themes—cultural rebellion and liberation, which often merged with political empowerment.

By investigating social activism, this book will also explore the sixties. That era challenges the Progressive years, the Great Depression, and World War II as the most important periods of the twentieth century, and one could argue that the most significant aspect of the sixties was social activism. After all, when most people contemplate that decade they recall demonstrations and protests. And when one considers the history of the

Republic it would be difficult to find more significant issues than those the activists raised and confronted: equality or inequality, war or peace, national interests versus individual rights, personal behavior versus community standards. Indeed, the protesters questioned the very nature and meaning of America.

Like all social activism, the movement was fluid and its participants diverse. Making generalizations is dangerous—but it also is necessary, for while various authors have written participant histories and books on certain aspects of the era, it now is time to put the pieces together and examine the significant events and issues of *The Movement and The Sixties*.

College Station, Texas   T. A.
May 1994

THE MOVEMENT AND THE SIXTIES

Spawning Ground: Cold War Culture

The seeds of the crisis of the 1960s lay in the 1940s.
Godfrey Hodgson, *America in Our Time*

I am going to look at the Fifties, then, as a seedbed as well as a cemetery.
Todd Gitlin, *The Sixties*

In January 1960 Tom Mathews was running for president of his high school class in California. His campaign slogan, he admitted, was not inspiring: "Vote for Tom—He's a Real Good Guy." "That's the way we were," Mathews reminisced, the "first stirrings of the '60s were innocent. . . . Around my high school, guys were still padding the halls in saddle shoes and humming 'Sh-Boom.' A nice girl was a virgin who didn't smoke cigarettes. Ideology? No one had even heard of it. There were no issues. We were suspended closer to the Age of Sinatra than the Age of Aquarius."

Since the sixties many have wondered about the reasons for social activism during that turbulent decade, and many activists have written memoirs or participant histories which begin by examining their early years, the postwar era, in an attempt to answer and examine what events or issues in the fifties had an impact on why they became activists in the sixties. This is a personal endeavor, for what seemed important to a black college student at North Carolina A&T College in 1960 might not be relevant to a white student at the University of Michigan teach-in during the spring semester of 1965, to a Yippie at the 1968 Democratic convention in Chicago, to a Chicano Brown Beret at the Los Angeles riot of 1970, or to a working woman marching for ratification of the Equal Rights Amendment in 1973. In their own ways, all thought of themselves as part of the movement. Why someone got involved, why individuals developed a social and political consciousness which guided them to respond to an issue, to protest, is a complex process that never can be fully understood. Everyone who demonstrated, who felt that they were part of the sixties generation, could express their own views on the origins of the movement. Yet no one lives in a vacuum. All activists experienced the fifties, and one must investigate the origins of the movement by examining some common characteristics of the postwar era that *affected* later activists. This approach, then, is not debating whether the fifties were "happy days," a good or bad decade, but instead is attempting to answer the question: What themes of the late forties and fifties created a climate for later change, or, What was the spawning ground that nurtured the development of the movement in the 1960s?

At the beginning of America's involvement in World War II, Henry Luce editorialized in *Life* that the next era of history would be the "American Century." That feeling of destiny, of purpose, expanded as our troops swept across the plains of Europe and as our navy steamed toward the Rising Sun. Most Americans were proud that their nation was poised on a new era, one of leadership and greatness. In the largest struggle in history, the United States had won: we had crushed the Axis Powers.

World War II was clear-cut. Hitler and Tojo were the aggressors, and they attacked us: Remember Pearl Harbor! We counterattacked and fought a war which was easy to comprehend—the first armies to capture the enemy's capital won. As our warships defeated the Japanese Navy in the Pacific and cruised toward Tokyo, our armies marched through North Africa, up the Italian peninsula, across France and into Berlin. We dictated the peace, demanding "unconditional surrender." We had met the enemy on the battlefield, beat them fair and square. The men returned as heroes, and for those who did not, the sacrifice was worth the price: No American died in vain.

In a sense, World War II was a "good war." It ended the Great Depression at home while allowing us to extend our power abroad. Furthermore, the overwhelming victory reinforced beliefs that most Americans held before the conflict, that supposedly were validated by the war, and that veterans defended during the postwar era. The United States was strong, so strong in fact that we could beat any enemy. All we had to do was to try hard enough, work as a team, and use our Yankee ingenuity. With our superior technology, winning was a matter of the proper application of our power, and of our will to use it. The victory in 1945 was so conclusive that Americans accepted the myth that the "United States has never lost a war." While that illusion whitewashed the circumstances of the War of 1812, it became creed as veterans taught it to their children and as presidents comforted the public by stating that they would not be the first to lose a war. The victory also reinforced the traditional American belief that in a world of good and evil our totalitarian enemies represented evil, and we exemplified good. The war enhanced America's self-appointed position as the beacon of freedom, the shining light, the "City upon a Hill."

These were "truths" for the men who grew up during the Great Depression and who fought the war, the World War II generation. Those veterans wanted their sons to learn these truths, to understand their lives, and so in the postwar era they took their boys to the movies. A large crop of baby boomers began their education about their dad's generation—and about America—by seeing films that glorified the good war: *Guadalcanal Diary, A Walk in the Sun, Bataan, Wake Island, Battle Ground, Gung Ho.* "I'll never forget Audie Murphy in *To Hell and Back,*" remembered Vietnam veteran Ron Kovic. "At the end he jumps on top of a flaming tank that's just about to explode and grabs the machine gun blasting it into the German lines. He was so brave I had chills running up and down my back, wishing it were me up there." John Wayne starred in scores of films, from *The Sands of Iwo Jima* (1949) to *The Green Berets* (1968), and as the others did they all stressed the same themes: American men meant just what they said, stood up for good against evil, and after a tough fight always won. The struggle for what was right was worth the sacrifice, for it preserved the American way of life. "As children," a Vietnam veteran later wrote, "when my friends and I played war, we imitated the movies. My Dad would buy me the guns and gear I asked for so I'd look the best in my part. I'd kill the imaginary Japanese and Nazis over and over, and I'd love it. If I got wounded, I'd take it stoically and fight on. If I got killed, I'd always have time for one last cigarette, time to tell a buddy to say goodbye to my Mom and Dad. Then my Mom would call me to dinner, and the war would be over until the next day, when I would kill more hated Japanese and Nazis. This was my first basic training course."[1]

The older generation had won their war, of course, but by the late 1940s it appeared that someone was losing the peace. A new enemy, the Soviet Union, turned the American Century into an illusion. Just months after V.J. Day, the Grand Alliance of Britain, America, and the Soviet Union was crumbling over issues in Europe and Asia. The Russians refused to allow democratic elections in the areas of Eastern Europe they liberated from Nazi Germany, and Communism spread to Hungary, Rumania, Bulgaria, Yugoslavia, Albania, Poland, and the eastern section of Germany. By March 1946 Prime Minister Winston Churchill declared: "From Stettin in the Baltic to Trieste in the Adriatic, an iron curtain has descended across the Continent." The next year, President Harry Truman aimed to "contain" Communist expansion into Greece and Turkey by pronouncing his declaration of the cold war, the Truman Doctrine, and the U.S. returned to defend and rebuild Europe with the Marshall Plan.

In 1948 the Communists seized the government of Czechoslovakia, the Soviets closed access routes into the German capital, and the U.S. responded by initiating the Berlin Airlift. In Asia, Communist forces were victorious in the Chinese civil war, and in 1950, after less than five years of peace, American troops again were in combat, this time in the hills of Korea.

America again was at war, and now it had more ominous implications because the world had entered the atomic age. In 1945 America began the era; in 1949 the Soviets dropped their first atomic device; and shortly thereafter both nations were developing intercontinental ballistic missiles. With the USSR armed with atomic bombs and rockets, the United States was no longer sequestered from its enemies by the Atlantic and Pacific. For the first time in history, Americans felt vulnerable to annihilation.

The atomic age and the subsequent nuclear arms race provoked many throughout the cold war era to wonder about the future of the American way of life. "Total war is now the only way war can be waged," wrote a social scientist, "and this calls for total defense and fosters totalitarian conceptions of life and government." Democracy might be threatened, and Norman Cousins wondered whether "free institutions as we understand them can be maintained." Other social thinkers wondered if the peril of nuclear holocaust would affect the independent nature of the American character, and an author predicted that the future would be an "uncomfortable place for the individual." Most seemed to agree, as journalists Joseph and Stewart Alsop commented on a future with "constant, aching, mounting fear." The atomic age would provide the conditions for a "world-wide nervous breakdown."

The bomb generated anxiety. The main character in the popular movie *Them* asked about the giant ants apparently taking over the nation, "If these monsters are a result of the first atomic bomb in 1945, what will we find in the future?" The scientist answered ominously, "I don't know. No one can predict."

International events also caused alarm as the cold war escalated. "Communists in the Kremlin are engaged in a monstrous conspiracy to stamp out freedom all over the world," declared President Truman, and to confront them he supplied allies with economic and military aid and adopted the policy of containment. Yet the president attempted to do more than just contain the red menace. After the North Koreans attacked their southern neighbors, he ordered American forces beyond the old boundary and into North Korea. While that brought Americans into conflict with the Communist Chinese, the move was supported at home, especially by conservatives. "There is no substitute for victory," declared Congressman Joseph Martin, and in 1953 President Eisenhower's secretary of state,

John Foster Dulles, advocated a more aggressive policy. Containment, he charged, was a treadmill which would "keep us in the same place until we drop exhausted." Republicans felt that it was "negative, futile and immoral" to abandon "countless human beings to a despotism and Godless terrorism." The United States should "roll back" the red tide, should "liberate" Eastern Europe from Moscow. Dulles spoke in tough terms about getting our way in world affairs, even if this meant confronting Russia and going "to the brink" of war. His policy advocated the idea that conventional forces were too expensive. The U.S. needed to take a "new look" at its policy, and that meant the nation should rely on nuclear weapons, on "massive retaliation." These weapons were cheaper, "more bang for the buck."

Dulles's diplomacy sounded tough, but its central basis was not action but fear. During the Eisenhower years, a historian later wrote, foreign policy was a "mixture of an almost unthinkingly anticommunist ideology with a remarkably practical reluctance to translate that ideology into action." The U.S. sounded the alarm, talked tough, and then began posturing by dividing the globe into two parts—the Communists versus the "free world"—and forming alliances with any nation that might be on our side. The United States joined so many security organizations that journalists dubbed the policy "pactomania," and by the 1960s the U.S. had military commitments to 47 nations. This reinforced the assumption that the world was bipolar: Moscow versus Washington. East Bloc against West Bloc. Reds versus Whites. There were few neutrals during the era, none that could be trusted, and magazines such as *Time* and *U.S. News and World Report* published maps in which most of the 140 nations of the world were colored either red or white: Friend or Foe. Us or Them. Communism was monolithic, it was believed, and like a spreading blob all those "red" nations aimed to conquer the world. Hollywood reinforced this idea by producing popular science-fiction movies with red enemies such as *War of the Worlds* (red Martians versus white Americans), while some national publications continued popularizing this mentality for years; as late as 1972 *U.S. News* still referred to enemy forces in Vietnam as "reds."

Few questioned this unsophisticated view of the world in the 1950s, for they never were able to disengage from what they felt were the lessons of World War II. War was caused by evil forces with unjust aims. We could not appease them. We had to stand up to all forms of aggression—Nazis or Commies—for if we did not, then one nation after another would "fall like dominoes" until the enemy was at our gate. "We are fighting in Korea," President Truman told the nation, "so we won't have to fight in Wichita, or in Chicago, or in New Orleans, or on San Francisco Bay." Eisenhower and his advisers agreed, for they were an "unreflective lot," a historian has concluded; for them the "transition from world war to cold war required only transferring what they had learned about Hitler and the fascists to Stalin and the communists. Hitler had aimed for world conquest; so, therefore, must Stalin."[2]

In a world frozen by cold war, most Americans began to accept another notion: there were no just causes for revolution. Americans apparently forgot about 1776 and arrived at the conclusion that revolts in colonies or developing nations were no longer caused by nationalism, poverty, or social and political oppression. Instead, all were "Communist-inspired." That being the case, most citizens felt that it was in the national interest to maintain the status quo, both abroad and at home. Almost two centuries earlier James Madison had put it like this: "Perhaps it is a universal truth that the loss of liberty at home is to be charged to the provisions against dangers, real or pretended, from abroad." Madison was referring to the Alien and Sedition Acts, but the same idea applied to the Red Scare following World War I and also to the cold war era.

The same month that President Truman declared his plan to fight Communism abroad, the Truman Doctrine, he announced his plan to fight it at home, Executive Order 9835. The order established procedures to investigate federal workers and dismiss them on the "reasonable grounds for belief in disloyalty." Such grounds naturally included crimes such as treason and espionage but also the new category of being affiliated with a fascist, Communist, totalitarian, or subversive organization. Testing for loyalty was simple to the Man from Missouri; as he once said, "You're either loyal to the United States, or you're not." By 1951 the order was expanded to allow dismissal if there was "reasonable doubt" of one's loyalty. Eisenhower agreed, and his administration enlarged the program so a worker could be fired if any of his "behavior, activities or associations . . . show that the individual is not reliable or trustworthy." During the fifties, personal behavior could be judged "not in the national interest."

The Truman and Eisenhower administrations established the most sweeping inquiry into employee loyalty in American history. From 1947 to 1956 the federal government fired approximately 2700 workers; fearing investigation and dismissal, another 12,000 employees resigned. After becoming vice president, Richard Nixon boasted: "We're kicking the Communists and fellow travelers and security risks out of the Government . . . by the thousands."

It was a purge, yet simply investigating the government was not sufficient for many, including Truman's attorney general, Tom Clark. To him, and to most Americans at that time, "Those who do not believe in the ideology of the United States shall not be allowed to stay in the

United States." Love it or leave it, and to find those who should leave it the government began investigating the public. They formed countless committees, subcommittees, and special boards. They increased the powers of the FBI, and they relied on informers. These informers often were paid, and they gave secret testimony, made allegations, and passed on hearsay behind closed doors. Informers supposedly had knowledge, and could answer the question, Who was and who was not a subversive, a red? The idea of informing on a friend or a neighbor was accepted; an opinion poll found that two-thirds of those asked agreed with the statement that one should inform on someone even if some innocent people got hurt. The government, I. F. Stone wrote in 1951, had turned a "whole generation of Americans into stool-pigeons."[3]

The government needed legal justification, and so officials used the Smith Act. Originally, the Smith Act had been passed in 1940 to stop Nazi infiltration, and it stated that it was a crime to teach or advocate overthrowing the federal government. The Truman administration used the act at the end of the decade to prosecute the leadership of the Communist Party of the United States. All eleven leaders were found guilty, and they paid fines and served terms in federal prisons during the 1950s. One party leader, Gus Hall, served over five years, and eventually over a hundred Communists were indicted, and sixty were jailed. In 1950 Congress passed the McCarran Act, stating that Communist Party members must register with the federal government, and two years later passed the McCarran-Walter Immigration Act that established 33 exclusionary provisions aimed to bar immigrants and even visitors from the land of the free. Tourists could not advocate "totalitarianism" or be "sexual deviants," and they had to sign declarations that they were not prostitutes, homosexuals, or Communists. In 1954 President Eisenhower signed the Communist Control Act, which terminated "all rights, privileges, and immunities" of the party. In addition, the government denied Communists their passports, terminated their social security and military disability payments, and deported those who were not citizens.

This search for the subversive, then, was under way when its greatest advocate joined the crusade, the junior Republican senator from Wisconsin, Joseph McCarthy. In February 1950 he announced to the Republican women's club of Wheeling, West Virginia: "I have here in my hand a list of 205 that were known to the secretary of state as being members of the Communist Party and are still making and shaping the policy of the State Department." When confronted by reporters, he played the numbers game, and the 205 became "bad security risks," while later in Salt Lake City he announced that only 57 were "card-carrying members of the Communist Party." Alarmed, Congress formed a committee to investigate the charges, and after months concluded that McCarthy's charges were "a hoax and a fraud . . . an effort to inflame the American people with a wave of hysteria and fear on an unbelievable scale."

In saner times the report would have ended McCarthy's career, but 1950 was not a sane time. In June, North Koreans attacked South Korea, and shortly thereafter American troops were engaged in combat against Communism. No politician, consequently, wanted to be known as "soft on Communism," which gave McCarthy a free hand to continue his reckless charges, red-baiting, and slandering anyone in his way. He attacked the Truman administration by denouncing the secretary of state, Dean Acheson, as the "Great Red Dean," and by charging that the "hard fact is that those who wear the label Democrat wear it with the stain of an historic betrayal." He mesmerized his audiences as he spoke of red spies involved in "a conspiracy on a scale so immense as to dwarf any previous such venture in the history of man."

Not to be outdone, the Democrats no longer questioned McCarthy's wild charges but joined the frenzy. Two months after McCarthy's West Virginia speech, Truman's last attorney general, J. Howard McGrath, claimed: "There are today many Communists in America. They are everywhere—in factories, offices, butcher shops, on street corners, in private businesses—and each carries in himself the germs of death for society. These Communists are busy at work—undermining your Government, plotting to destroy the liberties of every citizen, and feverishly trying, in whatever way they can, to aid the Soviet Union."[4]

The nation was riddled with commies, supposedly, and the only thing missing from a legion of charges was proof: the Republic sank into rule by innuendo which became known as McCarthyism.

State and local governments eagerly joined the cleansing crusades. Almost all states introduced loyalty pledges for state employees, especially for teachers. In Indiana even professional wrestlers had to take the oath. Most states also passed antisubversive or sedition laws. A party member in Pennsylvania, Steve Nelson, violated that state's sedition act and received a twenty-five-year sentence. States excluded the Communist Party from the ballot, and they passed laws making it a criminal offense to advocate overthrowing the government or to join such a group. A resident of Connecticut broke the law if he used "abusive words about the form of government in the United States, its military forces, flag or uniforms." The penalty for speaking or writing subversive words in Michigan could be life in prison; in Tennessee it could be death. Penalties for being a Communist Party member varied from absurd to draconic: in New York a member could not buy a fishing license; in Ohio they were ineligible for unemployment benefits; and in Texas the member could be sentenced to twenty years in prison. In Indiana the official aim of the state was to "extermi-nate communists."

How would the government find the "subversive" lurking in the Ameri-can society? The government began an inquisition; critics labeled it a witch hunt. During the Truman administration alone the FBI conducted 25,000 full-scale investigations, but that was a fraction compared with the number conducted by all state and federal agencies during those years: 6.5 million Americans were checked for loyalty. Accused officials bene-fited from neither judge nor jury—they were without legal recourse. Five hundred lost their jobs because of "questionable loyalty."[5]

The inquisition included universities and Hollywood. This should have been expected since they are similar in that both the university and Holly-wood create their own version of the American Dream, and both profes-sors and directors introduce ideas which often provoke audiences to ana-lyze their society and themselves. In reality, few in the audience remember the message the next day, but the average citizen usually thinks that great persuasive powers lurk in the classroom or on the silver screen.

Public pressure mounted and college administrators cowered. Universi-ties banned outside speakers from using their facilities and talking on their campuses. This was especially true of small state colleges, as well as more distinguished liberal institutions such as the universities of Michigan, Minnesota, and North Carolina. Ohio State imposed the most restrictions on speakers, even denying a platform for a Keynesian professor and a Quaker pacifist. As public concern grew, administrators initiated searches for subversive professors or former Communist Party members. In 1948 the University of Washington terminated three faculty members and the next year the University of California dismissed 26 for refusing to sign a loyalty pledge. Colleges allowed "security officers," usually former FBI agents, to sit in classes and listen to lectures. Those faculty members who were called to testify in front of congressional committees, and who re-fused or took the Fifth Amendment against self-incrimination, were ter-minated at most schools, including Ohio State, Temple, Columbia, Rutgers, MIT, and the universities of Michigan and New York. For that reason, Harvard dismissed or suspended 54 professors. When a psychology professor at San Diego State refused to testify before the House Un-American Activities Committee (HUAC), he was attacked by the local American Legion until the university fired him; for the next 26 years he received no legal redress or retirement payments.

It was carnage: One historian calculated that because of loyalty oaths, state laws, and institutional pressures, more than 600 teachers and profes-sors lost their jobs. In New York City alone, 380 were forced to resign. At the University of California the loyalty oath resulted in not only 26 terminations, but an additional 37 resignations in protest, 47 incidents in which outside scholars turned down job offers, and the elimination of 55 courses from the university. During the fifties, a historian has concluded, the academic community suffered a "collective failure of nerve." By allowing faculty dismissals, censorship, and countless investigations, the "academy did not fight McCarthyism. It contributed to it."[6]

Hollywood also suffered a nervous breakdown. HUAC chose the entertainment industry as a special target because the Communist Party membership in Los Angeles was large during the 1930s and the war, and because of its glamour and influence. Hollywood was the "dream factory," for not only did directors create dreams, but actors seemed to live them in fast cars and mansions. "They were our royalty," the director of the local civil liberties committee observed, "and if you want to scare a country you attack its royalty." HUAC attacked in 1947 by calling "friendly" witnesses, ones who would "name names" of actors they felt might be Communists, and "unfriendly" witnesses, ones who refused to cooperate with the committee. Of this latter group, HUAC subpoenaed a group who became known as the Hollywood Ten. Most of them were script writers, and they refused to answer questions about their political affiliations. Congress cited them for contempt, sending a chilling signal to Hollywood. The Association of Motion Picture Producers issued a statement claiming that the Ten had committed a "disservice to their employers" and they discharged them unless they declared under oath that they were not party members. While the Ten served six months to a year in prison, conservative actors, directors, and station managers employed pressure and vigilante groups such as the Motion Picture Alliance for the Preservation of American Ideals, whose president was John Wayne, and they introduced loyalty pledges and the blacklist. Although the president of the Screen Actors Guild, Ronald Reagan, proclaimed, "We will not be a party to a blacklist," his union adopted a "clearance system" and banned suspected Communists and unfriendly witnesses from membership. Eventually, television and radio producers joined in; they fired 1500 employees, while the blacklist made about 350 actors and writers unemployable in Hollywood. Even in the dream factory no one could escape the red nightmare.

Studios attempted to demonstrate their "patriotism" by producing anticommunist movies such as *The Iron Curtain, I Was a Communist for the FBI, This Deception, My Ten Years as a Counterspy, The Web of Subversion, Red Masquerade, I Married a Communist*, and *The Red Menace*. Ronald Reagan starred as an American in China observing the brutal red Chinese revolution in *Hong Kong*, and John Wayne played *Big Jim McClain*, an agent for HUAC who investigated a Communist network in Hawaii. More popular, however, was *My Son John*, the story of three sons, two who were high school football players eager to fight Communism in Korea, and John, who went to college to become an intellectual. John mocked conventional moral standards, ridiculed the local priest, and the plot hinted that he experimented with drugs and was a homosexual. Naturally, he joined the Communist Party, but by the end of the movie he had repented and confessed to the FBI. Realizing the betrayal, John's Communist comrades assassinated him, appropriately, on the steps of the Lincoln Memorial. All these films had the same moral plot and the same message: Soviet Russia was attempting to dominate the world, and to do that, their spies were subverting society and infiltrating the United States.

The new technology of the decade, television, played prime-time anti-communism. "The Big Picture" demonstrated how the Russians had double-crossed the U.S. and how the Red Army had crushed democracies and erected Soviet satellites. Much more popular was "I Led Three Lives," which was based on Herbert Philbrick's episodes as a FBI informant and which resulted in the 1949 trial of the Communist Party of the United States. Philbrick was an advertising agent during the day. "Evenings and holidays he worked with the Communists, and he spent the gray hours of the morning in a secret room in his house where he typed out reports and developed photographs for the FBI." The unscrupulous reds and devious fellow-travelers, unshaven and dressed in dark trench coats, concocted plots to cripple the Great Republic; Philbrick then would inform the G-men, clean-shaven and in white shirts and ties, who would save the nation during the last few minutes of the show. This melodrama played throughout the decade, and Philbrick's book was serialized in over 500 newspapers.[7]

Newspaper editors competed with television and radio and they eagerly published headlines such as "How Russians Spy on Their Allies"; "The Reds Are After Your Child"; "How Commies Take Over"; "Trained to Raise Hell in America: The International Lenin School in Moscow"; and even, "Communists Penetrate Wall Street." Such articles dominated the decade, and seeped into the next. In November 1960 *U.S. News & World Report* printed "Underground Railway for Reds Begins at U.S. Border." It claimed that a "highly efficient Communist underground railroad is operating next door to the U.S., in Mexico," in which the Russians are able to "spirit spies and defectors from the U.S. to Soviet protection" and to "move Communist agents back and forth between Mexico and Red bases in any part of the world."

Subversives, apparently, were everywhere: America became engulfed in Red Hysteria. One evening a reporter entered a Chinese restaurant in Houston. She wanted to write a story on recent Chinese history and asked the proprietor for information. A patron overheard the conversation, rushed to a telephone, called the police, and the reporter was arrested for "talking Communism" and thrown in jail for fourteen hours before the authorities concluded that they had no case. Monogram Pictures canceled a film on Longfellow explaining that Hiawatha had tried to stop Indian wars and the audience might think the film advocated a red "peace offensive." A foundation offered $100,000 to anyone who would create a device that could detect traitors. A three-year-old girl was hired as a model but was not paid because she could not sign her name to a loyalty pledge. In San Antonio, a member of Minutewomen of America listed 600 books in the local public library which were "subversive," including *Moby Dick* and Einstein's *Theory of Relativity*, while a citizen of Indiana demanded that the legislature ban *Robin Hood*. "He takes from the rich and gives to the poor. That's Communism." And in Bartlesville, Oklahoma, a local citizens' committee accused the public librarian of thirty years of loaning out "subversive literature" such as *New Republic* and *The Nation*. She was sacked, along with the magazines.

"Watch Out!" Sartre proclaimed, "America has the rabies." This was Red Hysteria, McCarthyism, and this Great Fear was the main reason for the development of the cold war culture.

Every generation is unique in some ways. Those growing up in 1930s and fighting the war in the 1940s transferred what they had learned fighting fascism and tyranny to the new nemesis—Communism. These parents of the baby boomers saw foreign policy in black and white terms. The world was filled with good and evil forces. We had been the good guys before, and we would be in the future. That was the "truth": My country right or wrong. Love it or leave it. This mentality set the stage for the most significant event in the sixties—America's involvement in Vietnam—which many of the older generation saw as another World War II or Korea, another obligation to stop aggression. When their sons and daughters questioned and protested American policy, they had a very difficult time understanding why, and they usually had trouble admitting that there might be some legitimate reasons for dissent. Instead, their first response was to do what they did in the fifties—search for a scapegoat. Some of this search became ridiculous, such as when parents charged that putting fluoride in water to prevent tooth decay was actually a Communist plot. But most of the quest was more serious, and the older generation developed what might be labeled a collective denial. When the postwar baby boom naturally resulted in an increase in juvenile delinquency and teenage pregnancy, parents occasionally blamed "working mothers," but more often factors outside the family such as television, comic books, films, and of course Communism.[8]

For the older generation "commie" became a generic term for anything disliked, anything perceived as anti-American. That was understandable because blaming national problems on the commies was sanctioned by national leaders. Who gave atomic bomb secrets to the Russians? The Rosenbergs. Who lost China? Fellow-travelers in the State Department. On and on. In 1958, FBI director J. Edgar Hoover published *Masters of Deceit*, which sold over two million copies, and in 1962 A *Study of Communism*. Hoover had become a national hero to the older generation since his famous G-men had put so many gangsters behind bars. His message then was law and order, but Hoover had a different enemy by the 1950s: "Communism is the major menace of our time," he wrote, "it threatens the very existence of our Western civilization." He and others declared that patriotic citizens had the responsibility of exposing subversives, for as Senator Barry Goldwater proclaimed in 1959, "I am not willing to accept the idea that there are no Communists left in this country; I think that if we lift enough rocks we will find some."[9]

The fear of Communism, along with cold war tensions, resulted in the older generation being unusually concerned with security, which also was a consequence of growing up during the Great Depression. During the postwar era, almost all parents remembered being hungry, and according to one author the "depression taught people to reduce risks." Most did that by accumulating wealth, by having money to save or to spend. For some in that generation frugality became almost spiritual, and it lingered as a habit for decades. "During the inflation of the 1970s," one baby boomer recalled, "my dad still could tell you the price of a Craftsman wrench in 1955. He was a walking Sears and Roebuck catalogue." Others of the 1930s generation flaunted their newly acquired postwar wealth, and bought the status symbols that they only dreamed about in the Depression. Much of the consumption was for the kids, and while the presents might have demonstrated love, they also increased the strength of the family unit, kept the kids in line and the family happy. Being a "happy family" was not just a good idea—it was a requirement. Parents would have "family nights" when they would duly ask their children questions to which they already knew the answers, or they would take the kids on weekends to the park or to the lake. During the cold war era, happy families acted to protect individuals. Secure families could face the threat, from within and without. The aim, then, was to achieve the "good life," and for the generation that grew up during the Depression and fought the war, the good life in the 1950s ultimately meant security.

The desire for security, reinforced by McCarthyism at home and the Korean War abroad, created a chilling climate in the nation during the first years of the 1950s—a *cold war culture*. Most Americans naturally became hesitant to take a stand, especially one which could be considered controversial. Autonomy and uniqueness were inhibited, and the traditional rugged individualism, one commentator noted, had become "Rugged American Collectivism." No one wanted to be suspect. As one suburbanite told a new resident, "If you have any brains, you keep them in your back pocket around here." A study based on almost 2500 interviews with social scientists at 165 colleges in 1955 revealed that two-thirds believed that a threat existed to intellectual activity, and more felt that the threat had little to do with specifics such as Communist Party membership but instead reflected nebulous concerns such as being a subversive or un-American. The message was clear: fit in, be part of the team. Most citizens embraced the eventual result—a culture of consensus and conformity, one which aimed to uphold the status quo.[10]

Americans conformed in many ways, and that was demonstrated by the rise of suburbs. To be sure, the development of an endless number of Levittowns, Richfields, or Daly Cities inexpensively housed returning veterans and their pregnant brides. The government supported the suburbanization of America by guaranteeing loans through the Federal Housing Authority and Veterans Administration. That resulted in a boom for the real estate industry, and during each day of the fifties developers bulldozed some 3000 acres of farmland into suburbia. Families rushed from urban neighborhoods. Suburban population doubled between 1950 and 1970, marking the fastest growth rate in the nation. Government policy also supported race segregation, for the FHA refused to guarantee loans for integrated housing projects. As a consequence, in 1957 some 60,000 people lived in Levittown, Pennsylvania, and not one was black. Instead, white couples with children resided in suburbs, middle-aged and middle-incomed, Catholics, Protestants, and Jews. Others were not welcomed. "At no time in American history," two authors have stated, "with the abnormal exceptions of army or dormitory life, had such uniform one-class communities existed." Rows of almost identical homes sprung up across the nation, and by 1962 folksinger Malvina Reynolds was strumming about "Little Boxes" that "all look just the same. . . . And the people in the houses All went to the university . . . And they all have pretty children. . . . And they come out all the same."

America seemed homogenized, classlessly middle-class. Surbanites felt comfortable belonging to a community of people who looked and acted like themselves. Men idolized John Wayne or perhaps William Holden, and women modeled themselves after June Allyson, Debbie Reynolds, or Audrey Hepburn, actresses who played sweet girls who became wholesome and cheerful wives like Dinah Shore. The fifties was the Wonder Bread decade: Campbell's soup, Spam, Velveeta. Suburbanites embraced sameness, while many of them feared changes. "It was a real classic little town I grew up in," musician Bruce Springsteen remembered, "very intent on maintaining the status quo. Everything was looked at as a threat."

To contain that threat, parents sent their offsprings to hundreds of new schools where they were taught to be good Americans. Teachers and their school boards faced the cold war by adopting a patriotic curriculum. In 1951, as U.S. troops were fighting "godless Communists" in Korea, New York inaugurated a morning prayer for its public schools which merged nationalism with reverence for authority: "Almighty God we acknowledge our dependence upon Thee, and we beg Thy blessings upon us, our parents, our teachers and our country." Many states passed similar laws, and so a daily exercise became prayers and the Pledge of Allegiance. President Eisenhower suggested that parents remind their children of the "proud deeds and idealistic traditions of our country" and educator Max Rafferty went further, warning that if we do not indoctrinate students with patriotic zeal then they will "turn traitor when confronted with the brutal reality of Red military force."[11] Civics, a term that no teacher ever defined, really was nationalism, and students spent hours memorizing the Bill of Rights and Declaration of Independence. When students studied history, their textbooks reported only about "great Presidents," "strong-willed pioneers who conquered the west," or "hard-working *men* who built America." History was in consensus, everyone apparently agreed, and high school history teachers sounded like coaches bragging about their teams as they told teenagers how these rich and powerful men, these best and brightest of the last century, had "made America what it is today—the greatest country on earth!"

It was soothing pabulum, comforting, and so was being part of a group during cold war culture. Americans joined organizations—clubs, lodges, corporations, fraternities, sororities, legions, and leagues. Church membership increased to record levels. The Reverend Billy Graham warned about godless communism, "master-minded by Satan," and urged citizens to be loyal Americans by being loyal Christians. After church, mothers attended clubs while fathers coached Little League or Babe Ruth. In high school virtually everyone wanted to make the team or be a cheerleader, for that was the key to being well rounded and well adjusted. "Be normal," dad would tell the kids, "and you will be popular." And play sports, for recreation called for the same type of teamwork and determination that fathers had employed to win the war. "I gotta make the team," teenage boys would say over and over again in an era when individual exercise was scorned; during the fifties the sight of a roadside jogger would have caused a traffic accident.

There was security in numbers, and no one lamented the demise of individualism more than William H. Whyte, Jr. In 1956 he published *The Organization Man*, in which he noted that the junior executive was an example of the organization man, but so were the seminary students preparing to work for the church hierarchy, the doctor in the corporate clinic, the Ph.D. in the government laboratory, the engineer in the huge drafting room at Lockheed, or the attorney at his practice on Wall Street.

Whyte wondered what had happened to ideas such as hard work, thrift, independence, and competition. He was concerned about the concentration of power in corporations and civil service bureaucracies, and the "possible emergence of a managerial hierarchy that might dominate the rest of us." Whyte feared that individuals had become isolated and meaningless, that the source of creativity had become the group, and that American universities were educating a generation of bureaucrats. The students, he claimed, were conservative, but not in the philosophical sense: "Their conservatism is passive. No cause seizes them." They were interested in enlisting in the corporate army. "I don't think AT&T is very exciting," one senior stated, "but that's the company I'd like to join. If a depression comes there will always be an AT&T." Another favorite, of course, was working for a giant food conglomerate, for "people always have to eat." Whyte lamented: "What price bitch goddess Success?"

Naturally, some students had been intimidated by McCarthyism. At the University of Michigan in 1952 nine out of ten students were afraid to sign a document; it was the Declaration of Independence without the first sentence. When one activist at Yale University organized a chapter of the Student League for Industrial Democracy he discovered that the few students who attended meetings would not place their names on membership roles. The group only had five active members and "everybody had prepared the speech he was going to deliver to the House Un-American Activities Committee."

But most students simply did not care about issues that could have stimulated debate, even protest—the relatively unpopular Korean War, growing nuclear arsenals, atmospheric atomic testing, curtailment of civil liberties, and inequality for women and minorities. The thought of 50,000 collegians marching on the Pentagon in the 1950s was preposterous. One student later wrote that although papers were filled with issues during her four years in college, 1954 to 1958, she only "glanced at headlines or skimmed an occasional article on these events; certainly, the issues they represented were never the subject of even a few moments' discussion among my friends." When a professor in 1957 confronted his students, and complained that they accepted conformity and security, one of them responded: "Why should we go out on a limb about anything? We know what happened to those who did." Another expressed gratitude to Senator McCarthy for teaching a valuable lesson to his generation: "to keep its mouth shut."

"American college students today," a social scientist wrote in 1957, "tend to think alike, feel alike and believe alike. . . . The great majority seem turned out of a common mold." That professor had conducted a survey at sixteen universities and he summarized that the "dominant characteristic of students in the current generation is that they are *gloriously contented.*" Their parents had taught them well—like father, like son. In a set of national interviews 40 percent of young men could think of no way in which they wanted to be different from their dad. They looked forward to a professional career, especially one which was "steady." These future organization men pledged fraternities; these future executives enrolled in business colleges, as more male students studied business and commerce than the sciences and liberal arts combined. When females were asked to write a short essay describing how they expected to be living in ten years, 46 of 50 sophomores outlined almost identical scenarios: married to a successful professional man or junior executive, living in a suburb, chauffeuring three or four children in a station wagon, and participating in various civic organizations. For most students, the exciting events on campus were football games, panty raids, or trips to drive-ins. As one later remembered: We "spray-painted the fraternity insignia on an overpass. In 1954 they called that rebellion." There was no revolt, and a professor in Texas lamented that his students were a "generation without responses—apathetic, laconic, no great loves, no profound hates, and pitifully few enthusiasms."

They became known as the Silent Generation. Professors called them "listeners," even "goalkeepers." One professor carped, "It's almost as if they were painted on the wall," and another wondered, "Are they really listening? Their minds are as quiet as mice." By the end of the decade a young professor attempted to demonstrate that students really were not silent, that they actually had views, so he interviewed college seniors at Princeton. "I want to rise in status as far as my abilities will carry me," one said. "But I'm a coward when it comes to taking a chance. I don't want to gamble. What I want is a stable order of things in which I can work without exposing myself to ruin." Another told of his plans: "I would like to have enough money to be comfortable and somewhat well-to-do. . . . I want a comfortable, friendly home where I can hang my hat, with a wife I can love, and be loved by, a couple of kids, and a dog whose ears I can scratch." With dogged stoicism these students soberly marched toward gray flannel adulthood. [12]

Perhaps their label—the Silent Generation—was unfair, for they did talk, but they sounded just like their parents, so void of thought that perhaps they should have held their breath. Appropriately, a decade or so later when the nation was inflamed with protest and when the Silent Generation was relaxing into middle age, many of them earned a new label— the Silent Majority.

Silence was particularly expected from "coeds," as male professors called their female students. As an increasing number of young women flocked to college, advisers carefully guided them toward education and nursing, traditional female disciplines, so they would not compete with men. College administrators also decided that coeds needed a curriculum that would serve society's demands that girls grow up to become happy homemakers: home economics. While the University of Illinois directed male students toward business and engineering classes, they advised females about Home Economics 182, "Clothing Selection." The professions were for men, and administrators at most universities employed quotas to reserve their seats. At the University of Texas, for example, 95 percent of those accepted to law and medical school were male, and of the one hundred students in each new dental class only two could be female. The reason for this, the male dean admitted as late as 1970, was "girls aren't strong enough to pull teeth." Females in that state could not become veterinarians because that school was located at Texas A&M, the only land grant university in the nation that admitted just men. Furthermore, if coeds received their degrees, then they faced unfair competition for jobs. Madeleine Kunin, who graduated with a journalism degree from Columbia, was offered a job at one paper in the cafeteria, not the newsroom, and another company refused to hire her because a female reporter had been raped in their parking lot. Women who were hired started at a lower salary than men, and in hard times they were the first fired.

Faced with limited educational and career opportunities, coeds realized that it was in their interest to embrace the traditional role. At Smith College the student newspaper noted in 1961, "Perhaps we are old-fashioned, but we feel that for the majority of women, their place is 'in the home.' " Marriage, the editors continued, was a career. It was an "inappropriate wish" to become a doctor, so "Why don't we stop competing with the men, and instead cooperate with them?" In an insecure era, Mr. Right was security, for he would be a good father and provider. One study demonstrated that coeds during the fifties married younger than their mothers, and that they left college more often without degrees but with husbands with degrees, and in fact, one-half of coeds in mid-decade dropped out of college to marry. An educator declared that college for women was the "world's best marriage mart," and a Smith senior got right to the point when asked about her future ambitions: "I would like to be married to a Princeton graduate." Not being engaged by their last year on campus meant "senior panic," and one coed admitted, "On every blind date we all hoped to meet the handsome, smart, witty young man—with shining prospects and a beautiful soul—we would marry." Seniors intensified their search, and one observer noted that the "new girl on campus confronts a legion of coeds far more intent on getting their man than the F.B.I."

Coeds learned these lessons from their mothers. After the war older women left defense plants, returned home, and found security in marriage and family. As one scholar noted, because of anxieties created by the cold war, women sought the warm hearth—home and family. The family provided security in an insecure world, a "sense of responsibility, a feeling of being a member of a group," one dad admitted, that always would "face its external enemies together."[13]

As a consequence teens were "going steady" at record rates during the fifties, women married younger than at any time in the century, and the divorce rate plummeted. Marriage equaled success. *Ladies' Home Journal, McCall's, Redbook,* and other women's magazines ran one article after another: "Marriage Is Here to Stay," "Making Marriage Work," "How to Stay Married Though Unhappy," "Can This Marriage Be Saved?" Divorce equaled failure. Opinion polls demonstrated in 1957 that only 9 percent of the public believed that an unmarried person could be happy: No female wanted to remain single and become an "old maid." "Except for the sick, the badly crippled, the deformed, the emotionally warped and mentally defective," one author wrote, "almost everyone has an opportunity to marry."

Then came children, which, according to the accepted message of the decade, gave females fulfillment. The momism myth was that every normal woman had a maternal instinct (but, curiously, the father did not have a paternal one), and that the mother should stay home to attend the children. As *Life* declared in the special Christmas issue of 1956, "of all accomplishments of the American woman, the one she brings off with the most spectacular success is having babies." And they did; the birth rate soared to four million births annually—the baby boom. The number of families with three kids doubled, with four kids tripled, and sitcoms and movies advocated that childbirth and family life was "cheaper by the dozen." Procreation to the average collegiate was nifty; as one Harvard business major said, "I'd like to have six kids. I don't know why I say that—it just sounds like a minimum production goal."

America embraced the traditional role, husband in the lead and wife at home. A survey found that concerning the repetitive but essential chores around the house of cleaning and washing, only ten percent of husbands helped their happy homemakers. She embellished the home and then created another recipe for dinner. In 1955 the two nonfiction best-sellers were *Better Homes & Gardens Decorating Book* and *Betty Crocker's Cookbook.* The result was the "Happy Home Corporation," as Pat Boone labeled his family in *'Twixt Twelve and Twenty.* Boone named his wife the executive vice president, and naturally saved the top job for himself, for "when the chips are down . . . it's got to be this way." Men had responsibilities, and they dutifully marched to their anointed role. As one recalled: "Those of us who came of age in the fifties had no choice. You had to be a husband, a provider, and a success."[14]

To many Americans, the fifties were Happy Days. From the perspective of the older generation, the decade was a vast improvement over the previous era of Depression and war. In 1957 a poll asked, "Taking all things together, how would you say things are these days—would you say you're very happy, pretty happy or not too happy?" A resounding 89 percent were either very or pretty happy.

Why? During the last half of the 1950s the Korean conflict was history and politics were returning to normalcy. McCarthyism was on the wane, and Grandfather Ike was on the golf course or relaxing at the White House. In addition, the fifties were happy because of two reasons—babies and bucks. "Kids: Built-In Recession Cure," proclaimed *Life*. "Rocketing Births: Business Bonanza." *Time* declared, "1955 showed the flowering of American capitalism," and it kept on blooming. The gross national product doubled during the decade, inflation remained low, and American consumption soared. As the babies grew up the five-and-dime era became a feast, "The Big Barbeque." The average home contained seven times more equipment than one in the 1920s. Parents showered themselves or their kids with gifts, resulting in a constant supply of fads—saddle shoes, Barbie dolls, and endless stacks of 45 records. During the last half of the fifties parents bought almost $300 million worth of toy guns, boots, chaps, lassos branded by the likes of Hopalong Cassidy, Gene Autry, Roy Rogers, Wyatt Earp, and the Cisco Kid. The Davy Crockett television series alone produced a market of a million coonskin hats, while kids bought 20 million Hula-Hoops in just a few months of 1958. More high school guys had cars, and their girls dressed better and could afford more cosmetics, than at any previous time in history. "We are the luckiest teenagers in the history of the world," wrote Geoffrey O'Brien. "We have been given cozy and well-protected suites. . . . We've inherited some fabulous floor space."

The surging market relieved cold war stress and provided a well-fed slumber for older citizens and a gushing optimism for many youngsters. "If you grew up in the 1950s," recalled Robert J. Samuelson, "you were constantly treated to the marvels of the time. At school, you were vaccinated against polio, until then a dread disease. At home, you watched television. Every so often, you looked up into the sky and saw the white vapor trails of a new jet. You stared until the plane vanished. There was an endless array of new gadgets and machines. No problem seemed beyond solution. Good times and the power of American technology: these were not lessons learned, they were experiences absorbed. You took prosperity for granted. . . . We came to believe that prosperity was inevitable."

The Happy Days idea was broadcast throughout the era on popular television shows, beginning with "I Love Lucy," "Topper," "Leave It to Beaver," "The Donna Reed Show," and ending with "My Three Sons" and "The Beverly Hillbillies." Two favorite sitcoms were "The Adventures of Ozzie and Harriet" and "Father Knows Best." Nicely dressed in his alpaca cardigan, Ozzie demonstrated the art of being DAD, and when joined by Harriet, David, and Ricky, the Nelsons exemplified the perfect family from 1952 until 1966. Here was American home life in the suburbs, complete with brick fireplace, eagle over the mantle, two sons, and a wife who always seemed to have a fresh plate of cookies or a hot pot of coffee. Nothing serious ever happened: Ricky would borrow David's sweater without asking, then refuse to give it back. It would take thirty minutes to resolve the crisis since Ozzie seemed to be as bright as a potato. Family battles were just simple misunderstandings, and one never had to think about the outcome in the suburbs. Just by watching it, one critic noted, the viewer automatically knew that "Ozzie and Harriet were Republican; she bought frozen vegetables; Ozzie never cheated on Harriet." The "Nelsons' adventures weren't very adventurous. Or very real." Yet that made little difference, for most viewers wanted to be like them.

So did the competition, which appeared in 1954 as "Father Knows Best." In an era of family togetherness, father was a super-daddy who could and would do anything. Jim Anderson (Robert Young) was wise, warm, and understanding; his wife Margaret (Jane Wyatt) was a perfect mother and thoughtful homemaker. The show, one critic wrote, "seemed to both epitomize and exploit the mood that prevailed throughout the country. Eisenhower was President and Robert Young was Father. They could have traded jobs at any time and no one would have noticed the difference. . . . 'Father Knows Best' reinforced American mythology in the '50s. It was the same reality that forced Jane Wyatt, in one bedroom scene with Robert Young, to wear a brassiere under her nightgown. That seemed to typify the program, which was about as realistic as a bra under a nightie."

Neither show was realistic, neither touched a social issue, but that did not matter. Audiences tuned in because television simply reflected what most people thought—or hoped—was real: there was an American Way. Everyone was the same, living in suburbs, married, and happy. Yet a minority of citizens were concerned about that picture of America. They realized that even during Happy Days there were problems in the nation, and in the late 1950s three issues gradually appeared: life in the atomic age, the role of women, and the status of blacks.

In 1955, because of above-ground atomic testing, radioactive rain fell on Chicago. Then, two years later, the Soviets shocked the world by launching a satellite, Sputnik. The vehicle rotated and reflected light from the heavens above the USA, and certain evenings radio stations would inform listeners where to view the satellite. A baby boomer remembered, " 'Look,' my mother would say to me in our suburb, 'there goes the Russians,' and seeing it floating above and blinking would send a shiver down my spine." Another added: "We might not remember Hiroshima, but we recall fallout shelters. Civil Defense. Air raid sirens. We hid beneath school desks, stored contingency rations. We set our dials on Conelrad. We lived in the backwash of nuclear holocaust without thinking such a condition absurd. . . . A nightmare was eternity spent underground, in a concrete bunker, alone."[15]

Sputnik renewed atomic fear. "The Russian success in launching the satellite has been something equivalent to Pearl Harbor," wrote British Ambassador Harold Macmillan. "The American cocksureness is shaken." Two years later, in 1959, deadly strontium-90 began to show up in milk, and two-thirds of Americans listed nuclear war as the nation's most urgent problem, a topic portrayed in successful books such as Walter Miller's *A Canticle for Leibowitz* and later in popular movies like *On the Beach*, *Fail-Safe*, and *Dr. Strangelove*. The last scene from *On the Beach* was an empty city with a banner waving in the radioactive breeze, "There is still time, Brother." The first issue of *Playboy* adopted a different approach: Marilyn Monroe's barely concealed breasts were on the cover, which the editors noted would provide men with "a little diversion from the anxieties of the Atomic Age."

For women there were few diversions, and some were beginning to question their role. After World War II, *Fortune* conducted a survey which asked women, If you could be reborn, would you rather return as a male or female? A surprising 25 percent marked male. It was "a man's world," according to a common saying, and during the fifties some women found themselves in a dilemma—they had educated themselves, many worked, but their only opportunity for management was in the home over the ironing board or at the dinner table. All the while they were bombarded with advice from "experts" such as psychologist Cleo Dawson, whose article "How to Manage a Woman" was published in *Reader's Digest*. Her research discovered "two truths: 1. All women like to work under a ceiling of authority. In short, they like to be bossed. 2. All women must feel that they are needed. These truths arise from the fact that, basically, women *feel* while men *think*." Dawson's report was one of hundreds of such articles, and such ideas compelled many women to question their popular image. Early in the 1960s, Betty Friedan challenged that

This strange discrepancy also appeared in studies on sexuality. During the late 1940s Alfred C. Kinsey conducted his famous research which demonstrated that sexual practices were more permissive than public morality. While this shocked the older generation, most future activists were too young to know what was going on behind closed doors. They were influenced by contemporary morals outside the bedroom, the "double standard," one for men and another for women. According to the double standard, a man had pent-up urges that occasionally had to be released. Late some night he visited the other side of the tracks for action with a loose girl; after she "serviced" him, he'd boast to his buddies and refer to her as a skag or slut. Like nations in the cold war, females were either good or bad. "Good girls" were different, for they carried the heavy responsibility of being virtuous, upholding the moral fiber of the boys— and of America. Good girls said, "No," "I'll lose my reputation," "Not 'til we're married," and while the hormones ran wild, they panted until wedding bells. Half the brides and grooms in the fifties were teen-agers.

This moral code was supported by the vast majority of Americans, and opinion polls demonstrated that 80 percent agreed with the statement that a woman should be a virgin when she married. After wedding bells, she was his property. As one young man explained: "After marriage, some guy taking out my wife would be like taking my car and putting on a few extra miles. It might improve through use, but I like to drive my own."

Such ideas were strictly enforced as authorities levied heavy fines for unsanctioned behavior. In high schools across the nation principals acted like policemen. "Our principal had one job," a baby boomer remembered, "to maintain law and order. He was bald, and we called him chromedome. He had the ability to dig his thumb between your muscles and hit the nerve, as if he had taken a course on how to give pain." Another wrote: "The administration's mistrust of students was very nearly paranoid. We were required to carry huge wooden passes if we left class to go to the bathroom. . . . Smoking was forbidden within a block of the school building, not because it was unhealthy but because it was considered unseemly behavior for teenagers." School boards expelled pregnant girls, who were not allowed to graduate. Universities monitored coed behavior in dorms or off campus. In 1960, Michigan State officials expelled a student who had been raped, and then went public by pressing charges against the assailant. At that time most Americans felt that females who endured such tragedy really had "asked for it." Two years later at Stanford a coed attended a party with her boyfriend. After both drank too much and passed out on a lawn, he was suspended for one quarter, but she for two. The charge: "leaving herself defenseless in the presence of a male."[17]

Governments passed laws, ordinances, and made rulings. The use of birth control, even between married couples, was banned in many states, and in Massachusetts the penalty for dispensing a can of contraceptive foam was five years in jail. Abortion was illegal nationally. Cohabitation among unmarried couples was unlawful in cities, and some states had laws similar to Alabama where it was criminal to participate in extramarital sexual intercourse. In Florida, nursing a baby in public was legally obscene, "indecent exposure, lewd and lascivious behavior." Some local governments even passed ordinances prohibiting the sale of bikinis as a way to "control promiscuity." As the federal government censored racy books such as *Fanny Hill*, *Tropic of Cancer*, and *Lady Chatterley's Lover*, television producers did the same with their media. In 1956, when Elvis Presley appeared on the "Ed Sullivan Show," the performer with the gyrating pelvis was broadcast as a half man, only from the waist up. In the early 1960s, Barbara Eden, who played a genie with a bare midriff in "I Dream of Jeanie," never appeared with a navel; her belly button was censored. Movies upheld the standard, as most citizens apparently felt that in the "battle of the sexes" there should never be sex, only *Pillow Talk*. After Otto Preminger produced *The Moon Is Blue*, a judge ordered an injunction, claiming that by contemporary standards the film contained vulgar language. The scandalous words were "seduction," "pregnant," and "virgin."

Sexual standards, of course, only demonstrated hypocrisy in 1950s America. Actually, half the teenage brides in the decade were pregnant— they "had to get married." Obviously, teens were doing something else besides watching the movie in the back seat of the '57 Chevy. Yet the older generation refused to face such facts. It was almost unpatriotic to see things unpleasant in America.

Some things were best left unsaid, many parents reminded their children, and that included discussions about race. During the fifties most blacks lived in the South, the vast majority in small towns or rural areas. For them the status quo was just a step away from slavery; it was a system of segregation called Jim Crow. Based on the 1896 Supreme Court ruling of *Plessy v. Ferguson* allowing "separate but equal" public facilities for the two races, 17 southern and border states had passed laws that established Jim Crow segregation. Public facilities were segregated. Concerning education, southerners saved money at the black schools, which often were shacks where teachers made about a third of white counterparts. In Clarendon County, South Carolina, officials spent $179 on every white student in 1950 and $43 on each black one; fourteen years later in Holly Bluff, Mississippi, those figures were over $190 for a white student and $1.26 for each black. The few blacks who remained in school and graduated faced the same situation in higher education. By Texas law, three-fourths of federal land grant funds were spent at white Texas A&M while a quarter went to black Prairie View A&M. This was the South's interpretation of "separate but equal."

Black voting rights were restricted throughout the South by legal gimicks such as white primaries, literacy tests, poll taxes, and even good character tests. White registrars simply would ask potential black voters an unanswerable question. "How many bubbles are in a four ounce bar of Ivory soap?" an official asked Carey Cauley in Alabama. When Cauley could not answer, he was deemed illiterate, unable to register. In 1958 the Civil Rights Commission found that in Alabama only 9 percent of blacks in the state were registered to vote, and that figure was only 4 percent for Mississippi. The commission also found 16 counties across the South which had a majority of black residents but not one black voter.

Jim Crow, however, reached beyond education and voting rights and seeped into society. Former Confederate states passed laws that established segregated hospitals, jails, and homes for the indigent, deaf, dumb, and even for the blind. "Whites Only" or "Colored" signs hung in bus and railway stations, sports arenas, swimming pools, and over toilets and water fountains. In Atlanta, white and black witnesses in court could not swear on the same Bible. In Alabama, a game of integrated checkers was illegal, while in New Orleans officials segregated prostitutes and red-light districts. The status of southern blacks was aptly described by signs the Texas Restaurant Association distributed for its members' windows: "We Do Not Serve Mexicans, Niggers, or Dogs."

To be sure, blacks had made some progress during the Truman administration, and their lives were better in the North. The Commander-in-Chief ordered the integration of the armed forces, which was implemented slowly, and the Supreme Court ruled that blacks could not be kept out of public graduate schools because of their race. In professional sports, Jackie Robinson broke the color line by taking the field for the Brooklyn Dodgers. Conditions were better in the North, but in no way equal. Schools usually were segregated in fact since school districts followed discriminatory housing practices; where there was a ghetto, there was a black school. Almost 90 percent of Chicago blacks attended all-black schools, while 27 public schools in Philadelphia were almost entirely segregated. Northern blacks did have voting rights, but since few politicians addressed their issues their registration rates were low, as was their usual turnout on election day.

In both the North and South, most white Americans were racists. Popular opinion polls revealed that 97 percent of southern and 90 percent of northern whites opposed interracial dating, while three-fourths of southern and half of northern whites opposed having a black neighbor. Country-western singers profited by recording tunes which were titled "Kajun Ku Klux Klan" or "Looking for a Handout," and one about how to chase blacks out of neighborhoods, "NAACP Flight No. 105," which sold a million copies. Racial slurs and "nigger jokes" were common throughout the nation. Whites might refer to the balcony as "nigger heaven" or Brazil nuts as "nigger toes"; they might respond to a generous act with "mighty white of you." If given the finger, young men might respond, "Is that your I.Q. or your number of white parents?" Once they became of age they were "free, white, and twenty-one." Racism even followed the black man into the grave for when he died a benevolent white might pay a compliment by writing in the obituary column, "He was a black man, but he had a white heart."

Such statements took their toll. Parents of light-skinned blacks did not want their children to date darker ones, and many felt shame at simply being black. Roger Wilkins later wrote about growing up in the 1950s: "I was ashamed of myself, my whole being. I was ashamed of my color, my kinky hair, my broad nose and my thick lips. . . . I would sometimes lie on my back and stare up at passing clouds and wonder why God had played such a dirty trick by making me a Negro."[18]

To a lesser extent, American society was intolerant toward all minorities. In ethnic cities, and especially in suburban homes filled only with white families, racial slurs were common: Mexicans = greasers; Puerto Ricans = spicks; Asians = chinks; and Jews = kikes, yids, or jewboys. Anyone who gave something and then wanted it back was an "indian giver," and there might have been more slurs about "injuns" but Americans did not know any more about "redskins" than they knew the next decade about "dinks" and "gooks," the Vietnamese. Racism infected even the wealthy and educated. Ivy League colleges often limited the number of Jewish students, and consequently the Jewish community established Brandeis University. Public universities allowed discriminatory practices. "There were more than forty sororities at Berkeley in 1961," Sara Davidson wrote, "but only three accepted Jewish girls." At the exclusive Choate School, one of the few Jewish students opened his geometry text and found the following note: "Fuck You, You Kike." "At Choate," he later wrote, "racist remarks were as much a part of our daily lives as the chapel services which we were required to attend each night."

Yet slurs were minor compared with the problem of making a living, for being black was being poor. In 1960 the Department of Labor reported that the average black worker made less than 60 percent of white counterparts. Blacks held the worst jobs. Fewer than 7 percent of them had professional or managerial positions, about a fourth of the figure for whites, while about half of black men were unskilled workers or laborers. In New York City, a third of black women were domestic servants. Those who became educated also found wage discrimination; in the South, black college graduates earned about half of white graduates, and in the north about two-thirds. "If all the discriminatory laws in the United States were immediately repealed," Michael Harrington wrote, "race would still remain as one of the most pressing moral and political problems in the nation. Negroes and other minorities are not simply the victims of a series of iniquitous statutes. The American economy, the American society, the American unconscious are all racist."[19]

Racism was a national problem, but it was more brutal in the South. Legions of politicians had made careers on "keepin' them in their place," while others were simply thoughtless. When Governor Luther Hodges of North Carolina appeared in 1955 as a guest speaker at a black college he mispronounced the word "Negro" as "nigra," not once, but three times. One might wonder how a southern politician speaking to a black group could not know enough about the other race to know how to pronounce Negro. John Howard Griffin, the white Texan who dyed his skin dark and traveled throughout the Deep South in 1959, provided the answer: "Though we lived side by side throughout the South, communication between the two races had simply ceased to exist. Neither really knew what went on with those of the other race. The Southern Negro will not tell the white man the truth. He long ago learned that if he speaks a truth unpleasing to the white, the white will make life miserable for him."

Those who tried to cross the "color line," who attempted to use the rights guaranteed by the Constitution, received a blunt warning or a vicious response. When blacks in Montgomery, Alabama, decided in 1955 to boycott the indignity of sitting in the back of the bus, local whites handed out a flyer: "When in the course of human events it becomes necessary to abolish the Negro race, proper methods should be used. Among these are guns, bows and arrows, sling shots and knives. We hold these truths to be self evident, that all whites are created equal with certain rights: among these are life, liberty and the pursuit of dead niggers." That was mild compared with the beatings, and compared with the killings. There were numerous examples, but one of the most flagrant miscarriages of justice was when a 14-year-old black from Chicago, Emmett Till, visited Mississippi. Unaware of "southern customs," he supposedly said "Bye, baby" to a white woman. Shortly thereafter, local whites captured him, cut off his testicles, shot him in the head, and then dumped his mangled body in a local river. Although the killers later confessed, the white jury acquitted them.[20] This brutal murder was not atypical—between the 1880s and the 1950s southerners lynched over 3800 blacks.

When journalist Walter Winchell asked a young black woman early in 1945 how Hitler should be punished for his war crimes, her answer was appropriate for the South before the civil rights movement: "Paint him black and send him over here."

The Supreme Court was aware of the plight of the African American, and in 1954 the justices made a landmark decision—*Brown v. Board of Education*. The National Association for the Advancement of Colored People (NAACP) filed on behalf of a black student, Linda Brown, who was *bused* out of her white neighborhood to attend a black school in

Topeka, Kansas. Chief Justice Earl Warren read the opinion: "Does segregation of children in public schools solely on the basis of race, even though the physical facilities and other tangible factors may be equal, deprive the children of the minority group of equal educational opportunities? We unanimously believe that it does." The court ruled that separate educational facilities were "inherently unequal," and the Chief Justice ordered segregated districts to integrate in "all deliberate speed."

The southern response was immediate and forceful—massive resistance. Mississippi Senator James O. Eastland warned that the South "will not abide by nor obey this legislative decision by a political court," and these words were confirmed by legislation, editorials, letters, and opinion polls. Southern congressmen stated their opposition by signing a "Declaration of Constitutional Principles" which proclaimed that the court had no power to demand an end to segregation while it reaffirmed states' rights by passing more than 450 laws and resolutions to prevent or limit integration. Southern states also passed laws aimed at crippling the NAACP. The attorney generals of Louisiana, Alabama, and Texas issued injunctions to prohibit the NAACP from operating in their states. Arkansas and Tennessee attempted to pass legislation that outlawed the organization, a law that was passed in Alabama. In Florida the legislature appropriated $50,000 to investigate "communist involvement" in the NAACP. Southern feelings appeared in the press. An engineer in Houston wrote that most "folks who have never lived down here in the South don't know the problems we have to cope with. There ought to be other ways of helping the colored folks than by living with them, going to church with them and having them in our schools." Opinion polls demonstrated that over 80 percent of white southerners opposed school desegregation, and a quarter felt that using violence was justified to maintain white supremacy. Southerners organized locally by joining vigilante committees, the Ku Klux Klan, or by forming White Citizens Councils. These councils raised money, held rallies and demonstrations, boycotted integrated businesses, and passed out handbills such as one circulating in Greenwood, Mississippi, that listed the black crime and illegitimate birth rates and asked, "How would integration affect the moral standards of our white children?" Or one Dallas flyer entitled "The Worst Horror on Earth," which was that after school integration white daughters would come home with black boyfriends.[21]

Southern racial feelings were dramatized throughout the decade. While blacks made some progress boycotting buses in Montgomery, Alabama, and other cities, and while they integrated a few school districts such as Central High School in Little Rock, those victories were only local triumphs. Much more typical was that southern states simply ignored federal court rulings, and that was allowed by the Justice Department during the Eisenhower presidency. Although the Supreme Court ruled in 1944 that white primaries were unconstitutional, the vast majority of southern blacks still were disfranchised in 1960. Although the Court ruled in 1958 that discrimination in interstate travel was unconstitutional, buses and trains throughout the South remained segregated. And although the Court ordered integration in the Brown case in 1954, only 1 percent of southern schools integrated per year—at that speed all black children finally would be attending integrated schools in the year 2054. Obviously, legal and legislative tactics for bringing about equality had limitations, a point not missed by activists of the sixties.

Southern reasons for maintaining white supremacy were always the same. They talked of maintaining the "Southern Way of Life," and of "Christian values." They were for "states' rights," and against "federal interference," "race mongrelization," and, of course, Communism. Southern politicians spoke out against subversives and state governments held hearings which were aimed to prove that Communists were responsible for blacks demanding their civil rights, or, in other words, that "colored folks" were happy with their plight but they were being manipulated by outside agitators. The White Citizens Council of Louisville handed out flyers: "EXPOSED! The Communist Plot to Integrate Public Schools, Pools and Housing Projects," and Louisiana conducted hearings in 1958 on the "Subversion in Racial Unrest: An Outline of a Strategic Weapon to Destroy the Governments of Louisiana and the United States." The committee chairman, W. M. Rainach, proclaimed that the publication presented the "first official outline of the Communist conspiracy originating with Joseph Stalin that is now widely acknowledged as the origin and guiding influence behind the move to integrate the public schools of the South."

Actually, Communism had nothing to do with the demands for civil rights, but that made little difference: many Americans believed that it did. The rationale seemed to fit cold war culture, especially in the South. The southern minority who did not agree, who questioned the racial status quo, were either local "liberals" or "outside agitators." Them not Us. After Mississippi newspaperman P. D. East published editorials asking for "fairness" toward blacks, subscriptions and advertisements were canceled, his friends turned against him, and he received telephone calls telling him that he was a "goddamn nigger-loving, Jew-loving, communist son-of-a-bitch." He began carrying a gun.[22] In the South at this time being a nigger-lover and Communist were synonymous.

Moreover, to most Americans, the "Negro Problem" was not their concern. "In the North," the saying went, "segregation was a Southern problem that only Southerners could solve. In the South, it was a problem only time could solve." During cold war culture, there would never be enough time, and blacks were not a concern because they were invisible. They did not appear in national, state, or local politics, unless one was elected from Harlem, and they did not appear on television, unless they played stereotypes on "The Amos 'n' Andy Show" or the "Jack Benny Show." Blacks were out of sight, out of mind, and in 1952 Ralph Ellison best described this in *The Invisible Man* when the black main character stated: "I am invisible, understand, simply because people refuse to see me."

More recently, in the conservative era that followed the sixties, a number of commentators have revised and rebutted the theme that the fifties were times of consensus and complacency. Instead, they have written that the decade was "when the going was good!" It was a proud time, a creative era in which a confident nation made great strides. Indeed, a historian has claimed, the fifties were an "American High . . . a time of hope, a time of growth, and in its best moments, even a time of glory." This argument might have some merit, or it might tell readers more about the 1980s when these books were published than about the 1950s, or it might say something about the authors—all of whom are white males born before the Second World War.[23]

What needs to be emphasized here is not the historical debate on the 1950s—but the future activist's *perception* of that decade. Kids growing up during those years who later became active in the movement did not view the fifties as a time of glory or a very creative era. Instead, they perceived the decade in terms of conformity and consensus, rules and regulations. As teenagers, many of them began to realize that they would rebel against the double standards, and against the lifestyle of their parents: "I loved them," Jane Alpert wrote, "yet it had been clear to me since I was thirteen that I would never be happy living as they did." For "young people like myself," wrote Tom Hayden, "the world of the fifties was largely a one-dimensional one . . . lacking in any real social conflict. There seemed to be only one reality, one set of values: those of the comfortable middle class. There being only that one reality, life was already programmed: You went to high school, then college, then got married and found a job. . . . It was the boring and prearranged nature of this existence that caused the first tiny irritations that would grow to rebellion later."[24]

Rebellion, of course, would not wait for the sixties. American society is not a monolith, and so there was some dissent, especially in the second half of the fifties after the death of the enemy, Joseph Stalin, and during the demise of McCarthyism.

A few brave academics stood up and fought the anti-Communist crusade. University of Wisconsin historian Merle Curti and his wife attempted to get residents to sign a recall petition against Senator McCarthy, but with little success, and Henry Steele Commager spoke out against the red scare in schools and universities. It betrayed the intellectual principles of a democracy, Commager stated, and he saw no evidence that Communist professors "actually did harm to students." College students were not "such nincompoops that they are unable to distinguish between truth and falsehood, between impartial teaching and propaganda." Nor do "they invariably believe all that their teachers tell them." Novelist Mary McCarthy agreed, writing that far from being in danger of Communist indoctrination, students should worry about "being stupefied by the complacent propaganda for democracy."

Yet cries in the academic wilderness were whispers compared with the growing roar from teenagers. In many cities teens formed gangs and conducted warfare. In suburbs the young grew restless, and parents became increasingly worried about one of the most important issues of the fifties—juvenile delinquency. Hollywood explored the topic in many perceptive movies such as *The Wild One, East of Eden, Splendor in the Grass,* and *Rebel Without a Cause.* In these movies the usual cause of youthful rebellion was that father had been fighting the war when the kids were young, and the message was clear: When Dad, the authority, the leader, was away, the kids rebeled, a threat to the family and therefore to the nation. In *Blackboard Jungle* Glenn Ford starred as a New York City teacher who was attacked by his students. Discouraged with teaching, Ford returned to his university and asked his mentor how he could get "crazy kids" to learn. As the National Anthem provided background music, the old sage pontificated about duty, honor, and patriotism. Juvenile delinquency, of course, had little to do with nationalism and instead demonstrated that the status quo was not so comfortable for everyone. Many teens sitting in theaters could relate to the characters portrayed by Montgomery Clift, Marlon Brando, and James Dean. When Judy (Natalie Wood) asked her new neighbor Jim Stark (James Dean) in *Rebel,* "Do you live around here?" Stark's response became a classic statement of teenage alienation for the decade: "Who lives?" "Whatever it was," said a later activist, "after you saw something like *Rebel Without a Cause,* you felt like going out and breaking a few windshields. And once in a while, you did, or at least you chucked a couple of water balloons at passing cars. That was you, man, a brooding nobody with something silent inside just seething to get out."

Other teenagers turned to an increasing number of new rebels without a cause. Jules Feiffer's cartoons, the comedy of Lenny Bruce or Mort Sahl satirized society while *Mad* magazine brutalized traditional values and mocked national leaders with their grinning, nuclear-age moron Alfred E. Neuman: "What, me worry?" More intellectual New York students might read the *Village Voice,* which covered bohemian life in Greenwich

Village, or Paul Krassner's *Realist*. The *Voice* was the first paper to break the barrier against publishing four-letter words, and by 1960 the *Realist* was destroying almost every other boundary of cold war morality. Krassner's "Magazine of Cherry Pie and Violence" shocked: "I Was an Abortionist for the FBI," "A Kick in the Inaugural Balls," and it attacked sacred cows, "The Sex Life of J. Edgar Hoover." Students also could read J. D. Salinger's *The Catcher in the Rye*, in which the antihero, Holden Caulfield, was kicked out of prep school and tells his story from a mental institution because he cannot adjust to the "phoniness" of American society.

Teenagers also tuned in their radios, for some bands were producing a different sound—one that Bill Haley popularized in 1954 with his hit "Rock Around the Clock." Chuck Berry followed with "Rock 'n' Roll Music," and during the last half of the decade the younger generation began to shake, rattle, and roll. Compared with adult popular music sung by Frank Sinatra, Andy Williams, Julie London, and Perry Como, rock was youthful, vibrant, exciting, as electric guitars and drums moved a younger generation to watch "American Bandstand," attend sock hops, and dance the jitterbug, stroll, walk, shag, and twist.

In a sense, rock demonstrated rebellion. It punched a hole in conformity, but more than that it was a generational revolt. Rock was reserved for teenagers, it "held us together like some kind of mystic glue," recalled a baby boomer. "We lived at 45 revolutions per minute and moved at a decibel range that put it all in code." Rock and roll certainly *sounded rebellious*, but if parents would have stopped yelling "Turn down that noise!" and listened to the lyrics, they would have realized that during the 1950s and early 1960s the message was not much different from their own music—romancing and dancing: Neil Sedaka's "Breaking Up Is Hard to Do"; the Dixie Cups' "Chapel of Love"; Dion's "Runaround Sue"; the Chiffons' "He's So Fine"; Dee Dee Sharp's "Mashed Potato Time"; Chubby Checker's "The Twist"; or Martha and the Vandellas' "Dancing in the Street." Elvis wiggled his hips more than Andy Williams but sang "Love Me Tender," and that message continued into the middle of the next decade with Diana Ross and the Supremes, Beach Boys, and the Beatles: "Love Me Do." Furthermore, musicians during the first decade of rock reinforced the status quo by expressing the contemporary ideas that girls were looking for security in Mr. Right (Shelley Fabares's "Johnny Angel"), that there was a double standard (Big Bopper's "Chantilly Lace"), and that it was a man's world (the Beach Boys' "I Get Around"). Rock demonstrated that Johnny and Sue were restless; the kids were bored, not rebelling, and in the 1950s and early 1960s the only disharmony most teenagers had with society was the jitterbug.

The kids, however, had fooled their parents; the typical adult response to rock was that the music and stars were leading youth toward juvenile delinquency. TV censors banned dances called the Alligator and the Dog from "American Bandstand" because they were "too sexy," and the Senate Subcommittee on Delinquency worried that Elvis Presley could be a dangerous symbol. "His strip-tease antics threaten to 'rock-n-roll' the juvenile world into open revolt against society. The gangster of tomorrow is the Elvis Presley type of today." That, of course, was the same response that parents had concerning fads, as Parent-Teacher Associations across the nation erected "proper" dress codes for local high schools. No jeans for boys, skirts for girls. Since stability was desired, teens looked remarkably like their parents. Girls wore hair that looked like mom's perma-press head, and dear ol' dad cropped his son's hair in World War II style, the crew cut. Parents unfailingly reminded restless teens that such appearance was "in your own best interest." In San Antonio, officials banned "tight blue jeans worn low, or ducktail haircuts, on the grounds that there is a connection between undisciplined dress and undisciplined behavior." [25]

The beatniks delighted in demonstrating undisciplined behavior. Allen Ginsberg realized that something was amiss in America by the late 1940s when he, Jack Kerouac, William Burroughs, and others attended Columbia University. He wondered about the official notion that it was America's Century, in which the national image, the "man of distinction," worked for the efficient, germ-free corporation in the "hyperrationalized skyscraper," agreed with the "dogmatic slumber," and worshipped the "square God of the Garden of Eden." In the late 1940s, Ginsberg worked on a ship and sailors introduced him to marijuana. Using the drug convinced him that personal consciousness was not standard, but variable, and that government statements about drugs and sensory perception were "a fraud, a con job." Authority should be challenged, for the "government didn't know anything, nor did newspapers, nor did the *New York Times*, nor did Texas oil millionaires, nor did elegant pompous senators, nor did giant preachers, nor did Adolf Hitler, nor did anybody actually."

Cold war culture appalled Ginsberg and his friends Gregory Corso, Lawrence Ferlinghetti, Gary Snyder, Jack Kerouac, and other beats who mingled in the Greenwich Village area of New York City or North Beach in San Francisco. To them, McCarthyism, cold war rhetoric, CIA-sponsored coups in Iran and Guatemala all demonstrated the Great Lie— the authorities could not be trusted. America disturbed the beats. John Clellon Holmes explained that the beats were the first generation raised with "peacetime military training as a fully accepted fact of life," to witness "genocide, brain-washing, cybernetics, motivational research," and to grow up with the possibility of atomic Armageddon as the "final answer to all questions." Beats, he concluded, are "specifically the *product* of this world."

This product had a novel, zany approach to literature and to life. In his introduction to *The Beats*, Seymour Krim wrote that "there should be enough here to turn on any reader who has been lusting for some real, unkidding, far-out, truly present-scene typewriter-jazz that *matches* the gone world we live and spin in. What follows is strictly for now, today, this minute, this second. In fact this is *it* and it's time I split." In *On the Road*, Kerouac described beatnik Rollo Greb: "He crawls like a big spider through the streets. His excitement blew out of his eyes in stabs of fiendish light. He rolled his neck in spastic ecstasy. He lisped, he writhed, he flopped, he moaned, he howled, he fell back in despair. He could hardly get a word out, he was so excited with life."[26]

Life to the beats was not the complacent suburbs, the organization man, the silent generation, for these young men wore black, grew beards, talked hip lingo, and frantically hitchhiked around the nation, smoking marijuana, reading poetry, having orgies. As they opted out of contemporary society they viciously attacked cold war culture. Ginsberg wrote a volume of poems entitled *Howl* and in the poem of the same name declared that America was "Moloch! Solitude! Filth! Ugliness! Ashcans and unobtainable dollars! Children screaming under stairways! Boys sobbing in armies! Old men weeping in the parks!" Appropriately for the decade, postal officials seized the volume and declared it obscene.

Beats ridiculed society; they dented the chrome 1950s. They provided a style of rebellion that lent momentum to the idea that a person could question and reject society. They probably influenced some future activists, and so did intellectuals and social critics, who also had a healthy distaste for cold war culture. Lewis Coser, Irving Howe, Erich Fromm, A. J. Muste, Dwight Macdonald, and other dissident social thinkers published their critiques in the *Partisan Review, Commentary, Dissent, Nation* and *New Republic*. Other creative thinkers joined the fray, so by the late 1950s and early 1960s interested students could read Vance Packard's *The Status Seekers*, John Kenneth Galbraith's *The Affluent Society*, William H. Whyte, Jr.'s *The Organization Man*, C. Wright Mills's *The Power Elite*, and Paul Goodman's *Growing Up Absurd*.

Goodman's book blasted the society of the 1950s. Consequently it was rejected by nineteen publishers. To Goodman, society was an "organized system" that avoided risks and relied on role playing and public relations. America was in a stupor: "We seem to have lost our genius for inventing changes to satisfy crying needs." And Goodman questioned: "*How* is it possible to have more meaning and honor in work? to put wealth to some real use? to have a high standard of living of whose quality we are not ashamed? to get social justice for those who have been shamefully left out?" The only hope, he proclaimed, was for youth to revolt against the organized system, the "impregnable feudalism." He issued a clarion call for the sixties: "One has the persistent thought that if ten thousand people in all walks of life will stand up on their two feet and talk out and insist, we shall get back our country."

Another call was issued by C. Wright Mills. A populist from Texas, this sociologist wrote a biting critique of the postwar American establishment, which he labeled "the power elite." He argued that the nation was run by a smug, self-righteous group composed of the chairmen of "two or three hundred giant corporations," the president and his staff, and senior officers at the Pentagon. The merger of economic, political, and military institutions that began during World War II continued afterward so that by the 1950s this elite controlled the fate of millions. Furthermore, they had convinced themselves that they were "The Ones Who Decide." In the privacy of their offices, not in public forum, they decided policy aimed at making the world safe for democracy and capitalism; they presided over "Pax Americana." What the power elite actually constructed, Mills contended, was "crackpot realism," an outlook that equated national security with global intervention; under their rule, democracy had become a hoax.

Historian William Appleman Williams agreed and in 1959 published *The Tragedy of American Diplomacy*, in which he challenged the contemporary idea that the Soviet Union was evil, was attempting to conquer the world, and that the United States was good, the bulwark of freedom. Instead, Williams charged that American foreign policy was based on short-sighted anti-Communism, an expansionist-frontier mentality, and the "open door" idea that U.S. multinational corporations should dominate international commerce. To him, corporate-military-political elites thought of the world as an endless frontier in which the United States had the divine right to expand, and to use its overwhelming power to cast the economies and politics of developing countries into "carbon copies of the United States." Furthermore, he claimed that America's possession of the atomic bomb led policymakers to believe that the weapon guaranteed that the U.S. could run "down that path to world domination."

Williams, Mills, Goodman, Whyte, Galbraith, Macdonald, Riesman questioned American society, as the novels of Albert Camus, Jean-Paul Sartre, Franz Kafka, Herman Hesse questioned Western culture. And in the early 1960s other authors produced influential books. Rachel Carson published *Silent Spring* in 1962, which stimulated Americans to think about the eventual impact of using chemicals such as DDT in soil and on the food supply. Michael Harrington's *The Other America* that year exposed the plight of the poor. Next year, Betty Friedan questioned the contemporary role of women in *The Feminine Mystique*, and in 1964 Herbert Marcuse wrote *One-Dimensional Man*, which suggested that youth should question capitalism and participate in "the great refusal": reject consumerism and conformism and experiment with new and more hopeful visions for future society. By the early sixties, then, many creative thinkers were publishing ideas that questioned cold war culture, and one scholar has claimed that these "postwar intellectuals became the parents and teachers—literally and spiritually—of the New Left, the partisans of the counterculture, the civil rights activists, and the movement to end the conflagration in Vietnam."[27]

One wonders. No doubt, these intellectuals planted seeds in the fertile minds of some young activists during the early 1960s. Williams influenced scores of graduate students, and Goodman and Whyte might have had some impact on the development of the new left. Yet their influence on most activists, on what developed into a mass movement, has been overemphasized. Southern blacks seeking civil rights did not have to read Mills, Harrington, or Galbraith to discover poverty and discrimination; all they had to do was walk down the street. College students faced with selective service did not have to read Williams to oppose American foreign policy or Whyte to be turned off by military organization; more likely they nervously scanned pamphlets on how to avoid the draft. Antiwar activists did not have to agree with A. J. Muste's ideas of radical pacifism to oppose the war, and in fact most who demonstrated probably never had heard of Muste, were not opposed to all wars (especially the "good war" of their father's generation), and objected only to their own participation in Vietnam. Feminists probably experienced discrimination and male chauvinism before they decided to read *The Feminine Mystique*. As we shall see, blacks in the South were provoked by racism and inequality, not by intellectuals writing articles in *Dissent* or *Commentary*. Essays were not going to get the crackers' attention—they were not going to stop beating peaceful blacks who demanded their Constitutional rights because a sage used multisyllabic words in an uptown review.

Consequently the intellectuals of the fifties would influence only a small group of future activists—students and professors who read and discussed their books at elite universities. There was such a group, and as shall be discussed, these young intellectuals brought about the rise of the new left.

Yet these students were the exception, not the rule, for during cold war culture Americans conformed. In January 1960, *Look* magazine published a Gallup poll that revealed that most citizens were satisfied with their home life, work, and community, that they expected to "go on enjoying their peaceable, plentiful existence—right through the sixties and maybe forever." The same was true on campus, where students embraced apathy. "The vast majority of my classmates just sat through four years," wrote a 1960 graduate of Hunter College. "They didn't challenge any authority, take any risks, or ask any questions. . . . They were bereft of passions, of dreams, of gods." A student survey supported that view, concluding that two themes were apparent on campus, "a remarkable absence of any intense or consuming political beliefs, interests or convictions" and "extreme political and economic conservatism." These polls convinced experts to predict calm on campus. "The employers will love this generation" of students, wrote the president of the University of California, Clark Kerr. "They aren't going to press many grievances. They are going to be easy to handle. There aren't going to be any riots."

Most Americans were satisfied with the status quo, and they wanted that for their children. As Philip Caputo wrote about his parents, "their vision of my future . . . consisted of my finding a respectable job after school, marrying a respectable girl, and then settling down in a respectable suburb."

That was the American Dream; who would question it? Only those who did not believe it, or those who did not live it. There were two groups in the spawning ground of the fifties that hatched during the sixties: in the North, a few alienated students and professors, and in the South, many blacks who were denied the dream. While these two might seem entirely different, they both were similar in that they revolted against the status quo of *their* 1950s. They rejected cold war culture, as did almost all future activists who became part of the movement. While all had individual reasons for their eventual participation in social activism, they all grew up during the foreign and domestic anti-Communist crusades which brought about a conformist society bent on consensus. There were issues in the fifties—American interference in the governments of Iran and Guatemala, the expanding military-industrial complex, the Montgomery bus boycott, atmospheric atomic bomb testing—but the vast majority of Americans refused to address them. With few exceptions, citizens were simply opposed to any public demonstrations because "political activism was not likely to keep the world steady." In an age of insecurity, a scholar continued, the more secure path was "adaptation rather than resistance as a means of feeling 'at home.' "[28]

Few had the nerve to question. "What did you learn in school today, dear little boys of mine?" sang Tom Paxton:

> I learned that Washington never told a lie,
> I learned that soldiers seldom die,
> I learned that everybody's free. . . .
> I learned our government must be strong
> It's always right, and never wrong,
> Our leaders are the finest men,
> And so we elect them again and again,
> And that's what I learned in school today. . . .

In 1960 some young Americans no longer accepted these notions, and when they questioned and confronted the American Dream, they began to crack cold war culture.

The Surge, 1960 to 1968

"We are trying to change society," said Tufts University student David Smith. "In the '50s, the beat generation ran away from it. My generation knows we have to strike at the system to make it respond."

The Struggle

Blood ran down my forehead, blood ran down my back,
Threw me in the jailhouse, face down on the rack,
Told Judge Jim Crow slowly, I may not be brave,
You can jail my body, but I'll never be your slave.
freedom song by Charles Sherrod

A new left must start controversy across the land, if national policies
and national apathy are to be reversed.
The Port Huron Statement

Al Haber, Bob Ross, Sharon Jeffrey, and Tom Hayden were friends at the
University of Michigan. They met regularly to discuss books and ideas.
Early in 1960 they were considering holding a conference on civil rights
when, as Hayden later wrote, the "historic events of the decade unexpect-
edly began."

On the afternoon of February 1, four black students at North Carolina
A&T College walked into the local Woolworth's in Greensboro, North
Carolina. Two of them bought toiletries and then they all walked over
and sat down at a lunch counter reserved for whites. When a white wait-
ress approached, Ezell Blair, Jr., ordered: "I'd like a cup of coffee,
please." The waitress answered, "I'm sorry. We don't serve Negroes here."
That was the typical answer throughout the South, and then blacks left.
This time, they remained. Blair continued: "I beg to disagree with you.
You just finished serving me at a counter only two feet away from here.
. . . This is a public place, isn't it? If it isn't, then why don't you sell
membership cards? If you do that, then I'll understand that this is a private concern." "Well," the waitress responded heatedly, "you won't get
any service here!" She refused to serve the black students for the remainder of the afternoon. When the store closed at 5:30 p.m., the students

left, and one of them said to the waitress, "I'll be back tomorrow with A&T College."

They became known as the Greensboro 4, and that evening on campus they spread the word of the sit-in. The next morning about thirty male and female black students walked into Woolworth's and sat at the lunch counter. They were dressed nicely, and they brought their books and started studying. Occasionally a student would try to order, but was not served. After two hours they ended the sit-in with a prayer. Next day a much larger group sat at the counter. This time they were joined by three white students from Greensboro College, and by the end of the week hundreds of black students from half a dozen nearby campuses appeared. "It spread to places like the shopping centers, the drugstores in the shopping centers, the drive-ins," said one of the Greensboro 4, Franklin McCain. "No place was going to be left untouched. The only criteria was that if it did not serve blacks, it was certainly going to be hit. . . . We actually got to the point where we had people going down in shifts . . . we took all the seats in the restaurants. We had people there in the mornings as soon as the doors were open," and the managers had to do something. "You just can't continue to have people come in and sit around. The cash registers have to ring." [1]

Greensboro became tense. Local white youths appeared at Woolworth's, threatened blacks, and attempted to hold the seats for white patrons. Eventually someone telephoned that if the sit-in did not stop, they would detonate a bomb. The manager closed the store, and the mayor called upon black students and local business leaders to halt the protests for two weeks in an attempt to find a solution.

This was not the first time in the postwar era that blacks confronted Jim Crow. During the 1940s activists affiliated with the Congress of Racial Equality campaigned against segregated public accommodations in the North, and the next decade a few members of the NAACP held small sit-ins at Durham, Wichita, Oklahoma City, and Louisville. The national press ignored these events, and it did the same during the 1953 bus boycott in Baton Rouge, which provided a model for the more important challenge to segregation in Montgomery, Alabama.

On December 1, 1955, a white bus driver demanded that a black woman, Rosa Parks, give up her seat to a white passenger. She refused and was arrested for violating Montgomery's segregated seating ordinance. A local black leader, E. D. Nixon, who had known Mrs. Parks because they both were active in the NAACP, had been waiting for the right situation to challenge the ordinance, and when he learned of the arrest, he bailed her out of jail and called local ministers Ralph Abernathy, H. H. Hubbard, and Martin Luther King, Jr. Mrs. Parks was tried and found guilty on December 5, and that night Nixon met with the ministers and they formed the Montgomery Improvement Association. Nixon wanted King to serve as president. Although King had been in Montgomery for only a year and was just 26 years old, he was educated, the best speaker, and a minister, all assets which would pull the black community together. The MIA started the bus boycott which lasted over a year. It focused black aspirations in the community, brought publicity and increased stature to local leaders, and promoted King's idea of nonviolent direct action, a disruptive tactic that demanded change "here and now." Also, the MIA forged a local coalition between black groups and churches which previously had been in competition, received financial aid from northern blacks and liberal whites, and eventually led to the formation of a larger southern organization which by 1957 became the Southern Christian Leadership Conference. Most important, the boycott was victorious: it demonstrated that average people could organize direct action. While the bus company lost revenue, the U.S. Supreme Court ruled against the Montgomery segregation ordinance and in favor of black demands for integrated seating. The buses desegregated, bruising Jim Crow in Montgomery.

Montgomery was a beginning. While scholars debate how much that boycott prepared blacks for the subsequent civil rights crusade, it did seem to stimulate action in other locales during the last half of the decade.[2] Blacks in Tallahassee, New Orleans, and some twenty smaller towns conducted boycotts while activists in over a dozen communities held sit-ins of some segregated businesses. These demonstrations were similar to Montgomery in that they were not led by national organizations, and if successful, they only were local victories. They did not inspire a massive civil rights movement.

That changed in February 1960 with the next stage of the black struggle, the lunch counter sit-ins, which were a decisive break with earlier civil rights demonstrations and with cold war culture. The sit-ins ignited a young generation of blacks to become activists, and more important, they stimulated some southern and many northern whites to participate in something they began calling "the movement."

In the weeks after the Greensboro sit-in, blacks used the college-church network to spread the news quickly throughout the South. Students started sit-ins at lunch counters in Winston-Salem, Durham, Raleigh, and other cities across North Carolina, and by the end of February activists were using the tactic in seven states and over 30 communities including Nashville, Tallahassee, Chattanooga, Richmond, and Baltimore. The stream of students sitting in during February became a flood by March and a torrent during the next months as activists employed the tactic in Charleston, Columbia, Miami, Houston, San Antonio, and even small towns such as Xenia, Ohio. Blacks also initiated new tactics against "white only" facilities, such as read-ins at public libraries, paint-ins at public art galleries, wade-ins at public beaches, kneel-ins at white churches, and in Philadelphia 400 ministers asked their congregations to boycott corporations that did not hire blacks. Throughout 1960 and the next year about 70,000 participated in thirteen states, and a newspaper in Raleigh noted that the "picket line now extends from the dime store to the United States Supreme Court and beyond that to national and world opinion."

Many southern whites reacted toward black demands for civil rights in the same manner that they had since the end of the Civil War. At first they attempted to ignore them. But the sit-in, unlike a court ruling, was impossible to disregard for it disrupted business and reduced profits. As a consequence, white officials formed committees to "study" proposals, applied pressure on older black leaders to control their youth, and demanded that black college presidents expel activists. During the first year of the sit-ins black college administrators expelled over 140 students and dismissed almost 60 faculty members.

Yet those tactics failed to stop the sit-ins, so some southerners began the unofficial response—violence. Police either conducted brutal arrests and threw thousands of peaceful black students in jail for "inciting a riot," or they looked the other way and allowed white thugs to attack. During demonstrations in Nashville white hecklers pushed lighted cigarettes into the backs of black coeds quietly sitting at the counter. They spit at black men, blew cigar smoke into their faces, and threw fried potatoes at them. They called white supporters "nigger lovers" and kicked and beat them. The demonstrators did not fight back, and when police eventually arrived they arrested scores of students, and not one assailant. In Atlanta, a white threw acid into a demonstrator's face, and during sit-ins in Houston, a white teenager slashed a black with a knife. Three others captured a protester, flogged him, carved "KKK" in his chest, and hung him by his knees from a tree. Whites in Biloxi, Mississippi, attacked blacks with clubs, chains, and guns, firing into a peaceful demonstration and wounding ten.

Repression in the past usually had worked, but during sit-ins it appalled many neutral white bystanders. When a heckler in Knoxville poured a soft drink over a black minister and then struck him in the face, a large, young white man intervened, "You fellows have gone far enough and now you'd better get out of here!" A white waitress at another store looked at the black students and said to her colleague, "I think they should be served. You know, you really have to admire their courage!"[3]

Nor did white violence repress the demonstrations. Just the opposite: It helped young blacks form a common bond, gave them a new sense of pride, and encouraged most of them to try harder to beat segregation. They were putting their lives on the line—this time there was no turning back. These activists played a catalytic role throughout the South: They launched the 1960s.

There were many reasons for this youthful activism, almost as many as there were participants, yet at the same time there were some common themes. Some had been inspired by parents, older civil rights workers, teachers, or by Martin Luther King, Jr. James Lawson, a student of theology at Vanderbilt University, reminded those engaged in Nashville sit-ins, "Remember the teachings of Jesus, Gandhi, Martin Luther King." Ezell Blair remarked that he had heard King preach two years before he joined the Greensboro sit-in, and recalled the sermon being "so strong that I could feel my heart palpitating. It brought tears to my eyes." Some students were inspired by decolonialization in Africa, where at that time a dozen nations were obtaining independence. Many others were determined to avoid what James Baldwin had predicted: "All of Africa will be free before we can get a lousy cup of coffee."

Young blacks were tired of the humiliation of discrimination, and in March 1960 students in Atlanta placed advertisements in local newspapers which explained their participation: "Every normal human being wants to walk the earth with dignity and abhors any and all proscriptions placed upon him because of race or color. In essence, this is the meaning of the sit-down protests that are sweeping this nation today." The ad warned that "Today's youth will not sit by submissively, while being denied all of the rights, privileges, and joys of life. We want to state clearly and unequivocally that we cannot tolerate, in a nation professing democracy and among people professing Christianity, the discriminatory conditions under which the Negro is living today in Atlanta." The sit-ins, one activist wrote, were a "mass vomit against the hypocrisy of segregation."[4]

"There is no power like the power of an idea whose time has come," wrote Thomas Paine at the beginning of the American Revolution, and to many black students in 1960 the time was Now! They were growing impatient, tired of procrastination. One of the Greensboro 4, David Richmond, explained that he and his companions realized "how black folks were mistreated and nobody was doing anything about it." They were tired of "many words and few deeds." These four freshmen challenged each other to do something, and the next day they began a sit-in. Two days later, after reading the paper in Atlanta, students at Morehouse College, Lonnie King and Julian Bond, discussed the possibility of holding their own sit-ins at the local Woolworth's, W. T. Grant's, and Kresge's. King remembered that his position was that the "situation in Greensboro would again be another isolated incident in black history if others didn't join in to make it become something," and that the "only people in the black community at that time who were free to take on the Establishment were college kids."

Students also were tired of listening to older middle-class blacks who were more satisfied with the status quo and their economic positions. Speaking of a principal of a black high school in Maryland, a young black activist stated: "Now he calls himself 'doctor' and uses fancy words, struts around and plays 'big nigger' in his own community while he Toms all the whites. Do you think that he wants to change a system that gives him such power?" James Bevel, a 19-year-old sophomore at American Baptist Theological Seminary in Nashville, was eager to face angry white mobs and participate in that city's first sit-in. "Why?" he was asked by a cautious minister. "I'm sick and tired of waiting," he responded. "If you asked us to wait until next week, then next week something would come up and you'd say wait until the next week and maybe we never will get our freedom." [5]

Joining the movement, in fact, often estranged students from their more cautious parents. Cleveland Sellers organized a youth group to hold sit-ins in his home town in South Carolina. Before the first big rally his father told him, "This demonstrating and rallying is no good. If you keep on, you're going to destroy everything." Sellers was enraged, and almost yelled at his dad, "Goddammit, nigger, you're scared! You're scared of what those candy-assed white crackers will do to you!" After one young man who joined a sit-in in Chapel Hill, North Carolina, suffered a beating which included being burned and kicked to the floor, and was arrested for "disturbing the peace," he was allowed one phone call from jail. He called his mother, told her the news, and she chided him: "Good Negroes don't go to jail."

These students were restless. Greensboro had demonstrated that they could challenge Jim Crow, and their actions were shown every evening on television news, another reason for the awakening of a national civil rights movement. It is difficult to overestimate the importance of TV in the 1960s. Numerous authors have debated the impact of the media on the Vietnam War and antiwar movement, and one wonders if bus boycotts during the fifties would have remained local incidents if more black and white homes had televisions, or if network coverage had been more extensive. By 1960, however, Americans had purchased 50 million TVs, and during the next years the network evening news expanded from fifteen minutes to half an hour. With more extensive coverage virtually every citizen could witness—and judge—the Southern Way of Life. "With the exception of the announcer's voice," black student Cleveland Sellers said, "the lounge would be so quiet you could hear a rat pissing on cotton. Hundreds of thoughts coursed through my head as I stood with my eyes transfixed on the television screen. My identification with the demonstrating students was so thorough that I would flinch every time one of the whites taunted them. On nights when I saw pictures of students being beaten and dragged through the streets by their hair, I would leave the lounge in a rage." Television not only provoked southern blacks to join the movement; it stimulated those residing in the North. As Robert Moses watched his set in Harlem he realized it was time to act: "They were kids my own age and I knew this had something to do with my life."

Student participation and leadership in 1960 set a pattern for the movement during the entire decade. Students were ideal protesters since compared with the rest of society they had little to lose. They usually did not have responsibilities such as families or careers, and often had more free time and more energy. Also, black students and ministers, unlike most blacks in the South in 1960, were relatively organized in colleges or congregations, and neither depended on the white society for their economic livelihood. When students or ministers demonstrated they could not be fired from their jobs; both could afford to fight Jim Crow.

Young activists in the early 1960s, both black and white, also had fewer concrete notions about what was possible and impossible, and they were more idealistic. Raised in cold war culture, their teachers had them memorize the words of the Constitution—"we the people"—and the Declaration of Independence—"all men are created equal." Yet such words rang hollow in the South. As Tom Hayden stated about his years as a civil rights worker, "We were imbued with very idealistic American values: a belief in racial integration, not just as a future ideal, but as an ideal to be practiced in the here and now; a belief that places like Mississippi were not part of the American dream, but nightmares that America would awaken from; a belief, finally, that the Constitution, the president, and the American people were really on our side. Our example would mobilize them."

"For the first time in our history," wrote a professor in the early 1960s, "a major social movement, shaking the nation to its bones, is being led by youngsters."[6] Yet as the movement was gaining momentum during spring 1960, older black leaders felt the need to form an organization that would consolidate the students and propagate their ideas. Ella Baker, the executive director of the Southern Christian Leadership Conference, also desired more cooperation among various student leaders. She called a conference in April at Raleigh, North Carolina, which resulted in the founding of SNCC, the Student Nonviolent Coordinating Committee. Baker assured young activists that the aim was "TO SHARE experiences gained in recent protest demonstrations and TO HELP chart future goals for effective action." The conference was going to be "youth centered," for Baker realized that students were willing to meet "on the basis of equality, but were intolerant of anything that smacked of manipulation or domination." About 120 students representing 50 colleges attended the conference. Martin Luther King, Jr., urged them to continue their commitment to nonviolent tactics and he preached love and Christian morality. Baker took the podium and urged students not just to integrate lunch counters, but to change the entire southern social structure—this crusade must be for "more than a hamburger."

In October a second conference was held in which SNCC organizers discussed aims and tactics. During the next few years SNCC became the most important organization in the civil rights campaign, but organization did not come easily to the movement then or throughout the decade. From the beginning there was friction between older leaders and younger activists. After the Greensboro sit-in, Franklin McCain remembered, "We were in the driver's seat . . . keenly aware that people would rush in and try to take over the Movement." He continued that the "Congress of Racial Equality offered a funny sort of help," which was: "If you let us control the show, we'll show you how the thing is supposed to be done." Four "seventeen-year-old guys were just not in the mood to let someone take their show. . . . Our position was, we are probably as much experts about this as anybody else. We were experts because we had had one experience already, and that's more than most people." Julian Bond recalled that "NAACP wanted us to be NAACP youth chapters, CORE wanted us to become CORE chapters, SCLC wanted us to become the youth wing of SCLC. We finally decided we'd be our own thing," which was SNCC. Moreover, many younger blacks resented elder leaders who had accepted years of segregation or who acquiesced to white demands. At Morehouse College, for example, black administrators discouraged sit-ins, and eager to avoid conflict with white businessmen who had been financial supporters, they prohibited their students from inviting white activists to campus.

SNCC became important, then, because it was run by young activists themselves. SNCC members wanted blacks in each community to develop their own struggle so they exchanged information and trained new participants in nonviolent tactics. The organization also aimed to revolutionize the struggle by inciting so many demonstrations across the South that Americans would realize that inequality was not just a southern problem, but a national issue.

The sit-ins continued in 1961 and by the end of that year the students had achieved impressive results. Activists had integrated lunch counters and theaters in Greensboro and nearly 200 other cities, including larger ones such as Houston and Atlanta. Success was contagious: more black and white students joined the movement, and that provoked participation from parents and many prominent blacks, such as Sidney Poitier, Harry Belafonte, and Sammy Davis, Jr. Comedian Dick Gregory led many sit-ins, and when whites told him, "We don't serve Negroes," he responded, "No problem, I don't eat Negroes."

Northern politicians spoke out in favor of civil rights, and so did some progressive southerners such as Frank P. Graham, former senator and president of the University of North Carolina, who proclaimed that black protesters were renewing the nation: "In sitting down they are standing up for the American dream." Black students had demonstrated in little over a year that change was possible, that some whites would accept integrated public facilities. The Southern Way of Life was not impregnable. Success also was exhilarating. "I walked the picket line and I sat in," said one activist, "and the walls of segregation toppled. . . . Nothing can stop us now."[7]

Nothing except the white man, for while black students might integrate lunch counters in border states and some towns, they now would get a lesson in the heartland of the old Confederacy, Alabama and Mississippi.

In May 1961 seven black and six white volunteers boarded two buses in Washington, D.C., and began the next phase of the movement—the Freedom Rides. The ride was organized by CORE to protest southern states continuing their custom of segregating buses and terminal waiting rooms, restaurants, and restrooms. The Supreme Court had declared such practices unconstitutional in interstate travel. CORE's new national director, James Farmer, wanted to test the situation in the Deep South, and extend sit-ins by "putting the movement on wheels." Farmer invited reporters to insure press coverage, and the two buses left Washington on May 4 and traveled without incident through Virginia and North Carolina. The freedom riders arrived at Rock Hill, South Carolina, and encountered their first taste of violence. Local whites assaulted John Lewis and another rider as they attempted to enter the white waiting room of the bus terminal. Both were knocked down but not seriously injured, and the bus continued to Atlanta. Then to Alabama, and when the first bus arrived in Anniston, whites armed with blackjacks, iron bars, clubs, and tire chains met the riders. They attacked the bus, broke windows and slashed tires before the driver could execute an escape. Whites followed, and when the bus was forced to stop eight miles out of town because of flat tires, the mob hurled a smoke bomb inside the vehicle. That forced the freedom riders out, into the hands of the angry crowd, and as the bus burst into flames, whites beat the riders. After the melee, local hospital workers refused to treat the riders, and when the second bus appeared in Anniston, whites forced their way aboard and beat the passengers. One white rider, a 61-year-old retired professor from Michigan, was left with brain damage.

The riders on the second bus decided to continue to Birmingham, where they were met by another white crowd. The police had been warned to expect trouble, but although their headquarters was only two blocks from the terminal, no policemen appeared. The chief of police later explained that it was Mother's Day, and that most of his boys were home "visiting their mothers" as the armed mob charged the bus. According to a CBS reporter who was on the scene, white toughs grabbed the passengers and dragged them into alleys, "pounding them with pipes, with key rings and with fists." When a white rider, James Peck, was pulled off the bus, he was knocked unconscious and later needed over fifty stitches to stop the bleeding. Police did not appear for ten minutes, and by that time local whites had left in waiting cars: no arrests. Riders wanted to continue on, but no bus driver would take them to Montgomery, Jackson, and New Orleans. Governor John Patterson told the riders to "get out of Alabama as quickly as possible," the Justice Department arranged a flight, and the first freedom ride ended bruised—but not defeated.

Events in Anniston and Birmingham were widely reported, which forced the Kennedy administration to order the FBI to investigate, to send more Justice Department officials, and to pressure Alabama officials to uphold the law. Also, television coverage enraged student activists and revitalized the movement during spring 1961. Students in Nashville immediately organized the second freedom ride, composed of eight blacks and two whites. As sit-in veterans, these activists realized the danger and several made out wills. All agreed, however, that the ride was something that they must do "because freedom was worth it."

Their bus left Nashville on May 17 and headed south for Birmingham. John Lewis, a veteran of the first freedom ride, explained that when their bus arrived in Birmingham they were met by the police commissioner, Eugene "Bull" Connor, who took them off the bus and put them in the city jail for the next two days. Then, in the middle of the night, Bull "took seven of us out of the jail, took us to the Alabama-Tennessee state line, and dropped us off. He said, 'There's a bus station around here somewhere, you can make it back to Nashville.' And I have never been so frightened in all my life."[8] They called friends in Nashville who picked them up and drove them back to the bus station in Birmingham. With a white mob chanting outside the station, they waited for the next eighteen hours until a bus driver could be found and until additional riders arrived from Nashville and Atlanta. Then they continued on to Montgomery. With a police escort, there was no violence, but when they arrived in the city, the police disappeared. Lewis recalled: It was an "eerie feeling," a weird silence in a "funny peace." No one was in sight until they got off the bus, then local whites charged. A Justice Department official on the scene immediately called Attorney General Robert Kennedy, shouting into the phone: "It's terrible. It's terrible. There's not a cop in sight. People are yelling, 'Get 'em, get 'em.' It's awful."

And they did get 'em. Armed with pipes and baseball bats, 300 whites attacked 21 freedom riders and a few newsmen. They clubbed Lewis to the ground, leaving him in a pool of blood with a brain concussion. When they spotted a white rider, a student from the University of Wisconsin, several local women screamed, "Kill the nigger-loving son of a bitch!" They almost did, bashing his head, kicking in his front teeth, and injuring his spinal cord. One rider suffered a broken leg, and another had gas poured on him and his clothes set aflame. Local men slapped two white female riders, and when a federal agent tried to help them into his car, the men beat him to the ground, knocking him unconscious. The crowd swelled to a thousand, and after twenty minutes of mob rule, the Montgomery police finally arrived and quelled the riot. When a newspaperman asked the police commissioner why ambulances had not been called, he responded that all were "broken down," and concerning why the police had not arrived sooner, he stated: "We have no intention of standing guard for a bunch of troublemakers coming into our city."

The freedom riders stayed overnight in local black homes, and participated in a Sunday church service in Ralph Abernathy's First Baptist Church. The Kennedy administration was informed that twelve activists intended to leave Montgomery in a bus the next day for Jackson, Mississippi. The president expressed his concern and asked blacks to cease rides for a while and to participate in a cooling off period. Black leaders said no. James Farmer replied that blacks had been "cooling off for a hundred years. . . . If we got any cooler we'd be in a deep freeze." The bus left Montgomery and this time it was protected by the National Guard, seven patrol cars, two helicopters, and three planes. There was no violence. But when the riders reached Jackson they were arrested for attempting to use the white restroom in the bus station, charged with "breach of peace," and jailed. They spent the next two months on a brutal Mississippi penal farm.

White repression during freedom rides did not stifle the movement, for throughout the summer activists continued arriving in Jackson. They were arrested, of course, for trying to desegregate the terminal, and by the end of summer over 300 were behind bars in Mississippi. Often jailed together, they made valuable contacts and shared a common bond forged by their experiences and by oppression in Mississippi. The student-prisoners usually worked in fields or along roads from sunrise to sunset, and when they returned they might be questioned, beaten, or tortured with cattle prods before being sent to filthy cells. This brutal treatment broke some activists and after release they quit the movement, but most found that the common suffering strengthened their ties to each other and increased their desire to challenge Jim Crow. The treatment also resulted in important discussions about future strategies and tactics in the movement. After being clobbered by white guards, activists began to wonder about nonviolent tactics advocated by Martin Luther King. The religious students were more inclined to support King, but many others began thinking about striking back, fighting fire with fire. The arrests, moreover, inspired others into action, and the movement spread from bus to railroad and airport terminals, creating more disruptions in interstate travel.

Activists had invited reporters on the freedom rides. The press widely publicized the savage events, not only in America but throughout the world, and that included newspapers in the new nations of Africa and other developing countries, ones filled with people of color. During the cold war the United States wanted those countries to look for guidance to Washington and not to Moscow. SNCC realized this, and informed the Kennedy administration that with the admission of thirteen new African and Asian nations into the United Nations it was time for America to "purge itself of the rabies of racism." An African seminarian visiting Yale University added: "For years the Statue of Liberty has faced out. It is time to face in." Most American editors agreed, and that included many in the South. The Atlanta *Constitution* wrote that "Any man in this free country has the right to demonstrate and assemble and make a fool of himself if he pleases without getting hurt. If the police, representing the people, refuse to intervene when a man—any man—is being beaten to the pavement of an American city, then this is not a nobel land at all. It is a jungle. . . . And it is time for the decent people in it to muzzle the jackals."

Freedom rides also were reported on television news. The chaplain of Yale University, William Sloane Coffin, Jr., remembered watching John Lewis "laying on the ground, his head split open, blood all over his face. . . . I doubt that I'd ever been angrier and certainly never more ashamed of the United States." Shortly thereafter, Coffin joined his first freedom ride.[9]

The activists again put pressure on the Kennedy administration. To be sure, the president was in a difficult position. In 1960 he barely won the election. With 68 million votes cast, he won by just over 100,000, and he split the South with his opponent. Kennedy naturally desired reelection, and could not afford to alienate the white vote in Dixie. Yet he realized that his narrow victory partly resulted from strong support from northern blacks. If he had not won two-thirds of the black vote, he would not have been elected.

The administration, therefore, acted cautiously. It ordered the Interstate Commerce Commission to issue rules prohibiting racial discrimination in interstate facilities, which were posted in terminals throughout the South that September. Although some terminals in the Deep South ignored the order, in general, by the end of 1962 the movement had won a qualified victory—most interstate travel and facilities were integrated. JFK also sent his brother, Attorney General Robert Kennedy, to meet with the leaders of the National Student Association, CORE, SCLC, and SNCC. The administration wanted the students to abandon direct and confrontational tactics and start voter registration drives which officials felt would be less threatening to whites and therefore less violent. If direct action was abandoned, Kennedy promised to obtain funds for voter registration from private foundations, and at one point said: "If you'll cut out this Freedom Riding and sitting-in stuff, and concentrate on voter registration, I'll get you a tax exemption." While some older blacks nodded, many younger activists gasped at the statement, complaining that the administration was trying to "buy off" the movement. Others yelled that they would be "selling out" their brothers and sisters, and one SNCC member jumped to his feet and charged the attorney general, shouting chest to chest before he could be restrained.

The administration had miscalculated. Their idea of easing tensions by abandoning direct action for voter registration backfired. The white response to the first registration drive was not less violent—it was vicious.

McComb, Mississippi, had a black population of 8000, and fewer than 200 had registered to vote in 1960. In two adjoining counties, there were 2500 blacks and various voting restrictions meant that not one had the right to vote. This was typical throughout the Deep South, and to challenge this system, SNCC sent a 26-year-old black from Harlem, Bob Moses. He had received his education at Hamilton College and Harvard University, returned to Harlem to teach school, and after witnessing the white reaction to the peaceful sit-ins on television, he moved to Atlanta and joined SNCC.

In August 1961 Moses and a few coworkers began the voter registration drive in McComb. On one of the first days on the job, Moses took three local blacks to the courthouse so they could fill out registration forms. While driving away he was arrested for interfering with police duties, and spent the next two days in jail. A week later he tried to register some other blacks, and was attacked and beaten by the cousin of the local sheriff. Moses needed eight stitches in his head to stop the bleeding, and then pressed charges—the first time in the history of the county that a black had pressed charges which questioned the white's "right" to beat him. The white jury found the assailant not guilty. In September, Moses again tried to register some blacks, this time with another SNCC worker, and they were attacked and beaten by a white mob in front of the courthouse. Two days later, one of Moses's colleagues took two blacks in the next county to the registration office. The white registrar pulled a gun, ordered them out of his office, and pistol-whipped the SNCC worker. The sheriff charged the activist with disorderly conduct. Later that month, a black man's body was found in the local river. Herbert Lee, who had helped Moses and had tried to register, was driving his truck when a Mississippi state representative, Eugene Hurst, pulled him over, took out a gun, and shot Lee in the head. Two black eyewitnesses told their story to the FBI, and afterward the local sheriff broke one's jaw, and the other was gunned down in his front yard. The white coroner's jury ruled that Hurst shot and killed the unarmed Lee in self-defense.

The repression continued. A few SNCC activists attempted direct action, a sit-in in McComb, and they were arrested and sentenced to thirty days in jail. That provoked a few brave black high school students to conduct another sit-in, and they were expelled from school and given jail terms ranging between eight months and one year. That outrage, and Lee's murder, provoked about 120 high school students and some SNCC members to march to the country courthouse. At the courthouse steps a white mob surrounded them, and while police beat students with billy sticks, the mob attacked SNCC workers. SNCC member Bob Zellner remembered a mob in the street "started screaming like banshees, just hysterically, 'Bring him to us. We'll kill him. Bring him here.'" They grabbed Zellner, and tried to carry him to the street, but he held onto the bannister. To pry him loose they "started hitting my fingers with baseball bats. . . . They got ahold of my belt and five or six guys got ahold of my legs, and they'd pull. They ripped practically all my clothes off. One guy started gouging deep into my eyes with his fingers. He pulled my eyeball out onto my cheek and tried to get it between his finger and his thumb, to pull my eye out. . . . I fell loose from the rail. The last thing I remember was somebody kicking me in the head repeatedly with a big boot. . . . This was raw, downright raw, violence."[10]

The police arrested 119 students. A few days later, Moses, Zellner, and ten others were sentenced to four months in jail for "disturbing the peace." The prison terms ended the voter registration drive in McComb, and the episode demonstrated the usual white response to activists and "outside agitators." It was a reign of terror, and the repression worked; without federal intervention, activists registered only a small percentage of blacks in the Deep South.

McComb was typical, but Zellner was not—he was white. He had joined the movement in summer 1961 and his initiation was McComb. Eventually he became the first and one of the only white field secretaries for SNCC. Like most whites in the crusade, he was a young, idealistic, college graduate. During that summer and throughout the next few years a number of white students began to participate, while older southern white progressives such as Anne and Carl Braden raised money, and attorneys Allard Lowenstein and William Kunstler defended activists in southern courts. Although few white students had sat in or been on freedom rides, the number expanded greatly after 1961, and by summer 1964 there were 150 whites working for or with SNCC and about a thousand who

volunteered for Mississippi Freedom Summer. Some whites were southerners, such as Zellner from Alabama, Connie Curry from North Carolina, Casey Hayden and later Sara Evans from Texas. Zellner and many
other activists were children of ministers. Evans was the daughter of a
Methodist minister who had attended Southern Methodist University and
discussed issues such as Christianity and civil rights in the Methodist Student Association. But most whites were from northern colleges. Ralph
Allen took leave from Trinity College in Connecticut, John Perdew and
Peter deLissovoy were from Harvard, Dennis Sweeney attended Stanford,
and Mary King graduated from Ohio Wesleyan University. Furthermore,
a number of whites who joined the struggle also represented northern,
predominately white organizations. About 30 percent of those attending
SNCC's conference in April 1962 were whites representing groups such
as the Northern Student Association, National Student Alliance, and Students for a Democratic Society, and activists often were members of many
groups such as Ann Arbor Friends of SNCC, which aimed to "support
SNCC activities through fund-raising and news dissemination." Bob Zellner, Tim Jenkins, Jim Monsonis, Robb and Dorothy Burlage, and Casey
and Tom Hayden were members of both SNCC and SDS, while SNCC's
second chairman, Chuck McDew, attended the SDS conference in 1962
at Port Huron.

They all came for different reasons, but most of them held common
views that segregation was morally wrong and not Christian and that the
status quo of the fifties was flawed if not intellectually bankrupt. "The
whole country was trapped in a lie," Casey Hayden said. "We were told
about equality but we discovered it didn't exist."

The struggle was a magnet; it pulled activists together and gave them a
cause, and working together they discovered they had many things in
common. They had been educated at liberal universities and colleges, as
had most of their parents, who earned good incomes, had provided a
secure and egalitarian home environment, and had raised democratic and
questioning children. While a small percentage of parents were political
leftists who raised "red diaper babies," most were liberals who voted Democratic. Their children obtained good grades, and were more tantalized
by ideas than typical students. These activists also read much more that
the average young adult. Some read unorthodox journals such as *Dissent,
Partisan Review, Liberation,* or the *Village Voice,* and most scorned intellectuals of the fifties unless they were like C. Wright Mills and Paul
Goodman, who criticized the establishment. Goodman's *Growing Up Absurd* became standard reading on many campuses during the decade,
eventually selling 100,000 copies. To Hayden, "Mills defied the drabness
of academic life and quickly became the oracle of the New Left, combin-
ing the rebel life-style of James Dean and the moral passion of Albert

Camus, with the comprehensive portrayal of the American condition we were all looking for." Mary King and Casey Hayden were intrigued by Camus's *The Plague, The Fall,* and *The Rebel,* fascinated that an author addressed an issue they confronted daily in the civil rights struggle—achieving a "balance between moral purity and political effectiveness." While others were influenced by William Appleman Williams, who questioned American foreign policy, Tom Hayden was so influenced by *The Power Elite* that he wrote a master's thesis on Mills, and Marcuse's *One-Dimensional Man* had such an impact on Wini Breines that a decade later she subtitled her doctoral dissertation with his phrase, "the great refusal."[11]

Students also became concerned with other issues after the McCarthy era. The bomb, and the atomic fear it produced, was critical in the late fifties since atmospheric testing resulted in traces of radioactivity in the nation's food supply and dairy products. A number of older peace activists responded by organizing the National Committee for a SANE Nuclear Policy, commonly called SANE. Some students joined SANE or Peacemakers, a group opposed to civil defense drills "since one H-bomb would end New York City." During spring semester 1960 a thousand Harvard students held a protest walk for nuclear disarmament, and three months after Greensboro hundreds of students participated with over 15,000 older citizens in a rally at Madison Square Garden aimed at ending the nuclear arms race and creating a test ban treaty. Peacemakers attributed the big turnout to the fact that "many students are now aware of and responding to an atmosphere of action resulting from the Southern sit-ins."

On campus, students began organizing or joining groups such as Turn Toward Peace, Committee for Nonviolent Action, the Student Peace Union, and they began publishing dissident journals and magazines such as *New University Thought* (Chicago), *New Freedom* (Cornell), *Studies on the Left* (Wisconsin), *Advance* (Harvard), *The Activist* (Oberlin), and *Alternatives* (Illinois). During the next two years over 25 of these journals appeared on almost 20 campuses. Some students also formed political parties concerned with civil rights, academic freedom, or campus issues: POLIT at Chicago, SCOPE at Illinois, VOICE at Michigan, ACTION at Columbia, Progressive Student League at Oberlin, Political Action Club at Swarthmore, and TOCSIN at Harvard. At Berkeley, progressives established a campus reform party called SLATE, and to support southern sit-ins, students began picketing Bay Area Woolworth's stores and conducting demonstrations against businesses they felt discriminated in employment practices.

On a few select campuses, then, the spring of 1960 witnessed the first pulse of student activism, and it troubled the older generation who remained steeped in cold war culture. The government responded in May

1960. HUAC held hearings in the Bay Area to investigate "Communist activities." That prompted a thousand Berkeley students to protest the investigations at city hall in San Francisco. The first day of the demonstration was peaceful, but not the second day. Students were singing "the land of the free, home of the brave," when police appeared with billy clubs and fire hoses, drenching the protesters. As Betty Denitch remembered, "Here were students being dragged by their hair, dragged by their arms and legs down the stairs so that their heads were bouncing off the stairs." Students labeled the affair "Black Friday," and Denitch later stated: "That was the start of the sixties for me."

For others the start of the sixties was more idealistic, and the standard bearer of that feeling in 1960 was John F. Kennedy. In speeches during his campaign and his first year in office JFK confronted the complacent 1950s. He proclaimed that the "torch has been passed to a new generation of Americans," and he pledged to move America forward with vigor. He challenged the nation to get involved, to make a commitment: "And so, my fellow Americans: ask not what your country can do for you—ask what you can do for your country." His administration would tackle "new frontiers," and he talked about a fix-it social agenda which would spread 1950s affluence and middle-class status to all. The president ushered in an era of rising expectations, and to lead the way he assembled a youthful group of advisers who eventually became known as the "best and the brightest." "We *knew* America was the best," an assistant attorney general later commented. "We *knew* we could change America for the better. We *knew we* could do it."

JFK resurrected "can do" politics that had been sidetracked during the cold war and McCarthyism, and with his flash and dash he stirred America out of its slumber. He appealed to liberals naturally, and to intellectuals. Philosopher Frithjof Benjamin of the University of Michigan remembered that "Kennedy created a climate of high idealism—it was evangelical. It was marvelous that we would make a beautiful world, a more compassionate world." And JFK excited a large crop of teenagers as they began thinking about their future. He aroused them by asking if they would give their time and energy in a "peace corps" aimed at helping people in emerging nations. He inspired them to think about a hopeful, bright future. "The whole idea," stated a teen, "was that you can make a difference. I was sixteen years old and I believed it. I really believed that I was going to be able to change the world."[12]

The Kennedy promise—you could make a difference—stimulated students to get involved. Less than two months after his inauguration JFK established the Peace Corps, the love child of his administration, and the immediate response demonstrated a new decade of students. "I'd never done anything political, patriotic, or unselfish," said one volunteer, "because nobody ever asked me to. Kennedy asked." Within an hour after the announcement the government switchboard could not handle all the calls from potential volunteers, and the press reported that the president received more inquiries about the corps than about any other issue: "some 6,000 letters of suggestion, inquiry and open application. None mentions salary."

Other students volunteered for tasks in campus organizations. The Student Peace Union only had 150 members in 1960 but boasted 4000 three years later. SANE also expanded, and the Young People's Socialist League tripled to 800 by 1962. By the standards of the 1950s, these organizations were "radical" because they no longer were afraid to state their views at a small demonstration; by the standards of the late 1960s, however, these were little more than debating societies. TOCSIN activities were the "most gentlemanly form of protest imaginable," one member remembered, "based on the assumption that a rational dialogue between Harvard faculty and Harvard students would save the world from destruction." Yet compared with the fifties, any dialogue seemed an improvement to young activists like Todd Gitlin, who stated his reason for becoming involved: "TOCSIN made me feel useful, gave me good company, books to read, intellectual energy."

Intellectual energy was important after the bland fifties. The "old left," socialists and Communists of the 1930s, had become disillusioned with postwar Soviet behavior in Eastern Europe and had been crippled by McCarthyism. The old left was on its deathbed, and so in 1956 Communist and Socialist party leaders Earl Browder and Norman Thomas held a meeting in which they discussed the possibilities of reviving the left. While they came up with few ideas, the discussion had one important result. The *National Guardian* published an article about it with the headline, "The New Left: What Should It Look Like?" It was the first time the term had been used, and it was an important question: What ideas and organizations should constitute a new left? During the next few years leftists debated the issue in a young British journal, the *New Left Review*. Yet they still were at an impasse in September 1960, demonstrated by the publication of C. Wright Mills's "Letter to the New Left." Like many intellectuals that year, Mills sensed the restlessness of the younger generation and was eager to "get on with it," to end the fifties and its "intellectual celebration of apathy." He raised questions, but more than half a year after the Greensboro sit-ins, months after the Madison Square Garden rally and "Black Friday," this leading leftist still could not "be definitive." He could not answer the question raised four years earlier, "The new left: What should it look like?" All he could do was suggest that leftists needed a new organization and then note that older intellectuals would have to look to the "young intelligentsia."[13]

Mills was not aware that during fall semester 1960 a growing number of young intelligentsia were attending select colleges such as the University of Michigan. Robert "Al" Haber, the son of a prominent professor, had been active on campus in the Political Issues Club, which eventually became VOICE. A visionary, Haber dreamed of resuscitating the old Student League for Industrial Democracy (SLID), a branch of the League for Industrial Democracy (LID), and making it a forceful student organization. At a time of expanding college enrollments, he also desired to change its name to something more appropriate, such as Students for a Democratic Society (SDS). To accomplish this he became a vice president of SLID in 1959 and negotiated with LID officials, who allowed the change to SDS in January 1960. Meanwhile, Haber began to enlist articulate and concerned students into SDS, such as sophomore Sharon Jeffrey, whose mother was a union and Democratic party activist, Robert Ross, an alienated New Yorker who played jazz, read beat poetry, and espoused leftist doctrines, and Tom Hayden, an energetic reporter and editor of the campus paper, the *Michigan Daily*.

From the start, SDS members demonstrated that they not only were interested in a broad range of issues but were eager to act on them. Soon after the Greensboro sit-in, Haber, Jeffrey, and Ross joined picket lines at the local Kresge chain store to support sit-ins at those stores in the South. In May they held a conference at the university on "Human Rights in the North," which included veterans of southern sit-ins, older leftists such as Bayard Rustin and Michael Harrington, and representatives from CORE, NAACP, and SNCC. The conference was a success, and the United Auto Workers donated $10,000, which resulted in employing Haber as field secretary and holding SDS's first conference that June. The 29 members of the new organization elected Haber president, and his statement signaled the future: "We have spoken at last, with vigor, idealism and urgency, supporting our words with picket lines, demonstrations, money and even our own bodies. . . . Pessimism and cynicism have given way to direct action."

SDS initiated physical and intellectual action the next two years. Haber managed the office and recruited members by visiting campuses and speaking out for civil rights and individual liberties. Hayden moved south and worked with SNCC, participating in voter registration drives and putting his body on the line: He was beaten by angry whites in McComb, Mississippi, and jailed in Albany, Georgia. By December 1961 the SDS steering committee realized that the organization needed to articulate its political positions and social values in a manifesto, so it called a conference for next June at Port Huron, a UAW camp forty miles north of Detroit at the southern end of Lake Huron. Only 59 attended, 43 SDS members, the rest older leftists or representatives of other student groups such as the Young Christian Students, Progressive Youth Organizing Committee, Young Democrats, and SNCC. They were intellectuals and activists who were hopeful that the meeting would have an impact. As Paul Booth later remembered, "Even though we weren't a political force yet—and we never dreamed of spawning a mass movement—we all thought we were making history."

Hayden had written a manifesto draft of almost 50 pages, and for five days the membership discussed what became known as *The Port Huron Statement*. They divided into small groups, sat around tables or under trees, drinking coffee and arguing about topics examined in the draft: American politics, economics, racism, and foreign policy; the nuclear issue; the role of students; communism; and the themes and values of SDS. The debates often were hot, and what resulted, Hayden later noted, was "clearly a generational appeal directed in particular to the middle class." The first lines: "We are people of this generation, bred in at least modest comfort, housed now in universities, looking uncomfortably to the world we inherit."[14]

Like black activists in the South, these and many other young intellectuals were uneasy because of the paradoxes in the nation, the inconsistencies between ideals and realities in America. *The Port Huron Statement* noted racial bigotry when the national creed declared "all men are created equal," growing national affluence while millions remained in poverty, possible benefits from atomic power with growing probability of nuclear destruction, and presidential statements about peaceful intentions while the administration maintained a costly cold war military budget. They were troubled by the anticommunism "paranoia" which had resulted in "finger-pointing and comical debate about the most serious of issues" instead of rational discussion on foreign policy. To them, contemporary society feared change, "all crusades are suspect, threatening," and they stated that the "remote control economy" had to be replaced by a new system.

The Port Huron Statement outlined SDS's new system, and could be interpreted in many ways. First, it was a radical document that clearly was a response to and a rejection of the immediate past, the 1950s. The authors repeated the ideas of older dissidents as they condemned the loneliness, isolation, "emptiness of life," the "powerlessness of ordinary people." They echoed Goodman's *Growing Up Absurd* and Mills's *Power Elite*, declaring that individuals—not the group—should make decisions that determine their futures, that society—not the power elites—should participate in the economic and political affairs of the Republic. The monolithic 1950s had alienated and provoked these young intellectuals, and the *Statement* was their strike against consensus, their declaration of war on cold war culture.

Also, the document was radical in proposing a new ideology for the 1960s—the new left. In the *Statement* these advocates condemned the continuation of the cold war and a U.S. foreign policy that supported dictators in the name of democracy, that brought the world to the brink of nuclear war, and they called for steps to replace the arms race with a disarmament race. Concerning emerging nations of the third world, they realized that representative government occurred only in the few nations with long traditions of democracy, and that while America might have to work with authoritarian governments, the aim should be to support other governments which "develop a reasonable theory of democracy" applicable to their own culture. They criticized the growth of the military-industrial establishment, the "permanent war economy," and the influence of multinational businesses: "a way must be found to subordinate private American foreign investment to a democratically constructed foreign policy. The influence of the same giants on domestic life is intolerable as well. . . . Corporations must be made publicly responsible," and as a countervailing force against the excesses of big business they called for a "revitalized labor movement." They demanded an end of racial bigotry, stating that "White, like might, makes right in America today," and they called for school integration, black voting rights, and equal opportunity "right now." They were appalled by a government that stifled dissent, that used the House Un-American Activities Committee to bring about an "atrophy of participation," and they wanted First Amendment rights seen as "guarantees, not threats, to national security." Ashamed by a silent generation of students who "don't even give a damn about apathy," they called for "participatory democracy" in which all Americans would decide national issues in a public forum and in which opposing views would illuminate diversity and choices in the Republic.

The Port Huron Statement also was a traditional reform document, especially when placed in larger historical context. These activists had been influenced by liberal policies of the past, and Hayden later wrote that the *Statement* was a "curious litany slightly to the left of the Democratic party." They demanded social programs to fight poverty, establish national health care, help family farmers, construct decent prisons and mental institutions, build more schools with smaller classes, and develop equal educational opportunities. Furthermore, and regardless of what some SDS members thought they were writing then or their revolutionary rhetoric later in the decade, the manifesto stated traditional themes of all American reform eras. Like the Jacksonian democrats, the populists, progressives, and new dealers, these SDS intellectuals wanted to increase popular influence and control of the economic and political system. Their document called for "a more reformed, more human capitalism," decried the "separation of people from power . . . from pinnacles of decision-making," and demanded participatory democracy. Hayden later wrote that "our democratic idealism flowed from a populist root, the belief that an informed public would make 'better' decisions about its own interest than anyone else."

The Port Huron Statement also was "unconnected with the past" in the sense that it was a break with the old left. The issues that had dominated the left since the 1930s—communism versus capitalism, labor versus management—were debated but were not as important to these younger intellectuals. Their document declared that "private enterprise is not inherently immoral or undemocratic," and stated new concerns: civil rights and personal liberties. They expected to recruit members not from labor unions but from universities where they would attempt to build a student movement which would challenge apathy, increase participation, and transform society. The old left, SDS activist Greg Calvert noted, wanted the capitalist system to change to socialism, while the new left desired people to change, to develop a "radical consciousness," which meant that individuals would become involved. As Calvert wrote, "the *personal* and the *political* could not be divorced. . . . The revolution is about our lives."

The Port Huron Statement, then, was the first commentary from a new generation of white students, and it was significant because it outlined new left ideology. How important the document and that ideology was to the sixties and the movement is a difficult question to answer, and depends on how broadly one defines the movement, what one considers the reasons for social activism, and whether one belonged to SDS. If one thinks that SDS and SNCC defined the movement, or that people are provoked to action because they read a manifesto, then the *Statement* provided, as the writers declared, the "Agenda for a Generation." Naturally, SDS members felt their role was very important—the vanguard of the movement. "We were launching something that had not happened among university students, ever," proclaimed Sharon Jeffrey. The activists at Port Huron were not shy. Being bright and aggressive after an era of apathy, these new lefters naturally felt that they were special, the "voice, conscience, and goad of its generation," wrote Todd Gitlin, the "movers and shakers of the Sixties." Many agreed. "By expressing their own utopian political vision they would inspire an entire generation," wrote former SDS member Jim Miller, and another declared about the author of the *Statement:* "Tom Hayden changed America. . . . He was father to the largest mass protests in American history."[15]

One wonders. The significance of a manifesto begs a classic question: Did Americans rebel against England in 1776 because Thomas Paine wrote *Common Sense* or because British laws and regulations discriminated against them? For the 1960s, what were the reasons for rebellion?

A manifesto, or a cold war culture which had not addressed pressing problems and a conformist white male society that discriminated against the rest of Americans? SDS itself provided the answer in the *Statement:* the "permeating and victimizing fact of human degradation, symbolized by the Southern struggle against racial bigotry, compelled most of us from silence to activism." Discrimination stimulated protest from a new generation. A survey of white Freedom Summer volunteers demonstrated that they went to Mississippi in 1964 because they were motivated by idealism, religion, optimism, and challenged by the aim of achieving equal rights and human dignity for African Americans. Virtually none mentioned ideology, politics, or the *Statement.* "I was apolitical," one stated, and another asked: "Politics? what the hell was that? . . . I was going to spend my summer 'helping Negroes' . . . sort of a domestic Peace Corps number." *The Port Huron Statement,* and hundreds of lesser-known manifestos written by other activists throughout the decade, were important because they announced existing problems in society, the inconsistency between the American dream and reality. Alone, however, they did not provoke many to act.[16]

While it is difficult to gauge the impact of *The Port Huron Statement* on the 1960s, it is easier to measure its meaning to SDS organizers. Todd Gitlin later wrote that the document was important because it fused SDS members into a "network joined in a common destiny." This network was a small circle of friends, a movement family, or what another former SDS member labeled "a very small and somewhat incestuous community" of young elites. During the next few years their energy would mobilize others to join SDS, making it the largest new left organization of the decade. In addition, the intensity of the conference itself was an awakening for many participants, one that deepened personal bonds through a shared experience. The final session lasted all night and then the delegates walked down to Lake Huron; some held hands as they watched the sun rise. "It felt like the dawn of a new age," Sharon Jeffery said: "It was exalting. . . . We thought that we knew what had to be done, and that we were going to do it." Bob Ross added, "It was a little like starting a journey."

The journey took these and other activists in three directions during the next year—some went to college campuses, others to northern slums, and many more back to the South. The efforts were related, for as one activist noted: "Creating a movement meant building a community in which people could trust each other and love each other enough to be able to carry on a collective fight." Also, many northern whites wanted to duplicate the activism of southern black students in northern universities and ghettos. Consequently SDS began the Peace Research and Educational Project (PREP) and the Economic Research and Action Project

(ERAP). PREP aimed to stimulate students and faculty to direct their education and research away from topics such as the cold war and military-industrial complex and toward issues of peace. SDS activists arrived on campuses during fall semester 1962 and also attempted to raise student awareness and activism, but with few tangible results. That year, Michael Harrington published *The Other America*, which stimulated many to consider the plight of the poor, and in 1963 Hayden and Carl Wittman published a SDS pamphlet that called for an "interracial movement of the poor" with the aim of developing an organization to improve conditions in impoverished neighborhoods. SDS established ERAP and by the next year a hundred of their members were working with the poor in many cities, achieving some results in Newark, Chicago, and Cleveland. At the same time PREP and ERAP created a debate in SDS: "campus versus the community," whether to spend energy and limited funds organizing students or the poor. The debate never was resolved, and eventually was one of many internal issues that divided SDS membership.[17]

All activists, however, could agree on the need to continue the struggle in the South. *The Port Huron Statement* declared the civil rights crusade "heartening" because it demanded justice and inspired activism—it was "a passage out of apathy."

The struggle continued to be the focus of the movement, and throughout 1962 an important venue was Albany, Georgia. A former slave-trading community in which 40 percent of the inhabitants were black, not one ever had been elected or appointed as a city official, policeman, or jury member. Strict segregation existed, and blacks were barred from parks, swimming pools, and the library. From the "colored waiting room" in the bus station it was eight blocks to a "colored restaurant" and six miles to a "colored motel." During the year activists marched, sat in, and attempted to register voters, but after months of demonstrations only a handful had won the right to vote. White officials maintained strict segregation of all public facilities and had thrown over a thousand protesters in jail, so many that they had to transport activists to other county jails, including Ralph Abernathy and Martin Luther King, Jr. Most of the repression was by arrest. When blacks peacefully marched out of their neighborhood and toward white districts, police simply charged them with disorderly conduct, parading without a permit, loitering, even "*tending* to create a disturbance."

The white response was similar in many southern towns. In Clinton, Louisiana, after twelve blacks wrote the mayor requesting the establishment of a biracial committee to ease racial tensions, they were arrested for "intimidating public officials." In Americus, Georgia, four students who peacefully protested segregation were charged with "insurrection," a capital offense in that state, and jailed without bond for four months.

Injustice was rampant in Mississippi. In Itta Bena, 60 blacks marched to the home of the deputy sheriff to ask for police protection for voter registration. His response was given the next day when all marchers over age 14 were tried, convicted, fined, and imprisoned for "disturbing the peace." In Ruleville, Fannie Lou Hamer's attempt to register led to losing her job, a jail sentence, and a $9000 water bill even though her house had no running water. In Holmes County, after someone threw a gasoline bomb at the home of a black activist, the resident and his wife were arrested and charged with arson, and in Clarksdale, officials arrested an activist who was wearing a T-shirt which read FREEDOM NOW. The charge: "parading without a permit." And when activists attempted to integrate restaurants in Chapel Hill, North Carolina, they were beaten and had ammonia poured down their throats at one cafe, and at another, an eyewitness reported: the "wife of the owner performed an act, which for its grossness, has not been equalled even in Mississippi. Lou Calhoun . . . was lying upon the floor protecting himself from flying broom handles. The owner's wife then urinated on his head. This even upset the local police, who then took Lou to the fire station and had him hosed off." [18]

To activists, "southern justice" meant one thing—federal intervention. Civil rights leaders demanded that the Kennedy administration protect them from racist attacks during peaceful sit-ins, voter registration drives, or any nonviolent activities aimed at achieving Constitutional rights. SNCC sent a telegram asking, "When will the federal government act to halt the Nazi-like forces operating against democracy in southwest Georgia?" After a white jury acquitted the local sheriff who had chased activists out of a small town in that state, Charles Sherrod asked, "What are we to tell the people down here? Must we die before the federal government stops compromising with bigots?" In frustration, he later confronted administration officials, shouting, "Your failure to throw the full weight of your offices behind our attempts, black and white together, to make the real tenets of democracy is a black mark for your administration. If we are murdered in our attempts, our blood will be on your hands."

The administration continued to act cautiously. Discrimination at lunch counters or in department stores at that time broke no federal statutes, and Justice Department officials questioned whether they had legal power to protect activists charged with breaking local ordinances or state laws. In 1962 Assistant Attorney General Burke Marshall wrote Martin Luther King, Jr., that "maintenance of law and order in any locality is the primary responsibility of local officials." While activists charged that the federal government did have power under numerous federal codes, the Kennedy administration did not want to irritate southern authorities by sending an occupation army into the old Confederacy. Robert

Kennedy later recalled, "What I was trying to avoid basically, was having to send troops and . . . having a federal presence in Mississippi." Consequently, and like Eisenhower during the Little Rock crisis, JFK sent troops only when the governor of Mississippi in 1962 refused federal court orders to allow blacks into the state university. Kennedy forced Old Miss to integrate, but meanwhile he continued to placate southern whites and enraged activists by appointing federal judges who were outspoken opponents of the struggle, who issued injunctions against peaceful demonstrators, threw them in jail, and gave them stiff sentences. "It is tragically ironic," wrote attorney William Kunstler, "that Kennedy's judicial appointments in the deep South included so many outright racists."

The administration's behavior meant that activists became increasingly disenchanted with Kennedy, who they charged was "racing in neutral." Mary King and her colleagues in SNCC were perplexed by a president who encouraged the young to do something to improve the country and then refused to use federal authority to stop white racists from beating them up. James Forman regarded Kennedy as "quick-talking, double-dealing," and many other activists were becoming disillusioned with white liberals who offered endless advice, desired leadership roles, and always talked about "both sides of the race issue," balancing black rights with white traditions and advocating gradual change. While admitting that white liberals had helped in the past, black attorney Loren Miller stated that activists were growing tired of advice and becoming more militant: "To liberals a fond farewell, with thanks for services rendered, until you are ready to re-enlist as foot soldiers and subordinates in a Negro-led, Negro-officered army under the banner of Freedom Now."[19]

Some northern activists also were becoming concerned with "liberal" policies, especially exhibited by the best and brightest during the first two years of the Kennedy administration. Without a doubt, most baby boomers think back on the Kennedy years as a thousand days of idealism and vigor, an era of Camelot. American youth were infatuated with the handsome and dashing leader, and thousands of students realized those feelings by volunteering for community projects or joining the Peace Corps. A small minority of young activists, however, especially outspoken ones associated with SDS or SNCC who felt part of an emerging movement, became increasingly disillusioned. To them, Kennedy's liberalism meant an unprecedented peacetime spending binge on weapons, cutting taxes for corporations, and continuing cold war rhetoric: "Let every nation know, whether it wishes us well or ill," the president declared in his inauguration speech, "that we shall pay any price, bear any burden, meet any hardship, support any friend, oppose any foes, in order to assure the survival and success of liberty. This much we pledge—and more." Some students became concerned as the president decided to make South Vietnam, a country thousands of miles away with no history of representative government, the "testing ground" for democracy in Southeast Asia, increasing the number of American military advisers to that country. Closer to home, more wondered about a president who supported the Bay of Pigs fiasco in an attempt to rid Cuba of its Marxist and anti-American leader, Fidel Castro, and were stunned in October 1962 when the commander-in-chief announced a "quarantine" of that island.

The Soviet Union had placed missiles in Cuba and Russian freighters on the high seas were en route with more. JFK responded by commanding the U.S. Navy to stop and inspect the cargo on Soviet ships before they reached Cuba, which could be interpreted as an act of war. The U.S. Armed Forces were put on alert; B-52 bombers began their wartime flight patterns, armed and loaded. As the public waited nervously, the freighters approached the island. After six long days, the Soviet Union ordered its freighters to turn around and head home: the Russians avoided a nuclear high noon.

While the vast majority of Americans rallied to the colors and supported the president, some activists felt that the crisis was unnecessary saber rattling and that JFK had created a "week of madness." Fearing atomic attack, a few students at New England colleges got in their cars and headed for Canada. Others at Cornell, Minnesota, and Wisconsin began questioning and even protested. At Indiana, fifteen students organized the Ad Hoc Committee to Oppose U.S. Aggression, called a rally, and were met by 3000 angry colleagues who supported JFK. At Michigan, 400 demonstrators passed out leaflets urging an end to the "game of Chicken, with mankind on the bumpers." Tom Hayden and many in SDS came to the conclusion that the Kennedys were not "liberals of a kind that we wanted to work with. They had brought us close to nuclear war," and Todd Gitlin and his companions "grew steadily more estranged from Kennedy liberalism." These students felt "not only endangered but insulted when power behaved stupidly."[20]

Civil rights activists also grew concerned about the missile crisis and the president. "The justification for risking the annihilation of the human race was always expressed in terms of America's willingness to go to any lengths to preserve freedom," wrote Martin Luther King, Jr. "To the Negro that readiness for heroic measures in the defense of liberty disappeared . . . when the threat was within our own borders and was concerned with the Negro's liberty." Consequently, in the months after the missile crisis King and his companions in SCLC aimed to steer the president's attention away from foreign policy and back to the struggle for civil rights. "The key to everything," King said, was "Federal commitment, full, unequivocal, and unremitting," and to provoke that he planned a dramatic crisis in Birmingham.

King and SCLC leadership wanted the white "oppressor to commit his brutality openly—in the light of day—with the rest of the world looking on." Birmingham was an appropriate choice. The city was so segregated that officials had removed a book from the library that featured white and black rabbits, so violent that local blacks called it "Bombingham" and their segregated neighborhood "Dynamite Hill." The police commissioner, Eugene T. "Bull" Connor, prided himself on "keeping the niggers in their place" and had predicted that "blood would run in the streets of Birmingham before it would be integrated." Local black activist the Reverend Fred Shuttlesworth informed the SCLC staff when they arrived in Birmingham: "You have to be prepared to die before you can begin to live."[21]

King realized the danger, but felt that the campaign might be able to "break the back of segregation all over the nation." He and his SCLC staff met with local black leaders and they issued a manifesto stating the grievances of black citizens. On April 3 the activists began sitting in and picketing restaurants and businesses. The police arrested them for trespassing. Next day, about fifty activists marched on city hall, and they too were arrested and thrown in jail. The same fate awaited King's brother, the Reverend A. D. King, when he led a march a few days later on Palm Sunday. The arrests did not deter the activists, for as comedian Dick Gregory shouted at the Mayor: "We will march through your dogs! And if you get some elephants, we'll march through them. And bring on your tigers and we'll march through them!" Each day more black citizens joined in, and the stream of marchers became a river which prompted officials to secured an injunction barring demonstrations. That did not work. King proclaimed it an "injunction from heaven," that it was his duty to violate immoral laws, and that he and his supporters would march to city hall on April 12, Good Friday. He had promised to lead demonstrations until "Pharaoh lets God's people go," and so accompanied by fifty volunteers, King and Ralph Abernathy marched and chanted "Freedom has come to Birmingham!" But it had not. Police this time were assisted with growling, snapping dogs, and they again arrested and jailed the marchers.

King used his jail time to compose his eloquent essay justifying his strategy and the movement, "Letter from the Birmingham Jail." Eight days later he was released and was planning the next confrontation with the establishment—the "children's crusade." On May 2 black children, most of them teenagers, met at the Sixteenth Street Baptist Church and then began marching toward city hall singing freedom songs. When Bull Connor's forces corralled them for the arrest, they prayed and then danced and skipped to the paddy wagons. The demonstration the next day, however, was different. As a thousand teens left the church, Connor ordered his men to charge: They did with nightsticks swinging, dogs snarling. Blacks responded by hurling stones, and the police turned on the high-pressure fire hoses, ripping into the crowd, blasting citizens off their feet.

Hundreds were arrested, but police brutality did not stifle the struggle. "I used to drive the church bus," stated Andrew Marrisett, "and I just happened to detour to go down by the park where the demonstrators would always be. What really sticks in my mind . . . is seeing a K-9 dog being sicced on a six-year-old girl. I went in front of the girl and grabbed her, and the dog jumped on me and I was arrested. That really was the spark . . . a big, burly two-hundred-and-eighty-five pound cop siccing a trained police dog on that little black girl. And then I got really involved in the Movement."

And so did others, for the next day several thousand blacks took to the streets, and the savage scenes again appeared on front pages of newspapers and on national television. *Time* reported: "There was the Negro youth, sprawled on his back and spinning across the pavement, while firemen battered him with streams of water so powerful that they could strip bark off trees. There was the Negro woman, pinned to the ground by cops, one of them with his knee dug into her throat. There was the white man who watched hymn-singing Negroes burst from a sweltering church and growled: 'We ought to shoot every damned one of them.' . . . The blaze of bombs, the flash of blades, the eerie glow of fire, the keening cries of hatred, the wild dance of terror in the night—all this was Birmingham, Ala." [22]

Birmingham prompted sit-ins and demonstrations in nearly 200 cities across the south, boosted King's reputation as the greatest black leader, and proved to be a turning point in the struggle: Black activists forced Kennedy to act. Like most Americans, the president and his brother watched the riots on television and were "sickened" by the police brutality. When King was jailed, the Kennedy brothers called Birmingham officials, and Bobby dispatched assistant attorney general Burke Marshall to negotiate a settlement. With more and more blacks marching in the streets, with jails overflowing, and as the city faced social disintegration and economic collapse, businessmen agreed to talk. For three days Marshall helped both sides worked out a compromise agreement which eventually integrated public facilities and provided jobs for blacks. In response, vengeful whites bombed King's motel headquarters and his brother's home, which forced Kennedy to announce that the agreement was "fair and just" and that the "federal government will not permit it to be sabotaged by a few extremists on either side." The president ordered 3000 federal troops into position near the city, and a few weeks later he federalized the state national guard and ordered it to protect two black students as they enrolled in the University of Alabama.

On June 11 the president delivered a nationally televised address. JFK told Americans that the nation was founded "on the principle that all men are created equal, and that the rights of every man are diminished when the rights of one man are threatened." He continued that the nation was confronted with a moral issue. "The heart of the question is whether all Americans are to be accorded equal rights and equal opportunities; whether we are going to treat our fellow Americans as we want to be treated." And the president asked citizens a question pertinent ever since: "Who among us would be content to have the color of his skin changed and stand in his place?"

A few hours after the address, JFK's question took on special meaning. A White Citizens Council organizer shot and killed NAACP field secretary Medgar Evers as the victim was stepping from his car at his home in Jackson, Mississippi. Later that summer, a white supremacist dynamited Birmingham's Sixteenth Street Baptist Church, killing four girls. It was the twenty-first bombing attack against blacks in that city during the previous eight years. Not one case had been solved.

As many white students pondered what it would be like to be black and to live in the South, JFK continued to speak out for civil rights. He asked Congress to pass the most comprehensive civil rights act in American history, a federal law granting the right of all citizens to be served in facilities open to the public. And the president finally put his administration behind the movement's aims to end school segregation and provide voting rights.

JFK's new position split the nation. King was elated over the president's speech: "He was really great," he told a colleague, and then wrote Kennedy that the speech constituted "one of the most eloquent, profound, and unequivocal pleas for justice and the freedom of all men ever made by any president." Southern politicians condemned it. Mississippi's Senator James Eastland called the proposed act a "complete blueprint for a totalitarian state," and a bumper-sticker seen in the South referred to the Republican hopeful for the 1964 presidential race while using a double entendre: "Kennedy for King—Goldwater for President." Many northern liberals praised the act and demanded that it be strengthened with provisions for federal registrars to aid and protect black voters and a permanent Fair Employment Practices Commission. Many college students felt the same way, for now the president had again rekindled idealism. JFK had spoken out for equality and for the American Dream. Activists on the picket lines, however, were more ambivalent. After two years of trying to provoke the administration to protect them, many SNCC activists felt that the speech was only "sound public relations," and Mary King continued that for a "couple of hundred staff members of SNCC and SCLC on the front lines in the Black Belt, this speech seemed too little and too late."

Nevertheless, almost all activists and liberals could agree that the proposed Civil Rights Act was a step in the right direction, and on August 28 they merged forces and demonstrated for its passage during the March on Washington. They came from all over the nation, some 200,000 blacks and whites. As they marched many held hands and sang, and as they walked past the Capitol they chanted: "Pass that bill! Pass that bill!" They continued on to the Lincoln Memorial, and on the steps Joan Baez greeted them with the struggle's anthem, "We Shall Overcome." She then joined Peter, Paul and Mary and sang "Blowin' in the Wind." Bob Dylan sang about the recent murder of black activist Medgar Evers, and Mahalia Jackson lead the massive crowd with spirituals. Then came the speeches. All the major black organizations were represented—NAACP, CORE, SCLC, the Urban League, and SNCC—and their leaders gave short addresses. SNCC's new chairman, John Lewis, had written a tough draft speech which criticized the administration, demanded immediate federal protection and stated that SNCC "will not wait for the President, the Justice Department, nor Congress, but we will take matters into our own hands." When the draft circulated before the march, other civil rights leaders objected, and for the sake of unity Lewis moderated his speech. He told of Mississippi sharecroppers who worked twelve hours for starvation wages, and of students in jail on trumped-up charges. He wondered about both the Republicans and Democrats and charged that American politics was "dominated by politicians who build their careers on immoral compromises," and he asked, "Where is the political party that will make it unnecessary to have Marches on Washington?" He warned those who advocated patience that blacks "do not want to be free gradually. We want our freedom and we want it now." And he urged blacks to join the great social revolution sweeping the nation, and to "stay in the streets of every city, every village and every hamlet of this nation . . . until the unfinished revolution of 1776 is complete."[23]

While Lewis's speech demonstrated the growing militancy of some activists in SNCC, it was overshadowed by the more hopeful and idealistic words of Martin Luther King, Jr. He began by recalling the "sacred obligation" promised by the Emancipation Proclamation and Declaration of Independence, and he stated that "Now is the time to make real the promises of Democracy. . . . Now is the time to open the doors of opportunity to all of God's children." He reminded Americans that blacks could not be satisfied as long as they "cannot gain lodging in the motels of the highways and the hotels of the cities . . . as long as the Negro's basic mobility is from a smaller ghetto to a larger one. We can never be satisfied as long as our children are stripped of their selfhood and robbed of their dignity by signs stating: 'For Whites Only.' " Instead, King had a dream:

> I have a dream that one day on the red hills of Georgia the sons of former slaves and the sons of former slaveowners will be able to sit down together at the table of brotherhood. I have a dream that one day even the State of Mississippi, a state sweltering with the heat of injustice, sweltering with the heart of oppression, will be transformed into an oasis of freedom and justice. I have a dream that my four little children will one day live in a nation where they will not be judged by the color of their skin but by the content of their character. I have a dream today. . . .
>
> When we let freedom ring, when we let it ring from every village and every hamlet, from every state and every city, we will be able to speed up that day when all God's children, black men and white men, Jews and Gentiles, Protestants and Catholics, will be able to join hands and sing in the words of that old Negro spiritual, "Free at last! Free at last! Thank God almighty, we are free at last!"

"At that moment," stated a listener, there was a "coming together of people with a man who . . . reached out to people. It was truly unbeliev-able. There'll never be another moment like that." It was the pinnacle of hope—for the civil rights struggle, and for the decade. While a few in the movement had grown militant, while some had advocated immediate change in revolutionary terms, King carried the day and a great sea of listeners roared their approval. The nation, finally, seemed to be moving forward, moving toward equality for all. After the speeches, President Kennedy invited civil rights leaders to the White House. He was glowing, and in his private quarters he complimented the activists on their march.

"It seemed like the beginning of a new era for America," recalled John Lewis, "And then, not long afterward, President Kennedy was killed. It was shattering."[24]

Kennedy's assassination on November 22 shocked the nation. "It was too big, too sudden, too overwhelming, and it meant too much," David Brinkley told a grieving television audience who watched three days and nights of images: a smiling president in a black limousine waving to crowds in Dallas . . . the slow-motion scene of JFK in the back seat, his head jerking forward and back to his wife's shoulder . . . secret service agents climbing on the car's trunk as it rushed off to the hospital . . . a distraught Vice President Johnson taking the oath of office on *Air Force One* . . . a crowded hallway in the Dallas jail as Jack Ruby suddenly stepped out, pointed a pistol, and shot suspect Lee Harvey Oswald . . . the riderless horses pulling the slain president's casket, a family in black, and the farewell salute from his son, John Jr.

To the nation, and to the emerging sixties generation, the assassination was a crucial event. After a few years of promising rhetoric, JFK's sudden death shattered hope and marked the end of innocence. In the first month after his death more than 700,000 mourners paid their respects at his grave in Arlington National Cemetery. One said to her friend, "We'll never laugh again." "No," the other responded, "We'll laugh again but we'll never be young again." For months, even years, there was sadness. "I truly felt I had lost a dear friend," wrote Ron Kovic. "I was deeply hurt for a long time afterward." Like Pearl Harbor for their parents, the assassination was one of those rare events that stirred the younger generation to remember where they were, what they were doing on that fateful day. "I'll never forget that cold drizzly day," one baby boomer recalled. "I was in high school study hall with two hundred other restless teenagers when we got the news. First there was shock, then disbelief, and in a few minutes the girl in front of me put her head down on her desk and started gently weeping. Within minutes, most of us joined her."

The assassination also provoked Americans to question the life of the young president. In death John Kennedy's stature grew to almost epic proportions, and by the 1980s citizens ranked him their favorite president. Even his critics noted that in foreign policy, the commander-in-chief during the Bay of Pigs and Cuban Missile Crisis seemingly had shifted from a cold warrior to a more thoughtful and progressive leader. In 1962 his administration was flexible in negotiating a coalition government in the Laos crisis and the next year he ended above-ground atomic testing by signing the Test Ban Treaty with the Soviet Union. Others, however, wondered about his infatuation with the Special Forces, and his continued increases of Green Berets and other advisers in Vietnam. In civil rights, JFK grew in the presidency and eventually became a supporter of the movement with his landmark speech in June. In a struggle filled with bigotry and resistance, Kennedy after his death became the martyr for the opposite—for equality and progress. His admirers boosted this view, and during the decade one could often find his portrait hanging in black homes. Yet later historians have demonstrated that JFK often was absent from civil rights decisions, and that he was more interested in politics and foreign affairs. Rarely has a president promised so much and accomplished so little, or as one biographer concluded: "At best he was an 'interim' President who had promised but not performed."[25] In fact, while the president was sympathetic to civil rights, the activists—young and old, black and white—put their lives on the line, confronted racial hypocrisy in the South, created the mood and demonstrated the need for civil rights, and that forced JFK to act, to uphold the basic tenants of democracy as expressed in the Constitution.

Lyndon Baines Johnson became president, and stated in his first address to Congress: "So let us here highly resolve that John Fitzgerald Kennedy did not live—or die—in vain," and then he ended his speech with:

> America, America,
> God shed his grace on thee
> And crown thy good
> With brotherhood
> From sea to shining sea.

Eight months later President Johnson signed the Civil Rights Act of 1964. After blacks had resided for three centuries in America, Congress finally recognized that they were citizens protected by the Constitution. This landmark legislation raised the issue of "public" verses "private." Contrary to conservatives, the administration supported the view that any privately owned enterprise that accepted taxpayers' funds or business was public. Consequently the act desegregated all public facilities and most companies, authorized the federal government to withhold funds to programs practicing discrimination, and it established an Equal Employment Opportunity Commission. The act also provided aid to school districts that integrated and prohibited discrimination in national elections, but failed to address another important issue for blacks—the right to vote in state and local elections—and so again activists pushed on, this time to Mississippi.

One can pass laws, but that doesn't change minds. Few blacks in the Deep South had ever voted, most had no say in who would be their local masters. SNCC activists had attempted to address this situation by working with local blacks to register voters, without much success. Mississippi was over 40 percent black, a third of its counties had black majorities, but in three years activists had registered only about 5 percent of those eligible voters. A coalition of movement organizations decided, therefore, to change tactics. They decided to invite about a thousand white northern students to invade Mississippi for summer 1964 to help register black citizens. They assumed that northern public opinion and federal officials would not tolerate southerners assaulting white college students from prominent families.

In June, students from over 200 universities and colleges met with representatives of the Council of Federated Organizations in Oxford, Ohio. Earlier, COFO flyers had been distributed on some northern campuses to advertise the Mississippi Project. "A Domestic Freedom Corps will be working in Mississippi this summer. Its only weapons will be youth and courage. We need your help now." Other flyers explained that they were not interested in students who were limited in their perspectives, knew all the answers, or disliked politics. They wanted activists who were realistic, flexible, responsible, and understanding. They sought to avoid young students who would try to transform older black sharecroppers: "We are *not* trying to make the Mississippi farmer just like us." The volunteers were not paid for the summer, and had to provide their own transportation and bond in case they landed in jail, thus most came from affluent families and attended the finest universities. In fact, almost 60 percent came from Harvard, Yale, Stanford, Princeton, Berkeley, Michigan, or Wisconsin, and so some felt that they represented the "counter power elite." Most also shared the optimism and idealism so prevalent in the early years of the 1960s. "There is so much to do, so many barriers between men to be broken, so much hate to be overcome," stated one volunteer, and another added, "There is a moral wave building among today's youth and I intend to catch it!"

As they arrived in Oxford, they were greeted by the COFO staff, which included Bob Moses, who told the first group of 300: "The guerilla war in Mississippi is not much different from that in Vietnam. But when we tried to see President Johnson, his secretary said that Vietnam was popping up all over his calendar and he hadn't time to talk to us." He paused, and then added, "Our goals are limited. If we can go and come back alive, then that is something. Mississippi has been called 'The Closed Society.' It is closed, locked. We think the key is in the vote."[26]

During the next week veteran activists trained new volunteers in voter registration and in nonviolent tactics, and naturally at that time and throughout the summer there were interpersonal problems. Many SNCC activists were black veterans who had developed a strong sense of racial pride and considered themselves militants or radicals, while many of the white students had just joined the movement or had been involved only in local civil rights issues and considered themselves more idealistic and liberal. At times, relations between SNCC veterans and the new white volunteers suffered, and one student lamented that blacks sometimes "treated us as brusquely as sergeants treat buck privates during the first month of basic training." Also there was tension between males and females of both races, especially concerning the forbidden fruit—black men dating and having sexual encounters with white women. All volunteers were part of the "beloved community." "If they really believed in equality," one white female later asked, "why shouldn't they sleep together?" While many relationships during that summer resulted in understanding, even marriages, many others increased tension and especially irritated young black female activists who felt neglected, and who eventually struck the first blow for women's liberation in the movement. Finally, some black activists resented the fact that although their lives had been in jeopardy for years, the only way to provoke the federal government to provide protection was for southerners to threaten the lives of affluent white students. As one black SNCC activist commented, "Wherever those white volunteers went, FBI agents followed."[27]

But the agents didn't follow too closely, nor did they protect the volunteers, and that was demonstrated just a few days after the first group of students arrived in Mississippi. During the evening of June 21, Michael Schwerner, Andrew Goodman, and James Chaney disappeared while driving away from the small town of Philadelphia, Mississippi. Schwerner and Goodman were whites from New York, the former a graduate of Cornell and the latter a student at Queens College. Chaney was a black Mississippian who along with Schwerner had been active in CORE. Since there had been four "mystery killings" of blacks in the state during the first half of 1964, activists feared for their coworkers' lives and immediately called for a search. Governor Paul Johnson scoffed at the idea and declared a publicity hoax: "They could be in Cuba." Two days later authorities found the volunteers' burned-out car. President Johnson ordered sailors from a nearby navy base to conduct a massive search with the help of the FBI. Federal agents searched for six weeks before they discovered the bodies buried in an earthen dam. Goodman and Schwerner had been shot in the heart, and a physician stated that Chaney "had been beaten to a pulp. . . . In my twenty-five years as a pathologist and medical examiner, I have never seen bones so severely shattered, except in tremendously high speed accidents or airplane crashes." A few days later Schwerner's widow told the nation: "We all know that this search with hundreds of sailors is because Andrew Goodman and my husband are white. If only Chaney was involved, nothing would've been done."[28]

Rita Schwerner was right, unfortunately, and her husband's death was just the beginning of violence. A selection from just the first week of the Mississippi Freedom Summer log:

June 23 **Jackson:** Shots fired at home of Rev. R. L. T. Smith. White man escapes on foot.

Moss Point: Knights of Pythias Hall fire-bombed.

June 24 **Canton:** Civil rights car hit by bullet.

June 25 **Ruleville:** Williams Chapel fire-bombed.

June 26 **Columbus:** Seven voter registration workers arrested for distributing literature without a city permit. Bond: $400 each.

Clinton: Church of Holy Ghost arson.

Jackson: CORE field secretary beaten at Hinds County jail while a federal prisoner.

June 27 **Greenwood:** Several phone harassments; bomb threat.

June 28 **Jackson:** "Hospitality Month" in Mississippi: white volunteer kicked over from behind, slugged on arrival from Oxford at local train station.

June 29   **Hattiesburg:** Two cars owned by volunteers shot by four whites in pickup truck at 1:00 a.m.

June 30   **Ruleville:** Man loses job for housing white volunteers.

Holly Springs: SNCC staff worker jumped by local white who threatens to shoot both him and his office with 12-gauge shotgun.

"Some day Mississippians are going to have to grow up," wrote historian James W. Silver of Old Miss in 1964, "to accept the judgments of civilization." Throughout the summer racists beat 80 civil rights workers and shot at 30 volunteers, killing four. Southern policemen arrested over a thousand on flimsy charges, and one coordinator, Hunter Morey, was arrested three times in the same city in less than four hours. Terrorists bombed or burned 30 black homes and businesses. In McComb there were 17 bombings in three months, and racists burned 37 black churches. Mississippi was burning.

"It was the longest nightmare of my life," Cleveland Sellers later said.[29] Nevertheless, volunteers continued working throughout the long, hot Mississippi Freedom Summer. They traveled throughout the state, on highways and byways, walking and talking to black croppers. They built "freedom schools" so that illiterate, poor blacks could learn to articulate their desires and demands, and community centers to "strengthen a home-grown freedom movement" which would survive as the volunteers returned to college campuses for fall semester. Activists also attempted to register blacks in the state's Democratic party, and soon realized that white Democrats would not budge. In fact, after a thousand volunteers worked an entire summer, they had registered less than 1600 black voters with the Mississippi Democratic party. That had been expected, so activists had prepared by developing another tactic: Following the rules of the Democratic National Committee they established an alternate party, the Mississippi Freedom Democratic party. The volunteers enrolled nearly 60,000 disenfranchised blacks into the MFDP, and those newly franchised voters elected 44 "freedom delegates" to attend the 1964 Democratic convention.

In August the Democratic party held their convention in Atlantic City. The "Freedom Democrats" stated that they would support the party's nomination and platform, whatever the outcome. White Mississippi delegates remained quiet, reminding others of the 1948 convention in which white southerners walked out and formed the Dixiecrats because of civil rights proposals of then mayor Hubert H. Humphrey and President Harry Truman. Black delegates testified in front of the party's credentials committee, stating that since they were not allowed to participate in state elections, the MFDP represented the only freely elected party in Mississippi.

They demanded to be seated as the true delegates for the state. On national television, James Farmer, Roy Wilkins, and many others described violence and intimidation in Mississippi. Fannie Lou Hamer, the granddaughter of slaves, revealed her efforts to register voters—being kicked off the plantation where she had been a sharecropper for eighteen years, shot at, beaten until she could no longer walk: "I question America, is this America, the land of the free and the home of the brave, where . . . our lives be threatened daily because we want to live as decent human beings?" Martin Luther King pleaded with the Democrats: "If you value your party, if you value your nation, if you value the democratic process, you must recognize the Freedom party delegation." Joseph Rauh, a white attorney and associate of Senator Hubert Humphrey, asked, "Are you going to throw out of here the people who want to work for Lyndon Johnson, who are willing to be beaten and shot and thrown in jail to work for Lyndon Johnson? Are we for the oppressor or the oppressed?"

The credentials committee voted for the oppressor: They refused to seat the Freedom Democrats. Southern white delegations had told LBJ that they would walk out of the convention if the committee, and the party, supported the MFDP, and that might bring about a Republican South and perhaps even throw the election to Republican Senator Barry Goldwater. The president could not take that chance. Furthermore, Johnson had signed legislation in 1964 that had given blacks and their liberal allies not only the Civil Rights Act but also new programs for food stamps, health, education, and an Office of Economic Opportunity to wage his War on Poverty. He would need some southern support to pass even more programs the next year which would result in the nation becoming his Great Society. To buy off the liberals, Johnson offered the vice presidency to their candidate, Senator Humphrey, and a compromise: MFDP would be allowed two seats while the white Mississippi delegation would be seated at the convention—but for the last time. In the future only state delegations that enfranchised all citizens would be allowed at the convention of the Democratic party.

The compromise meant that the 1968 Democratic convention would be a ruckus affair—for many unforeseen reasons—and that the 1964 convention was a watershed in the civil rights crusade. It highlighted a growing division within the movement. At Atlantic City some older activists saw progress in the compromise and continued to participate in coalition politics in an attempt to liberalize the Democratic party. King and most mainstream blacks in organizations such as the NAACP and Urban League agreed with Bayard Rustin that the compromise was "not what any of us wanted, but it's the best we could get." Change was possible; after four years of violent struggle the status of black citizens had jumped a light year when compared with their first three centuries in America.

Most blacks shared the optimism of white liberals, and they overwhelmingly supported the Democratic party; in the 1964 election over 90 percent of black voters cast their ballots for Johnson. The Democrats became the party of progress, and many activists attempted to gain more influence in the party, a tactic that eventually led to the presidential campaigns of Senators Eugene McCarthy, Robert Kennedy, and George McGovern.

Other activists, especially younger ones in SNCC and CORE, were discouraged at Atlantic City. Some had been on the picket line since the Greensboro sit-ins in 1960, and now after four years of dangerous struggle they had achieved only a compromise that in another four years, in 1968, southern blacks would be allowed to participate in the democracy. Freedom Now! had been their demand, and they grew disillusioned. "It makes me want to cry when I remember how we colored kids started in the Movement, some of us naive, yes; but we were purehearted," one veteran said in 1964. "All I'd better say is this Movement has got my soul to aching. And it hurts. God . . . how it hurts." The convention convinced many activists in SNCC that racism was not only a problem in Jackson or Birmingham; it was national, and it was institutionalized by liberals making compromises in Washington and Atlantic City. The federal government was not the solution; it was part of the problem. While they had demonstrated peacefully federal officials had refused to protect them. SNCC had informed the FBI of over 150 incidents of intimidation and violence and none resulted in a vigorous investigation until two whites were killed outside of Philadelphia, Mississippi. In fact, between the Greensboro sit-ins and the Selma March of 1965 at least 26 civil rights workers were murdered, but only one of the killers went to prison. This violence, combined with the disappointment at Atlantic City, resulted in frustration, rage, and eventually a new demand: "We want much more than 'token positions,' " proclaimed Charles Sherrod after the convention. "We want power for our people."[30]

The eventual emergence of black power was only one result of the four years of activism from Greensboro to Atlantic City. The struggle influenced the entire decade.

To the young generation the struggle demonstrated that there was trouble in paradise—America was not living up to its Dream. "We are in Mississippi this morning," one volunteer wrote, "because we believed what we learned in the schools of this country—freedom and justice for all—but we did not *see* freedom and justice. We are here *because* we believe in this nation. . . . We are your children, living what *you* taught us as Truth." Teenagers growing up during cold war culture had been drilled in school that "all men are created equal" only to realize upon graduation that their country was a class society in which some were equal and others were unequal, some had "unalienable rights" and others had few or no rights. "The high school civics you believed in," Stanford student David Harris said, "didn't apply to Mississippi." This discrepancy between the ideal and reality, between what was said and what was done, stimulated many students to become activists—and it provoked them to begin questioning authority. Freedom Summer volunteer Sally Belfrage remembered that her white colleagues "were changed for good; they had come to see how naked were their kings."

As these young Americans became involved, they also realized that hypocrisy and inequality were not just a "southern problem." When they returned home many were hurt and frustrated to hear the bigoted attitudes of their friends, and many came to agree with black lawyer Len Holt, who wrote then that the "nation is *not* composed of 49 states and a foreign island named Mississippi; damned or blessed, America is composed of 50 Mississippis which vary from each other in degrees."

These first activists exposed America, and the message was delivered to the nation's homes by the media, especially television, which played a momentous role throughout the sixties. TV became a courier of the struggle and activists realized it; they used it for their purposes and that was instructive for later advocates concerned with other causes. The media had the power to focus the nation on a problem and helped to make the struggle the nation's top news story in the first half of the decade. As the barrage of dramatic events flashed across the screen the sixties began to blur from a chronological experience to a psychological one: hefty white policemen with guns and clubs, firehoses blasting demonstrators off their feet, vicious dogs snapping at terrified marchers, tear gas and fire in the streets. All the while, the recurring vision of black and white clergy, arm and arm, leading youthful marchers and singing "We Shall Overcome." The message was clear. "I don't believe you could watch a poor black being hit by a big fat southern cop and have it ever leave you," said a baby boomer. "How could you not be moved by that image?" "And," another added, "how could you not know which side you wanted to be on?"[31]

Activists returning to campuses for fall semester 1964 knew what side they wanted to be on, then and throughout the sixties—the movement for change. The struggle encouraged them and demonstrated that it was possible to transform cold war culture. Nonviolent direct action had forced federal intervention, and it had wounded Jim Crow.

Yet activists also had learned that change meant struggle. "Power concedes nothing without a demand," stated Frederick Douglass in 1863, and a century later King wrote from the Birmingham jail: "We know through painful experience that freedom is never voluntarily given by the oppressor; it must be demanded by the oppressed." Many in the establishment would resist and would fight back throughout the decade. Maintaining

social control during cold war culture had been simple; the older generation searched for the scapegoat, smearing the few who advocated change
as disloyal or outside agitators.

The charade continued. In November 1964, FBI director J. Edgar
Hoover called King "the most notorious liar in the country" and he added
that SCLC was "spearheaded by Communists and moral degenerates."
Many southerners agreed, and they defended their way of life with other
worn justifications such as "states' rights" and "Christian values." All were
rationalizations for racism, and all were indefensible. The Bible did not
support segregation or racism, just the contrary, and when states joined
the union they lost their right to pick and choose which federal laws they
would enforce. As historians since have demonstrated, using FBI files,
and as many activists have confirmed, Communism had nothing to do
with the struggle for civil rights.

"We didn't need a foreign ideology," Mary King wrote, "we owed no
debt to any political theory other than Jeffersonian democracy." Freedom
Summer volunteer Mario Savio added, "We'd been raised on a diet of
anti-communism. America was anti-communist, anti-socialist, anti-
anything critical of society. . . . But you didn't need an ideology for
the civil rights movement—it was America contradicting itself on its own
best terms."[32]

Civil rights simply concerned power, and that was based on race. Were
all citizens—whites and blacks—going to have proportionate control of
the economy, society, and politics of the South, and ultimately of the
United States? Conservatives said, "Maintain the status quo," liberals said,
"Play the game by our rules," and activists demanded that the nation live
up to its Constitution: Freedom Now!

The struggle also demonstrated that national leaders often articulated
issues but did not lead the masses. Because the media focused on one
person, it had the ability to create "leaders" by searching for one spokesman in a movement that was sweeping through towns and villages all
over the South. The "white press's eternal search for a 'Negro leader' who
can account for everything that transpires is all but ludicrous," wrote black
author Louis Lomax. National spokespersons, of course, were important,
but their organizations often competed for funds and publicity while
scores of individuals and local organizers took a stand in communities
from Greensboro to Atlantic City. "The traditional left," Bob Moses explained in December 1964, "keeps talking about coalitions and leaders,
but always from the top; to them Mississippi is a chess board. . . . The
people don't need spokesmen or decision makers, just the confidence to
try to represent themselves." When considering the movement's achieve-
ments, a historian concluded, "the real accomplishments of the black
freedom struggle stemmed not so much from the activities of the

administrators and articulators as from the efforts of the grass roots organizers who actually built and directed the movement in the South."[33]
Marion Barry, Fannie Lou Hamer, Selyn McCollum, Diane Nash, Bernice Reagon, Willie Peacock, Michael Schwerner, Hosea Williams, Bob
Zellner, and hundreds of other "ordinary" citizens took the extraordinary
step of putting their lives on the line for something in which they believed. Leadership in the struggle and in the movement throughout the
sixties was best described by a statement Gandhi made during India's independence crusade: "There go my people. I must follow them for I am
their leader."

The experience of being part of the struggle changed most activists; the
South had been the boot camp for an emerging movement. They often
gained self-confidence, for they had confronted a major problem, organized and adopted aims, invented tactics, and had some impact on thaw-
ing cold war culture. A thousand students received their training during
Freedom Summer and so did some 250 northern clergymen and lawyers
who volunteered their services and made contacts that would be valuable
when addressing other problems later in the decade. Furthermore, the
relative success in the South increased the desire for change and provoked
more activism. For the first time since the 1930s a new generation of
Americans viewed activism as a legitimate part of the democracy. Activism would become fashionable, and in 1965 over 750 white northern
students volunteered to work in the South for the second Freedom Summer; thousands began to demonstrate against the Vietnam War; and many
more joined campus organizations.

As volunteers returned to college they discussed civil rights and questioned other issues, and some read manifestos such as *The Port Huron
Statement*. Some volunteers felt that they had experienced the new left's
view of America in the South—racial bigotry, growing white affluence
surrounded by black poverty, the powerlessness and fear of ordinary people, and a southern power elite that stifled dissent. More students realized
that they were the "people of this generation, bred in at least modest
comfort, housed now in universities, looking uncomfortably at the world
we inherit." SDS and other campus organizations grew, and after the
Atlantic City convention, it became obvious to those veterans of SDS and
SNCC that their earlier allies—liberals—would abandon them to compromise with the power elite. They became increasingly disillusioned with
"the Establishment," and some began turning left toward radicalism. "I
went from being a liberal Peace Corps-type Democrat," one volunteer
admitted, "to a raging, maniacal lefty."

The struggle also affected activists in another way: It forced many to
begin questioning their parents. Working in ghettos on ERAP projects or
teaching illiterate sharecroppers in southern freedom schools tended to

alienate activists from mainstream culture. "Coming out of Mississippi and into the 'civilized white' world was hard," a volunteer wrote after returning to her northern suburb. "It was like cultural shock or something. . . . I don't know quite what I am saying except that I am against much of what my family stands for." Many activists were disappointed by their parents and friends in the suburbs. After Debra Eisenberg returned to the North from the South, her parents asked, "Well, what was it like?" The young woman began telling them about the poverty, racism, and hopelessness, and then mom and dad blurted out, "No, no, it's not like that." Suburbanites could not stand to hear the reality of the South, just as many later would not listen to returning Vietnam veterans.

Some activists began changing their lifestyles. Many female volunteers wondered about the traditional role of women in society. After all, as Andrew Young later admitted, "Women were the spine of our movement. It was women going door to door, speaking with their neighbors, meeting in voter-registration classes together, organizing through their churches, that gave the vital momentum and energy to the movement, that made it a mass movement." Female activists had demanded equality for blacks, and some began to wonder why they did not insist on that for themselves, as the struggle planted the seeds that would bloom into women's liberation.

Female and male activists also began thinking of themselves as part of a different society, one more flexible and experimental which offered more personal liberty, an interracial community within their own generation. Some began wearing different clothing. One volunteer stated that although "six of us had to sleep sweating on the dirty floor" of the Freedom House in Mississippi, that was not the excuse for abandoning their collegiate dress for work shirts and blue jeans: "It was part of our personal rebellion, tied to the fact that the Summer Project was as much an effort to work free from our own pasts as to help black people build a better future for themselves." Some began to consider the values of their parents' generation, to begin searching for new beliefs, as they began a long walk toward a counterculture.[34]

This "community of believers" began to think of themselves as part of a "movement." Whether they were the few dozen intellectuals who had written *The Port Huron Statement*, the one hundred SDS members who worked on ERAP programs, the few hundred SNCC activists, the 1000 volunteers for Mississippi Freedom Summer, or the 200,000 who had attended the March on Washington, those who had participated felt a solidarity with other activists. The commitment, Mary King later wrote, resulted in an "intense feeling of interdependency" and the "spirit of comradeship" that became part of the sixties generation. This attitude also developed into another theme of the decade: us against them. "We could not trust anyone else. We had to trust each other and we did." They *belonged* to a movement, and to a new generation that was seizing the moral leadership of the nation, that was confronting cold war culture.

That feeling was exhilarating for the first wave of activists in the early sixties. "In this brief moment of time," Tom Hayden wrote, "the sixties generation entered its age of innocence, overflowing with hope." While the enthusiasm of some activists had been broken in the South, the generation as a whole seemed to have unlimited potential. As Howard Zinn wrote in 1964: these "young people are the nation's most vivid reminder that there is an unquenchable spirit alive in the world today, beyond race, beyond nationality, beyond class. It is a spirit which seeks to embrace all people everywhere."

For the generation, then, the early sixties was an era of expanding optimism, and that spirit often stayed with activists for the rest of their lives. Casey Hayden reminisced twenty-five years later that the movement "was everything: home and family, food and work, love and a reason to live. . . . It was outrageous, really. Exciting, liberating, spicy, when we were young and in the South. The movement—sometimes I have longed for it so profoundly. . . . It was a holy time." It was an era when ordinary people felt that they were doing their own small part to brighten the future of America.[35] "I know that I exaggerate the importance of that summer, and especially my role in it," said a Mississippi volunteer years later. "But those memories have served me well. The . . . purest moment of my life was in that little church in Hattiesburg, sweating like a pig and crying like a baby, singing, 'This Little Light of Mine.' Do you know the words? One part goes:

> The light that shines is the light of love,
> lights the darkness from above.
> It shines on me and it shines on you,
> shows what the power of love can do.
> This little light of mine, I'm gonna let it shine,
> Let it shine, let it shine, let it shine.

The Movement and the Sixties Generation

This is the winter of our discontent . . . and although we have been quiet in the past, now we are beginning to stir. For we are angry, and there is a point beyond we will not be pushed.

Roger Ebert, University of Illinois *Daily Illini*, January 1965

This civil rights movement is evolving from a protest movement into a full-fledged *social movement*.

Bayard Rustin, 1965

"Last summer I went to Mississippi to join the struggle there for civil rights," said Berkeley student Mario Savio in 1964. "This fall I am engaged in another phase of the same struggle, this time in Berkeley. In Mississippi an autocratic and powerful minority rules, through organized violence, to suppress the vast, virtually powerless majority. In California, the privileged minority manipulates the university bureaucracy to suppress the students' political expression."

That expression had been curtailed by the University of California as students arrived on the Berkeley campus for fall semester in September. As was typical for university officials during the cold war era, a dean simply informed all student organizations that from now on they were no longer permitted to set up tables on campus to promote "off-campus" causes such as civil rights, and this ban applied to the traditional area for such endeavors, a small strip of property at the campus's main entrance where Telegraph Avenue met Bancroft Way.[1]

Activism had long since arrived in Berkeley. In 1958 students organized Towards an Active Student Community, which later became SLATE, and a few dozen began discussing civil rights, capital punishment, and nuclear disarmament. "For us," student Michael Rossman later wrote, "the discovery was of each other. We began to realize we were not alone."

In spring 1960 they acted, holding silent vigils at San Quentin to protest the execution of Caryl Chessman and picketing the House Un-American Activities Committee investigation of Communist activities in the Bay Area, a demonstration that led to Black Friday. Activism increased, and by the 1963–64 academic year hundreds of students had become involved in civil rights demonstrations, picketing hotels, automobile dealerships, restaurants, and other businesses that had discriminatory employment practices. At Lucky food stores, activists held "shop-ins," filling grocery carts with food, and after going through the checkout line, saying, "Sorry, I forgot my money. If you would hire some Negroes I would remember it next time." They picketed the Oakland *Tribune*, whose conservative owner was on the university's board of regents, and in March the local campaign reached a crescendo when 2000 violated a court order restricting the number of protesters in front of the Sheraton Palace Hotel; police arrested 800.

Political debate also was mounting. The Republican convention was held during June 1964 in San Francisco and the candidacy of conservative Barry Goldwater inspired discussion as he faced Lyndon Johnson in the upcoming elections. Then, in August, just weeks before students returned to classes, President Johnson declared that North Vietnam had attacked U.S. ships in the Gulf of Tonkin. He asked for and received from Congress the Gulf of Tonkin Resolution, which stimulated more student debate about America's role in South Vietnam. And as fall semester began in September approximately fifty students returned from volunteer work during Mississippi Summer. At Berkeley and at other universities many of these students were welcomed back to campus as "civil rights heroes."

The university administration apparently was under pressure by conservatives in the state, community, and on the board of regents to curb activism when they issued the political ban. The students' response was dramatic. On September 21 campus organizations of all political persuasions united—from the Young Socialist Alliance to Youth for Goldwater—and they violated the ban. Two hundred students picketed on campus with signs such as "UC Manufactures Safe Minds," "Ban Political Birth Control," and "Bomb the Ban." To most, the issue was freedom of speech. "We're allowed to say why we think something is good or bad," said activist Jackie Goldberg, "but we're not allowed to distribute information as to what to do about it. Inaction is the rule, rather than the exception, in our society and on this campus." The movement gained support, and a week later some students set up political tables. Administrators took down names, and ordered civil rights veteran Jack Weinberg to appear in front of a dean. He did the next day, but he was followed by 500 supporters who packed into the administration building, Sproul Hall, and stayed until early the next morning. University of California president Clark Kerr suspended eight activists, but that did not stifle dissent as it would have in the 1950s. It only increased ill will and resulted in more protest. "A student who has been chased by the KKK in Mississippi," said student Roger Sandall, "is not easily scared by academic bureaucrats."

The Free Speech Movement it was called, and along with the civil rights protests the previous spring it demonstrated the emergence of a new generation. "How proud I felt," wrote Berkeley student Sara Davidson. "I belonged to a great new body of students who cared about the problems of the world. No longer would youth be apathetic. That was the fifties. We were *committed*."[2]

Ever since, Berkeley has been synonymous with student protest and campus rebellion in the 1960s. Historians have described the rise of student power by examining the events at Berkeley in 1964 and then those at Columbia University in 1968 as if little happened during those years on other campuses. Sociologists and psychologists have written a library of articles and books postulating numerous theories of why students were challenging the system—family affluence, permissive child rearing, developmental stress, the impending collapse of capitalism, and even that young male students were plagued with castration complexes.[3] These interpretations are misleading. During the mid-1960s the rise of student power was a national phenomenon concerning many more issues than just free speech on one prominent campus. Furthermore, social science theories might explain the behavior of some individuals, but will not account for the rise of campus turmoil. Instead, one must examine the massive new generation—the sixties generation—as a sizable percentage arrived on campuses, and then discovered that university administrators restricted their personal behavior and constitutional rights.

In 1964 and 1965 the first babies born after World War II were coming of age; they were celebrating their eighteenth birthdays. The enormous postwar birth rate lasted eighteen years, from 1946 to 1964, and it resulted in the largest generation in our history, over 70 million, the baby boomers. Their sheer numbers changed the face of the nation. In 1960, because of the low birth rate during depression and war, America had grown middle-aged; there were only 16 million youths, 18- to 24-year-olds. The baby boom, however, brought about a dramatic shift. By 1970, the number of youth soared to about 25 million. Suddenly, the nation was young. The "sixties generation" included baby boomers who were born in the late 1940s and early 1950s, and the generation also comprised older siblings, those born during World War II who became the "first wave" of activists in the early 1960s. Consequently the sixties generation could be defined to include anyone who turned eighteen during the era from 1960 to 1972. The oldest was born in 1942 and turned 30 in 1972, and the youngest was born in 1954 and turned 18 in 1972. This generation numbered over 45 million, about 33 million who also were part of the baby boom, and this group felt special, especially after the traumatic events of the decade. A 1969 survey revealed that 80 percent of youth felt part of "my generation."

America seemed young, and in mid-decade being part of the sixties generation was suddenly important. Businesses cashed in on youth as Ford Motor Company developed a car for kids, the Mustang, and as a soft drink company proclaimed the arrival of the "Pepsi Generation." To explain, exploit, or cater to the young became an obsession, and the number of commercials soared while articles on youth tripled during the decade. The Associated Press declared that youth "made more headlines than anybody. . . . 1964 would have to go down as the Year of the Kids." In 1965 *Newsweek* claimed that "America's future has always belonged to its youth but never before have the young staked out so large a claim to America's present." And *Time* proclaimed, "For the Man of the Year 1966 is a generation: the man—and woman—of 25 and under."

Furthermore, and because of postwar affluence, the sixties generation had an opportunity missed by their parents' depression generation. The children could spend years at college, even travel, before they "had to settle down." This increased the probability of a "generation gap" between parents and kids. The years between the late teens and early twenties usually are stressful, rebellious, as individuals search for themselves, a mate, a career. The decade was destined to be more rambunctious than earlier eras as baby boomers passed through growing pains. The large number of kids also meant that throughout the decade there always would be an abundant supply of young faces entering college, being drafted, or being examined by academics and journalists.

Yet in the mid-1960s what it meant to be part of the sixties generation was uncertain. Journalists labeled some youth "committed," but they named most the "explosive," "aloof" and especially the "cool" generation. Taking the term from jazz and the beatniks, the media declared that this generation felt that it was "cool" to be young.

The nation seemed flooded with the cool generation, and they began exhibiting youthful forms of rebellion as they dominated the American scene. Spring breaks at Fort Lauderdale became an annual pilgrimage for boys participating in the great hunt for "beach, broads and booze," while at Daytona Beach they searched for "sex, sand, suds and sun." On Easter weekend some 75,000 collegians held a huge bash at Daytona Beach. All was rather serene until one girl, who was being tossed on a blanket, lost her swimsuit. The riot was on. A Michigan State sophomore boasted, "I just came to have me some fun and get drunk," as police arrested almost 2000 for public promiscuity and drinking.

Labor Day weekend the party moved to Hampton Beach, New Hampshire. Some 10,000 teens arrived at the quiet seashore resort which prohibited beer and the new fad, "bundling," sleeping together on the beach. Kids naturally broke the law and a riot ensued. Police attempted to disperse the crowd with fire hoses, tear gas and dogs, but eventually the governor had to call in the National Guard. The ruckus lasted two nights, and the authorities drove the crowd three miles, literally across the state line and into Massachusetts. Those who did not get out of town were arrested, and the judge showed the older generations' displeasure by handing out stiff sentences of up to nine months in jail and $1000 fines. While the governor stated that the beach riot was a "symptom of the moral sickness in American youth," the kids disagreed. To many in the sixties generation, the decade was becoming one long party.

Meanwhile in California: Surf's Up! Golden girls and flexing boys apparently surfed an endless wave or played a continual game of volleyball before pizzas, nightly parties, and some heavy panting. Young love was celebrated in numerous movies between 1963 and 1965: *Beach Party, Muscle Beach Party, Bikini Beach, Beach Blanket Bingo.* By all appearances, the girls and guys of the "Mickey Mouse Club" had graduated from the show and were having a wonderful time, wiggling and giggling, bulging out of their swimsuits. It appeared that everyone was eager to learn "How to Stuff a Wild Bikini." As The Beach Boys sang "Surfin U.S.A." and drove their "Little Deuce Coupe," tanned "California Girls" exclaimed, "Life's so bitchin'!"

It was more than that, for the sixties generation was getting its first taste of the sexual revolution. Birth control pills became available for married women, and by mid-decade single coeds were flocking to family planning clinics, wearing a friend's wedding ring, and getting their monthly prescriptions of "the pill." Along with the diaphragm, the pill dramatically increased a woman's feeling of independence as it placed birth control in her hands and liberated her from the dreaded fear of getting pregnant. The press began writing about sexual mores of the young, and *Newsweek* explained to the older generation the new definition of a "technical virgin," a "boy or girl who has experienced almost all varieties of heterosexual sex—except intercourse."

Men made new demands on their girlfriends, turning up the pressure to "do it." A "boy used to date two girls simultaneously, a nice girl and a not-so-nice girl," a Michigan coed explained. "Now he wants two girls in one. The nice girl who doesn't want to go along has a problem." A Bennington female stated, "If a girl reaches 20 and she's still a virgin, she begins to wonder whether there's anything wrong with her," and a Vassar coed added, "It's a load off my mind, losing my virginity."

The older generation was shocked. "Morals don't mean a thing to them," a beach hotel manager said about the kids during spring break in Florida. In Darien, Connecticut, a suburban community that prided itself on wholesome children, church attendance, and propriety, parents were alarmed by reports of high school pregnancies, heavy drinking, and "sexual activity going on at the drive-in-theater of every kind and degree."

The kids were beginning to express values of their own generation. "We've discarded the idea that the loss of virginity is related to degeneracy," an Ohio State senior explained. "Premarital sex doesn't mean the down fall of society, at least not the kind of society that we're going to build."[4]

That society was becoming increasingly sexy as the sixties generation dominated the media. In fashion, the girls of the 1950s had grown out of their bobby sox and pedal-pushers and in 1964 began wearing mini-skirts. Hemlines never had revealed so much leg, and many older women quickly adopted the new fad, even Jackie Kennedy. Coeds, meanwhile, were taking off one-piece bathing suits and wearing smaller and smaller "itsy bitsy teenie weenie yellow polka dot" bikinis, while some models created a sensation by wearing topless swimsuits. Teenagers bought what parents called "a dirty magazine," *Playboy*. Hugh Hefner's sexual values were merged with the 1950s can-do masculinity and presented on film in numerous James Bond movies. Sean Connery became the John Wayne to the sixties generation as he merged technology and sex to pursue "Pussy Galore" in *Goldfinger*.

"Most of all," the Associated Press wrote about 1964, "it was the year of the Beatles." The Beatles did not just come to America; they invaded. In February the rock group arrived at Kennedy International Airport and were met by 3000 screaming fans, mostly teenage girls. The Fabulous Four could not get through the crowd without the help of 200 policemen. For a month the group performed to shrieking, squealing audiences, and when they made their American TV debut on the Ed Sullivan Show, the program received the highest ratings in history: 72 percent of the New York audience tuned in. Beatlemania was an instant fad, and soon many of the sixties generation were abandoning crew cuts for long bangs and black boots.

The Beatles' sound and lyrics were similar to American popular music at that time; it was as adolescent as the baby boomers. Top hits of the era included Leslie Gore whining "It's my party and I'll cry if I want to," the Angels sneering, "My Boyfriend's back and you're gonna be in trouble," the Kingsmen slurring, "Louie, Louie," or the Temptations talking about "My Girl," my girl. Most popular, however, were surfer groups such as Jan and Dean and the Beach Boys, or the Motown sound of the Supremes. Between summer 1963 and 1965 the Beach Boys had nine songs in the top ten and the themes were "I Get Around," "Surfer Girl," and

"Do You Wanna Dance." While Jan and Dean were squealing around "Dead Man's Curve" en route to "Surf City," the Supremes sang "Baby Love" and wondered "Where Did Our Love Go?" The Beatles had the answer: "I Want to Hold Your Hand," "All My Loving," "And I Love Her." If it was "A Hard Day's Night" for the Beatles, it was not for the Beach Boys, who just had "Fun, Fun, Fun," telling the generation to "Dance, Dance, Dance." Kids agreed, and performed what one reporter labeled, "touch-less, wildly tribalistic dances like the 'frug' and the 'swim' and the 'mashed potato.' " Everyone was having "good, goood, gooood, good vibrations."

Yet the Beatles were having more impact than other bands. They were part of the British Invasion which included many English bands and which demonstrated that rock and roll—although a uniquely American invention—was becoming the music of the international postwar baby boom: The sixties would not just be an American phenomenon. Also, the Beatles looked and acted differently than clean-cut American performers. After the crew-cut 1950s, the "Fab Four" had relatively long, shaggy hair. After an era of learning "to respect your elders," they seemed irreverent, even joking about the Queen of England. The Beatles movie in 1965, *A Hard Day's Night*, was "almost all joy," a student critic wrote, because "all the dreary old adults are mocked and brushed aside." To many young Americans, these musicians symbolized rejection of 1950s morality, a revolt against authority, and estrangement from parents. "My mother hates them, my father hates them, my teacher hates them," said a young fan. "Can you think of three better reasons why I love them?"

A subtle revolt was under way, a generational conflict in which many youth felt different from their parents. As adolescents sprouted into adulthood they realized that their values were unique; they were more idealistic and tolerant, less concerned with Communism. A third of these high school graduates headed off to college, three times the percentage as during their parents' generation, and that naturally began to create tensions between moms and dads and their collegiate sons and daughters. "We sent them to a university," parents would say, "that's more than we ever had. What more could they want?" The generation gap was becoming evident by 1965, and The Who expressed it in song:

> People try to put us down,
> Just because we get around,
> Things they do look awful cold
> I hope I die before I get old. . . .
> Why don't you all fade away
> Don't try to dig what we all say.

That alienation naturally appeared on campus. *Newsweek* noted, "The young successfully 'Beatle-ized' the nation, and many think they may be about to 'Berkeley-ize' it as well." [5]

On campuses and in coffeehouses a growing number of students had been listening to young folk singers declaring the dawn of a new era. The cover blurb on Peter, Paul and Mary's debut album in 1962 proclaimed that the record "is bright with enthusiasm. No gimmicks. There is just something *Good* about it all. . . . One thing is for sure in any case: Honesty is back. Tell your neighbor." Many did, and soon the generation was singing out with Phil Ochs, Joan Baez, Tom Paxton, Judy Collins, Leonard Cohen, the Chad Mitchell Trio, and the Brothers Four.

The folk musicians' message was popular; it stated the emerging values of the sixties generation. ABC began a show in 1963 that featured folk singers, "Hootenanny," and soon ten million watched each week. At the same time Bob Dylan produced *The Freewheelin' Bob Dylan*, which sold 200,000 copies in two months, a remarkable number then for a folk-singer. The album featured the first popular protest song about the military-industrial complex, "Masters of War," and one about nuclear apocalypse, "A Hard Rain's a Gonna Fall," and it questioned the older generation in "Blowin' in the Wind." Later that year Peter, Paul and Mary released a single of "Blowin' in the Wind" and it sold over 300,000 copies in less than two weeks, eventually over a million, making it the first protest song to make the hit parade.

Many folk songs concerned the most important issue of the day in the first half of the 1960s—civil rights. The Chad Mitchell Trio sang a satiric tune about segregation at the University of Mississippi entitled "Alma Mater"; Tom Paxton skewered segregationists in his "Dogs of Alabama"; and Phil Ochs decried the southern way of life in "Talking Birmingham Jam" and "Here's to the State of Mississippi." Peter, Paul and Mary sang "If I Had a Hammer," proclaiming that they did have a hammer, a bell, and a song: "It's the hammer of Justice, It's the bell of freedom, It's the song about love between my brothers and my sisters, all over this land." And in "Blowin' in the Wind" Dylan posed a moral choice to his generation:

How many roads must a man walk, before you call him a man?
Yes, 'n' how many times can a man turn his head
Pretending he just doesn't see?
The answer my friend is blowin' in the wind,
The answer is blowin' in the wind.

"The first way to answer these questions," said Dylan, "is by asking them. . . . I still say that some of the biggest criminals are those that turn their heads away when they see wrong and know it's wrong."[6] Folk-singers felt a warm wind of change blowing from the southern struggle, a breeze carrying new values, and in 1965 Dylan warned mothers and fathers:

> Your sons and your daughters are beyond your command
> Your old road is rapidly aging.
> Please get out of the new one
> If you can't lend a hand
> For the times they are a'changin'

Times were changing on campus as the first baby boomers began flooding classrooms in mid-decade. In the past, higher education had been reserved for wealthy Americans usually enrolled in private colleges. Before World War II more students attended private than public institutions, but that changed after the conflict. The government awarded veterans the GI Bill, which paid their tuition; a strong postwar economy meant that many more families could help their children enroll in state universities; and then, in 1957, the Soviets challenged America—the Russians launched Sputnik. The race for space was on! Parents in the suburbs began wondering if Little Ivan was smarter than Little Terry. Congress responded by passing the National Defense Education Act, which granted scholarships and some loans to science and engineering students, and in 1965 President Johnson dramatically enlarged the student loan program as part of his Great Society.

Education had been democratized. If the mind was willing, virtually anyone could enroll at a university. "Of course I went to college," said a baby boomer. "That was assumed." By the end of the 1960s three-quarters of university students were enrolled at public institutions and almost half of all kids 18 to 21 were attending college. Enrollments soared. In 1960 there were three million college students, but in autumn 1964 the first baby boomers hit campus and by the next year there were five million and that doubled to ten million by 1973. This meant the rise of a new form of higher education, the large public university. Before World War II there was not one university with over 15,000 students, yet by 1970 over fifty institutions had that enrollment and eight campuses were stuffed with over 30,000. Between 1958 and 1970, for example, the approximate number of students at North Carolina (Chapel Hill), Georgia (Athens), and LSU (Baton Rouge) almost tripled to about 17,000. Washington (Seattle) and Texas (Austin) expanded from about 15,000 to almost 27,000, while Michigan (Ann Arbor) and Ohio State (Columbus) each grew by 50 percent to about 34,000. Minnesota doubled to over 40,000, and Wisconsin soared from 14,000 to 35,000. In just the first five years of the

1960s Berkeley's enrollment increased 50 percent to over 27,000. The stunning increase in enrollment, the massive numbers at college, meant that if students became active then the media would quickly focus its attention on the campus. The national and local press would see any student activism as "a potential Berkeley."

As the size of the university increased, so did its functions. The university became the "generator of knowledge," the arena for analysis and data which would help America not only compete with other nations but win the cold war. "Experts" would save the day, and the "best" ideas apparently came from the "brightest" professors. Besides teaching and research, professors attended conferences, workshops, symposia, and they consulted government, industry, and business. Besides educating, colleges began competing with each other for the most distinguished faculty and for prestige. Some that had been "colleges" for generations, even centuries, changed their names to "universities." But that was not enough. "Multiversities," President Kerr labeled these institutions. They were a "prime instrument of national purpose . . . the focal point for national growth . . . at the center of the knowledge process." Competition became more intense, and administrators of multiversities fought for federal grants, research funds, endowment gifts, and organizational support. This called for a growing corps of officials, more deans and their assistants, all expanding at a faster pace than the professoriat. "Educational administrators," wrote professor Andrew Hacker in 1965, "are adept at discovering new services they can perform, new committees they can create, new reports they can write." Quantity became the new equation for prestige: students × deans × programs × research dollars. Bureaucracies expanded until administrators searching for funds became more important than professors teaching Aristotle. [7]

The quality of students arriving on campus each fall also improved. Suburban schools were meeting the cold war challenge and sending better educated kids to college. In June 1963 *Life* surveyed deans at twenty college campuses, from Yale to UCLA, from Miami to Denver, and then editorialized: "'63 is probably the best prepared, stablest and most promising college class in U.S. history. Instead of preaching to it, let's listen."

Yet that was the problem—university administrators were not listening. "Universities as a rule are less interested in what students are complaining about," wrote Yale chaplain William Sloane Coffin, Jr., in 1965, "than in how to stop their complaining." During the early years of the decade, University of California administrator William McGill admitted, "We were so involved with our own work and our own ambitions that at first we did not hear what students were trying to tell us."

Students had a lot on their minds. Each fall semester they found themselves in long lines at registration and in enormous classes, the "massclass." Four and five hundred students in a massclass became common at state universities. At Texas some 700 sat in freshman geology, but that was small compared with Minnesota, where almost 2000 students were enrolled in Psychology 2. The class was taught by one professor and a team of harried graduate students, who in fact were conducting most entry-level classes at research universities. At Berkeley, two-thirds of the smaller classes were taught by graduate students in 1965, and at Texas inexperienced teaching assistants, who had an average of only one semester classroom experience, taught 90 percent of all freshman classes in math and English and 70 percent of those courses in French and Italian. At Illinois an army of 130 graduate assistants taught almost all sections of first-year English.

College administrators responded to exploding enrollments by increasing class size and by relying on technology. Classes were televised; students were computerized. At Minnesota, 400 freshmen sat in an auditorium waiting for the bell. Then a dozen televisions went on, the professor appeared on screen and began the lesson in Sociology 101. Students never knew for the entire term if the man on TV was alive, for they never saw him in person. "Registration was accomplished with IBM cards," Sara Davidson recalled about Berkeley, "and papers frequently were returned bearing a grade and no comments, as if they had been read by a machine." The *Daily Californian* informed new students, "Welcome to lines, bureaucracy and crowds. The incoming freshman has much to learn—perhaps lesson number one is not to fold, spindle or mutilate his IBM card."

"The multiversity is a confusing place for the student," admitted Clark Kerr, and while the massclass has become standard since, it was frustrating then to a generation of students who had been raised in relative affluence and showered with parental attention. "They always seem to be wanting to make me into a number," said a Syracuse student. "I won't let them. I have a name and am important enough to be known by it. . . . I'll join any movement that comes along to help me."

To many students sitting in an auditorium listening to someone with a microphone, the university seemed like a service station, a factory where one matriculated before heading off to automated America. The multiversity became the "screwnaversity." The "rapid spread of conflict through other campuses was not like an army mobilizing under central command," noted Michael Rossman, "but like mushrooms after a fall rain: Today one, tomorrow a thousand, because conditions are similar and ripe everywhere."[8]

The condition that most irritated students in the first half of the decade was not only overcrowding, frustrating but understandable, but the way that colleges set rules and regulations for its students. *In loco parentis* was a term meaning "in the place of the parents." Historically, it gave academic officials authorization to act as the students' parents and issue discipline during college years. Philosophically, it meant that daddies and deans would continue to tell college kids how to behave, smiling and saying, "It's for your own good." Legally, it meant that unlike regular citizens, students between kindergarten and graduate school could be tried by civil and university authorities, and they could be found guilty, not just of breaking laws, but also of violating campus regulations. Thus, an underaged student who drank alcohol, smoked dope, or even had a traffic ticket could be fined or jailed by the judge and expelled by the dean. During the mid-1960s campus activists began raising the question: Are students full citizens, ones protected by the Constitution?

"No," said American society. In the 1640s Harvard College informed its students that they shall not speak "lies and uncertain rumors . . . bitter scoffing, frothy wanton words," or display "offensive gestures." For the next three centuries university administrators had not changed many rules—they set regulations which governed virtually all student behavior. Dorms were segregated by sex and visitation restricted. During spring semester 1964 a heated debate at Harvard was over the number of hours men and women could visit, and Earlham College revoked Sunday visiting privileges because too many dorm doors were being closed. Just how wide those doors had to be opened was discussed endlessly. Administrations usually stated the "width of a book," while students often interpreted that as a "book of matches." While newspapers ran racy headlines—"Collegiate Capers Behind Closed Doors Cause Chorus of Comment"—university administrators attempted to, as they called it, "hold the line" against sexual activity. The president of Vassar, Miss Sarah Blanding, was blunt, suggesting that girls who had engaged in sexual intercourse should not apply.

Students had curfews, especially the coeds, for the idea was, "If the girls are in, the boys will be too." The University of Illinois was similar to most colleges: at 10:30 p.m. on weekday nights, and 1 a.m. on weekends, women's dorm doors were shut and locked. In dry detail, college handbooks spelled out how to fill out white cards, blue cards, or yellow cards so one could stay until midnight at the library or go home for the weekend. The University of Massachusetts Student Handbook in 1964–65 listed penalties for females arriving late at her dorm: Five "minutes means loss of the next Friday night," ten eliminated Saturday night, and fifteen sent the wayward gal to women's judiciary. After all, the handbook stated, "Every woman student shall conduct herself at all times, in all places, so as to uphold her own good name and that of the University."

Rules bordered on the absurd. During dorm visitation hours at Barnard College, a man could visit a coed, but three of their four feet had to be on the floor at all times. The "three foot rule" also applied at Illinois dorms, but not just for rooms, also for the lounge. While with their dates in the lounge, coeds were prohibited from wearing raincoats which supposedly insured that they were not nude under their coats while snuggling with their dates. To maintain propriety during dorm closing, no couples were allowed to kiss goodnight while leaning up against the building, preventing couples from bumping and grinding. "The university campus is an urban community with a rural ethic," reported a journalist in 1965, "one of the final homes of the Puritan code."

Administrators treated students as if they were children. At Texas, coeds had to live on campus until they were 21 and had 90 semester hours. If they then applied for apartment residency, the dean of women would review the "total record of the girl" and decide whether off-campus living was appropriate for the applicant. To control expanding enrollments at Illinois, all freshmen had to take what was commonly known as a "flunk out class," Rhetoric 101. Three spelling or punctuation errors on one paper meant an automatic C for the semester, more resulted in a fail, and by the end of the first year a third of the new class had flunked out. At Michigan State the students' grades were not even their own. The administration sent grades for all students under 21 directly to parents, and also irritated students with petty harassment. Since drinking was not allowed on campus, students liked to blow off steam at the end of the week by having "grassers," keg parties in fields or backyards. Police would hold raids to stop the practice, and they would charge not only all under 21 with drinking as a minor, but anyone over age in the vicinity with contributing to the delinquency of a minor.

Regulations were even stricter at colleges affiliated with religions, at small institutions, and at those in the South. When two students at St. John's University were married in a civil ceremony in 1962, they were expelled for violating Roman Catholic law. Catholic colleges had dress codes that prohibited males from wearing T-shirts, shorts, sweatshirts, or jeans, and stricter rules for coeds, even limiting places where females could smoke. At Brigham Young University the same dress codes applied, and other rules for men mandated no beards or long hair. For females, strapless dresses, sleeveless shirts, and the "no bra look is unacceptable at B.Y.U." The student manual for one of the largest Catholic universities warned that if student conduct or attitudes did not conform to university standards then the administration was the "sole judge" for expulsion. As late as 1971, Sam Houston State University in Texas still enforced an 11 p.m. curfew for its coeds and compulsory class attendance, and closer to Houston, regulations at San Jacinto Junior College limited the length of students' sideburns and prohibited peace symbols.

Furthermore, students had virtually no say at the university which they supported with tuition. Administrators dictated course offerings, degree curriculums, and almost everything else on campus—dorm assignment, speakers, types of intramural sports, semester length and final exam dates. Faculty advisers acted as censors of most university student newspapers. Rules prohibited drinking, smoking, drugs, gambling, sex or public display of affection, and mandated class attendance, dress codes, dorm assignments, and for male students at most public institutions, Reserve Officer Training, ROTC. It was a "barracks culture," Tom Hayden recalled of the University of Michigan, "thirteen hundred young men were cramped into my sterile quad, arbitrarily assigned to roommates, whether we preferred each other's company or not."[9]

The role of the university in the first half of the 1960s, then, was not only to train students but to tame them to be conventional adults. To fit in, to become their parents. Students who did not play the game often were expelled or left in disgust; professors who did not teach the game usually were fired. Journalism major Phil Ochs at Ohio State was slated to become editor of the school paper, *The Lantern*, but faculty advisers rejected him because his views were "too controversial." He quit in his last year and became a folksinger. Illinois professor Leo Koch wrote in the *Daily Illini* that in his opinion premarital sex was all right for mature unmarried college students. The university president found the views "offensive and repugnant . . . contrary to the accepted standards of morality," and he fired Koch. For similar reasons St. John's University fired two dozen faculty members in 1966—none even received a hearing, for according to university rules the board of trustees could give or take away tenure at any time without explanation. *Newsweek* editorialized that "college must not abdicate its role in conserving, transmitting, and helping to mold both moral and intellectual values" of its students.

Yet many students by the mid-1960s had little desire to "be molded." This generation was different from older brothers and sisters who had been cowed by McCarthyism. That campaign was ancient history to them, hardly remembered and not taken seriously. Furthermore, these students had learned from the struggle. "If there is any one reason for increased student protest," a University of Utah journalist wrote, "it would probably be the civil rights movement. The movement . . . convinced many of them that non-violent demonstrations could be an effective device on the campus. It also served to make them more sensitive of their own civil rights."[10] Problems in society had to be confronted and resolved, not blamed on imaginary subversives or outside agitators, and that called for student activism.

The reasons for student power were stated by the activists themselves in their campus papers and in new student undergrounds. This generation felt *in loco parentis* rules were absurd. Texas student Jeff Shero complained that campus regulations were "aimed at maintaining a 'proper image' for the University, rather than protecting girls." The young editor of *The Paper* declared "Michigan State is the Mississippi of American universities," protesting the administration's "closed-mindedness, intolerance and back-woods McCarthyism." The *New Orleans Freedom Press* proclaimed that student discontent resulted from "administrative restrictions on student autonomy," while University of Florida activists were blunt in their campus underground, *Freedom Forum:* "The American university campus has become a ghetto. Like all ghettoes, it has its managers (the administration), its Uncle Toms (the intimidated, status-berserk faculty), its raw natural resources processed for outside exploitation and consumption (the students)." Their demand highlighted the reasons for student power: "NO RESTRICTIONS MAY BE PLACED ON STUDENT DRINKING, GAMBLING, SEXUAL ACTIVITY, OR ANY SUCH PRIVATE MORAL DECISION."

The sixties generation began to confront its university administrations in 1964, politely demanding to be heard. During spring semester the administration at Brandeis consulted no one and then instituted new, stricter dorm visitation rules. That prompted several hundred students to stage a two-day demonstration, and the campus newspaper declared that such regulations "makes impossible any meaningful relationship between boy and girl." That fall semester, Syracuse University students approached their administrators with a simple request—they felt that holiday break, which began on December 23, was too close to Christmas. A few dozen students asked for more travel time to get home by Christmas Eve. After officials turned down all petitions, the students called a rally in December, and they were surprised when 2000 appeared. They demanded a speech from the chancellor, and he gave a short address, again saying no. As he ended his talk, some students jeered and booed, which shocked elders. "The students were supposed to show proper respect," a journalist wrote, "to know their place and keep it." Student activists, however, had a different interpretation. They wanted some role in the university. "If today's demonstration proves nothing else," the student paper editorialized, "we are not ones to be ignored or taken lightly." [11]

Students at Berkeley certainly were not going to be taken lightly—they again challenged the ban on disseminating literature. On October 1, Jack Weinberg and others set up a few tables outside the administration building on Sproul Plaza and began passing out civil rights and political flyers. Before noon two university deans and a policeman approached Weinberg. "Are you prepared to remove yourself and the table from university property?" asked the dean. "I am not," replied Weinberg. After a brief discussion the official informed Weinberg of his arrest, and at this point several hundred students who were gathering for a free speech rally startled the officials by shouting, "Take us all, take us all!" Policemen drove a car onto the plaza and placed Weinberg inside, but suddenly someone shouted, "Sit down!" "I'm around the police car," recalled Michael Rossman. "I'm the first person to sit down. You will hear five hundred others who say that, and everyone is telling the truth." Students either laid or sat down around the car. They refused to move. The police could not drive their prisoner to jail as the crowd swelled to 3000. Mario Savio and many others climbed on top of the car and gave speeches, and later the crowd sang civil rights songs. They remained on the plaza all night. The next morning the area looked like a campsite, filled with sleeping bags, blankets, and even a pup tent. The crowd increased to 4000 that afternoon and President Kerr realized that the free speech issue was not going to disappear. After a thirty-hour sit-in, university administrators finally agreed to meet the activists.[12]

To university officials, and to most citizens after the law and order 1950s, Berkeley had been reduced to chaos. Although campus rebellion would become common later in the decade, this was the first major eruption, and administrators responded forcefully. Under pressure from conservatives in the community and state government, they allowed 500 police officers to appear on campus minutes before they met activists. The police were armed with nightsticks, and the sight shocked students who never could remember a police army on campus and who felt that the incident was novel in American educational history. As police stood by, civil rights veterans taught nonviolent arrest tactics and urged those with police records or children to leave. Administrators had the support of California Governor Edmund G. Brown, a Democrat who stated that the demonstration was "not a matter of freedom of speech" but was an attempt by the students to use the campus illegally. "This will not be tolerated." He continued, "We must have—and will continue to have—law and order on our campuses."

Negotiations with Kerr continued for two hours, and then Savio and other students emerged from Sproul Hall. Savio climbed on the police car and announced that an agreement had been reached. A student-faculty committee would examine the free speech issue and make recommendations to the president. The university would not press charges against Weinberg or FSM leaders, and the eight students suspended earlier would have their case reviewed. Kerr seemed to support establishing a small free speech area at the campus's main entrance where Telegraph Avenue met Bancroft Way.

The October 2 agreement collapsed by November. The administration filled the committee with their own supporters, and then stalled for weeks. Meanwhile, Kerr took the issue to the press. Under pressure from conservative regents and politicians, the president attacked activists by raising the old bugaboos: "Reds on Campus," Kerr told the *San Francisco Examiner*. The article reported that the president "declared flatly that a hard core of 'Castro-Mao-Tse-tung line' Communists were in the crowd of demonstrators." The president then rejected political activity, provoking students to petition the regents and to set up tables on Sproul Plaza. The regents refused to hear the case, and on November 29 Kerr surprised students by announcing that the university was going to press new charges against FSM leaders Art Goldberg and Savio for their actions during the October 1 demonstrations. Charges included "entrapping a police car," "packing in" Sproul Hall, and, against Savio alone, biting a policeman "on the left thigh, breaking the skin and causing bruises."

The administration's behavior only alienated more students, irritated many professors, and fueled more protest as students and faculty began to feel that the university all along had been negotiating in bad faith. "The Administration sees the free speech protest as a simple problem of disobedience," proclaimed an FSM steering committee statement. "By again arbitrarily singling out students for punishment, the Administration avoids facing the real issues. . . . We demand that these new charges be dropped." Thousands of activists took those demands to Sproul Plaza on December 2, and Savio voiced the students' frustration by telling the crowd: "There is a time when the operation of the machine becomes so odious, makes you so sick at heart, that you can't take part; you can't even tacitly take part, and you've got to put your bodies upon the gears and upon the wheels, upon the levers, upon all the apparatus and you've got to make it stop."

"We Shall Overcome," sang Joan Baez, and others joined in as they moved toward Sproul Hall. "We'll walk hand in hand," for "the truth will make us free." The activists shut down the university administration—again they confronted the establishment.

Governor Brown responded immediately: "We're not going to have anarchy in California." He informed Kerr that force must be used to oust the students and ordered police to arrest activists who refused to leave the administration building. At about 4 a.m. some 600 policemen entered Sproul Hall and began arresting students, eventually about 770, in the largest mass arrest in California history. Some 7000 students remained on the plaza, and that morning they began picketing all entrances to the campus, handing out flyers:

IT IS HAPPENING NOW!

In the middle of the night, the police began dragging 800 of your fellow students from Sproul Hall. Sproul Hall was turned into a booking station; the University has become an armed camp—armed against its own students! . . .

Now the police take over.

Instead of recognizing the legitimacy of the students' demands, the administration is attempting to destroy the FSM. . . . The administration position is clear. It is saying "We decide what is acceptable freedom of speech on this campus. Those who disagree will be ignored; when they can no longer be ignored, they will be destroyed.

We have not been defeated by the University's troops! Our protest will continue until the justice of our cause is acknowledged. You must take a stand now! No longer can the faculty attempt to mediate from the outskirts of the crowd. No longer can students on this campus afford to accept humbly administrative fiat. Raise your voice now!

WE SHALL OVERCOME.

The faculty met, and after a long and heated discussion in their senate, they declared their position: Professors overwhelmingly voted to condemn the use of police on campus and to support the FSM. As faculty left the meeting, students cheered, and on December 4 both students and faculty held a huge rally on Sproul Plaza. Arrested activists had been released on bail, many wore a large white "V" on black shirts, and they and several professors criticized Governor Brown, the regents, and President Kerr. Students declared a strike, and that week half the classes were canceled.[13]

With business as usual disrupted, Kerr called a special meeting for December 7 at the Greek Theater. About 16,000 students, faculty, and staff gathered, and the president condemned the sit-in but offered clemency for all acts of civil disobedience before December 2 and stated that the university would abide by "new and liberalized political action rules" then being developed by the faculty senate. The speech sounded conciliatory, and as the president left the podium Savio began walking across the stage apparently to make an announcement. Before he reached the microphone, campus police astonished the crowd by grabbing the activist and dragging him backstage. When other activists attempted to help, the police wrestled them off the stage.

"The crowd was stunned," wrote participant Bettina Aptheker, "then there was pandemonium." Students cried out "We Want Mario! We Want Mario!" Kerr, realizing that the police were ruining his efforts to reach an understanding, quickly agreed to let Savio make his announcement—a rally would be held at noon. Nevertheless, most spectators remembered the incident and its inescapable symbolism: authorities physically preventing a student committed to free speech from speaking on his own campus. As Aptheker later wrote: "That episode more than any other single event revolutionized the *thinking* of many thousands of students."

The next day the faculty met and overwhelmingly passed a motion affirming that "speech or advocacy should not be restricted by the university." While the administration and regents discussed the motion during the next two weeks, the FSM invited CORE national director James Farmer to address a rally on December 15. The administration was conciliatory, informing students that Farmer could talk on campus, but FSM activists decided to hold a legal rally off campus as a token of good faith. Farmer told the crowd that the "battle for free speech" could not be lost, for that would "turn off the faucet of the civil rights movement." When someone charged that he was an "outside agitator," he replied, "Every housewife knows the value of an agitator. It's the instrument inside the washing machine that bangs around and gets out all the dirt."

The administration eventually decided to accept the faculty's liberalized political rules. On January 4, 1965, the Free Speech Movement held its first legal rally on Sproul Plaza. The FSM was a success, Savio told the crowd, because "it was so obvious to everybody that it was right."

The FSM raised a philosophical debate that divided many students and administrators: What is the nature of a public university? While Kerr thought of himself as a liberal and had been praised for his stand favoring academic freedom, he stated the usual reasoning of cold war culture. The "university is an educational institution that has been given to the regents as a trust to administer for educational reasons, and not to be used for direct political actions." FSM advocates and many professors disagreed, arguing that the mission of higher education was much broader. "The university is the place where people begin seriously to question the conditions of their existence and raise the issue of whether they can be committed to the society they have been born into," wrote Savio. At a public institution supported by all taxpayers, activists felt that discussion should not be reserved only for campus issues but should be open to all concerns of the Republic.[14] Art Goldberg advocated making Berkeley "a marketplace of ideas" where citizens would be exposed to "new and creative solutions to the problems that every American realizes are facing this society in the mid-60s."

That idea was not original in 1964, for actually students had initiated free speech movements earlier at a few other campuses, including Ohio State and Indiana University. In March 1963 three students at Indiana, officers of the Young Socialist Alliance, sponsored a speech by a black socialist on the civil rights movement. In May, the county prosecuting attorney charged the students with violating the Indiana Anti-Communist Act, meeting with the purpose of "advocating the violent overthrow" of the governments of Indiana and the United States. The prosecutor also demanded that the university drop its recognition of YSA. "We may all be ten years away from Senator McCarthy," wrote one professor, "but I am ten blocks away from the office of the Prosecuting Attorney." Supporters of the three established the Committee to Aid the Bloomington Students, which eventually received assistance from 50 colleges in 15 states.

Over 140 faculty members signed a statement that the indictment was not "motivated by zeal for law enforcement, but by a desire to dictate to Indiana University that it shall not permit the use of University facilities for the expression of ideas repugnant to the Prosecutor." The university president agreed, and state courts found the law unconstitutional: The faculty continued supporting the students and broadly defined the university as a community where "debate, disagreement and the sharp confrontation of opposing ideas is a vital part of the attempt to come closer to the truth." [15]

The free speech episode at Indiana differed from that at Berkeley. The Indiana administration viewed the conservative attack as a threat to the institution, and eventually the president supported the First Amendment. If Berkeley administrators had subscribed to such views, the sit-in of Sproul Hall probably would have been avoided. Flexible officials could avoid most confrontations on campus—a point remembered by hundreds of successful university presidents throughout the 1960s.

Kerr and the regents could not overcome their authoritarian 1950s mentality. They treated the students like subordinates, gave orders to tuition-payers, which only increased resentment toward authority. Activists felt that "liberal" administrators, the "power elites" who ran the university in Berkeley, seemed more interested in maintaining the status quo than changing rules, even if those regulations denied rights guaranteed by the First Amendment of the U.S. Constitution. Looking back, Kerr's position was indefensible. During the 1950s he had supported academic freedom for professors, yet in 1964 his administration curtailed freedom of speech for students. Many students wondered, if they could not hand out political statements, if freedom of speech did not exist on a public campus, then where did it exist in the land of the free?

The administration brought on the crisis, handled it poorly, and lost to students. As in the civil rights struggle, the FSM students put another dent in the idea that those in charge should be in charge, that the older generation had some monopoly on determining the proper path for the present and future in America. "Don't trust anyone over thirty," said Jack Weinberg and others, meaning that the generation who grew up in the 1950s had a different view of the world than their parents. During cold war culture the older generation "told the truth" to students, but in the 1960s students were "discovering the truth" for themselves, and their younger siblings would continue the process throughout the decade. At Berkeley, the young began to realize that the older generation had no monopoly on truth or on virtue. Once students began to raise their voices and question policy, Michael Rossman wrote, then "the emperor had no clothes." President Kerr's decision to uphold an untenable regulation at Berkeley could be just as wrong as Chief of Police Bull Connor's enforcement of segregation rules in Birmingham.

The FSM was significant for many other reasons. Activists adopted a political style that reflected the ideas of the new left and some of the practices of SNCC. Unlike traditional organizations or political parties, Berkeley students "worked through direct personal involvement in small autonomous interest groups. Our groups were ad hoc," Rossman recalled, "problem-orientated, flexible. They strove to govern themselves by participatory democracy, and to come to consensus on decisions." They also were pragmatic. "We were experimental social scientists, placing practice before theory. . . . We also were cheerful and funny, and made art as we went."

Campus issues increased personal awareness as students focused on themselves, on their status at their college, and then decided to watch or to get involved—the personal again became the political. Like Freedom Summer participants, student activists began to feel part of a movement, a new generation. Bettina Aptheker remembered at Berkeley the "intense moment of connection between us which infused a spirit of overwhelming and enduring love." The experience became emotional as campus activity and turmoil unleashed a restless questioning of mainstream society. "For me personally it was a heavy turning, a rebeginning," wrote Rossman as he and others questioned their parents' generation. There was "born among us a new vision of community and of culture," a "vision of social justice that . . . moved us to action in the New Left. During the rest of that decade, in the Movement and the counterculture, we saw millions of young people moved by their versions of these visions."[16]

Most student activists at mid-decade had similar visions, backgrounds, and personality characteristics. Social scientists conducted many surveys and found that participants generally were bright and articulate, concerned about campus and national issues. At Berkeley, the university's ban shifted their concern from civil rights to their own freedom of speech. While the administration and local conservatives attempted to smear the activists as the weaker, less serious students, the opposite was the case. The activists' grades were above average and on personality tests they scored high on independence, maturity, and flexibility. Most considered themselves either political independents or Democrats and the vast majority were students of the liberal arts and humanities. Few were studying business, engineering, or agriculture, and of the 770 arrested for the sit-in of Sproul Hall, not one was a business administration major. Most of these students lived independently in apartments while only a few were in fraternities and sororities.

These generalizations held true for activists at other universities, and so did the fact that student activists always were a minority on every campus and concerning every issue throughout the decade. While organizing civil rights activities, Cleveland Sellers complained about his colleagues at

Howard University—how most were primarily interested in maintaining the Howard image, the impression that they were the well-dressed black elite. "My roommate was typical," Sellers recalled. Asked if he didn't feel some responsibility to improve racial conditions, the roommate responded, "Fuck it, man. . . . Don't confront me with that Martin Luther King shit. Everybody's gotta go for himself and I'm going for me. If niggas down South don't like the way they're being treated, they oughtta leave. I'm not going to join no picket lines and get the shit beat outta me by them crazy-ass Ku Klux-ers! I'm interested in four things. A degree, a good job, a good woman and a good living. That's all."[17] At Berkeley there were many such white students. Approximately a thousand participated actively in FSM, about 4 percent of student enrollment. Polls demonstrated that about a third of the students supported both tactics and aims of the movement while about two-thirds supported only the goal of free speech. At the largest rally on December 2 about 11,000 showed up out of over 27,500 students, and so at no time did a majority of students demonstrate for FSM.

Many were indifferent—a student silent majority—while a number opposed FSM for various reasons. About a third disagreed with disruptive tactics. After the October 1 incident on Sproul Plaza, the *Daily Californian* editorialized that the "demonstrations have dissolved into a morass of distorted goals. . . . We urge the students to think by themselves—not by the group." Charles Powell, the student body president, stated that the real target should not be university policy but state law, for "the only rational and proper action . . . is to seek changes in the law. Those opportunities are not here on the campus—but in the houses of the State Legislature." The University Young Republicans withdrew from the FSM during the December 2 sit-in of Sproul Hall, and a few conservative activists carried signs: "Throw the Bums Out." Conservatives also organized University Students for Law and Order, who handed out flyers condemning demonstrations, advocated taking the free speech issue to the courts, and asked of the FSM: "Where will their *putsch* end? WHAT VICTORY WILL BE GAINED BY THE DESTRUCTION OF OUR UNIVERSITY?"

Conservative students across the nation agreed, and some of them had joined the Young Americans for Freedom. During the late 1950s and the first half of the 1960s the National Student Association was the largest student organization, and many conservatives felt that it was too liberal, including Senator Barry Goldwater. In 1960 he published a book that was widely circulated on campuses, *The Conscience of a Conservative*, and he suggested an organization for young conservatives. William F. Buckley agreed, and in September he held a conference at his estate in Sharon, Connecticut. The Sharon Statement and their magazine, *New Guard*, attacked NSA. "You, Too, Can STOP NSA!" wrote young conservative Tom Huston, for "NSA is great at brainwashing student government leaders" with its "misrepresentations, half-truths, and vague generalities." Other articles noted that the greatest threat to American political liberties and free enterprise was international Communism, and that the United States should "stress victory over, rather than coexistence with, this menace." Conservative activists held a rally at Madison Square Garden in 1962 and 18,000 attended to hear Brent Bozell, editor of the *National Review*, call on the U.S. to tear down the Berlin Wall and immediately invade Communist Cuba.

YAF boosted an image of being "sensibly clean people," said one, "not liberal and dirty people." They opposed Kennedy and the "ludicrous array of bearded University of Chicago beatniks, self-righteous and militant pacifists and solemn-toned members of the corn-and-hog country intelligentsia" who fostered the Peace Corps, which they referred to as "A Spree de Corps . . . a grand exercise in self-denial and altruism, paid for by the American taxpayers and administered by the United Nations." The protests at Berkeley, YAF editorialized, were conducted by a filthy crowd of beatniks and liberals who had been raised and coddled by Communists. "Behind Campus, Youth Turmoil: The Red Diaper Babies Grow Up," proclaimed *New Guard:* It "seems to us that what the 'Free Speech' advocates are really demanding is that the administration allow students to run the university." [18]

A year after the Berkeley protests, YAF boasted a membership of 20,000 with 250 chapters across the nation; in 1970 they claimed twice as many chapters and 60,000 members. Their sponsors included John Wayne, Ronald Reagan, Senator Strom Thurmond, and the national board of directors included two students who would have an impact later during the Nixon and Reagan administrations—Tom Huston and Richard Allen. Throughout the decade YAF usually counted more members than SDS or SNCC, but membership figures never were a reliable measure of an organization's significance. During the free speech movement, for example, there were few or no YAF or SDS members at Berkeley. The issue of free speech—not an organization, not a leader—generated the activism, and that remained true throughout the sixties.

Americans today look back at the decade as a radical era but often forget that there was activism on both sides of the political spectrum. Like all generations, the one that came of age in the sixties was not a monolith. Coming out of cold war culture, the left naturally generated more media interest and received more press. The youthful revolt against the establishment—at lunch counters, on campuses, or in the streets—was dramatic, perfect for television news. Conservative students rarely took shocking action and instead remained on the defensive, responding to the leftists by writing articles or letters in campus papers or by initiating legal challenges.

Older, conservative newspaper editors responded quickly to the FSM, putting it on page one and making it the first student protest that was covered intensely by the media. While a few papers attempted to present all sides of the issue, such as the *New York Times* and *Los Angeles Times*, most editors demonstrated that while they might support black ministers peacefully asking for civil rights, they could not see any parallels with college students shouting for free speech. To many, it appeared that the older generation was losing control to unruly kids. "Who Runs the University of California?" asked the *San Francisco Examiner*. The paper declared that the FSM challenge was "intolerable and insufferable," that "UC Rebels" should be expelled, and that non-student activists should be somehow permanently barred from the campus. The *Oakland Tribune* wrote that the students really aimed to make Berkeley a radical campus to train revolutionaries and terrorists, like the University of Havana which schooled Fidel Castro, and the *U.S. News and World Report* proclaimed: "A Campus Uproar That Is Blamed on Reds." Berkeley had attracted members of the "beatnik generation" and the campus was under the specter of "educational anarchy."

Reading such articles, or watching the drama on the evening news, would convince many older Californians that in the future they should vote for "law and order" candidates who would uphold conventional values. "Observe the rules or get out," proclaimed conservative Ronald Reagan, and as he ran for governor in 1966 he proclaimed that "Beatniks, radicals and filthy speech advocates have brought shame on a great university." He promised to "clean up the mess at Berkeley," where he claimed were "sexual orgies so vile I cannot describe them." Many parents were horrified by what they considered was shocking behavior and appalling dress of the activists, and one wrote to FSM: "Go to Hell, all you Rotten Beatniks!"[19]

Such comments and especially the establishment's articles had a different impact on many youth. They began to realize that they could not count on the media to present their side of the story, their values, or news about their generation. Consequently, Art Kunkin began publishing an "underground" newspaper, the *Faire Free Press*, which eventually became the *Los Angeles Free Press*. In Berkeley, the FSM spawned temporary magazines such as *Spider*, *Wooden Shoe*, and *Root and Branch*. In San Francisco a "counter" to mainstream culture appeared in occasional issues of *Renaissance*, *Notes from the Underground*, and *Open City Press* as the Haight-Ashbury district began emerging as a "hip" enclave.

The first issues of these undergrounds usually presented cultural news for the young generation. During the early months of 1965, for example, *Free Press* printed articles on films, dance, and music: Ravi Shankar; An Evening with Lenny Bruce; Blues '65 Concert featuring Chuck Berry and Big Mama Thornton. But by March, the youth culture, civil rights, and student issues were merging. "I wanted the *Free Press* to build a local movement base," said Kunkin, and when the struggle was aflame in Selma, Alabama, he began reporting on protests in Los Angeles in which over 6000 marched to the federal building demanding "government action against racist violence and intimidation in the South." In Berkeley, *Open City Press* covered the arrest of local poet John Thompson. University officials claimed that Thompson had outraged public decency by carrying a sign on campus with his one-word poem: "FUCK." Thompson responded that he was protesting against hypocrisy: "I could walk around this campus for weeks with a sign that said MURDER or SHOOT or KILL and no one would pay the least attention. I write this one little word and BAM, into jail I go." University officials and older journalists were appalled, dubbing the incident the "filthy speech movement," but the writer for *Open City Press* took a different approach that demonstrated new values. He described how a few creative students had began the "Phuque Defense Fund."

During the remainder of the year others began undergrounds, such as the *Berkeley Barb*, and in New York City, the *East Village Other*, *Free Student*, and *Partisan*. In Detroit, teenager Harvey Ovshinsky offered a substitute to the so-called fourth estate of the press with his *Fifth Estate*, and a 21-year-old student at Michigan State established its first campus underground, *The Paper*, to present "an independent alternative to the 'established' news media of the university community."

The publication of these first undergrounds was a subtle but significant event. It demonstrated that a youth culture was emerging within the sixties generation. Some young Americans had different values from their parents, and that began to appear during Freedom Summer and as the movement spread into 1965. *Free Press* ran ads for the subculture, "girls to share housekeeping with lonely studs." And on campus, Sara Davidson wrote that Berkeley was "an enclave where things happened first, where the rules of middle-class society did not apply." Gerald Rosenfield recalled that Free Speech was "a swinging movement. The F.S.M., with its open mass meetings, its guitars and songs, its beards, and its long-haired chicks, made the aloofness and reserve of the administration . . . the formality of the coat and tie world, seem lifeless and dull in comparison." Authorities dressed like authorities, and styles began to make a statement. "Yes, my hair is long, and I haven't shaved in days," sang a folksinger at Berkeley, "But fighting for my freedom, while clean-cut kids just look the other way."

Cold war culture was over for many white students. "The Long Sleep Ends," proclaimed *Free Student* in spring 1965. Like the sit-ins in the South in 1960, the publicized events at Berkeley aroused other students to organize, to become part of a vague movement. "Student activists across the nation were shown by the Berkeley blow-up," declared a student in the *Daily Texan*, "that they could organize, protest, rally, sit-in, and strike—and get results. . . . And this means student power."[20]

That power appeared on many campuses during spring semester. In January, activists at Michigan State University formed the Committee for Student Rights to confront the administration concerning *in loco parentis* regulations. MSU approved or rejected student organizations, even distribution of all printed materials handed out on campus or in the dorms. All single students had to live in resident halls and abide by restrictive hours and regulations, even if they were over 21. Dorm officers enforced dress codes for evening meals: dresses for coeds, and for men, dress shirt and slacks, and no "denims, Levis, Bermudas, fatigues, knickers or beachcombers. . . . Corduroy pants may be worn only with a matching coat." The CSR maintained that regulations in some cases "superseded a student's civil rights," and as one activist proclaimed: "If Michigan State University . . . is anything more than a prison of the mind, we must move now to allow for individual freedom and dignity." In February, CSR distributed its pamphlet in dorms without approval, calling for more liberal housing regulations and the end of discriminatory rules against female students. The appeal struck a chord. A week later over 4200 students had signed an CSR petition, and they presented the 80-foot document to the director of student activities. He refused to accept the petition, which created hard feelings and more pressure. By April, the administration gave in, agreeing that students should "assume an increasing measure of responsibility" for their own behavior. Officials liberalized regulations concerning housing, dorm visitation, alcoholic beverages, and reduced punishments of students who had violated civil law. As the campus paper proclaimed, "The times must be a-changing."

They were at Ohio State, where free speech had been an issue since 1951 when the chairman of the board, a retired general, proclaimed, "As long as I'm a member of the Board of Trustees no Communist, fellow traveler, Fascist, or Nazi is going to have an invitation to speak here." In fact, the university established a gag rule and censored the appearance of numerous speakers during the next dozen years, including anyone who had publicly criticized the House Un-American Activities Committee. Students accepted this until spring semester 1962 when the president banned three speakers, one an alumnus of the university. With faculty assistance, activists formed the Students for Liberal Action and filed suit against the university in November. The response from the board was typical, as one trustee declared, "It is my personal feeling that the students who are trying to run the university rather than get an education had better move on." They remained, and for the next three years SLA continued to invite controversial speakers to campus and the president continued to ban them. After events in Berkeley, OSU students decided to take direct action. During spring semester they formed the Free Speech Front and in April held two rallies. About 450 students surrounded the administration building, and when attempts to talk with a vice president failed to produce any results, 270 began a sit-in, the first in the history of OSU. They eventually left without an arrest. Faculty members joined the fray by asking Communist Herbert Aptheker (father of Bettina), to speak on campus, which the administration quickly rejected. In May a hundred professors picketed a meeting of the trustees and four times that number petitioned the president to end the rule. Aptheker arrived on campus on May 21. He sat silently on the stage while professors read excerpts from his books to a crowd of almost 3000. The "non-speech" received national attention. While *Time* commented on "the futility of the ban," the Cleveland *Press* charged that the trustees could "blame themselves for the campus ruckus," and the Toledo *Blade* editorialized that the board had "ruled out reason and invited rebellion. It is our hope that a Berkeley can be avoided at OSU."

Like Berkeley, OSU's rule was unsupportable; unlike Berkeley, OSU students never had to break one university regulation or state law. They focused attention on a ridiculous rule, and that shifted public and political opinion behind them. Eventually, students, faculty, politicians, and judges called for reform, and the administration avoided a serious confrontation by abolishing the gag rule, which ended the free speech controversy and boosted student power at Ohio State.

A 1964–65 survey of 850 colleges, including the 50 largest public universities, demonstrated that students felt the most important issues on campus were various *in loco parentis* rules—dorm, dress, and living regulations, followed by free speech and food service. Like their parents, students stated that the most important off-campus issue was civil rights.[21]

That part of the movement was in the news almost daily during spring semester. In January, activists decided that it was time to provoke the nation again, to pressure the Johnson administration and Congress to pass a voting rights bill. Martin Luther King, Jr., and his assistants decided the venue was Selma, Alabama.

Selma epitomized white resistance to the struggle. Selma was the Black Belt. The city had a majority of black citizens, and Dallas County, Alabama, was almost 60 percent black, but less than 1 percent were registered to vote. In the two adjoining counties, Lowndes and Wilcox, not one black had the vote. Although SNCC activists had been attempting to register voters since 1963, little had been accomplished because the sheriff, Jim Clark, had allowed his men or local residents to intimidate black citizens. King wrote in the *New York Times*, "Selma has succeeded in limiting Negro registration to the snail's pace of about 145 persons a year. At this rate, it would take 103 years to register the 15,000 eligible Negro voters in Dallas County."

King and his colleagues realized that they had to repeat their tactics employed at Birmingham. SCLC activists had to provoke Sheriff Clark or local residents to unleash violence against them which would prick America's conscience, demand federal intervention, and result in a voting rights law. In January, King announced in Selma, "We are not asking, we are demanding the ballot," and then he led marches to the courthouse where blacks attempted to register. Clark responded by arresting King, briefly putting him in jail, and during the next month the sheriff arrested over 3000 demonstrators. White businessmen responded by firing black employees who attempted to register, eventually depriving 150 of their jobs. [22]

SCLC's tactic was not very successful. With the national press in Selma, the sheriff had lost his temper only a few times and had restrained his men from committing any shocking acts of violence. But that was not the case about thirty miles away in the small town of Marion. On February 17 a few hundred blacks held an evening church rally and decided to march around the courthouse to protest the arrest of one of their companions. As they began, local police reinforced by state troopers "turned out all the lights, shot the lights out, and they beat people at random," Albert Turner remembered. Willie Bolden saw one demonstrator run into the cops "and they hit him in the head, and it just bust his head wide open. Blood spewed all over." When Bolden tried to help the man, the sheriff pulled him away, and "stuck a .38 snubnose right in my mouth. . . . He cocked the hammer back, and he said, 'What I really need to do is blow your goddamn brains out, nigger.' Of course, I didn't say nothin'. I was *scared to death*, and all I could see was those rounds in that chamber." The police beat them bloody, and they shot Jimmie Lee Jackson. Several days later Jackson died, and local activists came up with a plan. As Turner recalled, "We had to do something else to point out to the nation the evils of the system. So we decided that we would walk all the way to Montgomery to protest. . . . Our first plan was to go to Montgomery with Jimmie Jackson, take his body and put it on the steps of the capitol."

King had other ideas. He was under pressure from the Johnson administration to abandon further demonstrations in Selma while the president attempted to pass social legislation, much of it aimed to help poor Americans. King left for Atlanta, but local activists decided to go ahead and march the 54 miles from Selma to Montgomery one week after Jackson's funeral. Governor Wallace stated that such a demonstration would not be tolerated, "not conducive to the orderly flow of traffic and commerce," but nevertheless on Sunday, March 7, almost 600 chanting and singing activists left Brown Chapel and began their trek, approaching Selma's Edmund Pettus Bridge, the gateway to Montgomery.

Sheriff Clark was ready. A hundred deputies lined the bridge, and another hundred state troopers, some on horseback, blocked the opposite end. The demonstrators walked across the bridge and stopped in front of a blue line of troops. An officer shouted that "for public safety" the crowd had two minutes to turn around and return to their chapel, but shortly thereafter the troops charged from all sides, swinging nightsticks and throwing tear gas canisters. "I saw those horsemen coming toward me and they had those awful masks on; they rode right through the cloud of tear gas," remembered young Sheyann Webb. "Some of them had clubs, others had ropes, or whips, which they swung about them like they were driving cattle." White spectators whooped approval as blacks panicked and fled in terror. Sheriff Clark yelled, "Get those god-damned niggers!" The troops did. "I saw a posse man raise his club," recalled J. L. Chestnut, Jr., "and smash it down on a woman's head as if he were splitting a watermelon." Police whipped and chased marchers all the way back to the chapel. "They even came up in the yard of the church, hittin' on folk," Willie Bolden recalled. "Ladies, men, babies, children—they didn't give a damn who they were."

Blacks labeled the day "Bloody Sunday," and that evening the nation saw it all on television. George Leonard and his wife watched from their living room in San Francisco:

> A shrill cry of terror, unlike any sound that had passed through a TV set, rose up as the troopers lumbered forward, stumbling sometimes on fallen bodies. The scene cut to charging horses, their hoofs flashing over the fallen. Another quick cut: a cloud of tear gas billowed over the highway. Periodically the top of a helmeted head emerged from the cloud, followed by a club on the upswing. The club and the head would disappear into the cloud of gas and another club would bob up and down. *Unhuman.* No other word can describe the motions. . . .
> It was at this point that my wife, sobbing, turned and walked away, saying, "I can't look any more."

"The news from Selma," the *Washington Post* wrote, "will shock and alarm the whole nation." Leonard left his home that evening, drove to the San Francisco airport, and boarded a plane for Alabama. Other concerned citizens were aboard—a lawyer from Palo Alto, a psychiatrist from Los Angeles, a young couple from Berkeley, and numerous black and white clergymen from the Bay Area. Civil rights organizations and individual activists placed calls to kindred souls throughout the nation. "It was informal," Robert Calvert remembered. A graduate student at the University of Texas, Calvert had volunteered to teach voter registration procedures for SCLC in Montgomery over Christmas break, and after he received the call, "Four of us piled into a car and headed for Selma. We arrived the next evening, and as we entered the city limits a local cop stopped our car, asked what we were doing in his town, told us that our tail light was out and suggested that we leave. That, of course, was aimed at keeping anyone sympathetic to the struggle, 'outside agitators,' out of Selma." Alabama troopers gave out tickets to whites with out-of-state license plates, even for "running red lights on an open highway where no such lights existed," reported law student Greg Lipscamb. "There were no citizens' rights or even states' rights. There were only Alabama white rights."[23]

Harassment did not stop the movement. The next morning Calvert and his friends returned to Selma and found a city filled with policemen, state troopers, and hundreds of activists. Black sharecroppers, ministers, and students mingled with white professors, doctors, and some 400 clergymen and nuns. Other Americans besieged the White House and Congress with calls and mail, and 4000 hurried to the nation's capital to demonstrate their support for voting rights. Across the nation, 10,000 joined sympathy marches.

While activists were arriving, SCLC planned a second march from Selma to Montgomery, but a judge issued an injunction that upheld the governor's ban on the march, and President Johnson quietly demanded that the activists cool off. LBJ's envoy and King met in Selma. Although King proclaimed to his followers, "We have the right to walk the highways, and we have the right to walk to Montgomery if our feet will get us there," he nevertheless agreed to a compromise.

Yet King did not tell the marchers, and many were eager for action after Bloody Sunday. SNCC members had rushed to Selma. "We were angry," wrote Cleveland Sellers. "And we wanted to show Governor Wallace, the Alabama State Highway Patrol, Sheriff Clark, Selma's whites, the federal government and poor Southern blacks in other Selmas that we didn't intend to take any more shit." On Tuesday, March 9, King led 3000 across Edmund Pettus Bridge as they sang "Ain't Gonna Let Nobody Turn Me 'Round." State troopers again blocked the route, but suddenly they moved off the road, clearing the highway to Montgomery. King knelt down and prayed, and then surprised the crowd by ordering them to turn around and return to the city. They did, ironically singing the same song back to the chapel. Militants were outraged, and quickly labeled the affair the "Tuesday turnaround." As for King, his biographer wrote, a "decisive turning point in his relations with the militants had now been reached."

The Selma struggle had intensified conflicts between SNCC and SCLC that had been growing since the 1964 Democratic convention. The Democratic party's rejection of the Mississippi Freedom Democrats at the convention "was to the civil rights movement what the Civil War was to American history," recalled activist Cleveland Sellers; "afterward, things could never be the same. Never again were we lulled into believing that our task was exposing injustices so that the 'good' people of America could eliminate them. We left Atlantic City with the knowledge that . . . our struggle was not for civil rights, but for liberation." SCLC disagreed, and again favored another dramatic demonstration calculated to spark national attention and pass liberal legislation. SNCC leaders voted not to be involved as an organization but to allow their members to participate as individuals.

One of those SNCC participants was John Lewis. Along with SCLC's Hosea Williams, Lewis walked in the front line across the bridge on Bloody Sunday. The police knocked Lewis to the ground and gave him a brain concussion. SCLC then ran an advertisement in the *New York Times*, picturing Lewis being hit and asking supporters to send money to SCLC. That "just burned us up," Julian Bond remembered, "SCLC was hoggin' all the publicity and all the money and doing very little to deserve it."

SNCC militants called SCLC "slick." King was losing control of young militant activists who had suffered at the hands of the Bull Connors and Jim Clarks. SNCC members were growing tired of nonviolent activism, and organizational jealousy was seething in Selma.

Again, white violence unified the groups, and sparked national attention. Local thugs attacked three northern white ministers, beating them with baseball bats. James Reeb, a Unitarian cleric from Boston, suffered multiple head wounds, and as he laid dying, nuns from St. Louis and local high school students led marches. When he died two days later, Sheyann Webb recalled that she and a friend "knelt down . . . and we prayed to ourselves for awhile. I didn't cry. I kept thinking how even though he had been white, he had been one of us, too."[24]

The death renewed demands for federal action. Thousands demonstrated across the nation and sent telegrams to Washington, and a dozen students held a sit-in at the White House. LBJ watched the reruns of the Selma confrontation on television and felt deep outrage. He sent yellow roses to Mrs. Reeb, discussed the situation with Governor Wallace at the White House, and on March 15 addressed a joint session of Congress and asked for the passage of a voting rights bill:

What happened in Selma is part of a far larger movement which reaches into every section and state of America. It is the effort of American Negroes to secure for themselves the full blessings of American life. This cause must be our cause too. It is not just Negroes, but all of us, who must overcome the crippling legacy of bigotry and injustice. And we *shall* overcome.

A week later the movement blossomed in Selma. On March 21 over 3000 white and black activists began the pilgrimage from Selma to Montgomery. LBJ informed Governor Wallace that citizens would be able to march on public highways, and for protection he federalized the Alabama National Guard. Accompanying a host of civil rights leaders was the president of the New York City Council, the Manhattan borough president, labor leader Walter Reuther, historians John Hope Franklin and William E. Leuchtenburg, and Jimmie Lee Jackson's grandfather, along with numerous ministers, rabbis, and a bishop from California. Most marchers were students, many of them eager to renew their commitment to the movement. They walked along U.S. 80, ironically known as Jeff Davis Highway, and averaged about ten miles a day, sometimes in heavy rain. They sang and talked, and camped out each night in tents on fields of supporters. A few whites heckled, and some waved Confederate flags or held up signs: "Nigger Lover," "Martin Luther Coon," "Yankee Trash Go Home." While "the march was incredibly disorganized," Robert Calvert recalled, "the mood was very upbeat, optimistic. The last two days were almost festive." The fourth day they were led by Jim Letherer, a white laborer and an amputee from Michigan, who made the entire walk on crutches. On his left and right were two young men, one black and the other white, each carrying the American flag, and behind them marched a black with his head bandaged in the style of 1776, playing on his fife "Yankee Doodle." The pilgrims spent their last night camped three miles outside of Montgomery, and there they intermingled with a platoon of celebrities: Leonard Bernstein, Floyd Patterson, Shelley Winters, Nina Simone, Tony Bennett, Sidney Poitier, Paul Newman, Harry Belafonte, Sammy Davis, Jr. The next day they were joined by thousands for the final procession to the state capital. The crowd cheered Dick Gregory, and they sang and walked along with the Chad Mitchell Trio, Mahalia Jackson, Ella Fitzgerald, Joan Baez, and Peter, Paul and Mary, who sang: "How many roads must a man walk, before you call him a man?"

The crowd swelled to 30,000, and on the speakers' platform assembled many of the most important civil rights figures since the 1963 March on Washington—Roy Wilkins of the NAACP, John Lewis of SNCC, and Whitney Young of the National Urban League, along with A. Philip Randolph, Ralph Bunche, Bayard Rustin, and Rosa Parks. King took the podium, and looking over toward Mrs. Parks recalled an episode from the Montgomery bus boycott a decade earlier. Sister Pollard, he said, was walking to work when a man asked her if she needed a ride. "No," she responded proudly, and then the person asked, "Well, aren't you tired?" King reminded the audience of Pollard's ungrammatical profundity: "My feets is tired, but my soul is rested."

"We are on the move now," King proclaimed. "Like an idea whose time has come, not even the marching of mighty armies can halt us. We are moving to the land of freedom."

While a hundred SNCC members in the audience thought they were moving much too slowly, thousands in the crowd and millions at home and on campus agreed with King. SCLC's tactic paid handsome dividends. "Let us march on ballot boxes," King continued, and they did. In August, LBJ signed the Voting Rights Act. The law placed federal examiners in states with a history of discrimination, eventually abolished the remnants of literacy tests and poll taxes, resulting in black voter registration. Two weeks later over 60 percent of blacks in Selma had registered to vote. By the 1966 elections over half of adult blacks in the South were registered, and they began electing their own officials. Selma transformed southern politics.

"Selma has become a shining monument in the conscience of man," King added as most of the audience started for home or back to campus for the remainder of spring semester. "We felt hopeful," Calvert recalled as he returned to the University of Texas. Most students of the sixties generation agreed. The few who had become active during the year could look back at successes in the South and on their campuses—they could make a difference.

Selma also provoked other students into action, not only at larger universities but also at smaller colleges. Approximately 150 activists from Beloit College in Wisconsin marched 50 miles to Madison to protest police brutality in Selma. In Minneapolis, Macalester College students formed Action Against Apartheid and raised money to rebuild destroyed freedom schools in Mississippi, and half the enrollment of Augsburg College marched to the state capital to protest events in Selma. At DePauw University in Indiana, Mary Ann Wynkoop and a few other students held a sympathy march; from then on she wore a button that proclaimed "I am an activist."

The day after Bloody Sunday, March 8, activists at the University of Kansas marched into the administration building and sat outside the office of Chancellor W. Clarke Wescoe. They demanded change. At that time, sororities and fraternities were segregated, dorms had de facto segregation, and not one black was employed as either a faculty member or administrator. The city of Lawrence did not have a municipal swimming pool, and some private clubs did not admit blacks. Wescoe had condemned exclusion, but stated that integration must come voluntarily. Activists, however, were tired of waiting for volunteers. They listed demands—end discrimination in housing, fraternities, and sororities, and change the advertising policy of the school paper, *University Daily Kansan*, so that it no longer accepted ads from businesses that practiced discrimination. After six hours, a dean informed the students that the office would be closed at 5 p.m., and those remaining would be arrested for trespassing. The police arrived at that time, and peacefully arrested over a hundred students. In a show of goodwill, the chancellor arranged for bond and bail money, writing a personal check.[25]

Before this incident, most K.U. students had been apathetic, but the episode sparked interest in civil rights. Thirty students volunteered to spend their spring break registering black voters in Louisiana, while others again took their demands to the chancellor, demonstrating in front of his home and office. Wescoe agreed to discussion, and within a month dropped all charges against the demonstrators; by autumn the regents prohibited all forms of discrimination at K.U.

During that spring semester another issue began to concern some students—United States' role in South Vietnam.

America's involvement there was logical. Americans had convinced themselves that Communism was monolithic, even though Yugoslavia had split from the Soviet bloc in the late 1940s and China was squabbling with Russia in the early 1960s. Aberrations, politicians said, another commie plot. The U.S. government continued expressing the view that all Communists wanted the same thing—world domination—and that our nemesis, Moscow, controlled "puppets" such as Mao Tse-tung in China, Fidel Castro in Cuba, and Ho Chi Minh in Vietnam. Third-world nations were pawns, "dominoes," and they would fall to Communism unless the bulwark of the "free world," the USA, stood firm. "Furthermore," declared Admiral U.S. Grant Sharp, "our stand in Vietnam will affect our other commitments all over the world—in NATO, Japan, Korea and Thailand." Vietnam, the argument went, was "a test of our reliability. We cannot back out of Vietnam without invalidating our position as a world leader." American troops had stopped the communist advance in Korea, so a decade later the question was: Would we make a commitment to the non-Communist government in Saigon in its attempt to prevent a victory by Communist forces of Ho Chi Minh? Would America stand up for South Vietnam?

The United States, supposedly, had little choice. "If we don't stop the Reds in South Vietnam," declared LBJ, "tomorrow they will be in Hawaii, and next week they will be in San Francisco." We must fight there, he said privately, or the United States "might as well give up everywhere else—pull out of Berlin, Japan, South America." At home or on campus, most Americans supported the president's views. A Kentucky farmer stated, "All Asia's at stake out there. I don't believe in looking down when you know you are right," and a West Virginia carpenter added, "If we don't stand up for people oppressed by Communism, we'll soon be oppressed ourselves." The first Harris survey on the conflict in 1963 found that by a two to one margin Americans felt that if the Communist threat to South Vietnam grew worse, then they would favor sending U.S. troops on a large scale.[26] After all, it was better to fight the commies on the Mekong than on the Mississippi.

The conflict started subtly—no declaration of war, no mass mobilization, no fanfare. For years the United States had been involved in Vietnam. In 1950 the Truman administration began supporting France's attempts to hold on to their colony of Indochina, and by 1954 the U.S. government was paying 80 percent of France's total military costs in their war against Ho's army. French troops had become our mercenaries. Massive American aid could not stave off military defeat, however, and that year Ho's forces annihilated the colonialist army at Dienbienphu. The world powers met at Geneva and the subsequent accords separated the colony into North and South Vietnam. National elections were to unite Vietnam under one government in 1956, but the ruler in the south, Ngo Dinh Diem, refused to participate since he would have lost overwhelmingly to the popular northern leader, Ho Chi Minh. Even Eisenhower admitted later that if elections were held in 1956, Ho would have won 80 percent of the vote.

"We the people," the democratic process, somehow did not seem important during cold war culture. Eisenhower did not force Diem to hold elections and the American government of the majority supported South Vietnam's government of the minority. The nation that had championed free elections against Soviet tyranny throughout the cold war now simply declared Diem "father of his country," while others joined in and proclaimed him the "Asian Liberator" and the "Winston Churchill of Southeast Asia." Consequently, Ho and his allies in the south, the Vietcong, began a guerrilla war to force unification. The U.S. responded by becoming the main benefactor of the Saigon regime. The president eventually sent about 700 advisers to train the Army of the Republic of South Vietnam (ARVN). To boost the economy, and to influence Vietnamese to support Diem, the administration pumped over a billion dollars into South Vietnam, even paying the salaries of ARVN. The economy improved, but by 1960 the little nation had become our welfare child.

Kennedy increased aid. A decade earlier the Republicans had won the presidency partly by asking "Who lost China?," and the Democratic president did not want to be blamed for losing Indochina. Although the

Vietnamese had no background or interest in democracy, the best and brightest declared that South Vietnam was America's "testing ground" to build democratic governments in developing nations and to stop the flow of Communism. South Vietnam, JFK declared earlier, was the "cornerstone of the Free World in Southeast Asia, the Keystone to the arch, the finger in the dike." Furthermore, the Soviets had built the Berlin Wall and the American-sponsored invasion of the Bay of Pigs had been a fiasco. Now, the young president told a reporter, "we have a problem in trying to make our power credible, and Vietnam looks like the place." [27] Kennedy sent helicopters and more advisers, including the Green Berets.

By 1963 the U.S. had about 16,000 advisers in South Vietnam. But they were not able to stop the Vietcong or strengthen the regime of Diem, a ruler whose "harsh and thoughtless rule," the CIA secretly reported, had alienated most South Vietnamese. By August the CIA chief in Saigon cabled the State Department: "Situation here has reached the point of no return." JFK then approved a plot to overthrow Diem, and in November, South Vietnamese generals conducted the coup d'état. The conspirators killed Diem. Saigon officials called the murder an "accidental suicide" as the sixties became the era of euphemisms.

ARVN generals, however, were no better democrats than Diem, and during the Johnson administration they fought over who would be the president of South Vietnam. For the next three years military governments came and went in Saigon. In one fourteen-month period there were seven different governments, so many coups d'état that the Texan president exclaimed, "I'm tired of hearing about this coup shit." Instability in Saigon meant that ARVN was not able to take the offensive against the Vietcong, leaving the task to the Americans. Finally, in 1967, two generals emerged as the cornerstones of democracy in Saigon, President Nguyen Chanh Thieu and Vice President Nguyen Cao Ky.

Meanwhile, in August 1964, North Vietnamese patrol boats attacked an American destroyer, the USS *Maddox*, in the Tonkin Gulf. The *Maddox* was helping ARVN conduct sabotage missions in the north, but LBJ kept that from the public. Instead, the president declared that our ship had been attacked in international waters, and that he was retaliating by ordering air strikes on naval installations in North Vietnam. The president then asked Congress to pass the Gulf of Tonkin Resolution, a vague charter that apparently gave him Constitutional authority to help our South Vietnam ally. "It's like Grandmother's shirt," press secretary George Reedy said privately, "it covers everything."

The nation rallied around the flag. The *New York Times* declared that the attack on the *Maddox* was the "beginning of a mad adventure by the North Vietnamese Communists" that the U.S. must "assure the independence of South Vietnam," and the *Washington Post* applauded LBJ's "careful and effective handling of the Viet-Nam crisis." The president's approval rating soared to over 70 percent, and Congress passed the resolution overwhelmingly. Two-thirds of the public supported the resolution, including at least that percentage of college students. A typical collegiate response was that of the *Michigan State News*, writing that LBJ "could hardly have chosen any other course of action. . . . Our announced intentions to defend southeast Asia from communist aggression would have rung pitifully false if we had patted North Vietnam's leaders on the head for launching an unprovoked attack on our ships."

LBJ assured the public that he had no intention of expanding America's role in the war. It "ought to be fought by the boys of Asia to help protect their own land," he said during the 1964 presidential campaign, continuing that the issue is "who can keep the peace." Johnson pledged moderation, and if Americans ever desired to become involved in a major war in Asia—or to declare war on North Vietnam—then they had a clear choice at the polls that November: Republican Senator Barry Goldwater. Instead, voters rejected the senator's hawkish stance and elected Johnson with the highest margin of victory in American history.

The Vietcong were not concerned about who occupied the White House and they continued attacking ARVN and its 20,000 U.S. advisers during winter 1964 and spring 1965. Although the American public was not aware of it, the South Vietnamese regime was on the verge of collapse; the enemy sensed victory. In December the VC conducted scattered attacks in Saigon, and by February they were bold enough to strike the U.S. Special Forces camp at Pleiku.

The attacks prompted LBJ to take action. He could not rely on the United Nations to become involved and stop the fighting, he said, because the organization "couldn't pour piss out of a boot if the instructions were printed on the heel." Johnson was convinced that if the U.S. did not send additional troops, then South Vietnam would be lost to Communism. "I'm not going to be the first president to lose a war," said LBJ, and he ordered Operation Rolling Thunder—the bombing of North Vietnam. During the ides of March the Texan decided that the only way to prevent a defeat was to change American policy. Shortly thereafter he sent the Marines, began increasing U.S. forces, and gave them new orders—they not only would advise ARVN but also could conduct combat missions with their ally in an attempt to search out and destroy the enemy. As the chairman of the Joint Chiefs of Staff said, "No one ever won a battle sitting on his ass."

Significantly, the administration also attempted to conceal the escalation and downplay involvement in Vietnam. LBJ was more concerned with civil rights and passing his Great Society legislation, and he did not want to provoke the Soviets, Chinese, or the Americans. A national security memorandum declared that the "President desires that . . . publicity be avoided by all possible precautions" and that subordinates should minimize any appearance that the U.S. was enlarging its commitment. The president, said one adviser, wanted to "go to war without arousing the public ire."

Americans either supported the president or knew little about the administration's policy. That spring, while events in Selma and the president's voting rights address dominated the evening news, opinion polls demonstrated that about 80 percent supported bombing North Vietnam. Surveys earlier revealed that two-thirds of the public had either not followed or had no opinion of LBJ's policy; a fourth did not even know that U.S. troops were fighting in Vietnam.[28]

Yet the bombing that spring also provoked some peace organizations, professors, and a few students to question American aims in Southeast Asia. Various liberal and peace groups began confronting congressmen and writing the White House, including Americans for Democratic Action, American Friends Service Committee, Students for a Democratic Society, and SANE. In February, over 300 activists in Women's International League for Peace and Freedom and Women Strike for Peace assembled at the Capitol for the "Mother's Lobby," an attempt to pressure congressmen to support a negotiated settlement in Vietnam. SDS called for an Easter Day peace march in Washington, and a handful of politicians expressed doubts about LBJ's policy. In New York, some 3000 activists protested the bombing at the United Nations Plaza.

During the winter months some students had conducted a few dozen small demonstrations, most of them organized locally, but the campus antiwar movement first received national attention when almost fifty professors decided to hold a "teach-in" at the University of Michigan. Inspired by civil rights sit-ins and freedom schools, and just days after the Selma march, 200 professors took out an ad in the *Michigan Daily* appealing to students to join them in a teach-in in an attempt to "search for a better policy." Throughout the night of March 24–25 more than 3000 students and faculty participated in lectures, debates, and discussions. As Professor Marc Pilisuk described it, "One honors student later told me that this was her first educational experience provided by the university during four year's attendance. . . . Some who had hardly ever spoken in class before argued for an hour in the halls with white-haired full professors." The next morning 600 remained, and they held a rally in front of the library. Like those who had participated in Mississippi Summer or the Free Speech Movement at Berkeley, Michigan activists noted that participating in the teach-in changed their lives, and they remembered a night when "people who really cared talked of things that really mattered."

The movement was growing, and it spread to other campuses. That spring teach-ins were held at about 35 universities, including Columbia, Illinois, Harvard, Michigan State, Rutgers, and even at usually sedate campuses such as Carleton in Minnesota, Marist College in New York, and Flint Junior College in Michigan. Berkeley held the largest and longest teach-in; 20,000 participated for 36 hours. At Wisconsin, a civil rights activist said the evening was not really a teach-in but the university's "first freedom school," for which he received a standing ovation. At Oregon, the teach-in was the first sign of social activism there since the 1930s. Some 3000 jammed into the student union and listened to speakers, poets, and folksingers, while they devoured hundreds of sandwiches and sixty gallons of coffee. One pretty coed wore a homemade card pinned to her sweater, "Let's make love, not war." "Raw freshmen argued fearlessly with senior professors," reported a journalist. "Never had the pleasant, placid campus of the University of Oregon been through anything like this."

In April, the peace movement arrived in the nation's capital. During the first half of the 1960s, peace groups had held annual disarmament marches on Easter Sunday. A few thousand usually appeared, but this year students passed out flyers: "The trip will be a great opportunity for all of us to get together to discuss ways of engaging in social action on many issues," wrote students at Carleton College. Bused in from campuses all over the country, some 20,000 appeared on that warm, beautiful Sunday. They picketed the White House and then began marching to the Washington Monument. "The times they are a-changin'," sang Judy Collins, and she was joined with songs by Joan Baez and Phil Ochs. Journalist I. F. Stone spoke, as did historian Staughton Lynd and civil rights activist Bob Moses before Senator Ernest Gruening called for an immediate bombing halt and peace negotiations. SDS president Paul Potter gave an inspired speech, calling for a "massive social movement" to change America. Activists waved signs: "Get Out of Saigon and into Selma," "Freedom Now in Vietnam," "War on Poverty Not on People."

A SNCC trio, the Freedom Voices, led the crowd in "We Shall Overcome" as the demonstrators marched down the Mall and to the Capitol where they presented Congress with a petition: "The problems of America cry out for attention, and our entanglement in South Vietnam postpones the confrontation of these issues while prolonging the misery of the people of that war-torn land. You must act now to reverse this sorry state of affairs. We call on you to end, not extend, the war in Vietnam."

A surge of energy from white and black activists appeared that spring, and it signaled that the struggle, student power, and now a small antiwar crusade could merge to become what civil rights advocate Bayard Rustin called a "full-fledged *social movement*." The teach-ins and various peace protests demonstrated that some Americans were going to question U.S.

foreign policy, even march against it, while a few other students began examining the role of their universities in the Vietnam War. In May, a hundred students at Hofstra held perhaps the first demonstration of the era against ROTC. Finally, protests and teach-ins identified a number of intellectuals who would challenge national policy. Over the years the professors would become important as alternative experts, an academic counterculture to the best and brightest in Washington.

But more important, the antiwar demonstrations that spring were significant because of what did not happen—the Johnson administration did not change policy in Vietnam. In fact, most Americans considered peace marchers beatniks, kooks, or Communists, and the demonstrators received little press and had little impact. On March 16 an elderly member of Women Strike for Peace, Alice Herz, protested the war in a sensational way—she set herself aflame on a Detroit street. Although she left a note protesting the bombing of North Vietnam, the administration made no statement on the suicide and the public showed little interest. In June, 17,000 activists attended an antiwar rally at Madison Square Garden that included speeches by Senator Wayne Morse, Bayard Rustin, Dr. Benjamin Spock, and even Coretta Scott King, who announced that she was a member of Women Strike for Peace. After the rally about 2000 followed Dr. Spock in a nighttime procession to the United Nations. The press neglected the affair. As a historian of the antiwar movement wrote, "it was clear that the administration had the support of the country's major opinion-shaping agencies. Antiwar activists quickly realized their limited effectiveness." [29]

Americans supported LBJ. When thirty activists at Kent State protested the bombing, an angry crowd five times larger pelted them with rocks. A teach-in at Wisconsin resulted in 6000 students signing a letter supporting the president's policy, and a fourth of the student body did the same thing at Yale. Some Michigan State professors condemned the teach-in on their campus as "deliberately one-sided," a "rally for indoctrination," and with the aid of students in Young Democrats and Young Americans for Freedom collected almost 16,000 signatures supporting U.S. policy. After twenty members of the Student Peace Union at Kansas demonstrated with signs that read "Negotiate not escalate!," the campus paper editorialized that the "SPU must surely be motivated by sincere feelings, but so was Chamberlain at the infamous Munich conference." A survey of student opinion demonstrated that only a quarter supported negotiations or withdrawal from Vietnam, and in January 1966 the *New York Times* reported that almost three-quarters of students at the University of Wisconsin supported LBJ's policies in Southeast Asia.

The spring teach-ins were a "short-lived phenomenon," a historian has concluded. Few American altered their views about LBJ's Vietnam policies, and few felt that Vietcong peasants or the North Vietnamese Army would be a match for the "greatest nation on earth." Faced with an army of John Waynes, the enemy would give up quickly. How could we lose? Furthermore, LBJ had assured the public that the nation should not get involved in an Asian land war and that he was not going to send "American boys to do the job that Asian boys should do" for themselves. The president announced in March and April that he was prepared to "go anywhere at any time" to talk peace, that he supported "unconditional negotiations" with Hanoi, and his subordinates added that while the administration shared the same goals as the dissidents, they had "secret information" that justified their policy.

By summer, as many of the sixties generation left their dorms and headed off to the beach, a survey demonstrated that most students felt that Vietnam would not be their concern. Almost all U.S. troops assigned to that country were volunteers, professional soldiers acting as advisers. It was a tiny nation, halfway around the world. When a teacher announced in David Christian's class that another coup d'état had taken place in that country, "We looked at each other and said, 'Where the hell is South Vietnam?'" Almost no one then would have thought that a few years later Christian would be leading men into battle in South Vietnam and Cambodia. [30]

Nevertheless, by the end of spring semester 1965 the climate on campus had shifted dramatically from the 1950s and early 1960s. "An End to Panty Raids," wrote a student at Kansas. The most important issues were civil and student rights; another continued that his generation was "fed up with their elders over such things as mass faceless education. . . . Students want to feel a sense of participation." With successes in the South and on their campuses, many students were optimistic about change, and as they became involved many began to think of themselves as part of a movement. "The thing for me right now is the movement," said Steven Block, an activist at Williams College. "That's an interesting word, if you think about it—movement. Because it is people in motion. It's not an end; it's not static. That's a very apt word for what we are doing."

The silent generation was history. *College Press Service* in December declared, "1964 Is Year of Protest on Nation's Campuses," and Professor Andrew Hacker called 1964–65 the "Year of the Demonstration." It was when compared with any time in memory.

But, more important, Hacker then placed the activists in context of the larger sixties generation. "Certainly, this year's protesters and demonstrators were not representative of their classmates, and it is instructive how quickly their ranks have tended to dwindle away after the first flamboyant outbursts. So long as a school will give an undergraduate his passport into the upper-middle-class without demanding more than . . . 15 weekly hours of studying, few are going to complain." Few indeed. Two years later, in 1967, professors Seymour Lipset and Philip Altbach flatly declared that it "should be made clear that . . . the scope of the American student 'revolution' has been greatly exaggerated by the mass media."

Newsweek confirmed such sentiments during spring 1965 when it conducted interviews and a poll of over 800 students at numerous universities. Over 90 percent expressed confidence in higher education, big corporations, and the federal government, while over 80 percent were satisfied with college and had positive views about the armed forces, organized religion, and the United Nations. When asked what students thought their lives would be like in fifteen years, most of them mimicked their older brothers: "I'll be secure, financially, married, have children, at least three," said one. Another aimed to be "upper middle class," and a third predicted, "I'll be living in a Long Island suburb." A journalist labeled the students "Flaming Moderates."[31]

In mid-decade only a few students were activists while the larger sixties generation was comfortably moderate. A conservative student at the University of Miami wrote about the "deadly infection called student apathy" and referred to his campus as a "hotbed of apathy." Fraternities and sororities still dominated campus life, and a coed at Kansas as late as 1967 admitted that the biggest craze on her campus was "to get your boyfriend's fraternity sweater." Most college papers were similar to the *Daily Illini*, printing regular features like "The Party Line" which announced lavalierings, pinnings, engagements, and marriages. "I have respect for the ones who went to Mississippi or joined the Peace Corps, who committed themselves," said an English professor at Illinois in 1965, "but there are very, very few of them. Very few on this campus."

While some students had been provoked out of apathy by campus issues and civil rights, most of the sixties generation sitting in crowded classes during spring semester of 1965 were optimistic and comfortable—still best defined as the cool generation—mildly alienated from their parents' values and eager to sing along and "let the good times roll." *Time* surveyed the generation then and reported conformity: "Almost everywhere boys dress in madras shirts and chinos, or perhaps green Levis, all trim and neat. The standard for girls is sweaters and skirts dyed to match, or shirtwaists and jumpers plus blazers, Weejun loafers, and knee socks or stockings." At that time no one would have predicted that just two years away were the Summer of Love and the March on the Pentagon. Campus life that spring semester was cool, the good life. As the student body president of University of Texas said, "We haven't really been tested by war or depression. We live very much in the present because we don't have to be overly concerned about the future."[32]

"There was that little conflict in Vietnam," Bob Calvert remembered, "but most of us in the movement felt optimistic during the summer of 1965." Indeed, most Americans felt that the nation was moving forward, and that mood was glowing in August when LBJ signed the Voting Rights Act. The president asked civil rights leaders to be present, and the signing ceremony included Bayard Rustin, Roy Wilkins, A. Philip Randolph, and Martin Luther King, Jr. LBJ had met with King the previous day and they discussed the remarkable advances during 1964 and 1965, not only in civil rights but also in the War on Poverty and Great Society programs—massive federal aid to education and job training, Headstart, Medicare, and Medicaid. King spoke of the president's "amazing sensitivity to the difficult problems that Negro Americans face in the stride toward freedom," and at the signing celebration the president declared, "Today is a triumph for freedom as huge as any victory that's ever been won on any battlefield." The civil rights leaders proclaimed LBJ the "greatest President" for blacks, even surpassing Abraham Lincoln.

"There was a religiosity about the meeting," recalled a presidential aide, "which was warm with emotion—a final celebration of an act so long desired and so long in achieving." Now liberals could sit back in their easy chairs and relax. In spring 1964 a new president had made his pledge, had declared his vision of the future. "This nation, this people, this generation, has man's first chance to create a Great Society: a society of success without squalor, beauty without barrenness, works of genius without the wretchedness of poverty. We can open the doors of learning. We can open the doors of fruitful labor and rewarding leisure, of open opportunity and close community—not just to the privileged few, but, thank God, we can open those doors to *everyone*." Now, just fifteen months later, it seemed that the liberals were delivering. The civil and voting rights acts had outlawed racial discrimination in public accommodations, employment, and the vote, and social programs were beginning to help the poor—white and black—to share the American Dream. On that day in August, liberalism reached its zenith in the 1960s.

Then, during the next two years, President Johnson gave the sixties generation a reason to be concerned about the future—he massively escalated America's role in the Vietnam War. The cool generation became history.

What would have happened to the sixties generation without the experience of Vietnam? Certainly, many would have continued to support and some would have demonstrated for civil rights. Five years of the struggle meant that it had become part of the generation's consciousness, and students began demanding classes on black literature and history at universities such as Stanford, Cornell, and San Francisco State. The "movement" would have been remembered as the civil rights struggle and the rise of student power. Increasing enrollments meant that the university was going to continue evolving in size and in substance, and that students would continue demanding and supporting change. In spring 1966 Stanford activist David Harris won election as student body president by calling for student control of regulations, equal policies for men and women, option of pass-fail grades, legalization of marijuana, elimination of the board of trustees, and the end of all university cooperation with the Vietnam War. The next year students challenged campus rules and regulations at Brown, Cornell, Oregon, Washington, and administrators at the best institutions were moving toward adopting the suggestion of a committee at Wisconsin that advocated "withdrawal by the University from its *in loco parentis* activities." By mid-decade it also was clear that 1950s morality was cracking and that the younger generation was revolting against the values of Ma and Pa. Most of this quest would be superficial, beer bashes and bundling at the beach as the sixties became a party decade. But for a few others, the questioning of morals would lead them to substantial changes as they became part of an emerging counterculture. Finally, the massive size of the generation alone meant that it would have modified society, and thus would have made an impact. [33]

What would have been remembered as the "sixties" without Vietnam? The Johnson administration would have continued civil rights legislation and Great Society programs, and along with the significant rulings of the Supreme Court of Chief Justice Earl Warren, the decade would have been taught today as another major reform era in American history.

Without the war, however, one wonders if the decade would have been as dramatic—would have been remembered as "the sixties." The decade had been a turning point for blacks since Greensboro in 1960. For white students and their parents the decade began to take shape in 1964 and 1965 as the young began to exhibit their new values and make demands on their campus administrators. Then, between autumn 1965 and the end of 1967, the Johnson administration escalated American involvement in Vietnam—and for the entire nation the decade became "the sixties."

ays of Decision

1966 shall be remembered as the year we left our imposed status as Negroes and became Black Men . . . 1966 is the year of the concept of Black Power.
Floyd McKissick, 1966

A new concert of human relations being developed within the youthful underground must emerge, become conscious, and be shared so that a revolution of form can be filled with a Renaissance of compassion, awareness and love . . .
Human Be-In announcement, 1967

Everything now revolves around Vietnam. . . . It's no longer a distant, bloodied, tedious spot half across the planet. Vietnam is here.
Dave McReynolds, 1967

During 1965 Phil Ochs sang to his generation:

> There's a change in the wind,
> a split in the road,
> You can do what is right
> or you can do what you're told,
> But the price of victory
> will belong to the bold,
> For these are the days of decision.

The days of decision were between autumn 1965 and the end of 1967. During that time the major issues that defined the first wave of the movement and the sixties—race and war—dominated the evening news. A more militant form of civil rights, an expanding conflict in Southeast Asia, and an emerging "counter" to mainstream culture all provoked citizens to question, to make decisions about their own views and about the direction of the nation. The political became the personal, especially for the sixties generation; they had been awakened by Kennedy's idealism, aroused by the struggle in the South, and confronted by campus regulations, and during the next years they would be educated by racial strife in America and by the war in Vietnam.

That education began just days after President Johnson signed the 1965 Voting Rights Act in August: the most destructive riot in the postwar era erupted in Watts, the black ghetto of Los Angeles. It began simply enough. A white policeman stopped a young black driver and began to arrest him for speeding and possible intoxication. At first the accused was polite, even joking, but the youth's mother appeared and an argument ensued. A crowd assembled, and the officer radioed for reinforcements. Other cars arrived, and when the police attempted to force the suspect into a car, he struggled, and his mother called for help. Bystanders began pelting police with rocks and bottles and within two hours an angry mob was attacking white drivers and setting cars aflame. By midnight a few thousand were in the streets, but by dawn it appeared that the riot had ended. Community leaders called for calm, but the next evening black hostility boiled over. Some 5000 roamed the streets. Many protested living conditions, others decried police brutality, some chanted civil rights slogans. The mob eventually began looting, and some attacked whites on the streets while others fire-bombed stores. The police and firemen moved in, but a few rioters shot at them from rooftops, forcing the police to call for the National Guard.

The riot raged on. As more white law enforcement officers appeared in Watts, more black citizens took to the streets. Fires burned out of control as some chanted, "Burn, baby, burn." Shots were exchanged. Eventually, authorities called in over 15,000 troops and police. The ghetto became a combat zone. Troops grew tense, shooting wildly. The President's National Advisory Commission on Civil Disorders reported: "Several persons were killed by mistake. Many more were injured." The troops restored law and order after six days, but at a high price: almost 4000 arrested, over 1000 injured, and 34 dead.

"Everything seemed to collapse," Ramsey Clark lamented. "The days of 'We Shall Overcome' were over." Indeed, Watts and riots a few days later in Chicago and Springfield, Massachusetts, did incalculable harm to the civil rights struggle. Many white Americans agreed with former President Eisenhower, who blamed the riot on "an increased lack of respect for law and order throughout the country." Ike continued that there was a feeling in the nation that "if you like a law, you obey it, if you don't like it you don't obey it."

The "white backlash" emerged, now even more forcefully than when

President Johnson first used the term after Alabama Governor George Wallace won about 30 percent of the vote in the 1964 Democratic primaries in Wisconsin and Indiana. Obviously, resistance to social change was buried deep in the heart of the body politic. Since Greensboro white conservatives had been losing control, watching the world change around them. They had been waiting to respond to the movement. Berkeley was their first opportunity, and they vehemently condemned student activists, and then Watts offered the first chance to strike at civil rights. Conservatives who had supported only local police protection for southern blacks and civil rights workers now demanded "whatever force is necessary" to stop the riots; to restore law and order the *Oakland Tribune* advocated employing the "full power of the Federal Government." William F. Buckley, Jr., paired "Mario Savio, hero of the anarchic beatniks," with the Reverend King, who advocates disobeying "laws he believes to be unjust." There will be more riots, Buckley predicted, "so long as the nation coddles the teachings of the Mario Savios and the Martin Luther Kings." Morrie Ryskind in the *Los Angeles Times* adopted another angle: "We have been proud of our race relations," he wrote. Some of the "richest Negroes in America—and that means the world—have made their wealth here." Under the leadership of King, however, "they have preached nonviolence but winked at violence. They have preached love but winked at hate. They have talked about rights but never responsibilities. . . . And where during the killing was the Nobel Peace Prize winner who takes all the bows when the going is good? Here, pleading with his followers? Wrong. He was busy drawing up plans for our peace negotiations with Hanoi. There may be a second peace prize in the offing."

Actually, King hurried to Watts. Along with Bayard Rustin and Andrew Young, he talked to the people, listened, and learned about life in the ghetto. Outside the South, urban blacks had the vote and had better opportunities—at least that is what most whites thought. In fact, a decade after the U.S. Supreme Court had ruled in the Brown case that school districts must integrate "with all deliberate speed," educational facilities remained segregated. White officials drew school districts lines that resulted in de facto segregation. The Civil Rights Commission found that between 1950 and 1965 segregation in fifteen large northern cities actually "rose sharply." In Los Angeles, for example, the student body at forty schools was made up of over 90 percent minority groups, and that situation existed in all major cities where blacks resided—New York, Chicago, Detroit, Cleveland, and Washington. Also in those cities, black unemployment was double that of whites, even in the booming economy of the 1960s, and black male workers earned 60 percent of white salaries. In Watts, the black unemployment rate was 30 percent, and nationally the majority of blacks were underemployed in unskilled and service jobs, the prescription for poverty. Over 40 percent of nonwhites were below the poverty line, and a federal study demonstrated that prices ghetto stores charged their customers actually were higher than in other areas of a city. Another study of poor neighborhoods demonstrated that the average combined underemployed and unemployed rate for blacks was almost nine times that of white citizens. The contrast with white America was startling. A black Watts resident told a white from Los Angeles: "You've got it made. Some nights on the roof of our rotten falling down buildings we can actually see your lights shining in the distance. So near and yet so far. We want to reach out and grab it and punch it on the nose."[1]

Even if blacks graduated from high school and acquired decent jobs, they still could not escape the misery of the ghetto. All the major cities in the nation had various housing restrictions: The better areas and the suburbs were reserved for whites. Unlike white America, then, the key to success—hard work—had little meaning for urban minorities. They were trapped. Someone wrote on a wall during the Harlem riot: "We had full employment on the plantation too, baby."

Furthermore, many city officials were racists, or they simply were not concerned about their black constituents. When black residents asked that anti-poverty funds from federal grants be spent in Watts, Los Angeles Mayor Sam Yorty said that such demands were caused by "Communist agitation." When King complained about housing restrictions, the mayor responded, "That's no indication of prejudice. That's personal choice." It was, but only for whites. When King asked the police chief why he referred to black rioters as "the criminal element" and as "monkeys," the chief declared, "That's the only language Negroes understand." City police forces were notorious. Before urban riots of the 1960s, almost all policemen in every major city were whites, graduates of high school only, and in the ghetto cops were known for racism and brutality. Policemen called sections of Watts "charcoal alley," and their billy clubs were "nigger knockers." In most cities black joggers were considered criminals running from a theft, and police routinely stopped and frisked them. During the Watts riot, President Johnson asked two trusted assistants to fly out and investigate. One was white, and the other was Roger Wilkins, a black assistant attorney general. The two men drove into Watts, and immediately were pulled over by two white policemen. While one cop asked the white official some questions and for identification, the other policeman pulled Wilkins from the car, frisked him roughly, drew his pistol, jammed the barrel into his stomach, and began asking questions to find out "why a nigger was riding with a white," Wilkins recalled. "My blood was boiling, and I came an inch of exploding—and losing my life—until the other policeman told his companion, 'Well, well, we've made a hell of a mistake.' "

Rage, frustration. As Wilkins walked down the filthy streets, past the shabby bars and gutted stores of Watts, he saw another culture: the ghetto. He reported that these were "the poor people, the voiceless people, the invisible people," that they "*had* been ignored, and they were enraged." A local black minister explained during the riot: "Here's the man who doesn't have any identity. But *tonight* he has the Los Angeles Police Department and the Los Angeles Fire Department upset. He has the National Guard called out. Tonight he is somebody."[2] That was the level of hopelessness and desperation in the American ghetto.

Other Americans were also beginning to feel desperate that autumn. They were not the poor and hopeless; just the opposite, they had been very successful during the last few years. They were activists in the movement, for after the Voting Rights Act and Watts many of them were wondering which paths to take—what was the future for the movement? Moderates in SCLC were discussing whether they should continue to concentrate on the South or take their marches to northern cities. Young SNCC volunteers argued over abandoning nonviolent activism and adopting a more militant stance, and many in SDS were considering ending urban projects and expanding their work on campuses. Activists argued endlessly over tactics, ideology, and almost everything. ERAP workers in Cleveland, for example, once spent twenty-four hours discussing whether or not they would take a day off from organizing and go to the beach. As Steve Max recalled, SDS was becoming "more and more movement and less and less organization. It was a situation of a movement looking for a place to happen."[3]

That place was on the other side of the world—Vietnam. Without the war, SDS and many other movement organizations would have dissolved into oblivion. And without the war the decade would have remained a liberal reform era, not a radical decade, not "the sixties."

Philosophers often wonder: What determines change, what is the engine of history? The Vietnam War became the engine of the sixties. While the civil rights struggle began the era and introduced the moral debate, the war, more than any other issue, defined and shaped the decade. Because of its length—over twice that of World War II—it eventually forced most Americans to wonder: Was South Vietnam worth the effort? For the younger generation the political question became more personal: Should I fight this war? Is this cause worth my injury, my death?

Apparently, the sixties generation had little choice. The president informed the public in May that the war was "guided by North Vietnam and it is spurred by Communist China. Its goal is to conquer the South, to defeat America, and to extend the Asiatic dominion of communism." At Johns Hopkins University he declared "our own security is at stake" and "we have promises to keep." He continued, "Tonight Americans and

Asians are dying for a world where each people may choose its own path to change. This is the principle for which our ancestors fought in the valleys of Pennsylvania. It is the principle for which our sons fight in the jungles of Vietnam."

The press hailed the speech. *Time* editors added that "No struggle in which Communism is involved is ever truly a civil war." Instead, the situation in Southeast Asia was like the conflicts in Greece after World War II or Malaya in the 1950s. Furthermore, the journalists continued, "A Viet Nam united under Communist rule would . . . remain a Peking satellite." To "surrender the Pacific to China now makes no more sense than surrendering it to Imperial Japan . . . in 1941."

False analogies, all of them. The Mekong Delta was not Valley Forge. Vietnam in 1965 was not Munich in 1938, Pearl Harbor in 1941, Greece in 1947, Korea in 1950, or Malaya in the mid-1950s. Vietnam was Vietnam. Ignorant about the Vietnamese or their war, the best and the brightest and the pundits urged the usual American masculine response—a show of strength. During the summer the Texan arrived at the conclusion that the U.S. had three choices: "Cut our losses and withdraw . . . almost certainly conditions humiliating the United States and very damaging to our future effectiveness on the world scene"; continue support "at about the present level . . . holding on and playing for the breaks while recognizing that our position will probably grow weaker"; or "expand substantially the U.S. military pressure against the Viet Cong in the South and the North Vietnamese in the North and at the same time launch a vigorous effort on the political side to get negotiations started."

With choices posed in such terms, there was little question that Americans would oppose being humiliated and rally behind the commander-in-chief when he announced in July that he was increasing the number of U.S. troops in Vietnam to 125,000. Significantly, he did not admit that he already had authorized a higher escalation to 200,000, and that he had given General Westmoreland permission to conduct independent combat missions against the enemy—clearing the way for the U.S. Army to replace ARVN and become the primary military organization in South Vietnam. When a reporter asked whether the buildup signaled a new policy, the president lied, stating that it "does not imply any change in policy whatever." Johnson now was guaranteeing the survival of South Vietnam by the Americanization of the war; yet he and his team walked across the Potomac and into the Mekong without getting their feet wet, without admitting that they were wading into a quagmire.

The public supported LBJ. What many have forgotten since was that Vietnam was a popular crusade in 1965. *Life* noted that "it is wiser and takes less bloodshed to stop a bid for world tyranny early rather that late. It is also wise as well as moral to fulfill a promise to defend a victim of

Sit-in in Jackson, Mississippi, and the response. State Historical Society of Wisconsin.

Kennedy idealism: more than 600 Peace Corps volunteers meet the president, 1962. John F. Kennedy Presidential Library.

Freedom Summer volunteer Edie Black from Smith College teaches in Mileston, Mississippi, 1964. © Matt Herron/Take Stock.

Berkeley Free Speech Movement, 1964. Bancroft Library, University of California.

The Selma march, spring 1965. © James H. Karales.

The movement's first antiwar march on Washington, April 1965. © Charles Harbutt/Actuality.

The civil rights struggle has an impact on other minorities: Cesar Chavez leads a United Farm Workers strike in Delano, California, 1966. © George Ballis/Take Stock.

The resistance: draft-card burning during Dow protests at the University of Washington, fall semester 1967. AP/Wide World.

Summer of Love, 1967, in Golden Gate Park. © Gene Anthony.

March on the Pentagon, October 1967. UPI/Bettmann.

Gene McCarthy on the campaign trail in Connecticut, spring 1968. UPI/Bettmann.

LBJ, 1968.
Lyndon Baines Johnson Library.

The Black Panther Party becomes more evident during summer 1968 when members protest the arrest and trial of Huey Newton in Oakland. UPI/Bettmann.

Bobby Kennedy takes his campaign to San Fernando Valley State College, California. UPI/Bettmann.

A divided nation, 1968. Pro-war supporters in New York. © Charles Gatewood/Magnum.

**Antiwar demonstrators at
the Democratic National
Convention in Chicago.**
UPI/Bettmann.

attack. . . . In this sense our Vietnam policy is a moral policy, and most Americans fortunately see it that way." *Time* editorialized that the war was "the crucial test of American policy and will," and the magazine proclaimed: "Vietnam: The Right War at the Right Time."

The president led, good citizens followed. They had done that in World War II and stopped the Nazis. They had done that in Korea and stopped the Communists. Now, veterans expected the same from their sons.

Forward, charge. Young men volunteered. Enlistments increased 70 percent in the army and almost doubled in the marine corps. "I was 17," one recalled, "reading the magazines and looking at those maps of Vietnam. The areas colored red were controlled by the enemy, white for the good guys, and red and white for the battlegrounds. I went to the recruiter to become a helicopter pilot so I could push the commies back, back into their end zone." Like their parents, the young generation saw the war in cold war terms; others had been influenced by JFK. "We believed in all the myths created by that most articulate and elegant mythmaker, John Kennedy," Lieutenant Philip Caputo remembered. "If he was the King of Camelot, then we were his knights and Vietnam was our crusade."

This crusade called for real men, a coming of age for the sixties generation. The U.S. Marine "would face it like a man," wrote Sergeant Ron Kovic. "He would not let his president, or his family, or any of them down. He could take it, he was tough, he knew it." And these tough young men would win their war swiftly. Like the Spanish-American conflict of 1898, Vietnam was a "splendid little war," wrote Lieut. Caputo. In 1965 when he and his men marched into the rice paddies, "we carried, along with our packs and rifles, the implicit convictions that the Viet Cong would be quickly beaten and that we were doing something altogether noble and good."[4]

"The most important single factor in the whole Vietnam problem," Ambassador Henry Cabot Lodge wrote from Saigon, "is support from the American home front." While that remained strong in 1965, there also was growing concern, especially from a few pacifists and intellectuals. Pacifists were concerned that escalation in Vietnam would draw China and even the Soviet Union into the war, increasing the potential for atomic Armageddon. "Wars have a way of getting out of hand," warned *Hiroshima* author John Hersey when he attended the White House Festival of the Arts. Other dissenters condemned the administration's military escalation, agreeing with the *New Republic* that the war "cannot be won by the United States. It can only be won by the Vietnamese." Still others felt that the conflict was a civil war, one that could be negotiated. Academicians such as Hans Morgenthau called upon the president to bring about a neutral Vietnam, to make the nation an "Asian Yugoslavia," and to ask Ho Chi Minh to become the "Tito of Southeast Asia."

Some of the first antiwar feelings had been expressed by students who felt part of the movement and had participated in civil rights demonstrations or in Freedom Summer. One volunteer wrote her parents, "For the first time in my life, I am seeing what it is like to be poor, oppressed, and hated. . . . The people we're killing in Viet Nam are the same people whom we've been killing for years in Mississippi." The casualties were the poor, the depossessed, those "of the Third World," Robert Moses told students in Berkeley. "You've got to learn from the South if you're going to do anything about this country in relation to Vietnam." In New York City a student attended a small rally and held a sign: "United States Troops Belong in Mississippi, not Vietnam."[5]

Some religious leaders and a few liberal politicians also questioned the war. In April, 2500 ministers, priests, and rabbis took out a full page ad in the New York Times: "In the Name of God, STOP IT!" At that year's governors' conference Mark Hatfield of Oregon was the only state leader to vote against the president's policy, feeling that the Vietnamese were trying to end foreign domination of their country and not expand Communism throughout Southeast Asia. Senators George Aiken, Edward Bartlett, Mike Mansfield, Ernest Gruening, and Wayne Morse privately warned the president against "another Korea." The conflict would end attempts at international disarmament and kill the Great Society. Gruening stated that the government in Saigon was riddled with corruption and so there was "no justification for murdering a single American boy in South Vietnam." One day the administration's policy would be "denounced as a crime." Morse charged that morally the escalation was indefensible, "stark, ugly imperialism," and furthermore that "McNamara's War" was illegal because it had not been declared by Congress. Vietnam was not in the national interest, Morse scoffed, and the U.S. did not have to fight for honor: "I have heard of 'throwing out the baby with the bath water,' but never before have I heard it suggested that we should blow off heads to save face."

Within the administration there was at least one critic. Under Secretary of State George Ball warned the president that in a few years the U.S. would have "300,000 American troops in Vietnam, fighting the Asian land war no one wanted to get into." LBJ laughed and said, "George, you're crazier than hell. That just isn't going to happen."[6]

Such warnings were cries in the wilderness. With vast popular support, the commander-in-chief plunged forward and continued the troop buildup in Vietnam. LBJ had the option of either increasing the draft or calling up the reserves. Not desiring to disrupt society by activating over

200,000 older reservists, the president opted to draft younger men. At that time the Selective Service system had been in operation since the Second World War, and over 60 percent of the public approved the draft, and that included college students. Baby boomers were coming of age, resulting in an enormous pool of potential draftees, some two million annually, and there were numerous ways men could obtain deferments. In July the president announced that draft calls would be doubled, yet because of the large number of volunteers the administration that autumn drafted only a fourth of the monthly number called during the Korean War, a tenth of World War II.

Draft calls doubled again by the end of the year, and while that did not result in significant protests, it did provoke the rise of another part of the movement—the Resistance—a "national movement which aims at undermining the Selective Service System by taking the position of complete and open noncooperation with the draft."

Few Americans had resisted the draft since World War II, and those who did usually were devotees of religions such as Jehovah's Witnesses or members of various peace groups such as the War Resisters League, Student Peace Union, Catholic Workers, or Committee for Nonviolent Action. During the first half of the 1960s when draft calls averaged about 100,000 a year, less than 200 citizens annually violated selective service laws, and the cases almost never appeared in the press. Yet with LBJ's announcement that draft calls would be increased, the media zoomed in on dissent, and the most celebrated case occurred in August when David Mitchell publicly refused to report for induction. A federal judge sentenced him to five years in prison.

Refusing induction was a personal statement, usually not a very dramatic one. Consequently, about 400 war activists picketed the Whitehall Street induction center in New York City. Christopher Kearns and some others dropped their draft cards into a flaming pot. Actually, Kearns and others such as Tom Cornell had destroyed many cards, having applied for duplicates. "I think I have a record," Cornell later said, "having burned ten." On this occasion Kearns was photographed and his action appeared in *Life*.

A "rash of draft-card burnings," *Life* declared, and the picture caused an uproar. Congressmen were outraged, calling draft-card burners a "sleazy beatnik gang," "filthy buzzards and vermin." Representative L. Mendel Rivers and Senator Strom Thurmond—both of South Carolina, the home state of General Westmoreland—sponsored legislation that proscribed up to five years' imprisonment and a $10,000 fine for willful destruction of a draft card or Selective Service documents. Rivers declared that sending a draft-card burner to prison "is the least we can do for our men in South Vietnam fighting to preserve freedom, while a vocal minority in this country thumb their noses at their own government." The law passed by a voice vote in the Senate, and in the House by 392 to 1.

The resistance to the draft had been born, but while only a few more activists burned their cards or refused induction until 1967, the press sensationalized the issue and the government attempted to suppress the "beat the draft movement." "No government can condone this kind of defiance and still govern," declared *Newsweek*. The *New York Times* reported that thousands of youths were trying to avoid the draft by burning their draft cards, by not registering, or by receiving selective service deferments "by feigning homosexuality, madness, or 'football knee,' by deliberately flunking a mental test, or simply by staying on in school or hastening marriage plans." Attorney General Nicholas Katzenbach announced an investigation, and local draft boards treated dissidents severely. After three dozen Michigan professors and students staged a sit-in at the Ann Arbor draft board, the state Selective Service director reviewed the protester's college deferments. A few weeks later a dozen of them lost their student deferments and were reclassified 1-A, ready for induction. Selective Service director General Lewis Hershey proclaimed, "I'm one of those old-fashioned fathers who never let pity interfere with a spanking."[7]

Nevertheless, the antiwar movement slowly expanded that August. In New York, a former Freedom Summer volunteer, Norma Becker, helped organize the Fifth Avenue Peace Parade Committee, and in Washington, activists from almost forty organizations formed the National Coordinating Committee to End the War in Vietnam. A thousand people held a vigil outside the White House between August 6 and 9, the twentieth anniversaries of the atomic bombings of Hiroshima and Nagasaki. On the last day, David Dellinger, Staughton Lynd, and Bob Moses led demonstrators down the mall toward the Capitol. When the marchers reached police, Lynd attempted to walk through their line and was arrested. Police then apprehended Moses, and Dellinger and the others held a sit-in, refusing to disband. Police arrested over 300. In Berkeley, activist Jerry Rubin and math professor Stephen Smale of the Vietnam Day Committee organized a troop train protest at the Oakland Army Terminal, an embarkation point for Vietnam. A few hundred attempted to stop or board the trains and hand out antiwar literature to soldiers. Some carried signs: "Peace Corps—not Marine Corps." At one point they placed a banner across the tracks: "STOP THE WAR MACHINE." A train rolled through it, blowing steam on demonstrators.

The antiwar crusade and struggle inched closer as Martin Luther King stated doubts about the war. The minister always had disliked war—"the madness of militarism," he called it—and he was appalled by the escalation in Southeast Asia. But many of his aides were deeply divided over the issue. King and LBJ were at the summit of their friendship that August, the president had moved forcefully for civil rights, and the people overwhelmingly supported the president's policy in Vietnam. If King announced his opposition, colleagues warned, he would alienate the president and SCLC would lose contributions that could be used to expand the civil rights struggle. King weighed these factors, and said on "Face the Nation" that the administration should stop bombing and start serious negotiations with Hanoi. As winner of the Nobel Peace Prize, King offered to mediate with the enemy, which was rejected sternly by the White House.

Other activists spoke out during autumn 1965, and they made their loudest demands during the weekend of October 15 and 16—the International Days of Protest. Nearly 100,000 activists participated in 80 cities and on campuses ranging from the University of California at Santa Barbara to Iowa State to Yale. In Madison, eleven protesters were jailed after they charged the commander of a local air force base with "war crimes" and tried to make a citizens' arrest. Students at the University of Colorado's football game formed a card section and flashed antiwar slogans at halftime. At Michigan, students held a forty-eight-hour peace vigil and hundreds picketed the local draft board. In New York, 20,000 participated in the Fifth Avenue Peace Parade to the U.N. Plaza, and 300 gathered for a "speak out" at the armed forces induction center on Whitehall Street. At dusk, David Miller climbed on top of a sound truck in front of the crowd. Earlier in the decade he had marched against atomic testing and volunteered in Mississippi. Now, he simply said, "I believe the napalming of villages is an immoral act. I hope this will be a significant political act." Miller lit his draft card and lifted the glowing card over his head. The crowd remained hushed. Television broadcast the event, and Miller became the first citizen indicted and imprisoned under the new Selective Service Act.[8]

In Berkeley, the Vietnam Day Committee held a teach-in on Friday, and that evening a crowd of over 10,000 left the campus on a "peace invasion" of the Oakland Army Base. The local district attorney declared the march treasonous, and the Oakland mayor refused to issue a parade permit. Consequently, when the activists reached city limits they were confronted with a wall of 300 policemen. VDC organizers argued whether they should continue on and force the issue, or avoid conflict and return to Berkeley. Eventually they decided to turn back, but the next afternoon activists attempted another march to the army base. This time they were confronted by another wall of police and a number of Hell's Angels who suddenly rushed the protesters and ripped up banners, one yelling, "Go back to Russia, you fucking Communists!" The bikers beat the activists. The police attacked the Hell's Angels. Order was restored.

During the march something else was happening. Max Scheer walked up and down the crowd selling copies of his new underground, the *Berkeley Barb*, laughing and shouting, "Read the *Barb*, it's a pleasure not a duty." Scheer first published the underground after the demonstrations against troop trains in August. The *Oakland Tribune* reported that at one "train-in" the activists jeered soldiers, and the troops gave the "thumbs-down or V-for-victory sign in response." The *Barb* contended that the "commercial press ignored the most revealing part of the story—the crudely lettered signs in the windows of one of the trains, put there by some of the troops on board, 'I don't want to go,' said one of them. Others said, 'Lucky civilians,' and 'Keep up the good work, we're with you.' " By that autumn in the Bay Area, it was becoming apparent that the movement was taking on a culture of its own.

"It's gotta be more fun to be in the revolution than out of it," declared Rubin, as a sixties culture began to sprout. Political activists appeared regularly at Berkeley, but so did cultural activists such as comedian Dick Gregory, Zen Buddhist scholar Alan Watts, musician Phil Ochs, and the San Francisco Mime Troupe. During the International Days of Protest, Joe McDonald sang his "I-Feel-Like-I'm-Fixin'-to Die Rag," Allen Ginsberg played cymbals and chanted, Lawrence Ferlinghetti read beat poetry, and author Ken Kesey spoke. Along with Joseph Heller's *Catch-22*, Kesey's *One Flew Over the Cuckoo's Nest* was becoming mandatory reading for the sixties generation. The young author appeared with a busload of wildly clothed folks, the Merry Pranksters, who had been living with a growing number of eccentric people in the Haight-Ashbury district of San Francisco. When he got on the stage it quickly became apparent that he was high on drugs. Kesey gave a rambling, incoherent address, occasionally taking time out to pick up his harmonica and play "Home on the Range." Abruptly, he concluded, "There's only one thing to do. . . . And that's everybody just look at it, look at the war, and turn your backs and say . . . fuck it."

Kesey irritated many. Berkeley activists had no desire to turn their backs on the war, to take drugs and forget the movement; in 1965 they wanted to organize, to demonstrate, to fight and change America. Older citizens were appalled by such language and behavior. Commenting on the demonstrations, Republican gubernatorial candidate Ronald Reagan stated: "If you ask me, the activities of those Vietnam Day teach-in people can be summed up in three words: Sex, Drugs, and Treason."[9]

Most Americans agreed, especially as U.S. troops that same month began their first major battle against the enemy at the Ia Drang Valley in Vietnam. "This is real war," said the president. After the Vietcong initiated some scattered engagements during the summer, the North Vietnamese Army launched an offensive in the central highlands in what appeared to be a plan to cut South Vietnam in half. General Westmoreland met the challenge by sending in the U.S. 1st Cavalry Division, Airmobile, to stop the advance in the Ia Drang Valley. The cavalry confronted three regiments of the NVA, and for three days just one U.S. battalion, outnumbered seven to one, withstood a dozen enemy human-wave attacks. U.S. officers called in massive air strikes, and artillerymen fired so fast that at times their barrels glowed red. Reinforcements arrived, and brief but violent engagements continued for five weeks. During the last fray at landing zone Albany in November, U.S. units suffered 60 percent casualties. A survivor recalled dead enemy snipers hanging from trees, piles of tangled bodies, the ground sticky with blood, and labeled the scene the "devil's butcher shop." The enemy retreated and both sides counted bodies: at least 2000 and perhaps 3000 enemy dead, and almost 240 Americans.

Ia Drang had an impact on the belligerents. The North Vietnamese Army avoided engaging U.S. troops in conventional warfare for over two years, until January 1968 and the Tet Offensive. The enemy, realizing that American soldiers were well trained and had massive firepower, shifted back to guerrilla warfare and employed tactics of ambush, hit and run, before vanishing into the jungle. For American policymakers, Ia Drang confirmed the search and destroy strategy of General Westmoreland. Days after the battle Westermoreland cabled the president that he now faced conventional war and that the way to win was to search out and then destroy the enemy with additional U.S. troops. A "policy of attrition," the general called it; the enemy would take heavy casualties and would give up first. LBJ agreed, and raised the ceiling of U.S. troops to 375,000 in Vietnam as Pentagon officials proclaimed Ia Drang a "resounding military success."

The battle also rallied the American people. "Fury at Ia Drang," *Newsweek* declared, and the magazine pictured two soldiers helping a wounded man with the caption "Red Badge of Courage." Journalist Joseph Alsop called Ia Drang a series of "remarkable victories," and *U.S. News* boasted about America's tenacious fighters who beat the "best the Communists could throw at them." Pollster Louis Harris reported a dramatic shift in favor of administration policy, with two-thirds approving of LBJ's handling of the war and only 11 percent favoring negotiations or withdrawal. Harris reported that the "most hotly debated issue among Americans was whether they should first carry the ground war North or destroy the Vietcong in the South." Supporting the war and the troops, citizens bought seven million copies of Sergeant Barry Sadler's patriotic album, *Green Berets*, making it one of the best-selling records in history.

"We'll lick them," declared Secretary of State Dean Rusk, and most Americans agreed.[10] Given the popular mood, the antiwar demonstrators in October provoked resentment. In Cleveland, a large crowd attacked antiwar marchers, and fighting erupted as they burned peace banners. In Austin, students threw water balloons at protesters, and in Ann Arbor 200 counterdemonstrators ripped apart an antiwar float. When a few students at Michigan State attempted to hand out antiwar flyers on campus, police arrested them for "trespassing," threw them in jail, and bound them in chains. War supporters in Washington, D.C., held signs: "Burn the Teach-in Professors," "More Police Brutality," and "Pink College Students Make Yellow Reds." In Boston, two dozen high school kids attacked four peace advocates, knocking them to the ground, and New York City policemen had to rescue one pacifist who had been beaten and stripped naked. Prowar New Yorkers tossed eggs, tomatoes, and red paint at demonstrators, and over 25,000 marched behind five winners of the Medal of Honor. A World War II veteran carried a sign, "Support our men in Vietnam—Don't stab them in the back." When pacifists attempted to hold a draft-card burning ceremony at Union Square, a young man bolted from the crowd with a fire extinguisher and doused them. While the pacifists attempted to light their soggy cards, hundreds of war supporters chanted, "Give us joy, bomb Hanoi," while waving signs, "Burn Yourselves, Not Your Cards!"

Politicians lambasted the protesters. Democratic Governor Edmund Brown of California proclaimed that demonstrations "gave aid and comfort to Hanoi," and Senator John Stennis of Mississippi declared that the government should "immediately move to jerk this movement up by the roots and grind it to bits." Congressman "Tiger" Teague of Texas agreed, and introduced a bill and a constitutional amendment that would have resulted in ten years' imprisonment for anyone who protested the war by "picketing, parades, rallies, or similar public demonstrations." Former president Eisenhower lamented the "moral decay" of the youthful protesters, and announced his support for Johnson's policy in Southeast Asia. When historian Eugene Genovese of Rutgers University stated that he "welcomed" a Vietcong victory, former vice president Richard Nixon demanded that the university fire the professor. If "Vietnam is lost," Nixon declared, "the right of free speech will be extinguished throughout the world."[11]

The press ridiculed demonstrators. *Life* called protesters "chronic show-offs" who failed to realize that the war was "a last stand for democracy or freedom or even that the destiny of the U.S. is at stake." The *Chicago Tribune* called on the government to "act in the toughest way possible," and the *New York Daily News* demanded that the "Communist-incited beatniks, pacifists and damned idiots" be tried for treason. The *Dallas Morning News* scoffed at the "transparent motives" of the "kooks and

Communists," and from Mississippi, the *Jackson Daily News* had a suggestion for demonstrators: "This is the time for police brutality if there ever was one."

Students and "some tweedy faculty members," *Time* wrote, "battered eardrums on campuses and street corners, but found in many cases that they were outnumbered and outshouted by supporters of their nation's foreign policy." In fact, that autumn less than one-tenth of 1 percent of the population participated in an antiwar demonstration, "hardly enough to merit a sneeze," wrote the *Boston Globe*, and on campus students overwhelmingly supported American policy in Vietnam. Prowar students held marches at Purdue, Cornell, Pittsburgh, and Brigham Young, while they lined up to sign petitions supporting LBJ's policy—approximately 16,000 at Michigan State, 9000 at Minnesota, 6000 at Wisconsin and at Boston, and 4000 at Texas and at Rutgers. A thousand Princetonians sent $400 to General Westmoreland and stated their appreciation of the sacrifices of his troops, and students at Stanford and Ohio State held "bleed-ins," giving blood for casualties in Vietnam. While 700 University of Texas coeds wrote to GIs in Vietnam, twice that at Harvard send a petition to LBJ: We "wish to disassociate ourselves from that vocal minority which . . . seeks to obstruct and misrepresent American policy." In Ann Arbor, over 2000 students sent the president a thirty-foot telegram supporting his efforts, and not to be outdone, Texas A&M students sent a sixty-foot telegram. The National Student Committee for Defense of Vietnam presented Vice President Humphrey with pledges of support from almost 500,000 students representating over 300 universities, and a Gallup poll reported that young people favored the war at higher rates than their parents.[12]

Still, even the small number of protesters concerned the government. In the mid-1960s, it was one thing to demonstrate for civil rights or student power, issues moderates and liberals could support, but it was another thing to question American foreign policy during the cold war. Who were these dissidents? Attorney General Katzenbach stated that there were "some Communists involved" and that the government "may very well have some prosecutions." FBI director J. Edgar Hoover declared that the party and other subversives supported and participated in the demonstrations. The Senate Internal Security Subcommittee held hearings, and then declared that the control of the antiwar movement had passed from the liberals to the "Communists and extremists who favor the victory of the Vietcong and are openly hostile to the United States."

Nonsense. Both liberals and radicals were active, and as historian Charles DeBenedetti demonstrated, "no one was in control of the antiwar movement." No one ever was in control, certainly not the Communists, although a number of groups were attempting to organize and lead a national movement. During 1965 these groups became polarized into liberal and radical camps.

On the liberal side were organizations such as the Fellowship for Reconciliation, American Friends Service Committee, Americans for Democratic Action, Catholic Worker, Committee for Nonviolent Action, Women's Strike for Peace, and SANE. In general, antiwar liberals worried about the morality of the war, agreeing with Norman Thomas: "I'd rather see America save her soul than her face." They opposed escalation and advocated some sort of cease-fire and negotiated settlement, but they were divided on other issues. Some supported the continuation of the containment policy while others advocated a fresh approach to foreign policy. Most were concerned that if they opposed their president publicly then he would not be able to pass more civil rights or Great Society legislation. SANE leaders stressed responsible criticism that would enlist broad support, and fearing a public blacklash, they refused to use the word "protest." Others were eager to confirm that they were not aligned with Soviet Russia. Before the Easter demonstration, A. J. Muste, Norman Thomas, and Bayard Rustin issued a statement calling for "an independent peace movement, not . . . drawing inspiration of direction from the foreign policy of any government." The *New York Post* added, "there is no justification for transforming the march into a frenzied, one-sided, anti-American show."

Radicals, however, advocated "Out Now!" Most of them felt part of the new left, and many were members of SNCC, May 2nd Movement, Progressive Labor Party, Socialist Workers Party, Northern Student Movement, W. E. B. DuBois Clubs, and SDS. They usually saw the war as another example of American imperialism in the cold war arena, like the CIA's involvement in toppling the governments of Guatemala and Iran during the Eisenhower years, the Bay of Pigs during Kennedy, or LBJ's intervention that April in the Dominican Republic. "Vietnam, like Mississippi, is not an aberration," declared the Vietnam Day Committee, "it is a mirror of America. Vietnam IS American foreign policy." The future choice was clear, stated SDS member Richard Flacks: the nation had to "choose between devoting its resources and energies to maintaining military superiority and international hegemony or rechanneling those resources and energies to meeting the desperate needs of its people."

The split between liberal and radical peace activists appeared throughout 1965. While planning for the Easter march, SDS and SANE argued over the participation of members viewed as Vietcong sympathizers or Communists, and eventually SANE refused to sponsor the demonstration. Differences emerged again in June when SANE and SDS participated in an antiwar rally at Madison Square Garden. Liberal speakers

Wayne Morse, Benjamin Spock, and Norman Thomas called for negotiations and regretted what they labeled LBJ's "mistaken policy of escalation." SDS spokesman Clark Kissinger disagreed, stating that the president's actions were not mistaken, but were part of a pattern of interventionism that demonstrated that the nation needed a "radical reconstruction" of foreign policy. Kissinger declared, "Our problem is in America, not in Vietnam."[13]

Indeed, the real problem for radicals for the next several years was in America. The majority of citizens would not be able to come to the conclusion that the U.S. should get "Out Now!" That was too extreme in 1965, or for the remainder of the decade. Citizens would increasingly feel that the conflict was a "mistake," but not until 1971, after six bloody years of war and over 50,000 American and perhaps one million Vietnamese deaths, would opinion polls reveal that the majority finally supported immediate withdrawal.

Most citizens during the last half of the 1960s could not face the agonizing reality—America had blundered, had become involved in a war that its citizens did not comprehend against people they did not understand. For the next few years policymakers and pundits wondered about the "inscrutable Oriental mind." "Why do they continue to fight?" someone would ask, and after head-scratching another would answer, "The inscrutable Orientals." The president said that if he could just sit down and talk with Ho he would be able to "cut a deal"—massive American aid and public works for a withdrawal of northern troops from South Vietnam—and as late as 1969 Pulitzer Prize-winning journalist Theodore H. White called LBJ's offer "one of the most generous gestures in any war." Not to the North Vietnamese. They were not interested in deals, not fighting for money or projects—they were fighting for the unification of their nation. Furthermore, citizens and officials would not be able to admit that whoever governed Vietnam was not important to U.S. national security. For the next eight years presidents remained more concerned about "credibility," about losing face in Vietnam, than most South Vietnamese ever were in becoming the American "cornerstone of democracy" in Southeast Asia.

Some students realized this, and increasingly they were drawn toward the new left. On the national scene that position was best articulated by SDS. The ranks of that organization grew as LBJ commenced his bombing campaign, and as SDS received the most credit for organizing demonstrations. The press zeroed in on SDS. Scripps-Howard papers editorialized that it was "highly suspect" that SDS was behind the peace movement. Andrew Kopkind published an article in *New Republic* and Jack Newfield declared in *Nation*, "A new generation of radicals has been spawned from the chrome womb of affluent America. . . . They are a new generation of dissenters, nourished not by Marx, Trotsky, Stalin or Schachtman but by Camus, Paul Goodman, Bob Dylan and SNCC." Hundreds of students wrote SDS and inquired about organizing campus chapters. Most of these activists attended institutions such as Antioch, Columbia, North Carolina, Oberlin, Princeton, or Stanford, but many also wrote from usually placid campuses such as Adelphi, Maine, North Texas State, even Dodge City Community College of Kansas. Membership soared to 2000 and campus chapters doubled to 80 that summer. As the historian of that organization wrote, "SDS had arrived."[14]

It had arrived, but where would SDS take the movement? In an attempt to answer that question, about 500 members held their annual conference near Kewadin, Michigan, in June. Many of the activists had just joined the organization that spring, and that resulted in some conflict between the old guard, the veterans of Port Huron, and many of the young Turks who often came from the Midwest and Texas and who became known as "prairie power" in SDS. Members wrote position papers, and in them, significantly, almost everyone was using the term "movement." But few read the papers. Instead, they meandered to and from sessions, discussed ideas, and used a new rhetoric—participate, organize, involvement, relevance, dialogue, alienation, consciousness, community—terms that were beginning to define the movement. They were building a community of equality, of participatory democracy, and there was a growing hostility to elitism. "Leaders mean organization," one member said, "organization means hierarchy, and hierarchy is undemocratic." In the sessions, some of the delegates argued that the Vietnam War was the most pressing issue and it offered the way to organize a mass radical movement. Yet others asked, "Where would we be if peace were to break out tomorrow?" They advocated building what Staughton Lynd called an "interracial organization of the poor directed toward basic social change," a long-term commitment that would end causes for conflict so they could prevent the "fifth and sixth and seventh war from now."

During the days of decision SDS activists continually discussed that issue. They did not want to be a single-issue organization, yet an increasing number of students were becoming concerned about one issue—Vietnam. Eventually, the members could not decide, and some agreed with Paul Booth, who recalled, "We really screwed up. We had the opportunity . . . to make SDS *the* organizational vehicle of the anti-war movement. It was ours. We had achieved it. Instead, we chose to go off in all kinds of different directions. . . . The main thrust of anti-war activity was left unorganized by us."

The antiwar movement remained an unorganized coalition of numerous groups. SDS members at Kewadin agreed that local chapters should set their own agendas based on the needs of their community, should operate without direction from a national headquarters. Thus, while more activists eagerly joined the organization, SDS's vision was blurred, unable to focus on a policy that might mobilize massive numbers of college students.

The Kewadin meeting had little impact on the sixties, yet it did reveal a new spirit in one organization of the movement. The prairie power activists looked, acted, and thought differently from older members. Many younger radicals had long hair and mustaches, and they wore blue work shirts, denim jackets, and boots. Many still were students, and this new breed brought with them a midwestern and southwestern creed of individualism as they talked about morals and values, honesty and courage, action not ideology. They had been influenced by the struggle and provoked by the escalation of the war. Jeff Shero had become involved at the University of Texas, where he and others integrated campus restrooms using the fitting slogan, "Let My People Go." Later he had been angered by the war. "Rage and disillusionment," said Shero, "and a moral impulse to create something better—that was our background." Time to confront; no time to theorize as eastern intellectuals had done. "They tended to be not only ignorant of the history of the left," Kirkpatrick Sale wrote, "but downright uninterested: they didn't know Dellinger from Dillinger, Rustin from Reston, Trotsky from Chomsky, *Liberation* from *Liberator*, the Socialist Workers Party from the Socialist Labor Party, and they didn't really care." For these new SDSers, "We Shall Overcome" had been replaced by "Blowin' in the Wind."

Something else was blowing in the wind at Kewadin. For the first time at an SDS convention, the smell of marijuana floated through the air. Veteran Steve Max complained that a raid on the meeting would have busted two-thirds of the members. It was a *"loony* convention," Paul Booth recalled, *"everyone* was loony," and after some of them returned to the University of Texas they established "Gentle Thursday," a day to relax and get high. Months later, in January 1966, police at the University of Oklahoma raided an SDS meeting and arrested members for possession of marijuana. Authorities immediately set high bail, and the two students with long hair were so unusual for the campus that police locked them up incommunicado in a state mental hospital.[15] The episode was covered by the national press, and the message was blunt: SDS = Drugs.

By autumn 1965, then, the themes revolving around the war were set, and they remained in place for the next two years. Citizens for and against the war had stated their positions, and antiwar activists had employed their tactics of marches and speeches. Some activists were dedicated peaceniks, others were students and professors, all were "elites" in the sense that they were educated. A handful of peace radicals had started the Resistance, and it was becoming apparent that the antiwar crusade was experiencing the same phenomenon that was occurring in the civil rights struggle and would happen in all phases of the movement—a split between liberal and radical groups advocating different methods to bring about the same goal.

That split was apparent at Berkeley. When the Vietnam Day Committee attempted to end the war by stopping troop trains, over two dozen prominent faculty members wrote an open letter to their colleagues stating that the VDC's "indiscriminate resort to extravagant tactics and the use of simplistic and violent slogans" hurt the reputation of the university and defeated the purpose of obtaining peace in Vietnam. They urged others to repudiate the methods of VDC. Liberals on the city council refused to support a VDC proposal that would have banned the passage of troop trains through Berkeley. As conflict rose, many new radicals in the Bay Area came to the same conclusion that others had learned in the struggle—youth could not trust "liberal compromisers." Radicals counterattacked. The VDC committee repudiated the professors' open letter, even calling it an "embarrassment to the University community because of its poor scholarship." Max Sheer chided liberals in the Berkeley Barb, quoting Lincoln Steffens: "A liberal is a person whose mind is so wide open all his brains have fallen out." Conflict only seemed to boost radical bravado. "Liberals are being flung off in all directions," boasted the Barb, and VDC coordinator Jerry Rubin later bragged, "We were fucking obnoxious, and dug every moment of it."[16]

But the average citizen did not dig it. Such behavior only appalled the public, and the tactic proved counterproductive. During the first year of the war most citizens accepted the notion that activists were beatniks, subversives, even Communists. Sitting in their suburbs they understood little about the war and had no idea how to win it. The president's policy won by default. Americans watched and waited, hoping for some sign of victory. A Gallup poll at the end of 1965 found that only 1 percent of those asked felt moved to demonstrate over Vietnam, and most of those would protest in support of the war.

Nor would many citizens be provoked to demonstrate in 1966. Although the president escalated troop strength during the year from about 180,000 to 385,000, although U.S. troop casualties tripled, most Americans felt that the president should be given the chance to win the war. Pollster Louis Harris noted that citizens were in a "get it over with" mood. "The key to understanding public opinion on this war," Harris wrote in September, "is that the American people want to honor this country's commitment to the South Vietnamese, but would also like to see the war come to an honorable end as rapidly as possible. The dialogue today is not really between so-called 'doves' and 'hawks,' but rather over what might be the most effective way to win our limited objective and end the fighting." While confidence in LBJ's war policies oscillated between 40 and 60 percent, about two-thirds of Americans felt a commitment to South Vietnam. In September, three-fourths supported and only a quarter opposed the war, and after LBJ ordered the bombing of oil depots around Hanoi and Haiphong, 80 percent approved the attacks. In fact, about the same percentage of Americans wanted to expand the war and attack North Vietnam as those who wanted to withdraw the troops. *Time* wrote in September, "Along with most other people, the politicians are letting Lyndon Johnson take the responsibility, and waiting for something to happen."

Throughout 1966, most Americans supported the president and were hostile to demonstrators. In Georgia, conservative politicians refused to allow Julian Bond to take his elected seat as a state representative because he opposed the war, but that was minor compared with the situation in Greenwood, Mississippi, where self-proclaimed patriots burned down a church after a peace prayer service, or Newark, where they ransacked the SDS office, or Berkeley, where they bombed the office of the Vietnam Day Committee. Again, minor episodes compared with Rochester, where two young men beat to death an antiwar demonstrator for expressing his views, or Richmond, where an assailant murdered an activist by shooting him in the back ten times, or Detroit, where thugs invaded the Socialist Workers Party office, pulled out shotguns, and wounded two and killed one pacifist.[17]

"Open Season on Dissenters," proclaimed *Christian Century*, as the antiwar movement sputtered through 1966. *Time* noted that many protesters "have begun to lose heart," and one disgruntled activist wrote A. J. Muste that the "peace movement in the United States hardly amounts to a hill of beans!" There were exceptions, of course, as some students protested what they felt was their university's involvement in the war effort or as others attended the We Won't Go conference in Chicago. But generally speaking, antiwar campus and street demonstrations slumped. At the second national days of protest in November, only 20,000 citizens demonstrated nationwide, a fifth of the number the previous year. On campus, *Newsweek* observed that "student activism may be on the wane, particularly in regard to national issues such as civil rights and Vietnam."[18] And a Berkeley activist complained, "More and more students would rather smoke pot than march in a Vietnam parade. We're going back to the 1950s."

Vietnam was still worth the price in 1966, but many activists were wondering about civil rights. The struggle appeared to be in disarray as they argued about tactics and location—should they continue concentrating on the rural South, or shift efforts to northern ghettos?

Suddenly, an individual brought the struggle back into focus, James Meredith. Four years earlier Meredith had been the first black to attend the University of Mississippi. By June he had graduated and decided to begin a "walk against fear" in his state, declaring that the 225-mile trek from Memphis to Jackson would demonstrate that a black man could walk on the highways without being harmed: "Nothing can be more enslaving than fear." With only 30 percent of eligible black Mississippians registered to vote, Meredith aimed to encourage black citizens to register. He began the march with only two companions, a minister and a journalist, for the major civil rights organizations had shied away from the walk—until the second day. Then, when he had marched only ten miles into his home state, a white man stepped out of the bushes, shouting, "James Meredith! I want only James Meredith!" He fired his shotgun three times, and Meredith, screaming, fell to the pavement. The activist was rushed to a hospital in Memphis, where doctors extracted a hundred pellets from his legs, back, and head.

Activists rushed to Memphis. Roy Wilkins of the NAACP, Whitney Young of the Urban League, Floyd McKissick of CORE, Stokely Carmichael of SNCC, and King and his SCLC aides began discussions on continuing the March Against Fear. But this march would be different from the last major event, Selma in 1965. Since then young blacks in CORE and SNCC had elected new leadership. Members of SNCC had replaced John Lewis with Carmichael, and CORE had replaced James Farmer with McKissick. The veterans had been voted out, and the new leadership reflected militant attitudes that had been emerging since the 1964 Mississippi Democratic Freedom Party and the Democratic convention. Many SNCC and CORE activists now were tired of taking the beatings. When Carmichael witnessed whites clubbing several blacks at Selma, he broke down, crying. "That day I knew I could never be hit again without hitting back," he said, and then he went to Lowndes County, Alabama, where 80 percent of the population was black, not one was registered to vote, and all elected officials were white. He formed a black freedom party with the symbol of a snarling black panther. "It's very simple," proclaimed a Black Panther flyer, "we intend to take over Lowndes County."

Young black activists also had been questioning whether whites should be in their organizations. Many wondered how they could become truly independent if they were "emotionally, socially, politically and economically dependent upon those individuals who are non-black." Without controlling their own destiny, a SNCC paper concluded, "Black people in this country will know no freedom, but only more subtle forms of slavery." Others were concerned with the new issue of racial identity, "blackness or black consciousness," and some felt that if SNCC or CORE excluded whites then they would also be eliminating those cultural values and beginning the search for their own, African roots. "If we are to proceed toward true liberation, we must cut ourselves off from white people.

We must form our own institutions, credit unions, co-ops, political parties, write our own histories." During 1965 the number of whites in SNCC and CORE plummeted, and the next year black SNCC members no longer appeared at the annual SDS convention. In 1966, SNCC and CORE took the final step—they expelled all white members.

"I have a lot of difficulty talking about that," Bob Zellner stated twenty years later. "It hurt. SNCC was the most important thing in my life."[19] Yet like other white members he realized that during the days of decision many young black activists were deciding to become more independent, more militant. And they were being influenced by the ideas of Malcolm X.

Malcolm had been outspoken throughout the early 1960s. He felt that Christianity was hypocritical, so he condemned segregated churches, converted to Islam, and became a leader of the Black Muslims in Harlem. After centuries of slavery and segregation, he felt the black man had no future in the United States. "I don't see any American dream; I see an American nightmare." He urged a "revolt of the American Negro," one part of a "global rebellion of the oppressed against the oppressor, the exploited against the exploiter." He enraged whites by labeling them "blue-eyed devils," and he demanded that since the United States was corrupt with racism, the United Nations should intervene and create separate black states, the only way they could obtain racial justice. "Separatism" naturally angered moderate blacks who had worked hard for integration, but to Malcolm, Martin Luther King was "just a twentieth century Uncle Tom." Furthermore, King's tactic of nonviolent activism was absurd. "If you think I'll bleed nonviolently," said Malcolm, "you'll be sticking me for the rest of my life. But, if I tell you I'll fight back, there will be less blood. I'm for reciprocal bleeding." Don't turn the other cheek, Malcolm declared, stand tall: "We're nonviolent with people who are nonviolent with us. But we are not nonviolent with anyone who is violent with us."

The idea was not original, not novel with the emergence of black power; such thinking came right out of frontier America. For centuries Anglos had treated everyone else on the continent by standing up and swinging back, often by swinging first. If such views had been stated by a white citizen, there would have been no interest, no media coverage, since whites felt that it was their "right" to arm and defend themselves. But Malcolm was not white; he was not a typical black politely asking for his rights. He was the first of a new phenomenon—a bold black man demanding self-determination and if necessary self-defense. That shocked white America. The *New York Times* labeled him an "extraordinary and twisted man." The *Los Angeles Times* editorialized about Malcolm's "sick personal hatreds" and called for an official investigation of the "structure, strength, operations, and financing of the entire Negro extremist movement."[20]

Whites had little to worry about in the first half of the decade, for few blacks were listening to Malcolm X. A *Newsweek* poll in 1963 found that blacks ranked King first and Malcolm last in popularity and effectiveness, but that changed in mid-decade. In 1964 Malcolm was becoming famous in Africa, touring and urging the development of a Pan-Africa movement. A few SNCC workers had traveled with him, and in February 1965 they asked him to join them during the demonstrations in Selma. Malcolm accepted, but by that time he and many young activists were moving in opposite directions. Malcolm was moderating his views, talking less about violence and more about brotherhood, and SNCC was becoming more militant. The meeting was cordial and brief, and Malcolm hurried back to New York. Then, just two weeks later, Black Muslims assassinated Malcolm X. The killing shocked many young blacks, and later that year, with the publication of his fascinating autobiography, Malcolm X became more famous in death than he had been in life. To many, he was a martyr, even a hero—a teacher of African heritage, a preacher of black pride, a militant who no longer would ask for his rights, but would take them.

Armed with such ideas by June 1966, SNCC and CORE activists arrived in Memphis to continue Meredith's March Against Fear. As they negotiated the terms of the march with leaders of other organizations, it became apparent that the civil rights movement was in disarray. Moderate organizers for the NAACP and the Urban League wanted another Selma, a call to white liberals to join them in a drive for voter registration and support for another civil rights bill, but the militants advocated a march of blacks only, urged condemning liberals and LBJ, and wanted to employ a black Louisiana group, Deacons for Defense, as an armed protection force. Moderates Roy Wilkins and Whitney Young were appalled, refused to participate, and left Memphis.

The civil rights movement continued melting in the hot summer sun of Mississippi. King, Carmichael, and McKissick led the march, and for the first time very few whites participated. Along the route, King was warmly received by local residents, but within the ranks the mood had changed. King overheard a young black, "I'm not for that nonviolence stuff anymore. If one of those damn white Mississippi crackers touches me, I'm gonna knock the hell out of him." The Reverend continued preaching love, but some young participants were saying, "Too much love, too much love, nothing kills a nigger like too much love." Carmichael, McKissick, and King discussed ideas and tactics. While they grew fond of each other, they also disagreed. "I'm not going to beg the white man for anything I deserve," declared Carmichael, "I'm going to take it."

Each night the marchers pitched camp and held a rally. King preached nonviolence and brotherhood, but when SCLC members attempted to sing, "We Shall Overcome," militants sang a new version, "We Shall Overrun." When the crowd reached Greenwood, Carmichael violated police orders and pitched a tent on the grounds of a black high school. State troopers arrested him. When the young radical was released, three times the number of blacks showed up for the rally. Carmichael jumped on a flatbed truck, shot his arm into the sky with a clenched fist, and shouted: "This is the twenty-seventh time I have been arrested—and I ain't going to jail no more! The only way we gonna stop them white men from whuppin' us is to take over. We been saying freedom for six years and we ain't got nothin'. What we gonna start saying now is Black Power!"

The crowd roared back, "Black Power!" Another activist, Willie Ricks, jumped on the platform, and yelled, "What do you want?" "Black Power!" they shouted, and then Carmichael yelled, "You know what to tell them. What do you want?" And they continued, "black power! Black Power! BLACK POWER!"

"Everything that happened afterward was a response to that moment," wrote participant Cleveland Sellers. "More than anything, it assured that the Meredith March Against Fear would go down in history as one of the major turning points in the black liberation struggle." Black Power was on television, made national headlines the next day, but what did it mean? Black activists bickered, continually defining and redefining the term. "We must come together around the issue that oppresses us—our blackness," stated Carmichael, and he later added: "It doesn't mean that you take over the country. Black power is the coming together of black people in the struggle for their liberation." To McKissick, it was an effort "to grab our bootstraps, consolidate our political power and act in the framework of this democracy to change our lives." Moderate blacks were alarmed. A. Philip Randolph saw the new creed as dangerous to integration and as "a menace to racial peace." Black power would result in black deaths. Roy Wilkins claimed that "black power means anti-white power. . . . It has to mean going it alone. It has to mean separatism. We of the NAACP will have none of this." Wilkins later added that black power was "the father of hatred and the mother of violence."

King also was alarmed. The following evening he responded to Carmichael's call for black power, telling the audience: "Some people are telling us to be like our oppressor, who has a history of using Molotov cocktails, who has a history of dropping the atomic bomb, who has a history of lynching Negroes. Now people are telling me to stoop down to that level. I'm sick and tired of violence! I'm tired of the war in Vietnam! I'm not going to use violence, no matter who says so!" As far as King was concerned, ethnic groups in America were influential because they used constructive means to amass economic and political power. They built group identity: "No one has ever heard the Jews publicly chant a slogan of Jewish power, but they have power. . . . The same thing is true of the Irish and Italians." Carmichael and McKissick countered, "How can you arouse people to unite around a program without a rallying cry? . . . What we need is a new slogan with 'black' in it."

The debate would have no victors, but a few days later the movement would have more victims. Southern whites again boosted the black militants' position, this time in Neshoba County, where two years earlier racists had murdered Chaney, Schwerner, and Goodman. King attempted to hold a memorial service, but whites encircled the activists, taunted them, and then charged, clubbing them with ax handles. Police stood by. Young blacks began swinging back, and only then did law enforcement officers intervene, stopping the clash. That evening whites and blacks exchanged gunfire, and King wired President Johnson asking for federal protection. LBJ did not respond, and the situation continued to deteriorate as the marchers entered Canton. In a driving rain, they tried to set up camp in a black schoolyard, but police refused permission. Soaked and tired, the marchers continued pitching tents in the darkness. The police fired tear gas, and then charged, whipping and clubbing. "Don't make your stand here," yelled Carmichael, "I just can't stand to see any more people get shot." As marchers hurried through a cloud of gas to a nearby black church, Andrew Young vomited, and he thought: "If I had a machine gun, I'd *show* these motherfuckers!"

"King himself had never witnessed anything so vicious," wrote his biographer. The brutal episode alienated young marchers against an unresponsive LBJ and increased cries for Black Power. On the last day of the march, when 15,000 rallied in Jackson, the crowd needed no coaching. The chant of "Freedom Now!" had been replaced: "Black Power!" McKissick ended the final rally with the declaration, "1966 shall be remembered as the year we left our imposed status as Negroes and became *Black Men.* . . 1966 is the year of the concept of Black Power."

Sitting in his living room in Washington, D.C., watching Carmichael chanting "Black Power" on the evening news, Roger Wilkins turned to his wife and said, "There's a whole lot of white people gonna have diarrhea tonight."[21] True, cries for Black Power sent a chill down many white spines. Whites had held power for centuries, so long that the thought of black power was foreign, provoking fear and insecurity.

Then, the summer riots of 1966 erupted. In the second wave of urban unrest, frustrated blacks revolted in Cleveland, Dayton, Milwaukee, and San Francisco—resulting in 3000 arrests, 400 injured, and at least seven dead. The sight of fires in the streets, of broken store windows, of looters running into the darkness became common on the evening news.

These were the days of decision concerning the future of civil rights. Perhaps conservative critics were right, many thought, maybe civil rights had gone too far, perhaps the struggle was inspired by subversives who aimed not to share power, but to take power, to dominate whites. Polls that autumn found that three-quarters of whites felt that the call for Black Power hurt civil rights, and over 80 percent felt that black marches were having the same effect.

Many whites recoiled, and the white backlash received more adherents who began demanding that local officials maintain law and order, and who, strangely, began demanding "white power." A day after a disturbance in Atlanta, white police appeared at the local SNCC office and arrested Carmichael. The charge was inciting a riot and disturbing the peace, even though he had not been at the scene; they set bail at $10,000.

A more vivid example of the white backlash was in Chicago. Since the early 1960s activists had been attempting to desegregate schools and end housing restrictions that kept most blacks in slums. They formed the Coordinating Council of Community Organizations and put pressure on city officials, but had few successes. King decided to lend his support in 1966. He, his assistant Jesse Jackson, and many local activists promoted an "open housing campaign" but again, achieved little. That summer, in an attempt to provoke the federal government to support a fair housing act, activists staged numerous marches into white neighborhoods. The response was vicious: scores of locals threw bottles and bricks, holding signs: "Nigger Go Home" and "White Power." In August, violence reached its peak as King and followers walked to Marquette Park. Whites waved Confederate flags and shouted: "We Hate Niggers!" "Martin Luther Coon!" And they hurled bottles and rocks, hitting King and knocking him to his knees. He called off further demonstrations, commenting, "I have never seen such hate, not in Mississippi or Alabama as I see here in Chicago."

King left Chicago, but young militants continued the desegregation campaign by announcing a march through Cicero. Not one black lived there, and the county sheriff called the plan "suicidal." Fearful of certain violence, only 200 blacks participated, and on the short route they had to be protected by 700 policemen and almost 3000 National Guardmen. Whites pursued the procession, throwing bottles and rocks, and the demonstration degenerated into street fighting. This three-mile walk against fear resulted in almost 40 arrests and a dozen injuries.

A few months later citizens had their day of decision; they voted in the November elections. While the war had little impact then, analysts stated that the white backlash was a prominent factor in the defeat of liberal Illinois Senator Paul Douglas, the election of Republican Ronald Reagan in California, and the surprising show of strength of segregationist Lester Maddox in his bid for governor of Georgia. Polls demonstrated that in two years the percentage of citizens who felt that LBJ was pushing too hard for civil rights doubled to over half, a mood apparent at the voting booth as the Republicans picked up almost fifty seats in the House of Representatives.

The sixties were shifting away from liberalism, and a contributing factor was the demand for Black Power. In a sense, one might wonder why it took six years of beatings before young blacks stood up and fought back. Perhaps because of the influence of King, or because of the initial successes of nonviolent activism, or maybe it says something about how centuries of slavery and segregation had drained the spirit of many African Americans. Whatever the reason, when young blacks behaved like whites and demanded their Constitutional rights, it not only alarmed many whites but also shocked many blacks. The idea divided many black moderates and militants, middle-class and poor, and increased the gap between the World War II and the sixties generations. This division hurt King. He remained in headlines, but never regained the position of leadership that the media granted to him in the early 1960s. Accordingly, there seemed to be no single tactic that blacks could employ to achieve civil rights. In September, A. Philip Randolph stated that "marches and demonstrations have about run their course." The veteran activist urged a shift in strategy "from the streets to the conference table."

The broad social movement that Bayard Rustin mentioned in 1965, a balance of civil rights, antiwar, and campus activists, entered a new phase by the last months of 1966. The focus of the movement continued to shift away from the struggle and toward the war in Vietnam.

There were some obvious connections between the war and civil rights. Some blacks were upset as federal funds declined for poverty programs and increased for the war, and others saw the irony in blacks fighting for South Vietnamese rights. After young civil rights activist John Shaw was killed in action in Vietnam in 1965, other blacks posted leaflets in McComb, Mississippi, urging mothers to encourage their sons to avoid the draft: "Our Fight Is Here at Home!" Next year, a candidate for the Mississippi Freedom Democratic Party proclaimed, "Not wanting to negotiate with the Viet Cong is like the power structure in Mississippi not wanting to negotiate with MFDP." Young militants fired more salvos during 1966, forming the Black Anti-Draft Union and Afro-Americans Against the War in Vietnam and demanding to know why the Selective Service drafted poor blacks from the ghettos and gave a hardship deferment to millionaire actor George Hamilton IV. "Wake Up Black People," proclaimed a Black United Action Front poster in spring 1967, drafting blacks "is part of the Anti-Poverty Program! The way to solve the poverty of the black people is to get them killed in foreign wars!" Carmichael blasted Selective Service as nothing more than "white people sending black people to make war on yellow people in order to defend the land they stole from red people."[22]

The draft was unfair. Blacks represented the poorest and least educated sector of society, and like poor whites, few were attending college during draft age, from 19 to 26. Local draft boards across the nation were composed of so-called "upstanding citizens," meaning that 99 percent of their members were white. In the South, local boards were notorious. After civil rights activists Bennie Tucker and Hubert Davis filed to run for city offices in Mississippi, they received their induction notices, and when Willie Jordan reported for his physical a few minutes late he was sentenced to five years in prison. Meanwhile, draft boards arbitrarily granted deferments to some fathers, for certain hardship cases, and to all those affluent enough to attend college. Until the summer of 1968 student deferments could be extended for graduate or professional school, and educational deferments could be granted to graduate teaching assistants, public school teachers, even Peace Corps volunteers. Professors did not like to flunk students because that grade might send the kid to Vietnam. With degree in hand, the graduate would be offered a job, often with defense contractors, engineering firms, and many other corporations who guaranteed an employment deferment. Selective Service considered most jobs at Lockheed, Dow Chemical, even at Honeywell designing thermostats as in the national interest. Or, if that was not possible, the graduate might continue his education or travel in another nation because the law stipulated that an American living outside his country could not be drafted. Wealthy young men were particularly immune to military service. Of 600 Harvard men surveyed from of the class of 1970, only 56 entered the military, and of the 30,000 male graduates from Harvard, Princeton, and MIT in the decade following 1962, only 20 died in Vietnam. As columnist James Reston wrote, Selective Service was "a system whereby poor boys are selected to go to Vietnam and rich boys are selected to go to college."[23]

Furthermore, because most blacks and poor whites did not have a skill or could not type upon induction, they were perfect candidates for infantry training and then for Vietnam. Once sent to the war zone, there was additional discrimination. A much higher proportion of whites held rear support positions while blacks were stationed in the front lines. While the U.S. had less than 12 percent black citizens, the army in Vietnam was a quarter black and many front line units were half. At times, forward bases were called "soulvilles," and those troops took a disproportionate percentage of casualties. In 1965 the government reported that black soldiers suffered a fourth of combat deaths, and the next year a quarter of the casualties while fighting the Vietcong.

"I got no quarrel with them Vietcong," declared boxing champion

Muhammad Ali, and Carmichael added, "If I'm going to do any fighting it's gonna be right here at home." SNCC and CORE flatly declared their opposition to the war in 1966 and the next spring Martin Luther King watched the horrors of war on the evening news and said to aides, "I can't be silent. Never again will I be silent." In February 1967 he spoke out, calling on all "creative dissenters to combine the *fervor* of the civil rights movement with the peace movement . . . until the very foundations of our nation are shaken." A month later he and Dr. Benjamin Spock led a procession of over 8000 in Chicago, and in April he gave a memorable address. The "Great Society has been shot down on the battlefields of Vietnam," and he merged the movements by declaring that the reason to support civil rights and peace was embodied in the motto of SCLC: "To save the soul of America."

King also revealed that he was shifting away from the liberal and toward the student radical position. Vietnam was "a symptom of a far deeper malady" in our democracy, he said, and unless the nation experienced "a true revolution of value" future U.S. troops would be marching from Guatemala to South Africa. "I could never again raise my voice against the violence of the oppressed in the ghettos without having first spoken clearly to the greatest purveyor of violence in the world today—my own country." And the Nobel Prize winner appealed to his countrymen: "We are at a moment when our lives must be placed on the line if our nation is to survive. Every man of humane convictions must decide on the protest that best suits his convictions—but we must all protest."

Many already were. "I didn't go to college in 1965 expecting to become a radical," recalled Judy Smith, "but I didn't expect the Vietnam War to develop the way it did either. My friends and I became committed to *no life as usual.* For us it would have been immoral to just go on with college and career plans when the war was still going on. If you weren't part of the solution, you were part of the problem."[24]

Judy Smith and thousands of other students began to consider the relationship of their university to the war, and during 1966 and 1967 they asked questions: Should male students have to participate in Reserve Officer Training Corps? Should university administrations cooperate with draft boards and release student grades to Selective Service officials? Should the CIA, military, or defense contractors be able to conduct job interviews on campus?

During 1966 a few students held local protests. Reserve Officer Training had been compulsory for decades at many colleges, and to some that requirement clashed with the ideals of student rights. During spring semester, some Columbia University students formed a human chain to block the final review of the Naval Reserve Officer Training Corps, provoking violence that had to be quelled by police, and perhaps for the first time, high school students protested, a hundred of them in the Bronx demonstrating against a military career day assembly. At the University of Chicago and at City College of New York activists protested because administrators decided to divulge grades to draft boards, meaning that if grades were substandard then the board might reclassify the student from 2-S, student deferment, to 1-A, ready for military induction. In May, 400 Chicago students took over the administration building and held it for three days. That autumn semester a handful of Maryland students protested the campus presence of Marine Corps recruiters, 400 Berkeley activists demonstrated against the navy, and nine students at Grinnell College in Iowa carried signs protesting job interviews by the Central Intelligence Agency: "What is the C.I.A. REALLY doing in Vietnam? Indonesia? Santo Domingo? etc., etc."

But it was during spring semester 1967 when it became obvious that the movement was spreading, for protesters no longer were what critics called fringe radicals or bearded pot smokers but increasingly were mainstream students. Early in the year college newspaper editors and student body presidents at 100 universities sent a letter to LBJ informing him that students were deeply troubled about a war "whose toll in property and life keeps escalating, but about whose purpose and value to the United States remain unclear." The campus leaders warned that unless this "conflict can be eased, the U.S. will continue to find some of her most loyal and courageous young people choosing to go to jail rather than bear their country's arms."

Students also were becoming concerned with defense companies that conducted job interviews on their campuses. There were campaigns against Honeywell, Lockeed, and General Dynamics, but the primary target was the largest manufacturer of napalm, Dow Chemical. A mixture of gasoline with naphthenic acid and palm oil, napalm stuck to whatever it contacted, burning or suffocating a victim. American military forces employed the weapon in massive quantities in Vietnam, and as napalm became a symbol of the war Dow became the symbol for "war profiteer." The campaign spread rapidly throughout spring semester, especially at the University of Wisconsin. Students picketed company recruiters and police arrested three activists for disrupting university business. The arrests of peaceful demonstrators encouraged more than 800 students to march, to hold a rambunctious sit-in, to obstruct interviews, to "do battle with Dow."

Dow's president, Herbert Dow Doan, was perplexed. Like many defense industry executives, he recalled that during World War II and the Korean conflict producing weapons to help American soldiers was patriotic; now that was being questioned, even called inhumane. He agreed to meet antiwar activists and stated the usual business response when the war

162

was still relatively popular: Dow was manufacturing napalm "because we feel that our company should produce those items which our fighting men need in time of war."[25]

Other Americans also were becoming perplexed with the war by spring 1967, and that certainly was true of those conducting it in Washington, D.C. The U.S. had almost half a million troops in South Vietnam. A massive American military machine that supposedly had superiority on land, in the air, and off shore, had been conducting combat operations for two years—yet victory remained illusive. In May, General Westmoreland stunned the Johnson administration by privately requesting an additional 200,000 troops.

The request ignited a fire of dissent within the Pentagon and the White House. By that time, Secretary McNamara had become disillusioned. When he heard of the request he leveled with the commander-in-chief, writing that the war was "becoming increasingly unpopular as it escalates. . . . Most Americans do not know how we got where we are, and most, without knowing why, but taking advantage of hindsight, are convinced that somehow we should not have gotten this deeply in. All want the war ended and expect their President to end it. Successfully. Or else." The secretary was more blunt with his staff, declaring that "Ho Chi Minh is a tough old S.O.B. And he won't quit no matter how much bombing we do."

What to do? In June, McNamara handed assistant Leslie H. Gelb a list of a hundred questions, and ordered him to establish a task force to answer them: How confident can we be about body counts of the enemy? Were programs to pacify the countryside working? Was Ho Chi Minh an Asian Tito? It was a clear indication that the blind in Washington were leading the blind in Saigon—a deadly policy for soldiers in the rice paddies. The subsequent report was leaked to the press in 1971 and became known as the "Pentagon Papers."

While U.S. policymakers were confused in 1967, the enemy knew what to do. They continued to avoid conventional battles and use guerrilla warfare in an attempt to prolong the war until the Americans tired and left Vietnam. Then the north and their Vietcong allies could defeat the regime in Saigon. That meant LBJ again faced the classic dilemma of the war. He had had the same choices in 1965; so did Kennedy earlier and so would Nixon later. The commander-in-chief could enlarge the war by increasing troop strength and by attacking enemy positions in Laos, Cambodia, even North Vietnam. That policy might bring China into the conflict, certainly would damage American-Soviet relations, and would provoke more domestic demonstrations. Second, he could limit troop size, stabilize the commitment, and hope that the South Vietnamese Army could be trained to assume more of the burden of fighting the enemy. That would mean a long conflict, with a limited chance of success. Or he could demobilize the war. The killing would stop, but that would be political suicide because of the eventual collapse of South Vietnam. The third choice was possible but unthinkable. From Kennedy to Ford, no president would be able to overcome his own cold war mentality. All became victims of their own rhetoric.

LBJ's advisers discussed the first two options. National security adviser W. W. Rostow and the Joint Chiefs of Staff argued for an immediate expansion of air and sea operations against North Vietnam. McNamara disagreed, stating that expansion of the conflict would not win the war "but only submerge it into a larger one." The defense secretary wrote the president, "There appears to be no attractive course of action." The enemy's "intention is a stalemate; he can get it at whatever level we choose to deploy." McNamara warned, "The war in Vietnam is acquiring a momentum of its own that must be stopped."

But the war continued. Casualties mounted. In 1965 less than 1400 Americans died in Vietnam, but the next year that number soared to over 5000, and in 1967 to over 9000 for a total of about 16,000. Draft calls again increased, and the president decided to expand troop strength to over 525,000. Furthermore, the war was hurting the economy. Massive federal expenditures for Vietnam resulted in higher deficits and inflationary pressures. "We must finance this war," LBJ said to his advisers, and he advocated a 10 percent income surtax.

Popular approval for the war and for the commander-in-chief declined during 1967. In July, a Harris poll found that 72 percent of citizens supported the war, in August that dropped to 61, and by October it slid to a new low of 58 percent. The proposed surtax was very unpopular and was overwhelmingly defeated in Congress: South Vietnam was not worth an increase in taxes. LBJ's overall approval rating declined to 39 percent in August and plummeted to just 28 percent in October. By November, those thinking that the war was a mistake equaled those who did not. Under-Secretary of State Nicholas Kazenbach wrote to the president: "Can the tortoise of progress in Vietnam stay ahead of the hare of dissent at home?"

The hare was running faster. The public had been waiting for two years for some sign of victory and what they sensed was growing frustration. Many wondered whether there was a "credibility gap" between the administration's statements and the reality in Vietnam. The press began asking questions, and many citizens were wondering what to do. Hawks said expand the effort, doves said de-escalate, but by 1967 if there was a bird that symbolized the growing disenchantment with Vietnam it was the albatross. As opinion analyst Samuel Lubell noted, Americans shared a "fervent drive to shake free of an unwanted burden." Citizens were confused, frustrated, and impatient. As one housewife commented, "I want to get out but I don't want to give in."[26]

Others simply wanted to get out. The antiwar movement blossomed in spring, and it continued merging with the civil rights struggle. James Bevel of SCLC joined A. J. Muste, Dave Dellinger, and many others to form the Spring Mobilization Committee to End the War in Vietnam. Based on the idea behind the March on Washington in 1963, to bring all activists together, the spring committee aimed to fuse a more unified movement and conduct a demonstration "so much more impressive than any previous effort" that it would force the Johnson administration to withdraw the troops. Although bickering ensued between various groups, the April turnout was phenomenal—the largest demonstration until that time. Coretta Scott King addressed 50,000 in San Francisco and in New York City some 200,000 marched with Bevel, Spock, Carmichael, McKissick, Pete Seeger, and Martin Luther King. The movement continued to expand, for crowds included students and workers, blacks and whites, ministers and rabbis, children and grandparents, cleancut businessmen and long-haired youths, even a few Vietnam veterans and small group of Native Americans, who held a sign: "Americans—Do Not Do to the Vietnamese What You Did to Us."

The spring march was "just the thing to pull the Movement out of the doldrums," said one activist, and it also rekindled the Resistance. A Cornell University group sent out a flyer to other campuses that demonstrated frustration and signaled a growing militancy in the movement:

> The armies of the United States have, through conscription, already oppressed or destroyed the lives and consciences of millions of Americans and Vietnamese. We have argued and demonstrated to stop this destruction. We have not succeeded. Murderers do not respond to reason. Powerful resistance is now demanded: radical, illegal, unpleasant, sustained. . . . Body and soul, we must resist in common. The undersigned believe that we should *begin* this mass resistance by publicly destroying our draft cards at the Spring Mobilization.

The antiwar movement was moving from protest to resistance. At Sheep's Meadow in Central Park about 175 young men burned their draft cards while protesters chanted, "We won't go!" Others formed RESIST, another anti-draft organization that helped young men learn about ways to avoid military service, and by the summer Midwest activists were organizing the Chicago Area Draft Resistance. "We call ourselves CADRE," wrote Gary Rader. "We speak of squads, escalation, campaigns. The terminology is no accident—it fits our attitude. We are no longer interested in merely protesting the war; we are out to stop it."[27]

To stop it activists began employing shocking behavior, especially after the regimented and polite 1950s. Harvard radicals confronted Secretary McNamara, surrounding his car, and when he attempted to answer questions some chanted, "Bullshit." At Howard University, students jeered the director of Selective Service, General Hershey, and burned his effigy while shouting, "Burn, baby, burn!" At Indiana, some students booed for so long when Secretary of State Rusk appeared at the podium that he left without making his address, and at Cornell the secretary spoke while looking at hundreds of students wearing death's head masks. Whenever LBJ went out in public he was greeted with, "Hey, Hey, LBJ, How Many Kids Did You Kill Today." Another shocking tactic appeared at Sheep's Meadow. Some demonstrators carried Vietcong flags—and one burned the Stars and Stripes.

"The American people are not going to let this go on," proclaimed Congressman L. Mendel Rivers. "They want this treason stopped." Was it treason? Many of the sixties generation asked, What is patriotism? General Westmoreland returned to Washington in April and spoke of the high morale of his troops but added that "they are dismayed, and so am I by recent unpatriotic acts here at home." The president added later that the nation must unite behind his policy as a "family of patriots." Dissidents disagreed. Senator William Fulbright stated that dissent "is more than a right; it is an act of patriotism, a higher form of patriotism," and the *New York Times* was concerned that the administration "insinuates that its critics are to blame for its own failures and that dissent borders on treason." Clergyman Robert McAfee Brown concluded, "The question is not what right have we to be speaking, but what right have we to be silent."[28]

Patriotism would be debated for the remainder of the era, but in 1967 most politicians still desired cold war obedience. A hint of disloyalty was outrageous, and Congress overwhelmingly passed a bill making desecration of the flag a federal crime. Millions of countrymen bought a record numbers of flags, and many put flag decals on their car bumpers. Prowar posters appeared: "My Country, Right or Wrong." "Love It or Leave It." "One Country, One Flag." Old Glory was becoming a symbol of the 1960s.

Conservatives talked about passing laws that would end military deferments for students who joined demonstrations, and some university administrators tightened screws on unruly students. The University of Texas withdrew recognition of the SDS chapter, kicking it off campus, and when students protested half a dozen were put on scholastic probation for failing to "show respect for properly constituted authority." Many parents gave stern warnings to their children: "You know, Chuck," said one impatient father. "I'm not spending a fortune sending you to school to have you making a fool out of yourself—and me—at some ridiculous leftie 'peace' protest. If you expect me to keep paying your tuition, you're going to have to straighten up and fly right."

Yet by 1967 many kids were beyond parents' control. The antiwar movement continued to expand as flyers appeared on campus during spring semester announcing: "Vietnam Summer, like the Mississippi Summer Project of 1964, needs thousands of student volunteers to make the project a success. Unlike the Mississippi Summer, however, this project anticipates that students will stay and work in their home or university communities." Activists devised a program of "teach-outs instead of teach-ins" aimed to organize workers, professionals, housewives, clergy, and anyone else in their communities who had doubts about the war.[29]

The movement seeped out into the greater society. The California Federation of Teachers passed a resolution opposing LBJ's policy in Vietnam, and concerned citizens in Minneapolis formed the Council for the Peaceful Use of Taxes and asked, "How much longer will we say yes to war and no to education?" Attorneys and law professors developed the Lawyers Committee on American Policy Towards Vietnam and petitioned the United Nations to stop the war. Housewives in Denver's Stop the War Committee passed out flyers proclaiming, "War Escalates Food Prices!!!" Over a hundred intellectuals published "A Call to Resist Illegitimate Authority" in the *New York Review of Books* pledging to aid anyone who resisted the draft. Liberal entrepreneurs organized Business Executives Move for Peace, and the former chairman of the Federal Reserve Board, Marriner S. Eccles, began speaking about the financial costs, rising interest rates, and future veterans' benefits. Their flyer asked: "Shall we kill— or build?" Other citizens formed Taxpayers Against War, claiming that the war was illegal and demanding tax refunds. "I am not going to volunteer the 60% of my year's income tax that goes to armaments," singer Joan Baez wrote to the Internal Revenue Service. Protestant, Catholic, and Jewish religious leaders prayed for peace and joined Clergy and Laymen Concerned About Vietnam and another group called Negotiations Now! The Committee for Non-Violent Action handed out flyers, "Suppose They Gave a War and No One Came." Those who fought in World War II and Korea organized Veterans and Reservists for Peace, and younger ones returning from Southeast Asia formed Vietnam Veterans Against the War.

Dissent also emerged within the military. While there had been a few cases earlier of servicemen refusing orders to Vietnam, such as the Fort Hood Three, the press rarely provided coverage until the trial of Private Andrew Stapp. An antiwar demonstrator who had burned his draft card, the army drafted Stapp anyway and stationed him at Fort Sill, Oklahoma, where he enraged his superiors by receiving antiwar literature and discussing his views with other soldiers. Officers ordered him to give up his literature. Stapp refused, claiming First Amendment rights, and the private was put on trial. Activists rushed to the fort and attended the trial, and when the military judges found Stapp guilty of disobeying an order, the civilians began chanting peace slogans in what was probably the first antiwar demonstration inside an army fort. Afterward, Stapp quickly broke a minor regulation, and was retried. Activists rushed back to Fort Sill, where local police arrested them in their paid motel room for "trespassing on private property." Stapp was restricted to the base, and with the help of civilian supporters, formed the first national GI union, the American Servicemen's Union, and a new legal defense organization, the Committee for GI Rights, and began publishing the first military underground, *The Bond.* All this was too much for the brass, and the army awarded Stapp an undesirable discharge.

Women mobilized and came out against the war. Women, of course, had been marching for all types of causes, playing a major role in the movement throughout the decade. Yet the mid-1960s preceded the national emergence of the women's liberation movement, and so seeing coeds, angry black women, or well-dressed ladies protesting on television made a significant impression. In October 1966 ten young women held the first draft board sit-in in Texas, disrupting the Selective Service headquarters in Austin for over four hours. That same year sisters in Harlem formed Black Women Enraged and urged their men to write letters to draft boards: "Refuse to Fight Whitey's War." Women Strike for Peace was much more prominent, for their members had demonstrated against atmospheric nuclear testing earlier in the decade. In January 1967 some 2500 members marched on the Pentagon, demanding to see "the generals who send our sons to Vietnam," and later that year the organization began "a woman's resistance" to the draft by marching to General Hershey's office with a coffin bearing the slogan, "Not Our Sons, Not Your Sons, Not Their Sons." Another Mother for Peace began printing up posters, buttons, and T-shirts with what became one of the most popular slogans of the era, "War Is Not Healthy for Children and Other Living Things."

Many demonstrations were individual actions. In Big Lake, Minnesota, Barry Bondhus broke into his local draft board office and destroyed files by pouring buckets of human feces over 1-A records; his action became known as "the movement that started the Movement." Recalling that in 1952 presidential candidate Eisenhower had offered to end the Korean conflict by flying there, some Tucson citizens bought LBJ a one-way ticket to Vietnam. The lead singer of the Beach Boys was indicted for refusing induction and so was the heavyweight boxing champion Muhammad Ali, who also was stripped of his crown. Retired officers began to question the war, such as former Marine Corps commandant General David M. Shoup, Rear Admiral Arnold True, and General Hugh Hester, and Vietnam veteran Donald Duncan quit the Green Berets and began speaking out against the conflict. One young man, Robert Dewart of Nashville, wrote to his draft board:

> Gentlemen:
>
> For some time now I have been receiving unsolicited mail from your office. You have sent me questionnaires that request information of such a personal nature as to be classified as indecent. You have made unheard of demands upon my person, requiring me to submit to a physical examination. Most recently you have pushed me to the limit of endurance by expecting me to prove my conscientiousness or face the consequences of indentured service in a dehumanizing machine of mass murder operating under the euphemism of the Department of Defense. I can no longer put up with your impertinence. Since I do not consider myself to be in any way obligated to your agency, and since I have more important matters to warrant my attention . . . , I would appreciate it if you would immediately delete my name from your mailing list.
>
> P.S.: As I cannot consider myself a member of your despicable little club, I have destroyed those silly membership cards which you sent me.

Some individual actions were more profound. During 1967, J. D. Copping, a navy veteran, burned himself to death, and so did Hiroko Hayashi of San Diego and Florence Beaumont of Los Angeles. "The match that Florence used to touch off her gasoline-soaked clothing," her husband reported, ignited "a fire that will not go out—ever—a fire under us complacent smug fat cats so damned secure in our ivory towers 9000 miles from exploding napalm."[30]

Back in America, the summer of 1967 also was exploding. For the third time in three years urban blacks rioted. From Boston to Tampa, Buffalo to Wilmington, fires in the streets burned in over a hundred cities. Then, there was Newark, a city with the nation's highest black unemployment rate and perhaps the most corrupt white city administration. The rumor of white police beating a black taxi driver was all it took to spark anarchy. The governor declared the city in "open rebellion" and ordered in the National Guard. The troops unloaded, firing 13,000 rounds of ammunition, wounding 1200 and killing 25 blacks. A week later Detroit exploded. The ghetto quickly turned into an inferno. The governor mobilized the National Guard as FBI Director Hoover reported to the president: "They have lost all control in Detroit. Harlem will break loose within thirty minutes. They plan to tear it to pieces." To stop the upheaval in Detroit, frightened guardsmen fired wildly, over 150,000 rounds of ammunition. The commander-in-chief sent the U.S. Army, who arrived with tanks, machine guns, and helicopters; with better leadership, the army cooled tensions and ended the upheaval. After six days and nights, a World War II veteran said, the city looked like Berlin in 1945. When the violence subsided, the press reported 4000 arrests, 2000 injuries, and 43 dead. Detroit, *Newsweek* wrote, was "An American Tragedy." Throughout the nation, the 1967 urban riots resulted in 4000 injured and at least 90 killed in action. At home and abroad, America was at war.

The riots clearly demonstrated that LBJ's guns-and-butter policy, fighting a war abroad and poverty at home, was a failure. While the administration spent over $300,000 to kill one Vietcong in 1967, it spent about $50 to help one American out of poverty. The Great Society, proclaimed Senator William Fulbright, had become the "sick society. . . . Each war feeds on the other, and, although the President assures us that we have the resources to win both wars, in fact we are not winning either of them."

The riots also demolished the myth that racism was only a southern problem, so the president appointed Illinois Governor Otto Kerner to establish a commission to investigate the reasons for the urban upheavals. The governor picked moderates, white and black, Democrats and Republicans, and after surveying twenty cities, the commission found that the primary grievances rioters stated were police brutality, unemployment or underemployment, and discrimination in housing and education. Every major riot was "precipitated by arrests of Negroes by white police for minor offenses. . . . Thus, to many Negroes police have come to symbolize white power, white racism and white repression. And the fact is that many police do reflect and express these white attitudes." Rioters, therefore, shot or threw stones at police, and destroyed businesses owned by absentee white landlords or ones they considered racist, hostile, or notorious for high prices. Rioters spared most black businesses, white stores that gave credit to black customers, and nearly all public facilities such as libraries and schools. The Kerner Commission summarized: "What white Americans have never fully understood—but what the Negro can never forget—is that white society is deeply implicated in the ghetto. White institutions created it, white institutions maintain it, and white society condones it." The commission concluded, "Our nation is moving toward two societies, one black, one white—separate and unequal."

President Johnson had announced after Watts that his administration would launch "an attack—mounted at every level—upon the conditions that breed despair and violence," yet two years later the fires continued to burn. The administration had become less concerned with the war on poverty than with the war in Vietnam.

All the while the liberal consensus crumbled, and the nation became more divided. Suburban whites demanded law and order; urban blacks demanded the end to police brutality. Black militants were shouting Black Power! Peace advocates were screaming Out Now! *Newsweek* declared the "Summer of Discontent."[31]

Yet not for all Americans. A growing number of young people had decided to drop out—to reject war, racism, and indeed, the entire American Way of Life.

In July *Time* published a cover story that introduced "The Hippies." Actually, the editors admitted, hippies had been emerging on the U.S. scene since the last months of 1965 as "a wholly new subculture, a bizarre permutation of the middle-class American ethos." A few had gravitated toward the Haight, the Haight-Ashbury district of San Francisco, near the Panhandle of Golden Gate Park. Dressed in anything unusual—granny gowns, pirate or Old West costumes, Victorian suits, British mod fashions with black boots—they attended "happenings" at the Fillmore Auditorium and danced to groups called the Charlatans, Great Society, Jefferson Airplane, Quicksilver Messenger Service, Grateful Dead, Moby Grape, and Big Brother and the Holding Company. Throughout 1966 more came to the Haight, smoking and selling marijuana, and joining in with Ken Kesey's group of Merry Pranksters and dropping LSD, or as they joked, participating in the Trips Festival and taking Acid Tests. They blew bubbles, wore beads and bells, looked into distorted mirrors, and chalked colorful designs on the sidewalks. Some adopted new names—Apache, Coyote, Superspade, Teddybear, Chocolate George, White Rabbit, Blue Flash, Black Preacher. A mailman was known as Admiral Love, a cop went by Sergeant Sunshine, and Ulysses S. Grant wore his dress uniform. They bought groceries at Far Fetched Foods, posters at the Blushing Peony, Zig Zag paper at the Psychedelic Shop, and drank coffee at I/Thou while reading the *Oracle*. They ate free food collected by older bohemians, the Diggers, who handed out flyers: "Free Food *Everyday* Free Food. It's Free Because It's Yours!" In autumn the Diggers held a Full Moon Public Celebration (Halloween), which attracted considerable attention from students in Berkeley and was reported in detail in the *Barb*, and they celebrated Thanksgiving with a "Meatfeast," a dinner for a few hundred in a garage know as the Free Frame of Reference. Haight had energy, vibrations, and for many questioning youth it became a spawning bed.

During 1966 most San Francisco newspapers referred to these people as beatniks, and in New York City author John Gruen labeled them "new bohemians" as he described the East Village. Long-haired girls, bearded guys, and interracial couples wore boots and bell bottom pants, went to poetry readings or experimental theater at Cafe La Mama, browsed at boutiques such as The Limbo, Khadejha Fashions, the Queen of Diamonds, or read a growing number of underground magazines such as *Clothes Line, Elephant, Mother, Nadada, Fuck You/ A Magazine of the*

Arts, or a new neighborhood paper, the *East Village Other*. The East Village was experiencing a Renaissance. Allen Ginsberg read poetry, LeRoi Jones wrote plays, Yoko Ono composed her "insound music," and the Fugs played their sexual tunes, "What Are You Doing After the Orgy?" Andy Warhol, Jim Dine, Red Grooms, and many others painted, while Dick Higgins, Claes Oldenburg, and Robert Rauschenberg put on "happenings," art in action. Freedom. Ed Sanders hung signs in his Peace Eye Book Store that read: "POT is FUN" and "Legalize Cunnilingus Now." "It can truly be said," reported Gruen, "that for New Bohemians every day is Independence Day."[32]

Hippies also began appearing in more antiwar demonstrations, especially in Berkeley and New York City. In November 1966 a few thousand joined a protest in Manhattan, giving it a different twist by singing Beatles songs and carrying a huge yellow submarine. By 1967 the sight of long-haired demonstrators was becoming more commonplace, walking alongside well-dressed members of Women Strike for Peace, clean-cut liberals, and student activists in jeans and blue work shirts.

Some of the sixties generation were beginning to feel alienated, part of a different society, a strange underground movement outside or below the Establishment. "Who is the Underground?" asked *Avatar*. "You are, if you think, dream, work, and build towards the improvements and changes in your life, your social and personal environments, towards the expectations of a better existence. . . . Think—look around—maybe in a mirror, maybe inside."

Looking different, behaving differently, was dangerous in cold war culture. Hair, of all things, provoked an incredible backlash. In San Francisco, the police routinely stopped anyone with long hair and harassed them. "Wow! All you have to do is walk down Haight Street," a young one complained. "The police stop and hassle you. They just bug you." Indeed, "A Record Haul—33 Beatniks," proclaimed the *San Francisco Chronicle*. *Life* ran a cover story that year, "LSD: The Exploding Threat of the Mind Drug That Got Out of Control," and in autumn California passed a law that made LSD illegal. The next year a writer for the *San Francisco Chronicle* informed citizens that smoking marijuana frequently caused "delirious rage which sometimes leads to serious crime." That's why, he claimed, marijuana is called the "killer drug."

Until the *Time* article, most citizens had no idea what these young people thought, just that they looked different, strange. To its credit, the magazine attempted to describe the behavior and philosophy, the "Highs & Lows of Hippiedom," from Acid to Zen. While that will be examined later, *Time* in 1967 concluded that "it could be argued that in their independence of material possessions and their emphasis on peacefulness and honesty, hippies lead considerably more virtuous lives than the great majority of their fellow citizens. . . . In the end it may be that the hippies have not so much dropped out of American society as given it something to think about."[33]

But during the rising frustrations of 1967 most citizens were not interested in thinking about unconventional behavior. "These people do not have the courage to face the reality of life," proclaimed San Francisco Police Chief Thomas Cahill. "They're trying to escape."

Indeed, they were trying to escape the problems of America and the values of police chiefs, ministers, generals, parents, and the state's new governor, Ronald Reagan. LSD made more sense than LBJ. Time for a "pow-wow," a "gathering of the tribes," said the Diggers, and after consulting an astrologer they set the date of January 14, 1967, for a "human be-in." *Oracle* editor Allen Cohen declared that it was time for a "union of love and activism" between "Berkeley political activists and hip community and San Francisco's spiritual generation. . . . A new concert of human relations being developed within the youthful underground must emerge, become conscious, and be shared so that a revolution of form can be filled with a Renaissance of compassion, awareness and love." On the other side of the Bay the *Barb* agreed: "In unity we shall shower the country with waves of ecstasy and purification. Fear will be washed away; ignorance will be exposed to sunlight; profits and empire will lie drying on deserted beaches; violence will be submerged and transmuted in rhythm and dancing."

Thousands appeared on that sunny Saturday, streaming into Golden Gate Park. Jerry Rubin called for an end to the war, Allen Ginsberg chanted mantras, LSD guru Tim Leary said, "Turn on, tune in, drop out," but the people themselves were the main event at the human be-in. They came in all shades, all colors, all costumes, "a polyglot mixture of Mod, Paladin, Ringling Brothers, Cochise and Hells Angels' Formal." Some held "gorgeous flowing sheets of color on the green as though knights were assembling on the Camelot plain," and others watched a parachutist float to the ground through rising yellow incense. The Diggers handed out thousands of turkey sandwiches, made from dozens of birds donated by LSD chemist Augustus Owsley Stanley III, who also donated ample amounts of his homemade White Lightning LSD. Music flowed all afternoon. People smiled.

That spring more youth wandered or hitch-hiked to San Francisco, where the hippies announced a Summer of Love: "This summer, the youth of the world are making a holy pilgrimage to our city, to affirm and celebrate a new spiritual dawn. . . . Kitchens are being made ready. Food is being gathered. Hotels and houses are being prepared to supply free lodging." Word spread. In New York City the *East Village Other* announced that a "love-guerilla training school for drop-outs from mainstream America" was being built in the Bay Area, "the new world, a human world of the 21st century."

The authorities were alarmed. Chief Cahill announced that "law and order" will be maintained: "Hippies are no asset to the community." The *San Francisco Chronicle* ran the headlines, "Mayor Warns Hippies to Stay Out of Town" and "Supervisors Back War on Hippies."

Warnings made no difference. Hippies did not listen to the Establishment—that was the point—and by spring they were flooding into the Haight. "If you go to San Francisco," they sang, "wear a flower in your hair."

The Haight was blooming. Hippies established new businesses—Weed Patch, Love Burgers, Xanadu Clothes, the Hobbit Hole—and residents were busy developing their own community complete with the Haight-Ashbury Settlement House, Neighborhood Legal Assistance, Job Co-op, Krishna Temple, and Haight-Ashbury Free Medical Clinic. While entrepreneurs established a business organization, the Haight Independent Proprietors, or HIP merchants, a far-out doctor, Eugene Schoenfeld, wrote a question and answer column in the underground press, HIPpocrates. The people grooved to the first FM stereo station that played psychedelic rock, KMPX, and when they tired of the city they visited Lou Gottlieb at Morning Star Ranch in Sonoma County. The music scene was thriving at the Fillmore and also at the Avalon—the usual San Francisco sounds plus visits by Otis Redding, Mothers of Invention, Pacific Gas & Electric, Country Joe and the Fish, and the Doors: "Break on Through to the Other Side."

More than ever, the music was becoming the message. During the summer of 1967 the sixties generation was buying more than romance or dance tunes, more than "Hey, hey, we're The Monkees." The top five albums on the charts included the Beatles, Rolling Stones, Doors, and Jefferson Airplane. Between 1964 and 1966 the Beatles had grown from "She Loves You" to "Yellow Submarine," and in the latter year they began tracing the alienation of the younger generation in "Nowhere Man" and "Eleanor Rigby." They continued the theme in 1967 by producing one of the most significant albums of rock, *Sgt. Pepper's Lonely Hearts Club Band*. "It's getting better all the time," they sang, and that was because of generational unity, "a little help from my friends," and because of other help, *Lucy in the Sky with Diamonds*, "a girl with kaleidoscope eyes." So if you were still part of the Establishment, they continued, it was rather hopeless, just another "day in the life." Give the new generation a chance, experiment; after all, "I'd love to turn you on." For the generation's dream world, the Jefferson Airplanes created a *Surrealistic Pillow*. Grace Slick wanted to get in bed, "I just want somebody to love," and the band mocked parents as they created their own version of Alice in Wonderland:

One pill makes you larger,
and one pill makes you small.
And the ones that mother gives you,
don't do anything at all.

Mainstream media rushed to the scene—the "Hashbury," as Gonzo journalist Hunter S. Thompson labeled it in a stunning article in the *New York Times* magazine. Not to be outdone, *Time, Life,* and most national newspapers ran stories on the hippies. TV crews caught flights to San Francisco, and film makers produced quicky movies, *The Love-Ins, The Trip, The Hallucination Generation.* Gray Line Bus Company instituted a "Hippie Hop" tour, advertising it as the "only foreign tour within the continental limits of the United States."

Hippies did not disappoint the older generation. While most newcomers sported long hair, dressed in colorful garb, and liberally puffed marijuana or did LSD, some were more exotic in behavior and dress. On one Gray Line tour a hippie boarded the bus, told the startled passengers, "You're all free! This bus has been taken over by the Diggers!" He took the bus to the house rented by the Grateful Dead and then to the Diggers' hangout. Allen Noonan and his Universal Millennium group created the Here and Now Air Research Club, which served vegetarian food and gave out free flying saucer information. Noonan declared himself Supreme Officer of the Galactic Command and World Messiah. Another fellow wore a poncho with one of his arms sticking out of one side, and a plastic baby's arm out the other, and one hippie wore a door knocker around his neck; he would not talk to anyone who did not knock first.

There were numerous happenings in the area that summer, almost daily and usually spontaneous, but one that was planned was in June, the first major music festival of the sixties, Monterey Pop. At the venue, the organizers provided a playground, projection room, shops and booths, a guitar workshop, and a Buddha. A producer filmed the event for a television special, which became a popular movie on campuses, and the crowd of about 30,000 for Friday evening swelled to 60,000 by Sunday. They came in peasant dresses, in bell bottoms, leather vests, in colors: mellow yellow, panama red, moby grape, deacon blue, acapulco gold. Owsley supplied a new batch of LSD called Monterey Purple, dubbed Purple Haze, and the bands merged the San Francisco sounds with American pop, rock, blues, soul, folk-rock, and the British Invasion. Groups for the three-day event included Eric Burdon and the Animals, Johnny Rivers, Simon and Garfunkel, Canned Heat, Otis Redding, Al Kooper, Ravi Shankar, The Byrds, Country Joe, Steve Miller, Paul Butterfield, Electric Flag, the Grateful Dead, Jefferson Airplane, Booker T. and the MGs, The Who, the Mamas and the Papas, Janis Joplin and Big Brother and the Holding Company, and a U.S. Army veteran making his first important American appearance, Jimi Hendrix.

Monterey Pop was the first major rock festival of the sixties. "It was one of the first times that we all felt together, interconnected," recalled Frank Christopher. "So innocent, we all touched each other. It was magical." Considering its size, the largest festival up to that time, it also was incredibly peaceful. The local police chief reported on Sunday that he had sent half his force home, and many other officers got in the spirit, draping their motorcycles with flowers. After dealing and rapping with organizers, the chief admitted, "I feel the hippies are my friends, and I am asking one of them to take me to the Haight-Ashbury."

Yet back in the Haight, the vibes were turning negative for the Summer of Love. The area was flooded, overwhelmed with youth. Authorities reported that they were picking up 200 runaway minors a month. In June the *Oracle* printed a record 100,000 copies; the editors noted that problems were mounting, and if one must come to San Francisco, then, "in addition to flowers," bring clothing, sleeping bags, food, even money. Easy living was getting expensive. Houses and crash pads were in short supply, and store-front rentals soared on Haight Street. Many hip businesses were in debt and the city was cracking down on building code violations. Life also was getting dangerous. Earlier, in April, a sixteen-year-old female runaway had been picked up by a street dealer, drugged heavily, and then raped repeatedly. "The politics & ethics of ecstasy," Communication Company hippies sarcastically called it. "Rape is as common as bullshit on Haight Street." Another complained, "Are you aware that Haight Street is just as bad as the squares say it is?" New drugs were introduced, some dangerous like STP, methedrine, and heroin, and with drug dealers competing for profits, violence mounted. In August, drug dealer John Kent Carter, alias Shob, was found dead in his apartment, stabbed a dozen times. A few days later, the body of black dealer Superspade was found. Some Diggers began carrying guns, and hippie Charles Perry wondered, "Acid dealers *killing* each other? This was what the New Age promised?"[34]

The editors of *Oracle* wondered. In August they asked, "Is community and brotherhood being built here? Is Haight Street going to take off before it is absorbed into the grade B movie of the American Mainstream, which is likely to turn into another bad Nazi flick?" Perhaps it was time to cool it, to try "Chanting Om or Hare Krishna or Peace in America, Peace in Vietnam, or staring with attention at a candle or water coloring or beading or reading or writing poetry or painting or building or studying ancient or new scriptures or practicing yoga."

Save the dream, time for cleansing, and so some people announced a ceremony, the Death of the Hippie. Some would shave, they claimed, and become the new "Free Man." Most residents ridiculed the idea, and only about eighty appeared for the event in October. They played Taps, burned beads, dope, and underground newspapers. Signs: "Be Free," "Don't Mourn for Me," "Nebraska Needs You More."

Hippies, of course, did not die, and in fact the highs and lows of Haight-Ashbury would be repeated in various forms and shapes in Nebraska and in most states of America. While hippies in 1967 were just a tiny fraction of the sixties generation, the 75,000 who visited the Haight that summer returned home or to their campuses with different values. With the help of the Establishment's media coverage, the anti-Establishment spread. *Time* declared in July, "Today hippie enclaves are blooming in every major U.S. city from Boston to Seattle, from Detroit to New Orleans; there is a 50-member cabal in, of all places, Austin, Texas." The magazine noted that there might be 300,000 hippies, and "by all estimates the cult is a growing phenomenon that has not yet reached its peak—and may not do so for years to come."

How prophetic. By mid-1967 more members of the sixties generation were listening to the music—questioning and rejecting mainstream values, dropping out. Yet this was not only the Summer of Love. It also was Vietnam Summer and the Summer of Discontent. Others in the sixties generation were shouting out, growing more frustrated and yelling louder as many activists continued shifting away from liberalism and toward radicalism.

The rhetoric got hot, especially from black militants. Earlier in the year, Huey Newton and Bobby Seale had formed the Black Panther Party for Self-Defense in Oakland. They wore black leather and saluted by raising their right hand stiff above their head, fist clenched, with black glove. Since the U.S. Army elites wore the green berets, they donned black berets. They published a paper and a program that for that time made startling demands—education that "teaches us our true history," black offenders tried by black juries, black men exempt from military service—and to insure racial justice they even called on the United Nations to intervene in America. They enlisted young supporters who established breakfast programs and self-defense groups to combat what they claimed was police or "pig" brutality. They held watch in their neighborhoods—armed—for that was legal then in California. "So we floated around the streets," wrote Seale, "and we patrolled pigs."

The Black Panthers were an obscure group—until May. In "one of the most amazing incidents in legislative history," declared the *Los Angeles Times*, thirty Panthers, twenty armed with rifles and shotguns, arrived at the capitol building in Sacramento to protest a bill restricting citizens from carrying loaded weapons in city limits. Seale, Bobby Hutton, Eldridge Cleaver, and the others marched into the building, and with a mob of journalists following and cameras flashing, Seale read Mandate

Number One: As "the aggression of the racist American government escalates in Vietnam, the police agencies of America escalate the repression of black people throughout the ghettos." Consequently, "the time has come for black people to arm themselves against this terror before it is too late." As the Panthers left, clamoring about repression, genocide, terror, some stunned whites mumbled the feared words, "Niggers with guns, niggers with guns."

Yet the next month whites were the ones with the guns in Prattville, Alabama; they unloaded their rifles into several black homes. SNCC chairman H. Rap Brown responded, "We will no longer sit back and let black people be killed. . . . We are calling on full retaliation. . . . It appears that Alabama has been chosen as the starting battleground for America's race war."[35]

The war was coming home, and some activists were becoming more militant. Tom Hayden called for a legion of "urban guerrillas" to change America, and concerning Vietnam, Carl Oglesby had arrived at the conclusion that the antiwar movement was becoming a "wilderness of warmed-over speeches and increasingly irrelevant demonstrations." The National Mobilization Committee to End the War in Vietnam, usually called the Mobe, announced Stop the Draft Week for October. The new aim—to "confront the warmakers," to "disrupt the war machine." As activist Dave McReynolds declared: "Vietnam is here."

Vietnam certainly was here, and on campuses tactics were becoming more provocative. At Ohio University, activists on a Monday presented their administration with "The 99 Demands," which included everything from beer on campus to coed dorms to an immediate end to the war. All demands, they proclaimed, must be met on Friday at noon—or else. At Oberlin, a hundred students trapped a navy recruiter in his car for four hours, passing him coffee and doughnuts, until police arrived and freed the stuffed sailor. At Wisconsin, there was turbulence when Dow recruiters appeared on campus. Some 300 students obstructed interviews while chanting "Down with Dow." After talks between officials and activists failed, the university called in police equipped with riot gear, tear gas, and billy clubs. "Everyone dropped to the floor, heads between legs, arms protecting heads, all glasses were removed," reported the campus paper. "Girls began to scream, and both men and women students staggered sobbing from the building, many with blood dripping from head wounds." The demonstration tore the community apart. While thousands of students and 300 faculty members condemned the "animalistic brutality" of police and boycotted classes, state assembly legislators passed a resolution 94 to 5 demanding that university expel protesters. One assemblyman called activists "long haired, greasy pigs," and another yelled, "Shoot them if necessary. I would . . . it's insurrection."

University officials suspended the company's interviews for the remainder of the semester, while students at twenty other universities joined the battle against Dow. Activists held company recruiters prisoner at Harvard, Illinois, Indiana, Minnesota, and Pennsylvania. At UCLA, protesters waved signs—"Making Money Burning Babies"—at Harvard students chanted, "Napalm is Johnson's baby powder." On other campuses activists handed out flyers inscribed: "Dow Shalt Not Kill."[36]

Antiwar fever in 1967 reached its peak on Saturday, October 21, when Stop the Draft Week climaxed with the March on the Pentagon. By all accounts, this event stunned the public, for this one demonstrated that the movement included a mixture of middle-class liberals, student radicals, hippies, civil rights workers, black power advocates, Vietnam veterans, even some federal workers and the "Time-Life Employees for Peace." The war continued to change and expand the movement.

While radicals proclaimed that they now were ready to fight, those of the counterculture joked that they planned to exorcise demons from the military control center by chanting "om" and levitating the Pentagon. About 50,000 assembled on the sunny Saturday in front of the Lincoln Memorial, watching a performance by the Bread and Puppet Theater and listening to Peter, Paul and Mary, followed by Phil Ochs singing "Days of Decision." David Dellinger announced that the march was the end of peaceful protest: "This is the beginning of a new stage in the American peace movement in which the cutting edge becomes active resistance."

Across the nation, 1400 young men returned their draft cards as the crowd in Washington began walking across the Arlington Bridge and toward the Pentagon. The federal government was prepared; for the first time since the Bonus March of 1932 it ordered its armed forces to protect the nation's capital against Americans. Upon arriving at the Pentagon, a few dozen radicals attacked. It was "a particularly American form of violence," reported eyewitness Martin Jezer. "Couples held hands and watched the action. They cheered and booed with the tide of the battle. . . . It reminded me not of insurrection but of spectators going after the goal posts at the end of a football game." The military repulsed, beat, and arrested some radicals.

At the same time, a few hundred others began a sit-down in the Pentagon parking lot. "Soon diggers started bringing in food and joints were in evidence," wrote Thorne Dreyer. "A real festival atmosphere was in the air. People laughed and hugged." Many talked to other troops, chanting "join us," singing out "we love you," or "we'd love to turn you on." A few put flowers in the troop's rifle barrels—flower power. Some used a new tactic, guerrilla theater, pretending to be soldiers acting out death in war. Some smoked dope into the evening, others sipped wine and built campfires. A few sang "Silent Night." Others sat in the lotus position and hummed "om." By most reports, the Pentagon did not levitate.

"Near midnight," reported Jezer, "paratroopers of the 82nd Division replaced the MPs on the line. With the marshals at the rear they began massing at the center of the sit-in preparing to attack. . . . The brutality was horrible. Nonresisting girls were kicked and clubbed by U.S. marshals old enough to be their fathers. The process was repeated over and over again. With the middle wiped out, the troopers and the marshals advanced down the flacks, cracking heads, bashing skulls." Eyewitness Margie Stamberg added, "They sang the Star Spangled Banner and other songs, but the troops at this point were non-men, the appeals were futile."

The March on the Pentagon was a success, most activists felt, "the best thing in American history since the Boston Tea Party," claimed Keith Lampe, because it created a spirit of community and because they talked with soldiers and supposedly two or three threw down their rifles and defected to the movement. Yet many also felt that the tactic of sitting down and taking the beating was getting old. "Saturday night's confrontation at the Pentagon was a last sit-down for us," stated Jezer, adding, "why the passivity?"[37]

Activists also wondered in Berkeley, where the day before some 10,000 marched on the draft induction center in Oakland. After they sat down at the center, "a flying wedge of helmeted cops tore into demonstrators," reported *Newsweek*, "flailing away with nightsticks and batons and firing spray cans of the paralyzing chemical Mace." Governor Reagan declared that the police action was in "the finest tradition of California law-enforcement agencies," yet this brutality provoked other activists the next day to adopt a new tactic—trashing. When police charged, activists dispersed to sidewalks or ran behind authorities in an attempt to "piss 'em off and run away," while others stopped traffic by pulling trash cans, newspaper racks, and unlocked cars into the streets. Stop business as usual: Shut It Down! Protesters disrupted the city and closed the induction center for four hours, without being the target of police bashings. Then, before the National Guard arrived, they ended the demonstration and held a victory march back to the campus. Said one activist, "Everyone in Berkeley today knows that we'll never sit down again."

Stop the Draft Week was a prologue to the explosions of 1968. Some in the peace movement were going on the warpath; former disciples of Gandhi were becoming guerrillas. While they realized that trashing would not stop the war, they aimed to disrupt the Establishment. "Glue in the keyholes," said participant Suzy Nelson, obstacles to the System.[38] Marvin Garson explained the tactic:

We are engaged, basically, in street theater rather than insurrection. Our barricades and shields and coke bottles, their tear gas and fire hoses and bayonets, function less as real weapons than as stage props. The refrain of our play is that if you need conscription to have an army, then you will need an army to have conscription. The moral of our play is that you cannot have imperialist war abroad and social peace at home.

Stop the Draft Week had an impact on the administration. LBJ believed that the peace movement was turning citizens against the war. That probably was not true—the frustrating war was turning Americans against the frustrating war. The president responded by announcing to his cabinet: "It is time that the Administration stopped sitting back and taking it from the Vietnam critics." LBJ took the offensive, publicly labeling dissidents "bearded oafs," and privately instructing government agencies to watch antiwar leaders and conduct investigations. The Internal Revenue Service examined tax returns of dissident publications such as *Ramparts*. The FBI sent phony letters to editors of national publications and leaked secret information to friendly journalists in an attempt to defame outspoken critics. The CIA began Operation Chaos, which violated federal law excluding that agency from domestic investigations, and in which agents infiltrated dissident groups such as SANE, CORE, even Women Strike for Peace in an attempt to find proof that they were controlled by foreign governments or Communists. When the administration found no such evidence, the president ordered more studies while he and his aides leaked fabrications to hawkish politicians. Some "superior forces," said Democratic Senator Frank Lausche, were the "architects behind closed doors watching innocent youth bring shame upon our nation." House Democratic Leader Carl Albert added that the march on the Pentagon was "basically organized by International Communism," and House Republican Leader Gerald Ford proclaimed that the administration had a secret report that confirmed that Stop the Draft Week was "cranked up" in Hanoi.

Johnson, therefore, attempted to change opinion in America instead of changing policy in Vietnam. Time to rally the nation. The president had not wanted the war, but once committed he could not back away. He would shoulder the burden. The president continued the same policy in 1967, historian George Herring has written, "for the same reasons he had gone to war in the first place—because he saw no alternative that did not require him to admit failure or defeat." For the Texan, the war had become a matter of pride.[39]

"We are not going to yield. We are not going to shimmy," the president proclaimed publicly, while privately informing his advisers: "We have got to sell our product to the American people." Administration officials became salesmen. With great fanfare, Johnson replaced the best and brightest with another group of experts, the "wise men," who like the former knew little about Vietnamese culture or nationalism. They held many publicized discussions while others began the second phase of the policy: predicting victory. In August, Army Chief of Staff General Harold Johnson declared, "We're winning the war," and that same month the president told congressmen that "Westmoreland has turned defeat into what we believe will be a victory. It's only a matter now of will."

America could will a victory—or at least fake one. The administration intensified the charade. In September, Walt Rostow cabled Westmoreland and directed him to "search urgently for occasions to present sound evidence of progress in Vietnam." U.S. officials began to fudge the numbers. Generals wanted results and lieutenants sent privates back out to recount the enemy dead. Enormous pro-American kill ratios and body counts appeared on television, and few realized that they were meaningless since to be victorious the enemy would—and did—sacrifice many times more than the U.S. In November, LBJ reminded his advisers, "The clock is ticking . . . the main front of the war is here in the United States." Accordingly, Ambassador Ellworth Bunker left Saigon and returned home to proclaim, "We are making steady progress in Vietnam, not only militarily, but in the pacification program. . . . There is every prospect, too, that the progress will accelerate." The president added a few days later, "We are pleased with the results that we are getting. We are inflicting greater losses than we are taking." Westmoreland declared, "It is significant that the enemy has not won a major battle in more than a year," and later he appeared with the ambassador on "Meet the Press," where they gave another premature victory speech: The U.S. now was "winning a war of attrition." The general reported that the conflict had entered a phase "when the end begins to come into view." The administration could see "the light at the end of the tunnel."

The first casualty in war is truth. We were not winning, simply sinking deeper into the quagmire. Yet most citizens wanted to believe their government in 1967. LBJ's approval ratings increased dramatically. Harris polls in December demonstrated that for the first time in six months more citizens approved than disapproved of the president's handling of the war, and the public also rallied behind Westmoreland. Almost 70 percent approved of him as commanding general, and almost 60 percent favored increasing military pressure against the enemy. Significantly, the public also disliked antiwar demonstrations, 70 percent feeling that they were acts of disloyalty and three-quarters stating that protests only encouraged the Communists.

The public had not done their democratic duty, had not educated themselves about the affairs of the Republic. They were simply confused.

At a time when half a million American sons were killing and being killed on the other side of the world, a *New York Times* poll discovered that nearly half of the respondents had no clear idea why their government was fighting a war in Vietnam.

These were the days of decision for the movement. Early in the decade activists had been relatively successful; they had changed America, but after the Voting Rights Act in 1965 there were few successes. True, activists won local victories on their campuses, but on the national scene it was becoming clear that civil rights marches, new federal laws, and court rulings would not end racism, and it was clear that peaceful protests would not end the war.

The result was frustration, a theme summarized in 1967 by Andrew Kopkind: "To be white and a radical in America this summer is to see horror and feel impotence." That also was true for blacks, as they grew increasingly angry over their plight in the ghetto and the continuation of racism, factors provoking many to consider new ideas—black power instead of nonviolent activism, separation, not integration, "we shall overrun" as opposed to "we shall overcome." Young blacks and whites were thinking about war and the draft, and students were bringing the war home to campuses. Realizing that they were having little or no impact on national policy, they began moving from protest to resistance. While some dropped out, others began shouting revolution! In November *Newsweek* noticed an ugly mood on campus and concluded, "The kind of protests that began with the Free Speech Movement at Berkeley only three years ago already appear as innocent as the panty raids of the previous generation."[40]

These also were the days of decision for the sixties. By the end of the year, a citizen looking back to the summer of 1965, an era of relative optimism and hope, would have been amazed at how far the nation had traveled in just over two years. The escalation of the war, civil rights marches, shrill calls for black power, endless urban riots, the angry white backlash, extensive campus demonstrations, strange young Americans flaunting mainstream values, and always the television images—fires in the streets, napalm in Vietnam—all blended together by the end of 1967. *Time* noted a "noxious atmosphere" in the country; the *Christian Century* mentioned a mood of "crisis and gloom"; and *Newsweek* noted "a sharp scent of crisis in the American air . . . a tension in society and a stress among men—not known since the 1930s." In the last week of December the *Nation* wrote about "a dimension of uncertainty about the present mood of the American electorate" and suggested that "almost anything *might* happen in 1968."

It did. During 1968 the movement and the sixties ended for some—and began for others.

1968: Rip Tides

There must be some way out of here,
  said the joker to the thief
There's too much confusion,
  I can't get no relief.
Bob Dylan, "All Along the Watchtower," 1968, sung by Jimi Hendrix

You've gotta be left or right,
  left or right.
The Sixties, Pyramid Films, 1970

Lyndon Johnson proclaimed that the United States was winning the war, and then he rallied the nation. What the Texan really did, unknowingly, was to set his ambush, his Alamo—the Tet Offensive.

On January 30, 1968, enemy troops launched a ferocious attack on almost every ARVN and American outpost and most towns and villages controlled by the South Vietnamese government. In Saigon, the Vietcong stormed into the city, blasted government positions, and broke into the symbols of security—Tan Son Nhut Airport, national radio station, presidential palace, and the courtyard of the U.S. Embassy. In Hue, more than 7000 troops overran the city and hoisted their flag above the Citadel, the historic capital of the Annam Emperors. Fighting was brutal, door to door, and the beautiful city was left a "shattered, stinking hulk, its streets choked with rubble and rotting bodies." The battle raged for over three weeks, and all the while the onslaught continued at Khe Sanh, an American outpost near the Laotian border. Since the end of 1967 crack units of the North Vietnamese Army had been assaulting the hill, conducting a diversion for Tet, and during February they intensified their attack in an attempt to repeat their famous victory over the French at Dienbienphu. The U.S. prevented its Dienbienphu by employing what the French did not have—massive B-52 strikes, perhaps the heaviest air raids in the history of warfare. Airpower blunted the onslaught and shell-shocked the enemy.

Tet produced sensational scenes, and they flashed across America in newspapers and on television: U.S. officials defending themselves, shooting out of embassy windows. Marines in Hue ducking for cover, firing at the enemy hiding behind scarred, ancient walls. American planes strafing villages, dropping napalm canisters that burst into rolling fireballs. A U.S. Army officer standing on the outskirts of what remained of a Mekong Delta village stating, "We had to destroy it, in order to save it." The haggard faces, the haunted eyes of defenders at Khe Sanh. The South Vietnam national police chief walking down the street with a ragged Vietcong suspect, stopping in front of reporters, nonchalantly lifting his pistol, pointing it at the man's temple—pulling the trigger.

WHAM! "Winning Hearts And Minds," the generals called U.S. policy, or "pacification," as television zoomed in and showed helicopters machine-gunning peasants running below in rice paddies. "If he's running," said a helicopter crewman, "he must be a Vietcong." These scenes, these statements, became symbolic for the war. Many Americans wondered whether all the brutality would bring victory, or whether it was just pointless. Editors of *Christian Century* wrote: "This is the genius of our war effort—to destroy Vietnam in order to save it." The twisted, tragic face of war confronted American viewers, and news anchormen began to warn viewers: "The following scenes might not be suitable viewing for children." Indeed, most citizens realized in 1968 that war really was hell. The myths created by John Wayne movies of the 1950s were devastated by the reality of one televised attack called Tet.

During Tet, General Westmoreland appeared on television and assured Americans that the enemy suffered heavy casualties and had been defeated. That was true, but it also was irrelevant. For America, Tet was a military victory and a psychological defeat. The enemy had miscalculated, thinking that peasants would join the battle and help throw out the Americans. Actually, the peasants only wanted to be left alone, and they ran for cover during the fight. Meanwhile, ARVN and American soldiers decimated North Vietnamese regulars and their Vietcong allies. While about 1100 U.S. and 2300 ARVN troops died, the enemy sacrificed as many as 40,000. The Vietcong never recovered, meaning that more of the fighting was taken over by the North Vietnamese Army. Remnants of the enemy retreated to the jungle, licked their wounds, and resumed guerrilla tactics for the next four years. At the same time the offensive stunned Americans. After hearing national leaders throughout 1967 proclaiming victory, the "light at the end of the tunnel," the public felt the enemy's ability to launch a massive attack was surely a defeat for the

United States. The attack forced citizens to consider the agonizing possibility that the conflict might go on for many years, even a decade, and more began to question: Is South Vietnam worth the price?

Many wondered, for the offensive also raised the question of the Johnson administration's credibility and policy. "I thought we were winning the war," CBS anchorman Walter Cronkite confessed to millions of viewers. Had the administration been telling the truth? "The American people have been pushed beyond the limits of gullibility," declared the *New York Times*. The credibility gap became a canyon. Who could Americans trust? Credibility became a major issue during the political campaign of 1968, and like most citizens, the previously supportive or neutral journalists now began to question and even demand a different policy. *Newsweek* declared that "a strategy of more of the same is intolerable," while columnist Joseph Kraft proclaimed the war "unwinnable." The conservative editors at the *Wall Street Journal* warned that "everyone had better be prepared for the bitter taste of a defeat," and *Fortune* blamed the war for the nation's growing economic problems. Late in February, Cronkite summarized the gloomy mood: "To say that we are mired in stalemate seems the only reasonable, yet unsatisfactory conclusion."

Tet shattered the myth. Throughout the century, and especially since World War II, Americans had assumed that their nation was invincible on the battlefield, a country with virtually unlimited power. No longer: disillusionment soared in the weeks after Tet. Polls from January to March recorded one of the most profound opinion shifts in history. Earlier, hawks had outnumbered doves 60 to 24 percent; a month later doves led hawks 42 to 41 percent. Furthermore, those approving LBJ's handling of the war plummeted to a record low, only 26 percent, and almost 80 percent felt that the U.S. was not making any progress in Vietnam. While various measures of opinion differed, and while questions asked always were too simple for the complex issues involved, it seemed clear that before Tet a majority of citizens supported the administration's policy, and that after a majority opposed it. Most Americans felt that the nation faced a hopeless stalemate in Vietnam.

The swing in opinion also was apparent in Congress. After the *New York Times* reported on March 10 that the administration was considering a request from General Westmoreland for an additional 206,000 troops, both congressional hawks and doves demanded an explanation. Next day, senators grilled Secretary of State Dean Rusk for hours on national television, demanding answers to the same questions being asked by their constituents. Conservative Senator Karl Mundt noted the bewilderment of the public and informed the secretary that those joining the dissenters were "not just street mobs." Senator Fulbright asked, "Can we afford the horrors which are being inflicted on the people of a poor and backward land to say nothing of our own people? Can we afford the alienation of our allies, the neglect of our own deep domestic problems and the disillusionment of our youth?" And the senator asked the most important question: "Can we afford the sacrifice of American lives in so dubious a cause?"

Again: What to do in Vietnam? The issue continued to divide the nation: left or right. Hawks again yelled—get tougher, stay the course! Former president Eisenhower lamented, "What has become of our courage? What has become of our loyalty to others?" More military pressure on North Vietnam, demanded conservative papers, even if that meant calling up the reserves. Privately, presidential aide Robert Murphy advised LBJ that the CIA should assassinate Ho Chi Minh, and General Westmoreland urged using atomic bombs to "send a message" to Hanoi, an idea publicly proclaimed by Congressman L. Mendel Rivers. Many others agreed with a World War II vet who stated: "My idea of peace in Vietnam is a small-sized atom bomb right in the middle of Hanoi." Doves screamed—negotiate! They urged the administration to talk peace with North Vietnam, consider withdrawing, and give much more of the war effort over to the South Vietnamese Army. As for the president, his exasperation was evident when he demanded of his secretary of defense: "Give me the lesser of evils."[1]

Tet also had an impact on the movement. The offensive radicalized a minority of activists, pushing them toward extremism, because it extinguished what remained of the Establishment's credibility. The president did not have the answer in Vietnam; again, the emperor had no clothes. Contempt grew, and a few responded by moving from resistance to rebellion and adopting more radical tactics to stop the war—sabotage. In February, Dennis Sweeney and a few others in the Bay Area attacked. In the middle of the night they carried cans of gasoline to the Stanford University ROTC clubhouse, struck a match, and escaped into the darkness as the building erupted into a "giant sheet of flame." The action was declared an unsolved arson, the first of many during the next few years.

Yet Tet provoked most activists in the opposite direction—to get involved in mainstream politics, to join the campaign of Senator Eugene McCarthy. As a Minnesota congressman in the 1950s, McCarthy had been one of the first to attack the anticommunist crusade of Senator Joe McCarthy. As a Democratic senator in the 1960s, he became the first to mount a political challenge against the commander-in-chief. McCarthy had criticized LBJ's war in 1967, and in November he announced his bid for the nomination. Most citizens laughed: no way, impossible, a joke. The last time an incumbent president had been seriously challenged was in 1912, and Republican Teddy Roosevelt eventually gave up his bid to unseat President Taft, formed his own party, split the Republicans, and handed the election to Democrat Woodrow Wilson.

Activists heeded McCarthy's call. The senator's supporters were not radicals, and in fact usually were not advocates of the new left. They were the more moderate, liberal wing of an expanding movement. The senator had been approached by Allard Lowenstein, who had worked for liberal causes in the 1950s, assisted Bob Moses and SNCC to develop Mississippi Summer and the Freedom Democratic Party, and understood the disastrous impact the war was having on the liberal agenda. Lowenstein had formed the Concerned Democrats in autumn 1967, and with the help of a young liberal, Curtis Gans, began searching for a candidate to oppose President Johnson. He approached Senators Robert Kennedy and George McGovern, who said no, and so he turned to McCarthy. The Minnesotan himself felt that Bobby Kennedy could make the strongest challenge, but RFK denied interest in a battle with the president. McCarthy's crusade, therefore, received the support of many establishment liberals— economist John Kenneth Galbraith, historian Barbara Tuchman, speech writer Richard Goodwin, actors Paul Newman and Joanne Woodward, and presidents of companies such as Dreyfus Fund and Green Shoe Manufacturing, who drove to New Hampshire, picked up phones, and began raising funds for the dissident senator.

McCarthy's most important supporters, however, were his army of volunteers. Student power moved from the campus to mainstream politics. Young and idealistic, they were similar to the Freedom Summer volunteers or early proponents of free speech on campus. As described by a McCarthy aide, they were excellent students who might romanticize popular revolutionaries, such as Malcolm X or Che Guevara, but who still remained optimistic about the nation. "Though they hated the war and the draft, they still believed that America could be beautiful—if it would live up to its own principles."[2]

In the weeks before the primary, college students climbed into their vans, bought bus tickets, or hitch-hiked to McCarthy's headquarters in New Hampshire. During the week there might be 3000 volunteers, and on the weekend the "congregation of brothers and sisters" might double or triple. "They all are arriving sober," remarked one staffer, "an unprecedented phenomenon in students." They came from nearby Ivy League colleges, and eventually from over one hundred universities from Columbia to California. Men with long hair or beards were asked to see the free barber, and the staff requested that females wearing stylish miniskirts search in their duffel bags for more traditional outfits, all in an attempt to quash any hint that these activists were radicals or hippies. "Clean for Gene" aimed to convince the state's moderate citizens that the volunteers were the boys and girls next door who wanted their neighbors to vote for peace. Remembering Birmingham, professional political workers referred to the volunteers as the "Children's Crusade," and the students spent long days ringing door bells, making phone calls, and distributing campaign literature. Late in the evening, "McCarthy's Kids" spread out their sleeping bags and crashed on the office floor or in church basements, empty gymnasiums, or at the homes of the candidate's supporters. With the exception of professional speech writer Richard Goodwin, the effort was run by students. Harvard graduate student Sam Brown directed the campaign, and one press secretary was a young reporter, Seymour Hersh. Returning Peace Corps veteran John Barbieri helped develop the mass mailings, and Joel Feigenbaum left Cornell to help organize the door-to-door campaign. Dianne Dumonoski, who had taught black children in the South and participated in the March on the Pentagon, left campus with a suitcase and a sleeping bag and soon was assigning tasks to new volunteers. As Goodwin wrote, these activists went to New Hampshire because they believed in the "terrible wrong of Vietnam" and in the possibility that they and McCarthy "could use the political system to alter the course of American history."

The activists did alter history, and that was partly because of their hard work and because their campaign literature addressed a theme of the 1960s that most of the public agreed with by 1968:

> In 1960 we started to get America moving again. Today, eight years later, the fabric of that great achievement is unraveling. . . .
> In 1963 our greatest cities were relatively tranquil. Today we look upon a period of virtual civil war.
> In 1963 our children in colleges and universities were concerned with the Peace Corps and Civil Rights. Today it is marijuana and draft protests.
> In 1963 were were at peace. Today we are at war.

The message struck home. By 1968 it appeared to most citizens that the nation was in decline, or at least much worse off than when the cool kids of the sixties generation were surfing and bundling on the beach. Then Tet and disillusionment. Many agreed with McCarthy's comment: "Only a few months ago we were told that 65 percent of the population was secure" in Vietnam. "Now we know that even the American embassy is not secure."

Frustration during the days of decision had been mounting, and two candidates exploited that theme, both McCarthy and Richard M. Nixon. The former vice president also was in New Hampshire running for the Republican nomination, and his message was simple: "Do you want four more years?" Nixon won the Republican primary overwhelmingly.

McCarthy's campaign was similar to Nixon's in the sense that a vote for the senator was a vote against the president. The children's crusade shifted into high gear to get out the vote on March 12. As a journalist quipped, "College students . . . have suddenly discovered a use for people over thirty—voting for McCarthy." Political analysts had stated in January that McCarthy would win a tenth of the Democratic vote, but on election day he won an astonishing 42 percent, 20 of the state's 24 delegates, a showing that was interpreted as a defeat for Johnson. "Dove bites Hawk," a journalist wrote. The joke in January became the miracle of March. McCarthy declared to his cheering supporters, "People have remarked that this campaign has brought young people back into the system. But it's the other way around. The young people have brought the country back into the system."[3]

Four days later, Bobby Kennedy announced that he was a candidate for the Democratic nomination. RFK had proclaimed in 1967 that he hated the war, stating on national television, "We're killing South Vietnamese, we're killing women, we're killing innocent people because they're 12,000 miles away and they might get 11,000 miles away." He felt that Tet "shattered the mask of official illusion," but he hesitated, contemplating a run in 1972, which appeased party bosses but irritated many young supporters. When he arrived to give a talk at Brooklyn College he faced a sign: "Bobby Kennedy: Hawk, Dove or Chicken?"

Kennedy's announcement surprised many in the movement. McCarthy had demonstrated that he had the courage to stand up to Johnson, and he was attracting much attention. When 750 students crammed into a small auditorium at St. Norbert's College in De Pere, Wisconsin, it was obvious that his movement was growing and the sixties generation was listening. Yet McCarthy was not a vivacious campaigner, too professorial. The *Village Voice* complained that his "speeches are dull, vague and without either poetry or balls." As for Kennedy, by waiting until after the New Hampshire primary before announcing, he looked like an opportunist, or as a McCarthy supporter quipped, a "Bobby-come-lately." RFK could generate enthusiasm, however, and he plunged into the body politic. "Kennedy exposed himself to crowds in an orgy of emotion," wrote supporter Jack Newfield.[4] Both candidates headed to the Midwest for the primaries.

The battle for the heartland was on, while in the nation's capital the Johnson administration appeared dizzy, on the verge of fainting. After Tet, the president named a new Secretary of Defense, Clark Clifford, who supposedly supported escalating the conflict, only to express his deep concern about continuing the present strategy. Westmoreland eventually was replaced as battlefield commander, or in the age of euphemism, "promoted" to duty in the Pentagon. In March, opinion polls revealed that Johnson's popularity was slipping fast, and by the end of the month had plummeted to its lowest level. Furthermore, it appeared that in the upcoming Wisconsin primary in which only McCarthy and the president were running, the senator might win by a two to one margin. LBJ again called in the "wise men," only to discover that most of them had changed their positions during the previous months and now felt that the U.S. could not guarantee a non-Communist, independent South Vietnam. Concerning the military, former secretary of state Dean Acheson was blunt: "The Joint Chiefs don't know what they're talking about." Clifford added that the legal and business community no longer supported the war, and the wise men suggested that the administration should eventually disengage. Johnson felt betrayed, bitterly complaining that the "establishment bastards have bailed out."

Yet by the end of the month he had arrived at a similar conclusion. During a private conversation with Generals Creighton Abrams and Earle Wheeler, the president admitted: "There has been a panic in the last three weeks. . . . The country is demoralized. . . . Senator McCarthy and Senator Kennedy and the left wing have informers in the departments. The *Times* and the *Post* is against us. Most of the press is against us. . . . We have no support for the war." Realizing "overwhelming disapproval in the polls," he predicted his fate in the upcoming election: "I will go down the drain."

On March 31, President Johnson announced that after three years of bombing North Vietnam, he was calling a limited halt. Then he became the war's most notable casualty by saying, "I shall not seek, and I will not accept, the nomination of my party for another term as your President."

Americans were shocked. Just three years earlier LBJ was one of the most popular presidents, had won an overwhelming electoral victory and so confidently told friends at his inaugural ball, "Don't stay up too late. We're on our way to the Great Society." He had reached so far, and now everything was crumbling.[5]

Most citizens felt that limiting the bombing was a positive step and hoped that peace would break out, perhaps later in 1968. Activists were ecstatic: "We did it!" cheered McCarthy workers as they flowed out of their hotel and into the chilly Milwaukee streets. Richard Goodwin remembered the announcement as "one gorgeously climactic moment." Although realizing that the war was not over, and that only strategy had changed, many felt that they had done the impossible—ended the wartime administration. Students at Wisconsin, Berkeley, Harvard, Columbia, Pennsylvania, and New York University left dorms and apartments to march and chant, "The hawk is dead!" "Peace now!" A hundred activists gathered in front of the White House. Some wore Kennedy or McCarthy buttons, and they began to sing a new version of the old civil rights song, "We *have* overcome."

It appeared that the movement again was having an impact, changing America. "Watching an exhausted LBJ withdraw his candidacy was like tasting blood," Geoffrey O'Brien later wrote. "Something was getting through. Maybe the young people could pull it off." During the first months of 1968, the spirit of the sixties seemed to be relit by the New Hampshire primary and LBJ's dramatic announcement.[6]

Then, four days later, the flickering flame of optimism again was extinguished: On April 4, a white drifter, James Earl Ray, assassinated Martin Luther King, Jr.

King had traveled to Memphis to lend support to striking sanitation workers, almost all of them black. He was aware of the potential for violence and wanted to avoid a tragedy such as the one that occurred earlier at Orangeburg, home of the predominately black college South Carolina State. For some time students there had protested a segregated bowling alley in town, illegal since the 1964 Civil Rights Act. In February, blacks began picketing, and after a few nights of demonstration police moved in, clubs swinging. The next evening students pelted cars driven by whites that passed their campus, and later they built a bonfire on campus. What followed was recorded in two different versions—the movement versus the Establishment. According to officials, when authorities arrived to extinguish the fire, snipers shot four times, wounding an officer. The authorities responded by opening fire, and the Associated Press reported, "Negro Students Trade Fire with Police and Troops." Not so, according to participant Cleveland Sellers: "The news media accepted and reported this lie as if it were gospel." According to him, the students were calm, huddled around the bonfire, confident that the authorities would do nothing as long as they remained on their campus. When one student stepped forward to place something in the fire, the cops started shooting, wounding many in the back or on the ground as they tried to crawl from the scene. Forty black students were wounded and three were killed. The police arrested Sellers for inciting to riot, and the governor claimed, "Black power advocates sparked the violence." Blacks disagreed. Roy Wilkins of the NAACP called for an investigation and H. Rap Brown proclaimed, "We will not forget the Orangeburg Massacre and we will revenge."

King wanted to avoid revenge in Memphis, and he also was publicizing his Poor People's Campaign, a forthcoming march on Washington by a coalition of poor from all races who would demand the next phase of the struggle—Congress must pass an "Economic Bill of Rights" that would vigorously enforce integration, quickly end housing discrimination, and most important, guarantee reasonable employment. "It didn't cost the nation anything to guarantee the right to vote, or to guarantee access to public accommodations," said King, "but we are dealing with issues now that will cost the nation something."

King was unusually somber in Memphis. He had been losing supporters for the last two years, attacked by conservative whites, black power advocates, and even many moderate blacks who were frustrated with his antiwar stance. By 1968, he had received fifty death threats, and as he told his audience on the night of April 3, "Well, I don't know what will happen now. But it really doesn't matter with me. Because I've been to the mountaintop. And I've seen the Promised Land. . . . Mine eyes have seen the glory of the coming of the Lord."

The next evening he was murdered, gunned down on the balcony of his motel. During the next few days, American restraint seemed to evaporate. Upon hearing the news, white students cheered in Arlington, Texas, and a delighted FBI agent in Atlanta declared, "They finally got the s.o.b.!" At the same time, Stokely Carmichael proclaimed, "When white America killed Dr. King, she declared war on us," and activist Alex Rodriquez felt, "White America killed Martin, and goddamit, you're gonna pay for this."[7]

Rioting swept the nation. Blacks poured out into the streets of over a hundred cities, venting their frustration. Sections of Boston, Detroit, and Harlem sank into chaos, but the worst was Washington. Over 700 fires turned the sky dark; smoke obscured the Capitol. Nationwide, officials called out more than 75,000 troops to patrol the streets, to keep the peace. The final casualty count was approximately 21,000 arrested, 3000 injured and 46 dead, all blacks but five. This because one violent white man slaughtered a nonviolent black man who had won the Nobel Peace Prize by calling on America to live up to its promise.

President Johnson declared a national day of mourning, and on that Sunday hundreds of thousands of Americans, black and white, marched together in their cities, many singing freedom songs in honor of Martin Luther King, Jr. The next day, his widow Coretta and her children conducted a silent memorial through the streets of Memphis with almost 20,000, and soon thereafter the city increased pay and benefits for sanitation workers, ending the strike. Tributes and condolences flowed in from all over the world, and on April 9 the funeral was held in Atlanta. A sea of humanity, perhaps 100,000 people, surrounded the Ebenezer Church. After the service, pallbearers placed the casket on a farm cart drawn by two mules, and a procession of 50,000 walked on Martin's last freedom march.

King's death shocked the nation and marked another turning point in the movement. Some 120 million Americans watched the funeral on television, saw the long lines of Democratic and Republican politicians, and witnessed the gentle weeping of average citizens, and of Mrs. John Fitzgerald Kennedy. The sixties generation had another event that they would never forget: "Where were you when . . .?" The assassination also killed one part of the movement, the phase of the civil rights struggle that began at Greensboro. More than any other person, King epitomized the dream of racial equality. He had inspired blacks and whites to become activists, to use nonviolent, dignified tactics to change the nation. Although he had been losing influence, he remained the only single focal point of the struggle. "For liberals, even for many black militants and radicals, he was the last black hope," wrote activist Todd Gitlin. "When he was murdered, it seemed that nonviolence went to the grave with him, and the movement was 'free at last' from restraint." A few radicals felt that with King dead, "the Panthers and the other militants would have a clear field to lead the revolution." Others were not so sure, for King also had an impact on other minorities who were beginning to flex their muscles and demand change. Mexican American organizer Cesar Chavez, who then was awakening the movement to the plight of farm workers in California, wrote to Mrs. King: "It is my belief that much of the courage which we have found in our struggle for justice in the fields has had its roots in the example set by your husband and by those multitudes who followed his non-violent leadership. We owe so much to Dr. Martin Luther King that words alone cannot express our gratefulness." Throughout the year there would be new calls for "brown power" and other forms of empowerment, while at the same time the black civil rights movement passed into another stage characterized by bickering and shouting. By the end of 1968, SNCC was dead, CORE was dying, and SCLC was disintegrating.

The assassination, along with the summer riots, also meant that understanding between black and white citizens began to deteriorate. Two black psychologists summed up race relations in 1968: Blacks "have had all they can stand. They will be harried no more. Turning from their tormentors, they are filled with rage. . . . White people have responded with a rage of their own. As the lines become more firmly drawn, exchange of information is the first casualty."[8]

King's death did have a legislative impact, however, for quickly thereafter Congress passed the Fair Housing Act, which began to fulfill King's dream of open housing by attacking racial discrimination in the sale or rental of property. Supported by blacks and Jews, both of whom had been kept out of many neighborhoods, the bill eventually would change the face of suburbs and allow all citizens who could afford good homes to move wherever they desired. Finally, eight years after the Greensboro 4 demanded a cup of coffee, the civil rights acts of 1964, 1965, 1968, along with the Twenty-fourth Amendment and numerous Supreme Court decisions, had ended the last legal vestiges of institutional racism in the Land of the Free. The nation began living up to its creed.

Yet all men are *not* created equal, and that was demonstrated time and again throughout the 1960s. Just a week after the burial of King it became apparent that those who shouted loudest were the most equal; they were the ones who received the most media attention. The cameras zoomed in on Columbia University.

During the mid-1960s student activism at Columbia was similar to that at many other fine universities across the nation. In fall semester 1966 some SDS members picketed military and CIA recruiters, and the next spring the students voted two to one not to have their class ranks released to draft boards, while some others confronted U.S. Marine recruiters. The number of campus activists had grown during those years, and many students participated in city marches that directed activism away from the campus.

Columbia was an appropriate target for student activism. The president, Grayson Kirk, a conservative by nature, epitomized the older generation. "He was doing Mozart, James Madison and Ralph Bunche," said a colleague, "while others were doing Bob Dylan, Che Guevara and Stokely Carmichael." Kirk also was a firm pillar of the establishment. He sat on the board of directors of many financial institutions, corporations such as Consolidated Edison and IBM, and on the Institute for Defense Analysis, which conducted weapons research at the university and was funded partly by the Defense Department and the CIA. To many students, IDA research on campus symbolized that the university was part of the industrial-military complex and supported the Vietnam War, but Kirk possessed little understanding of this and other student concerns, simply stating that young people "reject authority, take refuge in turbulent, inchoate nihilism." Also, and after years of campus demonstrations, Kirk's administration was strangely repressive. After activists confronted military recruiters in 1967, Kirk simply banned all indoor demonstrations. Although graduate students had been demanding some representation or role in their departments, the administration refused to budge. Many *in loco parentis* regulations still prevailed for undergraduates, and disciplinary action usually was handed out with little student participation. In March 1968 the university still was putting coeds on trial for "living with a boyfriend," a hearing that prompted sixty other females to demand the same charge.

Columbia also had a growing problem with its black students in the Student Afro-American Society and with local residents. Throughout its long history, few blacks had been admitted to the elite university, and that spring less than seventy were enrolled as undergraduates. Furthermore, the university was located in crowded Morningside Heights, close to Harlem, and it had been expanding by buying up old residential buildings and moving out tenants, almost all of them minorities. Tensions had been high since the 1964 Harlem riot, in which over a hundred blacks were injured and one killed, but apparently university administrators were oblivious to neighborhood concerns. Columbia intended to build a new gym in Morningside Park, and that raised additional issues: Should the neighborhood or university decide how to use the park, and should private concerns be able to use public land in crowded Manhattan? To many activists the gym idea smacked of racism—a rich, basically white corporation bullying poor, mostly black and Hispanic residents. The announcement prompted black students and neighbors to picket, some holding signs, "Gym Crow Must Go!"

Tension mounted during the spring semester. At a university memorial service for Martin Luther King, SDS campus chairman Mark Rudd and his cohorts rushed into the chapel, seized the pulpit, and shouted that it was hypocrisy for Columbia, a racist institution, to pay tribute to the great civil rights leader. These radicals also led an attack against Columbia's affiliation with the Institute for Defense Analysis. Six of them defied the ban on indoor protests and demonstrated in Low Library, the site of the president's office. When they were ordered to report to their college deans for disciplinary action, the six refused, were suspended, and Rudd proclaimed in an open letter to Kirk: "There is only one thing left to say. It may sound nihilistic to you, since it is the opening shot in a war of liberation. I'll use the words of Le Roi Jones, whom I'm sure you don't like a whole lot: 'Up against the wall, motherfucker, this is a stick-up.' "

The crude note, the vulgar rhetoric, set the tone for the upheaval at Columbia. Most students, however, paid little attention to the radicals until the spark on April 23. Then, approximately 500 activists, which included members from SDS and the Students Afro-American Society, held a rally at the campus sundial. At one point the crowd started to charge toward Low Library, but were repulsed by the more conservative Students for a Free Campus. What next? The demonstrators began marching to the proposed gym site, and some tore down a fence and briefly skirmished with police before they returned to the campus. Now what? While they were considering that, a black militant, Bill Sales, made a speech that revealed the radical thinking during spring 1968:

> If you're talking about revolution, if you're talking about identifying with the Vietnamese struggle, you don't need to go to Rockefeller Center, dig? There's one oppressor—in the White House, in Low Library, in Albany, New York. You strike a blow at the gym, you strike a blow for the Vietnamese people. You strike a blow at Low Library, you strike a blow for the freedom fighters in Angola, Mozambique, Portuguese Guinea, Zimbabwe, South Africa.

The radicals, obviously, were getting carried away by their own rhetoric. Yet placed in context of 1968, such statements seem more understandable. Many of these activists had been demonstrating for years against racism, war, and campus regulations; they had conducted hundreds of meetings and debates and participated in dozens of marches. The result? Nationally, racism and war continued, yet locally many universities were changing policies—but not Columbia. Kirk refused to budge. His response confronted these students with the agonizing feeling that they could not change the system. No matter how hard they tried, they could not succeed, and that depressing thought conflicted with their upbringing in the postwar era: "Son, in America you can do anything."

Frustrated, they lashed out against the Establishment—and the nearest target was their own Columbia. The radicals marched into Hamilton Hall. They took a dean hostage, proclaimed their demands, and prepared for the siege. In the middle of the night, black and white students argued, and black militants told white radicals to find their own building. The blacks remained in Hamilton and renamed it Malcolm X Hall. The disgruntled whites left and broke into Low Library, where they occupied President Kirk's office, sat at his desk and rifled some of his files. When the working day began, the phone rang as usual. James Kunen answered: "We are sorry, but Dr. Kirk will not be in today because Columbia is under new management."[9]

During the next two days a thousand students joined the occupation, entered and "liberated" three more buildings, barricaded themselves inside, and created communes. "The administration," the *Columbia Daily Spectator* declared, is "faced with its greatest challenge from the voices of student power in the history of the school." Students discussed politics, society, ideology, and the role of the university. Some became tired of endless discussions. "I wonder whether the Paris Commune was this boring," remarked Kunen, who like many also questioned his participation: "It's possible that I'm here to be cool or to meet people or to meet girls . . . or to get out of crew or to be arrested. Of course the possibility exists that I am here to precipitate some change at the University." Meanwhile, many occupiers entertained themselves. Some put on a strobe light show, others held a snake dance, and one couple even held a "movement marriage." The pastor pronounced them "children of the new age," and after a brief wedding procession around the campus they returned to their liberated building for the honeymoon. Communalism spread. Activists began calling each other "brother" and "friend." A student reported that his hall was a place "in which adult hypocrisies did not apply any longer, where people shared and shared alike," and another reported that her commune created a "society in which alienation is abnormal rather than normal." Friendly locals and students sent food, some of it delivered by Harlem's CORE office, and medical students from local hospitals set up an infirmary. Business as usual ceased at Columbia.

In response, President Kirk proclaimed that his administration would stay the course. "If these students succeed in disrupting the disciplinary procedure . . . then discipline at every university in America will be weakened. We are on trial here. Other universities will look to us for strength." Kirk had supporters, including a couple of thousand other students, conservatives who called themselves the Majority Coalition. They handed out flyers attacking the radicals' "tasteless, inconsiderate, and illegal" protest. Mostly composed of athletes and fraternity men, business or engineering majors, they demanded an end to the occupation and the resumption of classes, and even threatened to storm the buildings and evict the radicals.

All the while, an ad hoc faculty group attempted to negotiate between the occupiers and the administration. SDS members claimed to be spokesmen for the students, and they became as inflexible as President Kirk. The radicals made demands, the most important being that the university stop building the gym, sever ties with the Institute for Defense Analysis, establish an elected student-faculty disciplinary commission, and give amnesty for all those involved in the occupation. The faculty urged compromise. Kirk said no to amnesty, the regents said no to abandoning the gym, and Rudd called faculty efforts to mediate "bullshit."

The media tuned in, turned on. This was no rebellion in Austin, Madison, Seattle—even Berkeley—this was The City. The stage was colorful. Intellectuals rushed to Columbia to see revolution in action: Dwight Macdonald, Norman Mailer, Stephen Spender, Susan Sontag. Then came the leaders of the youth rebellion, proclaimed the press, the so-called movement heavies: Tom Hayden, Abbie Hoffman, H. Rap Brown, Stokely Carmichael. Music by the Grateful Dead. Journalists conducted interviews, papers sold, the great silent suburbs watched the action on TV. Meanwhile the press took no pictures of the IDA and were not interested in discussions about Columbia's ties with the Pentagon. Instead, stated one activist, the journalists noticed students who were the most "flamboyant, the ones who called for action, the ones whose rhetoric was 'Tear down the walls,' 'Seize buildings.' That was what the cameramen like to hear."[10]

Before sunrise on April 26 more than a thousand students and some faculty met in front of Low Library and chanted, "Kirk must go!" The administration called in plainclothes police, who charged into a line of faculty with billy clubs swinging. Many professors were hit, some knocked to the ground, prompting students to yell, "Fascist pigs!" and chant, "This is our university." Eventually, a vice president for the university addressed the crowd, announcing that plans to build the gym would be suspended, and that police would not be called in to evict the insurgents.

Four days later, after countless meetings, President Kirk ordered in the police. In the early morning hours of April 30 almost 300 students and some faculty stood in front of various occupied buildings, peacefully attempting to block the force of a thousand cops. To no avail: the men in blue marched forward with flashlights and blackjacks. As police entered some buildings, students gave up peacefully, or climbed out of windows to safety, and there was no violence. In other buildings, activists stood their ground. Some were belligerent, yelling "Up Against the Wall Mother-Fucker!" Others were peaceful and sang the school song or "The Star Spangled Banner." After the event, student Dionision Pabon reported:

> "We shall overcome" were the words that were being sung when the Gestapo came in. Circling us, our song got louder. The captain in charge held a piece of paper in front of him, looked at us, and then sicced his animals on us. They began beating, kicking, using crowbars and the debris from the barricades in their sadistic game. . . . After they had herded us, they then ran us through the gauntlet, stopping the flow of bodies as it got too much for them to handle. . . . I was called nigger and told to stand up and fight like a man. They then intensified so much around me that they began hitting each other trying to get to me. I was kicked in the head, face, back, stomach and groin. It felt like a herd of horses, instead of hooves—iron spikes.

The campus paper declared that the cops conducted a "brutal bloody show." Heads pounding, faces bleeding, students were dragged or walked out to waiting paddy wagons or ambulances. A hundred were injured, and over 700 were arrested, a tenth of the student body.

By 1968, one might have thought that a university president would have realized that relying on police force only resulted in violence and enraged the university community. If Berkeley's Free Speech Movement was too distant in the past, Wisconsin's Dow demonstration had occurred just the previous semester. But somehow these and dozens of other campus confrontations escaped Kirk. He called the cops, which played into the hands of the radicals and mobilized neutral professors and students who condemned the administration and police brutality. "Cops Out," declared the *Spectator*. "The police represent the lowest level to which Columbia has ever sunk," and the student strike committee flatly declared that by using force the administration "has forfeited its legitimate authority within this institution." Even many conservative students were appalled. "I had always respected the police," said one, "In this case the police action revolted me. I became a striker."

More students and many faculty joined the strike. Classes virtually ceased. The administration suspended radical leaders, which only resulted in a second occupation of Hamilton Hall in May. While most moderate students refused to become involved, some 250 radicals participated, and again Kirk called in the police. Violence erupted, a few radicals hurled bricks through windows and glass doors, and the police arrested approximately 170, again reuniting students against the administration. Almost half the students and faculty signed a petition demanding Kirk's resignation, and they continued boycotting classes. The administration suspended over seventy students and informed their draft boards that they had lost their deferments and were eligible for conscription. Meanwhile, the university canceled exams, and professors gave most students final grades of either pass or fail. Activists passed out flyers, "Grayson Kirk plans to hold Commencement as usual. We have other plans. A University which designs weapons for the Pentagon and the police, steals public park land to build a segregated gym, throws community residents out of their homes, and calls the cops to beat its own students cannot be allowed to carry out its business as usual. . . . The striking students will hold their own commencement ceremonies." [11]

The Columbia strike had national implications, for it contributed to the demise of the vital center of political life in America. Moderates of the older generation took a step to the right. The university trustees backed the administration and the use of force. "The police handled the situation very well," said one, and another added that the cops did "a magnificent job." From the House of Representatives, Republican Congressman Robert H. Michel declared that since "SDS tactics have succeeded in crippling a great university, the next target can be City Hall, the State Capitol, or even the White House." He added what many parents thought—university officials must "make clear that the schools are being run for purposes of education, not as field laboratories for revolution—domestic or imported." The liberal press also edged right. *Newsweek* trivialized the student demands and instead concentrated on their obscene language and unconventional behavior: the occupiers of President Kirk's office smoked his cigars, drank his sherry, and "urinated in a wastebasket." The *New York Times* labeled the radicals "extremist forces" and "disruptive nihilists" and called on students and faculty to isolate the radicals so they do not do "irreparable harm to the universities and to the whole democratic process." And conservative business journals declared war. *Barron's* proclaimed, "The scene might have been the University of Havana or Peking." The student's tactics "represented the latest assault by a revolutionary movement which aims to seize first the universities and then the industries of America." *Fortune* agreed, declaring that the students were "acting out a revolution—not a protest, and not a rebellion, but an honest-to-God revolution."

Many student activists took a step left. The *Spectator* blamed the upheaval on the administration, claiming that Kirk chose to ignore the students, and that the use of police only demonstrated that administrators were "too foolish to be called evil." Students across the nation read almost daily articles about the upheaval in their campus papers, and most sympathized with their counterparts at Columbia, especially after the brutal police attack. Furthermore, by 1968 underground papers had spread across America. Movement reporters from Liberated News Service rushed to the scene, "Berkeley East," and dispatched their articles and photographs to 300 underground subscribers. Many undergrounds also published documents from President Kirk's secret files that suggested that the university was grabbing land in Morningside Heights, that the establishment press did have close contacts with the university and was writing biased and even untrue reports. With movement information now flooding underground and campus press offices, "Columbia" increased a sense of cohesion in the sixties generation and symbolized "Us against Them." To many, Columbia again proved that the Establishment was corrupt. Time for "revolutionary social change," declared a writer in *Rat.* "What made Columbia happen and made it important was that hundreds of people saw that the needs of our generation and the goals of the world revolutionary struggle are one. We, the youth, have no place but a revolutionary one in the present-day decaying America. We must discover how to live human lives."[12]

The idea spread—revolution! Few stopped to define the term, for if one was young one understood what it meant. Activists hung pictures of their new heroes in dorm rooms and apartments: Che, Ho, Malcolm X, Castro, even Lenin. Students dressed in work shirts and army surplus jackets read Mao's mottos in his *Little Red Book.* The 1960s had moved from Greensboro and Thoreau to Columbia and Mao. Long-haired students rapped about conflict and change, evolution and revolution, about creating "two, three, many Columbias," and they began using the Germanic, or Nazi, spelling for their nation: "Amerika." A university's only function, proclaimed Mark Rudd, was "the creation and expansion of a revolutionary movement." Others rapped about radicalizing new students and used terms like "vanguard" and "cadre."

The revolution fantasy seemed to inch closer that spring as the youth revolt suddenly blossomed in numerous nations—French students rebelled against their antiquated educational establishment; Korean students threw fire bombs at military police; English students held sit-ins and demanded power at their universities; German radicals revolted at the Free University of Berlin; young Greeks clashed with their military regime; Japanese radicals battled with police and performed snake dances at Tokyo University; and Czechoslovakians took to the streets demanding the end of Soviet rule during Prague Spring.

The revolution was coming, at least that is what a few outspoken radicals proclaimed. Tom Hayden felt that violence "could not be ignored as an option," and he wrote that Columbia was a new tactical stage in the movement "from the overnight occupation of buildings to permanent occupations . . . from symbolic civil disobedience to barricaded resistance." Radical students would take over college buildings, bringing universities to a standstill, and that would force the government to change policy in Vietnam or send troops to occupy campuses. Then the student rebellion would spread to the cities, and create a crisis too massive for the police to control. Students were bringing the war home. "We are moving toward power—the power to stop the machine if it cannot be made to serve humane ends."

Other students began to consider another notion first proclaimed at Berkeley, "the issue is not the issue." As Todd Gitlin explained, the Free Speech Movement and other mass movements are "not simply 'about' free speech, nor even simply 'about' the right to organize for political action, but finally it is 'about' the necessity of revolt from the gargantuan, depersonalized, mass-production multiversity." By 1968, more activists were thinking that the purpose of any issue was ultimately to create a confrontation with authority. The establishment would respond, usually by instituting stern regulations or by employing police power. Demonstrators would get beaten, expelled, or arrested. That would create a sense of community among activists, and often radicalize moderate students. When a conservative Berkeley councilman asked Michael Rossman, "If we give in to your present demand will this satisfy you, or is this only one of a long list of demands?" Rossman replied, "Don't worry, we'll always be one demand ahead of you."[13]

After Columbia there would be new demands that never could be met, new issues that were not the issue, as America in 1968 became a Theater of the Absurd. Some SDS radicals, for example, opposed the Resistance movement, labeling resisters "sacrificial lambs," shouting that revolution would never come if activists accepted jail terms instead of creating ferment in the military. Others claimed that the ultimate radical resistance was to commit suicide, thus denying body and soul to the Establishment. As frustrations mounted, to shock, surprise, or be outlandish became the radical style. Tom Hayden approached a McCarthy activist and greeted him, "Why are you a whore for McCarthy?" Speaking of pacifist minister William Sloane Coffin, a radical declared, "Liberals like Coffin are the enemy. He must be destroyed." Jerry Rubin declared, "Open the jails, let everybody out, and then put the pigs in," and young father Abbie Hoffman screamed, "Kill your parents!" When Mark Rudd was asked about the issues at Columbia, he claimed on three different occasions, "The issues were symbolic. . . . I made them all up. . . . Every fucking issue was real." What was real? What was fantasy? A popular saying that year,

"Be Realistic—Demand the Impossible." It seemed strangely appropriate, therefore, that after a radical seized a dean and a building at Columbia he would proclaim, "We've got something going here and now we've just got to find out what it is." This was not revolution; this was 1968.

The outrageous rhetoric led many to assume, as one historian later wrote, that in 1968 the "goal of the movement became the seizure of power." No, the radicals called for revolution—but that was all. No students at Columbia picked up guns and shot at the cops, something true of virtually every student-police confrontation throughout the sixties. Jerry Rubin might have boasted during the March on the Pentagon that "crazy revolutionaries . . . are ready to burn the whole motherfucker down," but they never poured on the gas and lit the match. This was a Rhetorical Revolution, something most journalists and their middle-class readers did not seem to understand.

In the confusion, most activists did understand. "If there is a road to power," Gitlin realized, "we have no map for it." The movement raised issues, created activity, but because it was so diverse by 1968 it could not arrive at a common denominator, an answer for the nation's ills. Nor could it even agree on tactics. Frustrated, some shouted "Revolution!" or talked about violence. But "all of us knew," Paul Potter recalled, "the cops had almost all the force," and the *Spectator* added: "There is no question that the police are stronger and better-armed. . . . In any confrontation Columbia students can only lose." The shouting, Hayden later admitted, was a reflection of the "apparent failure of the liberal and non-violent strategies."[14] By 1968 the movement was composed of millions of Americans, and it was much more ingrained in the social fabric than a few movement heavies in blue work shirts and red bandanas shouting "Revolution!"

The radicals never had more than superficial influence within the broad movement. SDS received scores of headlines at Columbia, meaning that its campus membership soared that year and peaked in 1969. Yet the irony was that nationally the organization was disintegrating. Two months after Columbia SDS held its national conference, and the radical bravado of some of its members killed what remained of the organization. SDS splintered into factions, babbled into civil war, as many of its members became engrossed in bragging about who was the most revolutionary. Eager for a story, the establishment press rushed to the scene and reported that now the entire movement was being led by anarchists and radicals in organizations such as Progressive Labor, Spartacists, Trotskyites, and eventually the Weathermen.

Most activists were humored but not concerned about movement heavies calling for revolution. "Tom Hayden is in Chicago now," wrote James Kunen from his jail cell after being arrested for occupying Low Library.

"As an Outside Agitator, he has a lot of outsides to agitate in. Like the Lone Ranger, he didn't even wave good-bye, but quietly slipped away, taking his silver protest buttons to another beleaguered campus." At Columbia, as at other universities during the sixties, the vast majority of students in the occupation participated because they wanted to reform the university. Many more joined the Students for a Restructured University than SDS. The *Spectator* polled the student body and revealed broad support for the aims of the occupation and broad opposition to the tactics of the radicals. By three to one students wanted to end construction of the gym and all ties with the Institute for Defense Analysis, yet by the same margin they condemned infringing the rights of other students by shutting down the university. When asked whether Columbia was a good place to attend college, three-fourths said yes, and that response came from both strikers and non-strikers. The upheaval was more radical in form because of mounting frustration and subsequent alienation, most of it caused by the endless war. A Columbia vice president said that there were two wars, one in Vietnam and the other on campus, and a dean remarked, "If you could name a university where students aren't concerned with Vietnam and the cities, I'd be scared to death of the place."

At Columbia, pragmatism eventually won. The students continued to press for their demands, and by the beginning of fall semester their efforts resulted in victory. Kirk resigned, and so did his vice president. The new university administration asked the courts to dismiss criminal charges against building occupiers, pledged that the gym would not be built without the community's consent, ended its affiliation with the IDA, dropped the ban on indoor demonstrations, and granted students a "voice and representation at the highest level of decision-making."[15]

Nationally, antiwar activists also pressed for a pragmatic demand—end the war. In April the Student Mobilization Committee sponsored a national strike against the war, and a million college and high school students, faculty and teachers, boycotted classes. During spring semester, the last one for which graduate students had deferments, nearly 40,000 activists conducted over 200 demonstrations at over 100 campuses. Others resorted to more radical action. Nine men and women, most of them Catholic priests and sisters, walked into the Selective Service office of Catonsville, Maryland. As the staff continued working, they marched over to the draft files, pulled out all 1-A folders, and dumped them into trash baskets. Before the astonished workers could stop them, the nine were out in the street, lighting the files with homemade napalm. The Catonsville 9, as they became known, were led by Catholic priests Philip and Daniel Berrigan, who justified burning draft files by stating, "Some property has no right to exist."

Intemperate statements, massive antiwar marches, student strikes, and violent riots following King's assassination all created an uneasy atmosphere in the nation that spring as politicians campaigned for the presidency. While some radicals were forsaking politics, other activists and ordinary citizens watched the campaign, looked for someone, anyone, who could chart a path to domestic tranquility and out of Vietnam.

Vice President Hubert Humphrey announced his candidacy in April, pledging an end to the war without "humiliation or defeat," calling for a return to "the politics of joy." He appealed to organized labor and to older, traditional Democrats. At that time, only thirteen states had primaries, and so Humphrey began working behind the scene to gain the support of party regulars. So effective was the Democratic machine that within weeks the vice president could claim that he had the support of about 900 of the 1300 delegates needed to secure the presidential nomination.

Not many in the movement supported the vice president; for them the battle was between Eugene McCarthy and Bobby Kennedy. RFK's announcement to run for the nomination had split the movement, and activists wondered about the platform of the two candidates. Kennedy seemed more concerned about poverty, and both condemned racism. RFK appealed to minorities by stating that he wanted to rehabilitate ghettos by using private enterprise to help establish black businesses, and that he would follow the recommendations of the Kerner Commission, which the Johnson administration said were too expensive. McCarthy supported King's idea of expanding civil rights to include legislation for jobs, education, housing, and health care. Concerning the war, both candidates supported a bombing halt, negotiations, and granting the Vietcong's political partner, the National Liberation Front, some role in a future government of South Vietnam. The Minnesotan eventually went farther, stating that he was prepared to endorse a coalition government for South Vietnam that would include the NLF, and that it was time for American forces to disengage: "We shall take our steel out of the land of thatched huts." That was too radical for RFK, who was not willing to abandon America's commitment and who maintained that America should take retaliatory action if the negotiations failed. Both candidates criticized the cold war mentality that encouraged the United States to be the world judge and policeman, and McCarthy went farther, attacking the defense establishment. "If elected, I would go to the Pentagon," and he threatened to fire Secretary of State Rusk, Selective Service Director Hershey, and FBI Director Hoover. Kennedy was too much of an insider, too close to party heavyweights, to make such bold statements.

McCarthy's message, although expressed impassively, was more radical than Kennedy's. Nevertheless, the ideas of both candidates in 1968 came remarkably close to what young activists had declared six years earlier at

Port Huron: in effect, viable contenders for president of the United States were adopting the new left position, again demonstrating the rapid evolution of American politics during the 1960s. Volunteers for both RFK and McCarthy felt that their candidate would make a difference, that they were liberal politicians who not only would change their views but also would use the system to bring about a new America. What journalist Ward Just wrote about McCarthy during the New Hampshire primary also was true about Kennedy later that spring: the candidate was bringing alienated students "back into the traditional framework of American politics. That is, off the streets and into the electoral process."

Yet RFK usually *seemed* more radical, and that was because he and his advisers paved a colorful campaign trail into the ghettos and barrios and wrote speeches filled with rhetorical flourishes. Since the Nixon-Kennedy debate of 1960, these politicos were aware of the impact of television politics, the importance of "image" over "issues." Kennedy himself admitted that he got the support of the average and good students, while McCarthy won the intellectual ones who wrote the campus newspapers and led student organizations. Yet McCarthy seemed too bland, or as Norman Mailer quipped, not like a president but "like the dean of the finest English department in the land." McCarthy sounded like a philosopher; Kennedy appeared as an evangelist. RFK's relatively long hair and boyish face, attracted many young Americans, "the squealers," reported David Halberstam, the "shrieking teen-agers." Girls chased Bobby, tearing his tie, grabbing a foot, like their older sisters in 1963 had screamed after the Beatles. But many others of the sixties generation were drawn to the "Bobby phenomenon." New left intellectuals such as Staughton Lynd, Robert Scheer, Jack Newfield, Carl Oglesby, and Tom Hayden supported RFK, and so did activists such as Abbie Hoffman, John Lewis, and the leader of the United Farm Workers' Union, Cesar Chavez. The senator had read the writings of Camus and even of Hayden, had met with many radicals and black militants, had demonstrated sensitivity to the poor. These activists believed that Bobby could obtain the support of both students and workers, and that he had the best chance to win the presidency.[16] To many students, RFK represented hope. As he often said to college crowds, "Some people see things as they are and say 'why?' I see things that never were and say 'why not?' "

In May, Kennedy and McCarthy had their first political confrontation in the Indiana primary. RFK won. Kennedy had strong name recognition and afterward a Gallup poll found that nationally he attracted minorities, the poor, blue-collar workers, and many voters under thirty, while older, educated white suburbanites favored McCarthy. Kennedy also won in Nebraska, but then McCarthy dealt the first electoral loss to the Kennedy family, winning the primary in Oregon.

The stage was set for a showdown, and the venue was California. Kennedy called in all the family's political debts, and with a large staff of professionals he moved into the state and conducted a *Blitzkrieg*, shaking hands and grinning from San Francisco to San Diego, from Watts to Hollywood. Along the campaign trail supporters waved placards, "Bobby is Groovy," "Sock it to 'em, Bobby," "Go, Bobby, Go." RFK assembled scholars, novelists, actors—Arthur Schlesinger, Jr., Paul Samuelson, Norman Mailer, Truman Capote, Henry Fonda, Shirley MacLaine—and they spoke at universities while the candidate met with black militants in Oakland and jumped on a train for a whistle-stop tour through the Central Valley. Earlier in March, RFK had rushed to California to attend a large mass with Cesar Chavez, who had been organizing farm workers and protesting wages and labor conditions by boycotts, strikes, even fasting for twenty-five days. Upon the candidate's return, large Mexican American crowds cheered him enthusiastically. McCarthy also arrived in the Golden State and continued the Children's Crusade. "We hopped through sunny California," recalled an aide, "the airports, the campuses, the freeways and shopping centers. Everywhere we had bands and crowds of students who kept McCarthy happy." As bands played "When the Saints Come Marching In," students waved signs, including one of the senator's favorites: "We Believe You." McCarthy also assembled actors— Carl Reiner, Barbra Streisand, Walter Matthau—as students and even flower children answered telephones and sent out campaign literature. "What I remember is bright young faces," wrote the senator, "homemade posters, peace beads, and amulets."

The race was tight, and after the politicians made various charges, McCarthy challenged Kennedy to a debate. RFK agreed, and interest soared. Yet the debate was inconclusive, even anticlimactic. The candidates disagreed on little of substance, and neither at that time would demand an immediate withdrawal from Vietnam, disappointing many activists.

On June 5 the people voted: 46 percent for Kennedy and 42 for McCarthy. A narrow victory, but enough for RFK to tell an adviser, "I'm the only candidate against the war that can beat Humphrey." RFK left his hotel suite and went to the ballroom where he took the podium and waved to the cheering crowd. He attacked Humphrey for avoiding the primaries, and he appealed to McCarthy's followers to join him, congratulating the Minnesotan for making "citizen participation a new and powerful force in our political life." He called for an end to violence and division: "We can start to work together. We are a great country, an unselfish country, and a compassionate country. I intend to make that my basis for running."[17] The movement again was going to change America.

"KENNEDY SHOT" declared the headlines of the *Los Angeles Times*. Sirhan Sirhan, a deranged Jordanian, pulled out a pistol and fired eight times, wounding three others and shooting the candidate in the head. Kennedy died early the next morning. The body was put on a plane with his widow and two others—Jacqueline Kennedy and Coretta Scott King. Only eight weeks after the death of Martin Luther King, this time there were no riots, only a stunned, morbid silence. For a day the coffin rested at St. Patrick's Cathedral in New York City. Thousands waited for hours to pay their last respects, people of all races, all creeds, from the president to the poor. President Johnson proclaimed a day of mourning. One black woman mumbled, "Seems like anybody speaks up for us, they get killed," and another wept, "Our friend is gone. Oh, Jesus, he is gone."

The next day the coffin was placed in the last car of a train. Filled with admirers, it began the slow journey to Arlington Cemetery where Robert was buried next to his brother John. Along the way perhaps a million citizens waited. Arthur Schlesinger, Jr., reported, "Some stood at rigid attention, hand over heart. Some waved. Some buried their faces in their hands. Some knelt. Some held up hand-printed signs—REST IN PEACE, ROBERT. . . . Many cried. Some threw roses at the last car. Some as if in a daze followed the train down the roadbed."

"The sixties came to an end in a Los Angeles hospital on June 6, 1968," wrote Richard Goodwin. Jack Newfield left the campaign and went home, sat down and wondered about the death: "Why did it happen? What did it mean? What did I think about violence? My thoughts were not clear: they were not strong enough to support my feelings. I finally wrote down just three words on a lined yellow pad. 'He is irreplaceable.' "[18]

To many activists, especially the first wave of activists, RFK was the last hope. Many had worked in the system to support him, and now he was gone, the only man who might be able to bring about a new America. Todd Gitlin admitted, "We still wanted the system to work, and hated it for failing us." A writer in the *Berkeley Barb* noted that he and his friends were "badly shaken," and Tom Hayden shared the "feelings of loss and despair and grim, grim days ahead." The sixties were becoming the decade of frustration. Carl Oglesby remembered:

> Martin Luther King dead in April and just a couple months later Kennedy. What do you do? Go get a new hero and spend years teaching him and having the debates and doing the sit-ins . . . do it all over again while the people are dying in Vietnam? . . . That's why people started talking about revolution, because reform had been made to seem like a dead-end street. How many times do you climb that tree just to have it chopped down beneath you?

For the younger members of the sixties generation, the second wave, RFK had symbolized the renewal of hope. As nursing student Rose Eder recalled, "JFK's death was a tragedy for our generation, but Bobby was going to pull some meaning out of death. After Johnson, RFK was going to restore the magic and vision. He was going to relight the torch."[19]

The killing raised more agonizing questions for 1968: Why was America so violent? What type of people were we becoming? What was wrong with the nation? RFK in death became the great enigma of the 1960s: Would he have won the nomination in August, would he have won the presidency in November? If so, would he have ended the war honorably, would he have brought citizens together, would he have fulfilled the dream?

Questions pondered but never answered by many activists, questions simply not considered by most citizens, since by that summer middle America was becoming tired of 1968, yearning to escape from the tumultuous year.

Even during 1968 escape was possible. While the war was on television every night, while draft calls continued to increase, there still was no general mobilization as there was during World War II, no call-up of the reserves as during Korea. Furthermore, a relatively small number of the sixties generation were asked to fight. Of approximately 27 million young men who came of draft age from 1964 to 1973, little more than 2 million were drafted, while almost 9 million enlisted, meaning that about 40 percent of sixties generation men served in their nation's armed forces during its longest war. The majority of parents and sons, therefore, were not directly affected, and they had the option of tuning out the war, changing the channel, going to the high school football game.

This was true of most small towns across the land, including Millersburg, Pennsylvania. In 1968 a journalist visited and found that the majority of residents were "the indifferent" who thought little about Vietnam. As one admitted, concerning "who's right, who's wrong, what are we going to do about it . . . I really couldn't care less." But during America's war most citizens would not admit that, and at the same time they were foggy about Vietnam and held fuzzy ideas about the conflict. "I like to think of my country as Number One," said one resident. "If we are in a thing of this sort, we have to win it." Fight to Win: My Country Right or Wrong. Thus, they detested critics who challenged the government. Indeed, they hated protesters more than the Vietcong, and many locals supported the war only because many were demonstrating against it. In addition, residents in these Middletowns now had arrived at the conclusion that began surfacing in the press earlier—war protesters were synonymous with hippies, "a hairy youth with needle marks on his arm, wearing a blanket and flowers, who is more than likely also a Communist. A hippie does not believe in God, family, private property, good grooming, personal daintiness, Bing Crosby, Bart Starr or almost anything else that

Millersburg believes in." Such feelings were supported by a Harris survey that found that by three to one Americans felt that protesters were "peaceniks and hippies having a ball."

Millersburg citizens, and many others, had a ball by watching TV—which throughout 1968 not only was bringing chaos into the living room but also was providing the great escape from national problems. Millions tuned into "Bewitched," and Emmy awards were given to the "The Monkees" and to "Mission Impossible," which seemed the most appropriate program title for the year and perhaps for the decade. Bill Cosby of "I Spy" became the first black to win an Emmy, and Don Adams received an award for the best comedy show, "Get Smart." The "Lucy Show" still was popular and so was "The Andy Griffith Show." During the turbulence, more citizens tuned into the last episode of "Howdy Doody" than to the war, while fans watched an incredible spring and summer of sports: UCLA's NCAA basketball championship; Jim "Catfish" Hunter's perfectly pitched baseball game; the first Hispanic to win golf's U.S. Open, Lee Trevino; Bobby Unser's victory at the Indy 500; Billie Jean King's third singles championship at Wimbledon; the first African American to win the tennis U.S. Open, Arthur Ashe. As the Detroit Tigers slugged their way to a matchup against the St. Louis Cardinals in the World Series, athletes from all over the world prepared for the autumn Olympics in Mexico City. During the summer James Kunen recalled, "In the pennant year of 1967 I used to say that the Red Sox stood for all that's good in the world—happiness, enthusiasm, courage. Then I began to say they *were* all that's good in the world." [20]

Others escaped that summer by floating away from the mainstream. The youth culture had seized cities along the East Coast and began flooding into the heartland. In New York's Lower East Side, more hippies mingled with artistic bohemians as the area bloomed into flower power. Crowds of colorful people were reading Don McNeil's hip tales in the *Village Voice* or articles in the new undergrounds, *Other Scenes, Rat, Win,* and *New York Free Press*. Bill Graham had established Fillmore East and Bob Fass played "free form radio" on WBAI. The Diggers were giving away food and clothing at their Free Store, and while some were laughing at the satirical play about Lyndon Johnson, *MacBird,* others were singing along with the musical *Hair* which declared the dawning of the Age of Aquarius. In the nation's capital, a hippie might be reading *Washington Free Press* or an activist might peruse the *Student Mobilizer*. In Boston, kids were publishing *Avatar,* and in Philadelphia the *Distant Drummer*. More long-haired youth were appearing inland, speading the word in the Austin *Rag,* Champaign-Urbana *Walrus,* Chicago *Seed,* Detroit *Fifth Estate,* Madison *Connections,* Milwaukee *Kaleidoscope,* or Atlanta *Great Speckled Bird.*

Earlier, some of the sixties generation had been divided between activists and the counterculture, between the "fists" and the "heads." Activists complained that hippies were infantile escapists who could not face political reality and instead dreamed days away in purple haze, and hippies responded that the "New Left writes so many position papers that they have no time for sex. They just take a position." But by 1968 that division was receding because both sides realized that they had more in common with each other than they had with the Establishment.

The same was true for many young blacks, for the counterculture also was having some impact on them. There was a natural alliance between hippies and blacks, for both were attempting to escape from racism and both were disliked and distrusted by residents in the suburbs. The "poor Negro of whatever age," wrote one observer, "was apt to understand the young flower children, often better than their own parents or teachers." Furthermore, black power and African ideas were merging with the revolt against the image of the middle-class Negro. A few young blacks began to reject their parent's attempts to dress like white Americans and instead began experimenting with new styles such as African dress and Afro hair. Some also began using a new term to describe themselves: "BLACK IS BEAUTIFUL," proclaimed a "black person herself" in the *San Francisco Express Times*.[21] "Black is cool because it's dark trying to seek the light. That's why we call ourself BLACK because we are plain and trying to be ourself and not nobody else!!!!"

While some in the sixties generation were experimenting with their emerging culture, others were making one last attempt to work within the political system. RFK's assassination meant that the movement's last hope for that year was Eugene McCarthy. "He was the only man who was in a position to tell America what had happened," wrote one of his young aides, "to tell us who we were and what we must now do." But McCarthy was not up to the task. He had created a cause, but could not organize it around his candidacy. Perhaps he did not have the necessary character. Perhaps he did not want the responsibility. When a reporter asked him if he thought he could win the presidency, he replied: "Who would want the job?" Or perhaps he realized all along that he could not beat Humphrey, could not lure traditional Democratic delegates to cast their vote for a renegade at the convention. While the McCarthy movement grew that summer, his campaign sputtered. Again, the issue was more important than the leader. To crowds of 50,000 eager listeners in Boston and Chicago, the candidate delivered impassive lectures, leaving a trail of liberal suburbanites and college kids mumbling to themselves, "It was kind of vague, wasn't it?. . . . Yea, why didn't he tell us what to do?"

Other candidates were telling audiences exactly what to do, for the death of Bobby Kennedy also increased the chance that a conservative could win the presidency in November, ending what remained of liberalism in the 1960s. During the summer there were two contenders running for the conservative vote: George Wallace and Richard Nixon.

Wallace had been the Democratic governor of Alabama, and in that capacity was best known for standing up to the federal government in 1963 and attempting to stop the integration of the University of Alabama, pledging "Segregation now! Segregation tomorrow! Segregation forever!" "Forever" was brief in Alabama, lasting only a few weeks; nevertheless, many citizens saw Wallace as the last effort to preserve states' rights and the traditional racial order. Wallace became the symbol of the Southern Way of Life. In 1964 he took his message north, and during the Democratic presidential primaries in Wisconsin and Indiana he surprised pundits by winning more than a third of the vote against President Johnson, demonstrating white resentment toward federal orders to integrate schools in northern cities. The governor predicted, "By the fall of 1968 the people in Cleveland and Chicago and Gary and St. Louis will be so god-damn sick and tired of federal interference in their local schools, they'll be ready to vote for Wallace by the thousands."

The white backlash continued to grow in mid-decade as government implemented busing plans for integration, as students protested on campuses, as activists demonstrated against the war, as youths flaunted social norms, as blacks became more militant, and as cities burned. A Wallace staffer wrote: "Recent rioting and looting and the enactment of the so-called open housing bill have made thousands . . . realize that only Wallace has come forward with real solutions and he is the only man that will save our country from anarchy and its consequence—dictatorship." Law and order, Wallace demanded: Get Tough! "The people are going to be fed up with the sissy attitude of Lyndon Johnson and all the intellectual morons and theoreticians he has around him."[22]

The governor realized that he never could win the Democratic nomination, so he formed the American Independent party and declared his run for the White House. To spread the word, he enlisted numerous conservative activists to establish a grass-roots organization. Four were young southern lawyers who directed about thirty other Alabama attorneys. Labeling their task "Mission Impossible," they visited each state and researched election laws so they could get their candidate on the ballot. Others collected money or organized. In Alabama, for example, fifty residents of the small town of Eufaula dug deep and raised more than $11,000, while many students began to join Youth for Wallace. "He wants to get rid of Communists who are just waiting to overthrow what ever is good for the country," said one Houston teen, while older conservatives like Louisiana Congressman John Rarick joined the campaign. Claiming that young people were so confused that they "fall prey . . . to the empty philosophy and promises made to them by the vultures of the New Left," he urged students to support Wallace in his "movement toward patriotism, order, cleanliness, health and decency of spirit!" Liberal and radical students were appalled by Wallace, booing or jeering him on campus, but more conservative activists were almost religious in their devotion. By September, Youth for Wallace boasted 6000 members on over a hundred campuses and his activists collected nearly 3 million signatures, placing the governor on the ballot of all 50 states.

Wallace had many simple solutions to complex American problems. After Tet, all candidates shifted from escalation to de-escalation in Vietnam, all except for Wallace. "I think we've got to pour it on," proclaimed the governor, and then for his running mate he picked tough-talking, cigar-chewing retired Air Force General Curtis LeMay. The hero of strategic bombing in World War II, LeMay quickly became famous for his proposed strategy for victory: it would be "most efficient" to use nuclear weapons against the enemy. The U.S. should "bomb 'em back to the stone age."

Wallace also mastered the art of one-liners in his bid to become the spokesman of blue-collar populism. The "briefcase totin' bureaucrats, ivory-tower guideline writers, bearded anarchists, smart-aleck editorial writers and pointy-headed professors" knew nothing, he claimed; they "don't know how to park a bicycle straight." As for the secretary of state, "The other day Dean Rusk said the Vietnam protests had Communist elements in it. Well, the cab drivers of my state knew that five years ago." The workin' man should run the country, he said, and the Supreme Court should leave the states alone; Chief Justice Earl Warren "doesn't have enough legal brains in his head to try a chicken thief in my home county." His plan to stop rioting was simple: "We ought to turn this country over to the police for two or three years and everything would be all right." He lashed out at all those who demonstrated—"put a crease in their forehead"—and as for campus protests, "Any Alabama student who takes the extreme line like sending blood and money to the Vietcong, or burning his draft card, or urging our troops not to fight—we'll expel the sons-of-bitches."[23]

Wallace attracted attention, for he was a feisty speaker, and also because during summer 1968 he continually expanded his message, as he said, reaching out to "this average man on the street, this man in the textile mill, this man in the steel mill, this barber, this beautician, the policeman on the beat," even "the little businessman." The governor appealed to blue-collar workers and to what Nixon the next year would label the "great silent majority," all those who felt that they had been left out of the 1960s—whites who prided themselves for being god-fearing and law-abiding, who practiced "traditional values" and the Puritan ethic.

Many of these whites felt that LBJ's social programs did not help them and that the federal government was no longer on their side, and they were appalled that the administration was enforcing the Supreme Court's rulings on school prayer and desegregation. Especially in the South these whites charged that LBJ "took God out of the schools and put niggers in."

Wallace never had a chance to win, of course, but he might lose the presidency for Nixon. The Republican, therefore, devised his southern strategy. He campaigned in Dixie stressing traditional values, but unlike Wallace, Nixon behaved "presidential," a trait he promoted throughout the nation. Most citizens felt that during mid-decade he outgrew his earlier image of a rabid anti-communist who was vicious, untrustworthy, even unstable. Throughout 1968 he had presented himself as a moderate conservative, a mature leader, an honest family man who stood for law and order: the New Nixon.

In the first week of August the Republicans held their convention in Miami, or as a journalist labeled the affair, "a love-in on the beach." Delegates arrived to find the competition intense, not so much between the candidates but the female sideshows outside and inside the hotels. The "Rocky Girls" appeared, supporters of New York Governor Nelson Rockefeller. Posed in their miniskirts, radiant with golden tennis tans, these coeds from schools such as Sarah Lawrence and Wellesley chanted "We Want Rocky!" Not to be outdone, the "Nixonettes" marched in, a hundred off-duty stewardesses and dozens of New Orleans dancers in miniskirts, white boots, and blue jackets. Inside the convention hall the atmosphere was less exciting. The Reverend Billy Graham offered prayers and John Wayne gave an inspirational reading, "Why I Am Proud to Be an American," after which The Duke boosted his new movie *The Green Berets*, a typical western that happened to be set in Vietnam. That movie was more dramatic than the show on the floor, for the nomination was over before the first delegate arrived. The former vice president had won every primary and so he easily fought off challenges from liberal Rockefeller and conservative Governor Ronald Reagan. After the first ballot, placards proclaimed, Nixon's the One!

The nominee's acceptance speech was more serious, expressing themes felt by the silent majority during 1968:

> My Fellow Americans: When the strongest nation in the world can be tied down for four years in a war in Vietnam with no end in sight, when the richest nation in the world can't manage its own economy, when the nation with the greatest tradition of the rule of law is plagued by unprecedented lawlessness, when a nation that has been known for a century for equality of opportunity is torn by unprecedented racial violence, and when the President of the United States cannot travel abroad or to any major city at home without fear of a hostile

demonstration—then it's time for new leadership for the United States of America.

Nixon was concerned about support for Wallace, and that was one reason he nominated a Republican with a sharp tongue from a border state to be his running mate, Maryland Governor Spiro Agnew. The governor supported the war "100 percent," had a son in the U.S. Navy, and proclaimed that Humphrey was "squishy soft" on Communism. Agnew had won election running against a segregationist, had gained the support of moderate blacks while talking tough to black leaders and adopting a hard-line stance to squash rioting in Baltimore. "If one wants to pinpoint the cause of the riots," he proclaimed, "it would be this permissive climate," and he said that it would be justified for a policeman to shoot a looter. When black students staged an orderly sit-in at the state house to protest conditions at their campuses, the governor arrested over 200. "Governor Agnew has a good record for dealing firmly with rioters," said Ronald Reagan, and Nixon added, "That guy Agnew is really an impressive fellow. He's got guts."[24]

The Republicans left Miami. Sunburned and contented, they turned on their televisions to watch the Democratic delegates arrive at their convention in Chicago. They would be reminded of Napoleon's adage: "Never interfere with the enemy when he is in the process of destroying himself."

Liberals had been destroying themselves for three years, and the process climaxed in the Windy City. The venue was ripe for confrontation. In 1964 the Democrats had promised integrated delegations for all states, and now they were heading to Chicago. So were other types of Democrats, many of them associated with other parts of the movement such as the Assembly of Unrepresented People, or two groups developed by Allard Lowenstein, the Concerned Democrats and the Coalition for an Open Convention, all organizations that loosely fit into what was being called "new politics." These activists wanted to continue working in the system although, in effect, they had adopted the new left position: Democrats should turn from the war and military-industrial complex and move back to social programs for "the people" in an attempt to show more concern about "the quality of life." New politics was boosted in 1966 when Berkeley antiwar activist Robert Scheer ran in the Democratic primary and stunned the party machine by receiving 45 percent of the vote against the incumbent congressman supported by President Johnson. By September 1967 activists held the first National Conference of New Politics and by spring 1968 many supported the nomination of Eugene McCarthy or Bobby Kennedy and some favored Dr. Benjamin Spock or Martin Luther

King, Jr. They feared a campaign between Humphrey and Nixon, one that would fail to address the issues of war and race and result in a continuation of politics as usual. Some were below the voting age—21 at that time—as were many "McCarthy kids," and some were older local party workers, state legislators, county committee members, mayors, and obscure congressmen. "The Concerned Democrats were Concerned Americans," wrote a reporter, "all neat, well washed, bright and shining of face, few beards among them, fewer Negroes, no working-class types, and an extraordinarily large component of faculty and university types." Many drove Volkswagens, one of the only fuel-efficient cars at that time, and many had bumper stickers with the peace symbol or Peace Now! These Democrats were willing to buck their party for many reasons, but the most common one that year was stated by World War II veteran Donald Peterson: "I felt that my sons meant more to me than the Democratic Party. Everybody's willing to let other people's sons go off to the war, but not their own. But I can't commit myself to allow them to go off to that damned war. What am I in politics for, if I can't take care of my sons?"

Before the convention there was talk of 50,000, maybe 100,000 activists coming to the Windy City. Journalists reported that there would be all types—hippies and housewives, students and workers, slum dwellers and suburbanites, middle-class activists with peace buttons and scraggly revolutionaries carrying Vietcong flags, and of course, old and young. "The young have never before been so much involved in politics," penned a reporter in the *Washington Post*, "have never before invested so much hope in the political process." Women for Peace rented buses, and the National Mobilization Committee to End the War, the Mobe, announced a massive demonstration. There even was a rumor that the movement had mobilized a thousand women who would shed their brassieres in a march of the "Bare Breasts for Peace Brigade." [25]

Yet that was not to be. McCarthy urged his followers to stay home. He was aware of the tough reputation of the Chicago police and he did not want to be responsible for injuries or deaths. Other moderates and liberals lost interest, for there was little chance of a McCarthy nomination, and the Johnson administration was engaged in negotiations with the enemy in Paris. Also, city officials were uncooperative, refusing to grant parade permits to various movement organizations.

No more than 10,000 activists came to Chicago, some 5000 waiting for McCarthy's arrival on August 25. In an effort to keep his part of the movement away from any radical protests, the children's crusade was enlisted into small, peaceful demonstrations. The senator's plan for the convention was to demand that since he had about 800 delegates committed to him, his supporters should be able to reform how nominees are chosen and should have some say in the platform. The Democrats should have full discussions of all topics in an "open convention," not the nomination of Humphrey by the party machine behind closed doors.

Humphrey arrived, the second main character at Chicago. Over the years he had been a solid liberal. In the late 1940s he pounded a civil rights plank into the Democratic party platform and worked for federal aid to education. In the mid-1950s he supported a nuclear test-ban treaty, and in 1964 he pushed the Civil Rights Act through the Senate. He was the first to propose the Food for Peace program, the Peace Corps, and even Medicare. "Most senators are minnows," said LBJ. "Hubert Humphrey is among the whales." But liberals no longer were in favor with many activists, for they had sold out the Mississippi Freedom Party at the 1964 convention and they were responsible for the agonizing war. To many in the movement, Humphrey represented the old politics, a northern good ol' boy who coddled city bosses, made backroom deals, benefited from the political machine. In fact, without electoral victory in one state primary, the candidate had worked behind the scenes and had won almost 1500 delegates, securing the nomination. He also symbolized the administration, and appeared as the stand-in for the Democratic Establishment. As for the war, the vice president had sat in the wings, had gone along with his president, and to most activists he either supported the conflict or had compromised his values for his political career. By 1968, as an aide commented, "Nothing would bring the real peaceniks back to our side unless Hubert urinated on a portrait of Lyndon Johnson in Times Square before television—and then they'd say to him, why didn't you do it before?"

A more important character in the Democratic tragedy of 1968 was the man who controlled the streets of Chicago, Mayor Richard Daley. The mayor played by the rules—his rules. A man who had risen to political power through the machine, he had divvied out favors to the numerous ethnic groups and built a broad base of support in Chicago. Since he became mayor in 1955 he had been either loved or loathed as he ran "Fort Daley" with hardheaded determination. During the riot following the assassination of Martin Luther King, he ordered his police to "shoot to kill any arsonist" and "shoot to maim or cripple anyone looting a store in our city." Police wounded 48 and killed four blacks. When students marched against the war in April, Daley dispatched his police, who attacked the peaceful crowd. The mayor's spokesman declared that "these people have no right to demonstrate or express their views." After a few years of rising violence, and especially after the assassination of Bobby Kennedy, Daley was determined to maintain security at the convention. "As long as I am Mayor," he promised the local members of the American Legion, "there will be law and order in its streets." He placed his

12,000-man police force on twelve-hour shifts, stationed 6000 Illinois National Guardsmen outside the city and could call on the same number of regular army troops armed with rifles, bayonets, gas dispensers, flame throwers, grenade launchers, bazookas, and .30 caliber machine guns. A product of an older generation, Daley would "contain" the enemy, preventing the American Vietcong from disrupting his convention or conducting guerrilla tactics in his Chicago. He was the captain of his own ship holding firm the inner lines during the rip tides of 1968.

To many young activists the mayor symbolized the father, priest, general, corporate president, *Führer* of Fort Daley. "Chicago was an armed camp," recalled participant Paul Potter, "we just couldn't quite get it through our heads that all of that force was being lined up against us. It was too abstract; it was too absurd." Underground journalist Abe Peck added, "If you're going to Chicago, be sure to wear some armor in your hair."

Activists filtered into Chicago as the convention convened at the International Amphitheatre on August 26. This colorful mélange of people would make the 1968 Democratic convention like no other in American history. Some supported McCarthy, others had worked for Bobby Kennedy, a few had given up on liberal politics—all were against the war. Most felt that it was appropriate to go to Chicago and confront Johnson's party and his war, to hold a "People's Convention" in which the movement would march peacefully to the Amphitheatre and proclaim its issues in contrast to those of the Democrats. "We are not going to storm the convention with tanks or Mace," said David Dellinger of the Mobe. "But we are going to storm the hearts and minds of the American people." [26]

Most of these storm troopers were college kids, but the press zeroed in on a small number of the most outrageous—Yippies!

"Five conspirators lay scattered on the pillows adorning the postage-stamp living room of our Lower East Side flat" in January 1968, wrote Abbie Hoffman. "Paul Krassner, suffering from an acid hangover, staggered around asking, 'Why? Why? Why?' " Krassner then stated, "when you make the peace sign of the V the extension of your arm makes it a Y." Anita Hoffman exclaimed, "I, EYE! EYE! EYE! I love you very much." Jerry Rubin added, "PEE-PEE. You need a little pee-pee in every movement," and Nancy Kurshan proclaimed, "E is for everybody, energy." Suddenly, the chorus shouted, "Yippie!"

"The exclamation point would carry us to victory," Hoffman continued. "Its good vibes would conquer all question marks and get us to Chicago. If the press had created 'hippie,' could not we five hatch the 'yippie'? A political hippie. A flower child who's been busted. A stoned-out warrior of the Aquarian Age." Time for an alliance of activists and hippies, a "blending of pot and politics."

Some of the older generation tried to understand the yippies. "They are the cutting edge of something," wrote the *Washington Post*, "be it a true movement, a real rebellion, or simply a great and growing frustration that afflicts all young people these days in greater or lesser degree." J. Anthony Lukas of the *New York Times* stated that the yippies were "both protest and put-on."

But to most of the white-bread middle class the yippies were a disease, a strange illness that—like the Vietcong—were simply inscrutable. The authorities began harassment. In New York during March, when a few thousand yippies appeared at Grand Central Station to hold the first Yip-in (blowing bubbles, singing, dancing, popping balloons, removing the hands of a giant clock), the police charged into the crowd, clubs swinging. Charges dropped. In Chicago, police began arresting long-haired youth for no apparent reason; on one weekend in May they busted seventy for disorderly conduct. Charges dropped. In June, narcotic agents broke into Jerry Rubin's apartment, arrested him for possession of marijuana, beat him, injured his back. Again, charges dropped. Journalists also attacked. The establishment press began the assault just months after the Summer of Love. "Trouble in Hippieland," declared *Newsweek* after a hippie girl from a wealthy family died in New York's East Village. The magazine claimed that most flower children were "seriously disturbed youngsters" or "overprivileged products of the American dream." Early in 1968 *Reader's Digest* concluded for its 28 million readers: "Murder, rape, disease, suicide—the dark side of the hippie moon has become increasingly visible. Even its leaders admit that the movement has gone sour." By the Democratic convention many agreed with Theodore H. White, who labeled the yippies "lost and forlorn people seeking identity. They are a sad people, and when one examines the seasonal clusters where they come to roost, in Cambridge or San Francisco or New York, tears come to the eyes at their diseases (mainly venereal), their health (decayed from malnutrition and drugs) and the disturbances, rarely dangerous, of their minds."[27]

Such statements represented what the silent majority and Mayor Daley knew about the weird young people in the streets of Chicago, and it was all that they cared to know about those who looked, talked, and behaved differently. To the middle class in 1968, being different was being crazy. It was not American.

The yippies did not mind, and in fact reveled in the attention. Faced with the task of provoking young people to go to Chicago, they became creative. Yippie was a "myth that created free advertising for our Chicago confrontation. . . . Just do your thing; the press eats it up. MAKE NEWS." They sent out announcements that ran in underground papers: "This will be the first coming together of all people involved in the youth revolution. It should be a beautiful week. This is the first day in the rest of your life. See you in Chicago. YIPPIE!!!!!!!!!!" Since the Humphrey forces had already secured the nomination, yippies felt the convention was a Festival of Death. So they would put on a Celebration of Life, one with workshops, exhibits, demonstrations, rock concerts, pot, and plenty of gags.

They dropped rumors: Yippie potheads in Chicago had been busy all spring growing weed in vacant lots for a giant August smoke-in; yippie technologists were developing portable music equipment so they could fight cops and dance at the same time; yippie men were doing exercises to get in shape so they could seduce female Humphrey delegates while luscious yippie females were going to pose as hookers and then kidnap male delegates. Yippie cars would be painted yellow, pose as taxis, pick up delegates, and drive them to Wisconsin; yippies would put LSD in Chicago's water supply and would give free snake-dancing lessons; yippies dressed like Vietcong would blow up the baseball diamond in Lincoln Park and hijack the Chicago office of Nabisco and distribute free cookies; 100,000 yippies would protest the war by floating nude in Lake Michigan during the day and at night they would burn draft cards in unison creating a flame spelling: "BEAT ARMY."

What was the *truth?* Few knew after Tet, and so the yippies created politics of the put-on. The Rolling Stones would provide music, or maybe Dylan, or perhaps the Beatles. Vikings would surface their yellow submarines on the shores of Lake Michigan and rediscover America. They labeled their flyers "secret" and when journalists asked them to state their program, they handed out Mets scorecards or told them to check the yellow pages. They made up 20,000 buttons that read "Yippie Leader." Yippie proverbs: "Don't grow up. Growing up means *giving up your dreams.*" "Free Speech is the Right to Shout 'Theater' in a Crowded Fire." Yippie slogans: "Rise up and abandon the creeping meatball!" "Amerika says: *Don't!* The yippies say *Do It!*"

Their "platform" was a strange mélange of new left ideals and hucksterism called "REVOLUTION TOWARDS A FREE SOCIETY: YIPPIE!" They advocated an end to the war, freedom for all blacks, full employment, elimination of pollution, free birth control and abortion, promotion of the arts, and the legalization of marijuana and psychedelics. Yet they also demanded the total disarmament of police, that "people should fuck all the time, anytime, whomever they wish," and abolition of money, "pay housing, pay media, pay transportation, pay food, pay education, pay clothing, pay medical help, and pay toilets." The final demand was blank, with the words, "you can fill in what you want."[28]

Looking back, anyone listening to or reading these remarks would have laughed, but the authorities knew nothing about their enemy—just like in Vietnam—and this was 1968. After the assassinations of King and

Kennedy, few were interested in levity. The older generation reacted with force. Daley ordered his plainclothes police to infiltrate movement organizations, and the federal government placed a thousand agents in the city: for every six activists during the convention there was one undercover agent. The governor ordered troops to protect the water supply, and the *Chicago Tribune* published a series of alarmist articles: "How Cop Spied on the Yippies: Infiltrated Top Ranks to Gain Secrets"; how the paper had discovered a Yippie diary that contained the "inside story of disruptive plans by Communists and left-wing agitators to disrupt the city"; and how "Yippies Demand Cash from City" after Hoffman joked that if the city gave him $100,000 then he would leave town. Pundits wondered who was the "creeping meatball," and they decided it meant that the yippies would attempt a coup against President Johnson. Rubin replied, "We love LBJ. . . . Where would we be without LBJ?"

The establishment didn't get the joke—they were dead serious. Obviously, the nation was becoming so divided by August 1968 that entirely different world views were emerging. Some people respond to frustration with anger, some with humor, some with silence; some ignore the issue, others get drunk or stoned, and some use repression against those considered the enemy. Such responses were becoming apparent in mainstream society and in the movement. In a sense, then, the yippies were the most outrageous movement response to the overburdening frustration of 1968, and for the Establishment the most outrageous response would be forthcoming from Mayor Daley.

Conservatives lined up behind their mayor, but those in the movement bickered and remained divided. SDS headquarters in Chicago announced that it was not interested in demonstrating with liberals and did not want to be aligned with the "McCarthy kids." The Chicago Area Draft Resisters stated that they were "too individual" to participate in mass mobilizations. Except for a few veterans of the Poor People's Campaign, most blacks showed little interest in what they called "white man's politics." Other activists disliked the yippies, some seeing them as apolitical, irrational, freaks, while others viewed them as provocative radical New Yorkers on an ego trip. After all, local kids realized that there was potential danger in Chicago, and many did not feel a need for help from movement heavies. "Do not come to Chicago if you expect a five-day Festival of Life, music and love," warned Abe Peck in the *Seed*, and the *Berkeley Barb* added that activists will have to be tough for they might be radicalized by "having their heads busted by a cop's billy club."

Nevertheless, many activists came to Chicago, and so did a myriad of movement organizations who began applying for various city permits. A million fruitless meetings transpired; the officials stalled for weeks. Parade permits for marches? No, said Daley, traffic congestion. The Coalition for an Open Convention asked to use Soldier Field stadium for a rally. No, said Daley, it was booked the entire week for Lyndon Johnson's birthday party. Other activists applied to sleep in Grant Park, near the Conrad Hilton Hotel housing McCarthy and Humphrey. No, said Daley, too close to the Amphitheatre. They asked about Lincoln Park, three miles north near Old Town and ten miles from the Amphitheatre. No, said Daley, against city regulations. Many radicals wondered why a citizen would need a permit to protest a war that was being fought without a permit—a declaration of war—while liberals agreed with Allard Lowenstein, who concluded the authorities "seem determined to have a confrontation that can only produce violence and bloodshed."[29]

The summer before, San Francisco authorities had told hippies not to come to their city—to no avail—and so it was in the summer of 1968 in Chicago. Youth arrived in the city and pitched camp in Lincoln Park, listened to music, smoked weed, and a few yippies began their political campaign by obtaining a pig, naming him Pigasus, and transporting the squealing critter to the Civic Center. With cameras rolling, they attempted to nominate Pigasus for president with the campaign pledge: "They nominate a president and he eats the people. We nominate a president and the people eat him." His platform was "garbage," and the slogan: "Why take half a hog when you can have the whole hog?" The police moved in, and arrested the yippies—and the pig—before the candidate could utter an oink. The charge: disturbing the peace.

There would be little peace the entire week, and that was true outside and inside the convention hall. Humphrey and McCarthy forces argued over the Democratic platform, producing a majority and a minority plank on Vietnam, the first rejecting unilateral withdraw of U.S. troops and applauding LBJ's policy, and the second calling for withdrawal and an unconditional bombing halt of North Vietnam. Unfortunately for the peace delegates, a few days earlier the Soviet Union suddenly invaded Czechoslovakia and ended the reformist government that had been emerging since Prague Spring. The attack played into the hands of the hawks, boosting their position that the Soviets aimed at expansion and so the U.S. must continue to defend South Vietnam. While the invasion almost ensured the triumph of the Humphrey platform, the peace forces felt they had a right to be heard since during the primaries about 80 percent of Democrats had voted for either Kennedy or McCarthy. The two resolutions were introduced to the full convention and debate ensued, liberals contending that RFK would have supported the peace plank and conservative Congressman Wayne Hays declaring that the plank would play into the hands of radicals who want "pot instead of patriotism, sideburns instead of solutions. They would substitute riots for reason." The delegates defeated the peace plank and gave a victory to the Democratic machine.

The delegates continued quarreling in private as newscasters exposed the convention to the public. Americans turned on their televisions. Within hours after the opening remarks, some delegates decided that neither the old politics of Humphrey or the new politics of McCarthy should win the nomination or would win the November election. Young delegates began a campaign to draft Bobby's younger brother, Senator Edward M. Kennedy, and they waved banners: "We Want Kennedy." The senator from Massachusetts showed little interest, and the movement ebbed as the convention floor became rowdy. Black northern delegates sneered at white southerners, calling them racists, and when white Alabama delegates voted, other blacks marched out. A fist-fight erupted between delegates from Georgia, and tempers soared as conservatives and liberals shouted at each other and threw ice. More scuffles, and a few more fights erupted. CBS reporter Dan Rather rushed to the scene, and a policeman slugged him, knocking him to the floor. Astonished, anchorman Walter Cronkite called the police "thugs."

So ended the first evening of the convention. The confusion and madness continued for three more days, all of it sending a signal into American households—the Democrats were out of control. The party became a mirror of the nation, cracking over the issues of race and war.

Outside of the Amphitheatre, the party platform made little difference—most activists were not listening. They had made up their minds during the last three years that civil rights were mandatory and that the war was a disaster. About a thousand activists, hippies, yippies, and some street people were camping in Lincoln Park to prove it—or to prove something. When the 11 p.m. curfew passed, the police ordered them to leave. They stayed. Some taunted the cops. The authorities launched tear gas and charged into the park. Journalist Nicholas von Hoffman was on the scene: "Shrieks and screams all over the wooded encampment area. . . . Rivulets of running people came out of the woods across the lawn. . . . Next, the cops burst out of the woods in selective pursuit of news photographers. Pictures are unanswerable evidence in court. They'd taken off their badges, their name plates, even the unit patches on their shoulders to become a mob of identical, unidentifiable club swingers." They chased the kids through streets in Old Town, clubbing virtually anyone in the area, including onlookers and those going out to dinner. Sources reported that the police beat two dozen reporters and cameramen who were on the scene for the three national television networks and for *Newsweek*, *Life*, and three Chicago papers. "The Chicago police force understands very little about civil liberty," wrote the *Washington Post*, "and apparently cares even less." Dick Gregory added, "If you were in the streets, and if you moved, you were a yippie."

The next day a couple of thousand young people milled around in both Lincoln and Grant Parks, many singing along with Phil Ochs or listening to speeches by Abbie Hoffman, David Dellinger, and Black Panther Bobby Seale. "If a pig comes up and starts swinging a club," proclaimed Seale, "then put it over his head and lay him out on the ground." Others were more peaceful, sitting in a circle and chanting "Ommmm" while a few skeptics sang their own peace tune, "Ommmm Ommmm on the range." By evening, hundreds of clergy and other citizens came to Lincoln Park, expressed their concern, and some erected large wooden crosses and discussed tactics with radicals. A few militants stated that the clergy were "over thirty and totally irrelevant," but ministers reminded the youth that by "calling the police pigs and fighting with them you become as bad as they are." It was one of a million such conversations during the sixties that never would be resolved, and became immaterial at midnight as the police again launched tear gas and then attacked.

Just a few short months earlier, it had been a warm, sunny spring. Many of these activists then wondered which one would make a better president—Bobby Kennedy or Gene McCarthy. Then the assassination, McCarthy's faltering campaign, and the grim realization that the next president was going to be, as one activist remarked, either "The Humper or the Dick."[30]

Now, the last siege: the antiwar forces declared that they would assemble at Grant Park and march to the Amphitheatre on the day of Humphrey's nomination. As expected, Daley refused the parade permit. As expected, about 10,000 people assembled at Grant Park, and as expected, they were met by the police and the Illinois National Guard. CBS later reported that some 200 undercover agents were in the crowd. During the afternoon, as the activists listened to speeches, a group of young men—at least one an agent—approached the flagpole, took down Old Glory, and raised a red T-shirt. The action prompted police to charge, clubs swinging. "We see the way it is in Saigon," shouted Carl Oglesby to the battered activists, "we see the way it is in Bolivia, in Peru, in South Africa, we need no more illusions now." People scattered, and at twilight a few thousand gathered across the street from the Conrad Hilton which housed the candidates for the march to the Amphitheatre. The authorities were prepared. Hotel and building lights lit up the sky as television cameras recorded the events. The marchers began down Michigan Avenue, chanting "Peace Now! Peace Now!" "Dump the Hump." They approached the police line, and stopped. A few began taunting police, throwing garbage, yelling "Fuck You, LBJ," "Hell no, we won't go," "Fuck the pigs."

Bang! The police exploded into the crowd. Shouts, confusion, panic. Gas canisters exploding. Police clubbing. People screaming, bleeding. Some ran down streets, into hotel lobbies, back to the park. More cops arrived. Patrol wagons appeared. Tear gas floated into the Hilton, up the air vents, and into the suite of the vice president, who was preparing his acceptance speech. On the street, chanting: "Sieg Heil, Sieg Heil, Sieg Heil," and "The Whole World Is Watching."

The world was watching, or at least an estimated 90 million Americans, and those who did not have on their television could read national papers. The *New York Times* reported: "Even elderly bystanders were caught in the police onslaught. . . . For no reason that could be immediately determined, the blue-helmeted policemen charged the barriers, crushing the spectators against the windows of the Haymarket Inn, a restaurant in the hotel. Finally the window gave away, sending screaming middle-aged women and children backward through the broken shards of glass." On the street, the police chased and clubbed demonstrators, politicians, journalists, activists, and any doctors or nurses who attempted to help the injured. "Some tried to surrender by putting their hands on their heads," wrote another journalist. "As they were marched to vans to be arrested, they were rapped in the genitals by the cops' swinging billies." Richard Goodwin told young McCarthy supporters: "This is just the beginning. There'll be four more years of this."

NBC news commentator Chet Huntley declared: "Chicago police are going out of their way to injure newsmen, and prevent them from filming or gathering information on what is going on. The news profession in this city is now under assault by the Chicago police."

Police brutality provoked one of the first times that the moderate establishment press agreed with underground reporters. The "the power structure finally blew its cool," a writer proclaimed in *Rat*, while another noted in the *Barb* that one could watch TV, switch channels, and "while the police were beating up the demonstrators in Chicago, you could see the Russian soldiers chasing Czech civilians in Prague. . . . But, for the record, the Chicago police are much more brutal." At the convention, wrote an activist in *The Rag*, "America exposed herself. . . . Chicago is merely a domestic version of our foreign policy."

Later that evening, during nomination speeches for Humphrey, the televisions cut from the convention and played footage from the chaotic street scene. Allard Lowenstein told a TV interviewer, "This convention elected Richard Nixon President of the United States tonight." Humphrey left with the nomination, but recalled: "Chicago was a catastrophe. My wife and I went home heart-broken, battered and beaten." A few months later, lawyer Daniel Walker published a report based on 3500 eyewitness accounts: in the age of euphemisms he concluded that the events in Chicago constituted "a police riot."[31]

Chicago was "the place where all America was radicalized," wrote Tom Wicker, and historian David Farber later noted, "Chicago '68 marked a crisis in the nation's political and cultural order." It was as if the war between the states of mind, between left or right, finally had been declared. Who won the battle in the streets of Chicago depended on who was sitting in front of the television.

The events of that week outraged activists and many liberals. Antiwar students felt that the nomination of Humphrey demonstrated that the Democratic party was hopeless, controlled by a corrupt machine. Many now experienced the same disillusionment in liberalism that civil rights workers felt four years earlier at the convention in Atlantic City. Moreover, many young activists began to believe that the U.S. government was no longer a democracy; instead, they claimed, it had become illegitimate, an outlaw institution led by war criminals. American politics was bankrupt. More youths became alienated, attracted to the counterculture. Older liberals also were discouraged. During the next months McCarthy refused to support Humphrey for president and many others formed the New Democratic Coalition. Some citizens began to question the role of the police in society: Should taxpayers have more control over the men in blue? Senator George McGovern denounced Daley and his "Gestapo," labeled the convention a "blood bath," and the *New York Times* declared that the mayor's use of force "brought shame to the city, embarrassment to the country." Tom Wicker added, "The truth was these were our children in the streets, and the Chicago police beat them up," and columnist Mike Royko, noting that many cops had bruised hands and fingers, urged local citizens to stop smashing their faces against policeman's knuckles. As for radicals, police behavior only shifted many toward more militancy, toward more violent rhetoric and behavior. Repression did not suppress the radicals; on the contrary, as yippie Stew Albert said, Chicago was "a revolutionary wet dream come true." [32]

More conservative viewers said hit 'em again, harder. "The police stand was admirable," said a Chicago attorney, and a chemist added, "If other mayors followed Daley's action, then we'd have a much better society." A local woman agreed, "Ship all hippies, yippies, or whatever they call themselves to Russia. Everyone should fly the American flag to show these nit-wits what real Americans think." During the next weeks Daley proclaimed that he had received over 100,000 letters, and that 95 percent supported his tough stand. He was proud of his police, he said, for "no one was killed." He blamed the conflict on outside agitators and Communists who had been plotting to assassinate Humphrey, McCarthy, and perhaps a young female McCarthy worker and then blame it on the police. The protesters were "Communist stinkos, traitors and no-accounts," declared Democratic Senator Russell Long, and the *Chicago Tribune* labeled them "bearded, dirty, lawless rabble." Although Daley had at his disposal over 20,000 armed policemen and soldiers facing a few thousand unarmed activists, he declared that the behavior of his police was the only alternative to allowing "a lawless violent group of terrorists to menace the lives of millions of our people . . . and take over the streets of Chicago." Cars soon sported bumper stickers: WE SUPPORT MAYOR DALEY AND HIS CHICAGO POLICE.

The Windy City had a new breeze, a humid, heavy air. "From the statements of Humphrey, Nixon, Wallace and Co.," declared *The Rag*, "it is apparent that some sort of repression and increased militarization is in store for America in the coming years." The romantic idea that there would be a revolution in America in the late 1960s was beaten senseless in Chicago.[33]

Repression had been emerging during the previous year. During the waning weeks of 1967 the federal government indicted the Oakland 7—Berkeley radicals—for "conspiring" to commit trespassing during Stop the Draft Week. In New York, the FBI arrested 21 Black Panthers for "conspiring" to blow up department stores and botanical gardens, and early in 1968 the federal government indicted Dr. Spock and four others for "conspiring" to counsel and aid young men to evade the draft. Local officials joined the campaign. Oakland police randomly arrested Black Panthers, and there were numerous examples in LBJ's home state. As antiwar organizer Josh Gould drove to catch his plane to the Democratic convention, Killeen police stopped him, charged him with possession of "grains" of marijuana supposedly found on the car floor, and jailed him on $50,000 bail; authorities scheduled his trial for the day after the convention adjourned. In Houston, officials raided the SNCC freedom house, arrested black militant Lee Otis Johnson, charged him with giving an undercover agent one marijuana joint, and sentenced him to thirty years in prison.

As would be proven later, all of these measures were of dubious legality—but this was 1968 and most citizens were becoming disgusted with protesters. In January an 85-year-old federal judge sentenced Spock and his colleagues to two years in prison and a $5000 fine, a sentence later overruled, and Congress passed a law banning demonstrations of more than one hundred people at the White House. In April the House attached a rider to the Fair Housing Rights Act. Labeled the "H. Rap Brown Law," the statute made it illegal to cross state lines with the intention of inciting a riot, meaning that the federal government could define all national marches as "riots" and the organizers of such events could receive a ten-year sentence. "The government must be empowered to deal firmly and actively with those harbingers of anarchy," proclaimed Senator Strom Thurmond.

"A movement cannot grow without repression," said Rubin, and the older generation complied. While local authorities picked up activists and state governments began passing laws, the House Un-American Activities Committee subpoenaed Tom Hayden, David Dellinger, and Rennie Davis in an attempt to seek evidence that Communists helped lead the protest in Chicago. FBI Director J. Edgar Hoover ordered his field agents to use all their resources to publicize the "depraved nature and moral looseness of the New Left" and "to destroy this insidious movement." Early in 1969 the new Nixon administration ordered agents to arrest the "Chicago 8," the so-called leaders of the protests at the Democratic convention—Dave Dellinger, Tom Hayden, Rennie Davis, Abbie Hoffman, Jerry Rubin, Lee Weiner, John Froines, and Bobby Seale—for "conspiring" to cross state lines to incite a riot. The government kept the activists in and out of court until 1973, arresting them indiscriminately. Chicago police picked up Hayden when he was sitting under a tree in a park, charging him with resisting arrest, and they apprehended Hoffman three times in one day. In 1968 the federal authorities began treating antiwar protesters in the same manner that local southern sheriffs had been treating civil rights workers throughout the 1960s.

The long Chicago 8 trial proved little—except that the nation continued to polarize, left or right. The federal judge, Julius Hoffman, represented the Establishment. Seventy-four years of age, Judge Hoffman demanded respect for the bench. The co-conspirators showed none, dressing in wild costumes and yelling obscenities. The judge responded by restraining some of them, having others carried off. When two defense lawyers attempted to resign from the case, Judge Hoffman arrested them for contempt of court, prompting harassment charges from the defense and protests from 150 attorneys. Black Panther Bobby Seale wanted nothing to do with the defense lawyers, claiming that he deserved his usual attorney. Eventually the court agreed, but before the Chicago 8 became the Chicago 7, Seale called the judge "a blatant racist," shouted insults at the prosecutor, and the judge ordered him shackled and gagged.

It was the first time in years an American had been gagged in court, and to many activists it was fitting: a black man in a white man's court chained to his chair for shouting his views. To activists, and to most of the sixties generation, federal attempts to stifle dissent and protest by employing the legal system were preposterous. The term "fascism" to describe Establishment authoritarianism gained new currency on campus. By 1970 a Harris poll found that only 30 percent of college students, and only 17 percent of those who had been activists, felt that war protesters were given fair trials. Meanwhile, respect for authority continued to plummet. The "reason for claiming victory in Chicago," the *Seed* declared, was that "at last the country saw—though it took the beating of nearly thirty newsmen to provoke the media into covering it—that the most lawless and violent element in the society is the police." A word rarely used for police before

1968 now became common among the younger generation. "Some were reluctant at first to call cops 'pigs,' " wrote Rubin. " 'Pig' was a Berkeley–San Francisco thing, inspired by the Black Panthers. Also it was an insult to Pigasus. But we took one look at Czecago's big blue-and-white porkers: 'Man, those fat fuckers really do look like pigs!' "

Not to the silent majority. While most Americans had negative feelings toward southern cops earlier in the decade, by 1968 they felt that demonstrators placed the police in almost an impossible position. Mayor Daley explained: "If someone walks into you and shoves ya and spits in your face or calls you a four letter word, what would you do?" Many citizens began putting on bumper stickers—Support Your Local Police—and funding billboards that pictured an officer rescuing a child with the statement: "Some Call Him Pig." Referring to the activists, American Federation of Police founder Gerald Arenberg claimed, "We are at war with an enemy just as dangerous as the Viet Cong in Southeast Asia."[34]

Sometime between Columbia and Chicago the lines were drawn: "revolutionaries" versus "fascists." Both sides gritted their teeth in grim determination to win the war of the wills—that was what America was becoming by the waning months of 1968.

After the mayhem of the convention, many citizens hoped that the remainder of the year would quietly expire, but the discord continued. A week after the Democrats limped home, the Miss America Pageant began in Atlantic City. It was the most unusual one in U.S. history. "Miss America Pageant Is Picketed by 100 Women," declared the *New York Times*.

Before the pageant a few dozen New York women sent out flyers to friends:

> There will be: Picket Lines; Guerrilla Theater; Leafleting; Lobbying
> . . . to urge our sisters to join us and reject the Pageant Farce. . . .
> It should be a groovy day on the Boardwalk. . . . In case of arrest,
> however, we plan to reject all male authority and demand to be busted
> by policewomen only! . . . Male reporters will be refused interviews.
> . . . Only newswomen will be recognized.

Charlotte Curtis wrote the article for the *Times*: "Women armed with a giant bathing beauty puppet and a 'freedom trash can' in which they threw girdles, bras, hair curlers, false eyelashes, and anything else that smacked of 'enslavement' picketed the Miss American Pageant here today." The demonstrators, "mostly middle-aged careerists and housewives with a sprinkling of 20-year-olds and grandmothers in their 60's," marched around the convention hall, singing songs, carrying posters, and denouncing the all-white contest as racist. They insisted that women would not be free until they were "no longer enslaved by ludicrous beauty standards." Robin Morgan told the press that she had informed the mayor, "We wouldn't do anything dangerous—just a symbolic bra-burning. . . . We don't want another Chicago." As cameras rolled one protester threw liquid detergent into the can, proclaiming that she was against "such atrocities as having to wash the dishes," and another held a girdle over the can, stating, "No more girdles, no more pain. No more trying to hold the fat in vain." No one burned a bra, but some carried signs that demonstrated that various aspects of the broad movement were merging: "Up Against the Wall Miss America." "No More Beauty Standards—Everyone Is Beautiful!" "Girls Crowned—Boys Killed!" "Miss America Is Alive and Angry—in Harlem!" "I Am a Woman—Not a Toy, a Pet or Mascot!" Others ripped up a *Playboy* magazine and dumped it into the can, and danced around shouting "Liberation Now!" A few activists got into the convention hall during the telecast, one momentarily disrupting the event by throwing a stench bomb.

"The demonstrators," the *Times* continued, "belonged to what they called the Women's Liberation Movement." Unknown to mainstream society, that movement had been developing throughout the decade, but this was the first time the term was used in the national press. "Women's liberation" would not become part of America's lexicon for another year, and although a few feminists had founded the National Organization for Women in 1966, the first major article hinting that women were forming their own movement did not appear until March 1968, Martha Weinman Lear's "The Second Feminist Wave" in the *New York Times* magazine. The article asked, "What do these women *want?*" The answer, given by "theoretician" Betty Friedan and "analytic philosopher" Ti-Grace Atkinson, was a lot, including "wanting to be heard."

They would be heard much, much more during the second wave of activism. Yet at the pageant what these hundred women wanted became obscure as a crowd six times larger assembled and expressed their views. "They're vulgar," stated one man. A male shouted that the women should throw themselves in the trash can, and another told them, "go home and wash your bras." The runner-up in the 1967 pageant then appeared: the former Miss Green Bay, Wisconsin, who wore a sign, "There's Only One Thing Wrong with Miss America. She's Beautiful."[35]

Yet America was becoming increasingly ugly that autumn. In August, *Esquire* published a disturbing cover story on Private Andrew Stapp that demonstrated that the antiwar movement was seeping into—of all places—the U.S. Armed Forces. While dissidence in the military had grown slowly after escalation, it soared after Tet revealed the reality of American military policy in Vietnam. Antiwar organizations began to publish more undergrounds for servicemen, *Vietnam GI*, *About Face*, *Star Spangled Bummer*, and local activists and servicemen established a number of coffeehouses—Oleo Strut by Fort Hood, the Green Machine near Camp Pendleton, Red Herring by Chanute Air Force Base, Mad Anthony's Headquarters near Fort Leonard Wood, and DMZ for servicemen stationed in Washington, D.C. These establishments provided a place where GIs could discuss the war, gripe about the brass, or simply relax with others who felt part of the movement. More significant, active-duty GIs began printing their own undergrounds, usually after hours and sometimes using their base's typewriters and mimeograph machines. One of the most famous, and the first edited entirely by active-duty soldiers, was *FTA* from Fort Knox, Kentucky. The title was a play on words ridiculing the army advertisement that by joining the army an enlistee would have Fun, Travel, and Adventure. Actually, the letters stood for an old saying among draftees, Fuck The Army.

The "only way to stop the war," a dissident servicemen declared, "is to refuse to fight it!" While no GIs were doing that in Vietnam yet, a few were questioning orders in the U.S. During the Democratic national convention, the commanding officer of Fort Hood ordered his troops to prepare for possible departure to Chicago where they would be used as riot control against demonstrators. Over a hundred black soldiers held a meeting, and over forty refused orders, demanded discussions on army racism, and stated their opposition to using troops against civilians. They were charged with disobeying a direct order, and white soldiers and civilians collected money for their defense. Faced with growing dissidence, the Pentagon issued a new regulation banning uniformed military personnel from participating in demonstrations. But that did not stop some soldiers in the Bay Area. In October, some 15,000 civilians marched against the war, and citizens were amazed to see that in the crowd were 500 uniformed servicemen, including navy nurse Sue Schnall. This lieutenant also dropped antiwar leaflets from a plane on local military installations, and she became the first person tried under the new regulation, receiving a light sentence.

The act of drafting civilians and sending them to boot camp to make them "military" no longer was purging young adults of their antiwar views. The issues of race and war were so explosive that by 1968 they were busting out in unlikely places—even at the Olympics.

Just days after Americans read about servicemen marching in San Francisco, two black athletes on the U.S. Olympic team competing in Mexico City stunned the world. Tommie Smith wore a black glove on his right hand when he received his gold medal for breaking the world record and winning the 200 meter dash. John Carlos wore the glove on his left hand when he received the bronze medal. As the "Star Spangled Banner" played, both men looked down and raised their hands in the clenched fist that symbolized black power. "We are black," said Smith, "and we're proud to be black. White America will only give us credit for an Olympic victory. They'll say I'm an American, but if I did something bad, they'd say a Negro."

The elderly white men who composed the U.S. Olympic Committee were outraged, and they suspended Smith and Carlos from the games for boosting a political cause. The committee told the athletes to go home, and they apologized to Mexico for the "discourteous display" of "immature behavior."

In 1968 the vast majority of white Americans had little understanding of black power, and in the heartland most probably had never seen the salute. "Television has brought the glory and the anguish of the Games home to millions of Americans as never before," declared the *Washington Post*, when national newspapers still introduced the term "black power" in quotes. Smith and Carlos made their stand in front of an audience of hundreds of millions, and the Olympic Committee responded by making them martyrs, which placed their cause on the front pages of newspapers throughout the world and which rallied many young blacks. "That one act communicated to all of us," declared Stokely Carmichael, "and we knew precisely what it said."

The episode again divided the nation and the U.S. Olympic team. Tom Waddell, a decathlon athlete then serving in the U.S. Army, was asked if he thought the episode hurt the USA: "Our image is so bad it can't get any worse." Ron Freeman, a black sprinter, felt that the expulsion was terrible and predicted that many other blacks would leave the games. White hammer-thrower Harold Connolly agreed, and other black sprinters began wearing black berets. When they received their medals, they raised their arms, fists clenched, but since they were "smiling and apparently not defiant," reported the *New York Times*, they were not reprimanded. Many others were upset. White swimmer Barry Weisenberg called the incident "a disgrace. In my opinion, an act like that in the medal ceremony defiles the American flag." A day later, at the compound housing the U.S. athletes, a sign hung from the dorm window of the rifle team: "Win the War in Vietnam: Wallace for President."

"Bring Us Together!" was a Nixon campaign slogan, and most Americans were ready to end the discord. That autumn the candidate took to the campaign trail, calling for a "new voice . . . different from the old voices, the voices of hatred, the voices of dissension, the voices of riot and revolution." The Republicans blamed the Democrats for urban riots, crime in the streets, and student rebellion. With opinion polls demonstrating a large lead, the candidate avoided controversy. "Mr. Nixon has published a collection of positions he has taken on 167 issues," wrote the *New York Post*. "It seems a pity he could not have made it a round 170 by adding Vietnam, the cities, and civil rights." He remained vague while attacking Humphrey as a liberal big spender who had "his hand in your pocket." He appealed to "people who pay their taxes and go to work, people who send their children to school, who go to their churches, people who are not haters, people who love this country," indeed, all citizens who cry out, "That is enough, let's get some new leadership!"

But the campaign only continued to divide the nation, especially since there was an unknown variable, George Wallace. How many votes would he win? Popular opinion polls predicted during summer that he would win only 10 percent of the vote, but that figure quickly doubled after the chaos of the Democratic national convention. If that trend continued he might have 30 percent by the election and force the decision into the House of Representatives. Accordingly, Wallace moved into the suburbs and small towns with his message. Crowds swelled for the "Wallace Whitelash." In Cicero, Illinois, the scene of Martin Luther King, Jr.'s disastrous march two years before, many residents held their views in their hands: "Wallace Will Save America!" "Support Your Local Police." "Law and Wallace." Opposed to the Fair Housing Rights Act, Wallace told suburbanites, "I'm going to ask the Congress . . . to repeal this law about the sale of your own property and let them know that a man's home is still his castle." Posters waved: "I Worked to Buy My House, George, Protect Our Home."

In the crowd were five young dissenters, the oldest 20 and youngest 17, four girls and a boy. The young man carried a McCarthy sign, "Don't Let Wallace Make This a Police State," and a girl held a placard, "Love." An eyewitness reported that a man lunged at the kid, tearing at the sign, kicking. A hefty blond woman scratched his face as others yelled, "Look at those four lesbians and a homo!" A man pointed to one of the girls and added, "I bet she shacks with niggers!" Another added, "Take a bath, you dope addict!" [36]

Politics in America had made the full circle. In January bright young students, annoyed but still idealistic, had worked within the system to change the Establishment. Then the assassinations, the faltering candidacy of McCarthy, and frustrations exploding in the streets of Chicago. The movement limped back to the dorms, more alienated than ever, and replaced Bobby Kennedy or Gene McCarthy posters with Che Guevara, Malcolm X, or the great cynic W. C. Fields as they listened to the Rolling Stones wail about a "Street Fighting Man." On the other side, Spiro Agnew declared that demonstrations were out of control, that protesters should be "cast out" of America, and that the Republicans would "define permissible limits of dissent." At the same time the white backlash expanded, cheering George Wallace. Suburbanites put on bumper stickers, "America, Love It or Leave It," while pickup drivers in small towns were more blunt: "If Your Heart Is Not in America, Get Your Ass Out." This was 1968: Everyone was angry.

Everyone also wanted to know what the candidates would do about race and war. Nixon avoided civil rights questions, vaguely mentioning opportunity for all and law and order. Humphrey talked about continuing the liberal programs of the Democratic administrations. Since polls had shown for three years that Americans felt that Vietnam was the most important issue facing the nation, the media pressed the candidates. After Tet, both Nixon and Humphrey had to call for some sort of de-escalation. Nixon declared that he had a "secret plan" to bring about "peace with honor," but would not give out details because then he would reveal his scheme to the enemy. Actually, Nixon had no plan, possessed no knowledge about Vietnam, and had no idea how to bring about an honorable peace—but neither did most American voters, and neither did Humphrey. The Wallace-LeMay idea was too brutal for most Americans, and bombing had been used for three years with little success. After Tet it should have been obvious to the electorate that there was no way to bring about an honorable peace in Vietnam. But Americans would not face the cruel facts for a few more years—they *hoped* that political leaders knew something, some secret, that they did not.

Humphrey, trailing in the polls, went on the attack. He challenged Nixon to a debate. Remembering 1960, the Republican refused. Humphrey declared his liberal agenda and toured the nation to listless crowds, and to young hecklers chanting "Shame, Shame, Shame," and "Bull Shit, Bull Shit, Bull Shit." Humphrey then attempted to goad Nixon into making a political misstatement. "Nixon's firm positions would make an ad for Jello look like concrete. . . . Where do you stand, Mr. Nixon, where do you stand?" By October it was obvious that drastic action had to be taken to save the campaign, so the vice president began to distance himself from the Johnson administration, and he occasionally addressed the issue of Vietnam. If elected, he declared, he would propose an immediate cease-fire, stop bombing North Vietnam, and perhaps call on the United Nations to supervise the evacuation of all foreign troops from South Vietnam. Somehow, he would begin the "de-Americanization of the war."

The Democratic nominee was leaning closer to the movement's position, and the tactic had an impact. During the last few weeks of the campaign, Humphrey rarely was jeered as most activists returned to the Democrats. There was no alternative. Activists could sit out the election, as some radicals proposed, or support Humphrey and hope for the continuation of social programs and civil rights. During October more of "McCarthy's kids" helped the campaign, and so did older liberals such as

Allard Lowenstein and members of the Americans for Democratic Action. Senator McCarthy endorsed the candidate a week before the election, and at the same time President Johnson announced a bombing halt of North Vietnam.

As citizens went to vote, a Gallup poll showed that Humphrey trailed Nixon by only two percentage points, 42 to 40, and a Harris poll showed that the Democrat actually was ahead, 43 to 40. Too little, too late: Nixon was the One, just barely. Winning a little over 43 percent of the electorate, he beat Humphrey by half a million votes. Wallace won 13 percent.

Little was clear-cut in 1968, including the election. The Old South continued its transition away from the Democrats and toward any conservative that would stop the civil rights movement, including a third-party candidate. Wallace won in Dixie. Nixon won the border states. The southern vote demonstrated that the Old Confederacy was determined to oppose federal attempts to bring about racial equality. Considering the rest of the nation, since about 57 percent voted either for Nixon or Wallace and against the Democrats who had run the government since 1961, the election seemed like a repudiation of LBJ and liberalism, great society programs and civil rights acts, for the Democrats won 12 million votes fewer than they did in 1964. Yet the election also demonstrated confusion of the electorate. The people of Arkansas, for example, voted for hawk independent Wallace for president, liberal Republican Winthrop Rockefeller for governor, and dove Democrat William Fulbright for senator. In Iowa and California, the people voted for Democratic senators and a Republican president, and while more conservatives were elected to the House more liberals were voted into the Senate. Perhaps in the long run, one of the most important elections in the nation's history could be summarized by a bumper sticker that the Republican candidate recycled from his 1960 campaign and that in 1968 appealed to the beseiged electorate: "Nixon Is Safer."

Many pundits have contended that the election began the Age of Conservatism, and in a sense that is true. But more than an ideological shift, the electorate voted for something different, something that they felt had a better chance of ending the violence that had vexed the nation for three years. Since Wallace was an insult to thoughtful citizens, they only had one option—they voted for a Secret Plan, hoping that Nixon knew some way, any way to end the war at home and abroad. In a sense, then, the vote was a call for the return of the peaceful 1950s and a rejection of the movement and the 1960s. The silent majority voted for silence, for an end to the shouting. As students in the Free Speech Movement four years earlier had provoked the suburbs to vote for Governor Ronald Reagan, so did the yippies induce the average citizen to vote for Nixon.

The election, of course, did not heal the nation, did not "bring us together." The issues of war and race continued to divide citizens. By the end of 1968 residents of the various Millersbergs throughout the country were fed up. Many hated protesters, and agreed with the new vice president, who referred to them as "yippies, hippies, and the whole zoo." After CBS showed street violence during the Chicago convention, 9000 viewers called or wrote to complain—they no longer wanted to see that behavior on TV. Nationally, a poll showed that less than 20 percent of citizens felt that Mayor Daley used too much force. "Beat 'em, make 'em behave," many parents demanded, as their children lost faith, dropped out, or became more alienated. Marc Sarkady recalled being arrested by police: "I was kicked around, physically kicked. I was hit and slapped. . . . How could these people do this to me? What did I do to them? . . . It was a confusing and debilitating situation, and very radicalizing. I started to strongly question my earlier pacifistic views. Maybe it *was* important to push for revolution." Police brutality, in fact, created more radicals than all the pamphlets and books, all the speeches given by the new left vanguard.

Us versus Them. America was becoming two nations, divisible and divided. "You're either part of the solution," activists said, "or you're part of the problem." Paul Potter reflected, " 'Our' level of rationality and 'theirs' had drifted so far apart, that we just couldn't even guess at what theirs was anymore." David Harris added: "We become strangers in a strange land."

Left or Right. The division continued for the remainder of the era, sequestering the generations and even families. "My brother is in the National Guard," reported an activist in Madison. "When the Guard was out in the streets, I found him in one of their lines. He held his rifle out, his bayonet pointed right at my chest, brother against brother. America, whew!" A professor surveyed the press at the end of the year and concluded that there were two Americas: "On one hand the young, the disenchanted, the revolutionary, the pacifistic and idealistic, the draft resisting, the McCarthy-supporting and those concerned with the desperate plight of the blacks and of a nation in a horrendous war; on the other hand the complacent and the contented, the Nixonites and Humphreyites, the ones who have it made."[37]

To many of those who demanded change, the election signaled the end of the movement and the sixties. Activists knew that Nixon's policies would strive to contain the spread of Communism abroad, meaning that the war would continue for years. As one stated, the election only replaced "a venal Texan with a warlike Quaker." The new president also would contain the movement by employing massive police power, for according to Michael Rossman, Nixon was "the stern Daddy of an older frightened generation." Many activists also saw the end of poverty programs and, more important, the struggle for equality. For years the federal government had been supporting civil rights; now it appeared that the new agenda was law and order. The white blacklash, apparently, was victorious over the struggle. The part of the movement that began in Greensboro in 1960 seemed to die at the polls in 1968.

Such thoughts depressed many activists who had marched and demonstrated for years. Some continued the radical oratory. "The Resistance," David Harris claimed when he went to prison for evading the draft, "would carry on its struggle in jail and out. Our bodies might be locked up, but we would continue to organize." Harris later admitted that such statements were "typical of the well-intentioned but hollow rhetoric that seemed to overtake much of the Sixties that fall." For him and others apparent defeat was difficult to admit. Dreams die hard. Jack Newfield:

> Now I realize what makes our generation unique, what defines us apart from those who came before the hopeful winter of 1961, and those who came after the murderous spring of 1968. We are the first generation that learned from experience, in our innocent twenties, that things were not really getting better, that we shall *not* overcome. We felt, by the time we reached thirty, that we had already glimpsed the most compassionate leaders our nation could produce, and they had all been assassinated. And from this time forward, things would get worse: our best political leaders were part of memory now, not hope. [38]

Gripped by frustration, they wondered whether their movement failed, whether the new left was dead, whether the sixties were over. The Doors throughout the year had been "Waiting for the Sun,"

> At the first flash of freedom
> we raced down to the sea,
> standing there on freedom shore
> waiting for the sun . . .
>
> Waiting for you to hear my song,
> waiting for you to come along,
> waiting for you to tell me what went wrong. . . .

"This is the strangest life I've ever known," sang Jim Morrison, and Captain Billy America, the main character in the movie *Easy Rider*, simply added: "We blew it." That remark, many first-wave activists felt, could stand as an epitaph for the movement and the sixties.

Certainly, there were the casualties by the end of 1968. Gone was the innocence and idealism of the sixties generation, those in the community of believers who earlier had marched while singing "We Shall Overcome," those fresh young students who arrived on campus in 1964 and 1965 eager to participate, to change their university. Now, both groups were frustrated, the first too angry to carry on and the second looking forward to graduation—and to the draft. The nation had elected a conservative, the war continued, and organizations such as SDS and SNCC were in disarray. Yet that demonstrated again that activists always were a minority, and what the movement learned that election year was the first rule of democracy—the majority rules. The movement might be able to popularize issues and elect their candidates in liberal enclaves, but they never would win a national election. Furthermore, the movement and the sixties cannot be measured by the fate of organizations or the participation of the older wave of activists, many of whom retired from demonstrating and turned to other pursuits. The movement had become much broader, and in a sense it outgrew its early organizations as it flooded into American society. By 1968 many older citizens who had not participated before were joining ranks, and so was a new, second wave of younger brothers and sisters. Student Mike Wallace recalled his awakening while occupying a building during the Columbia strike: "My world had been very staid, very traditional, very frightened, very middle-class and respectable. And here I was doing these things that six months before I would have thought were just horrible. But I was in the midst of an enormous tide of people. . . . It wasn't just Columbia. There *was* a fucking war on in Vietnam, and a civil rights movement. These were profound forces that transcend that movement. 1968 just cracked the universe open for me."

Did the movement fail? "The most dangerous half-truth that came to be believed in 1968," two activists reflected, "was that the organizing of the 1960s had failed to accomplish anything, and that what was needed to change the system was an apocalyptic final conflict."[39] Indeed, since 1960 activists had changed society. They had provoked America's conscience and mobilized citizens, and in doing so they had contributed to the passage of major civil rights laws and programs, forced campus and educational reforms, and raised questions about a U.S. war and their obligation to serve in their nation's armed forces. As they propelled McCarthy to success in New Hampshire and boosted Bobby Kennedy's campaign, they had influenced mainstream politics, especially the Democratic party. The ideas that activists spawned in the early 1960s, that some wrote in *The Port Huron Statement*, had been co-opted by most liberals by 1968— a time, ironically, when the former authors of that document were farther down the ideological road, shouting "Revolution!"

The movement and the sixties did not end in 1968. In November black students at San Francisco State declared that they intended to shut down their university "by any means necessary," and various protests and demonstrations during the next few years were to be the largest in American history. Yet 1968 was momentous, for the rip tides of that year tore the social fabric, divided the nation, and floated the movement and the sixties down new currents of empowerment and liberation.

The Crest, 1968 to the early 1970s

During the autumn of 1968, Richard Goldstein, a writer for the *Village Voice*, asked Country Joe MacDonald to "rap about the revolution."

"There isn't going to be any revolution," the musician responded. "Let's be realistic."

"Why?" asked Goldstein.

"Because you have to control things," said Country Joe, "and most of the people I know aren't ready for that. They want a leaderless society."

"But," Goldstein continued, "what about the Guerrillas?"

"I don't know any," Country Joe responded. "I know a lot of people wearing Che Guevara T-shirts . . . what a bunch of tripped-out freaks. . . ."

Barry Melton, Country Joe's guitarist, added: "The revolution is just another word for working within the community."

"Hell," Goldstein protested, "you are the revolution."

"No," said Country Joe, shaking his head. "I'm just living my lifestyle. That's what you should be doing."

FIVE

Counterculture

Take a giant step outside your mind.
Taj Mahal

Does anybody really know what time it is?
Does anybody really care?
Chicago

Living your lifestyle, doing your own thing, was a significant theme of
the movement as it blended with the counterculture during the second
wave, the four or five years after Chicago. Some became involved in politics, working for causes that attacked the establishment and transferred
power to the people: *empowerment*. Others felt politics died with Martin
Luther King and Bobby Kennedy and they became consumed with personal pursuits that freed them from their past: *liberation*. All the while,
most experienced an individual transformation that made them "Sixties
People," different from the cold war generation. "Remember," Tuli Kupferberg told the emerging new culture: "The *first* revolution (but not of
course the last) is in yr own head. Dump out *their* irrational goals, desires, morality."

The counterculture must be defined broadly. The movement developed
as a counter to the political establishment: the counterculture was a
counter to the dominant cold war culture. After the rip tide the press
reported, somewhat ironically, that there were 200,000 "full time hippies"
and another 300,000 who shared the practices and beliefs, that some
20,000 were dropping out each year, and that "the number is accelerating
geometrically." By the end of the decade hippies had established thousands of communes, hip communities in almost every major city, and
they were hitch-hiking around the country and throughout the world—
from Marrakech to Kabul to Kathmandu. By the early years of the next

decade perhaps 3 million people felt part of the counterculture, yet they always were a minority within another minority—the movement. While it must be remembered that within the sixties generation were more conservative kids who were eager apprentices for the system, it was the hippies who confronted and disturbed the establishment, regardless of their numbers. "No one knows for sure just how large this massive generational upheaval really was," wrote a researcher. "We can only be sure that it took place on a scale unprecedented in our history."

During the second wave the counterculture became a phenomenon that affected many young Americans, and as baby boomers flooded campuses the division between activists and hippies faded like tie-dye. The underground was surfacing, gently infiltrating the movement. What started with blue jeans and work shirts during Freedom Summer had become bell bottoms and peasant dresses by Woodstock. Hip was a sign of the times, a symbol that the sixties generation had shifted from surfing and bundling on the beach to protesting and smoking dope, from "Love me do" to "Why don't we do it in the road." After the March on the Pentagon, participant Keith Lampe wrote, "Just two weeks ago we were talking about 'hippies' of 'the psychedelic movement' on the one hand, and 'straight peace activists' or 'resisters' as something quite distinct. Now the two are tightly communal aspects of the same thing—and who can hang a name on it? It's like wind, or water. Superbly leaderless. The bull horns at the Pentagon were passed around almost as freely as the joints and sandwiches and water jugs."[1]

Many commentators have discussed the origins of the counterculture. Most have mentioned that throughout American history there have been those who do not fit into the mainstream, misfits. In earlier times they might have been roamers, drifters, mountain men, or utopians at communities such as Oneida, New Harmony, or various Shaker or Hutterite settlements. As America urbanized they clustered in cities—bohemians after the First World War, student radicals during the Depression, beatniks during the cold war. Since future hippies were being raised during the postwar era, some were influenced by contemporary intellectuals and poets. Paul Goodman discussed *Growing Up Absurd*, William Whyte challenged students to "*fight* The Organization," and beat poets ridiculed society and urged readers to get "On the Road." "We gotta go and never stop going till we get there," said one of Jack Kerouac's characters, and in *Desolation Angels* the author spoke of "a 'rucksack revolution' with all over America 'millions of Dharma bums' going up to the hills to meditate and ignore society." Some writers emphasized that the counterculture was a response to technology, that during the atomic age America had become a "civilization sunk in an unshakeable commitment to genocide, gambling madly with the universal extermination of our species." Others viewed the growth of hippiedom as a result of a massive sixties generation that came of age. More kids meant more dissension from social norms. Throw in the Beatles, and presto: The Summer of Love.

Most of these writers were social scientists or journalists who traveled to Haight-Ashbury or the East Village, talked to a few weird kids, and then published dozens of academic essays and some 150 articles during the five years after the Summer of Love. Social scientists attempted to stuff hippies into paradigms, dichotomies, or theories, and divide them into categories (visionaries, heads, plastic hippies, communards), while conservatives railed that hippies were the result of "too permissive" child-rearing. Historians read those reports and then explained the hippies to the next generation of students.

It is not surprising that the resulting interpretation has been superficial—sex, drugs, and rock-and-roll. The second wave was such an emotional era that few could rise above silly arguments: Were the hippies good or bad? It never was that simple; just the opposite, for the counterculture came in many shapes and colors, which resulted in many inconsistencies. Three researchers examining the Jesus People wrote that they discovered "some things to praise and some to criticize, but the balance shifts, sometimes drastically, from element to element within the movement." It seemed easier for many to denigrate the counterculture than to explore it, resulting in many older commentators seeing what they were looking for. As a member of an Oregon commune stated: "Any family, any commune, is like a Rorschach test. What you see when you come here says more about who you are than what it is. Visitors . . . completely miss what's really going on because they don't see what these things mean to us."[2]

What was going on? *Why* did the counterculture flourish during the second wave? *What* were its values and social thought? *What* types of alternative societies did they attempt to build?

"Hippie," of course, often meant different things to the older and younger generations. Parents usually stated that hippies included everyone revolting against something, or simply revolting to them, and mainstream journalists simply labeled them "dirty, costumed protesters" who had long hair, smelled, and smoked dope. Marijuana was the "staple of hippiedom," declared *Time*, "L.S.D. its caviar," and Nicholas von Hoffman added, "if the word means anything, it means a hippie is a dope dealer." At the end of the decade a journalist summed up the older generations' level of knowledge of the counterculture when he gave his peers advise on how to spot a hippie: "Well, hippies look like hippies."

Americans like packages, labels. "Hippie" had been defined, so suburbanites turned away in disgust instead of trying to understand the rebellion. Actually, hippies considered themselves part of an alternative culture or underground, and they called each other many names, as a flyer proclaimed:

> The Paisley Power Caucus of the Peace and Freedom Party will hopefully prove congenial for hippies, Provos, anarchists, beatniks, Diggers, musicians, Zen monks, dealers, utopians, Wobblies, calligraphers, felons, Boo Hoos, and the many UNCLASSIFIABLE individuals who generally share our perspective.

Usage of these terms changed over time and varied with location. Some who felt part of the counterculture called themselves "seekers" or because they used dope, "heads." During the second wave many used "hippie" or another popular term, "freak," a "far out person" who was too odd, too abnormal to be part of the normal society. "Here come the 'freaks,' " declared the Ohio State paper when two were elected president and vice president of student government. The new president wore a red and white striped shirt with blue sleeves covered with white stars and proclaimed they were "freaks, not radicals," while his supporters blew bubbles and hummed "Hail to the Chief."

Freaks cannot be discarded as simply "sex, drugs, and rock-and-roll," because like the broader movement the counterculture included everyone, excluded no one. There were no hippie organizations, no membership cards, no meetings, no age limits, no perquisites. Being a hippie often was an individualistic journey. One did not *have to* drop out for a semester, a year, or a decade to "qualify" as a hippie, or *have to* take drugs, participate in sex orgies, live in a commune, listen to rock, grow long hair. No minimum requirements. No *have to*. While some hippies might not be able to articulate their thoughts or define their existence, most would agree that being part of the counterculture was a frame of mind, like being part of the movement. "Some of the most longhaired people I know are bald," laughed Jerry Rubin, and when a professor at the University of Utah criticized the counterculture, a student responded: "The hippie movement is not a beard, it is not a weird, colorful costume, it is not marijuana. The hippie movement . . . is a philosophy, a way of life, and a hippie is one who believes in this." Some dropped out and became as apolitical as possible, others participated in what they considered was a cultural revolution, but most rejected the values of the predominant culture and then developed and practiced different lifestyles. While this seemed difficult for the older generation to comprehend, it was readily understood by freaks all over the nation.

Moreover, hippies did not need older experts to explain the counterculture—they wrote about it constantly. Careful observers and later historians would have realized that by the end of the decade, as one thoughtful scholar noted: "The lesson to be learned from the turbulent youthquake is not that long hair or body odor or disrespect for traditional values are undermining the stability of America. The lesson for America is that *something is terribly wrong* with the systems that create such youthful unrest. And who are the most outspoken critics of these systems? Pick up an underground newspaper in Ann Arbor, Michigan, Jackson, Mississippi, Middle Earth, Iowa, New York, Chicago, or Los Angeles."[3]

The most appropriate sources on the counterculture are the articles and books the freaks wrote in underground newspapers and published with obscure presses. Read what they were writing, and listen to their music. Hippies did not put themselves in neat categories, for they dropped in and out of the fluid counterculture whenever they felt like it. Youth did not have to read Paul Goodman to discover that life was absurd, or David Riesman to learn that society was a lonely crowd, or Marcuse or Mills to know that there was injustice and war. All they had to do was to live through the sixties, consider the behavior of the establishment, and tune in to the couriers of the counterculture—the undergrounds and the music.

Underground papers flourished during the second wave. "There is a credibility gap between the press and the people," declared a former journalist for the United Press International and the *New York Times,* John Wilcock, "because the newspaper owners are plain and simple liars. . . . As a result, the Hippies just don't read the national papers." Wilcock began publishing *Other Scenes* while thousands of freaks and activists developed three national underground wire services and over 600 papers which eventually had a circulation of about 5 million. High school kids printed up some 3000 randomly printed tracts, while older siblings created a library of posters, leaflets, and newsletters. Armed with their undergrounds, the counterculture infiltrated the culture, and soon freaks could find each other and spread the word throughout the nation, "from the Heart of Old Dixie," Jackson, Mississippi *(The Kudzu)* to inside the Army security at Fort Knox *(FTA).* The message was Us versus Them, and the publishers knew what side they wanted to be on. Most never pretended to be accurate or to publish "All the News That's Fit to Print." Underground reporters were gonzo journalists; that is, they participated in the event and then wrote the article from their perspective. A sign in the *Berkeley Barb* office read, "Put down prejudice—unless it's on our side."

"Rock music," wrote a hippie in *Space City!,* "is responsible more than any other single factor in spreading the good news." Folksingers, of course, had bridged the musical canyon between the first decade of Elvis and the second one of the Beatles. Folk introduced many themes of the sixties, and then other musicians plugged in their guitars and blitzed the airways. While scholars argued whether the kids were really listening to the lyrics, the counterculture bought records and sang along. "Sound, like sex and the magic weed, is a turn-on," wrote a head, for not only did it forge a hip community but it challenged the establishment and liberated freaks from the older generation. "For our generation music is the most vital force in most of our lives," wrote Detroit cultural activist John Sinclair. "Its most beautiful aspect is that it gets to millions of people every day, telling them that they can dance and sing and holler and scream and FEEL GOOD even when they have to listen to all those jive commercials and death news reports."[4] To avoid the commercials and war reports—and to spread the word—freaks established and tuned into a few hip FM stereo stations. KMPX and KSAN in the Bay Area, WBAI or "radio unnameable" in New York, and Up Against the Wall FM in Madison were some of the first, and soon other listener-sponsored stations went on the air in many other cities, including Los Angeles, Houston, and Washington, D.C. All playing the music and all giving clues to the counterculture.

Why did a such a small part of the sixties generation during the Summer of Love—less than 100,000 kids—bloom into a garden of millions of flower people during the second wave? The behavior of the establishment stimulated the growth of the anti-establishment. The cool generation of mid-decade became the alienated generation during and after the rip tide.

It began as baby boomers entered "duck and cover" elementary schools, matriculated into crewcut high schools, and graduated into college, "the best years of your life," promised their parents. Instead, "Welcome to lines, bureaucracy and crowds," the *Daily Californian* editorialized as students were herded from advisers to classrooms down the maze toward matriculation. Welcome to rules and regulations. True, the situation at some universities improved, but for most students campus life resembled an article published by Jerry Farber and reprinted endlessly in undergrounds, "The Student as Nigger." Professors would not stand up for students, or to deans and politicians, because they were "short on balls." Instead, teachers terrorized students. "The grade is a hell of a weapon." A student smiles and shuffles for the professor, learning the most important rule of college: "Tell the man what he wants to hear or he'll fail your ass out of the course." Change was slow at many universities. Students, tuition-payers, demanded the end of puerile rules, and often confronted endless delays. Before the Columbia uprising, officials there were more concerned if a coed was sharing an apartment with her boyfriend and breaking rules than if the regulation was an invasion of her privacy. When articulate student journalists asked too many questions, or when they did not show proper respect, administrators fired or suspended them. Examples abound: *Florida Alligator* for writing editorials critical of state politicians; Queens College *Phoenix* for analyzing the power structure in the administration; Johns Hopkins's *Newsletter* for writing a parody ballot for Man of the Year that included three serial killers with Lyndon Johnson; the University of Texas at El Paso's *El Burro* for a fictitious interview between John Lennon and Jesus. When two students at Monmouth College wrote that a regent was a "political hack," they were suspended from college, and when they returned, arrested for trespassing.[5] Students felt powerless, and many dropped out in their own way. For 120 student government positions at the University of Minnesota not even a hundred ran for election in a university with 45,000 enrolled. Others moved off campus and established undergrounds without censors, or as hip writers for the Austin *Rag* proclaimed: "I'm not a student here, so you can go to hell." Buttons appeared:

I AM A HUMAN BEING
DO NOT FOLD, SPINDLE OR MUTILATE

There were other sayings that appeared on buttons, bumper stickers, and T-shirts that gave clues to the counterculture:

MAKE LOVE NOT WAR

The older generation was fighting a war, one that many younger citizens felt was illegal, inhumane, and immoral. For draft-age youth, the war forced a response. A young man could either go along with the establishment and join the military, fight the machine by protesting and resisting the draft, or drop out. The first two had not stopped the war, and after Nixon's election it was clear that the conflict would continue for years. What to do? Country Joe McDonald answered, "You take drugs, you turn up the music very loud, you dance around, you build yourself a fantasy world where everything's beautiful."

Most kids blamed the war on the older generation. "What's happening," wrote an activist, "is that a whole generation is starting to say to its parents, 'You can no longer get us to kill & be killed for your uptight archaic beliefs.' " Many returning soldiers agreed. Unlike fathers coming home after World War II, Vietnam veterans rarely talked of heroism, duty, honor. Instead, the "endless war" became an endless barrage of horror stories and disillusionment. "I just lost respect for everything after Vietnam," Lieut. Al Wilder commented. "Everything I learned as a kid turned out to be a damn lie." The agonizing onslaught of war tales and images repulsed more and more of the sixties generation. "From Vietnam," wrote Raymond Mungo, "I learned to despise my countrymen, my government, and the entire English-speaking world, with its history of genocide and international conquest. I was a normal kid."

Other kids were distressed by a nation that continued to discriminate against some of its own citizens. One son asked his parents: " 'What would you do if a Negro moved in next door?' and they'd say, 'Nothing! We don't mind.' And I'd say, 'What would you do if I wanted to marry a Negro?' and that was completely different. 'No. You can't marry a Negro. No, no. You can't do that.' And I couldn't understand why, because I'd been raised to believe Negroes were just like anyone else. Two and two just never made four."[6]

Young blacks and whites, of course, had been mingling throughout the decade. On civil rights marches and during Mississippi Freedom Summer many participants reported feelings of personal liberation mixed with community, and later interracial contacts increased on campuses, in liberal cities, and in Southeast Asia. "Vietnam aligned us with blacks after years of encountering them only through music," recalled Toby Thompson. "Our parents may have orchestrated Vietnam, but we played it, taking a curious dividend from that horror. We shook hands with black language, marijuana, G.I. hip. . . . The war to erase communism created a fresh sense of community." Naturally, there was some friction between hippies and "spades," as they first were called in Haight-Ashbury. The hippies had been ingrained with the values of the white suburbs and were attempting to lose those beliefs, while many blacks were working to escape poverty and to join the middle class. Nevertheless, black culture influenced many young whites, through not only jazz and soul music but Martin Luther King's emphasis on nonviolence and love, two important themes of the counterculture. Sexual rules and double standards were not as strict in the black community, which appealed to hippies. Young whites also began adopting some black lingo that came from the blues and jazz scene: "man," "get with it," "dig it," while often referring to young females as "chicks" and a girlfriend as one's "old lady."

Interracial dating became more commonplace and hip, for civil rights workers and freaks both advocated a culture that discriminated against no one—a community of brothers and sisters. A sign in the front of the Free Store in Haight-Ashbury read: "When you enter this door, you are a Digger." Everyone. The Youngbloods sang:

> Come on people now
> Smile on your brother
> Everybody get together
> Try to love one another right now

Thus, the behavior of the culture boosted the counterculture. Without racism, war, and campus paternalism, the population of hippiedom would have been proportionately about the same size as that of the beats in the postwar society. There would have been more hippies, of course, because of the enormous number of baby boomers, but the counter-culture would have been relatively small, confined to the usual bohemian enclaves of the East and West coasts and a few college towns.

In fact, hippies were a strange sight in most cities before the second wave. "To come to Chicago from New York," wrote an activist after the Democratic convention, "is to come into a town where people still stare at you if you are long-haired." And most citizens treated them with scorn. When hipsters first appeared in liberal cities like Seattle or Minneapolis many businesses were so shocked that they refused service. At a restaurant near the University of Washington a waitress declared, "We don't need or want your business," and called the police. An officer arrived immediately and proclaimed, "If they were niggers, they could get away with it!" But not hippies, who were taken down to the station for no reason.[7] In the South, few hippies would leave liberal enclaves such as Atlanta or New Orleans, and in the Southwest rednecks in Austin shouted obscenities while the Okies in Muskogee boasted that they used hippies for target practice.

Yet the counterculture expanded. National problems persisted, ran amok during the Nixon era, and that confirmed the hippie idea that the country was becoming a wasteland. By the end of the decade, surveys found that most citizens agreed with the statement, "Something is wrong with America."

To many youth, the great American institutions seemed to be failing, and that contradicted their upbringing. The military of the "greatest power on earth," a country that had "never lost a war," could not beat peasants in a tiny nation in Southeast Asia. The "experts" had supported this war. So had the political "leaders" in Washington and many "intellectuals" in New York. "The Right War at the Right Time." Students quickly realized that the draft was unfair. Harvard student James Fallows lost enough weight so his 6'1" frame was below minimum requirements, 120 pounds, while unaware working-class kids passed the physical and were shipped out for 'Nam. After graduation, many students felt that the future held out a job in a sterile corporation, perhaps one that made napalm or pol-luted the environment. And for solace, the younger generation could turn to their ministers—the older generation who preached love your neighbor in segregated churches and who flinched at the sight of young worshipers not dressed in their "Sunday best."

Furthermore, during the age of euphemism there seemed an overload of inconsistencies, ironies, and contradictions. The nation made a hero of rocket scientist Wernher Von Braun, a former Nazi and enemy, while putting young college graduates in jail for years because they resisted mili-tary service that would send them to kill Vietnamese. Young Americans were old enough, 18, to fight a war that they did not create, but not old enough, 21 then, to drink a beer or vote for their commander-in-chief. Doctors wrote 150 million prescriptions a year for tranquilizers and amphetamines, and parents who consumed caffeine, alcohol, and nicotine condemned youth for "using drugs."

Hippies turned the tables. It was not the younger generation that "blew it," but the older who behaved abnormally, who had lost touch with reality. Kids wondered, who was sane? As they watched popular films on campuses asking that question—*King of Hearts, A Thousand Clowns*—the establishment provided them with food for thought. The U.S. Supreme Court ruled that language was not obscene as long as it had "redeeming social value." A senator introduced a bill to "outlaw the Mafia." The federal Bureau of Reclamation announced plans to build dams on the Colorado River and flood the Grand Canyon. The federal government subsidized growing tobacco and at the same time paid for advertisements proclaiming that cigarettes were harmful to health and told college students that if they smoked marijuana they would "graduate to heroin." While some officials complained that a stamp picturing Henry David Thoreau made the author look too much like a hippie, President Nixon awarded Elvis Presley with a citation for the singer's contribution in the fight against drugs. The mayor of Cambridge banned the street sale of *Avatar*, claiming that the underground was not a newspaper but a "commodity." A 150 armed officers in Lawrence raided a hippie house near the University of Kansas, arresting 30 laid-back kids, while 200 cops stormed the sleeping campus of SUNY at Stony Brook, woke hundreds in dorm beds, and arrested 33 for possessing "evidence" such as tobacco pipes and psychedelic posters. The governor of New Mexico advocated expelling all freaks, and his counterpart in Tennessee was more blunt, declaring, "It's war. We want every long-hair in jail or out of the state." The forces of law and order left many to agree with David Harris: "If this is the law, then I want to be an outlaw." What happened to the Land of the Free? "I don't get it," wrote a freak in *Rat* after Senator Edward Kennedy drove off a bridge, killing his young female staff worker: "Kennedy has an accident that cuts a chick's life off and it was called a misdemeanor. You smoke tea and it's a fuckin' felony?"[8]

By the end of the sixties, then, the smiling baby boomers who had entered college at mid-decade and attended classes during the days of decision, had graduated into a sea of frustration. "We do not feel like a cool, swinging generation," declared a Radcliffe graduate, "we are eaten up inside by an intensity that we cannot name."

The name was alienation. "America," James Kunen jotted down, "Listen to it. *America*. I love the sound. I love what it could mean. I hate what it is."

Opinion polls revealed a startling growth of alienation among college students during the first Nixon administration. Researchers found that a third felt marriage was obsolete and that having children was not very important, and that the number of those responding that religion, patriotism, and "living a clean, moral life" were "important values" plummeted 20 percentage points. Half held no living American in high regard, and over 40 percent felt America was a "sick society," did not think that they shared the views of most citizens, and even considered moving to another country. During the entire American experience it would be difficult to find a more alienated people than the sixties generation during the second wave.

The counterculture believed that the nation had become a Steppenwolf, a berserk monster, a cruel society that made war on peasants abroad and at home beat up on minorities, dissidents, students, and hippies. America the Beautiful was no more; it had been replaced by Amerika the Death Culture. It was no coincidence that many youth no longer stood at sporting events as bands played the national anthem, or that one of their favorite groups took the name the Grateful Dead, or that more kids were using drugs. "What is increasingly clear," wrote one participant, "is that drugs are not a dangerous short-cut to ecstasy so much as they are a device used for coping with modern society. Drugs are . . . a desperate, futile flailing at a society that increasingly rejects humanitarian values." Many agreed with Timothy Leary: "Your only hope is dope."[9]

"There must be some way out of here," sang Jimi Hendrix. Alienation drove students toward the counterculture, for a hippie creed was that institutions and experts had failed. The emperor had been losing his clothes throughout the decade, and after Tet, Columbia, and Chicago, he was stark naked. Bumper stickers appeared on colorful VW minivans:

QUESTION AUTHORITY

Social ironies are always present in any culture, of course, but those paradoxes had an abnormal impact on the massive sixties generation. These kids had been raised in the cold war culture, where there were concrete rules of "normal behavior" and "right and wrong." Authority. When a teenage daughter questioned if God existed, her father retorted, "As long as you live in this house you'll believe what I tell you to believe." Don't question, play the game. Parents demanded that their children "fit in" and "be normal."

Kids did fit in, but then later critics complained that they were apathetic, that they lacked idealism and moral commitment. Students began to march, to demonstrate, and again the older generation complained. As

Benita Eisler recalled, "when young people became the romantic revolutionaries our elders blamed us for not being, they were confronted by guns and tear gas."

Hypocrisy. There were double standards, for boys and girls, for children and parents, for individuals and government. The struggle had cracked the consensus, student power revealed the contradictions, and the war killed the moral authority of the elders. "It is not only that parents are no longer guides," wrote Margaret Mead, "but that there are no guides."

Young against Old, but it never was that simple, for a number of elders understood the reasons for the counterculture. Martin Luther King felt that hippies resulted from the tragic debasement of American life, the slaughter in Southeast Asia, "the negative effect of society's evils on sensitive young minds." A bookstore manager said of hippies: "I don't blame these people for looking at us and shaking their heads. I think we handed them a lot of tough problems and I'm not sure what I'd be doing if I was growing up right now." A truck driver added, "I get a big kick outa hearin' about 'em, the drugs and shacking up together and given' the big guys hell," and a woman added: "Let 'em go their own way. They're not killing anybody. Our government's the one that's doin' that!"[10]

Many in the establishment criticized the status quo, boosting alienation and the counterculture. Senator J. William Fulbright denounced what he called the president's "arrogance of power," and James Ridgeway demonstrated that many of the finest universities were accepting enormous funds to do research for the Pentagon and CIA in *The Closed Corporation: American Universities in Crisis*. Many authors linked population growth with energy shortages and ecological disaster. The Club of Rome warned about overpopulation in *Limits to Growth* and so did Paul Ehrlich in *The Population Bomb*. Barry Commoner declared in *Closing Circle*, "The present course of environmental degradation . . . is so serious that, if continued, it will destroy the capability of the environment to support a reasonably civilized human society." The future was in peril, as Paul and Anne Ehrlich proclaimed in *The End of Affluence*. In a series of articles eventually published as *The Defeat of America*, historian Henry Steele Commager lamented a government that distorted the truth: "Bombing is 'protective reaction,' precision bombing is 'surgical strikes,' concentration camps are 'pacification centers' or 'refugee camps.' . . . Bombs dropped outside the target area are 'incontinent ordnance,' and those dropped on a South Vietnam village are excused as 'friendly fire'; a bombed house becomes automatically a 'military structure' and a lowly sampan sunk on the waterfront a 'waterborne logistic craft.' "

Students and freaks read novels and commentaries published earlier that became mandatory reading for the sixties generation: the black humor of Joseph Heller's *Catch-22* or Kurt Vonnegut's *Cat's Cradle;* Robert Rimmer's cult classic that advocated group marriages, *The Harrad Experiment;* novels inventing utopian worlds such as B. F. Skinner's *Walden Two,* Aldous Huxley's *Island,* or Robert Heinlein's *Stranger in a Strange Land;* and the science fiction of Isaac Asimov, Arthur C. Clark, C. S. Lewis, and J. R. R. Tolkien. Some young thinkers considered new age technology described by Buckminster Fuller and Marshall McLuhan, while others were interested in the cultural radicalism of Norman O. Brown or R. D. Laing. While some Americans protested, others pondered Viktor Frankl's *Man's Search for Meaning* or studied Erich Fromm's *The Art of Loving.* While U.S. troops fought a war in Asia, others became interested in Native American ideas traced in Carlos Castaneda's *The Teachings of Don Juan* or John Neihardt's editions of *Black Elk Speaks,* or in Eastern beliefs presented in the Chinese oracle *I Ching,* Alan Watts's *The Way of Zen,* Herman Hesse's *Siddhartha,* or Idries Shah's *The Way of the Sufi.* All of those were excellent sellers on campuses and in hip communities, and so were contemporary publications, such as the fables of Richard Brautigan and Richard Bach, or the social commentary of Philip Slater's *The Pursuit of Loneliness* and Charles A. Reich's *The Greening of America.* Regardless of the merits or demerits of these critiques, they boosted the hippie view of America—something was wrong, and a new culture was emerging.

By the second wave the sixties generation was clubbed into reality: The older generation was not practicing what it preached. Nor were some of the younger generation—the activists who had become revolutionaries, who clamored that there was no democracy in America and then shouted down other speakers while yelling Power to the People. As one demonstrator lamented, "the radicals always regard the people . . . as something to be manipulated, exploited, or ignored. 'Get out of the way, people,' they say, 'so we can have our revolution!' . . . Power trips are what we are trying to get away from." It wasn't that the emerging counterculture disagreed with the radical interpretation of America, it was that by the Nixon era that message was irrelevant. Fewer and fewer attended SDS meetings while more and more meandered to the smoke-in and lay in the grass. While the self-proclaimed vanguard was only a tiny percentage of the movement, it eventually provoked many to drop out. "Why did we start collectives?" asked members of the Canyon Collective. "Because we didn't dig being bossed around by bureaucrats whether on the job or in 'the movement.' We were tired of living and acting alone, and wanted to share more of our lives with each other."

"Some great wind was brewing as we breathed," Jacob Brackman wrote, "not a new generation, but a new notion of generation with new notions of its imperatives. We would not default, succumb to the certainties of age . . . compromise maturely. . . . We would not be normal. For normality was now disease."

What was normal? What was reality? As fires blazed in the ghetto politicians declared another program, and then voted $1 billion annually to attack the underlying causes of racism and riots and $30 billion to attack Vietnamese peasants. The best and the brightest, the wise men, the leaders declared we were winning the war, and weekly they "proved" it by body counts and kill ratios. Walter Cronkite would broadcast those figures to the nation, ending the evening news with "And that's the way it is." Many hippies thought, if that's the way it is, then:

DO YOUR OWN THING

What was their thing? As disillusionment soared after the assassination of Robert Kennedy, activist Marvin Garson wondered: "What's wrong with the New Left? What happened to all the magic in phrases like 'participatory democracy' and 'let the people decide'?" He answered his own question: "The heartbreaker has been that for some reason people don't WANT to go to meetings, don't WANT to participate."[11]

The stark realization that working in mainstream society would not change *the* world stimulated many activists to being looking inside to change *their* world. As Ten Years After sang:

I'd love to change the world,
but I don't know what to do,
so I'll leave it up to you.

During the second wave changing their world usually was done two different ways—some left the cities and began building their own communes and alternative societies, and others stayed in hip communities usually near campuses and became cultural activists.

Universities became filled with people who looked, acted, and talked like hippies. After the Columbia University upheaval, Carl Davidson of SDS suggested that three-fourths of the organization's national membership could be classified as hippies, and at Rutgers and Long Island universities professors noted interest waning from politics. "Now the talk has shifted to cultural revolution. Gentle grass is pushing up through the cement." Students who had been involved in protests began to look inward, and even occupying a campus building became part of a personal revolution. "The idea was to liberate yourself from the confining conventions of life, and to celebrate the irrational side of your nature, kind of let yourself go," recalled a University of Chicago student. "This was the counterculture coming to us, and it stirred people up and made us feel like doing something dramatic."

To many, doing something dramatic meant doing something *different*, rejecting the values drilled into them as they grew up during cold war culture. "The point is that it was the culture that was sick," said Jentri Anders. "One way to change that is to live it differently . . . just drop out and live it the way you think it ought to be."

Live differently, outside of the mainstream, but of course freaks never could drop out completely. They drove the roads and had to adhere to highway laws, bought land and had to comply with local ordinances. They paid rent, bills, and had to buy food and other goods. Some worked and paid taxes, others used social services, and some got drafted.

Dropping out, then, usually meant dropping the values of the older generation—developing ones for the New America—and counterculture values were a reaction to mainstream ones. If straights said, "My country right or wrong," then freaks shook their heads and said Fuck the War. The Fugs sang "Kill for Peace," the Doors "Unknown Soldier," and Country Joe and the Fish made war sound like a carnival farce:

> Come on, fathers, don't hesitate,
> Send your sons off before it's too late;
> You can be the first ones in your block
> To have your boy come home in a box.

All the while the movement chanted along, "All we are saying, is give peace a chance."

If World War II veterans proclaimed, "You have an obligation to serve your country," then freaks felt that they had an obligation to themselves. Arlo Guthrie derided selective service in "Alice's Restaurant Massacree," the story of a young man's draft physical. When the army psychiatrist asked what was his problem, the hippie answered: "Shrink, I wanna kill, kill, kill!" The doctor pinned a medal on him and proclaimed, "You're our boy."

When straights talked about "traditional values," freaks became the movement's cultural shock troops. During the first wave almost all activists had short hair and appeared and behaved rather clean-cut, but hippies delighted in upsetting the older generation with their dress, language, and especially hair. "I never could tell where my husband's sideburns ended and his mustache began," recalled a baby boomer, "but he didn't care as long as it irritated his mother."[12]

Language. What could be more vulgar, more filthy, most hippies thought, than racial hatred and the war. "What is obscene?" one wrote,

Is it obscene to fuck,
or
Is it obscene to kill? . . .

Is it more obscene to describe
fucking,
An act of love,
or
Is it more obscene to describe
killing,
An act of hate? . . .

Why is Free hate
socially acceptable
While Free Love
is socially unacceptable?

Which is really obscene?

The shock troops attacked the institutions held dear by most Americans. They ridiculed the military as the "armed farces," and skewered government in every underground. "Institutions—schools, hospitals, courts—not only do not do what they have been set up to do," wrote a participant, "but the opposite. They have become the ghouls, vampires, werewolves of our culture, the Frankensteins of our way of life." Hippies also blasted the church, an attack that had been initiated by many activist theologians such as James Groppi, Paul Moore, and the Berrigan brothers. The Reverend Malcolm Boyd spoke of a small but expanding group of committed men and women who were "forcing changes on the church from the middle and bottom," and he labeled it the Underground Church.[13] Hippies joined the crusade. While Arlo Guthrie claimed that "the streets of heaven have all been sold," actors in the rock musical *Jesus Christ Superstar* asked Christ, "Who are you, what have you sacrificed?"

The counterculture aimed to sacrifice the society's "bigger and better," "new and improved" thinking. What was progress? "At General Electric," the ad went, "progress is our most important product." Was new really improved, or was this progress simply the buy, buy ethic of the throw-away society, a way of life that hippies felt was wasteful and ravishing the environment? The question concerned not only hippies but a growing number of Americans who, like the musicians Spirit, were becoming concerned about the smelly breeze and dying trees. "It's nature's way of telling you something's wrong." The Guess Who demanded, "Don't give me no hand me down world," and Joni Mitchell lamented,

Don't it always seem to go
that you don't know what you've got 'till it's gone?
They paved paradise and put up a parking lot.

Counterculture paradise usually did not include the vinyl and aerosol institutions, the 9 to 5 gray-flannel day, the continual race for the Almighty Dollar. Freaks wanted to escape the suburban trap, the split-level house, the two kids and a dog, and they wanted to avoid becoming a "Nowhere Man," as the Beatles sang, who didn't have a point of view, "who knows not where he's going to." And since straights desired to make money, freaks scorned materialism and consumption, a career of mass production: "Plastics," said an older businessman in *The Graduate*—that was the key to the future. "All of us started to realize," wrote a hippie, "that the game of life played in school and the Supermarket U. leads only to styrofoam coffins and oblivious servitude. . . . All are well trained towards indiscriminate consumption. Yet the feeling persists—there must be something greater than this!" And so hippies aimed to be "free from property hang-ups, free from success fixations, free from positions, titles, names, hierarchies, responsibilities, schedules, rules, routines, regular habits." Free . . . Free . . . Free . . .

"I believe one of the major problems of our time is to teach people to do nothing," Lou Gottlieb stated. "Americans are all karma yogis, people who literally can't sit still. My mother, if she came upon a catatonic schizoid, would scream at him to get busy. I got that until it absolutely deformed my childhood. It was never enough just to sit still and scratch your balls, enjoying yourself." Sit back and relax. Think. Go with the flow.

Let It Be

Instead of the straight, normal life, Barry Melton recalled, "We were setting up a new world . . . that was going to run parallel to the old world but have as little to do with it as possible. We just weren't going to deal with straight people."[14]

Become a freak. Adopt different values. If the average guy took the straight and narrow road, the superhighway to suburbs, hippies sought a another path, dancing to a different drummer. Since mid-decade many had been exploring. Simon and Garfunkel "walked off to look for America," and later The Who asked the generation: "Who are you, who who, who who? . . . They call me the seeker, I've been searching low and high." Many became seekers, dropping out for a while, searching for themselves and for America. New spaces. New experiences. New thoughts. "Thinking is the best way to travel," sang the Moody Blues while Chicago was searching for an answer "to the question, 'who am I?' " Goodbye past. Time to take a giant step, to trip through the *doors* of perception.

Many did, as the second wave became the "Age of Aquarius," a joyous, bright time, a new morning. "Here comes the sun," proclaimed the Beatles, and the musicians in *Hair* sang out, "Let the sun shine." "The hippies have passed beyond American society," wrote an underground journalist. "They're not really living in the same society. It's not so much that they're living on the leftovers, on the waste of American society, as that they just don't give a damn."

They did give a damn about their own culture, however, and they began to build one that expressed values that they felt were positive, healthy—building a peaceful, gentle society that discriminated against no one and that practiced love. "All you need is love," they sang. "Love is other, love is being and letting be, love is gentle, love is giving and love is dropping out, love is turning on, love is a trip, a flower, a smile, a bell." Other values were honesty, tolerance, personal freedom, and fun. Hugh Romney of the Hog Farm stated a hippie truism: "Do anything you want as long as nobody gets hurt."[15]

IF IT FEELS GOOD, DO IT

A theme of cold war culture (and a later era) was "just say no." The creed was the Protestant Ethic: work. The motif of the sixties was "just say yes," and the canon was the Pleasure Ethic: fun. Live for the moment. Have a Happy Day.

Freaks said yes to many things that their parents had told them to reject—especially drugs and sex. Dope felt good: Dope was FUN. And "dope" was the usual name, as Tom Coffin explained in *Great Speckled Bird:*

> Dope not Drugs—alcohol is a drug, pot is DOPE; nicotine is a DRUG, acid is DOPE; DRUGS turn you off, dull your senses, give you the strength to face another day in Death America, DOPE turns you on, heightens sensory awareness, sometimes twists them out of shape and you experience that too, gives you vision and clarity, necessary to create Life from Death. . . . The difference between Stupor and Ecstasy is the difference between Jack Daniels and Orange Sunshine, between the Pentagon and Woodstock, between *The New York Times* and *Good Times*. We all have to make our choices.

While the older generation labeled it "drugs" and put up billboards asking their children, "Why do they call it Dope?," the younger genera-

tion sang along with the Rolling Stones who wailed about the older generations' dependency on tranquilizers, "Mother's Little Helper."

Dope was the freak's little helper that aided their escape from the establishment. "If it hadn't been for grass I'd still be wearing a crewcut and
saluting the flag." Escape was important. Frustrated people often relieve
anxieties by eating, smoking, drinking, even shopping away their worries:
"I Love to Shop!" But not hippies. "Smoke dope everywhere," proclaimed
one. "Dope is Great, it's fun, it's healthy. . . . Get every creature so
stoned they can't stand the plastic shit of American culture."

Dope, especially LSD, also helped them expand or alter their own consciousness. Timothy Leary recalled his first trip, the "most shattering experience of my life," for it "flipped my consciousness into a dance of
energy, where nothing existed except whirring vibrations and each illusory
form was simply a different frequency." Ram Dass added, "We've moved
in the direction of a whole new model of the human brain. . . . You
can travel anywhere, back into childhood, back through evolutionary history, cosmic history, down your own bloodstream or nervous system."

While the Byrds soared "Eight Miles High," others declared that their
cosmic trips brought them closer to religion or as an observer wrote, "a
spiritual agility and a gracefulness which leads them to believe that they
have achieved an unusual unification of the mind, the soul and the
senses."[16]

Thus, by taking dope hippies felt different, Heads versus Straights, another form of Us versus Them. "Grass opened up a new space for middle
class white kids," recalled Jay Stevens, "an inner space as well as outer
space. It became a ritual—sitting around with your friends, passing a joint
from person to person, listening to music, eating, talking, joking, maybe
making out—all the senses heightened." They felt community being part
of the underground. A daughter wrote:

> Dear Dad:
>
> Dope . . . potacidspeedmetheshitboojointtripped freakfiend. . . .
> Flip Out. It all runs together; indivisible, etc. etc. etc. from—if you
> can take it—the world in which we live. Real. World. REAL
> WORLD. Our world, not yours. The world of everything, dream
> dance escape thought and blood. A machine has cranked us out. And
> our father doesn't know how to stop it, much less fix it. . . . There's
> a LOVE in MY WORLD for the new exciting land that was always
> far off the map in fifth grade geography. Things aren't always knowable
> and certain and stifling. To walk through it is its essence, so, Dad,
> let's TAKE A TRIP.

But trip on certain helpers. While no two hippies would agree, in general they used marijuana and its more potent form, hashish, to obtain a

quiet euphoria and "get high," or they used hallucinogens or psychedelics such as psilocybin, peyote, and LSD to expand sensory perception and "blow the mind." Thus, dope that felt good or expanded experience was fine; others that made one sick or addicted were a "bad trip," a "bummer." Freaks might avoid depressants and substances that tended to be addicting such as amphetamines, or "speed," or narcotics such as heroin, or "smack." New drugs appeared endlessly, and underground editors ran columns like Dr. Eugene Schoenfeld's "HIPpocrates" and other articles which warned their readers, "Speed kills!" "I would like to suggest that you don't use speed, and here's why," cautioned musician Frank Zappa: "it is going to mess up your heart, mess up your liver, your kidneys, rot out your mind. In general, this drug will make you just like your mother and father."[17]

Hippies made their own decisions, of course, and they violated the norm because they were rebels and because they enjoyed experimenting. Nevertheless, various surveys reported that at the beginning of the sixties only 4 percent of youth aged 18 to 25 had tried marijuana, and that twelve years later that figure was almost 50 percent; 60 percent for college students; and much higher at some universities: 70 percent at the University of Kansas, and almost 90 percent at Boston University College of Law. Underground papers conducted their own unscientific surveys, and while unreliable, it appears that of those who responded usually 80 or 90 percent smoked marijuana, half to two-thirds had experimented with LSD, and perhaps 10 percent had tried heroin.

A majority of the sixties generation, then, tried marijuana, and many more attempted to liberate themselves from the older generation's sexual mores. Elders had taught children Puritan values, that sex was reserved for married adults. Youth must avoid premarital sex and promiscuity, and rumors abounded that masturbation caused everything from blindness to hand warts. The sledgehammer to prevent such behavior was GUILT. Hippies rebelled, calling those ideas "hang-ups" and advocating "free love." Of course, they did not invent the idea, for armed with birth control pills the sixties generation had been experimenting at college and sexual freedom leagues had been established earlier in the Bay Area and New York City. But freaks expanded the idea so sex seemed freer than at any time in memory. "Let's spend the night together" wailed the Rolling Stones, while Janis Joplin advised her sisters to "get it while you can." For the first time the airwaves were filled with blatant demands for sex, and while kids began wearing buttons—"Save Water, Shower with a Friend"—hippies clarified the idea of liberation. "A legal contract for a sexual relationship is, if not out of date, at least beside the point for most of us." This was different from a college kid "getting laid," they claimed; free love meant a couple "making love," any time, any form, out of wedlock, and especially without guilt. "Make love," wrote a freak, "not to one guy or chick who you grab onto and possess out of fear and loneliness— but to all beautiful people, all sexes, all ages." They watched the film *Harold and Maude*, where a zestful woman of 79 taught a young man to be sensual, to live, and they agreed with the idea that "If you can't be with the one you love, then love the one you're with."

Hippie writings often were sexist by later standards, since the counterculture developed before women's liberation. Sales of underground papers soared when they began publishing "personal" columns in which men would advertise for "groovy chicks who like to smoke weed and ball." In New York City, Underground Enterprises established a dating service called FUK, "For Turned-on people only. Heads Do the Matching." Guys could apply by sending five dollars, "girls apply free."[18]

The second wave, however, was influenced by the rise of feminism, and hippies became aware of equality in free love, and more tolerant of all forms of sexuality—masturbation, homosexuality, bisexuality. Sexual liberation meant that all private acts between consenting people should be legal and probably attempted. The underground press also rejected the elder's fear of nudity, dirty and shameful, and filled pages with nude couples skinny dipping in ponds, sunbathing, and holding hands and singing. Since nudity outraged the older generation, that was reason enough to take off clothes. "Here I am," proclaimed a freak, "see me; so what is new?" Hippies established nude beaches and communities. Freedom. Fun. Playfulness. One wanted to clean up politics so he ran for president nude with the slogan, "What have I got to hide?" To prevent police from attacking and beating demonstrators, the Shiva Fellowship in San Francisco advocated disrobing.

Free love was complemented by dope, for many hippies felt that psychedelics and marijuana were aphrodisiacs that heightened sexual pleasure. While that was debated endlessly, passing around a joint did decrease inhibitions and increase relaxation and intimacy, feelings that were attractive to youth raised during the uptight postwar era.

Making love and smoking dope was behavior usually conducted behind closed doors; dress was for the public, and it was a symbol. Hair represented rebellion from the crew-cut cold war era, and identity with the new generation. "Almost cut my hair," sang Crosby, Stills, and Nash, but instead they let their "freak flag fly," because, as Nash later stated, "if they had long hair you knew how they thought, that they were into good music, a reasonable life, that they probably hated the government." Hair, and dress, sequestered them from mom and pop, declared independence. Hip men threw out sport coats and ties, and hip women abandoned cosmetics and undergarments and for the first time in memory revealed the soft contours of unbound bodies. "Long hair, beards, no bras and freaky clothes represent a break from Prison Amerika," declared Jerry Rubin. Clothes became costumes and costumes became clothes.

The older generation was appalled, complaining, "you can't tell the boys from the girls," and oh, those "dirty, filthy, smelly hippies." During the veteran's era after World War II and Korea, the sight of a beard on a businessman even raised eyebrows. But freaks had different ideas about dress and cleanliness. While they did bathe, of course, they were not dismayed by the smell of the human body, for it was normal, part of getting back to nature and a revolt against middle-class TV-commercial values. They felt that deodorant, cosmetics, perfume, cologne were phony, Madison Avenue: "Aren't you glad you use Dial? Don't you wish everybody did?" Don't care, said the freaks, saying that people should smell their bodies, for each individual's scent was different. Learn about yourself: "You're beautiful." If they desired a scent then they lit incense or wore musk oil, a secretion of the male musk deer. Hippies also abandoned polyester clothing in favor of leather and cotton, and they ate fresh, natural foods without preservatives and grown organically.

Not "uptight," but "laid back" in dress and also in lifestyle. Many critics labeled hippies "lazy," and parents claimed, "You're throwing your life away. You don't know how hard it was for us. . . ." But that missed the point about hip ideas of work and play. "Life should be ecstasy," said Allen Ginsberg, and hippies worked to escape daily drudgery and to discover their own pleasureful existence. "What's your thing?" Many held jobs that they liked, and others labored to build their vision of the future, either part or full time. Margy Kittredge asked, "Why should we work 12 or 16 hours a day now when we don't have to? For a color TV? For wall-to-wall carpeting? An automatic ice-cube maker?" And Tuli Kupferberg summarized, "Believe me when I say, if you enjoy it, it can still be good; it can still be 'work' (only we'll call it 'play'). Play is as good as work. Work has been defined as something you *dislike* doing. Fuck that. Do the Beatles *work?* Who cares."[19]

Another counterculture value was brotherhood. "He ain't heavy, he's my brother," they sang, while *North Country News* editorialized, "You and I are part of the dawning of an age of sharing and co-operation." There were many problems facing the new culture, and the only way to resolve them was "working together and trying to—LOVE ONE ANOTHER RIGHT NOW." Neil Young advocated more understanding as he tried to bridge the gap between fathers and sons, crying out, "Old man take a look at my life, I'm a lot like you." "Come together," sang the Beatles, as they reminded their generation that "the love you take is equal to the love you make."

During the days of decision the activism was demanding, even violent, but during the second wave the idea was simple—live gentle. Crosby, Stills, Nash and Young:

> Our house is a very, very, very fine house
> with two cats in the yard
> life used to be so hard
> now everything is easy 'cause of you.

Counterculture values continued developing as the second wave flooded through the Gates of Eden and toward the Age of Aquarius. What resulted was a vague social thought that merged values with other ideas, a social thought that was never static but always flowing and bubbling since one of the ideas was the continual need to experiment. "Change jobs, spouses, hairstyles, clothes; change religion, politics, values, even the personality; try everything, experiment constantly, accept nothing as given." An endless experiment: How? Search out, seek what had not been allowed, what was not real. As Tim Leary said, "it becomes necessary for us to go out of our minds in order to use our heads." Far Out, wrote a hippie,

> BLOW YOUR MINDS!
> dont hang all day in the closet
> with your hats . . .
> FOR CHRIST'S SAKE allow yourselves
> to be a little crazy
> stop making so
> much sense . . .
> do something wrong . . .
> wear unmatched socks . . .
> go ride an elevator just for fun . . .
> think about trees . . .
> imagine how the sun would taste . . .
> smash your transistor radios . . .
> go out to the airport and wave goodbye
> to people you dont know . . .
> throw away your tubes of suntan lotion . . .
> unzip your faces and let the sun
> reach your grey minds . . .

Hippies agreed with Plato's ancient maxim that a life unexamined is not worth living. "Never forget that the greatest battlefield of them all is right within you, in that treasure-room called consciousness, where all future developments lie hidden, sometimes to be revealed in all their glorious magnificence!" While searching for the sun, Ramon Sender and Alicia Bay Laurel wrote:

> Open yourself to the possibility of having visions. Then prepare for them by feeling your own being and your own environment. The wisdom of all ancient teachings lives in your heart. When you relax enough to hear it, this wisdom can rename you, reclothe you, give you dances, exercises & meditations, ceremonies & recognitions of divinity in everyday life that make your whole day an act of being radiantly blissful.

Hippiedom was gentle for some, groping on a sunny afternoon, throwing frisbees with friends, and for others it was a continual excursion as they donned backpacks, put out their thumbs, and caught the disease—wanderlust. "If the vibes are good, I'll stay on," Joanie said about New Jerusalem commune, "if not, I've heard about a Zen group in the Sierras I'd like to look into." The quest did not end at U.S. borders. The demand for passports doubled, and by the end of the decade about 800,000 young Americans were traveling in Europe while over a million were thumbing throughout the nation. "We weren't fleeing home," said one, "we were seeking one."[20]

Another aspect of hip social thought was humor. Freaks smoked dope and giggled, ate hashish brownies and giggled, drank homemade wine and giggled. After the straight and narrow 1950s, freaks celebrated the weird. Buttons: "Reality is a nice place to visit, but I wouldn't want to live there," "People who live in glass houses shouldn't get stoned." At Cornell they challenged the mayor of Ithaca to an arm-wrestling match because they believed in "armed struggle," while the "Manhattan Indians" at Columbia demanded the return of the Indian head nickel, no classes on Sitting Bull's birthday, and complete amnesty for Geronimo. Freaky students attended ROTC drills where they lampooned the cadets by playing leap frog or blowing bubbles. New York hippies advocated a "loot-in" of Macy's department store, and the *Barb* spread the Great Banana Conspiracy, claiming that kids could get a legal high by drying banana peels, and smoking the inside scrapings; the Food and Drug Administration did experiments and declared that the fruit was a good source of potassium and fiber. While activists wore buttons demanding "Free the Chicago 7," freaks pinned on "Free the Indianapolis 500," and others delighted in making preposterous statements: "It will be an LSD country in fifteen years," claimed Tim Leary, and the "Supreme Court will be smoking marijuana." Freaks laughed all the way to the Cheech and Chong movies. "As for this 'don't trust-anyone-over-30' shit," wrote James Kunen, "I agree in principle, but I think they ought to drop the zero."

Hippies desired an anti-materialistic lifestyle. "I wanted to simplify my life as much as possible," one communard stated. "It wasn't hard to drop out. I had a lot of things to get rid of—a car, a hi-fi, a million useless things. . . . I got rid of it all. It was like getting a good load off." Living cheap became an art, and being poor was hip in America's throw-away society. Stores traditionally selling second-hand goods, Salvation Army and Goodwill Industries, witnessed scores of longhairs in their check-out lines. Freaks also scavenged. When residents at Drop City commune needed metal to build their geodesic domed homes, they dismantled an entire unused bridge. The Heathcote Community wrote about "The Fine Art of Trashmongering," finding useful things in the neighborhood or at the junk yard, and reported the free plunder from just one evening: an elegant stuffed lion, needing only a wash; a pencil and watering can; and a "blue blazer, nearly new condition, and emblazoned with the words 'College Bound,' which we removed."[21]

Some freaks were employed, usually holding temporary jobs to earn "bread," saving up for a few weeks, and then retiring, which became a familiar pattern during the second wave. With the economy growing and jobs plentiful, it was easy to find temporary employment, and as hip became style small businessmen grew less antagonistic toward hiring long-hair helpers. Also, many could find employment in an expanding number of hip business or social services that were not concerned about appearance. Soon freaks were selling records and delivering the mail.

Then they got paid, and hippies argued about money and profit. Critics often mocked them for denouncing capitalism while establishing hip businesses or working for a paycheck. This seemed like an inconsistency, but freaks came in all types and could not completely drop out of American society. Usually they felt that capitalism equaled greed, and so a few advocated "ripping off the system," meaning that it was all right for poor freaks to accept food stamps from the government, even to steal from private businesses as if they were Robin Hoods. The "Peoples Operators" informed readers of *Quicksilver Times* how to cheat the phone company and give the "largest pig monopoly in the world another big headache." But others disagreed. "I just don't trust a ripoff mentality. . . . Once a guy starts ripping off the phone company, or welfare, or a foundation, or a supermarket, he kind of gets the habit, and he'll be ripping you off next thing you know." Instead, most hippies attempted to live a simple, antimaterialistic existence, and to promote this many underground publishers sold for cost or gave away their papers. *Contempt's* price was "from each, to each," *Leviathan* was free to political prisoners, and *Little Free Press* was "totally free. . . . If we want freedom, let's quit using money because the rich control the money; so they control us." Others, however, were not so sure. "Make all the money you want. Make billions!" wrote a hippie in *Planet*. Money equaled energy, and "if WE don't get that energy, someone else will."

Such debates were never resolved, and they were most vicious when they concerned selling hippie culture. After the Psychedelic Shop in San Francisco opened it received a note: "You're selling out the revolution. . . . You're putting it on the market." But more offensive were hip promoters and musicians cashing in, because that conflicted with a cardinal belief—the music should be free. Underground journalists realized that rock festivals symbolized the struggle between two cultures, capitalism versus hippiedom, but freaks felt that promoters turned "festivals of love" into "festivals for profit." By the end of the decade the *Seed* reported that "freaks are getting more and more uptight with the rampant shucksterism involved in most of the festivals," complaining that a "whole swarm of sideburned entrepreneurs is preparing to capitalize on the hip culture's twin addictions: rock music and tribal gatherings."

Some freaks became activists when they felt that they were being "ripped off." They picketed theater chains that raised prices for the popular movies, *Easy Rider* and *Woodstock*, and instead of paying admission fees for concerts a few began to "gate crash." Others boycotted expensive concerts. The $14 admission price for a festival at Carbondale, Illinois, was condemned by an underground reporter who realized that musicians needed "bread" but questioned Sly and the Family Stone and The Band demanding $25,000 "in small bills, in advance" for a forty-five-minute set. "Holy shit, who was that that first said rock is getting a little commercial?" Indeed, as one hippie capitalist lamented, "Being a promoter these days is a bummer deal. You take it from the straights on one side and the crazies on the other."[22]

While issues concerning money and profit were debated endlessly, social thought about the environment was not: Hippies were environmentalists. They did not invent the movement, of course, for many citizens became concerned about pollution throughout the decade, but hippies boosted ecology and practiced such values. In Eugene, cultural activists created Cyclists Revolting Against Pollution, CRAP, "clean-air guerrillas" who drove in groups "to show people there are ways to move other than foul automobiles spewing death." But more often they established "people's parks." "HEAD for the Park," wrote a Seattle hippie, "a park is for living things, squirrels, children, growing things, turned-on things, people, love, food, lush green colors, laughter, kites, music, God, the smell of life." Hippies formed a coalition with the Hog Farm, Wartoke Unlimited, Ecology Action Council, Sierra Club, and numerous underground papers to establish Earth People's Park. The idea was that all "the people" would send one dollar, and a permanent living space for the generation would be purchased and built in New Mexico or Colorado.[23] The flyer proclaimed:

EARTH PEOPLE'S PARK

is not a music festival
is work and love and generosity and devotion and play
is you doing it whoever you think you are
is not being negative
has no time schedule
is immediate and spontaneous
is not possessive nor possessed
is great humility
is as serious as the universe and the life it sustains
will last as long as your hair. . . .

Counterculture social thought also included a spiritual quest. As institutions and authorities appeared to be faltering, many asked: What is moral? What is amoral? Their answers and experiments took them on a voyage that ranged from Astrology, to Hare Krishna, to LSD, to Taoism, to Zen—and back to Jesus. The idea of an underground church appealed to hippies. It was not that the new generation no longer believed in a supreme being, but that they felt that answers to salvation no longer could be found at the established altars. Hip Protestants in the Bay Area proclaimed that they were "actively involved in creating the alternative church in the alternative culture. . . . Submarine Church Action Network is one expression of the hope shared by that motley assortment of youth, issue-oriented churches, switch-boards, liturgy-freaks, communards and other assorted folk who are the church saying yes to the future. . . . The submarine church is surfacing."

During the Summer of Love, Christian freaks opened a coffee shop in Haight-Ashbury, the Living Room, where they helped kids on dope and talked about Jesus and the Bible. The idea spread rapidly because some hippies identified with Christianity, especially the primitive type practiced in the first century when it was an anti-establishment religion. They noted this in undergrounds and flyers:

FOLLOWERS OF JESUS
WANTED
Jesus Christ

Alias: The Messiah, The Son of
God, King of Kings, Lord of
Lords, Prince of Peace, etc.

Notorious leader of an underground liberation movement.

The notorious leader was wanted for food distribution without a license, interfering with businessmen in the temple, associating with known criminals, radicals, subversives, street people, and for claiming to have the authority to make people into God's children. His appearance was the "typical hippie type—long hair, beard, robe, sandals," and he was listed as "extremely dangerous." As one freak commented, "Did you ever happen to think what would happen if Jesus were to come down to earth again. What would the typical American think? He would probably be thinking, 'Look at that disgusting hippy. Probably high on something, preaching peace, happiness and good will.'"

Many freaks were attracted to underground religions because they felt unwelcome at their parents' church, which they thought was hypocritical. Long-hair members of the Submarine Church attended a Methodist service in St. Louis. When one rose to give witness, the pastor stopped the proceedings and called the police, who apprehended all bearded youth; 30 were led out of the church and 20 were arrested for "disrupting a religious ceremony." Christian singers Love Song put such episodes to music: "Long hair, short hair, some coats and ties. People finally comin' around. Lookin' past the hair and straight into the eyes."

During the turmoil of the second wave, many youth found comfort in the saying, "Jesus loves you," and they became known as Jesus People or Jesus Freaks. While never a unified movement, most agreed with the daughter of a wealthy businessman, "I'd been searching for an answer, something to give meaning to my life. I tried drugs, Zen, a dozen other things, but none of it worked. Then I met the Children of God, and I just gave up everything and joined them. I knew this wasn't just a way of passing time on Sunday, this was God's truth being lived."[24]

God's truth usually meant that Jesus People were religious fundamentalists but not social conservatives, while other hip religions usually preached a much more liberal theology. Catholic laymen at Duquesne and Notre Dame universities formed small study groups and began questioning doctrine and formalities, and many began thinking about St. Francis of Assisi, who left a wealthy Italian family to live in poverty. Some Jewish youth began considering Hillel, the first-century B.C. prophet who urged modesty and peace, while others joined the *havurot* movement, fellowships that emphasized experimental worship and communal living. Other hippies developed an interest in Hare Krishna, Zen Buddhism, and the beliefs of Native Americans. "A day will come when a people with white skin will walk our lands," stated a Native American prophecy, "their hair and clothing will be as ours and they will adopt our customs. We will know them because even their name will sound like our name . . . Hopi." Most hip religions usually were tolerant of other creeds and did not have a rigid deity. They often emphasized the discovery of the inner self, helping one to "get it together," while seeking affirmation and individualism within a group of brothers. *I Ching:* "What is required is that we untie with others, in order that we may complement and aid one another through holding together. . . . Common experiences strengthen these ties."

Counterculture social thought generally had two parallel themes that often appeared in the lives of many hippies. Some revolted and searched for personal liberation, and the freedom that they practiced often was unstructured, libertarian, even anarchistic. Through experimentation, they often grew into what they felt was a more independent and holistic person. Others rebelled, tasted freedom, and rushed to a more authoritarian form of counterculture. These freaks often joined others in spiritual retreats or ashrams, where leaders developed a more structured, disciplined day, and where members practiced religious beliefs aimed at personal growth or inner development. Both of these avenues aimed to balance self-realization and fulfillment with community, and the eventual results depended on each individual.

All the while, hippies developed their alternative society—some dropping out by going to the country while a larger number remained in the city and became involved in cultural activism. Both built various types of hip enclaves that they called communes, cooperatives, collectives, or experimental communities, all difficult to define because freaks interchanged these names and because those living arrangements always were evolving. While there probably were over 2000 rural and at least 5000 urban communes by the end of the decade, no one knows the number because most communards wanted to be left alone and usually would not reply to surveys.

Earlier in the decade pioneers established a few rural communes. Gorda Mountain at Big Sur, California, was an open-land community where everyone was accepted; Heathcote was an educational experiment, a school of living, in Maryland; while psychedelic artists outside of Trinidad, Colorado, constructed Drop City, a community of geodesic domes. By the Summer of Love, Lou Gottlieb had established Morning Star outside of San Francisco for anyone who wanted to practice "voluntary primitivism," and other colorful freaks established the Hog Farm, "an expanded family, a mobile hallucination, a sociological experiment, an army of clowns."

But the stunning growth of communes appeared during and after the rip tide. Assassinations, demonstrations, strikes, beatings—violence—all blended together and provoked many more to drop out, and that included many former activists like Raymond Mungo, Marvin Garson, and Marty Jezer. A communard at Grant's Pass in Oregon recalled "innocent people getting clubbed. Then we began to understand that all those protests just weren't going to do anything except breed hate." Another added, "I had done the political trip for a while, but I got to the point where I couldn't just advocate social change, I had to live it."

Activists such as Tom Hayden called them escapists—dropping out meant copping out—but these builders of the dawn were not listening. Aware that they were politically powerless, they no longer cared about changing the establishment. "Like it's so obvious that civilization is doomed," a communard said, "and we don't want to go with it. . . . We're retribalizing . . . it's the beginning of a whole new age." The new age would be different, said Jezer, for they were building communities, "learning self-sufficiency and rediscovering old technologies that are not destructive to themselves and the land. . . . And we are doing this, as much as possible, outside the existing structures, saying, as we progress, a fond farewell to the system, to Harvard, Selective Service, General Motors, Bank of America, IBM, A&P, ..., IRS, CBS, DDT, USA and Vietnam."

Eventually, many different types of people joined the "back to the land" movement—artists, visionaries, ecologists, radicals, academics, vegetarians, gays, organic farmers, Vietnam veterans, urban professionals, and women searching for more liberation, along with some who left personal problems behind such as a past of drug abuse or a bad marriage. Many were students. At the end of the decade a survey of college youth found that a third were interested in spending time in a commune or collective and almost half wanted to live for a while in a rural setting. Most communards were in their twenties, middle-class, had attended some college. Almost everyone felt trapped in mainstream society, alienated from the policies of their government and from materialistic, technological America. They usually were searching for new values in their own community. "What they all had in common was the highest human aspiration," stated one observer, "to be free."[25]

They adopted a very American approach. They headed for the wide-open spaces that held the bare promise of a fresh start. As they looked forward, they also looked back, hoping for a more primitive way of life, and along the way they developed many types of communes. Some hippies took over abandoned towns, such as Georgeville Trading Post in Minnesota, while others developed new villages such as Pandanaram in Indiana, and 300 moved from the West Coast and established The Farm in Tennessee. But most communes were much smaller, a few buildings. Hip professionals and architects constructed Libre, futuristic homes located beneath the mountains of southern Colorado, and others created two dozen fresh-air communes near Taos, New Mexico. Urban escapees established numerous cooperative farms in southern Oregon that aimed to become completely self-sufficient, while seven farmers annoyed by "the life-style typified by electric toothbrushes and BHT additives" formed Active Acres Co-operative in Wisconsin. Followers of psychologist B. F. Skinner began building a society based on behavioral principles at Twin Oaks in Virginia. Hare Krishna disciples developed New Vrindabsn in West Virginia, while fundamentalist Christians established a Children of God settlement on a ranch near Brenham, Texas. Maharaj Ashram in New Mexico practiced yoga techniques and concepts, and The Farm blended Zen Buddhism with Hindu philosophy and a touch of Christianity. In fact, during the second wave there were so many communes that the North American Student Cooperative Organization, Alternatives! Foundation, and many other groups published directories, newsletters, bulletins, and undergrounds such as *New Harbinger*.

Lifestyles varied at the communes, but in general counterculture values were practiced, or at least attempted. Work and play was a community effort, sacrifice and sharing was encouraged, and eventually some form of pattern or organization developed. "If you are lucky," Stephen Diamond wrote during his third year at Chestnut Hill, "a natural order and rhythm will develop. But it takes time, time to work out painfully all the personal hassles and complications that result from a structureless society, a community that has no previous textbooks to follow as guidelines." Communards naturally experimented with personal freedom and liberation. Some of the early communes advocated completely free love, where all members engaged in sexual encounters and where group sex or bisexuality might be accepted. Harrad West in Berkeley and Talsen in Oregon were "group marriages," spouses or singles who switched partners, and Bryn Athyn in Vermont practiced "sexual coziness" where members supposedly "played with each other's sexual parts without fear or guilt." But much more common were communes where hippies became partners, agreeing on various sexual arrangements, while at some only monogamous couples could reside. Many communards used dope, and perfected the idea of "grow your own," while some later settlements abstained from using any drugs in an attempt to become completely natural or self-reliant. Daily routine varied from anarchy at Wheeler Ranch to structured schedules at Lama Foundation. Visitors were welcome anytime at some communes and they became little more than "crash pads" for hitch-hiking freaks. To prevent that, other communes established visiting hours, some restricting guests to the weekends, while others only allowed those who adhered to their strict rules.

Most of those heading back to the land had been college kids or urban dwellers, and they soon realized that they knew little about rural living. To help them build their New America, Steward Brand published one of the most popular manuals, *The Whole Earth Catalog*. The first page declared that the establishment had failed, and that the catalog was aimed to supply tools that would help an individual "conduct his own education, find his own inspiration, shape his own environment, and share his adventure with whoever is interested." The catalog was filled with goods that could be ordered by mail—American wood stoves, Danish earth shoes, Australian wind generators—and it gave practical advice about tools, resources, and books that could help one become an organic gardener, give a good massage, learn to meditate, construct a tepee, or perform a do-it-yourself burial: "Human bodies are an organic part of the whole earth and at death must return to the ongoing stream of life." There was advice on helpful books to order: *Livestock and Poultry Production, The Book of Country Crafts, The Natural Foods Cookbook, The New Religions, The Old Farmer's Almanack, Champagne Living on a Beer Budget, Over 2000 Free Publications, Volkswagen Technical Manual.* And letters from readers told others how to make vinyl cement, mix up a batch of molasses-based plastic, or find free lumber. Brand included poems and directions: "Choose one: [ ] Bang [ ] Whimper." The book helped the new generation "get into something," learn a new hobby or trade. "The total effect is evangelical," wrote one reviewer, "conjuring up a way of life." Eventually, the catalogue went through four editions and even won the National Book Award.[26]

Burns also inspired others to publish guides. Alicia Bay Laurel wrote *Living on the Earth* for "people who would rather chop wood than work behind a desk." Written with the help of communards at Wheeler Ranch, the book contained celebrations, storm warnings, formulas, recipes, rumors, and country dances. *Domebook* discussed plans for constructing alternative homes and structures while *The Foxfire Book* and *Mother Earth News* explained aspects of rural life. To help freaks form or find an appropriate commune, one could read *The Modern Utopian*, which had a Communal Matchmaking Service. Urban cooperatives also developed important guides, such as various handbooks printed by the Communication Company in Columbus, Ohio.

Many times more freaks resided in urban hip communities where a counter-society flourished. Old Town in Chicago, Peach Street in Atlanta, West Bank in Minneapolis, Pearl Street in Austin, near Dupont Circle in Washington, D.C., and other areas in university towns such as Ann Arbor, Boulder, Eugene, Isla Vista, Ithaca, Lawrence, and many, many more that resembled Berzerkly or Miffland in Mad City. These communities were easy to find. Ask any longhair, and soon one would be walking down a street where below the STOP sign was painted WAR, where someone was throwing a frisbee for a dog, and where a few freaks would be rapping—talking—on the porch of a brightly painted old house. American flag curtains floating in the breeze. Crosby, Stills, Nash and

Young melodies drifting out to the street, along with the smell of musk or grass.

During the second wave urban communes proliferated in large American cities. Hippies shared apartments, rooming houses, or large homes, often in older districts or close to universities. As a hippie said about Madison, "the frats are dying fast . . . and some of them have been taken over by collectives—frats turning into communes!" Shared living arrangements always had been part of college life; it was convenient and appropriate for an era of antimaterialism. "Money's your problem?" asked Raymond Mungo. "Move in with thirteen other people, it's cheaper. And more interesting."

Although sharing was the rule, money usually was a problem. In the country, many communes survived by growing crops and selling or bartering their natural foods with locals; others had wealthy benefactors; a few close to liberal communities collected unemployment or food stamps. Bear Tribe adopted Native American methods and attempted to live off the land, while members of The Family took a hundred dollars to Las Vegas and won thousands, enough to begin their commune in New Mexico. Some communes developed around rock groups; the Grateful Dead supported one in northern California near Mendocino. Many established some sort of business. The Canyon Collective published and was supported by *Workforce*, and Bitterroot Co-op in Montana made and sold pottery. Mount Olive in Missouri raised livestock and manufactured fence posts, and Twin Oaks sold hammocks. The Farm established a construction and a publishing company, and Ananda Cooperative Village, a "self-realization community" in California, sold incense, crafts, luggage, and rented rooms on their 70-acre retreat to those studying yoga. In town, freaks often worked and lived in craft or trade cooperatives. Many hippies sold underground papers and lived at the press, such as at the *Washington Free Press* or Atlanta's *Great Speckled Bird*. The Yellow Submarine in Oregon made granola, while Maharaj Ashram opened a whole-foods restaurant, Nanak's Conscious Cookery, in Santa Fe. Freaks also resided at their head shops, bookstores, garages, or at their workshops for films, records, or papers. The Lama Foundation published religious books. Young architects in Sausalito, California, developed the Ant Farm, and south in Menlo Park others formed the Portola Institute as a "nonprofit cooperative to encourage, organize, and conduct innovative educational projects."

There were many other types of urban collectives, and the inhabitants of each dwelling worked out arrangements to share various aspects of daily living. Many were political collectives, such as the Kate Richards O'Hare Collective near Cornell University, which was based on socialistic ideals; the South End commune, formed by SDS members in Boston; or Reba

Place, a Christian social action commune in Evanston. Members worked in their communities on various programs, and at times formed umbrella groups such as the Seattle Liberation Front. Many hippies developed college communes or collectives, where some went to school and others worked, both usually part time, and where they organized for campus reform. Religious adherents established numerous spiritual communes. Feminists eager to discuss women's issues and work toward radical democracy developed Bread and Roses Collective in Boston and gay men formed the 95th Street Collective in New York. Soldiers returning from Vietnam organized the Veteran's Collective in San Francisco.

Many city hippies, thus, were cultural activists. They were concerned about war and race, of course, but also about building their alternative culture. The Trans-Love Energies Unlimited, "a total tribal living and working commune" in Detroit, was developed by John and Leni Sinclair with artist Gary Grimshaw. The commune produced rock dances and concerts, light shows, posters and pamphlets, and the underground *Sun*. It also served as a cooperative booking agency for rock groups, and Sinclair became the manager of the rock group, MC-5. Eventually, the commune moved to Ann Arbor and formed the White Panther Party, a cultural revolutionary group devoted to an assault upon mainstream culture "by any means necessary, including rock and roll, dope, and fucking in the streets."

In each hippie community there were some common themes, and one was the idea of free services. Free universities expanded in campus towns, an idea that Free Speech Movement activists began earlier at Berkeley. "Prerequisite: Curiosity" was the sign at the University of Man at Kansas State, as teachers throughout the nation volunteered lessons on everything from abstract art to mechanics. Sinclair taught jazz and contemporary poetry at the Artists' Workshop's Free University of Detroit, and Steve Gaskin gave classes in the Bay Area on "North American White Witchcraft," "Magic, Einstein and God," and to help hippies get into shape, "Meta-P.E." Others volunteered. A hip San Francisco directory listed 30 free services—including crash pads, a foot clinic, a drug hotline, the Animal Switchboard—while volunteers in Minneapolis established YES, Youth Emergency Service, and others in Milwaukee developed Pathfinders for Runaways. Hip attorneys organized legal aid services such as the Counterculture Law Project in Chicago.

Another theme in these communities was hip businesses. Freaks consumed, of course, and that meant that goods had to be bought and sold. They usually tried to be selective when purchasing goods, favoring businesses that appeared sympathetic to their values and did not discriminate or pollute, that supplied meaningful employment, or that contributed to improving society. While they would boycott or picket a corporation like

Safeway for buying grapes or vegetables from farms which paid migrant workers piecemeal, they would make their purchases at local family-owned stores, farmers' markets, or cooperatives. If the marketplace did not offer companies that sold their type of goods, then it was natural that some of these children of businessmen would establish their own ventures: record, book, or clothing stores; "head shops" that sold drug paraphernalia, posters, buttons, and almost anything weird; farm and food cooperatives; even a few construction companies and FM stereo radio stations.

Hip capitalists were the merchants of novelty, and they established many businesses. Since they did not trust the establishment media, they printed their own. One of the most successful was *Rolling Stone*, which had a circulation of a quarter million by the end of the decade and lucrative advertising contracts with national record companies. Ten years later *Mother Earth News* boasted a circulation of a million. Other undergrounds also had large circulations, such as the *Berkeley Barb, Fifth Estate, Great Speckled Bird, L.A. Free Press, The Rag,* and the *Las Vegas Free Press* boasted that with 25,000 readers they were the largest weekly newspaper in Nevada. While a few young musicians profited from singing their message on records, many others sold their values on T-shirts, buttons, and posters. A hippie could make a purchase in person at the Love Poster shop in New Orleans or by mail order from the Dirty Linen: "Here's a little something for Mother's Day. . . . Send for five posters ($5) and we'll send a sixth one free to the mother of your choice," which included Madame Ngo Dinh Nhu, Lady Bird Johnson, or General William Westmoreland. The Edward Horn company advertised a thousand buttons for $70. One could design her own, or pick from the standard "Peace Now" to the more timely "Majority for a Silent Agnew" to "I Am Cured, I'm Not a Hippie Anymore."

Some eked out a living by writing or publishing sarcasm and humor. Robert Crumb produced Motor City comics and LSD-inspired characters in Zap Comix; he invented a popular symbol for the age, the "Keep on Truckin" slogan. Gilbert Shelton thought that he had hit the big money when the *Los Angeles Free Press* paid him a hundred dollars a week. Shelton and three friends invested $600, bought a printing press, and began an "underground publishing empire" called Rip Off Press. Gonzo journalist Hunter S. Thompson published books, including his classic *Fear and Loathing in Las Vegas,* and Calipso Joe of Los Angeles established Handicap Pictures since "Everyone of our pictures is a 'Handicap.'" Produced in "True Bloody Color," these short films included titles such as "President Johnson the Defoliate President" and "Damn the Constitution-Undeclared Wars—Full Speed Ahead." Satirist General Hershey Bar spoke at rallies to "give war no quarter" because it "ain't worth a dime."[27]

Freaks established free markets on some campuses and many clothing and especially food co-ops in their urban enclaves. The "Great Food Conspiracy," the *Plain Dealer* called the "Madison Avenue-Pen Fruit-Kelloggs Korn Flake . . . chemical coated plastics in fancy boxes." During the era of white bread and preservatives the undergrounds urged readers to buy at movement food stores such as Willamette People's Food Cooperative in Eugene, Ecology Food Co-op in Madison, Cambridgeport Food Co-op near Harvard, or the Liberated Area in Richmond, Virginia. Hip cooperatives specialized in natural, organically raised foods with no preservatives—bulk honey, pearl barley, rolled oats, stone-ground wheat flour, herbal teas, fruits, vegetables, and new mixtures of cereals such as Crunchy Granola, the "Breakfast of Revolutionaries!"

Dope, naturally, was a movement business. Undergrounds from *The Mystic* (Fargo-Moorhead, North Dakota) to *Monolith* (Huntsville, Texas) ran articles on availability of the best local marijuana. The "Spring Market Report" in *The Spectator* (Bloomington, Indiana) put it like this: "The Market picture is bullish over all, with a falling off of activity in some commodity exchanges due to seasonal scarcities, and recent busts across the country, of some production centers." Head shops selling drug paraphernalia proliferated. The Entrepreneur in Chicago, Family Dog in San Francisco, Pipefitter in Madison, Third Eye in Los Angeles, and The Trance in Columbia, Missouri, all sold pipes and cigarette papers made from rice, maize, licorice, even hemp—the brand name was "Acapulco Gold." A thousand tabs of acid could be bought for a dollar each, transported inland from the coast, and sold to street vendors, for double or triple the price. Abbie Hoffman informed the masses how to deal dope in his underground best-seller *Steal This Book.*

Most movement businesses just survived financially, but a few made healthy profits. Various editions of *The Whole Earth Catalog* sold a million copies, and sales of the Family Dog head shop in the Haight topped $300,000 during the Summer of Love. Celestial Seasonings, founded by hippies who enjoyed drinking their own tea, eventually sold $16 million of natural teas and herbs annually, making one of their founders a youthful millionaire. Ticket sales at Bill Graham's Fillmore and Winterland auditoriums in San Francisco could reach $35,000 a week, and the Middle Earth Light & Power Co. grossed about $25,000 a month staging light shows at the Electric Circus in New York.[28]

Hip business merged with the counterculture, of course, at the rock festivals. Music was important, but so was the feeling—a gathering of the tribes doing their own thing beyond the customs and laws of the Establishment. After the success at Monterey, festivals spread, and during the next year they were staged at Newport, California, Sky River in Washington, and Miami, and during the last summer of the decade, the carnivals moved inland to Denver and south to Georgia, Texas, and New Orleans. The Atlanta Pop Festival attracted over 100,000, and the same number appeared at the Atlantic City Pop Festival. The Seattle Pop Festival offered additional attractions such as parachutists, helicopter flower-drops, and nightly fireworks.

But it was Woodstock that was destined to become the most famous of the era, to live on in mythology. "It was like balling the first time," wrote a participant after the festival; "historians will have to reckon with it" for "these young revolutionaries are on their way . . . to slough away the life-style that isn't theirs . . . and find one that is."

Woodstock began as a commercial enterprise. The four producers offered Max Yasgur $50,000 to use his thousand-acre farm near Bethel, New York. They hoped that 50,000 people would come to "The Woodstock Music and Art Fair: An Aquarian Exposition," and pay $18 for three days to hear over two dozen bands, including Jimi Hendrix, Janis Joplin, Joan Baez, Arlo Guthrie, Canned Heat, The Who, the Grateful Dead, Jefferson Airplane, Creedence Clearwater Revival, Country Joe and the Fish, Ten Years After, and Crosby, Stills, Nash and Young.

Yet Woodstock became much, much more. Before the first band began to play, a pilgrimage of young people streamed toward Yasgur's farm in unprecedented numbers, clogging the roads for miles, creating the most massive traffic jam in New York history. The kids rarely honked, and instead took out their guitars and tambourines and played songs, shared foods and drinks, and passed joints in perhaps the most patient jam of the decade. Vehicles slowly passed by: Volkswagens with riders hanging outside, a microbus with freaks on the roof smoking a gigantic water pipe, psychedelic motorcycles, a van painted like a tiger, another like a speckled trout. The generation streamed onto the farm, to alfalfa fields and pastures, pitched tents and tepees. Eventually 400,000 were camping, and as far as any one could see there were young people "walking, lying down, drinking, eating, reading, singing. Kids were sleeping, making love, wading in the marshes, trying to milk the local cows and trying to cook the local corn."

"We were exhilarated," one participant recalled. "We felt as though we were in liberated territory." They were, and since their numbers overwhelmed local authorities, the young quickly established their own culture with their own rules, rituals, costumes, and standards of behavior. An observer noted that the cops were like "isolated strangers in a foreign country," and they made little attempt to enforce drug or nudity laws as the counterculture blossomed. "We used to think of ourselves as little clumps of weirdos," said Janis Joplin. "But now we're a whole new minority group."[29]

The gathering of the tribe, however, also was ripe for disaster. Overcrowding created nightmares. Sanitation facilities were inadequate and some waited an hour to relieve themselves. Toilets overflowed. The hungry crowd consumed half a million hamburgers and hot dogs on the first day and food ran out, as did almost all drinkable water. Dope was sold and given away openly, and many consumed too much. Medical supplies became dangerously low. All the while the traffic jam meant that musicians, medicine, doctors, and food had to be flown in by helicopter at tremendous expense. Officials grew concerned, and thinking there would be a riot, the governor considered sending in the national guard. Then, the rains came, and came, and people huddled and slept in meadows that turned to mud.

Before the music began the first evening, a voice boomed out of the speakers: "We're going to need each other to help each other work this out, because we're taxing the systems that we've set up. We're going to be bringing the food in. But the one major thing that you have to remember tonight is that the man next to you is your brother." For many participants, the growing sense of community turned this rock festival into an unforgettable countercultural experience. "Everyone needed other people's help, and everyone was ready to share what he had as many ways as it could be split up. Everyone could feel the good vibrations."

That included many of the older generation. Bethel residents had feared a hippie invasion, but after watching the kids their dread dissipated and townspeople lent a hand. They opened soup and sandwich kitchens, left their hoses on for drinking and bathing, and donated medical supplies. *Life* admitted, "For three days nearly half a million people lived elbow to elbow in the most exposed, crowded, rain-drenched, uncomfortable kind of community and there wasn't so much as a fist fight." And the *New York Times* added, "Hippies have never been so successful . . . never before had they so impressed the world that watched."

Woodstock, of course, affected each participant differently. Twenty years later some recalled that it changed their life, others remembered only rain and mud. One recalled "Sunny, a nursing student from Boston. We shared love with each other in a way I have never forgotten and never bettered. Sunny, if you are out there, write." In a vague way, most leaving the rainy festival felt warm, and they sang along with Joni Mitchell,

> We are stardust
> We are golden
> And we've got to get ourselves
> Back to the garden

If freaks could stay in the garden, cultivating their culture, many thought that it could happen—a cultural revolution. "Woodstock is the great example of how it is going to be in the future," Tim Leary wrote to John Sinclair. "We have the numbers. The loving and the peaceful are the majority. The violent and the authoritarian are the minority. We are winning. And soon." Hippie culture was having an impact on the idea of revolution, for cultural activists began talking about the development of a Youth Nation committed to nonviolence concerned about one another, an idea popularized by Abbie Hoffman in his *Woodstock Nation*. Steve Haines of the *Berkeley Tribe* advocated more festivals, using the receipts to buy land and supplies to build large regional communes for one to two thousand freaks, and Sinclair talked about various tribes of black militants and white cultural activists signing treaties as the first step in developing a Sun Dance Nation. During the Indian summer after Woodstock it appeared to many that some sort of cultural upheaval finally was under way that would bring about a New America.[30]

Whatever fantasies were being toked up that autumn, they floated away as the mainstream press broke a cold-blooded story from California: "Sharon Tate, Four Others Murdered," proclaimed the *Los Angeles Times*: "Ritualistic Slayings." To many in the establishment, this was the beginning of the end of the hippies—and of the sixties.

During the next months police reported crimes committed "by a group of hippies known as 'The Family' under the leadership of Charles Manson." *Newsweek* labeled the trial the "Case of the Hypnotic Hippie." *Time* wrote about "a weird story of a mystical, semi-religious hippie drug-and-murder cult led by a bearded, demonic Mahdi," and ran an article about "Hippies and Violence," quoting a doctor that hippies "can be totally devoid of true compassion. That is the reason why they can kill so matter-of-factly. . . . Many hippies are socially almost dead inside." Presto: millions of American were convinced. Manson was a hippie, and longhairs could be killers.

Most citizens did not read the fine print, for as the trial continued other reporters uncovered many disturbing facts. Manson's mother was a prostitute, a heavy drinker, and he never knew his father. During his first 35 years he spent more than 20 either in foster homes, juvenile detention centers, or in prison. By the time he was 20 a state psychiatrist labeled him a sociopathic personality, "very unstable emotionally and very insecure," not a good candidate for probation. Nevertheless, he was paroled, and drifted to Haight-Ashbury after the Summer of Love. Older than many others, he could impress and control young, unstable kids. Eventually, he had about twenty followers, all of them from unhappy families and mostly teenage runaways. Manson had a large sexual appetite, often having intercourse three times a day. He had the ability not only to lure young girls into bed, but to convince them to find more for him as proof of their devotion. He and his followers drifted down the coast to Los

Angeles, and then out to the desert where they resided, occasionally going back to see friends in the city. The year of the Tate murders he had been arrested four times, and had made a point of stopping priests and claiming that he was Jesus Christ. Manson and his followers—as demonstrated by numerous psychological reports, court documents, some articles, and subsequent books—were mentally ill.[31]

Most of the counterculture could identify psychosis and were appalled by Manson's actions. *Rolling Stone* writers David Felton and David Dalton loathed him, and they leveled the blame for his behavior on the "society's perverted system of penal 'rehabilitation,' its lusts for vengeance and cruelty, that created him." Members of a Topanga Canyon community complained to the *Los Angeles Times* that hippies "pride themselves on their reputation for mutual love and peacefulness and they curse Manson for the notoriety he has brought the 'long-haired people.' " Another freak complained that the mass media lived "on sensationalism and scapegoats" and that Manson "has become the fall guy in the political battle between conservative America and the radical youth movement. He is now a social category, a demon hippie, a symbol of 'What can happen to your son or daughter.' "

The silent majority remained fascinated with the Manson story. It raised a horrific possibility—"hippies with guns"—and it also had another ingredient that lured readers—sex. After visiting numerous hip enclaves, a social scientist observed, "The idea that communal life is a sexual smorgasbord is a myth created and sustained by the media. Much of the media fascination with Charles Manson and his covey of willing women can be explained by the fact that he personally staged many men's fondest sexual fantasies." That seemed to be the case, and it was experienced by a 36-year-old journalist who went undercover by growing long hair and a beard to report on the counterculture. Instead of *Black Like Me*, Richard Atcheson wrote, his report should have been called *Hairy Like Me*, for men of his age dressed in "Brooks Brothers suits, with heavy brogans, attache cases and short hair, would approach me in bus stations or rail terminals or hotel lobbies, pick up conversations with me, and start almost at once to inquire into my sexual habits: did I get much, did I give it to them in the mouth, how many inches did I have. . . . These guys just seemed to assume that because I was hairy I was some kind of incredible stud, getting laid constantly." Atcheson's experiences helped him to understand why so many citizens loathed hippies: "They are presumed to be sexually free, and they have to be hated for that."[32]

Manson remained in the headlines that December as the Rolling Stones announced a free concert at Altamont Speedway near Livermore, California, a festival that many older citizens felt was the second example that proved a point that they suspected all along—the counterculture was going mad.

Just four months after already famous Woodstock, hip Californians were eager to have "Woodstock West." "We're all headed the same way," Andy Gordon wrote, "drawn by the power of the Woodstock myth. Gotta make it to that historic get-together. Altamont! The magic hits me—it's like Shangri-La. Xanadu."

But nirvana did not appear for most participants, and some described a reality closer to Hades. The audience was enormous, about 300,000, and most were good-natured, sitting on the surrounding hills, far from the stage. People got high, and there were very few arrests. The problems appeared closer to the stage, where about fifty became violent. Shari Horowitz reported: "Scanning the audience, I could see the chaos mounting—drunken brawls and bad acid trips. . . . I felt a sense of loss. My people hadn't the strength to transcend rudeness and get it all together." Numerous bands played in the afternoon, and the scene became more chaotic. In perhaps the most short-sighted move in the history of rock concerts, the Stones gave $500 worth of beer to the Hell's Angels with orders to guard the stage. When the crowd moved closer to the music, when some drugged kids began to dance wildly, the motorcycle thugs beat them, busting pool cues over heads, causing so much commotion that bands stopped the music and asked for peace. "Please people," said Grace Slick of Jefferson Airplane, "please stop hurting each other." At dusk, the Stones finally appeared, and while Mick Jagger sang "Street Fighting Man," the Angels grabbed a young black, Meredith Hunter. Reports conflicted; he did or did not have a gun at the love-in. Never mind, the black-leather gang stabbed him repeatedly and kicked in his face. Horrified and stunned, the crowd did nothing. Hunter died in a pool of blood.

Altamont disgusted many, especially those in the counterculture. "Pearl Harbor to the Woodstock Nation" wrote one participant, and Gordon noted just how far down the psychedelic path the counterculture had stumbled in almost three years since the Human Be-in: "scabrous, syphilitic Hell's Angels, and a few luscious random teenie-chiclets, with a hippier-than-thou look. And not a smile in a carload." After the music began, "I saw they were no longer joining hands and dancing together in spontaneous joy, as at the first gathering of the tribes." Commercialization had massacred the tribes, for at Altamont the magic between the hip community and musicians had evaporated. The people no longer were the show; they simply were the audience, and that agonized many. The younger generation was acting like the older one. A cultural activist wrote that the concert "exploded the myth of innocence," and many other underground writers felt that Altamont signaled "The Failure of the Counter

Culture." Robert Somma lamented that it was the "last gasp from a dying decade. . . . It made you want to go home. It made you want to puke."[33]

Three weeks later the decade chronologically ended and during the next year, *Business Week* claimed, "Middle America has come to view festivals as harbingers of dope, debauchery, and destruction." State and county officials drafted regulations aimed at preventing rock festivals, and conservatives turned up their attack on the counterculture. "You can be the irresponsible creature you are, the drones living off the work of others," the editor of *Christian Economics* told hippies, "only because most people are not like you." Conservative Tom Anderson was more livid: "Dear spoiled, deluded, arrogant, brainwashed brats and know-it-alls: I am sick of you," and he gave some advice: "Learn to speak Russian. And Chinese." Oddly enough, the Russians agreed and became strange bedfellows with conservative Americans. One Soviet historian referred to hippies as bourgeois bloodsuckers living off society, adding that "no one with any common sense can believe that the hippies and Yippies are capable of effecting any changes in American society." And even more odd, the negative interpretation was promoted by many older scholars who wrote popular books assigned in college classrooms during subsequent years. "No one was more of the 'love generation' than Manson," an expert on American youth declared, while a historian described hippies as "countless thousand disturbed youngsters" whose experiences generally were "stupid, pointless, and self-defeating." Altamont was "another disaster" similar to Charlie Manson: "Of course hippies were not murderers usually."[34]

Obviously, the older generation was fuming by the end of the decade, for after the law and order fifties, the rebellious kids naturally aggravated parents. "I'm tired of the tyranny of spoiled brats," proclaimed a professor, and closer to home a father complained about his son:

> First, he resisted efforts to get his hair cut (that's a mild statement of the fact) and showed an unusual fascination with anything to do with drugs. Next thing, he started going out of his way to look like a refugee from the Nigerian War (I later discovered he was adopting the bum style which had just begun to catch on). One afternoon, I found out he was the editor of an underground newspaper at the high school, which . . . had an offensive and obscene name. During the discussion of that project, he informed me that he had joined a Marxist group at the college nearby and soon we started receiving "The Militant" at home. As soon as school was out that year, he announced that he was leaving home to form a commune. He returned after four days "to regroup," but the short absence caused his mother great distress. About that time, he told me that he could not stay in the evenings because he had to be at a prayer meeting. This I interpreted as an insult to my

intelligence and a slur at religion. I lost my temper and took a poke at him.

The younger generation swung back. A mother pleaded with her daughter, "Our lines of communication are down, but I still hope for a way to get through to you." And then she asked her child to explain her freaky behavior, requesting, "I feel this is a personal letter not to be shared with your friends. Tear it up, throw it away or keep it; but don't put it on display." The daughter responded by sending the letter to *Second Coming*, and the editor printed it because "We feel that our parents have something to say: READ THIS STONED!!!!"

The middle continued to collapse. The generation gap expanded, perhaps to the largest size since the 1920s. When two researchers asked a mother if she would like to comment on her hippie son who lived in Kabul, Afghanistan, she responded: "I have nothing to say about him. He's gone. Far away. Dead."[35] An opinion poll asked citizens to list the most harmful groups in the nation, and the result: Communists, prostitutes, and hippies.

Citizens reacted to the hippie threat in many ways. Country-western singer Merle Haggard condemned the counterculture in his hit tune, "Okie from Muskogee," and singer Anita Bryant held "rallies for decency." Southern Methodist University officials attempted to stop mail posted to the campus address of *Notes from the Underground*, while a group of alumni and students threatened violence if the "filthy sheet causing embarrassment" did not stop publication. Businessmen across the country put up door signs, "No Shirt, No Shoes, No Service," while Marc's Big Boy in Milwaukee hired a cop to make sure that no one with beads, beards, flowers, sandals, long hair, or funny glasses was allowed inside to buy a double hamburger. Police harassment was common. In Charlotte, North Carolina, officers raided hippie houses, searched them without warrants, made numerous vagrancy arrests, and stopped only after so ordered by a federal judge. Boston cops arrested 200 freaks on the Commons for "idleness," and officers in Nevada arrested three long-hairs with money for vagrancy and held them for fifty days before the trial. Police routinely frisked, fined, or arrested young hitch-hikers while commuters yelled "Go to work!" In Milwaukee authorities raided underground newspaper collectives and arrested staffers for printing "offensive" material, and in New Orleans they even arrested a hip female in jeans for "wearing the clothes of the opposite sex." Hip life was particularly tough in the South and some rural areas where appearance alone seemed enough to provoke attacks. While filming *Easy Rider*, Dennis Hopper and other hairy actors were harassed in southern cafes, but two long-haired journalists also noted: "It didn't seem to matter much where we went in the country, we were never more than one or two words away from a fight. In Arizona it was *'You can't come in here like that!'* In a restaurant outside Indianapolis the waitresses plastered themselves against the walls and shrieked: *'We're closed! We're closed!'* It was doubly amazing because the two of us together scarcely weigh two hundred pounds, we're just skinny little guys and . . . we spent the whole summer obviously scaring people to death."[36]

More serious repression ensued, and an easy target was arresting freaks on drug charges. Earlier in the decade the federal government had assembled the Ad Hoc Panel on Drug Abuse, which reached the conclusion that "the hazards of marihuana *per se* have been exaggerated and that long criminal sentences imposed on an occasional user or possessor are in poor social perspective." Nevertheless, state and federal officials commenced a massive campaign. Authorities busted editors of *Raisin Bread* and *Fifth Estate* for possession of marijuana, but a more famous incident concerned John Sinclair. He gave some grass to an undercover agent in Detroit, and a month later was charged with "dispensing and possessing two marijuana cigarettes." After two and a half years of judicial wrangling the trial came to court and he was declared guilty after an hour of jury deliberation and sentenced to ten years in the state prison. Sinclair appealed, but the judge would not free him on bond, deeming him a security risk and transferring him to a prison almost 300 miles from his wife and friends. The treatment was so severe that the publisher of the mainstream *Detroit Free Press* wrote Sinclair's mother a letter of sympathy and a state representative informed the prisoner, "I have introduced a bill which would repeal all penalties for drug use." John Lennon and Yoko Ono participated in a rally that drew 15,000 people chanting, "Free John Now," and after he spent two years in prison, federal courts threw out the case.

Communes also were attacked. Bikers raided Oz, a rural commune in Pennsylvania, and they beat and tortured the males and then sexually assaulted the females. After residents complained, authorities in Sonoma County, California, descended on Morning Star, charging violation of building and health codes, and demanding that owner Lou Gottlieb make expensive changes in facilities. When he balked, officials ordered all persons to clear the land or pay $500 a day in fines. Eventually legal fees cost Gottlieb $14,000, and he deeded the land to God. The county declared the deed invalid and brought in bulldozers and leveled the buildings. The "War of Sonoma County" was waged against Wheeler Ranch. "We are very much like the Vietcong," said Bill Wheeler. "We're an underground movement. We're going to take some very hard blows," and they did. Supposedly searching for runaways and military deserters, two dozen policemen and narcotic agents invaded the commune without a search warrant, arrested one young female, and charged four men who objected with assaulting an officer. That was one of many raids during the next few years, as Wheeler said, climaxing with "150 pigs in a predawn assault. Many people were awakened staring up the barrel of a gun. . . . Some seventeen people were arrested on drug charges alone, mostly for cultivating marijuana. One person got arrested for ginseng root in a capsule, another for vitamin pills." Although the warrant was deemed illegal, and most arrested were acquitted, the legal and psychological expense of the war was too high and the commune disintegrated.

The reaction could be brutal. Someone bombed Trans-Love Energies Commune in Detroit; others did the same to the office of Houston's *Space City News*; someone else shot out the windows of *San Diego Street Journal*, prompting a hippie to declare: "Freedom-loving law'n Order Amerika is showing its true colors." Rednecks in Atlanta occasionally drove past hippie crowds and sprayed them with buckshot, and young Hispanics tried to drive hitching freaks off roads in New Mexico. At the outskirts of Taos was the General Store, a hip information center and clinic where commune members posted a message: "The locals aren't smiling, especially at hippies. You may have heard stories of violence in Taos—believe them." Thugs brutalized hippies, castrating some and even killing one. "Don't come to New Mexico," communards warned, "and if you are already here with nothing to do—LEAVE!"

"It's a nightmare," said Dennis Hopper about the violence. Then he urged the kids to "go and try to change America, but if you're gonna wear a badge, whether it's long hair, or black skin, learn to protect yourself."[37]

Regardless of the reaction, hippies did not fade away during the second wave. Repression might make them move on to more friendly communities, but it did not bring them back into the mainstream. Just the opposite. Nor did the counterculture end because of Altamont or Charlie Manson or the demise of hippiedom in Haight-Ashbury. Most freaks were not interested in a long-haired psychotic; the millions who did not go to Woodstock or Altamont were not concerned about what happened at music festivals; and the rise and fall of the Haight did not define the entire counterculture experience. Instead, hippiedom expanded exponentially. Freaks did their own thing. Wayne State's *South End* put it like this: "We are a generation that is sucking in life in gulps while others are trying to swallow. We are making the American cultural revolution." And as we shall see, these cultural activists infiltrated the very foundations of the Establishment—business, religion, even the United States Armed Forces. During the early 1970s hippies were participating in public "smoke-ins" in many communities, while cultural activists were establishing nude beaches and people's parks, running for city councils, and holding university conferences on their own lifestyles. "Flower Power," wrote an observer, "is as revolutionary as Black Power, and after it America will never be the same again."[38]

Nor would many young Americans. They were changing, some hoping, and some singing along with John Lennon. If they could make "Imagine" a reality, then, as the Moody Blues told the new generation, they were "On the Threshold of a Dream."

What was dream? What was reality in the counterculture? Did they get back to the garden? Some times. Some places. Other times and other places they did not. As mundane as it sounds, hippies were simply people who possessed all the human frailties as those in the Establishment.

Yet it was true that for many of the sixties generation, the counterculture was just a lark, a time to smoke weed and get laid, a long party. The hippie lifestyle of dope, free love, music, and values of brotherhood and sharing invited phonies, freeloaders, runaways, drug dealers, smackheads, and various self-appointed preachers and zealots. There were weak people who were lost, who could not think for themselves, those who would allow others to boss them, those who would join cults and submit to various hip heroes and gurus. A thousand rock stars, a hundred thousand lost groupies. And there were the criminals who grew long hair, the vicious bikers and drug runners who stalked teens searching for a free high and free love. Ed Sanders noted that the counterculture was a noble experiment but that so many were vulnerable, "like a valley of thousands of plump white rabbits surrounded by wounded coyotes."

There were many casualties who never understood "freedom." "Freedom is a difficult thing to handle," wrote communard Richard Fairfield. "Give people freedom and they'll do all the things they thought they never had a chance to do. But that won't take very long. And after that? After that, my friend, it'll be time to make your life meaningful." Freedom was not free, it took responsibility to make a meaningful life. It was easy, even vogue, to revolt against authority, but then what? Many never answered, and to them freedom meant any behavior, no matter how self-destructive, rude, amoral, or crazy. Examples were legion: Bored teens strung out on endless trips, picking up pills on the street and popping them. Young mothers who blew marijuana smoke into the faces of their infants. The guy who claimed that sexual liberation meant that it was far out that he taught a five-year-old girl to give him oral sex, or men who walked up to unknown females and asked, "Do you want to fuck?" That word itself became a verb, noun, gerund—became meaningless in overuse. To some, sexual freedom meant little more than getting laid, using another person for their own gratification. "We called it the free fuck club," one female recalled. "These guys talked about love, screwed us, and then zoomed off for more cultural revolution," often leaving behind a "pregnant old lady." To some others, freedom meant any kind of behavior at any time. "It was the only commune I ever felt forced to leave for fear of my safety," wrote Hugh Gardner about New Buffalo, "after a night spent in a sweat-filled sleeping bag while one of several psychopathic personalities in residence at the time walked around in the dark randomly shooting a rifle at targets unknown, some not very far from my head." A social scientist observed, "Part of the problem is that hippies, like all movements, attract a disproportionate number of followers who are genuine misfits—persons who are poorly equipped to survive in any culture." [39]

While mainstream citizens condemned hip behavior, so did the hippies. Ed Sanders wrote about an army of sick youth in *The Family*, and David Felton condemned numerous Mansons, or what the counterculture referred to as "control freaks" or "acid fascists," in *Mindfuckers*. Many others were disappointed about the phonies—the outside agitators of the counterculture—the "young hoods, alias transient hippies, alias teenyboppers, alias kick-kids . . . who were intent upon wrecking their minds and bodies in order to give all hip people a bad name." Self-criticism mounted after Altamont, and many wrote about their culture's behavior, about disparity between rhetoric and values. "I think we have fallen prey to the sickness which we fight," lamented Jon Eisen, and Jon Landau added: "We tell ourselves we are a counterculture. And yet are we really so different from the culture against which we rebel?"

Part of the hip problem was a common attitude. An "illusion of superiority," Eisen continued. "It was almost as though identification with the new culture, with long hair and serious differences with your parents meant that somehow you possessed a superior way of life and a superior insight into the nature of the universe. . . . It hurts a little to write this, for I'm writing about myself and my friends, my people." The attitude led some to think that *anyone* outside of the straight world was part of some Woodstock Nation where everyone loved one another. "We are not One," a freak in Dallas admitted, "we never have been One, there is conflict Within Us and Without Us." The attitude led many others to pervert hippie values. Frauds declared that it was all right to "rip off capitalist pigs" when they stole from merchants, or cried "power to the people" and gate-crashed rock festivals, or spoke of "free love" as they wrestled females to the ground—eventually they created a thousand rationalizations for selfishness. [40]

More than attitude, hip behavior caused problems. The emphasis on experimentation often meant pushing life to extremes. Eventually, most freaks realized that dope had diminishing returns, was no longer an experiment, but others found the ultimate downer. Too many overdosed in too many ways: Mama Cass, Jim Morrison, Janis Joplin, Jimi Hendrix, Al Wilson of Canned Heat, Brian Jones of the Rolling Stones, Keith Moon of The Who, and Pigpen of the Grateful Dead. Those were only the most famous, for untold numbers had bad trips, or worse. Some still are scared. No alien to drugs, Neil Young warned his generation that "every junkie is like a setting sun." Some never left the endless line of dope peddlers on Telegraph Avenue; others could never leave their own Haight-Ashburys.

Problems became apparent at communes and collectives. Many freaks admitted that they had a difficult time sharing everything, overcoming jealousies and hatred, and at times stronger personalities often dominated the weaker as free-flowing anarchy slipped toward authoritarianism. Youth reported bickering and ego trips at many underground papers, and interpersonal relations strained quickly at free-love communes where one shared soul and body. Talsen, for example, lasted only a year and eventually became a settlement of Jesus People. Neil Young closed his open ranch because he had too many people hanging around who "lived off me, used my money to buy things, used my telephone to make their calls. General leeching." Freeloading forced many communes to build gates, even post guards, and communards wrote to *The Modern Utopian* asking that their addresses be deleted from directories.

Some communes lasted weeks, others lasted years, some still exist. At most of them, however, life was much more difficult than hippies imagined when they left the city. "I remember having soybeans for breakfast, lunch and dinner, and nothing else," recalled Cynthia Bates of The Farm. "Having kids made you more sensitive to the lack of necessities . . . how long could you live in a house with 50 other people?" Especially a house with no running water, no flush toilet, no electricity. After a while, many began to ask, What's the point?

Communal life was hard physically and also psychologically. "In the commune there is nothing you can hide," a member admitted. "Some people can't take it," and Elaine Sundancer added, "We need some way to come together. We speak of a gathering of the tribes, but the Indians were supported by traditions from since the world began, and we're out here on our own."

Moreover, hip became fad. Like the freaks themselves, this trend began on the coasts and spread inland. Some hippie fashion, uniforms of leather and brass, cost more than business suits from Brooks Brothers. Radical chic became hip chic, meaning that more longhairs looked the part or preached counterculture values, but fewer practiced them. When businessmen marched to work in suits with flared trousers wearing paisley ties, when pick-up drivers grew ponytails, the cultural revolution was in demise, and with it the community and its values of sharing and trust. Communes and collectives locked doors as theft became too common in hip communities. After a someone stole radio and taping equipment from Abbie Hoffman, he announced his resignation from the counterculture:

"I know one thing. I don't use the phrase 'brothers and sisters' much anymore, except among real close friends and you'll never hear me use the word 'movement' except in a sarcastic sense."

Perhaps this should have been expected. These children of the postwar era often tried, but usually could not escape their past. Most had a very difficult time reversing twenty years of upbringing, conditioning, and socialization. While they dreamt about becoming a tribe, sharing body and soul, a communard at Cold Mountain Farm in rural New York admitted "we probably made love less than when we lived in separate apartments in the city. . . . Even though we created our own environment at the farm, we still carried with us the repressions of the old environment, in our bodies and our minds." After the demise of commune LILA, Charles Lonsdale recalled, "Much was learned by many people about sharing, love, and trust, but it was all too far in advance of our skills in human relations and understanding."[41]

How can the counterculture be evaluated? Reliable surveys and statistics on this amorphous blob do not exist, so it is difficult to judge. Subsequently, most assessments have been personal and emotional. Many of the older generation loathed the children for rejecting traditional values, and many kids loathed the parents for holding on to what they considered archaic beliefs. To some, the sight of a longhair or one death from an overdose was too much and they condemned the entire cultural experiment. To others, just seeing a policeman or another death in Vietnam was too much and they condemned the entire Establishment. The result was the largest generational gap in memory—the "war at home," one observer labeled it, who suggested that the nation's greatest internal conflict was "not between the rich and the poor, or the black and the white, or even the young and the old, but the people with long hair and the people with short hair."

To the longhairs, the question of whether the counterculture was a failure or success missed the point. Hippies were not taking a college course, trying to pass an exam, earn a grade, get ahead. The counterculture looked at it a different way. "How good were communes?" Compared with what, they asked, the best or the worst families in America? The fact that they experimented with their lifestyle was success enough for most of them, for they no longer were normal. They were different, had dropped out of the rat race, challenged their past. They had considered their existence on planet Earth, and in some ways, many had changed their lives. "If, through participation in the communal experience, individuals feel more alive and fulfilled (greater awareness of self and others, etc.), such a commune must be deemed a success," wrote Richard Fairfield. To hippies, then, the political revolution shifted to an individual revolution, and some felt proud that they had taken the chance, such as the communards at Twin Oaks who published a booklet declaring *The Revolution Is Over: We Won!*

Those people probably had won—for themselves—while others were not so sure. From his commune in Vermont, Marty Jezer described the pros and cons of the counterculture:

> At its best the amorphous and vaguely defined movement we call the counter-culture is working, and that there exists now, in cities and on farms everywhere in the country, a visible alternative community that is creating new ways of living out of a tired, frightened, and dying land. (There is another, darker side to the counter-culture symbolized by Altamont and Manson; rock-star millionaires; the dehumanizing attitudes longhaired men still have for women; the heavy consumer-trip so many people are on, buying bellbottoms and beads, records, tape machines, flashy new cars with peace stickers on the bumpers to make it all seem all right; the continued high price of dope and the availability of speed, smack, and other bummers; the ambitious and competitive ego-tripping, disguised in groovy garb and mystical language, but still a mirrored reflection of the dominant values of the old way; and more: all the baggage, possessions, psychic junk and garbage we carry with us from the past.) But despite the glorification of a life-style that so often manifests style at the expense of life, there are people moving ahead, experimenting with and leading lives that a few years ago they'd never have dreamed possible.

The counterculture eventually changed the sixties by altering cold war culture, but it also had a more immediate impact on the movement during the second wave. Jerry Rubin mused that "grass destroyed the left" and created a youth culture, and in a sense dope clouded the political focus. "The New Left no longer exists," SDS founder Richard Flacks said at the end of the decade. "The ideals of the New Left have now merged into whole new cultural situations in enclaves like Isla Vista, the youth communities outside the system, which may or may not have coherent politics." Little seemed coherent as the movement splintered into numerous factions, as earlier organizations and initial leaders continued to fade. Some older activists grew frustrated, dropped out, and began building their own society. As former SDS president Carl Oglesby recalled: "There were a lot of good, righteous people showing up in places like Vermont and New Hampshire in those days. Lots of parties, great reefer, good acid. Lovely friends . . . I remember it with great fondness. It was almost the best part of the struggle. The best part of the struggle was the surrender."

Some surrendered. Some did not, for many baby boomers were coming of age during the second wave and the counterculture idea of continual experimentation created different possibilities and activities. Cultural rebellion and political activism continued to merge and flourish. The underground *Win* described the budding alliance:

> Win was originally just for the peace movement
> but how can you separate the peace movement from the people
> On the streets
> On the farms
> in Canada
> in prison?
> how can you write about the peace movement without writing
>> about drugs, astrology, communal farms, rock music, painting the Con Ed building black?

A community was emerging, "the people" cooperating for a common goal that usually concerned their empowerment or liberation in a New America. While some activists remained concerned with national affairs, others shifted their involvement toward themselves, their people, their neighborhoods. A new motto appeared for the movement: Think Global, Act Local. "Back in the city, it was like you were a Weatherman type or a plastic hippie or you didn't do anything but talk revolution," said a freak who left Brooklyn for Eugene. "Here . . . all these alternatives have come into being. They may be small, they may not be all that new, but there is some progress you can put your finger on. Beginnings rather than endings."

And as they built their communities, they continued searching for alternatives, experimenting, considering their existence. "I'm hip!" said one veteran hippie, sitting under a tree, reading a book.[42] "But lately I'm beginning to wonder just what hip is, you know, what is it all about. I get this feeling I'm just not where it's at anymore. Maybe none of us here is where it's at. . . . Mind you, I don't know what it is, but . . . leave everyone to his own dreams. . . ."

Power and Liberation

Our purpose is to abolish the system (call it the Greed Machine,
capitalism, the Great Hamburger Grinder, Babylon, Do-Your-Job-ism)
and learn to live cooperatively, intelligently, gracefully (call it the New
Awareness, anarchism, The Aquarian Age, communism, whatever
you wish).

Marvin Garson, 1969

What is women's liberation? It is simply organized rage against real
oppression.

Marilyn Salzman Webb, 1970

Many commentators have ended histories of the sixties during or after
1968 because the election of Nixon is a convenient break and because the
focus of the movement blurred. Just what was the movement during 1969
and 1970, from the Third World Strike at San Francisco State to the
tragedy at Kent State? Streets became flooded with activists advocating a
myriad of causes as the movement swelled into the second wave.

The confusion was evident to participants themselves, who defined and
redefined the movement. Perhaps its evolution was best described by veterans Michael Ferber and Staughton Lynd:

> As an expression, "the movement" still enjoys wide currency in
> America, but it no longer refers to an existing entity. Until 1968, per-
> haps, someone "in the movement" could travel almost anywhere in the
> country and with little trouble find a group that would recognize him
> as one of its own. They might be in different factions, and stay up late
> arguing, but they would still be intuitive comrades; he would have
> friends, food, and bed. Now, two or three discouraging years later, it
> is no longer correct to speak of a single movement, and if we do . . .
> it should be understood as referring to a set of movements, some over-
> lapping, some mutually exclusive, many hostile to one another. The

very survival of the expression and idea of a single movement, however, points to a strong urge that American young people still feel,
perhaps more than ever, and certainly still in growing numbers. It is
an urge to make plans and theories, organizations and life styles,
dreams and "trips" that will take us out of the murderous wasteland of
America. Its existence may remain our only hope.

The movement expanded, becoming more difficult to define and to
chronicle. Michael Rossman noted that when "the movement got too diverse to cover, the mass media lost interest even in the kind of reductive,
superficial coverage they'd been doing." But the movement did not end—
in fact, social activism reached its zenith during the second wave as millions of baby boomers attended campuses and took to the streets. More
Americans participated after 1968 than during the first wave, and in 1970
Kenneth Keniston observed that it appeared that student demonstrations
would not end for years since the "trends in American culture . . . argue
for a continuation of protests."

The movement evolved into many different shapes and forms, and so
the second wave needs a focus. That was stated by many, including Bob
Gibbs, an organizer for one of hundreds of new organizations, Vocations
for Social Change. Gibbs declared that the movement had two insepara-
ble goals: "To build new things good for our own heads and to work
equally hard toward making a more humane and non-oppressive society."[1] That usually was the meaning of "revolution," one inside, another
outside. Some participants freed themselves from the silent majority's social norms—"liberation"—and created their own lifestyles or counterculture. Others organized and confronted the establishment in an attempt to
change the system—"empowerment." Many did both. Personal liberation
and political empowerment became the dual themes of the second wave,
and combined they resulted in a massive assault on the white males who
traditionally governed the nation's institutions.

That attack was under way, and it had been gaining national attention
and focus at San Francisco State College by the end of 1968 and during
early 1969. Black power had not been idle as the counterculture bloomed,
and in fact was reaching a crescendo.

Tensions had been high for two years at San Francisco State. With
18,000 students, the college only had about 700 black students, less than
4 percent in a city with a black population of 20 percent. A hundred had
banded together to form the Black Students Union, and they felt the rising tide of black consciousness and supported the idea of a "third world
revolution" in which all nonwhite peoples would revolt and empower
themselves in their own communities. In 1967, after the white editor of
the campus paper allegedly mocked Muhammad Ali, a dozen blacks
marched into his office and attacked him. The president suspended the

blacks, and also two white students who published a poem about masturbation. Both actions prompted black militants and white radicals to begin
angry demonstrations and building occupations, and that in turn stirred
conservatives to join the fray. Superintendent of Public Schools Max Rafferty declared that he would like "to go into those buildings and bounce
those people out like ping-pong balls," and when the president did not
call on the police, some politicians called for his dismissal.

The black students had a close relationship with local activists and the
Black Panthers. The BSU and the local state representative, Willie
Brown, demanded that the university establish a black studies department.
After prodding, administrators hired some black instructors on a temporary basis who gave a few African American classes. George Murray was
one lecturer, and he also was a graduate student and the Black Panther
Minister of Education. He and others grew tired of meetings with officials
and numerous delays, and by autumn semester 1968 many students and
local blacks felt that the university was stalling.

Perhaps, perhaps not, for university administrators across the nation
were facing a similar situation. At that time, many college officials were
aware of rising black consciousness and they began searching frantically
for African American instructors with advanced degrees from reputable
institutions. Yet because few had been encouraged to go to college and
especially to graduate school, there was a shortage of black scholars to
teach African American studies. That problem could be alleviated by admitting more black students, but since they often came from segregated
neighborhood schools many had weak educations and could not gain normal admittance to the better undergraduate institutions, the door for graduate study and a professorship. It would take years to overcome that situation, but the civil rights campaign had sparked a demand for classes on
the entire African American experience, and activists demanded that
black faculty teach those classes *now*.

The BSU wanted a dozen faculty members as the core for a black studies department. The administration talked about a program of courses that
eventually would be developed into a department, and they agreed to hire
one full-time professor and a secretary. The BSU demanded that admission standards for blacks be lowered, even abolished, and that scholarships
be increased or tuition reduced. The administration considered the proposals, and after they agreed to admit 400 black students who normally
would not qualify, the BSU upped the ante, demanding that all blacks
applying be admitted—with no tuition. Tempers grew short, and meetings
were filled with wild statements, name-calling, and angry denials.

BSU members began excluding radical whites from their meetings,
claiming they were only for nonwhite, "third world students," and militants promoted ideas such as "cultural nationalism" and "separatism." "In

the search for educational relevance," wrote student Nathan Hare, "black today is revolutionary and nationalistic." He condemned the "white-washed education" that taught racial stereotypes and demanded a separate black history and educational experience "designed to regenerate the mor-tified ego of the black child."

Race relations on campus soured, and Murray again added to the ten-sion by declaring that third world students should "bring guns on campus to defend themselves against racist administrators." In response, a local paper charged that Murray had traveled to Cuba and had allegedly de-clared that every time a Vietcong killed an American soldier it meant one less enemy for blacks in the United States. During a demonstration in October, a hundred blacks converged on the administration building chanting: "Revolution has come. Off the pig. Time to pick up the gun."

That was too much for the trustees of the state college system, and Chancellor Glen Dumke demanded that Murray be fired, or at least reas-signed to a nonteaching position for the remainder of his one-year con-tract. President Robert Smith was not eager to make that announcement because he realized that such action without following the proper proce-dure of hearings and due process would only enrage students and offend many faculty members. Nevertheless, Smith suspended Murray from teaching responsibilities, an action that prompted the BSU to declare that they would begin a general strike from classes in November. They invited numerous speakers, but the most popular was Stokely Carmichael, who reminded the audience that they must struggle. "We must go now for the *real* control. That's got to be the word, the real control. We want the power to pick, to hire, and to fire. That's the attitude." He concluded his speech in ominous terms: "Then we prepare for the confrontation so that when the confrontation does come we become victorious. It is easy to die for one's people," and he lowered his voice: "It is much more difficult to live, to work, and to kill for one's people." The audience stood up, ap-plauding.

The stage was set for confrontation. Black radicals roamed the campus, disrupting classes, shouting that faculty who continued teaching were rac-ists, irritating many students. A few stormed department offices, turning over files, setting small fires, and breaking windows in front of frightened secretaries. The president called the police to campus, but that tactic irri-tated some faculty members who joined the strike while blacks taunted the cops, "Pigs off campus!" The police exploded into the students, nightclubs swinging. George Murray declared to television cameras: "You can tell every racist pig in the world, including Richard Milhous Nixon, that we're not going to negotiate until our demands are met."

"Stormy Negro Students Force San Francisco State to Close," declared the *Los Angeles Times* as the board of trustees demanded that President

Smith meet them and that the campus remain open for classes—regardless of the cost. Like so many college administrators during the era, Smith was caught in the middle, for he did not want to irritate either the striking students or faculty members, and he feared more violence with the police on campus. At the meeting, he offered to resign. The chancellor and board supported the idea, and then without consulting with the faculty they appointed a man with no administrative experience to be acting president, conservative professor and semanticist S. I. Hayakawa.

Hayakawa had spoken out against radical students before, as early as the Free Speech Movement in Berkeley, and now five years later he had publicly denounced his liberal colleagues who supported the strike and BSU. He had little faculty support, and was seen by many as a puppet for the conservative trustees and Governor Ronald Reagan. Immediately, Hayakawa took a tough law and order stance and declared a "state of emergency." He announced that the campus would not be shut down by the strike, that it would be kept open by police, that professors supporting student strikers would be fired, and then he terminated an economics professor against the wishes of the faculty and vice president for academic affairs. He also declared that no students could give speeches with microphones, and on the morning of December 2, as radical students broke that order, he marched out of his office and stunned demonstrators by climbing on their truck and pulling the wires out of their amplifier. A pushing match ensued, and the subsequent press coverage prompted Reagan to declare, "I think we have found our man."[2]

Yet the bravado solved little, and by the afternoon radicals were throwing rocks, breaking windows, and police were chasing them all over campus. The next day, Hayakawa announced that five were suspended, which only encouraged a larger rally of about 2000 students. Local black politicians and community leaders came to campus and announced their support for the strike. The Rev. Cecil Williams blasted Hayakawa and his "police state" as the "most deplorable situation I've seen, and I'm from the South." Berkeley councilman Ron Dellums declared, "Principles are not negotiable, not discussable, not compromisable," and BSU coordinator Jerry Varnado spelled out the course of action: "We've got to put Hayakawa up against the wall. We must rip off the slavemaster." The crowd began shouting outside of Hayakawa's office, "Up against the wall . . . this is no longer a school, it's an armed camp." The administration responded by trying to drown out the strikers by turning on their loudspeakers and playing the radio full blast. Some radicals began hurling stones and bricks, many at the office, provoking 300 police to march into the crowd. The scene turned bloody. A policeman was knocked unconscious and many students were beaten; officers arrested about 30.

The strike was not repressed, and instead it expanded throughout

December. Students continued almost daily demonstrations. Classroom attendance plummeted to 20 percent, and only about a third of scheduled classes met. Outraged by Hayakawa's behavior, faculty who were members of the American Federation of Teachers also threatened to go on strike. Nevertheless, Hayakawa continued strong-arm tactics. About 600 police occupied the campus, at a tremendous expense to the city, and they arrested 150 students that month. Meanwhile, the acting president consulted with the chancellor, board of trustees, and the governor, and then tried to defuse the situation by announcing that the college would close a week early, increasing the holiday break to almost a month.

The ploy did not work. Although Governor Reagan had pledged to keep the campus open "at the point of bayonet if necessary," when classes resumed in January the strike continued, and this time students were joined with the AFT professors, who declared their own strike. Class attendance was about 50 percent, and many faculty members called in sick. The campus paper, *Daily Gater*, blasted the acting president. "Through a series of blunderous dictum and statements, Hayakawa has succeeded only in radicalizing more students while extending his own credibility gap. Driven into a corner of desperation on campus (he can no longer go anywhere on SF State without an armed guard), the new champion of law and order has issued various scattered charges in a feeble attempt to discredit strikers." Hayakawa responded by ordering mass arrests at demonstrations. During a rally in January the police jailed 450 students and professors. A few days later the acting president announced that any student arrested on campus since the beginning of the strike would be suspended immediately.

By the end of the month, repression and weariness began to take a toll. Posting bail demoralized radicals, who also realized that the faculty were more interested in compromising with the administration. With help from the mayor and community leaders, the striking students and professors began meeting with Hayakawa and his administrators and to work out an agreement. Meanwhile, the board of trustees sent all faculty members a sample of over 180,000 letters they claimed they had received from angry taxpayers. The silent majority was speaking and their message was clear, as one citizen wrote: "The only possible answer to the present campus unrest is swift, sure (and if necessary violent) action against the demonstrators, including suspension, expulsion, firings, revocation of tenure, fines, arrests and/or jail terms." The California legislature proposed two dozen bills, including ones that would immediately dismiss any university employee or faculty member for striking, and another aimed at students for disrupting normal campus activities—an action that could result in a five-year prison sentence.

Eventually, the administration agreed to a black studies department of eleven, and to waive admission requirements and allow numerous "third world" students into the college. Furthermore, a black administration officer was appointed who granted much more financial aid for minority students. Yet the price was high. Police charges against 700 arrested activists were not dropped, and a few such as George Murray eventually served six months in jail. The administration also fired about two dozen faculty members. Frankly, considering the tense situation during a strike lasting 134 school days, it was amazing that no one was killed.

Calm returned to San Francisco State during spring semester, but the affair demonstrated how divided the campus, and the nation, had become by 1969. While there was some compromise, there also was little middle ground. Both sides now were digging in for the remainder of the second wave: an increasingly frustrated and bold student movement versus a more irritated silent majority that was demanding more repression. Hayakawa became a symbol, the tough little administrator who had the will to stand up to the students, and that image eventually contributed to his election to the U.S. Senate. Yet to the students, as one noted, Hayakawa's stance "played an important part in causing a large number of courageous and idealistic young Americans to come to despise the major institutions of their country."[3]

San Francisco State also inspired more minority student militancy, and throughout 1969 they began advocating a "third world revolution" against the white college establishment. Asian Americans, Chicanos, and Native Americans joined African Americans and demanded classes on their history and culture. During the spring semester, students protested at over 230 colleges across the nation, from Harvard to Memphis State to Yakima Valley College in Washington. Previous concerns of ROTC on campus and greater student participation in university policies were eclipsed by issues concerning minority students. At Rutgers campus in Newark, the Black Organization of Students took over the main classroom building and renamed it "Liberation Hall," while at Texas the Afro Americans for Black Liberation insisted on converting the Lyndon B. Johnson Presidential Library to a black studies building and renaming it for Malcolm X. At the University of California at San Diego, Angela Davis, a black radical studying with Marxist philosopher Herbert Marcuse, organized a coalition of black and brown students who advocated a Third World College named for the African and Mexican revolutionaries Patrice Lumumba and Emiliano Zapata. And such demands at Wisconsin and Berkeley resulted in riots, forcing governors to call on the national guard to occupy the campuses.

Yet the most stunning demonstration of the emerging third world revolution was in usually placid upstate New York. "About 100 black students at Cornell University staged a surprise raid on the student union building at dawn today," reported the *New York Times*. On parents' weekend they ran through the halls shouting "fire" and after people evacuated they chained the doors shut and seized the building. Tensions had been rising since December when the Afro-American Society charged that the curriculum was white, middle-class, and racist. With an enrollment of 14,000 the university only had 250 black students, and a hundred of them launched demonstrations demanding black studies. The administration threatened the suspension of half a dozen demonstrators while they studied the idea. In April, officials approved funding for a center of Afro-American studies, but that prompted resentment from some white fraternity men. Someone burned a cross at a black women's cooperative, set off numerous fire alarms, and made two bomb threats. The next day the blacks marched into the union and seized the building. The university administration negotiated quickly, and within 36 hours agreed to demands that no charges would be pressed against activists in the December or April demonstrations, and that they would continue to support the Afro-American center. Then, the black militants marched out of the building and shocked the nation—they were armed with shotguns and rifles.

The scene epitomized the word "militant" and demonstrated how far black empowerment had spread in two years. It was one thing in 1967 to see armed Black Panthers march into the California state legislature. White suburbanites could say that the militants were simply ghetto thugs. But it was something else to see black students waving shotguns at an elite white university—confronting white authorities. Black power seemed to be reaching an ominous phase as militants escalated their words and deeds. James Forman, for example, took the pulpit of New York's Riverside Church and demanded that churches and synagogues pay millions in "reparations" for segregating their institutions and exploiting people of color. Union men in Detroit formed the League of Revolutionary Black Workers and picketed the United Auto Workers, shutting down a Chrysler plant and charging the union and managers with a conspiracy that "reduced the black worker to a superexploited, supersubjugated beast of burden, with less rights than a common street dog."[4] Militants proclaimed that they had to defend themselves, that they would achieve their aims by any means necessary, including "armed self defense," for as H. Rap Brown declared: "if America chooses to play Nazis, black folks ain't going to play Jews."

Cornell also demonstrated that the idea of "third world liberation" was sweeping across the nation. "The emergence of yellow power," wrote Amy Uyematsu. "A yellow movement has been set into motion by the black power movement." Indeed, African American students were having an impact on others, and that included the other large minority in the nation, Mexican Americans. "The Chicano Rebellion," announced a cover story in *The Nation*. "Now it's the Mexican Americans—Chicanos, they are called in California—who are appearing on the scene of protest, with a self-evaluation that breaks radically away from the old, degrading stereotype of fatalistic loafer asleep under a sombrero."

For the first time the term "Chicano" was being printed in the mainstream press, but feelings behind the term had been developing for years, and one of the main reasons was Cesar Chavez. During his early years, Chavez had been a migrant worker, and by the 1950s he worked for the Community Service Organization in California, developed by veteran organizer Saul Alinsky. In the 1960s Chavez organized an agriculture workers' union, the United Farm Workers. Until he began this task, union leaders had considered it impossible to unite these workers because they usually were illiterate, indigent migrants. They had little support from local communities and virtually no political benefactors. Consequently, when New Deal politicians wrote laws that gave most laborers the right to collective bargaining and receive a minimum wage, migrant workers were excluded.

The result was that the majority of the 5 million Hispanic American citizens lived in poverty. In California, their median annual wage was half the poverty level, family income was a third of the state average. Like most migrant workers, Jessie De La Cruz worked ten-hour days for ten cents an hour before such conditions convinced her to become an activist for the UFW. In south Texas counties, almost two-thirds lived below the poverty line, while in some northern counties of New Mexico almost half the families existed on $2000 a year. Living conditions were substandard; most Mexican Americans lived in barrios of large cities or in squalid conditions on farms. Growers usually kept shabby accommodations for field hands and local citizens wanted the migrants to work and then move on to another harvest since the community did not want to pay taxes to support additional schools and services. Half of Mexican American homes in the Rio Grande Valley had neither hot water nor plumbing. Migrant work also was dangerous. In California, the job accident rate was three times and infant mortality double the national average; life expectancy was under fifty, and since there were few controls then on farm pesticides and other chemicals, thousands of workers were poisoned. Furthermore, Hispanics received a poor education. Nationally, about 40 percent of adults were functional illiterates, having less than a fifth grade education, and in Texas almost 90 percent had not graduated from high school. In that state, the average Hispanic finished just six years of schooling, eight in California, while blacks in those states had nine or ten, and whites had eleven or twelve. Uneducated and poor, they had little hope for escaping poverty. Father Theodore Hesburgh, chairman of the U.S. Commission on Civil Rights, toured the Rio Grande Valley and was shocked, reporting that many farm workers were "living under conditions close to peonage or slavery."[5]

While public racism toward African Americans had decreased during the decade, that was not the case with Mexican Americans. Anglos commonly referred to them as lazy, dirty, or sneaky, and called them "greasers," "spicks," "wetbacks," "meskin"; they were either too fast—"Speedy Gonzalez"—or too slow—"Pancho." Stereotypes were rampant on television and in advertisements. A popular TV program baby boomers grew up with was the "Cisco Kid," a sort of Robin Hood of the West. The Kid was portrayed as a suave, articulate Spaniard, and his sidekick was Pancho, the chubby, happy-go-lucky Mexican speaking in broken English. Ads were filled with negative images. Thomas Martinez claimed that Frito-Lay Company's use of Frito Bandito to sell corn chips really conveyed the message that "Mexicans = sneaky, thieves," and that Arid Company's ad with a Mexican bandit spraying his underarms while the announcer was saying, "If it works for him, it will work for you," really meant "Mexicans = stink the most." As Armando Rendon wrote, "from the Chicano's viewpoint, we are being made the communication industry's new 'nigger.' Since they can no longer denigrate the Negro, they turn to safer prey such as the Chicano and the Indian."

Hispanics also suffered discrimination. While there were few Jim Crow laws against Hispanics, there was ample de facto segregation. In many rural California schools, lunch periods were segregated, whites first then blacks and browns. At harvest time police picked up Hispanic truants, and ignoring compulsory attendance laws, delivered them to growers for field work. Local customs often meant that it was difficult for Mexican Americans to go to the movies or use public facilities such as swimming pools. Many schools were segregated by the way whites had drawn district lines, and most school officials prohibited speaking Spanish. In California and Texas, teaching classes in that language was illegal. President Johnson reversed these state laws by signing the Bilingual Education Act in 1968, but the English custom continued for years. As East Los Angeles teacher Sal Castro stated, "If a kid speaks in Spanish, he is criticized. If a kid has a Mexican accent, he is ridiculed. If a kid talks back, in any language, he is arrested. . . . We have a gun-point education. The school is a prison."

In politics Mexican Americans had made some progress in the Southwest, much more than African Americans in the South. While representation varied between regions, political power increased during the 1940s when the League of United Latin American Citizens, LULAC, and the G.I. Forum challenged Texas laws concerning school segregation and voting rights, and the Supreme Court ruled in their favor. Hispanics began building a political base, especially in New Mexico, and in Texas, where in 1961 they achieved a breakthrough by electing Henry B. Gonzales to the U.S. Congress. Yet progress was slow. Although they made up a large percentage of the population in cities such as El Paso, San Antonio, Albuquerque, Phoenix, and San Diego, election districts were so gerrymandered that few were elected to the city councils and none had become mayor. In Los Angeles, a city with a million Hispanic citizens, not one was on the city council, and although California had about two million in 1968, not one was elected to the state government.

In front of the law Mexican Americans were second-class citizens. The United States Commission on Civil Rights exposed numerous cases in which white police gave brown suspects unduly harsh treatment, arrested them on insufficient grounds, and then dispensed penalties "disproportionately severe." The commission cited a case in which a white officer shot and killed a Mexican American resident in San Antonio. The Justice Department investigated the case for two years and then closed it, admitting that "prosecution of a white police officer for the shooting of a Mexican would have little chance of successful prosecution in the Southern District of Texas." There were few Hispanic policemen in the Southwest, and only six of over a thousand agents working that area for the FBI. Also, they seldom served on juries. An attorney who had practiced trial law for a decade in south Texas admitted that in his community, which was 85 percent Chicano, he had never seen a Hispanic juror. Anglo attitudes were revealed when a Los Angeles police official stated that people of Mexican descent were "biologically crime prone," and when a young Chicano stood trial for incest in another California city, the judge blurted out, "Mexican people, after 13 years of age, think it is perfectly all right to go out and act like an animal. We ought to send you out of the country—send you back to Mexico. . . . You are lower than animals and haven't the right to live in organized society—just miserable, lousy, rotten people. Maybe Hitler was right."[6]

Rodolfo "Corky" Gonzales described the Mexican-American despair in a poem:

> I am Joaquin,
> Lost in a world of confusion,
> Caught up in a whirl of an
>   Anglo society,
> Confused by the rules,
> Scorned by attitudes,
> Suppressed by manipulations,
> And destroyed by modern society.

Chavez was aware of this plight, of course, and he also had been in-spired by the civil rights struggle. He began La Causa, the movement, by organizing farm workers in Delano in the San Joaquin Valley, an area known for fruit and especially grapes. From the beginning Chavez was building more than a labor union. He and colleagues began developing a community with a credit union, co-op store, newspaper, insurance club, and services to help Spanish-speaking workers get everything from driver's licenses to welfare assistance, and eventually supported a culture center and El Teatro Campesino. He also was preparing for the eventual strike. In September 1965, local Filipino farm workers announced that they would no longer work because growers lowered wages. Chavez felt that his union was still too small, about 1200 members, but this opportunity provoked him to announce *"Huelga!"*—strike—and a month later they announced the national boycott of grapes. A disciple of Gandhi and an admirer of Martin Luther King, Chavez taught nonviolent activism, and the strike soon resembled the early years of the black struggle. Chavez invited clergy, CORE, and SNCC activists to Delano, and he asked for student help at Stanford, San Francisco State, and Berkeley. Chavez was not just interested in winning better wage contracts, noted a journalist, he was "out to develop a community of farm workers." He also was igniting the Mexican American civil rights movement.

The wealthy growers responded promptly. While some claimed that Chavez was a Communist, others stated that he aimed to ruin agribusi-ness, and one even proclaimed that this citizen's ultimate goal was to take over California and give it back to Mexico. Meanwhile, the growers bused in other poor Hispanics to work the fields in an attempt to break the will of the strikers. They pressured the federal government, which allowed more Mexicans to cross the border for the harvest season, and they re-sorted to intimidation and occasionally to violence, beating strikers, spray-ing them with pesticides, and firing shotguns over their heads. The local police intervened on the side of the landowners. Dolores Huerta, the vice president of the union, was arrested for trespassing and released only after the union received enough donations to provide the $12,000 bail. Offi-cials apprehended Chavez and a priest for "violating air space" of a grower, and they arrested over forty activists for chanting *"Huelga! Huelga! Huelga!"*

The growers' behavior reflected their fear of losing their powerful posi-tion in states that depended heavily on migrant labor. In one congres-sional district in Texas, for example, the U.S. Department of Agriculture in 1966 supplied less than $250,000 for food stamps to feed all the poor in eleven counties—about 150,000 residents—while the same agency paid 400 wealthy farmers over $5 million in crop subsidies and benefits. "In short," Rodolfo Acuna wrote, "the political and economic realities in

Texas were that Chicanos were controlled by an oligarchy of white Anglo capitalists."[7]

The strike received very little attention as the national media focused on civil rights and war between 1965 and 1968, but that was not true in the Mexican American press. During those years other Hispanics became active. In Denver, Corky Gonzales and his colleagues formed the first Mexican American civil rights organization in the nation, the Crusade for Justice, to protest unfair treatment by the city government. In Albuquerque, 50 disgruntled citizens staged a walk out of the Equal Employment Opportunity Commission, charging paternalism and declaring that the EEOC did not have one Hispanic member. In Texas, 6000 melon pickers declared a strike in the Rio Grande Valley, and they walked 400 miles to Austin demanding a state minimum wage law. The first militant behavior appeared in New Mexico in 1967 when Reies "Tiger" Tijerina and six cars of armed followers descended on the Tierra Amarilla courthouse, claiming that Anglos had stolen millions of acres from Hispanics after 1848 when Mexico ceded the Southwest to the United States. A shootout erupted. Tijerina was captured, and while he was in and out of court, his supporters developed the Alianza movement. Next spring, students at Lincoln High School in East Los Angeles shouted "Blow Out!" Conceived by teacher Sal Castro, the action quickly resulted in 15,000 students walking out of five schools to protest poor educational facilities and racist teachers. Authorities responded by calling police, who conducted mass arrests. Shortly thereafter, students in Denver and San Antonio conducted blowouts, many holding signs: "Teachers, Sí, Bigots, No!" The Los Angeles event was the first mass protest explicitly against racism ever taken by Hispanic students, and as a journalist declared, it marked "the beginning of a revolution—the Mexican-American revolution of 1968."

The blowouts were significant that spring, but during the Tet Offensive and the New Hampshire primary, they received only local attention. That was not the case, however, for a simple yet profound action by Cesar Chavez. To publicize La Causa, he began a hunger strike, a fast. It was a gamble, and it paid dividends. Senator Robert Kennedy sent a wire: "I want you to know that I fully and unswervingly support the principles which led you to undertake your fast." The press rushed to Delano. After 25 days, three longer than Gandhi's famous fast for India's independence, Chavez agreed with his friends and doctor and ended the hunger strike. Thousands appeared with him at mass, and Bobby Kennedy symbolically broke the bread. Too weak to speak, Chavez had a friend read his speech: "I am convinced that the truest act of courage, the strongest act of manliness is to sacrifice ourselves for others in a totally non-violent struggle for justice. To be a man is to suffer for others. God help us to be men!"

Chavez finally had provoked the national press. *Time* wrote about "Cesar's War," the *New York Times* labeled Chavez "Man in the News," and next year Chavez was the topic of a cover article for *Time*, "The Grapes of Wrath, 1969: Mexican-Americans on the March." He changed tactics, emphasizing the grape boycott, and that stimulated more support from activists who picketed national chain stores, forcing many to stop stocking grapes. By summer sales and prices dropped and one grower admitted, "We have to settle this thing to survive." Ten growers who produced about 12 percent of the state's crop signed contracts with the United Farm Workers, symbolizing that the grower's united resistance was starting to crumble. By next July growers who produced half the state's crop of table grapes signed an agreement with the union. Chavez described the accord as "the beginning of a new day," and shortly thereafter announced the next phase—the lettuce boycott.[8]

Chicano awareness also had been aroused by black power. "We found that the colleges were paying attention to the blacks because they were militant," Lee Polanco stated at San Jose City College, "so we started to get as militant as the blacks."

And as they did, Chicano consciousness expanded. In East Los Angeles, David Sanchez and others founded the Brown Berets, a "highly disciplined paramilitary organization" to fight police brutality, while some militants in New Mexico organized *Los Comancheros:* "We need guys with fresh blood and fresh ideas who can go all the way in the struggle and by any means necessary." Brown students organized, especially in California where more were enrolled in college than in any other state, forming the United Mexican American Students, the Mexican American Student Association, and MEChA, Movimiento Estudiantil Chicano de Aztlan, while others in San Antonio founded the Mexican American Youth Organization, MAYO. Chicanos began demanding Mexican American studies at universities throughout the Southwest, from California State at Hayward to Metropolitan State College in Denver to the University of Texas. At Berkeley, a hundred occupied the president's office during spring semester 1969, and another group invaded the chambers of the Los Angeles Board of Education. For six days and nights they conducted a sit-in and sleep-in, an event that Ralph Guzman labeled "the first important public appearance of something called Brown Power."

Brown pride swelled in 1969. "Our main goal is to orient the Chicano to *think* Chicano so as to achieve equal status with other groups, not to emulate the Anglo," proclaimed an activist at San Jose City College. *Viva la revolucion!* declared posters in high school lockers, or *Viva Zapata!*, referring to the great Mexican revolutionary. A new, dynamic sense of community was obvious as Mexican Americans began saying, "brown is beautiful," as young men grew angry mustaches and *guerrillero* beards, as females demanded to be called Chicana. Brown Berets and MAYO membership soared, and while cultural activists created Teatro Chicano in the barrios of Los Angeles, Fresno, and Denver, others formed the Chicano Press Association and began publishing movement newspapers such as *Compass* in Houston, *Inferno* in San Antonio, *El Gallo* in Denver, *El Papel* in Albuquerque, *Bronz* in San Jose, and *La Raza* in Los Angeles. Large crowds of kids attended conferences held in cities from Albuquerque to Kansas City to Santa Barbara.

The most significant meeting of the year was the Chicano Youth Liberation Conference organized by Corky Gonzales and held in Denver. There, the term "Chicano" became vogue among the 1500 delegates, and there, Gonzales gave the movement a homeland, Aztlan, the mythical fatherland of the Aztecs. Alberto Alurista declared that all present were "the Chicano inhabitants and civilizers of the northern land of *Aztlan*. . . . Brotherhood unites us, love for our brothers makes us a people whose time has come and who struggles against the foreigner 'gabacho' who exploits our riches and destroys our culture. With our heart in our hand and our hands in the soil, we declare the independence of our mestizo Nation. We are a bronze people with a bronze culture." The event was much more than a conference, said Maria Varela, it was "a fiesta: Days of celebrating what sings in the blood of a people who, taught to believe they are ugly, discover the true beauty in their souls during the years of occupation and intimidation. . . . We are beautiful."

Armed with a new pride, Chicanos demanded empowerment, and they confronted the Anglo establishment with new issues. "We teach our children about Joaquin Murieta, not Robin Hood, about Zapata, not Kit Carson," wrote La Coronela, who advocated the end of "Anglo education" and beginning of cultural heritage classes. School blowouts expanded as many students and parents demanded bilingual education, not only in large cities such as Houston, Los Angeles, Denver, and San Antonio, but also in smaller towns. In Visalia, California, students gave their principal 21 demands which included mandatory classes for teachers on Hispanic culture and serving Mexican food. In Oakland, 200 browns and blacks boycotted classes, insisting on the elimination of a tracking system that was "geared to direct all Third World people into vocational programs." Confrontations erupted in Phoenix, where parents insisted on more Hispanic teachers, counselors, and a citizens' committee to select personnel and resolve grievances. By autumn, Chicano power was a movement. On September 16, Mexican Independence Day, thousands of students throughout the Southwest were absent from their high schools in the First National Chicano Boycott.[9]

Besides education, another issue that excited both Hispanics and African Americans was equal employment opportunity—another assault on the white male establishment. As part of his Great Society, President Johnson revived and expanded affirmative action. Generally speaking, all citizens pay taxes, which then fund government, education, construction, and other services performed by thousands of private companies. Traditionally, those jobs had been held by white males, but the Johnson administration felt that those occupations should be opened to all taxpayers, regardless of race: if you receive public money you must employ the public. Taken one step further, liberal politicians began demanding that if minorities made up 20 percent of a certain community, then there should be about that same percentage holding tax-supported jobs. Eventually, activists demanded that affirmative action be extended to hirings at all levels, freeing up new positions for minorities—and eventually for women.

Affirmative action and equal opportunity became battle cries for empowerment during the second wave, and that was apparent when the U.S. Commission on Civil Rights convened a hearing devoted to Mexican American issues in San Antonio. The problem was obvious throughout the Southwest. Although Hispanics made up 10 percent of the population of California, they held only about 3 percent of federal jobs in the state. And there was another issue: the quality of those jobs. In San Antonio, a commissioner asked a disturbing question. Noting that Hispanics made up about 45 percent of the work force in the area, and that they represented about 30 percent of government employees at Kelly Air Force Base, he wondered why they held only 12 percent of the better jobs at the base. "Would you consider that a broad and glaring inequity?"

The scene would be replayed for years in almost every American city, challenging the establishment, but a more immediate demonstration of empowerment appeared in Del Rio, Texas. In March, 2000 activists arrived in that city to condemn Governor Preston Smith and county commissioners for their role in canceling War on Poverty projects that aided local Mexican Americans. The repeal, authorities charged, was because funds were supporting political groups such as MAYO, which in turn were spreading hate literature about Anglos. Mexican American organizers from all over the Southwest attended the morning meeting on Palm Sunday, and then they began a procession through the city to the county courthouse. The demonstration, some participants felt, was a "Chicano Selma," an event that finally would expose Anglo injustices to the nation. "We have crossed that bridge today," Albert Pena declared, "and we're not looking back. We have raised the cactus curtain."

Upon arriving at the courthouse, a founder of MAYO, Jose Angel Gutierrez, read the Del Rio Mexican American Manifesto to the Nation. "Recent events in this city have made it amply clear that our minority continues to be oppressed by men and institutions using the language of

democracy while resorting to totalitarian methods." He described the Anglo establishment as one of hypocrisy: they "preach brotherhood and practice racism"; they "built a multi-million school for their children, then
built barracks for ours"; they have a "double standard of justice—minimum penalty for gringo and maximum for Chicano." Hispanics warned
that if the governor and local authorities did not reverse their position,
then the activists were prepared to be "as aggressive as it may be necessary," even to "lay down our lives to preserve the culture and language of
our ancestors. . . . On this day, Mexican Americans commit themselves
to struggle ceaselessly until the promise of this country is realized for us
and our fellow Americans: *one* nation, under God, *indivisible*, with liberty and justice for *all*."

The Del Rio event was important on many levels. Brown power had
arrived, but significantly—except for Chavez's movement—it still was not
receiving much national attention. There were many reasons. Mexican
Americans were divided over the Chicano movement. Ralph Guzman
noted that compared with blacks, "the Mexican American has many more
options available to him," and many had worked hard to be assimilated
into the dominant culture. In Los Angeles, for example, "middle-class
Mexicans in the modest homes of Montebello and Monterey Park have
no intention whatever of proclaiming themselves beautiful Indian brown
and persuading their sons and daughters to walk out of school." Also, by
the second wave civil rights had been in the news for many years, and so
the public and mass media were beginning to tire of the topic and of
marches. And by spring 1969 there were many new issues in the headlines, meaning that only a shocking event would attract national attention—such as bloody violence at San Francisco State or students waving
shotguns at Cornell. Finally, local authorities also had been viewing television during the decade and they were learning from those confrontations. Even though Del Rio marchers strayed from the legal parade route,
police were flexible; they did not attack, avoiding a Chicano Selma.

For militants at the end of the decade, then, there were only two ways
to make news—violent behavior or vicious proclamations. "The black,
the brown and the Indios have been selected by the forces of nature to
march together, fight together, even die together," Tiger Tijerina declared
at a Black Panther rally, later adding, "Yes, there will be a war of races."
A Brown Beret warned that "students today have the guts our parents
didn't," and after the Del Rio demonstration Gutierrez announced that
the enemy was the "racist gringo." If he could not change, then Chicanos
might have to "eliminate" him.

Yet this rhetoric repelled other Hispanics. Much more than blacks,
Mexican Americans were divided by class and generation. For years,
many had worked hard to assimilate into middle-class Anglo society;

confrontation, they feared, only would retard assimilation. Senator Joseph Montoya of New Mexico called Tijerina a charlatan, impostor, racist, liar, "and if he doesn't like the nation and what it stands for he can get the hell out." U.S. Representative Henry Gonzales charged that "Cuban-trained revolutionaries" had infiltrated the Del Rio marchers. To older moderates, "Chicano" was a pejorative, like wetback, but to militants, these establishment Hispanics were traitors to la raza, *malinches*, sellouts *vendidos*, Uncle Toms *Tio Tacos* or "coconuts," brown outside white inside.

During 1969 the Mexican American movement was developing along similar lines as civil rights and student power, and that was reflected in a rising generational conflict and the inevitable rift between moderates and militants. As *Newsweek* noted, "the Brown Power Movement . . . is moving down the track in the footsteps of black power—with little more than a shade of difference." Nor did the brown revolutionaries have any more of a plan for the future than the black power advocates or the few college students shouting "Revolution." After Tijerina spoke at the rally, a reporter asked a black militant what a black-brown alliance was supposed to accomplish. He shrugged and said, "Those who know don't say. Those who say don't know." As Ralph Guzman concluded, brown militants "really don't know" their exact goals, but "they *do* know, vaguely, that they want full equality everywhere and possibly some rectification of past wrongs." [10]

Many other citizens that spring were becoming concerned about past wrongs as empowerment began mixing with liberation. "When the man can look upon 'his' woman as human and with the love of brotherhood and equality," Enriqueta Vasquez wrote in *El Grito del Norte*, "then and only then, can he feel the true meaning of liberation and equality himself. When we talk of equality in the Mexican American movement we better be talking about total equality beginning where it all starts, at home."

Some American women had been talking about equality since Freedom Summer, a few others since the 1950s. As examined earlier, women during cold war culture had roles, and they were traditional—girlfriend, wife, mother, homemaker. Men had been raised to think of themselves as decision makers and providers in a man's world. After providing a romantic courtship and participating in holy matrimony, husbands expected wives to serve them, and in many states laws mandated males head of the household and primary guardian of the children. In return, they pledged to "take care of the little lady" for life, 'til death do us part. Her most important decision was to find the right man, the best possible provider. Her man—not her*self*—was her future, for there were few other opportunities. "If anybody had asked me to marry them between April and September of 1962," Elizabeth Holtzman said of the year she graduated from Radcliffe, "I would have said yes. It appeared to solve so many problems."

Such was the norm, and when some women decided that they were not happy in those roles, that they might want to break the mold, they met considerable opposition. The male authors of *Modern Woman, the Lost Sex* equated higher education with female frigidity and urged coeds to return home so they could find sexual fulfillment; as for working women, author Merle Miller wrote that a "strident minority of women are doing their damndest to wreck marriage and home life in America— those who insist on having both husband and career. They are a menace and they have to be stopped." Many citizens agreed, for a working mother supposedly posed a serious danger to the family. *Life* assembled four doctors—all men—to discuss the "fatal error," the career woman, in its 1956 issue devoted to American women. The psychologizing that followed exemplified the era: "The children are *her* responsibility: Daddy is busy, he understands business, she understands children." She has a "primitive biological urge toward reproduction, toward homemaking and nurturing. And however much she might scoff at the idea intellectually (being 'independent'), she would deeply want to be able to submit to her husband." On and on. Eventually these experts warned that the "disease" of working women led to democratic households, and worse, to children who become juvenile delinquents, atheists, Communists, even homosexuals.[11]

All this was meant to intimidate females, to keep them in their place. Yet during the early 1960s a number of factors merged to provoke change. Simone de Beauvoir had written an important book that stimulated American women to consider why they were "the second sex." Betty Friedan completed hundreds of interviews with educated women and published *The Feminine Mystique*, a best-seller that began portentously: "The problem lay buried, unspoken, for many years in the minds of American women. It was a strange stirring, a sense of dissatisfaction. . . . Each suburban wife struggled with it alone. As she made the beds, shopped for groceries, matched slipcover material, ate peanut butter sandwiches with her children, chauffeured Cub Scouts and Brownies, lay beside her husband at night—she was afraid to ask even of herself the silent question— 'Is this all?' "

While some were considering that question, others were becoming concerned about radioactivity from above-ground weapons testing, provoking Dagmar Wilson to organize Women Strike for Peace. Some 50,000 women in 60 cities held a national peace strike in 1961, marching with placards such as "Let the Children Grow," and "End the Arms Race, Not the Human Race." President Kennedy signed the Test Ban Treaty, and urged by these activists he also established a commission on women that brought together professional females from all over the country. The commission revealed discrimination in salaries, recommended equal employment opportunity, and after returning home these women created state committees that gave them a forum to express their cause and publicize local grievances. Kennedy signed the Equal Pay Act of 1963 and Johnson did the same for Title VII of the Civil Rights Act of 1964, laws which excluded many professional workers but generally banned discrimination in hiring and hourly wages.

But the enforcing agency, the Equal Employment Opportunity Commission, showed little interest in past wrongs of sex discrimination cases. The male commissioners joked about the issue, and refused to condemn the common newspaper practice of segregating job want-ads by gender, usually meaning that women need not apply for professional positions. In 1966, therefore, female delegates on the EEOC presented a resolution demanding enforcement of Title VII. Conference officials responded by blocking a vote, prompting two dozen angry females to walk out. Delegates Betty Friedan, Pauli Murray, Mary Eastwood, and Kathryn Clarenbach decided to form NOW—the National Organization for Women.

NOW aimed "to take action to bring women into full participation in the mainstream of American society now," and that included equal opportunities for women, ending stereotypes, and a "truly equal partnership with men." The activists also opposed the custom that men must carry the sole burden of supporting the family and that married women were entitled life-long support. NOW wanted to reform the system, and this became the position of moderate feminism. NOW wrote a Bill of Rights for Women that was presented to politicians during the 1968 election year, and which also provoked some of its conservative members to drop out and form their own organization, the Women's Equity Action League. NOW demanded equal access to education and jobs, enforcement of laws banning sex discrimination, maternity leave for working mothers, federally funded day-care centers, and they presented two issues that would dominate politics for years—a woman's right to control her own reproductive life, including abortion, and adoption of a proposal first introduced by an older generation of feminists in 1923, the Equal Rights Amendment to the U.S. Constitution.

NOW grew rapidly, and while older women were setting the political agenda, daughters were smashing the social one of cold war culture. The pill became available in 1960, placing birth control in the hands of the female and giving her a powerful tool to control not only birth but her own sexuality. Then at mid-decade, medical researchers William Masters and Virginia Johnson completed their extensive experiments and published a classic work concerning the physiology of sexual intercourse, *Human Sexual Response*. Describing the four phases of intercourse—excitement, plateau, orgasm, recovery—the book became a best-seller, and more important, it exploded numerous myths about sexuality, such as: it was difficult for women to have orgasms; women did not enjoy intercourse as much as men; and women were "frigid" if they did not have vaginal orgasms with their husbands, thus they were dependant on males for climax (when in reality they could have multiple orgasms by stimulation of the clitoris). The book demonstrated that males and especially females had the physical ability to obtain a mutually satisfying sex life, and young women began publishing articles about their sexual awakening in college and underground papers: "When my guy first wanted to undo my bra I was completely stymied. I felt so guilty and embarrassed. This is not the way to feel. . . . I am saying something very specific. Listen to yourself carefully—your body, your mind. Learn to masturbate yourself. If the chance to develop a relationship with a man comes your way, be sensitive to yourself, to him and develop your potential together."[12]

Sexual double standards faded while numerous young women were participating in the civil rights struggle, sometimes with ample discrimination. As early as 1964 Casey Hayden and Mary King presented an unsigned memo on the "woman question" that raised the issue of male superiority in SNCC—"this is no more of a man's world than it is a white world"—and the next year they circulated a letter to females in SDS and SNCC that claimed: "There seem to be many parallels that can be drawn between treatment of Negroes and treatment of women in our society as a whole. . . . It is a caste system which, at its worst, uses and exploits women." Working for civil rights or with poor people in SDS urban projects "allowed women to develop a strong sense of their own capabilities," wrote Sara Evans, and in 1965 a few introduced the woman question at the national SDS conference. The result was male booing and catcalls: "She just needs a good screw," "She's a castrating female." The next year when female activists at the conference demanded a plank on women's liberation, men pelted them with tomatoes, provoking the females to wonder whether they were included in "participatory democracy."

Women's liberation spread in the larger movement, and so did male sexism. A popular button in the movement concerned draft resistance: "Girls Say Yes to Men Who Say No." Some young men considered themselves revolutionaries, and in some circles female submission became "revolutionary duty." Marge Piercy complained that a "man can bring a woman into an organization by sleeping with her and remove her by ceasing to do so. A man can purge a woman for no other reason than that he has tired of her, knocked her up, or is after someone else: and that purge is accepted without a ripple. . . . The etiquette that governs is one of master-servant."

This behavior provoked a few females in 1967 to discuss their status and popularize their concerns. In June SDS feminists arrived at the annual meeting, where they announced that the "struggle for liberation of women must be part of the larger fight for human freedom." A few months later others headed for the National Conference for New Politics in Chicago, which was an attempt to forge black and white radicals into some type of political party. Jo Freeman and Shulamith Firestone demanded a discussion about developing a "civil rights for women" statement, but male leaders refused, calling their issue "trivial," even patting Firestone on the head, saying "calm down, little girl."

To the "girls," there seemed to be a paradox, for as Mary King wrote, "civil rights issues are at the core of the women's movement." Yet the Vietnam War also provoked females to consider their status. In January 1968, some female activists introduced the issue of liberation at the first all-female antiwar demonstration organized by the Jeannette Rankin Brigade and Women's Strike for Peace, held in Washington, D.C. Most of the 5000 participants were older liberals, including Friedan, Coretta Scott King, and Jeannette Rankin herself, the 87-year-old pacifist who as a congresswoman had voted against U.S. entrance into World Wars I and II. They were joined by about 500 younger radicals. The procession marched on Congress, but was barred from entering. While the moderates sang along with Judy Collins, "We Shall Overcome," the younger radicals marched to Arlington National Cemetery to conduct a symbolic burial of Traditional Womanhood. "We cannot hope to move toward a better world or even a truly democratic society at home until we begin to solve our own problems," declared Kathie Amatniek. Females were "powerless and ineffective over war, peace, and our own lives." Thus, it was time to raise the consciousness of women, to unite, for according to their new slogan, "Sisterhood Is Powerful."[13]

Liberation spread throughout the movement, where it continued to meet considerable resistance from male activists. Earlier, these men had complained that bigots had responded to black demands for civil rights with violence; now some movement males reacted with ridicule to women demanding equality. Something seemed funny. They could not hit the females, so they laughed, or worse. At the "inHOGuration" of Richard Nixon protest in January 1969, Marilyn Salzman Webb, Shulamith Firestone, and Ellen Willis attempted to make comparisons between the war, black power, *and* women's liberation. "We as women are oppressed," Webb stated, and when she began denouncing viewing women as "objects and property," some men began catcalling: "Take her down a dark alley!" "Take her off the stage and fuck her."

Such conduct shocked Willis to wonder, "If radical men can so easily be provoked into acting like rednecks, what can we expect from others?" Indeed, during the next months many female activists discussed whether they should remain in the male-dominated new left and antiwar movement or split and form their own movement. Some felt they should remain as an "arm of the new left," while others asked, "Are we to be the 'arm' of a revolution, without asking who is the head?" Many called for "women's meetings" in their cities, and they began small organizations such as Cell 16 and Bread and Roses in Boston, Sudsofloppen in San Francisco, Redstockings and New York Radical Women, Berkeley Women's Liberation Group, Women's Radical Action Project in Chicago, and numerous other groups in Detroit, Toronto, and Washington, D.C.

These activists published their views and stimulated discussion, yet they constituted a small number in the sixties generation, perhaps a few hundred; thousands more were influenced by the rise of student power and the counterculture. Liberation naturally meant ending *in loco parentis* campus regulations that restricted coed but not male behavior. Male administrators remained concerned about morals of coeds, and they usually put only female students on trial for violating social norms such as sleeping or living with boyfriends. He was considered smart—getting something for nothing, the pleasures of sex without the responsibilities of marriage. Coed activists also were confronted by male students holding traditional stereotypes about females capabilities. At the Columbia strike in 1968, when coeds were participating in the occupation of a building, males made the proclamations to television cameras and gave the females tasks of answering phones, typing statements, making dinner. "For many of us women in the strike," wrote Nancy Biberman, "liberation has applied only to buildings, not to ourselves."[14]

Women also were being influenced by the counterculture. Hippie ideas of rejecting contemporary moral values prompted youth to question ideas of virginity and marriage—"If it feels good, do it." The emphasis on communal living provoked others to think about lifestyle and family—"Do your own thing." These values stimulated many to become introspective, to live with boyfriends, or to have many sex partners. "Men may have let their hair grow long," recalled a female baby boomer, "but I could and did unloose my breasts. Going braless was letting my freak flag fly."

Yet such manifestations of freedom left many women feeling used or exploited. As in most American homes, a female communard wrote, "the guys would gather around at about five o'clock and say, 'When's supper going to be ready?' " Others complained about insatiable demands on "hippie chicks" to give "free love," and underground papers were filled with semi-nude women and males advertising for companions, without strings, of course. Hippie button: "Peace, Pussy, Pot." Sexism was rampant in the music scene. In "cock rock" culture, feminists complained in *Rat*, "men always seem to end up on top." Bill Wyman of the Rolling

Stones coined the word "groupie" for female admirers of the band, and the members added up the number of women that they had slept with in two years: 444, from the band who appropriately sang about a "Stupid Girl" who should be kept "Under My Thumb," a "Honky Tonk Woman" who should give her man "Satisfaction."

Men in the rock culture, or in the movement, were only a reflection of men in society and traditional relations between the sexes—and all citizens suddenly were confronted at the 1968 Miss America Pageant by a protest that for the first time in memory provoked them to think about the role of women in society. While some might have recalled reading about the first women's rights conference at Seneca Falls, New York, in 1848, or about the flappers of the 1920s, the postwar generation had not experienced a feminist movement. This protest merged many aspects of the movement, as Robin Morgan explained, for the pageant was "degrading to women (in propagating the Mindless Sex Object Image); it has always been a lily-white, racist contest (there has never been a black finalist); the winner tours Vietnam, entertaining the troops as a Murder Mascot; the whole gimmick of the million-dollar Pageant Corporation is one commercial shill-game to sell the sponsors' products. Where else could one find such a perfect combination of American values—racism, militarism, capitalism—all packaged in one 'ideal' symbol, a woman."

The protest stunned the nation, and during 1969 women's liberation became a household word and flourished, partly because female baby boomers flooded the ranks of the movement, but more so because women were confronted with stereotypes, sexism, and especially discrimination.

As men told "women driver" jokes, popular magazines belittled females with a continual barrage of caricatures: "For years I saved for a rainy day," said one man to another. "Then I met a girl who wiped it out with one monsoon." Male activists lamented, "Life's a bitch, then you marry one." Ha, ha, some laughed, as male officials of famous races such as the Boston Marathon refused female entrants, declaring "it is unhealthy for women to run long distances." Women were excluded from men's clubs and bars, even in hotels that catered to the public, a violation of the Civil Rights Act. At Heinemann's Restaurant in Milwaukee, for example, women were prohibited from sitting at the *lunch counter* because "men needed faster service than women because they have important business to do." And the myths: it was *natural* that women were weak, passive, emotional, and a legion of experts from Sigmund Freud to Erik Erikson told them that they could avoid suffering from "penis envy" if they realized that they were different and if they did not attempt to do things beyond their "female dispositions." And the names, the scores of sexist terms that men used to describe women, as feminists in San Francisco noted in their flyer:

WOMEN are people . . .
Although some think they are:

a different species	chicks, pussies, kittens, cats, dogs, bitches, cows, foxes, pigs, birds
something good to eat	cookies, honey, tarts, tomatoes, sweeties
a mindless sex object	cunts, pieces, whores, nymphs, sluts, teases, sex pots, tramps, ball breakers, nutcrackers
or anything but people	babies, old ladies, little women, dears, old maids, "girls," mothers, hags, shrews, broads, dolls, wives, darlings, "the better half," counter-revolutionaries . . .

Feelings were beginning to simmer, and for radicals they were boiling over in 1969. Gayle Rubin wrote "Woman as Nigger" in the *Ann Arbor Argus* and at Cornell feminists handed out flyers proclaiming "The Chick as Nigger." "Here they come," Leni Wildflower declared. "Those strutting roosters, those pathetic male chauvinists, egocentric, pompous and ridiculous bastards. Here come the freaks in those tight bell-bottoms, tie-dyed T-shirts which their 'old lady' (would you believe it?) made for them. . . . Male liberators, *you* are stepping on my neck." Time had come. "FREE ALL SISTERS," wrote Robin Morgan, for "like every other oppressed people rising up today, we're out for our freedom—*by any means necessary*."[15]

So was another group—homosexuals. "Hundreds of young men went on a rampage in Greenwich Village," reported the *New York Times* in June, "after a force of plain clothes men raided a bar that the police said was well known for its homosexual clientele. Thirteen persons were arrested and four policemen injured." The Stonewall Inn was a famous gay bar. Police often raided such businesses and harassed patrons; this time officers said the club was selling liquor without a license. For the first time in memory, gay men stood and fought back.

The next night police again swept the area, and they were met by 400 young men and women, many hurling bottles and coins. The Stonewall Inn had boarded up windows with the graffiti, "Legalize gay bars," and some shouted, "I'm a faggot, and I'm proud of it!" The police broke ranks, charging into the crowd, making arrests, beating some, as the crowd chanted "Gay Power!"

Gays never had been liberated into the mainstream of American society; just the opposite—they were ridiculed and demonized, their sexual behavior labeled "deviant" and illegal in every state. A generation earlier the Kinsey survey reported that 4 percent of males were exclusively homosexual, and about 2 percent of females. Nevertheless, some citizens refused to admit that gays existed in America, rather like those who denied racial injustice or the mistake of fighting in Vietnam. Others admitted it, and then ridiculed them as fags or queers; kids growing up could always get a laugh by calling someone a homo. Physicians and psychologists labeled homosexuality an illness and they treated it with massive dosages of drugs, psychoanalysis, hypnotism, and electroshock. One team of experts even suggested lobotomy while another wrote, "Therapeutic castration . . . seems to be a valid subject for research." Police turned the other way as toughs drove into gay neighborhoods and beat or "rolled gays," and when some California gays advocated moving to the Lake Tahoe area and establishing a community, a local tavern hung a sign: "Homo Hunting Licenses Sold Here." Public pressure was severe, and if discovered, gays were dishonorably discharged from the military and usually fired from the federal government. To avoid such sanctions many would suffer unhappy marriages, such as actor Rock Hudson. Even in the movement, gays could be outcasts, and Black Panther Eldridge Cleaver denounced homosexuality as an evil. Thus, very few would admit it, or "come out of the closet." As Jonathan Katz lamented, "We have been the silent minority, the silenced minority—invisible women, invisible men."

During cold war culture homosexuals had established organizations such as the Mattachine Society and Daughters of Bilitis, and then the social activism of the 1960s provoked many to march for various causes. The counterculture stimulated more freedom and tolerance of different lifestyles, and student protests inspired gays on campus. Like the movement underground, they also began developing their own network and a few campus organizations. Robert Martin formed a Student Homophile League at Columbia, and Rita Mae Brown did the same at New York University. They discussed being gay. "As the personal and political came together in our lives," Katz recalled, "so it merged in our heads, and we came to see the previously hidden connections between our private lives and public selves; we were politicized, body and soul. In one quick, bright flash we experienced a secular revelation: we too were among America's mistreated."

Gay activity usually was going on behind closed doors, but that ended at Stonewall. Immediately after the confrontation, gay activists met, and then announced in the underground *Rat*: "We are a revolutionary homosexual group of men and women formed with the realization that complete sexual liberation for all people cannot come about unless existing social institutions are abolished. . . . We are creating new social forms and relations, that is, relations based upon brotherhood, cooperation, human love, and uninhibited sexuality. Babylon has forced us to commit ourselves to one thing . . . revolution."[16]

Gays began busting down the doors. They quickly developed some 50 groups, one of the most outspoken the Gay Liberation Front, and they began picketing companies that discriminated against them and publishing undergrounds, such as *Gay Power* and *Come Out!* Many did; that year New York had 50 gay bars, about 70 in San Francisco, and the Gay Liberation Front held the first street dances in New York, Chicago, and Berkeley—an action that earlier would have led to arrest. In October *Time* featured a cover story on homosexuals, contending that gays had been encouraged by a "national climate of openness about sex of all kinds and the spirit of protest," and it concluded, "Though they still seem fairly bizarre to most Americans, homosexuals have never been so visible." That was the case on the first anniversary of the Stonewall incident when 10,000 paraded down Sixth Avenue in New York. Some chanted "Two, four, six, eight! Gay is just as good as straight!" Others held signs, "Hi Mom!" "Me Too!"

Gay liberation shocked citizens, and so did the behavior of an increasing number of other men—soldiers in the U.S. Army. In 1969, the army was not only losing a war, it was turning the guns around on itself as some soldiers began the long march to empowerment.

At the beginning of the year eight soldiers assigned to Fort Jackson, South Carolina, circulated a petition asking their commander, Brigadier General James Hollingsworth, for permission to hold an open meeting on base to "freely discuss legal and moral questions related to the war in Vietnam and the civil rights of American citizens within and outside the armed forces." In a growing sign of discontent, 300 soldiers signed the petition. The general refused. In March, a hundred gathered outside their barracks and began discussing the war. Officers appeared, observed, and left, returning later that evening and restricting seven soldiers and placing four in the stockade. A few days later the army charged eight soldiers with breach of peace, inciting a riot, and disrespect to an officer.

The issue was G.I. rights, and many activists quickly came to the aid of the Fort Jackson 8. Prominent lawyers offered free counsel, students from Harvard to San Francisco State sent telegrams, antiwar actress Jane Fonda traveled to the base, and soldiers from other duty stations signed petitions and sent them to Hollingsworth. A gutsy officer with a brilliant combat record in World War II, Korea, and Vietnam, Hollingsworth received the command because his superiors knew that he did not back down from a difficult task. He later admitted that he was prepared to take a strong hand toward dissidents he felt were simply trying to be disruptive to the armed forces and who were perpetuated "by the Communist elements in this country . . . the Jane Fonda's and all the other types." Furthermore, the army knew the backgrounds of the eight soldiers and intentionally sent them to Hollingsworth's command. The FBI and local authorities placed informants among the eight and within the local movement, and when Fonda arrived, the general stated that he would keep her off his base even if he had to "arm every soldier."

The subsequent court-martial of the Fort Jackson 8 was closed to the press, but the case drew national attention after a reporter wrote an article in the *New York Times* magazine entitled: "Must the Citizen Give Up His Civil Liberties When He Joins the Army?" Under intense scrutiny, the army dropped most of the charges and got rid of the problem by giving most of the soldiers undesirable discharges; the movement declared victory.

The Fort Jackson affair demonstrated a new aggressive tone of the G.I. revolt while raising additional issues. After the trial ten Fort Jackson soldiers sued Hollingsworth and the Secretary of the Army for harassment and intimidation, and demanded the same rights to protest on-base as civilians had off-base. While the general joked with his army lawyer to "let me know when I'm supposed to go to jail with the Secretary of the Army," the Defense Department was more concerned. A spokesman described the suit as serious, "without parallel in American military history." Eventually, the army won the case in federal court, but meanwhile 80 soldiers on base signed a statement declaring that the "Army continues to trample on our rights as well as our lives," and that Vietnam "is the most unpopular war in our history. Yet the government's policy threatens to continue this tragedy for many years to come." [17]

Troops in Vietnam began voicing such sentiments that same spring, which became apparent after an incident in May when soldiers of the 101st Airborne Division were ordered to attack Hill 937. The commanding colonel ordered two battalions up the heavily fortified hill, which was defended by the North Vietnamese Army. Deeply entrenched in bunkers, the enemy continually repelled the onslaught. Officers called in an artillery attack that lasted 36 hours, and then ordered another attack. It too was repulsed, again with heavy casualties. After ten days the men grew tense and irritable, but the colonel obtained reinforcements and ordered another attack. Soldiers grumbled, but complied, and four battalions finally drove the enemy off the position, an area where troops had been so bloodied, so ground up, that they called it "Hamburger Hill." After controlling the position for a few days, the colonel ordered a withdrawal, commenting to the press that the "only significance of Hill 937 was the fact that there were North Vietnamese on it." After all, it was a war for hearts and minds, not for real estate. Shortly thereafter the enemy reoccupied Hamburger Hill.

The sacrifice, and the withdrawal, led to a political debate in America, enraged many troops, and boosted the antiwar movement. The *GI Press Service* proclaimed that "Hamburger Hill is Nixon's 'secret plan' for ending the war," and another G.I. underground advised soldiers, "Don't desert. Go to Vietnam and kill your commanding officer." "Fragging" became a new word in Vietnam as soldiers advertised a $10,000 bounty for anyone who killed the colonel who ordered the attack. Numerous soldiers attempted to frag him before the Army shipped him back to the United States. It was a lesson learned, for as one combat officer stated, "Another Hamburger Hill is definitely out."

Indeed, a few months later, a lieutenant 30 miles south of Danang radioed his commander, "I'm sorry sir, but my men refuse to go—we cannot move out." Company A of the 196th Light Infantry Brigade's Third Battalion had been ordered at dawn to move on a labyrinth of North Vietnamese bunkers and trench lines in Songchang Valley. They had done so for five days, and each time they had been thrown back by an invisible enemy which methodically waited until they advanced and then accurately picked them off. Company strength had been cut in half, most squad and platoon leaders had been killed or wounded. The commander ordered one of his trusted sergeants to fly to the scene and to "give them a pep talk and a kick in the butt." The sergeant found 60 exhausted men, lying in the tall elephant grass, uniforms ripped and caked with dirt; one was weeping. He asked them why they would not move, and it poured out of them—they were sick of the endless battle in torrid heat with sudden firefights in day and constant mortar attacks by night. It was a nightmare. Sixty colleagues had perished, and they too would be annihilated. After a long talk, some cajoling, the sergeant began walking toward the ridge line. The men began to stir, and slowly followed.

Although a few individual soldiers had refused orders in Vietnam, Company A was the first sign of a unit mutiny. Later that year soldiers in another unit flatly refused to advance down a dangerous trail, an act captured and aired on CBS-TV, and in 1970 about 30 units rejected orders to advance on the enemy, a year with so many cases of troop disobedience that the army developed an official euphemism, "combat refusal."

There were many reasons for combat refusal, such as the frustration created by living in and fighting an alien culture, the inability to tell friend from foe, and the one-year tour of duty that meant few wanted to risk their lives in the final months before going back to "the world," the USA. Yet these factors had existed for years; more important was President Nixon's secret plan, his policy of Vietnamization. Accordingly, the president would negotiate peace while U.S. troops continued training and supporting the South Vietnamese Army. Gradually, Nixon would bring U.S. troops home and ARVN would fight their own war against North Vietnam, resulting in "peace with honor." The idea sounded good, but the enemy never was interested in Nixon's definition of a "just peace" and the plan could succeed only if ARVN had the desire to fight for the regime in Saigon. Few of them did, especially when compared with the determination of the enemy. This had been apparent for years, and was the reason why LBJ had to send half a million troops in the first place and why Westmoreland had to order them out of secure bases and into combat. Vietnamization, then, was a policy for America, for President Nixon, not for South Vietnam. Nixon brought home enough troops so he could claim that he was "winding down the war," and of course secure his re-election in 1972. For Vietnam, the policy demonstrated that despite all Nixon's rhetoric, the slow withdrawal meant that the U.S. no longer aimed to "win" the war for the hapless Saigon government. ARVN desertion rates climbed and corruption soared in South Vietnam. For the U.S. military, the policy meant that the hoax was up: instead of fighting to win, the objective for the troops naturally became staying alive. "What we're doing now," said one soldier in 1970, "won't change the outcome of the war at all." Instead of conducting search and destroy missions, troops improvised, going out to "search and avoid" the enemy. As one soldier stated, using the racist term for his ARVN ally, "I don't want to get killed buying time for the gooks."

Vietnamization killed what remained of American troop morale in Vietnam. By the end of 1969 in some units, during 1970 in others, the army stopped fighting—and began surviving—in Vietnam. The army itself documented that fact, citing dozens of cases of combat refusal. While in previous wars refusing orders was one of the most serious offenses, "treason" punishable by death, that was not the case during Vietnamization. Faced with demoralized troops who wanted to go home, generals did not even give reprimands to most soldiers refusing orders, or to the men in Company A. Vietnamization had changed the mission. As James Reston wrote, Nixon was asking "Company A to fight for time to negotiate a settlement with Hanoi that will save his face but may very well lose their lives. . . . He wants out on the installment plan, but the weekly installments are the lives of one or two hundred American soldiers, and he cannot get away from the insistent question: Why?" [18]

More Americans were asking that question. After Tet the number of men trying to avoid serving in Vietnam soared—and that included youth of all political persuasions. While defense contractors were encouraging students to accept a job by guaranteeing deferments, family doctors and ministers were writing about their clients' flat feet or religious opposition to war. The number of young men who could not pass the induction physical or who claimed to be conscientious objectors climbed to record levels. College graduates avoided service by studying or traveling overseas, and perhaps as many as 100,000 young Americans moved to Canada, including as many as 10,000 deserters from the U.S. Armed Forces. Other youths flocked to national guard and armed forces reserve units, where they would have to spend only six months on active duty. A Maryland national guard general admitted that whenever the Baltimore Colts "have a player with a military problem, they send him to us," and the Dallas Cowboys had ten players assigned to the same national guard division while promoting themselves as "America's team." Thus, of the 27 million young Americans who came of draft age during the long war, 16 million avoided military service, 11 million served in some capacity, while just over 2 million went to the war zone: only 6 percent of sixties generation males saw combat in Vietnam.

As enlistment rates dropped to historic lows, antiwar sentiments soared to new highs. On Easter Sunday 1969, hundreds of thousands took to the streets for the first major antiwar demonstration during the Nixon administration. While thousands marched in New York and San Francisco, pacifists in Philadelphia read the names of all Americans killed in Vietnam, and the largest parades to date were held in Chicago, Atlanta, and Austin. In Washington, D.C., four young men were symbolically crucified on crosses planted in front of the White House, for as they said, "as long as the war continues, it is always Good Friday."

The Nixon administration at first tried to placate critics. "Give us six months," National Security Adviser Henry Kissinger told peace activists, "and if we haven't ended the war by then, you can come back and tear down the White House fence." Nixon pledged to end the unfair Selective Service system and replace it with a lottery, and to cut draft rolls. He told his supporters that Vietnamization would bring lasting peace and that the enemy was "counting on the collapse of American will." Again, the complexity of the Vietnam imbroglio was reduced to a simple application of American will. The president declared the Nixon Doctrine—less involvement in revolutionary wars—and he announced the first withdrawal, 25,000 troops. While activists felt the pullout was too small, signaling many more years of war, most citizens supported Nixon's initial policy toward Vietnam.

The administration also began a domestic policy, one aimed to crush the movement. Although the president-elect had advocated an administration "open to new ideas, open to men and women of both political parties, open to critics as well as to those who support us," that lasted only until the first dissenters appeared. "If people demonstrate in a manner to interfere with others," declared Deputy Attorney General Richard Kleindienst, "they should be rounded up and put in a detention camp." In March, the government began rounding them up by indicting the Chicago 7 for violation of the federal anti-riot or Rap Brown Act, charging them with conspiring to travel across state lines "with the intent to incite, organize, promote, encourage, participate in, and carry on a riot." The trial lasted throughout the year, and by autumn students called it "The World Series of American Injustice." Aside from the obvious issue of freedom of speech, the idea of "conspiracy" conveyed the impression that the eight plotted with each other when in fact some of them had never met. But justice was not the point of the trial; it was detention, an attempt to curtail the activists by legal wrangling that eventually cost them and their supporters half a million dollars during the next five years before the case was thrown out of court. During that time the government kept them under surveillance and harassed them. When Abbie Hoffman arrived for the trial he was given a search that uncovered a penknife, resulting in additional state and federal charges of carrying a concealed weapon. In one five-week period Hoffman was questioned once by the Internal Revenue Service, twice by the Justice Department, and five times by the FBI. While he sat in jail, the sheriff ordered his head shaved and displayed the long mane as a trophy. As for the defense attorney for the activists, William Kunstler, Judge Hoffman slapped him with a four-year sentence for contempt of court—later reversed—while most of the defendants were subpoenaed to testify before the House Un-American Activities Committee.

The administration was determined to demonstrate that the movement had links with Hanoi or Moscow. As during the Johnson years, the CIA could not find any foreign or Communist ties, but Nixon was tenacious and ordered additional covert actions. The administration formed the Committee of Six. Composed of young conservatives such as presidential speech writer Patrick Buchanan and a former president of the Young Americans for Freedom, Tom Charles Huston, the committee encouraged the IRS to harass liberal and antiwar organizations. The administration ordered the FBI to monitor the movement, and the bureau's counter-intelligence or COINTELPRO program eventually employed 2000 agents that infiltrated, provoked disturbances, and began a massive program of "disinformation," a euphemism for spreading lies.

As would be revealed later, the administration's behavior was shocking. FBI informers provoked fights and shootouts between black power groups. Agent Eustacio Martinez, who infiltrated the Brown Berets and MAYO, even attacked a U.S. Senator, smashing his car and kicking him, as part of his job to "start hassles among the people to divide them, create incidents and do crazy things" to give a bad reputation to the Chicano movement. The White House also ordered the CIA to break the law and begin domestic infiltration and disruption of antiwar organizations, code name Operation Chaos. After someone in the administration disclosed the secret U.S. bombing of Cambodia, the White House instructed the FBI to conduct illegal wiretaps of several government officials, journalists, and activists—from National Security Council staffer Morton Halperin to musician John Lennon.[19]

"A bad moon rising," Credence Clearwater Revival sang to the sixties generation, but to Nixon and millions of citizens the federal government's behavior was appropriate because America was under siege. The campus upheaval at San Francisco State began 1969 on an ominous note followed by armed black militants at Cornell, which *Time* predicted "may have been the turning point after considerable national tolerance toward the radicals." But Cornell was just the beginning. Students demonstrated at about 300 campuses during spring semester and officials now reported attempted arson and bombings. Campus confrontations, reported the National Commission on the Causes and Prevention of Violence, were at record levels, and it warned against the "escalating risk of assassination," declaring that political violence was "more intense than it has been since the turn of the century." Some militants conducted "trashing" raids, with the idea that the only way to get the nation to change policy was to vandalize public buildings, stopping business as usual. A few others advocated bombings. The Justice Department reported an unprecedented number, and some 35,000 threatened attacks as it appeared that 1969 would be the "year of the bombings." In Denver a militant was charged with a series of explosions that destroyed electric transmission towers of the Colorado Public Service Company, and later, a group called Revolutionary Force 9 claimed responsibility for bombing the New York headquarters of IBM, General Telephone & Electronics, and Mobil Oil. The next year, an angry mob in Isla Vista, California, burnt down a branch of Bank of America. Racial tension also remained high, and the number of ghetto gang fights and sniping at police tripled in 1969. *Time* reporters wondered whether the nation was heading toward "Guerrilla Summer." At UCLA, two black power groups, Black Panthers and United Slaves, had a shootout, leaving two dead, and when Sacramento police stormed Panther offices a hundred shots were fired, resulting in 15 wounded.

Race and politics were not the only cause of the mounting violence, for the government announced rising crime statistics in all categories, even transportation. Hijackers seized 40 planes, setting a record and prompting the federal government to pass a law installing metal detectors in airports. Random violence soared. " 'Maniac' Sought in Five L.A. Murders," declared the *Los Angeles Times* at the beginning of a year that ended with the bizarre murders by Charles Manson. The commission lamented that Americans "have become a rather bloody-minded people."

"Anarchy," said Nixon, "this is the way civilizations begin to die," and one of his subordinates added that America was "facing the most severe internal security threat . . . since the depression." Most parents agreed that it was time to get tough with the younger generation, and especially with the radicals. A Gallup poll found that 80 percent supported the idea that student protesters should be expelled and over half opposed even peaceful and legal demonstrations on campus. As for professors who protested—"Fire them," demanded columnist James J. Kilpatrick, "and turn a deaf ear to blubbering of 'tenure' and 'academic freedom.' " *Time* concluded, "If there was one word that summarized the feelings of much of the U.S. toward the radical it was: 'Enough!' " While the president demanded that university administrators show more backbone, federal and state governments proposed hundreds of bills aimed at curtailing student demonstrations, terminating financial aid to protesters, and jailing anyone who attempted to prevent faculty or students from attending classes. Attorney General John Mitchell stated what many citizens wanted to hear: "The time has come for an end to patience." [20]

Patience certainly had run out at the University of California in Berkeley. Spring semester had witnessed a violent confrontation as the Third World Liberation Front clashed with administrators and then police over establishing a department of ethnic studies. By April, tempers began to cool when about 200 students, hippies, and community activists brought shovels, rakes, and topsoil to an area about the size of a football field situated south of campus and began planting. They were "sod brothers," and according to one, "We tended it, loved it, planted trees, grass, and flowers on it, made it into People's Park." Officially, the university owned the land, but they had delayed its development and so the area had been home to street people, stray cats, and mud. Planting changed that, and during the next month the park became symbolic. "For all of us, hip and straight, the Park was something tangible that we had done, something that drew our community together. The Park was common ground." But not to the university; it was trespassing, and the chancellor announced that construction would begin for a playing field and parking lot and that a fence would be built "to exclude unauthorized persons from the site." Activists held a large campus rally, but to no avail, and on the early morning of May 15 police entered the park, dispersed about 50 people, and within hours workers had constructed an eight-foot cyclone fence.

All hell broke loose. At noon, a few thousand people met on Sproul Plaza, and they began marching to retake the park. They confronted police lines. Rocks and bottles. Tear gas. Street fighting. Armed with shotguns, police fired buckshot into the crowds, ripping flesh. By nightfall 20 police officers had been injured and 100 activists, and 30 protesters had been shot, including one fatally, student James Rector. "It is of paramount importance that law and order be upheld," declared the regents. Governor Reagan sent the national guard in full battle gear—they established martial law, made random arrests, and occupied the campus. Students still conducted rallies and marches; about 80 percent of faculty and students voted in favor of developing a park, a stance even accepted by the Berkeley City Council. No, no more tolerance. The governor sent helicopters, which sprayed potent tear gas on the campus. Some students vomited, others in classes cried, as the noxious cloud spread over the community. "If it takes a bloodbath," Reagan had declared, "let's get it over with. No more appeasement."[21]

Appeasement was an appropriate word for the World War II genera-tion, and the gathering storm continued for the remainder of 1969. Fed-eral officials charged Tim Leary with drug possession and sentenced him to ten years while they indicted Tiger Tijerina for burning two forest ser-vice signs and condemned him to three years in prison. Four states filed a dozen charges against H. Rap Brown, who also was appealing a five-year federal sentence for a gun possession violation; Stokely Carmichael was fighting a ten-year sentence. Many black radicals were charged with Selective Service evasion, such as Fred Brooks and Cleveland Sellers, and Willie Ricks faced riot charges in Atlanta. The FBI infiltrated the Brown Berets and Black Panthers, disrupting programs and harassing members. Agents arrested Panther David Hilliard on charges of threatening the pres-ident, and released him only after his supporters could raise the $30,000 bail. Eldridge Cleaver supposedly was drawn into a gun battle with Oak-land police, and he went into exile in Algeria. Huey Newton was in prison for allegedly killing a police officer, and Bobby Seale was on re-strictive probation. Almost all of these charges would be dropped, but like the Chicago 7 Trial, only after the activists had spent time and money in court—away from demonstrations.

Sometimes the crackdown was brutal, as in Chicago when police at-tacked the local Black Panther headquarters, wounding four and killing Mark Clark and Fred Hampton. Officers claimed the militants engaged them in a "fierce gun battle" in which about 90 shots were sprayed throughout the apartment. The Panther's lawyer was outraged, countering that authorities nationwide were conducting raids to exterminate the group, resulting in the deaths of 28 Panthers. The attorney was near the truth, for during a later Senate investigation FBI documents confirmed that the raid was part of COINTELPRO, that an informer gave officials a floor plan of the apartment, and that the ensuing gun battle was one-sided: Ballistics experts determined that the police shot all shells but one and that holes going out of the front door were made not by bullets but by the police who pounded nails through the door. The bureau was crim-inally complicit in increasing violence between organizations in the movement, and eventually authorities agreed to a settlement with the families of Clark and Hampton, awarding them almost $2 million. While these facts were not known after the raid, Chicago police tactics and state-ments then were so questionable that nine congressman called for a fed-eral investigation and the *New York Times* wondered whether "authorities there and elsewhere are engaged in search-and-destroy campaigns rather than in legitimate law enforcement."[22]

It was a purge, yet ironically, one that some militants provoked by their behavior throughout 1969. In June, SDS held its ninth and last annual convention at the Chicago Coliseum. The organization had to pay a large rental fee because some 50 universities refused their request to use campus facilities. About 1500 members arrived, including delegates from the Black Panthers and Brown Berets, not to mention hundreds of journalists, undercover agents, and policemen. Quickly, the meeting disintegrated into shouting gangs of revolutionaries—Progressive Labor, Revolutionary Youth Movement, the Weathermen. Some fantasized about "guerrillas" and "cadres" in the liberation struggle that would crush imperialism and bring about the "third world revolution." Others called for a "vanguard" that would lead working-class kids to power after the imminent collapse of the establishment. Black Panthers referred to women's liberation as "pussy power." Feminists shouted "Fight Male Chauvinism!" The next month, white and black militants formed the United Front Against Fascism, and at their meeting in Oakland whites talked about "sabotaging" the establishment and armed Panthers clamored that they should "off the pig." Eventually, the conference dissolved into macho rhetoric. Panther David Hilliard proclaimed, "We don't see SDS as being so revolutionary. . . . We'll beat those sissies, those little schoolboys' ass if they don't straighten up their politics."

SDS disintegrated. The most important student organization of the decade had traveled far during the seven turbulent years since its founders wrote *The Port Huron Statement*. That document had called for more citizens to participate in democracy, for students to work peacefully to change the system and to open the doors of democracy for all Americans. Now, the shouting remnants called for a militant elite to destroy, apparently, whatever lay in the way.

The first target was Chicago. The Weathermen would lead the attack, a group that, surprisingly, had among its members the sons and daughters of many prominent liberal and conservative families—Bill Ayers, Kathy Boudin, Bernardine Dohrn, David Gilbert, Cathy Wilkerson. They had adopted their name from a Bob Dylan song stating, "You don't need a weatherman to know which way the wind blows," and to them, the wind was howling from the left. They boasted that their "Days of Rage" in October would lure 20,000 angry youths to "pig city." In a stark demonstration of how much support militants ever had in the movement, about 300 appeared—while two months earlier 400,000 went to Woodstock and a month later a few million would participate in the antiwar Moratorium. Dressed in denim or leather jackets, some with football helmets or gas masks, the Weathermen met in Lincoln Park and chanted, "Revolution's begun! Off the pig! Pick up the gun!" They put on helmets and pulled out pipes and chains. "We began to feel the Vietnamese in ourselves," said Shin'ya Ono, and Susan Stren added: "We were the Americong."

Then, they attacked Chicago. They ran down streets smashing windows, knocking people down, until they met the police. Fifty were injured, a hundred arrested, and the entire affair was denounced by the establishment—and by the movement. SDS condemned the Weathermen, another activist labeled them "kamikazes," and the Black Panthers called the attack "Custeristic."

This was not revolution, simply nihilism. The Days of Rage revealed the character of the tiny band of white militants who always yelled the loudest and thus received much media attention. They shouted "revolution," yet rarely acted so: They shouted "smash the state," and only smashed a few windows. Only a handful of them actually acted in a way to hurt the "enemy," the Establishment. Bombing targets were buildings, not police chiefs, and in America where anyone could walk into a sporting goods store and buy a gun, these radicals did not do it—they did not shoot at the authorities. With rare exception, "by any means necessary" was only violent rhetoric. The militants' greatest act of revolution was screaming vulgar language, taunting cops, and offending the silent majority.

They also offended the movement. Gallup polls demonstrated that students "deplored violence," and among those who demonstrated very few supported militant tactics. After the Bank of America went up in flames near U.C. Santa Barbara, 7000 students signed a petition opposing the destruction. Many activists began mocking the Weathermen by saying "you don't need a rectal thermometer to know who the ass-holes are." Marty Jezer lamented, "The Movement, like society, has run amok. Fighting cops. Killing pigs. Hurray! Our vision for the future. A new age soaked in blood. I'm crying." Others were singing, most with the Beatles who proclaimed that they too wanted to change the world, but when you talk about violence and destruction, "Don't you know that you can count me out."[23]

The rhetoric and behavior of the militants convinced many activists that they had to redouble their efforts to divorce themselves from violence, behave peacefully, and appear patriotic. Now that Nixon had declared Vietnamization, activists aimed to convince citizens that it was patriotic to bring the boys home—withdrawal was morally right. That autumn journalist Seymour Hersh helped the antiwar movement by revealing a disturbing tale. The year before soldiers under the command of First Lieutenant William Calley, Jr., apparently had herded hundreds of old men, women, and children together in the village of My Lai, Vietnam, and slaughtered them. After assembling evidence, the army announced in November that Calley was going to stand trial. Weeks later, investigators also announced that some noncommissioned officers were skimming millions of dollars from the profits of post exchanges in

Southeast Asia. This revelation, and especially the subsequent My Lai trials, cast aspersions on the U.S. Armed Forces and became symbols for activists: A dishonest U.S. military was aiding a corrupt Saigon regime by killing innocent civilians to obtain peace with honor.

As citizens began questioning the military, activists prepared for the Moratorium of October 15. Former McCarthy activists Sam Brown and David Hawk originated the idea: To counter Nixon's slow withdrawal, peace advocates would conduct a one-day pause in their usual business, a moratorium, for the purpose of generating popular support for either immediate withdrawal or at least a fixed timetable. The moratorium would be conducted peacefully, with reverence and respect, and the idea gained vast liberal support from religious and university leaders, students and workers, and from an increasing number of local, state, and national politicians. Numerous congressmen and two dozen senators endorsed the demonstration. Republican Senator Charles Goodell sponsored a resolution calling on the president to withdraw troops by the end of 1970 or face a cutoff of funding for the war, and senators Church, Hatfield, and McGovern offered companion bills, one proposing the termination of the Gulf of Tonkin Resolution. Although none passed, the proposals demonstrated that demands for peace had become a responsible crusade in Congress.

"Bells Toll and Crosses Are Planted Around U.S. as Students Say 'Enough!' to War," reported the *New York Times*, and the *Los Angeles Times* added, "Prayers in Many Cities Mark Day of Dedication." The Moratorium was the largest demonstration held in a western democracy, and according to historian Mel Small, "the single most important one-day demonstration of the entire war." Millions participated, some attending church services or joining processions through their cities, others simply wearing black armbands symbolizing peace or boycotting classes. Activists conducted teach-ins, vigils, and rallies and handed out leaflets across the country. An airplane skywrote a peace symbol over Boston. Actors held a moment of silence during plays in New York, while 90 percent of high school students in that city boycotted classes. A Baltimore judge interrupted court proceedings for reflection. Students at Bethel College in Kansas struck a bell every four seconds for each death in Vietnam, and 200 Vassar coeds walked through the gates of the military academy at West Point, handed flowers to cadets, and sang "America the Beautiful." Women planted flowers at veterans' cemeteries. In Vietnam, some troops went on patrol wearing black armbands, and at home thousands conducted quiet candlelight processions, one of the largest from the Washington Monument to the White House. About 600,000 activists converged on the Mall for the rally. A "Political Woodstock," declared the Boston *Globe*, for more than ever before the massive, peaceful Moratorium revealed a yearning in America—solemnly, many more citizens were beginning to sing, "All we are saying, is give peace a chance."

Nixon declared war—on the peace movement. After telling colleagues that he was "not going to be pushed around by the demonstrators and the rabble in the streets," he unleashed his allies. Vice President Agnew attacked the "strident minority," the "mob," who did not support the president. "A spirit of national masochism prevails," he declared, "encouraged by an effete corps of impudent snobs who characterize themselves as intellectuals." As for the "malcontents, radicals, incendiaries, civil and uncivil disobedients among our young," he continued, "I would swap the whole damn zoo for a single platoon of the kind of Americans I saw in Vietnam." Agnew then went after the press, charging that the liberal media, "a small and unelected elite," distorted the news, raised doubts about the president's policies, and promoted dissent. Congressman Gerald Ford denounced those who would "cut and run" from Vietnam, and Senator Goldwater proclaimed that the Moratorium was "playing into the hands of people whose business it is to kill American fighting men." On November 3 the president launched his own attack, his "silent majority" speech. Although the term had been used before, that evening it became part of the 1960s lexicon. Nixon asked for time to "wind down the war," and then turned up the heat on "a minority" who were attempting to impose their will on the nation by mounting demonstrations which threaten America's "future as a free society." The enemy, apparently, really was at home: "North Vietnam cannot defeat or humiliate the United States. Only Americans can do that." And "to you, the great silent majority of my fellow Americans, I ask for your support."

Nixon claimed that he received that support, and Kissinger boasted that the president's speech "turned public opinion around completely." He certainly won the support of those who had voted for Wallace the year before, and conservatives embraced the president, from the American Legion and Veterans of Foreign Wars to the Christian Crusade for Christ and Young Americans for Freedom. But as for the mainstream, opinion polls revealed a people desiring peace but confused about how to obtain it. Half of citizens now felt that the war was "morally indefensible"; 60 percent said that the war had been a "mistake"; and 80 percent were "fed up and tired of the war." Although half felt that South Vietnam would fall without U.S. support, a third now demanded an immediate withdrawal—a position advocated by the movement but unthinkable to political leaders just a year earlier. Other polls showed contradictions. Three-fourths of Americans would give the president time to wind down the war as long as he continued to negotiate with the enemy, decrease draft calls, and withdraw U.S. troops. And while 80 percent felt activists raised important issues that should be discussed, 60 percent agreed with Nixon that demonstrations harmed the prospects for peace. By the end of 1969, then, Americans were frustrated, angry, and confused; they simply wanted peace, preferably with honor.

Activists were less concerned with honor in what they considered a dishonorable war: They wanted peace now. "I would like to live for my country," said one Penn State student, "not die for it." He, and many more like him, headed for Washington in mid-November for the next demonstration, the Mobilization Against the War. The first evening they began the March Against Death. Over 40,000 participated, each carrying a candle and a placard with the name of an American killed in Vietnam. The father of one dead soldier grieved that Vietnam was "a war we didn't have the courage to win, and now that we've failed, don't have the courage to pull out of." For two nights they walked from Arlington National Cemetery to the White House, pausing to state the name, and then continuing on to the Capitol in the nation's longest single-file parade. On Saturday, more activists streamed into Washington and flooded the Mall, including several hundred members of the U.S. Armed Forces. A week before the G.I. Press Service placed a full-page antiwar ad in the *New York Times* which was signed by over 1300 active duty servicemen, including almost 200 stationed in Vietnam. Some G.I.s climbed on to the speakers' platform, one proclaiming that Nixon was worried about not just "being the first president to lose a war, but to lose the army," and others boasted that their "whole company went AWOL for the demonstration." As the afternoon continued, numerous bands played peace music while activists held the usual banners, "Peace Now," and a new one: "Silent Majority for Peace." Eventually, the crowd swelled to almost 700,000, in the largest single demonstration in American history.[24]

That same month, other activists took dramatic action that refocused the movement from war to empowerment—and that demonstrated that power was shifting from the Establishment to the movement.

Crystal City, Texas, was a rather typical migrant worker town. The "spinach capital of America," complete with a statue of Popeye, it was located in the winter garden area a hundred miles southwest of San Antonio. Local Mexican Americans had made progress during the decade, but while they constituted over 80 percent of the population, Anglo landowners and agribusinessmen dominated the power behind the government and school board. Education had slowly improved during the decade, but by national standards it was disastrous, resulting in a median schooling for Mexican Americans of less than three years and an 80 percent dropout rate. The high school strictly enforced a no Spanish speaking regulation, although the student body was almost 90 percent Hispanic. But discrimination reached even deeper levels in small-town Texas, affecting the selection of cheerleaders, baton twirlers, and homecoming queen. The faculty, itself three-fourths Anglo, chose the cheerleaders. The teachers erected a quota of one Mexican American for the four cheerleaders, and the homecoming queen had to have a parent who was an alumni, meaning Anglo. To keep the peace, the Texas Rangers patrolled the area, an organization with a reputation captured in an old saying, "Every Texas Ranger has some Mexican blood. He has it on his boots."

In November, Jose Angel Gutierrez, who grew up in Crystal City, joined parents and students and presented demands to the school board for classes on the Mexican American experience, more Hispanic teachers and counselors, bilingual instruction, and no punishment for students who spoke Spanish. The board did not respond. A month later, therefore, 1700 Chicano students in all grades, almost three-fourths of the student body, began the blowout. As students walked out of classes, parents picketed the school. Some local businessmen then fired striking student workers, and that prompted Chicanos to boycott those stores. With the school in deadlock, students asked U.S. Senator Ralph Yarborough, a liberal Democrat, to ask federal authorities to cut off funds to the district, claiming that the board continued segregation and thus violated the Civil Rights Act. State and federal officials flocked to the scene and began an investigation. By January, the school board capitulated. The students won all demands. Crystal City became known as the most successful Chicano walkout in history, stimulating Mexican Americans in four other counties to confront their school boards. Shortly thereafter Gutierrez and his supporters began planning for the next phase of empowerment—forming a political organization, La Raza Unita party, and winning control of the school board in the elections of 1970 and eventually of the government of Crystal City.[25]

Empowerment spread to other communities, to East Harlem where the Young Lords, a Puerto Rican group, occupied a church demanding a breakfast program for children, declaring a school of liberation—and to the Bay Area.

That same November, eleven braves and three squaws landed on Alcatraz Island, the prison facility that the federal government had abandoned in 1963. They approached the caretakers and offered to buy the island for "$24 in glass beads and cloth" and they announced that the island should be made into a Native American institute and museum. They departed, but two weeks later about 80 returned and declared, "We have come to stay," making themselves at home in the fortress. Bay Area students and activists manned boats and provided food and water, and more Indians boarded rafts to join the occupation. On Thanksgiving, 300 celebrated, and citing an old Sioux treaty that gave Indians the right to occupy unused federal land, they announced that they wanted funds for the cultural complex and that they would give the U.S. government two weeks to surrender Alcatraz. "Keep Off U.S. Property" signs were repainted "Keep Off Indian Property," and they took down Old Glory and raised their own flag, a red teepee under a broken peace pipe on a field of blue. Negotiations began and continued into 1970. By then, *Newsweek* declared, Alcatraz had become "a symbol of the red man's liberation."Alcatraz was not the first symbol that decade, for earlier Washington tribes had held "fish-ins" demanding that the state recognize their treaty rights for salmon, and during 1969 two important books were published that revealed the plight of the Native American—Edgar Cahn's *Our Brother's Keeper* and Vine Deloria, Jr.'s *Custer Died for Your Sins*. But Alcatraz was on another level, as *Look* proclaimed, "The beginning of the warpath!"

During the next months over 10,000 Indians from dozens of tribes and every state visited the island, and a few began broadcasting "Radio Free Alcatraz," an evening interview program that explored the status of their group, which *The Nation* labeled "Our Most Silent Minority." Life was hard on the reservations, home to about half of the 700,000 Native Americans. Housing was pathetic, 80 percent did not have running water and sanitary toilet facilities, and disease was rampant. Compared with average citizens, Indians were eight times more likely to suffer from tuberculosis and ten times more likely to have rheumatic fever and hepatitis. Poverty prevailed, and unemployment rates on reservations ranged from a low of 20 to a high of 80 percent. The income of Native American families on the reservation was the lowest for any ethnic group in the nation, while life expectancy was 44 years compared with the national average of 64. Boredom and depression was widespread, and Indians had abnormally high rates of alcoholism and suicide. Educational opportunities were limited; the average Native American completed less than six years of schooling. Films and television shows were filled with prejudice—the murdering, scalping, raping savage—and so were history texts, one declaring that tribes "lived for some generations on the frozen wastes of Alaska. This experience deadened their minds and killed their imagination and initiative." Nor did most universities have courses on Native Americans, for as one student said, "We can learn more about our past and about our future right here on Alcatraz." Another added, "Even the name Indian is not ours. It was given to us by some dumb honky who got lost and thought he'd landed in India."

Native American grievances were specific to their tribe and reservation and long-term aims were diffuse because there were some 200 tribes and no apparent national leaders. Their movement never would be as united as the black or even the brown struggles. Nevertheless, there were some common grievances. Most were bitter toward the nation that had cheated and double-crossed their forefathers, and they were angry at the agency that dealt with their concerns, the Bureau of Indian Affairs. They criticized the BIA for being paternalistic, treating them as wards of the state, constantly interfering with their lives and giving unwanted advice. Over the last century the BIA had become the Great White Father, issuing their money, educating their children, relocating them from reservation to city, and determining the use of their land. Officials had a history of granting white developers and corporations special rights on reservations, or selling their lands at ridiculously low prices, especially in attractive areas like New England and California. In 1964, for example, Californian tribes were given 47 cents an acre as compensation for millions of acres stolen from them during the century, a price based on fair market value in 1851. To control Native Americans, officials had erected a web of thousands of rules, regulations, laws, and court decisions that governed only the tribes. Most of the BIA employees were white; the Indian employees who went along with the agency were called Apples, red outside and white inside, or "Uncle Tomahawks." On the reservations Native Americans complained that they were "prisoners of war," and Cherokee Robert Thomas declared that the BIA had created "the most complete colonial system in the world."[26]

These complaints ignited Red Power. "We are learning how to work together, tribe with tribe," said an activist. "It hasn't happened before like this. This is where our new nation will begin." Red Power spread like wildfire throughout the first half of 1970. "We don't use the language of the New Left," declared a Cherokee, "but that doesn't mean we're not militant." Native Americans peacefully raided federal properties—a lighthouse in Michigan's Hiawatha National Forest, Ellis Island in New York Harbor, and 20 attempted to establish a permanent camp in California's Mount Lassen National Park while 100 invaded Fort Lawton in Seattle. Angered at whites who littered their beaches, Indians in Washington State set up road blocks and closed 50 miles of seashore, and Tulalip Janet McCloud and others violated fishing regulations because restrictions on salmon, she claimed, reduced them to "savages with no more rights than a bear." In Maine, Passamaquoddy tribe members charged motorists fees on a busy highway that passed through their land. Other activists protested the Indian dress of the Dartmouth College mascot, and Iroquois demanded that New York state museums return their wampum belts and other cultural artifacts. In Minneapolis, one of the few cities with an Indian ghetto, Chippewa Clyde Bellecourt formed the "Indian Patrol." Dressed in red jackets and berets, they observed police on duty, and arrests of Indians dropped significantly. "Goodbye to Tonto," declared a *Time* cover story, now Indian activists were chanting new slogans, "Custer Had It Coming," "Better Red than Dead," and "Kemo Sabe Means Honky, RED POWER!"

Indians continued the attack, adopting a new call for "Integrity, Not

Integration." The United Native Americans demanded the establishment of cultural centers, "fishing and hunting rights, the right to survival," and *Indian-oriented education."* The Native American Rights Fund and others filed suits against state and the federal governments involving trespass, employment discrimination, misuse of school funds, and breach of treaty agreements, while others conducted sit-ins at BIA offices in Denver, Cleveland, and Chicago. Sixty members of the American Indian Movement invaded the BIA office in Minneapolis demanding good jobs; the Intertribal Councils of Michigan insisted that the governor appoint a Native American as state commissioner of Indian affairs; and the National Indian Youth Council filed a discrimination suit against the BIA in Denver and called for "the eventual Indian takeover of the BIA." Alaskan Indians filed to prevent the construction of the Trans-Alaska oil pipeline, and a Navajo squaw filed against the Arizona Tax Commission claiming that because she was living on the reservation she did not have to pay state taxes. Other tribal councils avoided the local BIA offices and went directly to Washington, where they presented their grievances to the Interior Department and to Congress. A Senate subcommittee held hearings, and after testimony from members of tribes across the nation, the chairman, Senator Edward Kennedy, wrote that in the future the government's program must be: "Let the Indians run Indian policy."[27]

The statement defined empowerment—let the people decide—and as the decade of the 1960s ended and as 1970s began, "the people" was being defined as *all the people* who had felt powerless before and during cold war culture. Now for the first time, the people included the majority of Americans—women.

Women's liberation surged in 1970. While Native Americans occupied Alcatraz that spring, feminists were busy spreading the news and developing networks. In 1968 the first two feminist underground papers appeared; three years later there were over a hundred journals, newsletters, and newspapers, from Boston's *No More Fun and Games* to Austin's *The Second Coming* to Seattle's *Pandora.* In 1970 feminists published *Notes from the Second Year* and it quickly sold 40,000 copies.

The flood of publications provoked more women to read, discuss, and consider their plight. They formed small support, affinity, or rap groups and participated in "consciousness-raising." They met in living and dorm rooms, anywhere comfortable, and explored feelings, ideas, oppression, and questions that were startling for the times: Should we wear makeup or bras? Does your husband help clean the house? Should I live with my man, or marry him, and if the latter then should I keep my name or take his? Should I use Miss, Mrs., which connote marital status, or Ms.? What are the father's responsibilities with the children? Should women love other women? How aggressive should females be with men? Would your man change jobs or move for your career? Does your man satisfy you sexually, or do you fake orgasms to make him feel adequate? Can my marriage be saved, or should it be saved? Women often followed a four-stage process of opening up, sharing, analyzing, and abstracting. To Pamela Allen, her group was "free space," a place "to think about our lives, our society, and our potential for being creative individuals and for building a women's movement." Experiencing a support group or liberation conference and discussing personal problems often struck a chord—other women shared the same feelings and ideas—and that resulted in great emotion. "The week after the conference was spent in euphoria. It was very mystical," stated a participant. "I felt my whole life had changed. It has." In 1969 there were about 40 consciousness-raising groups in the nation, and the next year there were three times that just in New York, Chicago, and San Francisco.[28]

Yet like the broader movement, the number of groups and the size of organizations never was a clear indicator of women's liberation. As Robin Morgan wrote in 1970 for her introduction to *Sisterhood Is Powerful*:

> You, sister, reading this . . . you are women's liberation. This is not a movement one "joins." There are no rigid structures or membership cards. The Women's Liberation Movement exists where three or four friends or neighbors decide to meet regularly over coffee and talk about their personal lives. It also exists in the cell of women's jails, on the welfare lines, in the supermarket, the factory, the convent, the farm, the maternity ward, the streetcorner, the old ladies' home, the kitchen, the steno pool, the bed. It exists in your mind. . . . It is frightening. It is very exhilarating. It is creating history, or rather, *her*story. And anyway, you cannot escape it.

Nor could women escape stereotypes, sexism, or their status, topics that were being discussed in groups and now being examined on the front pages of the national press. While journalists had published only a few articles about women's rights in national magazines at mid-decade, in 1970 they printed 30 on that topic and double that on women's liberation, and every major broadcast network ran special programs. What did this barrage reveal? Not only stereotypes and sexism, but more important, legal, educational, and economic discrimination that resulted in second-class citizenship—or what Mary King labeled the "caste system for women."

Discrimination became the most important woman's issue during the Nixon administration.[29] The Johnson administration had begun investigating violations of Title VII, but the Republicans stalled, even though the number of equal pay complaints soared. Instead, the administration announced in 1970 that it would enforce affirmative action guidelines only to eliminate race—not gender—discrimination in the workplace. Secretary of Labor James Hodgson stated that women were "different" from minorities, and that his department had no intention of making contractors hire female workers or enforcing Title VII. The Equal Employment Opportunity Commission also took little action, and in fact the EEOC still was using "his" while describing job functions for their own directors and investigators and "her" for all clerks and secretaries; almost all their regional directors charged with investigating gender and race discrimination were white males. NOW concluded: "In the seven years since Title VII was passed, the EEOC has compiled a record on combating sex discrimination so dismal that its negative effects far outweigh the one or two positive items on its record." Shortly thereafter, federal officials met with a few hundred citizens in Wisconsin, and the only time the men referred to women was to tell jokes about "a flat-chested cocktail waitress who filed a Title VII complaint."

Jokes instead of enforcing the law became increasingly maddening as a record number of women attended college and looked for work. The percentage of women working outside the home climbed during the decade, reaching over 40 percent by 1970. There were more wives and mothers working than ever before, and more baby boomer females attending college, if they were admitted. The University of North Carolina and other public institutions, for example, set higher entrance standards for female applicants than for men. On campus, coeds often found doors closed, as advisers steered them away from "male professions" such as business, science, engineering, and toward "female occupations" such as nursing, teaching, and home economics. Deans had erected quotas to maintain male dominance in medical, dental, law, and graduate schools, and so only 1 percent of engineers were women, 2 of dentists, 3 of lawyers, and 7 percent of physicians. There were very few female professors, journalists, and executives. Nevertheless, by the end of the decade millions of females stood in line for interviews. Armed with diplomas, they sought an opportunity, perhaps a career at a time when the economy was booming. What did they find? Scores were denied interviews, or male interviewers asked, "Are you engaged?" and if not, then, "Can you type?"

Most women with college degrees had three opportunities—teach, type, and take temperatures—all meaning lower pay and little chance for advancement. A Harvard Business School survey of a thousand male executives found that 80 percent of them felt that women made valuable contributions to management, but only a third favored giving them such opportunities. That seemed to be the case for female law school graduates, for 1300 of them cited almost 2000 cases in which they had been told by law firms, banks, corporations, unions, and agencies, "We do not hire women." Ruth Bader Ginsburg, who graduated first in her class at

Columbia, could not get a job offer nor a judicial clerkship. "Does she wear skirts?" inquired Supreme Court Justice Felix Frankfurter when he was asked to consider Ginsburg. He refused, saying, "I can't stand girls in pants!" For the few women hired as professionals, they started work at a salary about 10 percent lower than their male classmates with the same degree and at the same company, a practice followed by the federal government—by law an equal opportunity and pay employer. Some 80 percent of females held low GS-1 to GS-6 jobs, and only 1 percent held higher GS-13 and above positions, and for the same work men made an average of $1500 more a year.

On the job discrimination was pervasive. In higher education female professors filled the lower ranks, and took much longer to be promoted—if they could get a job, for women were the last hired. University advertisements asked men to apply, and for many educated women the future looked bleak. Unemployed with a Ph.D. in Chinese history, thinking about her plight as a faculty wife, Marilyn Young wrote in her journal, "I have no proper work, and for me that is hard. And I grow lazier, mentally, by the hour." Thus, at UCLA only 7 percent of professors were female and at Stanford only 5, and at Columbia while about 25 percent of doctorates were granted to women, they made up only 2 percent of tenured faculty. Harvard's faculty consisted of almost 600 male tenured full professors, and 3 women. Although women made up over 40 percent of students at the top 100 universities, they comprised only 10 percent of faculty. Female taxpayers partly funded the U.S. military academies, but no women were allowed to enroll. Discrimination even existed in the so-called traditional female occupations. Women made up about 80 percent of teachers, yet only about 10 percent of school principals and 3 percent of superintendents. Female airline flight attendants were fired when they married or reached age 32, but not male attendants, prompting Congresswoman Martha Griffiths to write the personnel director of United Air Lines, "You are asking . . . that a stewardess be young, attractive and single. What are you running, an airline or a whorehouse?"[30]

Many women felt that their work was little more than prostitution when it came time for payday. A survey found that only half of men favored equal pay for equal work. White men with an eighth-grade education in 1965 made almost $4000 annually, while white women with a high school degree made $2400, and a survey three years later demonstrated wage discrimination within occupations. Male professionals earned about $10,200 and women $6700, and for clerical workers the difference was $7300 versus $4800; in sales the discrepancy was very high, $8500 versus $3500.

All the while legal discrimination continued in the land where "All men are created equal." Eighteen states exempted only women from serving on juries, increasing the probability that a female suspect would face an all-male jury. Factory health and safety "protective laws" in some states applied only to women, rewarding businessmen who avoided such regulations and hired only men. In 17 states women could not work in mines, in 10 they could not tend bar, while other states "protected ladies" from lifting more than 15 pounds (the weight of a one-year-old child) and from working nights, except if they were nurses or telephone operators. In half a dozen states women were considered incapable of handling their finances. Without a male co-signer they could not establish a business, buy stocks or bonds, or get a loan, meaning that it was difficult for a single female to purchase a car or home. In four other states a married couple's earnings were joint property, and all the earnings were controlled by him. In most states the double standard was legally institutionalized. Only a woman in Arizona using obscene language was committing a crime, and only a female juvenile in New York could be put in jail for promiscuous behavior. Schools expelled pregnant school girls, not their boyfriends, and rape laws usually stated that the woman must physically resist; if she was not a virgin, attorneys were allowed to present evidence of her previous sexual behavior to discredit her testimony. In state law it was inconceivable that a husband could rape his wife. In most cities, women prostitutes were entrapped and fined for participating in illegal behavior but not male prostitutes nor customers. In Kentucky, a husband could get a divorce after proving that his wife committed adultery, but not vice versa, and in Connecticut if a man killed his wife over an extra-marital affair he could plea "passion shooting," while a woman could only plea murder if she shot his mistress. In Rhode Island a husband could physically "chastise" his wife. Some states prohibited single women from obtaining contraception, and all forbade her from making the choice herself and then obtaining an abortion. The result, according to the President's Crime Commission Report in 1968, was that nationally there were one million illegal abortions a year, and at least 1000 women died annually from botched attempts.

By the end of the decade *Time* noted that the "status of American women is, in many ways, deteriorating." Female workers in the 1950s earned about 64 cents for every dollar earned by a male, and during the 1960s that figure *declined* to about 58 cents. Politically, women lost 50 seats in state legislatures and the number of congresswomen decreased from 17 to 10. In education, they held fewer faculty positions at the end of the decade, received a lower percentage of doctorates, and made up a smaller percentage of elementary school principals.

Conditions were worse for minority women. Elvira Saragoza declared that Chicanas were tired of being treated like "inferior beings," and Armando Rendon admitted that the "Chicano macho has to concede that he has usually relegated la mujer to the kitchen or to having kids and has never allowed her to express herself." As for black women, Pauli Murray declared that they were "doubly victimized by the twin immoralities of Jim Crow and Jane Crow." While most black females were concerned more about issues of race than gender, they became increasingly aware of the dual burdens of racism and sexism that had made them, according to Angela Davis, "the most oppressed sector of society." In fact, they were the least educated and the poorest in the nation. For every dollar earned by a white male a black female made about 45 cents. And like white activists, black males belittled females. Black Power was stated in male terms, tough and aggressive, and although women had been on picket lines for years, the men accepted stereotypes about the "weaker sex." When civil rights activist James Farmer ran for Congress in 1968 against Shirley Chisholm, his campaign literature stressed the need for a "strong male image" and a "man's voice" in Washington. Black females were stereotyped as "bossy" or "matriarchal," and told that they should help their man re-establish black manhood because he, supposedly, had suffered more during slavery. To that, Murray answered: "If black males suffered from real and psychological castration, black females bore the burden of real or psychological rape."[31]

"What is women's liberation?" Marilyn Salzman Webb declared to the movement: "It is simply organized rage against real oppression." Women began to realize, and then declare, that opportunities and thus destiny in America were shaped not only by race and class but also by gender. The publicized facts struck home: Awakening. A Gallup poll early in the 1960s revealed that less than a third of females felt discriminated against, but by 1970 that percentage was over half, and it climbed to two-thirds by the end of the second wave.

How to attack that oppression? Like the other movements of the decade, feminists divided; the schism had erupted in 1968 at a meeting of NOW. Moderates such as Betty Friedan advocated reforming the system, demanding rights, obtaining equal opportunity, and integrating women into the positions of power in the establishment. Radicals like Ti-Grace Atkinson responded that they should aim "to destroy the positions of power," and that women would not be liberated without a economic and social revolution. As Bonnie Kreps declared, "we must eradicate the sexual division on which our society is based." While moderates defined the problem as their exclusion from the boardroom, radicals defined it in terms of sexual politics and personal life in the bedroom. Even the very personal was political.

Other radical women spoke out. Ellen Willis, a founder of Redstockings, published an article which declared independence from the male radical movement and emphasized separatism: "We have come to see women's liberation as an independent revolutionary movement." A radical interpretation developed in which some felt that women were colonized people and thus part of the Third World Liberation Front. To them, liberation would come only through class struggle overthrowing capitalism. Other radicals disagreed. The economic system was not the real oppressor, men were, and some advocated separatism from men, even excluding sexual affairs. After all, Roxanne Dunbar proclaimed, "Sex is just a commodity." Robin Morgan began calling the male left "the boys' movement," with the "serious, ceaseless, degrading, and pervasive sexism. . . . We were used to such an approach from the Establishment, but here, too?"

No! they yelled, and they acted. Kathy Amatniek and a dozen compatriots disrupted a New York legislative committee abortion hearing by standing up, shouting down stunned elderly legislators, demanding immediate repeal of the state law, and asking, "Why are 14 men and only one woman on your list of speakers—and she's a nun?" Feminists at Grinnell College, Iowa, stripped naked in front of a representative of *Playboy*, held a nude-in, and demanded the end of commercializing the female body. Radicals invaded the offices of *Rat*, taking over the paper from males in January 1970 and establishing a women's collective. In their first issue, Morgan declared "Goodbye to All That." In an article reprinted in numerous undergrounds, she continued: "No more, brothers. No more well-meaning ignorance, no more co-optation, no more assuming that this thing we're all fighting for is the same; one revolution under *man*, with liberty and justice for all. No More. . . . goodbye to the dream that being in the leadership collective will get you anything but gonorrhea."

Women radicals, therefore, turned the tables on radical men: They acted like the men, confronting the culture, shocking the movement, shouting out for liberation, calling for separatism, and along the way they became radical women.

Moderates acted in other ways. Friedan berated "female chauvinism," the "pseudoradical copout which talks about test-tube babies, eliminating men, and the one-sex society." Such appeals would force both sexes into adversarial positions and repel male opinion makers and the media. NOW resolved that "the movement is aimed at changing not only discriminatory laws, but the entire concept of man as the bread-winning, decision-making head of household and women as his subordinate helpmate. It envisions a society where men and women would share equal opportunities for supporting their families and taking care of their children." NOW, WEAL, and other moderates acted, organizing campus chapters, pushing for abortion rights in liberal states, attacking universities and corporations with lawsuits and demanding the end of discrimination in admission quotas, student aid, and practices of hiring, promotions, and salary.[32]

During spring 1970 the emerging women's movement took direct action as female employees began confronting their male employers. A hundred women working for *Ladies' Home Journal* conducted a sit-in at the office of editor John Mack Carter, demanding an end to "exploitative" advertisements in the magazine, a free day-care center, and a special feature section on women's liberation for a future issue. Carter agreed, while those working for *Time* and *Newsweek* rebelled, the latter filing a complaint with the EEOC charging that the magazine discriminated against them. Their attorney, Eleanor Holmes Norton, declared that the "statistics speak for themselves. There are more than 50 men writing at *Newsweek*, but only one woman." Bread and Roses feminists in Boston converged on radio station WBCN and demanded the end of an ad which announced, "If you're a chick, we need typists." *Liberation News Service* joined the cause, asking, "Could a radio station get away with an ad that ran, 'And if you're a black, we need janitors'?" The feminists presented the station manager with six live baby chicks, and the manager changed the ad. In March, *Newsweek* summarized the situation in the nation with a cover story: "Women in Revolt."

The revolt was significant: More than any other crusade of the sixties era, female activists were mixing the two themes of the second wave—liberation and empowerment. Women expanded the movement, and they were joined by others who became interested in issues such as community, consumerism, and conservation. During spring 1970 the sixties bloomed; the evening news became a pageant of demonstrators.

"You can't fight city hall," citizens said during cold war culture, but during the second wave activists throughout the nation were doing just that, fighting local government and businesses. That activism was as old as American democracy itself, of course, and during the 1960s the Kennedy and Johnson administrations had encouraged various community action programs which became part of the War on Poverty. Yet government agencies directed those programs, and then the Nixon administration abolished them or shifted funding to law enforcement. Local activists initiated a new "backyard or neighborhood revolution" with a new saying, "Think Global, Act Local."

Neighborhood activists realized that many issues they faced were not created in their own backyards but were determined outside by powerful economic forces; one such issue was highway construction. During the 1960s city planners were attempting to join growing suburbs with the downtown by building freeways. While white suburbanites applauded such plans and contractors and city hall calculated profits and jobs, ethnic workers and minorities en route grew alarmed as plans often slated demolishing their older neighborhoods. Two famous battles during the second half of the decade were waged in Baltimore and Philadelphia. In the former, the city council planned a six-lane highway through the southeast part of the city, which would force the relocation of some 100,000 residents whose families had lived in the area for generations. Activists formed SCAR, Southeast Council Against the Road, and they were able to stop construction by getting part of the neighborhood named to the national register of historic places. In Philadelphia, the chamber of commerce joined the city and state highway departments and proposed an eight-lane crosstown expressway that would have destroyed South Street and basically sequestered black residents from the newer downtown while uprooting 5000 from their older neighborhood. Black community organizer George Dukes dubbed the project Philly's "Mason-Dixon line," and he joined forces with Alice Lipscomb and Robert Sugarman. They established a citizens' coalition which mobilized support and blocked construction.

The backyard revolt expanded, and in spring 1970 activists were protesting many issues and marching on city halls across the nation, including Chicago. Like most cities then, Chicago had a pollution problem, mostly created by the soft coal–burning utility, Commonwealth Edison. Columnist Mike Royko asked the veteran activist Saul Alinsky to do something about mounting pollution, and Alinsky asked the journalist to write a column, which created a flood of letters. When Mayor Daley denied there was a problem, Alinsky shot back: "What in hell does he breathe with, his ears?" Alinsky held a meeting, and a diverse group appeared—scientists, hippies, workers, students, housewives. They decided to protest at the company's rate request hearing, and after guards refused to let most of them attend, they formed CAP, Citizens Action Program. The co-chairs, Paul Booth and Father Leonard Dubi, had been activists for years, the former a founder of SDS and the latter involved in civil rights, and both had read Alinsky's classic on organizing, *Rules for Radicals*. CAP demanded that the local government force the company to cut sulfur emissions and electricity rates, and that the city council pass a clean-air ordinance. During spring the activists began applying pressure. Fifty women appeared at the company's offices, delivered their demands to the president, and passed out flyers telling consumers to delay paying their electric bills. A thousand demonstrated at the mayor's office, and others applied "proxy power," an idea devised by Alinsky that meant buying stock in the corporation so they could be allowed into the annual meeting of the board of directors. At that gathering Father Dubi led a band of senior citizens up the center aisle, some singing "The Star Spangled Banner." An older woman did a tambourine dance, and writer Studs

The massive 1969 Moratorium; this march is in San Francisco. AP/Wide World.

Black power spreads to campuses: Cornell University, spring 1969.
Division of Rare and Manuscript Collections, Cornell University Library.

Native Americans make demands at Alcatraz Island, spring 1970. AP/Wide World.

Women Strike for Equality in Washington, D.C., August 1970. UPI/Bettmann.

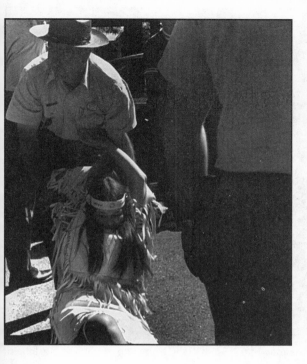

Passamaquoddy Indians protest: blocking traffic through their reservation in Maine. UPI/Bettmann.

Black Panther headquarters in Chicago after police raid. UPI/Bettmann.

The counterculture expands. Brotherhood of the Spirit hippies canning produce in Northfield, Massachusetts. AP/Wide World.

Kent State, May 4, 1970. Kent State University.

John Sinclair of the White Panthers. One of many during the second wave who merged political activism with counter-culture values.
Courtesy of John and Leni Sinclair Collection, Bentley Library.

Antiwar feelings dominate American campuses. Graduation at the University of Massachusetts, May 1970. UPI/Bettmann.

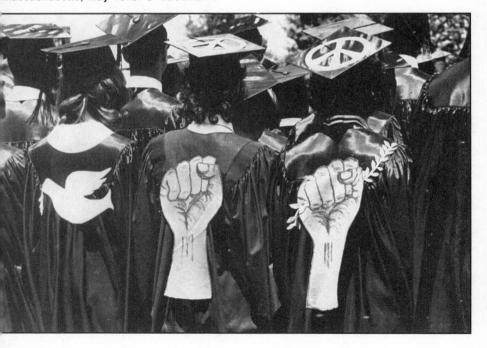

Women liberationists take over a building at Harvard, spring 1971. AP/Wide World.

Senator George McGovern captured movement support by demanding immediate U.S. withdrawal from Vietnam, and then was crushed in the 1972 election. UPI/Bettmann.

Dewey Canyon III: Vietnam veterans throw their medals at the Capitol, spring 1971. AP/Wide World.

Wounded Knee, spring 1973. UPI/Bettmann.

One of the last causes: a few anti-Nixon protesters in Boston, autumn 1973. AP/Wide World.

Political activism declined, but many continued their new cultural values: communards near Takima, Oregon, in the mid-1970s. Courtesy Jim Shames.

Terkel led 800 others in a chant, "Let Us Breathe!" The *Sun-Times* reported, "The young people had made it seem like a civil rights or anti-war rally; the middle aged like a union meeting, and the old people like a Golden Agers outing. Nobody . . . made it seem like an annual meeting of a big corporation."[33]

By summer, CAP had won all demands, and other activists were becoming more involved in this form of empowerment—community organizing—which was destined to become one of the most important aspects of the expanding movement during the early 1970s. The movement was becoming more concerned with consumer and environmental issues, and CAP's next target was the pollution emitted and taxes paid by the local U.S. Steel plant. Activists began putting pressure on businesses to reconsider the old idea of "social responsibility." How powerful should business be? What is more important, personal and community or private and corporate rights? What is legitimate corporate behavior? Ultimately, activists challenged the business establishment by asking: Who should have the power?

Father Dubi felt there should be more "people power," an idea that had been promoted for years by Ralph Nader. A young graduate of Harvard Law School, Nader had moved to Washington, D.C., in the early 1960s to become the self-appointed guardian of the American consumer. He attacked General Motors in his book on the Corvair, *Unsafe at Any Speed*, prompting a debate about automobile safety features and resulting in numerous automobile regulations and seat belts. Nader enlisted student interns, "raiders," who conducted investigations and pressured politicians, and Congress again responded by passing the Truth in Lending and Fair Packaging and Labeling acts, signed by President Johnson. That was the beginning. "My job is to bring issues out in the open where they cannot be ignored," declared Nader in 1969. "There is a revolt against the aristocratic uses of technology and a demand for democratic uses." *Time* labeled him "The U.S.'s Toughest Customer" who had fostered a movement that "goes by the awkward name of 'consumerism,'" and when he called for more student participation the response was overwhelming. From Texas law schools alone he received 700 applicants to be a raider for summer 1970, a position that lasted ten weeks and paid between $500 and $1000.

Fight the System, said consumer activists, and they fought in many ways. Activists employed economic pressure such as sit-ins, picketing, and boycotts against numerous companies that they felt paid low wages, practiced discrimination, or ripped off the consumer—Gallo Wine, Polaroid, Levis, Farah, AT&T, Coors, Coca-Cola, and Philip Morris. Locally, they often used direct action. In Minneapolis, for example, students and community leaders protested a fast-food hamburger franchise, Red Barn.

The company purchased a building in Dinkytown, an area of older brick structures, demolished it, and began erecting one of their drive-ins, which resembled a large red plastic barn. After a turbulent spring 1970, in which activists occupied the site and proclaimed a "people's park," Red Barn abandoned its plans, and the nearby McDonald's franchise eventually began remodeling its original yellow plastic exterior to brown brick.

The consumer movement blended many aspects of the broad movement—minority and women's rights, the war, and concern about the environment. Activists united behind consumerism because they perceived job discrimination, war production, and pollution as symptoms of a sick business establishment. Business was greedy and kept wages and opportunities low for women and minorities while profiting from making bombs; it was irresponsible and poured refuse into streams. *Liberated News Service* condemned defense contractor General Motors as the company that "put more smog, dirt, and poison into the air than any other industry or corporation in the country." Another Mother for Peace charged that Standard Oil supported the war so it could obtain oil leases in Southeast Asia, and *The Common Woman* claimed that the corporation was pumping out "smog at a killing level in California," spilling petroleum in the Pacific, and thus was guilty of "slick imperialism." All the while journalists were reporting that the army was using a chemical spray, Agent Orange, that declared war on foliage in Vietnam.

The movement continued expanding as baby boomers graduated from college and law schools. "Rebels in Grey Flannel Suits" *Forbes* labeled the 1970 graduates being hired by businesses—a new breed of trainees interested not only in profits but also in corporate social responsibility and the "quality of life." While young attorneys organized groups such as the Center for Constitutional Rights, Ralph Nader formed Public Interest Research Groups on campuses, and hundreds of law students went to court filing suits, usually in cooperation with new organizations such as Common Cause, Environmental Action, and Friends of the Earth. Activists demanded that corporations profiting from the youth market speak out against the war, and flyers advised readers to take the war to financial institutions by withdrawing their funds from corporations such as the Bank of America. They formed corporate responsibility action groups and watchdog organizations such as Businessmen for the Public Interest, Council on Economic Priorities, and Project on Corporate Responsibility. Demonstrators appeared at corporate headquarters and handed out flyers mocking company slogans—"At GE, Profits Is Their most Important Product"—or they picketed local stores that sold plastic guns—"War Toys for Christmas?"

Activists were making so many demands on business that spring that *Forbes* editorialized that future profits will be linked to listening to ecologists and young consumers, and *Business Week* proclaimed, "No longer can a company officer live a cloistered life behind the walls of private enterprise, concerning himself solely with turning out a product and a profit. These days, tenacious demonstrators and persistent consumers are insisting that he do something about the worldly issues of minority rights and the environment." [34]

To be sure, the environment had been a popular issue throughout the decade, since radioactive fallout and since Rachael Carson published *Silent Spring* in 1962. While the Surgeon General linked cigarette smoking and lung cancer, smog alerts in Los Angeles kept environmental problems in the news. President Johnson and the Democratic Congress responded by passing an impressive number of air and water quality acts as well as the Wilderness Act.

Nixon had a different agenda, of course, but environmental problems continued generating interest on campuses and in communes. In 1969, an oil-rig line ruptured off of Santa Barbara, California. Petroleum gushed into the ocean for two weeks, creating an enormous slick that eventually fouled 200 miles of valuable coastline. Activists formed GOO, Get Oil Out, and 100,000 citizens signed a petition to end drilling off Santa Barbara. Next year, Chevron oil wells off Louisiana caught fire, burning out of control and creating the largest spill yet in American history. As the secretary of the interior charged the company with 347 drilling violations, a tanker off Florida punctured and an oil slick spread across Tampa Bay. Meanwhile, Cleveland authorities declared that there was so much oil and chemical pollution on the Cuyahoga River that it was a "fire hazard," and Ohio officials proclaimed that Lake Erie was "almost dead," a result of companies and municipalities dumping 11 million pounds of chlorides and sulfates each day. "If you fall in," locals joked, "you won't drown, you'll decay." In January 1970 *Newsweek* publicized the cause with a long cover story—"The Ravaged Environment"—that proclaimed the "Dawn for the Age of Ecology."

The rise of Green Power. "We haven't forgotten Vietnam or the problems of the blacks," stated Berkeley student Ruthann Corwin. "Vietnam is a big environmental problem in itself. We're concerned with better living for all people. What we're talking about is total survival." Berkeley students formed Ecology Action and membership soared on campuses nationwide. Youth began damning the "throw-away culture" of America with its creed of growth and consumption. "Growth is God," declared a student, and another added, "I'm tired of scientists talking to scientists seeking a solution. It's political and we'll take to the streets." They did. Northwestern students staged an environmental teach-out that attracted 10,000, and those at MIT, Harvard, and Brandeis demanded stricter water controls and marched on the statehouse. Berkeley and Stanford students ignited the "Save the Bay" campaign, and those at Texas filed almost 60 complaints against their university for polluting a creek. "The impending 'eco-catastrophe' is now the focus of student protest," reported *Business Week* in spring 1970, "nowhere is the quality-of-life issue more alive than on the U.S. campus."[35]

During the spring polls showed that Americans were more concerned about the environment than any other domestic issue, and that became apparent as they participated in the largest demonstration of the sixties era—Earth Day. Senator Gaylord Nelson of Wisconsin and Representative Pete McCloskey of California had proposed that citizens conduct a moratorium to discuss the environment, and Denis Allen Hayes became the national coordinator, a young man who earlier had hitchhiked around the world. Thousands of students heeded the call, working on their campuses to devise programs aimed at ecological awareness. On April 22, students and hippies, workers and professionals, urbanites and surburbanites, mingled at hundreds of parks, 2000 colleges, and 10,000 high schools. At Indiana University coeds handed out birth control pills while Louisville high school students crowded into a hall to illustrate overpopulation, a topic popularized by Paul Ehrlich's best-selling book *The Population Bomb*. Crafts, music, and spirituality was the theme at U.C. Davis while Cal Tech held an Ecological Fair and Minnesota had a Festival of Life Week. Nursing students at Connecticut cleaned a pond adjacent to their school, while Girl Scouts in canoes dredged up garbage from the Potomac River. At Tulsa University they conducted a walking tour of a "pollution trail" while at Michigan a few protested auto emissions by smashing a Ford. In Madison, students handed out flyers advocating recycling and the use of returnable bottles and biodegradable detergent. Thousands picked up trash along the roads in Vermont for Green Up Day, while "survival walkers" in California marched from Sacramento to Los Angeles. Blacks in St. Louis conducted guerrilla theater, dramatizing problems created by poor garbage collection and poisonous lead paint, and hundreds of New Yorkers took brooms and dust pans to clean Central Park. In the Bay Area citizens participated in the Berkeley Environmental Teach-in or planted trees in the Earth Rebirth Celebration. The media published articles, from the underground *Survival*'s suggestions on how to "re-order *your own* priorities" to *Mademoiselle*'s "40 Ways You Can Depollute the Earth" to the University of Texas's mock article dated 1990 with the headline, "Noxious Smog Hits Houston: 6,000 Dead."

"It was Earth Day," reported the *New York Times*, "and like Mother's Day, no man in public office could be against it." Indeed, during the months before and after Earth Day, Congress passed more clean air and water acts and mandated environmental impact statements. States followed, as many governors signed legislation creating state environmental protection agencies. Companies pledged buying pollution control equipment for plants and establishing environmental departments, and Henry Ford II called for a "virtually emission-free car." At the Washington Monument on April 22, 5000 sang along with Pete Seeger and Phil Ochs and about half marched on the Interior Department chanting "Off Oil" or singing, "All we are saying is give earth a chance." Many activists wore a new button: a green peace symbol.

By the end of the week about 20 million had participated, and it appeared that this celebration might indicate the blooming of the Woodstock Nation. E-Day created a mellow, gentle glow, rekindled hope for the second wave. "Should the campaign to clean up our air, water, and soil fizzle—for whatever reason—and destroy the faith or idealism of the young people again," said newsman Murray Fromson, "I would not like to imagine the scope of disenchantment and cynicism that will emerge on our campuses."

A week later President Nixon suddenly extinguished the glow of E-Day with his D-Day. On April 30 he announced that ARVN and U.S. troops were crossing the border into Cambodia. Since the Geneva Agreement, Nixon declared, American policy "has been to scrupulously respect the neutrality of the Cambodian people." The North Vietnamese had not, for they had set up headquarters and supply bases. "This is not an invasion of Cambodia," declared Nixon, claiming the action did not expand the war. Rather, he continued, the attack was necessary to destroy the enemy's bases and supplies, and thus speed the pace of American withdrawal and Vietnamization. Nixon proclaimed that he would rather be a one-term president than see "America become a second-rate power" and have the "nation accept the first defeat in its proud 190-year history." America must have the will, the character to stay the course. "If, when the chips are down, the world's most powerful nation, the United States of America, acts like a pitiful, helpless giant, the forces of totalitarianism and anarchy will threaten free nations and free institutions throughout the world."

Nixon's invasion reignited an antiwar movement that had been smoldering that spring. After all, Congress had passed the lottery for military service, meaning that all men age 19 stood for the draft without discrimination. The president was cutting draft calls and had announced the withdrawal of another 150,000 troops while continuing negotiations with the North Vietnamese. And after five years of war many activists were tired of marching, turning toward other causes or dropping into the counterculture. But the invasion of Cambodia, more than any other event of the era, provoked the sixties generation out of their dorms and into the street. Most felt betrayed. Nixon had promised students that he would not enlarge the war by invading neighbors of South Vietnam, claimed that he was winding down the war, but then he expanded it into Cambodia. "That's the same anti-communist bullshit they taught us in elementary school," declared the underground *Plain Dealer*. "We're not buying it any more."

Minutes after the president's address activists took to the streets in Philadelphia and New York, and the next day students began demonstrations on campuses from Maryland to UCLA. After the president referred to demonstrators as "bums blowing up the campuses," more students participated, some calling for a national strike and others advocating a massive demonstration in Washington. Many congressmen were outraged and some began talking about an "impending constitutional crisis." The invasion also alienated many in the Establishment; over 200 State Department officers and workers resigned in protest while several hundred federal employees marched with a banner, "Federal Bums Against the War." Strikes spread to 60 colleges across the nation—and then into the cities. Activists rallied at federal buildings in Nashville and Chicago, and 1000 students blocked traffic in downtown Cincinnati. Most rallies were peaceful, but violence erupted at the University of Maryland, Ohio State, and Stanford.

Then, Kent State. On May 4, Ohio national guardsmen fired over 60 times into a crowd of about 200 students, wounding nine and killing four.

"My God, they're killing us!" cried one coed, as blood ran from the wounded. May turned red. The nation erupted into the most revolutionary mood since 1776. In "ten terrifying seconds," *Time* reported, the usually placid campus was converted "into a bloodstained symbol of the rising student rebellion against the Nixon Administration and the war in Southeast Asia."

Us against Them. Students, and a surprising number of their administrators, were enraged. Some 35 university presidents called for withdrawal from Cambodia, and 225 student body presidents called for the impeachment of President Nixon. In the week after Kent State, students at 350 universities went on strike, and protests resulted in closing about 500 campuses, 50 for the remainder of the semester. Protests were so common that wire services began reporting campuses that did not have demonstrations.

Frustration became rage, and it erupted into violence. Students and police clashed at two dozen institutions, even at tranquil campuses such as Alabama, Eastern Michigan, New Mexico, and South Carolina. Students attacked and damaged ROTC buildings at over 30 universities, including Berkeley, Nebraska, Virginia, Case Western Reserve, Central Michigan, even DePauw and St. Norbert. Authorities reported almost 200 possible bombings or arsons, half that number on campuses, and another three dozen aimed at corporations or government buildings. At Temple University, students smashed the windows of military trucks. In Buffalo, 2000 blocked traffic and smashed windows of local banks while activists in Madison and Iowa City shattered storefront windows. The Bank of America eventually reported two dozen fires or bombings of their branches in California. The governors of Ohio, Michigan, Kentucky, and South Carolina declared their universities in a state of emergency, and governors of 16 states activated the national guard to curb rioting at 20 universities. In other words—the government was forced to employ its military to occupy the nation's campuses to quell the insurrection of its own youth.

Then, Jackson State. Just as the fires in the streets began to smolder, white state troopers in Mississippi opened fire on black students, shooting 300 bullets into a dormitory, wounding 12 and killing two coeds who were watching events from their window. Amid cries of racism students again rebelled, demonstrating at 50 campuses.

Tired, exhausted, students limped home, only to find most citizens staunchly opposed—not to the killings, but to them, those who demonstrated against America's foreign policy. Numerous moderate and conservative students were enraged that they had not been able to attend classes, and most parents agreed. Opinion polls showed that a majority supported the invasion of Cambodia and now felt that campus demonstrations were the nation's primary domestic problem. Three-fourths opposed protests against the government and even would support restricting basic freedoms guaranteed by the Bill of Rights. The mother of one Kent State student declared, "It would have been a good thing if all those students had been shot." Alarmed, her son responded, "Hey Mom! That's me you're talking about," and she replied, "It would have been better for the country if you had all been mowed down."

The tragic events of May 1970 ended another chapter in the movement and the sixties.

The Cambodian invasion resolved little in Vietnam. From spies in the Saigon government, the enemy knew about the attack weeks in advance and they had fled. U.S. troops captured supplies, withdrew, and months later the enemy again controlled the area: another Hamburger Hill.

The invasion had more impact at home. Few could be neutral any longer. Conservatives lined up behind their president and his calls for law and order. Construction workers in New York City attacked antiwar students, injuring 70, prompting an observer to note: "They went through those demonstrators like Sherman went through Atlanta." Students at Brigham Young held a prowar rally, as did 20,000 citizens in St. Louis, and staunch Republicans proclaimed the "raw personal courage" of the commander-in-chief. At Kent State, a grand jury indicted not the national guard troops who fired into an unarmed crowd, but two dozen faculty and students, claiming that the soldiers fired in self-defense. The Nixon administration supported a bill that would make it illegal to "utter loud, threatening or abusive language" near the president. More important, the administration also expanded its covert activities against the movement, directing not only agents of the FBI and CIA but also the U.S. Armed Forces, National Security Agency, and Internal Revenue Service to conduct additional wiretappings, surveillance, disinformation, even "surreptitious entry," a euphemism for burglary. By 1970, the Nixon administration was walking down the long path that would lead to Watergate.

Left or Right. "The crisis has roots in division of American society as deep as any since the Civil War," reported the presidential commission investigating the upheaval. "If this trend continues, if this crisis of understanding endures, the very survival of the nation will be threatened. A nation driven to use the weapons of war upon its youth is a nation on the edge of chaos."

The liberal establishment condemned the events, from politicians to ministers to university presidents. "This is madness," declared Senator Edward Kennedy, and while the Young Democrats declared the "Nixon-Agnew Dictatorship," the Senate overwhelmingly repealed the Gulf of Tonkin Resolution. The office of the president of the University of Wisconsin proclaimed, "We clearly oppose the U.S. involvement in southeast Asia and the murder of over 500,000 Asian civilians. We also oppose the increasing repression of legitimate dissent ending in events like persecution of the Black Panther Party and left leaders and the Kent State massacre."

Most college students were appalled. Harris campus surveys found a major shift in opinion after Cambodia. The percentage of students calling themselves conservatives halved to 15 while liberals doubled to over 40 and radicals reached the highest percentage of the era at 11. Some 80 percent of students felt that new laws were needed to restrict the president's power to make war and 60 felt that the nation had become a "highly repressive society, intolerant of dissent."

The invasion and subsequent tragedies were the last straw, removing any lingering doubts in the movement about the president—Nixon was the enemy. The administration was Orwellian, wrote the *Minnesota Daily*, "more war is less war, less peace is more peace, escalation is peace initiative . . . freedom is repression, criticism is praise, dissent is agreement." *Rat* called him "Super Pig," while other undergrounds replaced the x in his name with a swastika. To activists, "Tricky Dick" would use any means necessary to crush dissidents and the youth culture. "And America convulsed, killing its children, who had lost all respect," wrote Michael Rossman, "trying to tighten the old lines of control; trying to pretend that the 1950s were back again, stable and familiar, with everyone in his or her place."[36]

Alienation soared, and hatred for authorities seethed out of tight smiles—families and friendships dissolved. Aware that they could not influence the Nixon administration, activists faced three options: go underground and fight the establishment by any means necessary, drop out and do their own thing, or turn their energies toward other causes. A tiny fraction did the first, a suicidal option. Many more did the second, for it eased the pain and could result in personal liberation. The vast majority adopted the third, empowerment, or they mixed the personal and the political.

Thus, the movement spread into new currents. The second wave surged forward, churning the waters, cresting on the themes of empowerment and liberation—which in the early 1970s were changing the white male face of America.

The Movement Toward a New America

The Sixties have seen the dawn of a new culture. The Seventies will see its flowering.
The Second Coming, 1970

The new American revolution has begun.
Saturday Review, 1971

During the month of the Kent State tragedy, activist Mitchell Goodman and his friends published a massive collage of documents from hundreds of underground papers. These members of the Great Conspiracy commune entitled their book *The Movement Toward a New America: The Beginnings of a Long Revolution.*

This movement, of course, had been under way since Greensboro. The first wave crested in 1968 when Paul Booth wrote, "We are the young people of the new American left, educated in the social movements of the sixties, now attempting to define a politics appropriate to our ambition of building a new America." That ambition appeared to be on the verge of becoming reality in the two years after Kent State, for during the early 1970s the second wave crested, broke, and splashed against the bedrock of the American establishment, creating a cultural and political whirlpool that had not been seen since the progressive era of the early twentieth century.

Most citizens realized during those years that "something is happening," as Goodman wrote. "It goes deep, deeper than we know. Some call it revolution. Too easily, at times. . . . Yet it persists." Underground journalists employed various terms for this phenomenon—Woodstock Nation, Aquarian Age, Alternative Society, New Awareness, New Consciousness, the New Nation—and many readers hoped for a New America. "The Sixties have seen the dawn of a new culture," wrote activists in *The Second Coming*. "The Seventies will see its flowering." Establishment commentators also felt the winds of change. "There is a revolution coming," declared professor Charles Reich, one which he labeled *The Greening of America*. Students bought the book as the president of Columbia University estimated that half of all collegians belonged to "an alienated culture . . . which is growing at a very rapid pace." Commentator Gresham Sykes declared that "the seventies may well make the sixties look like a picnic" and Emmet John Hughes wrote that the politics of the sixties had gone "from the New Frontier to the New Revolution." *Time* labeled it a youthquake that would continue even if the war ended immediately, and discussing the movement's assault on the establishment, *Saturday Review* concluded, "The new American revolution has begun."[1]

The movement toward a New America was exemplified by a *kaleidoscope of activism* during the early 1970s. The themes were political empowerment and personal liberation—but beyond that there was little that focused the movement. The second wave witnessed a series of demonstrations and protests, but with the exception of a few remaining national marches for women's liberation or against the war, most of these actions were unrelated to each other, often addressing local concerns. The movement fractured, making social activism more difficult to describe, but it also spread as participants turned toward other concerns and confronted the establishment on almost every level and at almost every institution: the university and even high schools, the church, business, military, and all forms of government, from city hall to the White House.

At the same time, the sixties generation continued developing their counterculture, which set the *ambience* for the New America. The cultural revolution flourished after Kent State, for that episode again reminded youth that the mainstream was corrupt and that they should drop into the counterculture. The government reported in 1970 that border agents were seizing massive quantities of marijuana and hashish, that 120,000 had been arrested for possession and sale of those substances, and they estimated between eight and twelve million drug users—all setting records. During the next two years thousands of young professionals established "counter-institutions" such as law collectives, day-care cooperatives, or free schools. Medical professionals volunteered at almost 350 free health clinics nationwide while activists developed alternative food stores near most universities, from the New Haven Food Co-op to St. Paul's Green Grass Grocery, from Denver's Common Market to Fresno's Our Store. Some 50,000 people took classes at free universities annually, while daily a larger number of young Bostonians read the *Real Paper* or listened to the underground message on WBCN. Many others headed for conferences aimed at creating the New America. "We spent five days attending workshops and getting down with the people," wrote Don Peyote about the New Nation Convention held in Madison in 1971. Some 800 learned about self-defense, oppressive sex roles, and pollution in America and Agent Orange in Vietnam.

Thousands more flocked to communes. *Time* estimated 2000 communes nationwide in 1970, and the Associated Press declared that the "movement reached massive proportions in 1971," with 3000 communes and perhaps 3 million communards. "We are trying to create a whole new culture," said a freak in New Haven, "with its own economics and values."[2]

The New America expanded, as its youthful inhabitants frolicked from the Atlantic to the Adriatic. During summers, promoters held rock festivals from Atlanta to Portland and at many areas in between: Carbondale, Illinois; Love Valley, North Carolina; Goose Lake, Michigan. Some 600,000 attended the largest festival in history, at Watkins Glen, New York, in July 1973 to listen to The Band, the Allman Brothers, and the Grateful Dead, a group that already had a massive following of DEAD-HEADS. "People can you feel it, love is everywhere," the Allman Brothers sang, as the Woodstock Nation spread to other countries, as hippies held festivals in Australia, Canada, England, France, Germany, Japan, Sweden, even in South Vietnam. When some American festivals became unruly, states and communities banned them, and so music freaks created a myriad of smaller events—blues, bluegrass, folk, jazz, and classical festivals—while others worked with city officials and institutionalized the music into affairs such as Summerfest in Milwaukee. All the while, 2 million youth hitchhiked, searching for America, while hundreds of thousands were on the beaches of Mikonos or thumbing from Istanbul to London, from Allahabad to Zagreb, riding their own Marrakech Express.

Liberal cities turned exotic as freaks and ethnics created a hip cultural renaissance. Street art flourished; color flooded the nation. Chicanos painted murals at high schools and "walls of fire" on buildings. Black men wore jumbo Afros and the women sported vivid African dress. Young men with shaved heads and robes beat tambourines and chanted on corners, "Krishna, Krishna, Hare Krishna." Hip capitalists invaded the streets, setting up shops: Artisans wearing bandanas and bellbottoms sold jewelry, bells, and leather, as sunlight streamed through cut glass. Communards in ragged bib overalls sold loaves of whole-wheat bread at co-ops and organically grown vegetables at farmers' markets. Freak flags flew, curling, waving across America. Carpenters wearing ponytails moved into decaying neighborhoods, paint and lumber in hand, and began urban homesteading. Longhairs blew bubbles or lofted frisbees in the park. Tribes of young men and women skinny-dipped at beaches and hippie hollows.

A New America, or *something new*, was emerging. "When my students talk about the Sixties," a professor stated a generation later, "they really mean the early 1970s," and that was the case. Pictures of youth in the mainstream press before the 1968 Chicago convention are radically different from those during the two years after Kent State—it was the second wave that looked and sounded so unusual as a massive number of baby boomers at least *appeared* so freaky, so different from their predecessors.

Counterculture beliefs and behavior were infiltrating mainstream society, diluting or polluting traditional American values. In 1971 the National Commission on Marijuana and Drug Abuse stunned the older generation and President Nixon, who appointed the committee, by their recommendation of ending prosecution for possession of marijuana for private use, which is what governments were doing in cities like Ann Arbor, Berkeley, and Madison. A surprising number of older citizens lost inhibitions, joined demonstrations, questioned their nation, and considered new values. The movie *Harold and Maude* stated the message, "You can do what you want." The film confirmed that "age" ceased to have much to do with date of birth. And many Americans abandoned standard dress. Plain, white T-shirts became passé, and almost everyone wore a button, from the peace symbol to the crucifix, or a proclamation on their chest, from "Mother Earth" to "Keep on Truckin" to "Swede Power." One observer noticed in 1972:

> All sorts of people suddenly appeared as other than they were: stockbrokers dressed as if for African safari; sociologists came as greasers, motorcycle drop-outs; English professors looked like stevedores; businessmen like circus trainers; accountants like Jesse James; grandmothers were in pants suits, young girls in granny dresses. Others came disguised as farmers, housepainters, telephone linesmen, American Indians, Gypsies, Pancho Villa gunmen, or people from old photographs. Who was giving the masquerade, where was the costume party?

The movement was throwing the party.[3] The expansion of the counterculture was a form of liberation—a colorful, free, New America, one that many women participated in by liberating themselves and by striking out for political empowerment. Feminists again merged the dual themes of the second wave, and the union appeared forcefully on August 26, 1970, at the Women's Strike for Equality.

NOW had declared a national women's mobilization to mark the fiftieth anniversary of the Nineteenth Amendment, and activists urged women throughout the nation to cover their typewriters, unplug switchboards, and put down mops until male bosses at their companies guaranteed that all jobs were open to female employees—with equal pay. Other aims included equal educational opportunities, child-care centers, and abortion on demand. NOW formed a massive coalition with all feminist organizations, from radical lesbians to moderate businesswomen, in an attempt to demonstrate "how powerful we are."

Woman power had arrived. With the slogan, "Don't Iron While the Strike Is Hot," thousands boycotted work, invaded offices, deposited children at husband's desks, and marched down main streets in the first major feminist demonstration in half a century. Some 5000 marched to Boston Commons, a few thousand to San Francisco's Union Square and the same number in Washington, D.C., where they demanded the passage of the Equal Rights Amendment. "We Shall Overcome," they sang in Los Angeles, and while hundreds more marched in Denver and Baltimore, others in Seattle held an open house in the mayor's office and in Miami staged a mock coffee cup–breaking garden party. At the Pentagon, secretaries filled a trash basket with bras, girdles, and pink panties to protest being treated like sex objects. In Chicago they held sit-ins at restaurants that barred them, and in Indianapolis they staged a street performance entitled "Male Ego." But the largest demonstration was in New York City. Thousands joined Betty Friedan, who marched down Fifth Avenue between a young radical in blue jeans and Dorothy Kenyon, age 82, who had demonstrated for her vote on the same route fifty years earlier. Grandmothers, mothers, and daughters held hands. Husbands carried kids on their shoulders. A group called Men for Women's Rights marched next to Older Women's Liberation and High School Women Unite! Some handed out flyers—"You and Your Marriage"—while others held banners: "Women Strike for Peace—and Equality." They defied police orders to remain on the sidewalk, overflowing into the avenue. Female employees waved from office windows, and activists yelled, "Come join us, Sisters!"

"It made all women feel beautiful," wrote a marcher. "It made me feel ten feet tall." The message was clear, as Kate Millett declared to a crowd of almost 40,000 in New York: "Today is the beginning of a new movement." It was, for generally speaking the strike was a resounding success. The *New York Times* declared that liberation was a "serious revolution," that the Equal Rights Amendment was an "idea whose time has come." The *Los Angeles Times* felt that equality was long overdue, and so did Congress. The House of Representatives, which had not held a hearing on the measure for twenty years, suddenly began debating the ERA. The strike cast NOW into the spotlight as the leading feminist organization, and three years later its membership had soared to 40,000 in 700 local community and campus groups.

There was a backlash, of course, especially from older and more conservative Americans. During the strike a few New York men jeered marchers as "bra-less traitors" and held a sign "Draft Women NOW." A Los Angeles male held a placard demanding "Repeal the 19th Amendment," and another shouted, "The man is the king of the house, and we want our wives to be queens, not partners." An elderly representative in the House attempted to block debate of the "blunderbuss amendment," and a West Virginia senator labeled strikers a "small band of bra-less bubbleheads." Many conservative females and housewives agreed. Mrs. Saul Schary of the National Council of Women contended that the feminists did not have a legitimate purpose because there was "no discrimination against women like they say there is. . . . And so many of them are just so unattractive. I wonder if they're completely well." Lucille Shriver of the National Federation of Business and Professional Women's Clubs refused to join the strike. "We're going to be dignified and ladylike," she said. "We're not exhibitionists, and we don't carry signs." The strike appalled other traditionalists. "I don't know what those women are thinking," declared real estate agent Posey Carpenter. "I love the idea of looking delectable and having men whistle at me." Author Helen Andelin publicized the "Celebration of Womanhood," urging females to commemorate their gender by wearing their most feminine dresses and serving their husbands breakfast in bed. Thousands of other conservatives joined HOW, Happiness of Womanhood, or FAF, Feminine Anti-Feminists, the latter informing members, "If your husband wants to go out . . . don't do the FAF work. You drop it and go out with your husband."[4] Phyllis Schlafly had a larger aim in mind, and organized Stop ERA.

The strike also provoked many male activists, as women's liberation was changing the movement, juggling traditional roles. "This is an uncomfortable period to live through," wrote Susi Kaplow, for many young feminists were angry at male activists—and also at the grocer who called them "honey" or the construction worker who whistled. Time to get assertive, Kaplow declared, tell them to "fuck off, or, if you're brave, a knee in the right place." Men recoiled from being called "sexists" or "chauvinist pigs," from feminist banners declaring, "Don't Cook Dinner Tonight—Starve a Rat Today." Raymond Mungo wrote that at one rally he "agreed with most of their arguments, but when the Liberated Women threw me out of the room, shouting 'Oppressor!' and stuff, I felt a lot like a white liberal getting unwelcomed at SNCC." Sex roles became ambiguous, uncertainty prevailed, as men began to wonder if they should open doors for their dates or if that was patronizing.

The early 1970s were an awkward time of adjustment, but many men got the point. Paul Potter noted that liberation confronted him and taught him "to be far more self-conscious of my own chauvinism." The mostly male editorial board at the University of Minnesota *Daily* noted that although feminism had "attracted its share of fanatics, kooks, and man haters, the goals beneath their rhetoric would benefit both men and women," and men at the Madison Defense League wrote that all relationships should be reevaluated in an attempt to build a "People's Liberation Movement."[5] The definition of liberation was being expanded, and soon it would include all aspects of self-fulfillment.

Meanwhile, no topic received as much national attention as women's liberation. The *Los Angeles Times*, for example, devoted 50 times more coverage to the topic in the year of the strike than the previous year. The media also stopped joking and seriously examined women's issues—abortion, discrimination, opportunity, sexism.

A growing number of feminists debated new topics such as bisexuality, lesbianism, pornography, rape, and women as colonized people. While they supported equality, students and radicals often demanded liberation, and older career females advocated rights. Strains naturally erupted, as groups developed that ranged from the Anarcho-Feminists to Older Women's Liberation to WASP, Women Armed for Self Defense. Rhetoric escalated. A "Women's Revolutionary Movement must . . . destroy all vestiges of the male-dominated power structure, including the State itself," declared one group, while some female Black Panthers demanded that abortion law repeal was a "genocidal policy aimed at Black People," and the lesbian commune Furies called for separatism from the straight society. Heated debates, in-fighting, and conference walkouts became so common that a New York feminist group circulated a flyer calling for the "end of male-like tactics" and a call to "cure our schism-syndrome." Feminists have written volumes about these conflicts. In the short run they hurt feelings and ended friendships, yet in the long run they had much less impact on the woman's movement, for while moderates and radicals sounded different, a historian concluded, "the overlap was *enormous*." That was because feminists could focus on a common target—discrimination.[6]

Activists confronted discrimination at American institutions with a torrent of lawsuits. "Newest Campus Crusade," reported *U.S. News* in 1971: "Equal Rights for Women." WEAL lawyers sued 350 universities for sex discrimination, including the entire state college systems of California, Florida, New Jersey, and New York—and all of the nation's medical and law schools. NOW filed a class-action suit against all public schools on the grounds that they discriminated in salaries, promotion, and maternity benefits. Feminists filed complaints against 1300 major corporations that received federal funds, demanding goals and timetables for equal employment, and they sued numerous companies—Southern Pacific, General Motors, Colgate-Palmolive, Martin-Marietta, Libby-Owens, American Airlines, and Northwest Airlines, as well as the Ceramic Workers union of the AFL-CIO.

Liberation expanded throughout the year, and new participants broadened the attack. Servicewomen formed support groups on bases and WACs Against the War, and nuns also organized, 2000 meeting in Cleveland. Sister Albertus Magnus McGrath declared: "Father says this is a clerical church. I say it's a male church. . . . Under canon law, women are not permitted to testify—nor are children or imbeciles." Baptist, Episcopalian, Jewish, Lutheran, and Presbyterian women began making demands, challenging the ideas of sin based on Eve, and addressing God as "Father." When priests said, "God bless you," feminists responded, "Thank you, She will." That July, half a million workers declared a strike against the largest employer of women in the nation, American Telegraph and Telephone. The strike reflected that the movement was sweeping into the rank and file. Over half of AT&T's Bell System employees were females, yet they were paid less than men for the same job and were excluded from management and craft jobs; 99.9 percent of operators were women. "Maybe it's about time for a little more women's lib" in the union, said one operator, and feminists in Madison printed flyers urging support, claiming that at Wisconsin Bell "women are relegated to the dullest jobs, paid sub-standard wages, and are treated like both small children and slaves. . . . Ma Bell Is a Cheap Mother!"

Other females challenged state laws. They formed NARAL, the National Abortion Rights Action League, and along with a new group, Zero Population Growth, they pressured legislatures to begin reviewing abortion laws. "When we talk about women's rights," declared an activist, "we can get all the rights in the world . . . and none of them means a doggone thing if we don't own the flesh we stand in, if we can't control what happens to us, if the whole course of our lives can be changed by somebody else that can get us pregnant by accident, or by deceit, or by force." After a series of rapes in Ann Arbor, activists formed the Women's Crisis Center and began advocating legal revision as part of its "war on rape." And while the few congresswomen introduced a record number of bills concerning women's issues in the House of Representatives, other feminists warned political leaders that their issues would be addressed in 1972. If not by the two traditional parties, then by the Feminist party and their "favorite daughter" for president, Congresswoman Shirley Chisholm.[7]

The Nixon administration resisted women's liberation, even appointing a housewife who never had held a professional position to the EEOC, but the feminist wave was too powerful—within a year after the strike, women activists could count a surprising number of victories. The administration began enforcing Title VII of the Civil Rights Act and holding up college grants and contracts while conducting investigations of 40 institutions, including Harvard, Chicago, Michigan, and Pennsylvania. The government discontinued advertising "male" or "female" positions, began hiring women to all careers, from park rangers to security guards. The Department of Health, Education and Welfare pledged to appoint more women to senior offices, and the Federal Communications Commission responded to discrimination charges in broadcasting, such as one leveled by Jean Hunter that the "last famous woman disc jockey was Tokyo Rose." FCC added women to its equal employment rule, opening new jobs in radio and television, while Madison Avenue executives began considering if their commercials were sexist. The Supreme Court ruled unanimously that "equal protection" guaranteed by the Fourteenth Amendment applied to female citizens. And while the U.S. Senate began debating the ERA, Congresswoman Martha Griffiths maneuvered it to a vote and the House passed it overwhelmingly, 354 to 23. State legislatures began discussing liberalization of their abortion laws, and by the end of 1970 abortion reform laws were passed in 17 states. Companies ranging from Newsweek to Colgate-Palmolive to NBC signed agreements promising equal opportunities, and the United Automobile Workers reversed policy and issued a strong endorsement of women's equality. Protestant churches discussed the role of women in their congregations, some liberalizing policies, and Sandra Eisenberg became the first female rabbinical student at the Hebrew Seminary in Philadelphia. Universities and professional schools nationwide re-evaluated their policies. The University of Wisconsin granted 600 female employees $500,000 to equalize salaries, while Maine, Oberlin, and others abrogated their nepotism rules to allow wives and husbands to work in the same department. San Diego State College set up the first women's studies program in 1970, and by the end of the decade such classes were being taught at 500 campuses. Universities changed health-center services to include gynecological examinations and contraception. Previously male colleges Dartmouth, Notre Dame, and Princeton began admitting women. So did Yale, and the university elected women to the board of trustees for the first time since its founding in 1701.

The early 1970s became a Feminist Renaissance. The first television sitcom that concerned a professional woman, "The Mary Tyler Moore Show," appeared in 1970 and within two years Moore was followed by other unique females, "Maude" and "Rhoda." The message also was on the airwaves. Helen Reddy's "I Am Woman" soared to the top of the charts, Carole King's *Tapestry* became the best-selling album of the decade, and Holly Near sang folk feminism while the Chicago Women's Liberation Rock Band turned up the volume with "agit-rock." Feminists published provocative best-sellers: Ingrid Bengis, *Combat in the Erogenous Zone*; Kate Millett, *Sexual Politics*; Shulamith Firestone, *The Dialectic of Sex*; Germaine Greer, *The Female Eunuch*; and popular novels such as Rita Mae Brown's *Rubyfruit Jungle*, Erica Jong's *Fear of Flying*, and Sylvia Plath's *The Bell Jar.* A new breed of female scholars produced exciting books ranging from *The Southern Lady: From Pedestal to Politics* to *The Rebirth of Feminism,* while others were printing hundreds of new publications, from *Women: A Journal of Liberation* to *Ms.,* a magazine "owned by and honest about women," which soon had a circulation of 200,000. The Boston Women's Health Book Collective challenged the male medical establishment by publishing *Our Bodies Ourselves,* which became a best-seller and was translated into eleven languages.

Clearly, during the early 1970s feminists shocked and challenged Male America. Throughout the history of the Republic, men had defined gender roles. Female activists now shouted, No more! "The whole *point* of the feminist movement," wrote Vivian Gornick, "is that each and every woman shall recognize that the burden and the glory of her feminism lie with defining herself honestly *in any terms she shall choose.*"[8]

The strike again provoked the nation to consider the status of American women, and three days later Chicanos in East Los Angeles aroused citizens to consider the plight of Mexican Americans.

The National Chicano Moratorium aimed to demonstrate that brown empowerment was merging with the antiwar movement by protesting the high proportion of Hispanics killed in Vietnam. Like blacks, Chicanos felt that the draft discriminated against them, or as former UCLA student body president and draft resister Rosalio Munoz declared, it "funneled" them to the war because they were poor and felt a special burden to prove their loyalty to America. Their casualties in Vietnam were 50 percent greater than the ratio of that minority group in the overall population. Munoz, Brown Beret David Sanchez, Corky Gonzales, and Cesar Chavez organized the march to end the war and to urge Chicanos to resist the draft and fight for social justice at home.

August 29 was a warm, sunny day. About 20,000 appeared for the demonstration, from grandparents to children, and they marched down Whittier Boulevard and headed to the speakers' platform at Laguna Park. As they filed into the park, an incident occurred at a liquor store where some thirsty demonstrators were either attempting to buy or steal soda and beer. Moratorium officials went to the scene to cool tempers, when about 50 police left their cars, pulled nightsticks, and marched toward the store and into the park. As people were listening to speakers, police apparently declared the entire assembly unlawful, ordered the park vacated, and began firing tear gas into the crowd: chaos ensued. Mothers picked up their children and ran. Fathers rushed to the scene of the fighting. Tempers boiled over. As officers chased marchers through the streets, demonstrators smashed storefront windows. Within two hours, buildings were aflame, dozens of fires burned out of control. Protesters, officers, and residents exchanged gunfire. Police arrested over 100 including 30 in a truck armed with rifles, and Gonzales, who was booked on suspicion of robbery. More significant, police had wounded over 70 Hispanics and killed two, including Ruben Salazar.

A popular columnist for the *Los Angeles Times* and spokesman for Mexican American rights, Salazar was having a beer in a tavern when an officer suspected foul play and fired a tear gas projectile into the establishment. The missile smashed the journalist's head. It was a tragic mistake, claimed the police, but many local residents declared that Salazar was murdered because he had been critical of police brutality. He quickly became a martyr, especially after the district attorney refused to indict the officer responsible for the death. That decision was condemned by the usually conservative *Times*, and the Mexican American community was enraged, claiming that the verdict "once again proves that the system of justice is perverted." Charles Chavez of LULAC continued that "law and order is not synonymous with justice but merely represents the violence required to uphold the interests of the establishment."

As usual, police behavior did not dampen the movement; it encouraged more Hispanics to become activists and challenge the Anglo establishment. "The Chicano lives in a totalitarian-like atmosphere" within the Los Angeles community, wrote Rosalio Munoz:

> Our behavior can only be seen as a normal response to an abnormal condition created by those in political power. The police brutality that occurs 10 to 20 times a month in East Los Angeles again communicates to us our worth to the broader society that does not seem to care. We desperately wish to be a part of this society but your powerful sentry repeatedly sends us away bleeding. We are now directly protesting against the sentry.

Chicanos continued demonstrating in East Los Angeles that autumn, resulting in more violence. In January 1971 police shot into an angry crowd, wounding 35 and killing one, setting off another round of marches. During that year, at least four marches turned into riots, and a group calling itself the Chicano Liberation Front took credit for a series of bombings. After months of conflict, many activists looked back with bitterness, claiming no substantial improvements in the barrio, while conservative Hispanics called demonstrators "a pack of raving radicals devoid of human feelings." Many other citizens agreed with Richard Martinez, who lamented, "I sometimes feel that out of the ashes just came more ashes."[9]

Perhaps, but also out of the fires in the streets came greater Chicano pride, solidarity, political consciousness, and eventually, empowerment. Shaken by the riots, artists Charlie Felix and Judy Baca organized local gang members into squads of designers and painters who soon were painting murals depicting Mexican and Aztec legends as street art became a craze in Los Angeles, quickly spreading to the Bay Area and throughout the nation. Chicanos in the Southwest challenged the political establishment and the party that they had supported for years, the Democrats. "We have been political whores," declared one, "Or, maybe, virgins! And what do we have to show for giving ourselves so freely? Nothing! So now we say no more." In Los Angeles, Hispanics organized and supported their own political activists for county positions, forming an alliance with blacks that would result in the election of a liberal black mayor, Tom Bradley. In Texas, Jose Angel Gutierrez organized La Raza Unida party, registered voters, and won control of the school board in Crystal City. He instituted a bilingual program, adopted culturally relevant textbooks, and hired more Hispanic teachers. The party also won city council seats and the mayoral race, and that encouraged Chicanos to become involved in the political process and nominate candidates in many counties in south Texas and also in Colorado and California. La Raza Unida began pulling votes from the Democrats, as Hispanics flexed their political muscles and changed the establishment. When a couple of hundred marched in Houston to demand paved streets, improved sewer facilities, and parks in their barrio, the new mayor, an Anglo who won the election with their support, declared that he considered such services "not demands but necessities that are long overdue."

"What is essential to recognize and understand," wrote Armando Rendon, "is that a revolution is now in progress in the Southwest. It has a Spanish accent." And it had many other accents, for the movement toward political empowerment was provoking a significant question for all minorities: Was progress measured by assimilation into, or separation from, the dominant white culture? Many ethnic groups debated the question during the second wave. "We have been trying to become American for too long," declared a Puerto Rican woman, "and we are forgetting our roots, culture and values." The debate had heavy overtones, confronting the establishment and raising the issue of cultural superiority. Professor Rafael Guzman argued for a new pluralism that meant "something other than forcing minorities into the established Anglo-Saxon mold; each group should be free to develop its own culture while contributing to the whole."[10] The movement was provoking new questions for the New America, ones that during the next generation would stir public debate over topics labeled cultural diversity and multiculturalism.

Confronting the white establishment often led to friction and violence, and that again was demonstrated in the months before the November 1970 elections. During the third quarter of the year officials announced over 500 attacks on authorities, allegedly by Chicanos and black militants, resulting in the deaths of over 20 policemen. In Detroit, 100 cops battled

15 blacks for nine hours, resulting in two police deaths, and in Cairo, Illinois, militants attacked the police station three times in one night. "What we have had tonight in Cairo," stated the mayor, "is open, armed insurrection." In California, armed blacks stormed the San Rafael courthouse and jail in an attempt to free inmates. They took hostages and a gun battle erupted, resulting in the deaths of two convicts, their accomplice, and a superior court judge. The federal government issued a warrant for Angela Davis, a popular black Communist activist and feminist who was not on the scene. Officials charged that she had bought shotguns used in the escape attempt. Under California law, an accomplice who supplied weapons used in a homicide could be charged as those who fired the shots. Across the nation an FBI poster showed mug shots of Davis. The charge: murder. After a month, authorities captured her in New York.

"Free Angela!" activists shouted, while a few white militants conducted a campaign of bomb threats. Officials announced thousands of threats and over 140 bombings. During autumn semester Boston University had to vacate classrooms and dormitories 80 times, and radicals made over 175 threats at Rutgers, disrupting operations on almost a daily basis. Explosions were rare on campuses, but just one could have a lasting impact, and that was the case at the University of Wisconsin. During the early morning of August 24, four militants led by Dwight and Karl Armstrong bombed the Army Mathematics Research Center. Karl had been radicalized as a McCarthy supporter during the Chicago Democratic convention. Earlier at Wisconsin, activists contended that researchers at the center were conducting secret military projects which allegedly helped the U.S. Armed Forces in Vietnam, making the facility a target. "To bring the war home," recalled Karl, "we had to make a dent in the war machine." They did, loading a stolen van with almost a ton of explosives, parking it alongside the building that housed the center, and before 4 a.m. lighting a seven-minute fuse.

The blast could be heard for 30 miles. Windows shattered for blocks. The six-story building was gutted, one side demolished and walls collapsed, resulting in the single most destructive act of sabotage in U.S. history. The van was blown to bits, and parts of it were found on top of an eight-story building three blocks away. The human toll was more tragic: three injured and one killed, a post-doctoral researcher with a wife and three children.

The bombing shook Madison, and also the nation. The death forced people to contemplate the consequences of militant rhetoric. A few radicals might consider it heroic to bring the war home by destroying military property, or disrupting business by smashing storefront windows, but what about the injury and death of innocents? Or what about a few militants disrupting discussions, lectures, and activities of thousands of students on campus? Moderates were raising those issues, and rising discontent with radicals was obvious in electoral victories that year of groups such as the Student Committee for a Responsible University at Penn State, the Non-violent Action Party at Berkeley, Students for Columbia University, or the Thomas Jefferson Club at UCLA, who boosted the slogan "Dialogues Not Diatribes."

A team of correspondents visited numerous colleges during the autumn semester to assess student opinion. They discovered that the Cambodia invasion had renewed interest in working for liberal candidates, and that most students agreed that institutions were repressive. Moreover, collegiates felt activists turned fugitives such as Angela Davis were victims of oppression and should be supported, even helped. But the journalists also found that bombings were "alienating large numbers of radicals and many college youths . . . and are hurting the chance for any meaningful political change." As Detroit radical Harvey Ovshinsky stated, "Blowing up the CIA building will not bring home the troops. . . . Bombings are suicidal and are not bringing any change except more repression."[11]

That was the case. Although the Campus Commission on Student Unrest, led by Republican William Scranton, reported that the main reason for student demonstrations was the president's policies in Vietnam, the administration quickly rebuffed the report and went on the attack. The president reversed his position after the Wisconsin bombing and called for federal intervention at universities, and for a thousand new FBI agents to investigate campus disorder. In an attempt to boost Republican support for the November elections, Nixon traveled to Kansas State University. He asked the generally conservative students there to help him win a just peace and so "avoid an American defeat which would bring on another war." He called for the end of terrorism, blaming the "violent and radical few, the rock throwers and the obscenity shouters" who were not for lasting peace, but wanted to "tear America down." As the audience applauded, he chided weak college administrators for not standing up to students. Later, Attorney General Mitchell joined the chorus, stating that students and "these stupid bastards who are running our educational institutions" are uninformed about the nation's problems and about Vietnam, and his wife added that liberal educators were "responsible for all our troubles" and "destroying our country."

The autumn political campaign degenerated into an ugly slugfest. Activists met Nixon and Agnew at every stop, taunting and heckling, shouting obscenities. In Burlington, Vermont, demonstrators threw trash at the vice president, and in San Jose, California, a thousand chanting youths tossed stones, bottles, and eggs at the president's limousine, almost hitting him with a rock. Such behavior played into the administration's plans as spokesmen deflected criticism away from their policies and toward college students and administrators. The president called the San Jose incident "the action of an unruly mob that represents the worst in America." Agnew blamed "radical liberals" for national problems, and he declared that "little groups of intellectual bully boys" on campus were infecting other students with the "virus of political violence." The Republicans equal law and order, he said, the Democrats equal permissiveness and violence. As Democrats complained that the campaign was not addressing the real issues, Nixon declared that it was "time to draw the line." Agnew put it bluntly, urging blue-collar Democrats to prove their patriotism by voting Republican. As for protesters, he said, it was "time to sweep that kind of garbage out of our society."

The administration's campaign failed. Although citizens were concerned about campus unrest and frustrated with demonstrations, opinion polls found that beside local items important in all congressional elections, the war remained the most significant issue that fall followed by new concerns about the economy. On the state level, Republicans were battered, losing 11 governorships, and conservative Georgia elected a moderate Democrat who promised equal rights, Jimmy Carter. Nationally the Republicans could not beat seven of eight Democratic senators who they had labeled "extremists"—peace candidates—and the conservatives won only two seats in the Senate while antiwar liberals were easily reelected. In the House, 24 peace candidates won and five lost. Democrats picked up nine seats, including one by feminist Bella Abzug of New York City, a founder of Women Strike for Peace, and another by black militant Ronald Dellums of Berkeley, resulting in a more liberal and antiwar House. While election results were cloudy, it seemed that citizens were tired of the war and wanted their government to address domestic problems.

Instead, the administration amplified its attack on the movement, and that became public two months after the election. In January 1971 the *New York Times* reported that 1000 U.S. Army agents were using computers to collect the names of civilians in operation Continental US Intelligence, or Conus Intel. While LBJ began the operation, the newspaper noted, it had been greatly expanded by Nixon. Congress began investigations, and during hearings Pentagon officials admitted that the military had dossiers on 25 million Americans. After this revelation, someone anonymously mailed FBI documents to several newspapers, and activists broke into a bureau office in Medina, Pennsylvania, and stole files. The records revealed that director Hoover had ordered surveillance of student and peace groups, including black organizations at all the nation's colleges because they "pose a definite threat to the nation's stability and security." Other memoranda disclosed that the agency had compiled massive files on citizens, some with no criminal record, such as ecologists at Earth Day, a pilot who criticized the agency's handling of a hijacking, and a Boy Scout leader who planned to take his troop to visit the Soviet Union. As for known activists, the FBI had boxes of information, 17,000 pages on Tom Hayden, and they had bugged the phones of the Michigan activist group the White Panthers. The bureau urged its agents to interview and intimidate those in the movement because "it will enhance the paranoia endemic in these circles and will further serve to get the point across that there is an F.B.I. agent behind every mailbox."

The surveillance was far more extensive than generally known, and it concerned many in Congress who demanded an explanation and threatened legislation to curtail the practice. Attorney General Mitchell stated that the government had "inherent power" to wiretap dissident groups without a court order. Assistant Attorney General William Rehnquist testified his opposition to any limits on the administration's power because "self-discipline on the part of the executive branch" will prohibit illegal activities. Democratic senators McGovern and Ed Muskie and Republican Charles Mathias disagreed, calling for more controls to prevent the abuse of power. House of Representative majority leader Hale Boggs demanded that Hoover, age 76, resign, accusing him of tapping phones of congressional members and of using "tactics of the Soviet Union and Hitler's Gestapo." The administration cried foul, demanding an apology, and House Republican leader Gerald Ford defended Hoover. But Boggs declared that Hoover had him under surveillance, which Mitchell charged a "reckless and cruel attack on a dedicated American." Deputy Attorney General Kleindienst added that Boggs was "either sick or not in possession of his faculties."

The accusations placed the administration on the defensive during spring 1971. Congress began probing the FBI, soon advocating a limited tenure for the FBI director, while movement groups sued the administration. Concerning the White Panthers, a federal court rejected Mitchell's stance on wiretapping, noting that there was "not one written phrase" in the Constitution supporting the position of the Justice Department.[12]

The administration also was under fire concerning its policy in Vietnam. Since the Cambodian invasion, support for the war had been disintegrating. By the November elections 60 percent favored a withdrawal—even if that meant the collapse of South Vietnam—and half wanted to bring American troops home immediately. After two years in office Nixon was under increasing pressure to win peace with honor, and so he announced more troop withdrawals while quietly escalating the bombing campaign. Eventually the U.S. dropped three times the bomb tonnage in Southeast Asia as was used in all theaters during World War II. In February, the administration announced that the South Vietnamese Army was invading Laos. The aim was to stop supplies flowing from north to south in an attempt to cut the Ho Chi Minh Trail, and to prove that Vietnamization was working—that ARVN could stand alone and beat the North Vietnamese Army. During the first week the operation appeared successful, but then it turned ominous. NVA troops attacked, and ARVN retreated, forcing American B-52s to pound Laos. U.S. helicopters ferried in fresh troops and supplies, but in the third week the battle degenerated into a rout. Helicopters evacuated the remnants of ARVN before it was decimated. North Vietnamese moved back and took control: another Hamburger Hill.

The jig was up. Although the vice president attacked anyone who criticized the invasion as a "movement to plead America guilty" that will "destroy us as a nation," most citizens realized that it might be many years, if ever, before ARVN would be able to fight on its own. Veterans wondered if their younger brothers would be drafted; parents thought about their young sons. The invasion prompted protests, of course; some 50,000 converged on Washington, and the Weathermen claimed credit for a bomb that demolished a restroom in the Capitol. Other activists began planning for a major demonstration in April.

To make matters worse for the administration, some Vietnam veterans came forward with shocking revelations. Ever since the My Lai story broke in autumn 1969, and the subsequent investigation and trial of Lieut. Calley, there had been agonizing rumors about the conduct of America troops in Vietnam. In December 1970 the Calley trial was on nightly news, and a group of activists began what they called the "war crimes hearings" in Washington. Thirty veterans testified, and that month another vet, Philip Balboni, published a number of interviews in an article, "What Every Vietnam Veteran Knows: Mylai Was Not an Isolated Incident." The writer noted, "All the men seemed to want their recollections publicized. They were disturbed, angry." In February, the Vietnam Veterans Against the War conducted its own "Winter Soldier Investigation." More than 130 vets testified. One after another they came before the camera:

> *Specialist 5th Class Nathan Hale* . . . my job was to elicit information. This meant that I could elicit information in any means possible. . . . I could cut 'em—I never shot anyone—just don't beat them in the presence of a non-unit member or person. That's someone like a visiting of-

ficer or perhaps the Red Cross. And I personally used clubs, rifle butts, pistols, knives. . . .

Pfc. Charles Stephens . . . they didn't believe our body counts. So we had to cut off the right ear of everybody we killed to prove our body count.

Sergeant Scott Camil . . . I saw one case where a woman was shot by a sniper, one of our snipers. When we got up to her she was asking for water. And the lieutenant said to kill her. So he ripped off her clothes, they stabbed her in both breasts, they spread her eagle and shoved an E tool up her vagina, an entrenching tool, and she was still asking for water. And then they took that out and they used a tree limb and then she was shot.

Moderator Did the men in your outfit . . . did they seem to think that it was all right to do anything to the Vietnamese?

Sgt. Camil . . . when you shot someone you didn't think you were shooting at a human. They were a gook or a Commie and it was okay.

Horror stories poured out—rapes, beatings, maiming, strafing, defoliating, napalming, body counts, free-fire zones, tossing enemy prisoners out of helicopters: "Don't count prisoners when loading, only upon landing."

By April the veterans were marching on Washington: Operation Dewey Canyon III. The first Dewey Canyon engagement was in February 1969 when U.S. Marines secretly invaded Laos, remaining for a week; the second was the first week of the recent Laos invasion. This was the third, a week of "limited incursion into the country of Congress." On Monday, April 19, a thousand veterans marched to Arlington National Cemetery, some in wheelchairs or on crutches, and at the head of the procession were mothers who had lost sons in Vietnam. Cemetery personnel refused to admit them, and the demonstrators marched on the Capitol. Jan Crumb of Vietnam Veterans Against the War presented their demands calling for an immediate end of the war and major reforms in the armed forces. Then they set up camp on the Mall.

They came in peace; the warriors committed no violence, but the Justice Department responded by asking for an injunction to break up the camp. The administration had tried to debunk the veteran's stories, claiming that these men were frauds, that they had never served in Vietnam. Conservatives called them traitors, unpatriotic cowards. "Son," a member of the Daughters of the American Revolution said to one of the veterans, "I don't think what you're doing is good for the troops." "Lady," he responded, "we are the troops." A court granted the injunction, but at the time of eviction, the administration got cold feet. Perhaps officials remembered the popular outrage in 1932 when President Hoover ordered unemployed World War I veterans in the "Bonus Army" routed out of the capital. Whatever the reason, the Nixon administration did not order police to carry out the expulsion order, and the police did not arrest anyone. "Camping?" said one cop. "I don't see any camping." The vets went about Washington, staging guerrilla theater at the Capitol, marching to the Pentagon and demanding to be arrested for "war crimes," and to the Supreme Court where they asked for justices to rule on the war's constitutionality. The vets were joined by other activists and sympathetic politicians on the Mall, at times being entertained by singers and the cast of the musical *Hair*.

The climax of the demonstration came on Friday. About 800 angry vets made a profound statement—they threw their medals and ribbons on the steps of the Capitol. One threw a bronze star, a silver star, and nine purple hearts; another called his medals "merit badges for murder" before one proclaimed, "We don't want to fight anymore, but if we have to fight again it will be to take these steps." "Right On!" the crowd roared back, "Right On!" Ron Ferrizzi explained that if he participated then his parents never wanted to see him again, and that his wife

> said she would divorce me . . . because she wanted my medals for our son. . . . I'm not proud of these medals. I'm not proud of what I did to receive them. I was in Vietnam for a year and our company policy was to take no prisoners. A whole year we never took one prisoner alive. Just wasted them with the door gun, dropped down to check their bodies for maps or valuables, and split. If it was dead and Vietnamese, it was a VC.

Inside the Senate, the Foreign Affairs Committee was holding hearings, and the rage of young veterans overflowed. "We didn't dodge the draft," said Mike Milligan. "Nobody is going to doubt the sincerity of a guy who got both his legs blown off in the Nam. We're finally bringing the war home."[13] Paraplegic Robert Muller added, "I'm bitter because I gave to my country myself, 100 percent, and they used me," and Lieut. John Kerry turned the guns on the Nixon administration:

THE SECOND WAVE: THE CREST, 1968 TO THE EARLY 1970S

. . . this Administration has done us the ultimate dishonor. They have attempted to disown us and the sacrifices we made for this country. In their blindness and fear they have tried to deny that we are veterans or that we served in Nam. We do not need their testimony. Our own scars and stumps or limbs are witness enough for others and for ourselves. We wish that a merciful God could wipe away our own memories of that service as easily as this Administration has wiped away their memories of us. But all that they have done and all that they can do by this denial is to make more clear than ever our own determination to undertake one last mission—to search out and destroy the last vestige of this barbaric war, to pacify our own hearts, to conquer the hate and the fear that have driven this country these last ten years. . . .

Citizens did not want to hear it; Vietnam had become too painful. The silent majority tried to switch channels, turn off the bad news, but they could no longer ignore the endless revelations. Law student and antiwar activist Tom Harkin visited South Vietnam with a congressional delegation earlier and discovered that the Thieu regime was holding thousands of its own citizens as political prisoners in tiny bamboo pens, or "tiger cages." The disgusting photographs appeared in *Life*, but that was just the beginning, for by spring 1971 there was a torrent of bad news. "More Atrocities?" asked *Newsweek*, while *Time* reported "a sprawling $40 million consortium of corruption that reached all the way to MACV headquarters," and *U.S. News* declared a "Breakdown in GI Discipline." The public learned that U.S. troops had been conducting a secret war in Laos, Cambodia, even crossing into North Vietnam. A jury of combat veterans ruled that Lieut. Calley was guilty of murder of at least 22 villagers. The army admitted that drug abuse in South Vietnam was rampant, that usage during the previous three years had increased six times, that half the troops were using marijuana. And the Pentagon admitted "fragging" in the war zone. Soldiers were turning the guns around, killing commanders who were too gung ho and who forced them to engage in combat. The number of such incidents had doubled to over 200 during the last year. Many commanders felt that their own troops could not be trusted and they began restricting access to explosives and rifles. Eventually the army admitted that fragging had resulted in about 600 murders, 80 percent of them officers, and they could not account for the deaths of another 1500—the army was at war with itself over the war in Vietnam.[14]

Back home, American men would no longer serve in the military. Re-enlistments fell to the lowest on record, and ROTC enrollment plummeted as the number of men filing for conscientious objector status soared to record levels: over 60,000 in 1971. That year the government reported that 15,000 men refused induction and 100,000 did not appear for their physicals, and there were 190 attacks on local Selective Service offices.

And so again activists confronted the administration, this time on April 24. Half a million people joined the veterans and appeared in Washington, and about 125,000 in San Francisco, marking the second largest gathering in the nation's capital and the largest on the West Coast. Americans of almost all backgrounds demanded peace, from businessmen to unionmen, from clergy to veterans, from Democrats to Republicans. Demonstrators urged Nixon to "set a date" for the end of American participation in the war; some wanted the Fourth of July and others advocated December 31. The peace movement reached out and expanded into the heartland, while in Washington the Reverend Ralph Abernathy of SCLC, Congresswoman Bella Abzug, and Lieut. John Kerry gave speeches, and Phil Ochs again sang, "I Ain't Marchin' Any More."

The demonstration was very peaceful, gentle, and most activists returned home; yet about 30,000 stayed in the capital and camped in Potomac Park. The May Day Tribe, they called themselves, and organizer Rennie Davis declared that on Monday, May 3, they would force the administration to sign the "People's Peace Treaty" by using a new type of nonviolent direct action: "Unless the Government of the United States stops the war in Vietnam, we will stop the Government of the United States."

Nixon struck first. At dawn on Sunday, federal officials appeared at the encampment and arrested a couple of hundred. The May Day Tribe regrouped, and on Monday converged downtown, putting up barricades, letting air out of tires, momentarily impeding traffic.

The administration's response was overwhelming: City police and 10,000 soldiers quickly swept the downtown and occupied federal buildings. In battle dress, many armed with machine guns, soldiers patrolled the streets while helicopters whirred overhead. Police shot tear gas and chased virtually everyone who looked like a protester. A few scattered skirmishes erupted, resulting in 150 injured activists. But mostly officials conducted mass arrests, some 7000—the most in one day in the nation's history. On Tuesday, May Day forces tried to protest the severe treatment by marching on the Justice Building, again resulting in mass arrests which included unlucky shoppers, jaywalkers, and even federal employees. By that evening 12,000 people were incarcerated in the Washington Coliseum or at a practice field near RFK Stadium.

The administration was playing hardball. Attorney General Mitchell urged communities to use such tactics against demonstrators, who he compared to "Hitler's Brown Shirts," later commenting that some of them had "Communist-oriented or related backgrounds" and were funded by "Communist sources." The president would not tolerate critics of his Vietnam policy, proclaiming to aides: "We'll get them on the ground where we want them. And we'll stick our heels in, step on them hard and twist . . . crush them, show them no mercy." To Nixon, obviously, dissidents were the enemy, the Vietcong, and his pre-emptive strike was the domestic equivalent of the invasions of Cambodia or Laos. To keep the government functioning, the president of the United States had to rely on draconic measures, employing over 10,000 troops and police, rounding up everyone with long hair, and throwing them in what activists charged were concentration camps. Nixon then had to assure citizens that the nation "isn't a police state and it isn't going to become one." The FBI arrested Rennie Davis, holding him on $25,000 bond and charging conspiracy, but most demonstrators never were charged with any crime. In the subsequent trials that kept activists occupied and paying court fees, only 63 of the 12,000 were found guilty of any offense, and eventually a class-action suit forced the taxpayers to give $10,000 to each one improperly arrested.[15]

The May Day Tribe, of course, failed to stop the government, but just the attempt demonstrated that some in the movement were very serious about their attempt to bring about a New America, one at peace. And so were some others who had been drafted into the military, as G.I. activists increased their attack on another pillar of the establishment—the U.S. Armed Forces.

Two weeks after May Day, G.I. activists staged a demonstration that they dubbed Armed Farces Day. Several hundred active duty personnel marched and held antiwar fairs at almost 20 bases, including Fort Bliss, Fort Lewis, Fort Hood, and Fort Bragg, which they now called Fort Fragg. In San Diego, 1500 sailors on the carrier USS *Constellation* signed a petition demanding that antiwar actress Jane Fonda be allowed to perform her Fuck The Army show on the ship, and when the captain rejected that, some 4000 appeared at her rally in the city.

The movement infiltrated the military. G.I. activism and antiwar sentiments were apparent on virtually every American installation—at home, abroad, and on the high seas. The number of G.I. undergrounds soared. The Defense Department reported at least 250 such papers published on bases, a few with circulations of 5000, and activists were printing dozens more on ships and installations in Germany, Japan, Korea, and Vietnam.

Furthermore, many in the military no longer looked or acted military. Black soldiers abandoned the crew cut and began wearing Afros; they often refused orders and demanded that the military open all positions to them and dismiss racist officers. In the war zone, some soldiers gave the Black Power salute while many wore love beads and peace symbols, and of course, smoked dope. Hippies who had been drafted received their G.I. hair cut but that did not change their behavior. Freaky sailors on the USS *Constellation* disrupted procedures by initiating the "Peanut Butter

Conspiracy." For three days they called the captain, tied up communication lines, and demanded that "peanut butter be served at every meal." On the submarine tender USS *Huntley*, sailors published an underground entitled the *Huntley Hemorrhoid* that informed officers: "We serve to preserve the pain in your ass." Hippies in the USAF decided to take as much time as possible on all tasks, to "slow down the great and powerful Air Farce machine," and they even demanded a second opinion on haircuts. And when the army recruited two soldiers at Fort Bliss, Texas, to monitor antiwar G.I.s, the spies organized the base chapter of GIs for Peace and used army funds to fill its treasury. Officers realized something was amiss when half the troops under surveillance deserted and their two agents filed for conscientious objector status. Nevertheless, the brass was relieved to grant their agents discharges after one of them claimed to be "on a continual trip," hearing "heavenly hosts" and seeing "nursery rhymes." The man actually was given a medical discharge because, as he claimed, "Someone injected LSD in my brain."

During 1971 the movement was winning the war against the military. With an unpopular war, receiving less than an honorable discharge no longer determined a young man's future. Thus, G.I. activists abandoned duty and refused orders. That year some 25,000 personnel took undesirable discharges as desertions increased to a stunning rate: for every 100 soldiers that year, 17 went AWOL and 7 deserted, the highest numbers in army history. In fact, over half a million soldiers deserted during the war—again, record numbers. For those who remained, discipline plummeted. An army survey found that over *half* of troops had participated in either drug offenses or acts of dissidence or disobedience. Officers formed the Concerned Officers Movement, published *COMmon Sense*, and COM even had a small chapter at the Pentagon. As the commander-in-chief shifted more of the war burden from land to air and sea, some sailors rioted on ships and a few pilots refused to fly missions. The navy reported almost 500 cases of arson, sabotage, or wrongful destruction on its ships, while 1000 sailors on the USS *Coral Sea* petitioned Congress to stop its cruise to Vietnam. These "flattop revolts" expanded the next year, as sailors signed petitions or disrupted operations on the *Kitty Hawk, Oriskany, Ticonderoga, America,* and *Enterprise*. Sabotage on the *Ranger* and *Forrestal* prevented their scheduled port departures while pilots and airmen became increasingly concerned about their role in the bombing campaign and questioned the war openly. Captain Michael Heck, who had flown 175 missions, refused to fly more because "a man has to answer to himself first." In Vietnam, troops signed petitions, joined VVAW, and even marched against the war in 1971. On July 4, over 1000 G.I.s at Chu Lai held a peace rally which they reported as the "largest pot party in the history of the Army." The troops hated the war, and as one veteran predicted, "If Nixon doesn't hurry up and bring the GIs home, they are going to come home by themselves."

The brass knew it. "The Army's prestige is at the lowest ebb in memory," stated the commanding general of Fort Bragg. "There's never been a more unpopular war and it's had its effect." After returning from the war zone, retired Colonel Robert Heinl published a stunning exposé in *Armed Forces Journal:* "The morale, discipline and battleworthiness of the of the U.S. Armed Forces are, with few exceptions, lower and worse than at any time in this century and possibly in the history of the United States." Heinl reported drugged soldiers dispirited and near mutiny. "By every conceivable indicator," he summarized, "our army that now remains in Vietnam is in a state approaching collapse." Marine Major H. L. Seay agreed, declaring, "Unit leaders are faced with more problems today than ever before in the history of the Marine Corps."[16] Vietnam and Vietnamization were killing the U.S. Armed Forces.

The movement was laying siege to the military, and then in June the press fired another salvo at the Vietnam War. The *New York Times* and *Washington Post* began publishing the secret history of the war, *The Pentagon Papers.* In 1967, Secretary of Defense McNamara put together a team of 40 researchers to examine how the U.S. became involved in the war in the first place; that in itself was an incredible admission while soldiers were giving their lives for their country. One of the researchers, Daniel Ellsberg, copied the documents and delivered them to the *Times,* who along with the *Post,* began publishing them. Alarmed, the Justice Department issued a restraining order to block publication, citing "national interest." The *Times* took the issue to the Supreme Court, arguing that the government had failed to prove its case. The court agreed, six to three, and allowed publication.

The secret history was "deeply disturbing," said *Newsweek,* for it exposed the delusions and deceptions of previous leaders, especially in the Kennedy and Johnson administrations. The documents revealed a war kept secret from Americans—covert military operations against North Vietnam and bombing missions in Laos, while such actions were being denied by the U.S. Memoranda contradicted official statements: JFK knew of and approved the plot that led to the coup d'état against Diem in 1963; the next year the CIA reported that it did not believe the domino theory was relevant to Asia; intelligence experts in Vietnam had informed LBJ then that the insurgency against the Saigon regime was primarily indigenous instead of being directed from Hanoi; the administration knew that air strikes did not soften but had hardened the attitude of the enemy; the various Saigon regimes were not free and democratic but generally controlled by Washington. The *Papers* exposed how Johnson did not tell congressmen or the people the full details of the attack in the Gulf of

Tonkin, how in 1965 he wanted to avoid publicity about his expansion of American involvement. It was clear, as activists had said all along— elected officials had lied about the war to their electorate.

In the hearts and minds of most Americans, the Vietnam War ended during the first half of 1971. The deception and lies disclosed in *The Pentagon Papers*, the revelations about the U.S. military, ARVN's failure in Laos, and the nature of the Thieu government in Saigon all revealed the dark underside of the war, and ended lingering doubts. The effort was no longer worth the cost. Opinion polls between March and June revealed that only 15 percent wanted to continue the war, almost 60 percent thought U.S. involvement was "immoral," and over 70 percent thought the war was a "mistake" and favored withdrawal. Opposition reached the highest levels yet, while the president's approval ratings fell to the lowest of his first term; his "credibility" problem was becoming ominously close to that of LBJ in 1968. Even the few conservatives who still supported the effort phrased their position as supporting their president's policy, not the war, while other former proponents simply abandoned the crusade. "Everybody's just sick and tired of the war," said a conservative, and Republican Senator Hugh Scott told Secretary of Defense Melvin Laird, "You don't see any hawks around here. The hawks are all ex-hawks. There's a feeling that the Senate ought to tell the President that we should get the hell out of the war." Businessmen complained that the war was hurting profits and creating labor unrest. Unions said it was fueling inflation and hurting workers. The foreign policy establishment preached that it was no longer strengthening but weakening our credibility and alliances. As for the average citizen, most could sympathize with columnist Arthur Hoppe, who admitted his reaction when he heard about ARVN's failure in Laos: "Good. And having said it, I realized the bitter truth: Now I root against my own country. . . . I don't root for the enemy. I doubt they are any better than we. I don't give a damn any more who wins the war. But because I hate what my country is doing in Vietnam, I emotionally and often irrationally hope that it fails."[17]

It was failing, but Nixon could not admit it. He was in an impossible situation. He had promised "peace with honor" to Americans and to South Vietnam, but that meant different things to both nations. Americans wanted out, the South Vietnamese government needed us to stay. Yet vast antiwar feelings meant that the administration had little recourse. Kissinger felt constant pressure to continue troop withdrawals and negotiate with the enemy in Paris. In June, with 240,000 troops in the war zone, the president announced the withdrawal of 100,000 by the end of the year. The administration also played the trump card—fear. If the U.S. pulled out, officials stated, the enemy would win and would conduct a bloodbath against the South Vietnamese. More persuasively, the administration declared that the U.S. could not entirely withdraw until the enemy returned all American prisoners of war. Meanwhile, Nixon privately promised Thieu that the United States would never abandon their ally, and he made secret contacts with the Soviet Union and his old adversary, the People's Republic of China, which he hoped would pressure North Vietnam to curtail their attacks in the south.

As the administration scrambled for a way out of an unpopular war, the antiwar movement naturally faded. April 24 was the last major *national* antiwar demonstration. On campus, fewer joined protests against the war. A journalist surveyed 40 universities and found that "while student opposition to the war and the Nixon Administration is as monolithic as it ever was," the second wave of activists were no longer enthusiastic for mass demonstrations, especially at colleges that had witnessed years of upheaval. Many students felt or hoped that Vietnamization was working; troops were coming home, draft calls and American casualties were declining, and they supported the fairness of the lottery. Other students were more cynical, noting that 200,000 still remained in the war zone and that every week massive bombings killed untold hundreds of Vietnamese. Yet activists admitted being tired of marches—and feeling powerless. "The problem," one organizer said, "is that students feel totally alienated from the Administration, that it has never listened and that it will not now."

The assessment was correct. A year later, in spring 1972, Nixon ordered the mining of North Vietnam's Haiphong harbor and intensified the bombing campaign, prompting scattered protests in New York City, San Francisco, and Los Angeles but no major occupation of Washington. Fewer students demonstrated, although some clashes were significant. In Albuquerque, the governor had to declare a state of emergency to quell a riot at the University of New Mexico, and for the first time officials at Minnesota had to call on the national guard to occupy the campus. Ohio State and Wisconsin reported property damage, and the president of Columbia labeled the protests "the roughest I ever experienced." Significantly, the national media ignored the demonstrations, for they no longer were "news." A newspaper editor stated that with the war "scaling down . . . it's hard to justify front-page coverage."[18]

The antiwar movement dissipated during 1971, but another way to look at it is that such activism was no longer necessary. The call for peace, which a majority considered unpatriotic as late as 1968, now was patriotic. After all, the president was trying to end the war, and in June about 40 senators attempted to tie Nixon to a date for total withdrawal when they voted for the McGovern-Hatfield amendment. Although the measure failed to win a majority, the idea of Peace Now had become in the national interest. The only question was, "When?" Across the nation the political center shifted; frustrated by the endless conflict, former support-ers eventually adopted the position advocated by the movement. The anti-war crusade became obsolete, and as it declined, the second wave contin-ued flowing along the theme that began after the election of Nixon. Many activists turned away from national matters and toward personal self-fulfillment and local political issues, broadening empowerment while confronting the establishment.

One pillar of the establishment was organized religion, and during the early 1970s the sixties generation deserted not only the military in record numbers but also mainstream religious denominations. Surveys demon-strated that a quarter of respondents either rejected their parent's religion or chose none at all, while at the same time church membership plum-meted, especially on college campuses.

The religious current of the movement had many tributaries that had been flowing throughout the 1960s. Christian and Jewish clergy had been at the forefront of the civil rights struggle and had made up a significant part of the antiwar crusade. Meanwhile, many Catholics were discussing radical theology, the idea that priests should behave more like Jesus and act on behalf of the alienated, poor, or outcast. To many clergy activists, being "committed" was being "religious," and being a religious person often meant direct action based on conscience, often without regard to the church hierarchy or American law. So activists such as priests Leo-nard Dubi of Chicago, James Groppi of Milwaukee, and Daniel and Philip Berrigan protested for social justice—which in turn often con-fronted and irritated the elders. As early as 1967 U.S. News reported "Un-rest in U.S. Churches" as activist priests were being arrested. Because of his antiwar activities, elders exiled Daniel Berrigan to a ministry in South America, which only resulted in an outcry for his return. Protestants had their own problems, for during the decade many conservative domina-tions maintained segregated churches, condemned the counterculture, and supported U.S. policy in Vietnam. The Reverend Billy Graham did not criticize the war effort and often was a guest at the Nixon White House where he proclaimed that protesters were trying to "destroy the nation."

While many felt alienated by mainstream religion, an alternative reli-gious movement was flourishing. "Man, God turned me around from the darkness to the light," said a former speed freak. "That's all I know. That's all I want to know." This new surge in religion was expanding so rapidly in 1971 that Time and Newsweek had cover stories, the former declaring, "The New Rebel Cry: Jesus Is Coming!" The magazine noted a "startl-ing development for a generation that has been constantly accused of tripping out or copping out with sex, drugs and violence. Now, embracing the most persistent symbol of purity, selflessness and brotherly love in the history of Western man, they are afire with a Pentecostal passion for sharing their new vision with others."

The Jesus Freaks, also known as Jesus People, Street Christians, the God Squad, Children of God, or Straight People, were busy building their New America, one based on first-century or primitive Christianity. They established several hundred small communes throughout the nation, 200 just in California, and opened coffeehouses such as I Am in Spokane, the Way Word in Greenwich Village, or the Catacombs in Seattle. They converted a strip joint into a nightclub in San Antonio where rock groups such as the Joyful Noise or Crimson Bridge played Christian rock. Musicians spread the message: 8000 attended the "Sweet Jesus Rock Concert" at Stanford, while others flocked to see the plays *Godspell* and *Jesus Christ Superstar*, or bought 6 million of copies of Nicky Cruz's *The Cross and the Switchblade*. They established 24-hour hotlines and published about 50 underground newspapers, from *Oil & Wine* in New Orleans with a small circulation to the *Hollywood Free Paper*, which printed up to 400,000 copies of each issue. Christian businessmen sold T-shirts, posters, buttons, bumper stickers: "Smile, God Loves You." Activists adopted a Jesus Power salute—a raised arm, clenched fist with the index finger pointing toward heaven. And they spread the word the old-fashioned way. In Houston, they held revival meetings, and as the young pastor declared "Outta sight, man," 11,000 declared themselves for Jesus. At Corona del Mar, California, they held a mass baptism, ending the event at twilight by singing the Lord's Prayer. In Chicago's Grant Park, an evangelist led 1000 converts in Jesus cheers, and then the crowd marched through the Loop, surprising authorities by handing them a box of drugs and shouting, "Police, we love you! Jesus loves you!"

The Jesus revival invaded campuses. By 1971 neatly dressed, well-groomed, evangelical Straight People were active on over 450 campuses through organizations such as Young Life, Campus Life, Navigators, Youth for Christ, and the Fellowship of Christian Athletes. The two largest organizations were the Campus Crusade for Christ and Inter-Varsity Christian Fellowship. Campus Crusade held "Operation Sunshine" at Daytona Beach as part of their "Revolution for Jesus Christ," and they established a folk-rock band called Armageddon. Some 12,000 attended a Campus Crusade missionary convention at the University of Illinois, and the organization attracted 75,000 to the Cotton Bowl in Dallas for an event they billed a "Fundamentalist Woodstock."

The religious movement came in many colors. Rabbi Arthur Green organized Havurot Shalom near Boston, where young Jews joined the *havurot* movement, fellowships that rejected traditional authorities and fundamental beliefs and emphasized experimental worship, communal living, and political action. Some Catholics were swept into fervor, joining the Catholic Pentecostal or Catholic Charismatic Renewal. They worshiped emotionally in prayer meetings by shouting, rolling on the floor, even speaking in tongues. Some 1400 attended the national conference at Notre Dame University in 1970, a number that soared to 20,000 by 1973. At the University of Michigan a few hundred joined the Word of God community, and by mid-decade some 30,000 received a papal blessing in Rome.

While critics complained that the Jesus revolution was "spiritually chic" or a "cult," the young flock was not listening. Religious activists were creating another Great American Revival. "All I know is that kids are turning on to Jesus," declared a evangelical pastor. "My concern is that the staid, traditional churches will reject these kids and miss the most genuine revival of our lifetime."[19] Like the previous revivals, this one presented a challenge to established religion. Indeed, the movement advocated the dawning of a new age, a New America, or as they called it, a New Consciousness, in which the failed dreams of the sixties could be fulfilled in the seventies.

To other activists, however, the New America was less personal and more political, and some became active in the growing consumer movement which aimed to confront the business establishment. "Is the corporation next to fall?" asked a university lecturer. Other business observers began to predict internal revolts when corporations hired activists graduating from college, and in 1971 that apparently was becoming reality. *Fortune* noted that new trainees "reflect the passionate concerns of youth" such as "individuality, openness, humanism, concern, and change."

Many activists held similar and vague ideas about business: capitalism equaled greed; big business was too powerful; and multinationals were imperialistic. Such rhetoric scared businessmen and their journals lost little time condemning the entire movement. But in fact, most college students held ambivalent feelings toward capitalism and the overwhelming majority—85 percent in one survey—felt that business was entitled to make a profit, clearly demonstrating that only a few radicals were aiming to dismantle free enterprise.[20] Like previous reformers of the populist-progressive era and of the 1930s, the sixties generation condemned the "remote control economy" that excluded workers and citizens from decisions affecting jobs and the community. *The Port Huron Statement* continued by advocating "a more reformed, more human capitalism."

To bring about reform, activists employed "proxie power." Saul Alinsky solicited the movement and liberal foundations, churches, and universities to buy stock in corporations and then vote their proxies in a block to compel the business to pursue social goals. Activists demonstrated at annual stockholder meetings of numerous corporations—General Electric,

Union Carbide, American Telephone & Telegraph, Columbia Broadcasting System—and they sponsored the "Honeywell Stock Buy-In." They purchased about 40 shares which they claimed were tickets of entry to the stockholders meeting at the Minneapolis headquarters. Some 3000 assembled, and while officers allowed a few into the meeting, demonstrators in the parking lot held a "people's stockholders meeting." Inside, the president called the meeting to order, ran through all official business, and adjourned in ten minutes over protests of dissidents. Philip W. Moore established the Project on Corporate Responsibility, bought General Motors stock, and demanded that the corporation give him names of the other million stockholders so he could solicit their help in forcing GM to place three "public directors" on the board who would support social and anti-pollution policies. Students adopted these tactics and demanded that their universities divest their stocks in defense contractors, polluting corporations, and those doing business in South Africa.

Some employees participated by ridiculing their bosses. As firms hired the sixties generation, some young workers formed "corporate underground" groups. The black power Polaroid Workers' Revolutionary Movement demanded that the company quit business in South Africa, and they handed out leaflets claiming "Polaroid imprisons blacks in 60 seconds." Radical workers derided corporate policies by printing underground papers such as *AT&T Express*, *Met Lifer* at Metropolitan Life Insurance Company, and *Stranded Oiler* at Standard Oil of California. Edited by "Scarlet Punpernickle," *Stranded Oiler* was "written on company time, using a company IBM typewriter, while . . . listening to KSAN at high volume," and like all the corporate undergrounds it aimed to raise the "consciousness of the modern day galley slaves," mock management, and ridicule corporation hypocrisy, such as Standard's statements about their concern for the environment while they vigorously opposed California's clean coastline acts.

Throughout 1971 consumer activists appeared on campuses, even at work. Students at dozens of universities volunteered at Ralph Nader's Public Interest Research Groups, conducting research on local business issues, comparing prices, or checking pollution. Nader also urged the rise of "employee power," and publicized the idea at a "Whistle-Blowers' Conference." He encouraged workers to become "on-the-job conscientious objectors" by refusing to carry out tasks they considered illegal or immoral and by leaking corrupt or unethical practices of their corporate bosses, what consumer activists called "crime in the suites."[21]

The economy in 1971 also fueled the fires of consumer activism. Wartime spending resulted in inflation, and provoked many housewives to become activists. When Jewel Food Stores in Chicago increased meat prices, CAP, the Citizen Action Program, demanded that the president of the supermarket chain account for new prices by meeting activists at check-out lanes of one of his stores. He declined, so housewives entered a Jewel store, packed their shopping carts with meats, proceeded through the check-out lanes, and refused to pay until the president appeared to discuss prices. Outside, activists picketed, waving signs—"Honk for Lower Meat Prices"—and the street became a cacophony of noisy vehicles at the beginning of what became known as the meat boycott.

Rate hikes by energy companies stimulated more citizens to activism. Some 1500 marched in Fayetteville, North Carolina, while in one county of the state two-thirds of the residents signed a petition to the governor. In Philadelphia, 15,000 signed cards pledging to withhold utility payments, and in New York, when the Consolidated Edison board met, they were confronted with a huge picket line and a banner: "Con Ed Is Robbing Us—We're Fighting Mad."

The movement, then, was raising questions about the way America did business, and that concerned the establishment. While citizens were losing faith in all institutions during the second wave, surveys found that the percentage of those expressing confidence in corporate leadership and agreeing that "business tries to strike a fair balance between profits and the interest of the public," plummeted 50 percent. In 1971 David Rockefeller of Chase Manhattan Bank told an audience of businessmen, "It is scarcely an exaggeration to say that right now American business is facing its most severe public disfavor since the 1930s. We are assailed for demeaning the worker, deceiving the consumer, destroying the environment and disillusioning the younger generation."[22]

City hall also was facing public disfavor, and that appeared during the early 1970s as a movement some called the backyard revolution, the new localism, or the neighborhood rebellion. "We tried to get back to real, everyday things," recalled former Black Power advocate Bill Thompson. "We switched issues from Vietnam and Cambodia and just moved in with the community." Thompson became an organizer fighting rising insurance rates and eventually helped organize Massachusetts Fair Share, while Toby Moffett established coalitions with other activists and eventually organized Connecticut Citizen Action Group. Former national secretary of SDS Lee Webb fought utility company rate hikes and often joined forces with Bernard Sanders and a new party called Liberty Union that supported progressive causes in Vermont. Martha Ballou switched from marching against the war to organizing the elderly into the Metropolitan Senior Federation in Minneapolis, while Berkeley activist Michael Rossman began a campaign to establish free universities and reform public schools. Freedom Summer veteran and feminist Heather Booth founded the Midwest Academy in Chicago, and along with former SDS activist Steve Max trained future community organizers and worked closely with

CAP. A graduate from Midwest, Ellen Cassedy, went to Boston and helped establish one of the first groups for working women, 9 to 5, while Ernesto Cortes left his work with Cesar Chavez and returned to San Antonio where he began transforming politics in the city by developing Communities Organizing for Public Service, COPS. Ira Magaziner, who had been at Brown University fighting successfully for curriculum reform, moved to Brockton, Massachusetts, where he and others established a food cooperative, tenants' rights group, and a nonprofit corporation to repair dilapidated housing. Wade Rathke left draft counseling and welfare rights organizing and went to Little Rock where he attempted to unify many of the new groups into what eventually was named the Association of Community Organizations for Reform Now, ACORN. Soon, ACORN had a staff of 20, almost all 1960s activists, such as John Beam, who had organized food co-ops near Northwestern University, Steve Kest, a former worker for the New American Movement, and Judy Rosenkrantz, a founder of the Berkeley Women's Health Collective. "Almost every week we'd hear about a new organizing effort starting up," recalled Bert De-Leeuw. "Welfare rights organizers, civil rights activists and an assorted array of lefties—we were making it happen in local communities across the country. We had wounded the great beast of state in the 60's and we were convinced that in the 70's we were going to blow it away!"

While coordinators differed over how to confront city hall and organize neighborhood residents, most tried to avoid the rhetoric and ideology of the 1960s. If there was an ideology, then it was a blend of the old American idea of popular sovereignty stated in contemporary parlance, participatory democracy, with the populist idea that the little guy should stand up and be counted. Community activists were pragmatic. Realizing that social change was a long process, they focused on one goal at a time as they attacked the establishment, demanding to be in on the decisions that affected their lives. They mobilized "the people," overcoming race and gender issues as minorities and whites worked together to improve their neighborhoods. The ultimate aim was empowerment, common in all American reform eras, and was best stated by ACORN's slogan, "The People Shall Rule."[23]

That idea was becoming contagious. "We saw what the kids were doing," declared a middle-aged resident, "and we decided to protest too." Increasingly, citizens became activists. They took on the usual urban issues of water and sewage, schools and parks, tenant's rights and utility rates, welfare and public housing, and they asked new questions: Who controls the police? Who causes local pollution, and who should pay for clean up? Who sets zoning policy?

You *can* fight city hall, activists proved. During the early 1970s "citizen participation" was demonstrated in hundreds of struggles nationwide concerning urban freeway plans. In Los Angeles, retiree Ralph Keith mobilized the Freeway Fighters and formed a coalition with the NAACP, Sierra Club, and Environmental Defense Fund, and they filed a suit against the state highway department, delaying construction of the Century Freeway for a decade. The "freeway revolt" also quashed planned construction on the Beverly Hills and Malibu freeways and other roadways in Boston, New York, Memphis, New Orleans, and San Francisco. In Toledo, residents of a Hungarian neighborhood stopped a road project that would have divided their community, and St. Louis activists fought off officials who threatened to destroy the Italian district known as The Hill. When Mayor Richard Daley supported the crosstown expressway in Chicago, citizens launched a massive educational campaign and printed half a million flyers supporting their gubernatorial candidate who opposed the project, and was elected. "We took on the city, the state, and the federal government," recalled Joyce Zick, "and we won. . . . It was not an easy battle, there were many ups and downs . . . but that gave many of us the courage to move on to other issues."

They did, and another issue was redlining—the custom of banks avoiding mortgages or home improvement loans, insurance companies refusing to sell policies, or real estate companies rejecting business in what they consider high-risk districts. The result, naturally, was the deterioration of neighborhoods, white flight to the suburbs, and urban blight, which in turn resulted in demolition and urban renewal. This pattern was supported by construction companies, real estate brokers, lending institutions, and most politicians, all talking about jobs and profits. In 1971 Gail Cincotta and others in the West Side Coalition decided to stop the redlining of their districts of Chicago. She and 600 activists marched on the city council, and when they did not get results, 1200 demonstrated at the local office of the Department of Housing and Urban Development. They demanded an investigation, and by the end of the year HUD handed down 70 federal indictments against real estate agents, building inspectors, even HUD officials for discriminatory business practices. Jeanine Stump and others then attacked the local bank. When the residents heard that the bank intended to move to a suburb, that it had been receiving almost 70 percent of its deposits from the neighborhood but only investing 15 percent there, she and 150 others held a "bank-in." Scores of children cashed in pennies, parents opened new accounts for one dollar, and others bought one dollar money orders, tying up business until the bank president agreed to negotiate. The bank not only decided to stay, but agreed to invest $3 million in the neighborhood.

Small but important local victories prompted more citizen participation, and such was the case in Southeast Baltimore. To protect the neighborhood from degeneration, more than 1000 residents appeared at a meeting in 1971 and formed SECO, Southeast Baltimore Community Organization. SECO demonstrated how much the movement had expanded since the first wave, for it represented over 90 groups, from hippies to small businessmen, from welfare mothers to union men, from churches to the Little League. "We knew we had to be tough and militant," stated former civil rights activist Barbara Mikulski. Mothers with baby carriages blocked trucks to keep them off residential streets. A wheelchair march prevented closure of the only public nursing home, and a demonstration kept the library open. Protests at city hall discouraged officials from allowing subdivision of homes into rental units, and pressure on authorities resulted in a health cooperative, two public schools, a youth program, and an investigation of redlining resulted in a compromise with the banks.

The people were taking back democracy, becoming involved. "National politicians are completely out of touch with us," declared Mikulski. "They are even starting to believe the myths they created about us. We are *not* the Silent Majority. We're getting pretty vocal." And by the election year of 1972 national politicians were listening. The West Side Coalition sponsored a national housing conference in Chicago that year, drawing 2000 neighborhood representatives from almost 40 states. Politicians attending included Mayor Daley and Democratic presidential contender George McGovern. The representatives formed a network, the National People's Action, directed by Gail Cincotta, and they proposed federal legislation inhibiting redlining by requiring lending institutions to disclose where they make home loans.

The backyard rebellion also boosted a resurgence of neighborhood pride. One demonstration was street art, and another was historic preservation, which became a craze. Citizens became involved from Savannah, Georgia, to Granbury, Texas, to La Grange, California, refurbishing old buildings instead of destroying them. America came home, looked around, and got involved. Mary Lou Watkins of Granbury put it this way: "The nation has been through a rootless period of alienation, and many of us are trying to re-establish our sense of place."[24]

Older citizens were re-establishing a sense of pride. In October 1970, *Newsweek* noted that "an increasing number of senior groups are gradually joining the growing ranks of the country's demonstrators in an effort to publicize their demands." Indeed, the magazine declared, elderly "citizens have recently begun to organize across the country, creating the latest pressure group to appear upon the American political scene—Senior Power."

The press quickly labeled the movement "Gray Power," and it formed a natural alliance with other activists. Although the elderly had Social Security and Medicare, a forth of those over 65, half of minority seniors, lived in poverty, and unlike all other age groups then, the percentage was increasing. Furthermore, too many citizens held the opinion that anyone retired was "used up," useless. "The old and young have three common traits," stated an official for the American Association of Retired Persons, "both have no money, no power and no identity." Like many blacks, browns, reds, and women, some gray Americans felt injustices and began to challenge the white middle-aged establishment.

The movement was becoming ageless. "We want to give old folks a new sense of power and worth," declared Maggie Kuhn. She and five friends, all forced into retirement, formed a organization which the media dubbed the Gray Panthers. "We don't have organized chapters," said Kuhn. "Our operation is more like guerrilla warfare. Panthers are organizers, enablers, catalysts—on a national level." In San Francisco, gray activists picketed cafeterias that raised prices on their so-called senior lunch special. In Miami, they demonstrated at overpriced grocery stores and held sit-ins at expensive medical offices. In Chicago, Margaret Person noticed that an elderly couple on her block was forced out of their home because of increasing residential taxes, and she became active, organizing the Senior Coalition in CAP and beginning a crusade for tax relief. She soon was confronting local politicians and corporate bosses, and she led a delegation of 250 to discuss generic drugs with the president of Abbot Laboratories. In Philadelphia 600 Gray Panthers mobilized, staged demonstrations, and held meetings with the mayor to get lower mass transit fares, better routes, and easier access to buses. That "really shook 'em up," said Kuhn. "And the old folks got such a bang out of it. They really felt they had some power for the first time."

"We're not settling for crumbs," Kuhn continued, "This is a massive assault," as Gray Power broadened the attack from city hall to state house to the federal government. In Illinois, seniors held a rally in Springfield that resulted in the governor creating a post for elderly affairs. In New York, they pressured state legislators to abolish mandatory retirement laws. In Washington, Gray Panthers joined forces with Ralph Nader and pushed the government to inspect nursing homes and fraudulent retirement land sales and to improve health care and reconsider retirement laws. "Political action makes old people feel important again," stated the director of the National Council of Senior Citizens. "It gives them a psychological uplift."

Gray pride and power was not lost on politicians. They were very aware that the elderly voted at a higher percentage than any other age group in the nation, and they responded throughout 1971. A Senate panel that had been studying aging painted a grim picture of millions of older citizens living in poverty, concluding that the "retirement income problem has reached crisis stage." Politicians designated May as Senior Citizens'

Month and the Nixon administration announced that for the first time in ten years it would hold a White House Conference on Aging. Before the event, Senator Frank Church advocated that government stop "timid tinkering" and "stop-gap proposals" and instead develop a national policy on aging, a topic discussed at the conference in November. Some 3500 delegates appeared, politicians pledged increasing Social Security, and the president called on local governments to reduce taxes for the elderly. The conference inspired states and communities. Within a year, Oregon, Florida, and many other states began special transportation services, reducing fares and adding routes. Hawaii began senior day-care centers. Washington reduced fees for community colleges, and Colorado, Virginia, and other states began "meals-on-wheels." About 20 states established new commissions on aging while a dozen considered and passed bills lowering property tax relief. "There has been a great awakening of interest in older persons and their problems," declared a Nebraska official, "and a renewed commitment at the State and local levels to attempt to deal with those concerns."[25]

Farmers also had concerns, and they began expressing them and organizing, a phenomenon that one journalist eventually labeled "Barnyard Radicals. . . . Protest tactics used on city streets in the 1960s have moved to country roads in the 1970s." A young political scientist, Paul Wellstone, enlisted a number of students at Carleton College and founded the Organization for a Better Rice County in southern Minnesota. Concerned about rural poverty, the students joined farmers and the poor, who challenged the county commissioners, winning concessions concerning food stamps and welfare rights, and a few years later Wellstone and others successfully fought power companies who proposed building one of the nation's largest power lines across farmers' land in North Dakota and Minnesota. In Washington, D.C., Jim Hightower, Susan DeMarco, and others organized the Agribusiness Accountability Project and began investigating food processing, profits, and preservatives while boosting the idea of organic gardening. Farmers began fighting corporate land buying and utility company expansion to prime lands, and they were supported by populist senators such as Fred Harris of Oklahoma. And merging with the consumer movement, urban activists invited farmers back to towns to sell their produce, cutting out the middleman while re-establishing farmers' markets in cities from Bangor to Seattle.

Ecologists continued the attack on the establishment. "The drive against pollution catches on at the local level," reported Life in 1971, as "concerned citizens all over the country are waging individual and community battles to control the nation's growing mountain of waste." Armed with the 1970 amendments to the Clean Air Act which allowed communities to issue more restrictive environmental standards, ecologists confronted city halls and applied pressure on developers, winning significant victories. In Eugene, activists got the city council to restrict development—"Save Oregon for the Oregonians"—while in Boulder they discussed limiting growth, and in numerous cities they began recycling programs. After activists rallied in San Francisco, the board of supervisors killed plans for a massive U.S. Steel office and hotel building. "Developers have been just too darn greedy in the past," declared a supervisor. "People across the country feel they've got to do something to stop this promiscuous growth."

The movement reached the state level. Ecologists saved wetlands from development in New Jersey and they blocked construction of the Everglades jetport in Florida. "We are tightening up our restrictions for commercial development," stated Florida's governor. "We want to make sure that we aren't simply attempting to grow for growth's sake." The governor of West Virginia canceled permits for strip mines and his counterpart in Delaware signed a law restricting potentially polluting industries from the coast. In the wide open spaces, locals joined ecologists and restricted open-pit mining in Montana and Arizona, and forced smelters to meet pollution standards in Texas and Washington. The movement even reached into the desert. In the California Mojave, citizens in Barstow blocked construction of a coal power plant, one official commenting, "We're not against industry. We just don't want that coal fouling our air." The ecology movement swelled, challenging business so often that in 1971 *Forbes* concluded, "Today it is nearly impossible to build an electric-power plant, a jet airport, an open-pit mine or a resort community without strong protests. . . . The intent is clear: A pleasant environment is at least as important as industrial expansion. Maybe more so."

These activists aimed to improve "quality of life," an idea that affected and stimulated many more citizens. Margaret Person and many others were older, "retired," when they became activists. Gail Cincotta was mother of six. Jeanine Stump was the wife of a truck driver and had four children. As a journalist noted, "Women who once apologized, 'I'm just a housewife,' have . . . become involved in their neighborhoods, and now are halting highways, sitting on city school boards, negotiating with bank presidents, and engineering the reconstruction of town squares." The people were gaining more control over their lives, bringing about what they considered was a more humane society, a New America.[26]

By 1972, then, the movement had become a kaleidoscope of activism—disconnected, unfocused, often local—making it difficult for journalists to examine and summarize for the national media. Instead, the press declared the sixties upheaval over, dead: RIP. Yet social activism did not die, it shifted again, confronting some of the old and many more new issues. "I keep hearing that everything's dead and there's no big cause since civil rights and the Vietnam War. But that's a myth," stated Gail Cincotta. "There's a neighborhood movement that started in the sixties. It's not as dramatic with everybody out in the streets, but it's steadily gaining strength in every city and state."

Some observers realized Cincotta was right, and in the mid-1970s they began revising the "sixties is dead" myth by publishing books and articles. "A movement for social reform in America exists today without a leader and without a party," declared Stephen Schlesinger in his book *The New Reformers.* Journalist Steward Dill McBride agreed, noting that "a crazy-quilt alliance of 'longhairs' and 'hardhats,' black and white, young and old" was confronting the establishment.[27] Activists had created a new localism that was "sweeping neighborhoods across the United States. It is a groundswell movement of citizens calling for the return of political and economic power to the local level. . . . Neighborhoods have become the 'politics of the '70s.' "

There were other politics of the 1970s, of course, and the beginning of the end of the second wave was the 1972 election.

For many activists, that election began a day after the Chicago convention in 1968. After that debacle, party reformers, or "New Democrats," many of whom had participated in the campaigns of Eugene McCarthy and Bobby Kennedy, demanded changes in delegate selection for the next convention with the aim of enlarging youth, minority, and woman representation. Many party rules had not been revised since the last century, meaning that in some states Democrats did not hold primary elections, in two southern states the governor picked all delegates, and in ten states there were no written rules. For the most part, then, Democratic (and Republican) delegates made up a White Male Club.

New Democrats responded to the demand for more representation by advocating a commission. Party regulars agreed and named George McGovern the chairman; he appointed a staff of young activists. Eli Segal was a recent law school graduate who had volunteered for McCarthy in 1968, and so had Ken Bode, who eventually joined Robert Nelson as aides to Senator McGovern. These men saw the commission as a crusade against the Democratic establishment, the force that for years had cut deals behind closed doors, had refused black representation at Atlantic City, had led the nation into a disastrous war, and had clubbed activists in the streets of Chicago. The commission held months of hearings and interviewed 500 witnesses, who were mostly women, minorities, and local party organizers. The staff then wrote a report advocating a more open process and more primaries, basically calling for more participatory democracy. The result was a "quiet revolution," a scholar has claimed, the most significant change in delegate selection in American history.

During the quiet revolution the movement began converting the Democratic party, and that became obvious during the primaries for the election of 1970. Activists volunteered for and supported New Democrat candidates who surprised party regulars by winning primaries for governor in California, Michigan, Ohio, Pennsylvania, and Wisconsin. Other progressives won congressional primaries in Manhattan, Berkeley, Denver, and Newton-Cambridge. New Democrats also began influencing party caucuses. In Oklahoma City, for example, an antiwar chairman packed his convention with activists and they wrote a platform favoring abortion, reduced penalties for marijuana, and a date to quit Vietnam. Activists in Washington did the same, and they upped the ante by calling for nationalization of the railroads and a moratorium on building missiles, while New Democrats in Michigan added unconditional amnesty for draft evaders to the state platform, even reparations for North Vietnam.

Two months after the elections, in January 1971, George McGovern announced his candidacy for the Democratic nomination. Aware of the painful alienation in the nation, he pledged to "seek a way out of the wilderness," to "call America home to those principles that gave us birth." The announcement was made a year before the usual declaration time, and eventually he had rivals. New York mayor John Lindsay looked appealing and held many movement views, but had trouble mounting a credible campaign, as did Congresswoman Shirley Chisholm, for it was doubtful then that a majority of the nation would vote for a black woman who was outspoken enough to tell congressmen in the Black Caucus: "I'm the only one among you who has the balls to run for President." Governor George Wallace declared that this time he would run as a Democrat, and began his attempt to capture the conservative wing of the party. Senator Hubert Humphrey had support from establishment Democrats and he eventually announced his intentions by declaring, "Had I been elected in 1968, we would now be out of that war." But the most important contender was Senator Edmund Muskie of Maine, who was the vice presidential candidate in 1968. Like McGovern, Muskie was eager to end the war, and was known for honesty. Unlike McGovern, Muskie was a moderate who could work with all factions within the party. Thus, by early 1972, the Maine senator had lined up a remarkable number of endorsements, and a Harris opinion poll found that he was as popular as President Nixon, while McGovern ranked last in the possible pack of contenders. Muskie's campaign was based on trust. "Trusty Muskie" was his campaign slogan, and he would slay "Tricky Dick," but during the next months there was little mention of specific proposals, leaving voters to say, "I trust Muskie, but to do what?"

Citizens knew where McGovern stood on the issues, and the two most important remained race and war, now thinly disguised in terms such as busing and quotas, and peace with honor. He gave more speeches at universities than any other candidate, drawing large crowds, seeking the youth vote that had been enlarged because the Twenty-sixth Amendment lowered the voting age to 18 for the upcoming national election. He supported busing to bring about school integration as "a way to reverse a hundred years of segregation." He told minorities that he would set up guidelines to hire them to governmental posts in reasonable relationship to their presence in the population. He was generally liberal on abortion, and he had made his reputation as the most outspoken critic of the war. This World War II bomber pilot was blunt, calling Vietnam "a moral and political disaster—a terrible cancer eating away the soul of the nation." McGovern had spoken at the Moratorium in 1969, and the next year in the Senate he introduced an "End the War" resolution that would have put a termination date on American participation. He confronted his colleagues: "Every senator in this Chamber is partly responsible for sending fifty thousand young Americans to an early grave. This Chamber reeks of blood." The resolution was defeated, but McGovern was not; he continued attacking the war, eventually stating that if he was elected then he would bring the soldiers home and end the war "in ninety days or less."

Such proclamations made McGovern popular with the movement. "The themes of the McGovern campaign had been accepted as given— the themes of the Movement," wrote journalist Theodore White, "the first objective was to seize control of the Movement, of its manpower and womanpower now adrift." McGovern went to work, assembling a campaign staff directed by former spokesman for Robert Kennedy Frank Mankiewicz and managed by young Denver attorney Gary Hart, who also had been a volunteer for RFK. They were advised by historian Richard Wade and civil rights activist and lawyer Morris Dees, while others eventually joined the cause. Eugene Pokorny, a McCarthy volunteer in 1968, directed the campaigns in Wisconsin and Massachusetts. Actors Shirley MacLaine and Warren Beatty raised funds by putting on benefit concerts with musicians such as James Taylor, Carole King, Simon and Garfunkel, Dionne Warwick, and Peter, Paul and Mary. The campaign was in place long before the New Hampshire primary, and students from universities throughout the Northeast volunteered in what White labeled a "guerrilla army on the move. . . . The army had an idea that could snare souls. The idea was that politics could bring peace and establish justice."

The New Hampshire campaign of 1972 never captured the imagination of the nation like Eugene McCarthy's crusade four years earlier—no second time around ever does. Plus, alienation was running at record levels; hope and passion were withering as cynicism became the national malaise. But volunteers and students manned the phone banks, knocked on doors, and got out the vote. Pollsters had predicted that Muskie would win 60 percent of the vote in his neighboring state, but when he did not obtain a majority and beat the South Dakotan by only eight points, pundits declared a psychological victory for McGovern. On to Wisconsin, where McGovern won easily, and the same in Massachusetts, tossing Muskie out of the race and demonstrating that there was no center of the Democratic party. The primaries revealed, wrote gonzo journalist Hunter S. Thompson, that the "race would boil down to a quick civil war, a running death-battle between the Old Guard on the Right and a gang of Young Strangers on the Left." Humphrey represented the bulls, and he won in Ohio and gained momentum for the big prize, California. Humphrey called in the IOUs, while 10,000 McGovern volunteers walked precincts and rang doorbells. McGovern barely won, and then he was victorious in New York and New Jersey, making him the man to beat, attracting what Thompson called a "mind-bending coalition: a weird mix of peace freaks and hardhats, farmers and film stars, along with urban blacks, rural Chicanos, the 'youth vote.' " The senator later noted the reason for his success was his "highly motivated *grassroots army.*"[28]

Grassroots versus the Establishment was a theme of the 1972 campaign, and Nixon adopted the latter role, acting presidential, being above politics, and remaining in the headlines as the world statesman. Earlier, the president had sent Henry Kissinger to Paris to negotiate peace, but the North Vietnamese were not interested, stalling for the Americans to withdraw so they could launch a conventional attack in South Vietnam. To pressure Hanoi, the administration held secret talks with China and the Soviet Union, and in February the president stunned the world by flying to Beijing. A man who had made his career lashing out against Communism and "Red China," Nixon now grinned and gingerly shook the hand of Chairman Mao Tse-tung. The meeting itself was significant since the United States did not have diplomatic relations with the People's Republic, and soon trade began flowing while discussions began on eventual recognition. Yet little else was achieved. The Chinese and Americans agreed to relax tension in Asia, but then ignored the issue of Vietnam. "We have been here a week," the president proclaimed upon departure. "This was the week that changed the world."

Not to the North Vietnamese. A month later they launched a conventional attack, their first major assault since Tet. During the Easter Offensive they stormed into South Vietnam in another test of Vietnamization. Only 60,000 U.S. troops remained in that country, and they reported a rout, ARVN in disarray. Within a few weeks the enemy threatened the survival of the Saigon regime. Nixon responded by ordering another massive escalation in the air war, and B-52s pulverized enemy positions and North Vietnam. The president ordered Kissinger to shock the North Vietnamese: "You tell those sons of bitches that the President is a madman and you don't know how to deal with him. Once re-elected I'll be a mad bomber." Nixon raised the stakes. He ordered the armed forces to mine Haiphong harbor and bomb rail lines from China, thereby blocking trade into Hanoi. "It was one of the finest hours in the Nixon presidency," wrote Kissinger, and the president told his daughter that if his plan did not work then "the United States would cease to be a respected great power." Nixon and Kissinger then went to Moscow. They negotiated strategic arms and continued their attempts at easing tensions with the big powers, while proposing that the Soviets pressure North Vietnam to stop fighting in the south.[29]

Activists commenced scattered protests, resulting in over 2000 arrests that included the presidents of Amherst and Smith colleges; by spring 1972 the peace movement had become so mainstream that establishment Democrats fired the main shots at Nixon's escalation of the war. "The president is an international lawbreaker," declared New York Congressman Ed Koch, while Iowa Senator Harold Hughes called the episode a tragedy and Senator Edward Kennedy labeled it ominous folly. Presidential contenders weighed in, Senator Muskie warning that Nixon was risking a "confrontation with the Soviet Union and with China and is jeopardizing the major security interest of the United States." Humphrey declared the action "filled with unpredictable danger," and McGovern was more harsh: "This new escalation is reckless, unnecessary, and unworkable, a flirtation with World War III."

George Wallace had other views, of course, but while he was stressing his conservative stance an assassin critically wounded the candidate, gunning him down and his campaign. Wallace's misfortune was Nixon's fortune, for now the president would face only one adversary in the election. There would be no third party battle for the South and for the hearts and minds of conservatives. Even before the Democrats assembled for their convention, the election was shaping up as a fight between the status quo and the New America.

McGovern's grassroots army arrived at the convention in July and began working on the Democratic platform. "There won't be any riots in Miami," stated observer Ben Wattenberg, "because the people who rioted in Chicago are on the Platform Committee." Indeed. State parties had adopted the new rules and had elected delegates, and those who attended the convention were not the same old group of white males from unions, universities, and city machines. Instead, what appeared were the New Democrats. Professionals, teachers, and housewives made up half of the delegation; 80 percent had never attended a convention. There were students from the East, farmers from the Midwest, Native Americans from the Great Plains, Chicanos from the Southwest, African Americans from the Deep South, and females from everywhere who now called themselves "Ms." Fannie Lou Hamer represented Mississippi, and gave her support to vice presidential hopeful Frances "Sissy" Farenthold of Texas, while Jesse Jackson represented Illinois, instead of Mayor Richard Daley. New York, which had more union members than any other state, had only three labor men in its delegation while it included nine associated with the Gay Liberation Front. Also from the Empire State were Congresswoman Bella Abzug, *Ms.* editor Gloria Steinem, and Betty Friedan. Even more striking was the group from California, which included young men with long hair, women with short hair, and numerous Asians, Hispanics, and African Americans. In a state where minorities made up less than 30 percent, they made up almost 40 percent of a delegation led by Shirley MacLaine and two young blacks, Willie Brown and Yvonne Braithwaite. Compared with 1968, the ratio of female delegates at the 1972 convention tripled to almost 40 percent, blacks tripled to 15, and those under the age of 30 soared from 2 to over 20 percent. "Where was the bourbon and broads of yesteryear?" asked Norman Mailer. "Yes, every sense of power in the Democratic party had shifted."

After a bitter fight with the Humphrey forces over delegate selection, McGovern won the nomination: The movement captured the Democratic party. Union leaders, urban bosses, white ethnics, and many moderate blacks resented the new party. One black union man stated that Jesse Jackson "couldn't lead a vampire to a blood bank." AFL-CIO boss George Meany labeled the delegates "hippies, women liberationists, gays, kooks, and draft dodgers," and columnist Mike Royko wrote, "Anybody who would reform Chicago's Democratic party by dropping the white ethnic would probably begin a diet by shooting himself in the stomach." Soon, opinion polls noted an unprecedented defection of mainline Democrats to President Nixon.

The Republican convention next month was a stark contrast. Clearly, there were two Americas: Left versus Right. Nixon championed those who were satisfied with the status quo. John Wayne appeared in Miami, as did Jimmy Stewart, Pat Boone, and Frank Sinatra, and "black power" was represented by Sammy Davis, Jr., who hugged the president after singing "Dixie." The Republican delegates were professional politicians—congressmen, senators, governors; over 80 percent had been officeholders. Most were older white folks from the suburbs and country clubs. Journalist White counted just three beards in the entire group, no longhairs, and as for the California delegation, they "came from paintings by Norman Rockwell—stately, big-bosomed clubwomen; silver-haired men with pince-nez eyeglasses . . . and the young men all looking as if they had showered and come in fresh, with neckties, from a workout with the track team." There was little to discuss at the convention since no one seriously ran against the president. Nixon stood on stage with his arms making a V for victory while hundreds of Young Voters for the President screamed on cue, "Four More Years! Four More Years!"

But it was not that easy, for activists appeared to protest Four More Years. "Welcome to Flamingo Park," declared a flyer, "the people's liberated zone of revolutionary living, organizing and nonviolent direct action. Here we shall work to expose, confront and defeat the oppressive Nixon Administration." Over 3000 eventually camped in the five-acre park, sat in shade, smoked dope, and listened to music. They set up tents along "Ho Chi Minh Trail." The Free Gays, Jesus Freaks, Miami Women's Coalition, the People's Pot Park, SDS, Yippies, and Zippies: "Put the Zip back into Yip!" Zippies declared Dishonor Amerika Day, THE SECOND COMING: "Jesus in a Zippie T-shirt will descend and lead a march to Convention Hall bearing a cross with Billy Graham on it." At the hall Zippies promised a "piss-in," a flag-burning, a Free Marijuana rally with a twenty-foot joint, and an Om-out where they would serve Jell-O. Some performed guerrilla theater. Freaky women in Vietnamese costumes held disemboweled dolls and moaned funeral chants. Young men held a "puke-in," vomiting because "Nixon makes us sick." Back at the park, a fundamentalist preacher chanted "Christ is coming" as Jesus Freaks tried to convince militants to join the Christian army. A young woman, topless, climbed a lightpole and a few others strolled nude, arm in arm, under palm trees. Some 1200 Vietnam Veterans Against the War arrived and set up camp, complete with guarded perimeter. The Miami Women's Coalition organized WARS, Women's Anti-Rape Squad, and patrolled the park to prevent harassment. They declared, "A fresh wind is blowing against the empire."

The empire stood firm, again, as bands of demonstrators took to the streets and attempted to disrupt the convention and delay the president's acceptance speech. Some militants tried to prevent delegates from assembling by blocking traffic. A few slashed tires and hurled rocks, others laid down in front of cars or pounded on limousines screaming, "War criminals!" That behavior prompted pacifists to condemn the militants, and heated arguments ensued. Police counterattacked. Officials fired pepper gas, a stinging irritant that immobilized, and they arrested 900 weeping militants.

The sixties were smoldering. Chicago '68 could not be repeated—once was enough—and likewise there would be only one March on the Pentagon, one Woodstock, one time that the sixties generation would properly mix the political and cultural ingredients into a historical Happening. Militants had proclaimed that 10,000 would come to Miami, but only a third of that appeared. Many activists were working for McGovern, others feared violence, some were wondering, "What's the point?" With the exception of the Vietnam veterans, activists were disorganized, "stoned street crazies and screaming teenyboppers," wrote Hunter Thompson, "whose only accomplishment was to embarrass the whole tradition of public protest." Former Yippies Abbie Hoffman and Jerry Rubin were reporters for movement magazines; the younger Zippies said that older Yippies were over thirty, retired, irrelevant. Who was relevant anymore? "Failure to create chaos at Convention," declared *U.S. News*, "showed the waning strength of antiwar protest."

Furthermore, the establishment had learned from the sixties. The police chief gave the kids a permit to camp, supplied tents and medical supplies, and ordered his officers to treat demonstrators humanely. Officials surrounded the convention hall with a barricade of buses, bumper to bumper, and when violence erupted they effectively used massive quantities of pepper gas. The Republicans relocated their convention from San Diego, a pleasant climate within thumbing distance of the hoards in the Bay Area, to Miami, as far away from activist universities as one could get and insufferably hot in August. And the Nixon administration attempted to immobilize the only group that might receive press attention and public support, the Vietnam Veterans Against the War. Before the convention the Justice Department subpoenaed two dozen VVAW coordinators, charging "conspiracy to cause disorder," keeping those citizens occupied by a grand jury 500 miles from Miami.

Nevertheless, on the day of the nomination the VVAW held an extraordinary demonstration. "It is our last patrol together," wrote ex-marine Ron Kovic. "It is war and we are soldiers again, as tight as we have ever been, a whole lost generation of dope-smoking kids in worn jungle boots coming from all over the country to tell Nixon a thing or two. We know we are fighting the real enemies this time—the ones who have made profit off our very lives." Twelve hundred of them slowly marched toward the delegate's hotel, the Fontainebleau. They marched in silence, using hand signals, some in wheelchairs or on crutches, most dressed in battle fatigues, helmets, boots, some carrying plastic rifles, many wearing peace symbols. The Republican street crowd said nothing—no jeers, nothing. They arrived at the hotel, came to parade rest, maintained silence as if saying: Witness us, America, we are your crippled sons. Five hundred armed policemen stood between them and the hotel. Nobody moved. Hunter Thompson noted, "I have been covering anti-war demonstrations with depressing regularity since the winter of 1964 and I have never seen cops so intimidated." Attacking silent veterans was out of the question for police, not standard operating procedure. Eventually, a platoon leader picked up a bullhorn and said: "We want to come inside."

Were the vets going to try to take over the Republican convention hotel? There was a eerie silence, restless movement in police lines. The vets held their ground. Congressman Pete McCloskey, an antiwar Republican, came out of the hotel and rushed through police lines to the vets. No, they told him, they came in peace—no violence. But they did want to make some speeches, which they did. McCloskey agreed to get passes for a few vets to attend Nixon's acceptance speech.

That evening, Kovic, Robert Muller, and Bill Wieman, all in wheelchairs, were sitting in the center aisle, far back from the podium. Nixon appeared to roars of "Four More Years," and the vets raised a sign: Stop the War. A man quickly tore it down, yelling, "You lousy commie sonofabitch." As the crowd chanted for the president, the vets screamed as loud as they could, "Stop the bombing, stop the war!" Guards quickly grabbed their chairs and pulled them toward the door. A man rushed up to Kovic, spit in his face, and screamed, "Traitor!"

Traitor or patriot? Those terms had been defined so easily years before, and America had become more confusing ever since. "I gave three-quarters of my body for America," Kovic declared to a newsman, "And what do I get? Spit in the face! . . . What more was there left to do but go home? I sat in my chair still shaking and began to cry." [30]

As the last patrol went home, Richard Nixon headed for the campaign trail. The result of the election was never in doubt. Opinion polls demonstrated that voters usually supported Nixon two to one over McGovern. The only hope for the Democrat was to convince citizens that Nixon could not be trusted, and McGovern's slim chance appeared after a bizarre incident: the break-in of the Democratic National Headquarters at the Watergate Hotel. In June, a security guard had caught five men apparently burglarizing the Democrats' offices. Two of them had notebooks with telephone numbers traced to the White House and to E. Howard Hunt, who worked for the Committee to Re-elect the President, CREEP. Nixon denied knowledge, claiming that the affair was some sort of political prank conducted by zealots, privately stating at the White House, "I don't think you're going to see a great, great uproar in this country about the Republican committee trying to bug the Democratic headquarters." McGovern pounded away that autumn, mentioning Watergate in every speech, but most citizens felt the denial was plausible. Two-thirds thought the matter was "just politics," and 80 percent saw no reason to change their support to McGovern. After all, citizens thought, Nixon was going to win. Why would the President of the United States know anything about a botched break-in at Watergate?

The McGovern campaign never could muster the support necessary to lead the New Democrats to the White House. Although the senator won his nomination with support of the left, he had to move back toward the political center to win the election, and his attempt was not credible. He irritated many feminists when he would not support an abortion plank in the Democratic platform, stating that the issue should be left to the states. Some peace activists were turned off when he stated that America needed "military capability—in Thailand and on the seas," for that sounded too much like another tired plea for defending Southeast Asia. Furthermore, and after numerous national politicians had turned down the offer to run as his running mate, McGovern chose moderate Senator Thomas Eagleton of Missouri. Eagleton had been hospitalized three times for depression, but failed to inform McGovern, and when the medical problem was revealed, the presidential nominee declared his support "1000 percent" for his running mate. Yet opinion polls revealed Eagleton as a liability, and 1000 suddenly became 0. McGovern changed his mind, and chose a relative of the Kennedy family, former Peace Corps director Sargent Shriver. The reversal raised questions about McGovern's character, and estranged supporters who already were alienated from the establishment now saw the antiwar candidate as an opportunist, just another politician.

The "Eagleton affair destroyed any chance I had of being elected President in 1972," McGovern later wrote, but he never had a chance. McGovern was the most liberal candidate ever nominated by a major party. His views reflected the values and ideas of the movement, and since the movement always was a minority of citizens, McGovern was doomed. His army at the convention paraded to the microphone and into American living rooms, shocking the mainstream. Women demanded liberation, equality, and abortion. Gays advocated the end of all discrimination against homosexuals, even the right to marry. The candidate stated that he favored "decriminalizing the use of marijuana," which rallied some youth who hoped he said legalization, while just mentioning drugs enraged most parents. If elected, he said, he would consider amnesty for draft resisters, which was popular with a few hundred thousand dissidents but angered millions of veterans. He would slash defense spending 40 percent, and to reform welfare he would give every man, women, and child $1000 annually, a Demogrant. He advocated major increases in taxes on corporations and on inheritance. He supported busing at a time when about 60 percent of white citizens opposed it and when a Detroit suburb voted against it fourteen to one. He attacked American foreign policy as imperialistic, supporting any "dictators, dope-runners and gangsters," and on the war he was scathing: "The Nixon bombing policy on Indochina is the most barbaric action that any country has committed since Hitler's effort to exterminate Jews in Germany." While such declarations heartened many activists, they also irritated millions who considered such words unpatriotic, who did not want their nation compared to Nazi Germany, and who did not want to take the blame for Vietnam.

Aware of the mood of their constituents, many Democrats refused to endorse their party's ticket. As Governor Jimmy Carter explained, McGovern's views were "completely unacceptable to the majority of the voters."

The Republicans knew that and launched their attack. McGovern was the "candidate of the 3 A's: acid, abortion, and amnesty." His grassroots army was "a small group of radicals and extremists" who would "abandon prisoners of war and friends in Saigon . . . cripple our Army, Navy and Air Force," resulting in the United States "begging, crawling to the negotiation table." The Republican platform ran against the 1960s, "a nightmarish time in which the torch of free America was virtually snuffed out in a storm of violence and protest." Nixon declared that he supported law and order, neighborhood schools, prayer in school, and that he opposed abortion. He vigorously campaigned for the white backlash vote, urging Congress to defeat an enforcement provision for the Fair Housing Act and an extension to the Voting Rights Act. The Republican was against hiring minorities to government in relation to their numbers in society, labeling that "quotas," and his southern strategy of opposing busing, slowing school integration, was not only working in the South but gaining heavy support in the suburbs. His administration pleaded before the Supreme Court to postpone the desegregation of schools in Mississippi. "Nixon is doing what I advocated," stated George Wallace, "and he said I was unfit to be President."

Nixon emphasized his "New American Revolution." Since almost everyone was talking some sort of revolution then, the president declared that his aim was to return "power to the people." He would do that by establishing revenue sharing with states, reorganizing the federal government, and reforming welfare. He also said that he would bring about detente with the USSR and China and would end the war, and announced another troop withdrawal from Vietnam. Although candidate Nixon in 1968 had told voters that he would win peace with honor, and that no one should vote a second time for a president who had not ended the war, the message was different in 1972. Now, he was the best hope of peace, and voters agreed. Opinion polls found that citizens, two to one, felt that Nixon could do a better job ending the war than McGovern. Then, twelve days before the election, Henry Kissinger returned from Paris and proclaimed, "Peace is at hand," a statement that made headlines around the world. Peace was not at hand, of course; the statement was a campaign stunt. Neither South nor North Vietnam agreed to U.S. terms, and it would take months of pressure on Saigon and the most intensive bombing of Hanoi of the entire war, during Christmas, to force all parties to sign the Paris Peace Accords—an agreement which all quickly violated.[31] Nevertheless, Kissinger's pronouncement was what Americans had wanted to hear for years. And so again, Americans voted for hope.

Nixon won in a landslide. Liberal enclaves supported McGovern. The antiwar candidate did well on campuses, winning majorities in university towns such as Ann Arbor, Berkeley, Madison, Iowa City, and he captured almost 90 percent of the minority vote. Nixon won everything else. Females voted overwhelmingly for him, for women's liberation was still a movement, not a political reality at the ballot box. The Republican won two-thirds of the white male vote, 70 percent of southerners, and even a majority of the blue-collar and union vote. The white voter agreed with Nixon's views on civil rights, which became a dream deferred. Nixon won 49 states, but he had no coattails; the Republicans were not successful in Congress. They picked up only a dozen seats in the House, where they remained a distant minority, and the same was true in the Senate, where they lost two seats. Nixon would spend the remainder of his presidency battling moderate and liberal Democrats. They would cut off all funds for the war and would begin investigations of the administration; eventually, the Senate Judicial Committee would cripple the president over Watergate.

The election also demonstrated alienation. In 1960 almost 64 percent of the electorate voted, a figure that remained over 60 in 1968, but by 1972 only 55 percent took the time to vote, a disturbing trend that would continue for the next four national elections. Youth did not vote in large numbers; many potential McGovern supporters were turned off by politics, joking, "Don't Change Dicks in the Middle of a Screw: Vote Dick Nixon in '72." Furthermore, millions of citizens went to the polls to vote for representatives, senators, and governors, but did not cast a ballot for either presidential nominee. The election, then, was not so much a mandate for Richard Nixon as it was a defeat for George McGovern, the standard bearer of the movement toward a New America.

To some activists, the electoral rejection of the movement was depressing, especially to those who for years had been on the picket line. As early as autumn 1970 radicals Greg Calvert and Carol Neiman grumbled that the new left had "failed miserably" to "turn America-the-Obscene into America-the-Beautiful," and looking back later, Bo Burlingham felt that the few accomplishments seemed pedestrian: "To those of us who rode the historical wave of the '60s, there is a sense perhaps of the mundane in starting co-ops when our purpose had been to stop a war, or electing a mayor when we had set out to unseat a President, or lowering utility rates when we had planned to transform America." Naturally, those who had fought so long wondered, questioned, and often felt disappointed. "Social movements ultimately fail, at least in minds of many committed participants," wrote historian Clayborn Carson. "As radicals and revolutionaries have discovered throughout history, even the most successful movements generate aspirations that cannot be fulfilled."[32]

Yet the nomination of a man with McGovern's views was in itself a success. In just twelve years since four black students ordered a cup of coffee in Greensboro a major political party had been transformed. Naturally, after the defeat the party moved back toward the center of the body politic, but at the same time New Democrats won elections. Voters that year sent Andrew Young of Georgia and Barbara Jordan of Texas to the House of Representatives, and by mid-decade some 200 activists had been elected as state, city, or local officials. Eventually, many of them would become prominent, such as John Lewis and Julian Bond in Georgia, Sam Brown and Gary Hart in Colorado, Willie Brown and Tom Hayden in California, Jim Hightower in Texas, Bob Kerrey in Nebraska, John Kerry in Massachusetts, Toby Moffett in Connecticut, and Barbara Mikulski in Maryland, along with many others such as mayors Paul Soglin of Madison and Jeff Friedman of Austin, council members Marion Berry of Washington, D.C., and Loni Hancock of Berkeley, judges Justin Ravitz of Detroit and Jose Angel Gutierrez of Zavala County, Texas. Furthermore, delegate selection reforms meant that four years later an obscure southern governor would be able to drive around the Northeast, stopping at small towns, shaking hands and saying, "Trust me," and Jimmy Carter would win the nomination—and the White House. The activists had brought politics out of back rooms, and along the way they had demonstrated that there was little need for revolution—the Republic still was what Lincoln called the "last best hope," because it had the capacity to change.

That capacity was demonstrated in the early 1970s as activists won significant victories, as a New America began to emerge. Concerning the environment, Congress passed strict amendments to air and water quality laws, and more important, enacted the National Environmental Policy Act which required government agencies to file environmental impact statements for public projects and created the Environmental Protection Agency, destined to become the largest regulatory agency ever established by the U.S. government. By 1972 Congress had passed the Pesticide Control Act, banning DDT, and had proposed the Endangered Species Act. "The astonishing thing, two years into the Age of Ecology," *Newsweek* noted, "is how much is being done." The same was true concerning consumerism, noted *Business Week*. An "increasingly militant attitude among state and local consumerists" had resulted in 50 cities and half the states establishing consumer protection offices.

Women, too, obtained stunning victories in 1972. In March, the Equal Rights Amendment, first introduced in Congress almost 50 years earlier, was passed by the Senate overwhelmingly, 84 to 8, and sent out to the states for ratification. By the end of the year 22 states had ratified it, most pundits predicted victory, and numerous states were adopting their own ERAs. The federal government passed Title IX of the Higher Education Act which forbid discrimination in any public university program or activity, opening the door to women in all programs, including athletics, and another congressional act made it illegal for administrators to expel pregnant girls from public high schools. The Equal Employment Opportunity Act strengthened the enforcement powers of the EEOC, and the amendments to the 1963 Equal Pay Act prohibited sexual discrimination in federally supported programs and expanded the jurisdiction of the EEOC to include local government agencies and educational institutions. Representative Bella Abzug called 1972 a "watershed year" and Jo Freeman proclaimed a "bumper crop" of legislation, "considerably more than the sum total of all relevant legislation previously passed in the history of this country."

Also significant, feminist attorneys won notable cases at the Supreme Court. Beginning in 1971 the court began striking down numerous laws that discriminated against women in unemployment insurance, maternity leave, Social Security benefits, and dependency benefits for military personnel. Then, in January 1973, the court stunned the nation with the *Roe v. Wade* decision, ruling a Texas law unconstitutional that made abortion a crime except to save a pregnant woman's life. The court ruled the law discriminatory, and that the Constitution provided the right to privacy which encompassed a woman's decision to terminate a pregnancy. Soon afterward, the court struck down restrictions on places that could be used to perform abortions, giving rise to abortion clinics.

The 1970s became the decade of women's liberation. Compared with minorities, change was relatively quick, probably because females had more leverage with those in power—white men—and because it seemed the logical conclusion of the era. Ruth Rosen recalled: "Throughout the sixties we were trying to imagine how to live differently, how to change the world. And the women's movement took much from the civil rights movement, from the new left, from the antiwar movement—but we brought it home. We brought it into the kitchen. We brought it into the bedroom. We brought it into the most personal and intimate aspects of people's lives. It was hard to deny there. It was hard to ignore those issues."

And it was hard to ignore other activists who clamored for their vision of a New America. Gays succeeded in establishing homosexual rights ordinances in at least ten cities, including Minneapolis and Washington, and after years of demonstrating at meetings of the American Psychiatric Association, the organization agreed to no longer label homosexuality a disease. Physically disabled citizens organized, and Congress responded by passing a civil rights bill for them, the Rehabilitation Act of 1973, later mandating free, appropriate public education for all handicapped children in the least restrictive environment. Gray power was even more success-ful. Congress passed laws protecting private pension plans, began financing service programs for the elderly, and prohibited mandatory retirement before the age of 70, up from 65. California, Pennsylvania, New Jersey, Illinois, Montana, and other states exempted the elderly from state income taxes, mandated lower utility rates, passed generic drug laws or nursing home regulations, and experimented with home visits. By the mid-1970s, the *New York Times* noted that the "elderly have a better legislative record than almost any other group," and a New Jersey woman added, "Everybody has parents. When those legislators look at those old people, they all have guilt feelings. How can you say no to your mother?"

Nor could local politicians say no to the new crowds of citizens knocking on the gates of city hall; the backyard rebellion had renewed faith in populist, democratic action. Activists questioned development, city officials listened to zoning requests, and the federal government attacked redlining by passing the Home Mortgage Disclosure Act. Throughout the decade millions became involved in neighborhood organizations. Think Global, Act Local. Activists established several thousand block clubs just in New York City, and by the end of the decade there were 8000 community organizations in America. All the while, local organizers were taking control of their environment—from the Clamshell Alliance in New Hampshire to the Abalone Alliance in northern California, fighting nuclear power corporations from Seabrook to Diablo Canyon. While confronting the power elites of the community would have been suspect during cold war culture, the movement had legitimatized social activism, which became "normal behavior" not just for activists but for citizens. As Tom Hayden stated, "The radicalism of the 1960s has become the common sense of the 1970s."

In fact, activism became so normal that it was co-opted by conservative citizens. Neighborhood organizing touched on issues that had a more direct impact on most individuals and families than the struggle in the South, campus regulations, or a war in Southeast Asia. The majority of citizens did not have a son in uniform, a daughter marching for liberation, or a college student in revolt. But they did have an opinion about building public housing next door, or busing their children across town to a ghetto school for something called integration. George Wallace had touched this chord throughout the 1960s, and the white backlash expanded while supporting Nixon and strengthening the Republican party. Conservatives organized into block clubs aimed at maintaining their status quo and protecting their ethnic neighborhoods and white suburbs. In Boston, Catholic Irish and Italian citizens established Restore Our Alienated Rights, or ROAR, and conducted the ABC campaign: anti-abortion, antibusing, anti-Communism. In an ironic twist, the movement inspired popular participation that contributed to the rise of the New Right.[33]

Activism continued throughout the seventies on a local level and on a state level, as feminists marched for ratification of the ERA, but in 1973 an event clearly demonstrated that nationally the movement was in demise—Wounded Knee. In February, about 300 members of the American Indian Movement occupied the small village of Wounded Knee, South Dakota, the site where in 1890 the U.S. cavalry had massacred a few hundred Sioux in the last conquest of the Native American. The militants took 11 hostages, ransacked the trading post, and barricaded the church. One activist declared "a liberation struggle and the birth of a new nation." Journalists rushed to the scene, television crews arriving from New York, London, and Tokyo, and to the world AIM announced its demands: an investigation of the broken treaties made by the federal government; immediate improvement of conditions on reservations; and "sovereignty" over their own affairs, including the idea that Indian nations be considered independent. AIM had made such demands the previous November when members donned war paint and occupied the Washington office of the Bureau of Indian Affairs. That time they disrupted and vandalized the BIA; this time they were armed, ready for the eventual confrontation with the White Man. While they talked to reporters, they fired on federal marshals who attempted to approach. "We've got the whole Wounded Knee Valley," declared Russell Means, "and we definitely are going to hold it until death do us part."

The siege dragged on for weeks, and it degenerated into a feud that again revealed the division between radical and moderate activists. Militants Russell Means and Dennis Banks charged corruption on the Oglala Sioux reservation, and advocated the resignation of the tribal chairman, moderate Richard Wilson, whom they called a half-breed, an apple, a puppet of the BIA. Wilson refused, charging that AIM members were outsiders who were interfering in local tribal affairs. As friction intensified between Indians, negotiations with the government broke down, ultimatums were issued, and both sides commenced sporadic gunfire. In the seventh week, the militants shot at a helicopter, wounding a marshal, and officials responded with more gunfire before a cease-fire was declared. Eventually, authorities agreed to supply the militants with food and medicine, but that enraged Wilson, who rounded up a band of Oglala and tried to blockade the road and stop delivery. AIM members began to slip away from the reservation, including Dennis Banks, who went on a speaking tour, and Russell Means, arrested in Los Angeles. Wounded Knee lost meaning. "This is guerrilla theater," said one government official. After 70 days, *Newsweek* concluded, "Wounded Knee faded away last week, leaving a shattered and vandalized village, two Indians dead and one FBI agent paralyzed, and a pervasive inconclusiveness about what had been accomplished."[34]

Wounded Knee paralleled another event that symbolized the end of the sixties. The Nixon administration signed the Paris Peace Accords, which ended U.S. involvement in South Vietnam and withdrew remaining troops. Commentators naturally made comparisons between the 1890 massacre and the events in Vietnam—U.S. soldiers burning villages, abusing prisoners, slaughtering women and children, destroying an indigenous population. Officials also described the 1973 battle in South Dakota in military terms. Indians set up a demilitarized zone. The authorities established a command post and appointed cease-fire observers. The army drove troops around in armored personnel carriers while the air force flew Phantom jets low overhead on reconnaissance missions. Gunfire: Tracer shells screaming into the dark. As the Indians evacuated Wounded Knee and gave up to the authorities, the American prisoners of war were returning from Vietnam: The battle, and the war, were over.

Wounded Knee generated surprisingly little activism. Unlike the Alcatraz incident three years earlier, other tribe members did not rush to the scene. While Native Americans did win concessions from the federal government later, including much more self-determination on their reservations, it appeared in 1973 that Red Power was on the wane. So was student activism. Even though surveys demonstrated that college students ranked Native Americans with homosexuals as the groups most oppressed in the nation, there was no outpouring of support, no mass marches, no bus brigades heading for Wounded Knee.

There was no "end" to the movement: no announcement, no last call, no final bell. The sixties generation had graduated. Opinion polls demonstrated that younger students were more moderate, that they were less inclined to protest, and that discrimination was not as pressing to them as the environment, consumer protection, and women's equality. Students were turning away from sixties issues and toward self-fulfillment. "The students I've seen have been talking about more personal issues," said the president of Oberlin College. "There is a desire for greater quality of life."

The 1970s was becoming the Me Decade. A sociologist in the Bay Area noted that the "burned-out activist was almost as common in the early 1970s as the burned-out drug user," that many activists "have turned to quiet politics or withdrawn from politics altogether," and that their first priority had become "getting my head together." After a chaotic era, many re-evaluated, reconsidered their lives, and began their own pursuit of happiness. Thousands left cities, and went to the country to tend, literally, their own gardens, and the number of food co-ops soared. Others considered their physical selves and began jogging or more stimulating forms of exercise as the decade became synonymous with sexual liberation. Millions turned to personal reflection, seeking awareness and growth in the human potential movement, employing a smorgasbord of approaches: Arica training, astral projection, biofeedback, EST, Gestalt, Hare Krishna, humanistic psychology, massage, psycho-cybernetics, primal therapy, rolfing, Scientology, sensitivity training, Sufism, T'ai Chi, transcendental meditation, yoga, Zen. Sufi saying: "The one who know his self knows God." And many found their God, as the decade eventually became a time of religious awakening, when individuals en masse were "born again." Tom Hayden told a group of students, "There is a race going on between religion and revolution to capture people's minds, and I'm afraid we're losing to the occult."[35]

The decline of the movement was logical. The one focal point during the second wave—the war—was over in 1973, and that meant, said activist David Mixner, that the movement would "split into a thousand directions." The dissolution was assisted by a shaky economy that resulted from military demobilization and rising unemployment. Then, the OPEC oil embargo that year suddenly forced citizens into long lines at gas stations. Petroleum prices quickly doubled and eventually quadrupled, sending inflation rates into the stratosphere, dismissing workers from assembly to unemployment lines, and resulting in the worst economic downturn since the Great Depression. Production was disrupted, then stagnant, and citizens learned a new economic term: stagflation. In addition, the baby boomers, the massive generation that had flooded into colleges, was aging. The mean age of the nation was beginning to shift upward as the huge bubble of postwar boomers were graduating from college and record numbers of them were looking for jobs. Moreover, not only white men with degrees were starting careers, so were more minorities and females than at any time in American history. The nation slipped into recession, and many activists—exhausted after a decade of revolt, fearful of Nixon administration repression, frustrated by ideological feuds and organizational bickering—naturally turned away from public protest and toward personal interests and employment. Finally, the movement declined because activists had changed America. The sixties were over because, compared with 1960, there was much less to protest against. Activists had exposed hypocrisies, and they had won victories. Jack Weinberg looked back on the era and summarized, "We had taken what we had as far as we could go."[36]

The generation knew the movement and the sixties were over, and they sang about the demise, from "The Day the Music Died" to "Hotel California," to "The Last Waltz." Jackson Browne sang it best, telling the story of The Pretender, a young man who sold out his hippie values, his hope, and love:

I'm going to be a happy idiot
And struggle for the legal tender
Where the ads take aim and lay their claim
To the heart and the soul of the spender
And believe in whatever may lie
In those things that money can buy
Thought true love could have been a contender
Are you there?
Say a prayer for the pretender
Who started out so young and strong
Only to surrender.

Not everyone surrendered, of course, but sometime, early in the decade, the second wave washed upon the beach, and depending on the local tides and shifting sands, it began receding, leaving in its wake a nation that had experienced a sea change.

The Sea Change

But doth suffer a sea change
Into something rich and strange.
Shakespeare, *The Tempest*

What a long, strange trip it's been.
The Grateful Dead, "Truckin' "

"Someday we may look back on these times and laugh," wrote activist Jesse Kornbluth in 1968. "And then again, we may not." Whatever the case, the sixties generation certainly would not be able to forget those times, as Don Henley reminded them in the 1980s:

> Out on the road today, I saw a DEADHEAD
>   sticker on a Cadillac
> A little voice inside my head said, "Don't
>   look back. You can never look back."
> I thought I knew what love was
> What did I know?
> Those days are gone forever
> I should just let them go but—

But . . . how difficult for a baby boomer to let go; how difficult to summarize an era that changed the lives of so many Americans. Writing legacies of any recent era is fraught with peril. Consider this: How different would an evaluation of the movement be if this chapter had been written after the electoral triumphs of Jimmy Carter, or Ronald Reagan, or Bill Clinton? Or consider this: How differently do Americans evaluate the sixties? Conservatives generally loathe the instability of the era, the extreme behavior, the "permissiveness." They might agree with George

411

Will, who in the 1990s bashed away: "Has there ever been such politically barren radicalism as that of the Sixties? . . . The Sixties are dead. Not a moment too soon." Liberals often dislike the excesses and violence but feel that many changes eventually were beneficial to the nation, labeling it a progressive era. College students then and parents now most likely recall a period of excitement, challenges, hopes, disappointments, new values, and they might agree with Todd Gitlin: "Unraveling, rethinking, refusing to take for granted, thinking without limits—that calling was some of what I loved most in the spirit of the Sixties." Minorities might agree with Roger Wilkins, who when asked what he thought of the sixties simply answered, "Wonderful. It was the time that freed my people." Former hippies might chuckle along with Carl Gottlieb—"Anyone who remembers the sixties wasn't there"—or they might wink and say, "Far out."

Whatever one thinks of the sixties, the tumultuous era cracked the cold war culture and the nation experienced a sea change—a significant transformation in politics, society, culture, and foreign policy. The legacies of that era are worthy of another book, one that would detail recent trends in the nation's history, and thus be as controversial as the popular debate over whether the sixties were "good or bad" or the academic arguments over race, gender, and equality. Since that book is not possible here, this chapter will offer some generalizations about the legacies of the movement and the sixties.[1]

The political legacies of the sixties were apparent to anyone watching the 1976 Democratic National Convention in New York City. African American Congresswoman Barbara Jordan of Houston gave a stirring opening address, and black Mayor Tom Bradley of Los Angeles and Chicano Governor Jerry Apodaca of New Mexico were selected as two cochairs of the convention. Grace Olivarez, a Chicana feminist from New Mexico, presented the welfare reform plank to the platform. Cesar Chavez delivered the nominating speech for youthful California Governor Jerry Brown, and also from that state was delegate Tom Hayden. The eventual nominee, Governor Jimmy Carter of Georgia, represented the end of Jim Crow—in the November election both white and black southerners voted for the same candidate for the first time, delivering the presidency to the first man from the Deep South since before the Civil War.

That bicentennial year also revealed the impact of the new left, although those activists had been grumbling since the 1968 election that they had failed to bring about a "revolution," a New America. In 1962 they had set a course for the nation in *The Port Huron Statement*, which condemned racial bigotry, anti-Communist paranoia, popular complacency, corporate irresponsibility, and a remote control government and economy controlled by power elites. Those activists failed to interest the majority in long-term efforts to reduce poverty, reform welfare, or curtail the military-industrial complex. Nevertheless, they succeeded in destroying cold war political culture. Americans no longer live in a society that fears change, that suspects dissent. Activists buried McCarthyism. Demonstrations have become routine. Authorities are questioned, scrutinized, and that has changed official behavior. Government offices are open for public inspection, and activists altered police tactics. No longer are protesters beaten. Police are more educated and integrated; they are trained in crowd control, and they work at improving their relations with all in the community. Because of political activists, empowerment is taken for granted.

The new left also influenced the Democratic party. In 1896, William Jennings Bryan co-opted the Populist party platform of 1892 and thus transformed the Democrats into the party of reform. Eighty years later the Democrats did the same, embracing ideas expressed in *The Port Huron Statement*. Since then, they have become the party of civil rights, personal freedom, environmentalism, corporate responsibility, and a foreign policy emphasizing human rights. Moreover, political activists of the 1960s pried open democracy, which earlier reformers had done by extending the vote during the Jacksonian and progressive eras. This time, the movement wrestled political control from white males who for years had been negotiating alone behind closed doors. Activists revived the old progressive idea, You *can* fight city hall, and what activist Bo Burlingham noted in 1976 will remain pertinent for some years: "The convulsions of the last decade have produced something that has fundamentally altered the terms of American politics . . . change is both possible and necessary."

The movement inspired citizens of all types to express their democratic rights, to demand change, and that included conservatives. The backlash began as a response to blacks marching for their civil rights and to students making demands on campus. The struggle raised issues of integration and equal employment opportunity, and that contributed to white flight to the suburbs and charges of "reverse discrimination." Because of race issues, many white working men deserted the party that had boosted and represented them, the Democratic, and became conservatives who voted Republican. The counterculture and women's movement shocked other citizens and they joined the backlash: Phyllis Schlafly and her campaign Stop ERA; Anita Bryant and her crusade against sexual liberation; and a host of others who appeared as televangelists on the "700 Club," "Praise the Lord Club," and "The Old-Time Gospel Hour"—conservatives who reached the zenith of their popularity during the first administration of the "Reagan Revolution."

Ronald Reagan's triumph in 1980 did not overturn the 1960s; there was no return to 1950s America. While the president was very popular, the majority of citizens did not honor his call for traditional social roles or support his environmental views, cold war foreign policy, or attempts to dismantle civil rights legislation and defeat the Equal Rights Amendment.[2]

In fact, sixties political values marched on during the 1980s, and a central theme since has been inclusion. Every primary campaign and convention since has included delegates representing all Americans. Jimmy Carter named more women and minorities to his administration than any previous president, and by 1984 civil rights activist Jesse Jackson had formed his Rainbow Coalition and was running for the Democratic nomination for president. That year female Representative Geraldine Ferraro accepted the party's vice presidential nomination. Republican presidents during the 1980s named Hispanics, African Americans, and women to their Cabinets and to the Supreme Court, and a member of the sixties generation, Bill Clinton, pledged and then appointed a Cabinet that would "look more like America." The long era of white men exclusively controlling the body politic was over.

America became multicultural—a legacy of the struggle. For minorities, the sixties were a legal and political revolution. In just a few years minorities overturned centuries of legal inferiority and discrimination and obtained their rights guaranteed by the Constitution—an astounding achievement for any society. President Johnson proposed and Congress passed the Civil Rights Act of 1964, Voting Rights Act of 1965, Fair Housing Rights Act of 1968. With the support of the Supreme Court, the nation integrated public facilities, ended all voting restrictions, and accepted the idea that men and women charged with a crime should be judged by a jury of their peers. The 1960s killed the legal system called Jim Crow, and since then citizens have witnessed the unprecedented election of people of all races and the rise of minority political power, from mayors and police chiefs of predominately white cities, to governors, Congress, the Cabinet, and the Supreme Court. Furthermore, Black Power advocates stimulated a flourishing of cultural pride that spread to Hispanics, Native Americans, and other ethnic groups, all of whom have embraced empowerment. The federal government answered ethnic demands by ruling against discriminatory practices by businesses and agencies and by enforcing bilingual ballots and education. Ultimately, the struggle challenged Anglo America, and the result was a new definition of "American."

The struggle also diminished stereotyping and racism. That was apparent as early as 1975 when a Cabinet member, Earl Butz, made a racist joke and was forced to resign. Since then, a black leader who was hated by millions, mistrusted by presidents, harassed by the FBI, and assassinated—Martin Luther King, Jr.—has become a national icon. Congress established a federal holiday observing his birthday, placing him on equal footing with Washington, Jefferson, and Lincoln. Numerous opinion polls since have demonstrated that racism as measured by slurs and stereotypes has declined, especially among the young. Compare white racial convictions before and after the 1960s. Attitudes that had been held for centuries have changed considerably, have become more tolerant. Television programs and movies today depicting minorities would not have been possible without the struggle, and school textbooks are more inclusive than at any time in our history. Opinion polls in the 1990s demonstrated that whites and blacks, three to one, felt that race relations have improved since the 1960s and two-thirds felt that the nation has made significant progress. "There's room for improvement," stated black restaurant owner W. A. Mathis in 1994 about race relations in Mississippi, "but it's 99 percent better than it used to be."

Minorities won their constitutional rights—but not their equality. To address centuries of discrimination, President Johnson established social programs and boosted affirmative action. King advocated an "Economic Bill of Rights" that would result in reasonable education and employment: "It didn't cost the nation anything to guarantee the right to vote, or to guarantee access to public accommodations, but we are dealing with issues now that will cost the nation something." Although slavery and discrimination lasted for centuries, the voters supported those programs only for a few years. Then the economic slump of the 1970s, slashing employment and educational opportunities. The majority elected representatives who opposed special programs, who would not enforce the law, and who made careers publicizing the myth that hiring in the nation was based on federally mandated quotas. Affirmative action, equal employment, and educational loans did help some minorities attend college and obtain good jobs, but generally, those programs had little impact on the vast number of poor and uneducated, and even on the professions. In 1970 the percentage of African American attorneys was about 1 percent and by 1990 that had risen only to 3, from 2 to 3 in medicine, and from about 3 to not even 5 percent of college professors. During those 20 years, white flight to the suburbs accelerated, resulting in larger urban ghettos and resegregation of schools and residential areas; black unemployment remained double that of whites and the poverty rate three times higher. At least half of all black children grow up in poverty. Moreover, rates have soared for minority teenage births, drug addiction, and violent crime. A generation after the struggle there are as many young black men in prison as in college. The hopelessness behind those discouraging statistics exploded in 1992 in South Central Los Angeles. "The riots were a powerful reminder of the rage of the dispossessed," wrote *Newsweek* in "The Price of Neglect." And court files demonstrate that young minorities continue to receive stiffer penalties than whites for the same crime, prompting one to wonder when the nation's legal system will adhere to the colorblind words engraved on the Supreme Court Building: "Equal Justice Under Law."

In 1963 John Kennedy called on the nation to pass an equal rights law. He looked into the television camera and asked his mostly white audience, "Who among us would be content to have the color of his skin changed?" While there is more racial sensitivity than ever before in the nation, Kennedy's question remains relevant. Race still matters. There remains the "burden of double consciousness of being black in America," said Jesse Jackson. "You belong and yet you don't. . . . it's like we have almost to be superior just to be equal." The burden was personalized when the first African American to win Wimbledon, Arthur Ashe, was dying from AIDS received from a blood transfusion. The tennis champion, captain of the U.S. Davis Cup team, was by all standards a success story. Near death, he was asked if the disease was the heaviest burden of his life. Ashe thought, and said, No, "being black is the greatest burden I've had to bear. . . . No question about it. Having to live as a minority in America. Even now it continues to feel like an extra weight tied around me."[3]

The legacy of the struggle is clouded by the issue of race, but the impact made by student activism on the American university is more apparent. The sixties generation of students raised fundamental questions: Who controls the university? What rights do students have? What are appropriate courses for a college degree? Activism disrupted and then changed campus life, and at most colleges, gone are the days of *in loco parentis*, the barracks regimented dormitory life, the mandate that the administration rules and the students are ruled. What Mount Holyoke College activist Julie Van Camp stated in 1969 remains valid: "After Columbia a lot of administrators got a rude awakening, but they also realized that many of the student grievances were valid. So now when we want change we aren't going up against a stone wall any more. It's more like a mattress." Administrators became more flexible, students received more choice, and activism has been apparent whenever moral issues arise, as demonstrated by the anti-apartheid crusades of the 1980s.

Furthermore, students in the various power movements challenged an education based on male European civilization, provoking administrators to develop new classes on African American, Chicano, Native American, Jewish, and women's studies. That prompted a debate. "About the sixties it is now fashionable to say that although there were indeed excesses, many good things resulted," wrote professor Allan Bloom in 1987. "But, so far as universities are concerned, I know of nothing positive coming from that period; it was an unmitigated disaster for them."[4] Conservatives complain about a seemingly endless debate over what is and what is not politically correct. Others, however, note that the debate demonstrates that the movement brought about more sensitivity about language, and they note that activists forced changes in the educational experience that resulted in new scholarship on new topics for a multicultural America. Whatever the case, students of the sixties confronted the educational establishment, and the result was more personal freedom on campus, and a broader college curriculum, than at any time in history.

The legacies of the antiwar movement also are mired in debate. As North Vietnamese tanks rolled into Saigon in 1975, Americans sank into resentment, cynicism, the willed attempt to forget the long nightmare. Depression and denial. "The United States did not lose the war," proclaimed Hubert Humphrey in 1975. "The South Vietnamese did." Within a few years neo-conservatives were adopting a new approach. Actually, the war was, President Reagan declared in 1982, a "noble cause," and a few years later Richard Nixon reinterpreted his own policy: "On January 27, 1973, when Secretary of State William Rogers signed the Paris peace agreements, we had won the war in Vietnam. We had attained the one political goal for which we had fought the war: The South Vietnamese people would have the right to determine their own political future." He and many conservatives claimed that the United States lost the war because wimpy liberals forced his administration to end aid to South Vietnam. Our troops were stabbed in the back by cowardly congressmen, an idea popularized after every defeat, and one boosted this time by actors in numerous "Rambo" and "missing in action" movies. Although these actors and almost all of the young neo-conservatives avoided service in Vietnam, their ideas were warmly received by many who wanted someone to blame and by those who desired to accept another nationalistic myth instead of cruel fact. But in fact, by 1970 two-thirds of citizens wanted to withdraw from South Vietnam even if that nation fell to the North, a figure that increased to 80 percent as the last U.S. troops came home in 1973. Congress was only representing the views of the electorate. Furthermore, after the Cambodian invasion there were no Rambos in the U.S. Army in Vietnam. "By '70," recalled General Norman Schwartzkopf, "it was over. . . . Everyone wanted to get out." Indeed, antiwar activism inside the military was rampant. Americans at home did not want to continue the conflict, and G.I.s in the war zone had little desire to risk their lives. Eventually, even to the great silent majority, Vietnam was not a noble cause, but a lost one. "Nobody was sorry to hear the war was over," wrote Jerry Rubin. "And even more amazing, nobody asked, 'Who won?' Nobody gave a fuck."

But citizens did care about future foreign policy, for Vietnam taught two lessons: America is not invincible; in that sense, the Vietnamese killed the John Waynes. Second, the presidents and their wise men who direct foreign policy cannot be trusted. While Americans have supported the commander-in-chief in short military operations, they also have continually expressed skepticism about intervention in foreign lands. Citizens had cast aside the 1950s ideas of containment and the Domino Theory even before the demise of the Soviet Union. Despite Ronald Reagan's popularity, citizens two to one opposed his attempts to overthrow the Sandinista government in Nicaragua and his stationing of only 55 army advisers in El Salvador. George Bush understood the popular mood, promising that the *allied* intervention to liberate Kuwait was "not another Vietnam," and then withdrawing U.S. troops as soon as feasible, ending Desert Storm.

The antiwar movement alone did not end U.S. participation in Vietnam, but it did provoke citizens out of cold war allegiance, it generated and focused public opposition, and influenced presidents Johnson and Nixon. After all, LBJ quit his job and Nixon withdrew from Vietnam, actions incompatible with their personalities and inconceivable without the antiwar movement. Protesters also prompted citizens to raise questions about their nation's foreign policy, and so, the sixties killed the Imperial Presidency. The commander-in-chief since has not had the power to order U.S. troops to fight in foreign lands without citizens asking, Why? Is U.S. involvement necessary, is it in the national interest? True, the quick Desert Storm war was popular. It also had international support and was approved by Congress, itself a legacy of the movement. But one wonders how much activism and counterculture behavior would have resurfaced if the desert campaign would have forced the reintroduction of the draft and lasted three years, just a third of the length of Vietnam. In this sense then, the antiwar movement was victorious, for as historian George Herring stated: "The conventional wisdom in the military is that the United States won every battle but lost the war. It could be said of the antiwar movement that it lost every battle but *eventually* won the war—the war for America's minds and especially for its soul."

The movement also won a new armed forces. The resistance publicized a discriminatory Selective Service, and that along with an unpopular war, forced Nixon to abolish the system and establish a lottery, eventually leading to a volunteer armed forces that has freed young men from a staple of cold war culture—two years of military service. On campus, ROTC training is no longer mandatory. Because of G.I. resistance within the services, the brass tossed out numerous "Mickey Mouse regulations" and erected a more flexible and especially professional U.S. military. The Old Army became the New Army.[5]

The movement changed other American institutions. Many religious denominations today are more concerned about social ills, more active in their communities, and more integrated, while the number of alternative beliefs has expanded and is more accepted. Sixties activists raised old questions concerning business: What is more important, personal and community or private and corporate rights? What is legitimate corporate behavior? By challenging the establishment, the movement provoked a return to business social responsibility. Corporations since have increased their visibility in communities, and their advertisements often attempt to convince the public that they are environmentally aware and good citizens. Executives of old companies and some new businesses have become involved in progressive politics, from Ben and Jerry's to Working Assets. Finally, companies have changed their hiring patterns. Giving applicants an equal opportunity was a fundamental change in business practices, affecting many occupations, and according to one business journal, new positions for minorities and women were "clearly a response to social protest."

The establishment today includes more women than ever before—a legacy of the women's movement. At the beginning of the new wave of feminism, editor John Mack Carter of *Ladies' Home Journal* published a statement that raised eyebrows. "The point is: this is 1970. All peoples and both sexes are free to reexamine their roles. They are free to grow where they have been stunted, to move forward where they have been held back, to find dignity and self-fulfillment on their own terms." Radical as it seemed then, the statement now is taken for granted. Since then, a "woman's place" is *her* decision. On television, gone are the days of June Cleaver. Sitcoms since have portrayed numerous career females, from "Hill Street Blues" to "Murphy Brown." Heroines can be as complex as heroes. Feminists confronted sexism, provoked men to reconsider their views, and along the way brought about men's liberation. Men have the freedom to choose whether to be the provider, the decision-maker, to stay at home with the children, or to remain single. Roles shifted, as demonstrated by polls in the 1980s that a majority of citizens agreed that men and women should share housework and child-rearing equally. Feminists also changed the family. In the 1950s about 70 percent of families were traditional: a dad who was the breadwinner, and a mom who was the wife, mother, and homemaker. By 1990 only 15 percent of families fit that description. More women than ever before are working, and while the economy was significant in pushing them out of the house and into the office, contemporary opinion polls demonstrate that a majority of females want marriage, children, *and career.* Naturally, that strained the family. Divorce rates have doubled since 1970, but another view is that people no longer feel obligated to spend their entire lives in loveless marriages. "It now appears," pollster Louis Harris noted in 1987, "that the country is witnessing a radical and even revolutionary change in the basic role of women within the family unit." Sex roles have not ended, of course, but because of the movement, America has become a more androgynous society with more flexible views on those roles than at any time, and of any nation.

Activists also were successful in winning legal and political power. Although feminists did not succeed in getting the Equal Rights Amendment ratified, they utilized civil rights acts and decimated discriminatory state and federal laws. During the 1970s most states revised divorce laws, established the idea of common property and no-fault divorce, and accepted the notion that women were full and equal partners in marriage, not subordinate to the husband. Women also revolutionized American politics. While very few had been elected before 1970, by 1990 women had become mayors, governors, congresswomen, senators, and Supreme Court Justices. Two decades after the Strike for Equality, Texas elected a female governor and senator, California elected two such senators, and they had become prime ministers in nations such as Britain, Canada, Norway, Poland, and Turkey. By the time a female becomes president, few will be concerned about the question, "Would you vote for a woman?"

Feminists liberated occupations and the professions. Females sued states, universities, and corporations, resulting in major victories and job opportunities. Almost all states and hundreds of local governments legalized the concept of equal pay for comparable worth, and since then the amount females make compared with males, the earnings gap, has been slowly narrowing. While critics charge that there is a "glass ceiling," that most top positions still are held by white men, feminists nevertheless punched open the door of opportunity. Quotas keeping women out of colleges and professional schools have been abolished, and clearly, women—not minorities—were the main beneficiaries of affirmative action and equal opportunity; they are the ones competing against white males for appointments in colleges and professional schools and for jobs. Between 1970 and 1990 the percentage of female attorneys, professors, physicians, and business managers increased from approximately 5 percent to one-third. Supreme Court Justice Ruth Bader Ginsburg noted: "When I began teaching law in 1963, few women appeared on the roster of students, no more than four of five in a class of over one hundred. . . . Law school textbooks in that decade contained such handy advice as 'land, like women, was meant to be possessed.' . . . The changes we have witnessed since that time are considerable. Women are no longer locked out, they are not curiosities in any part of the profession."

The argument here is not that the women's movement brought about complete equality, a condition reserved for utopia. In fact, as feminist scholars note, liberation generally helped white, middle-class women, having much less impact on the poor, and it contributed to the feminization of poverty since new laws made it easier for husbands to abandon their families. The number of single mothers living in poverty has soared. Since liberation, women do more, often receiving the double burdens of home and work, while they listen to the media discuss the so-called burdens of being independent.[6]

Nevertheless, activists exposed private matters long suppressed—abortion, harassment, incest, lesbianism, rape, wife and child beating—forcing public discussion that resulted in a more open society. They challenged the traditional system of education and brought about more sensitivity in the classroom and in textbooks, and they inspired female writers who flooded the nation with new, exciting literature and scholarship. Moreover, in a relatively short time, feminists revolutionized the legal status of women while they changed relations between males and females that had existed for centuries, resulting in more freedom to define their own lives. Because of feminists, women have more opportunities, more equality, more freedom, than at any time. "It changed my life," Betty Friedan simply wrote. The women's movement resulted in changes so profound, and so accepted, that to the ire of many older activists, young females today often take their rights for granted and have to be reminded of their mothers' status. Women's liberation was the most successful social movement of the sixties—and of American history.

Feminists changed the meaning of "traditional values," and that also is the legacy of the counterculture. Since the first hippies walked down the streets of Haight-Ashbury, critics have castigated them, blaming them for everything from the decline of the American family, to the drug and venereal disease epidemics, even for AIDS. Sex, drugs, rock and roll. To most citizens since, the word "hippie" is similar to "Communist" in the 1950s—anyone undesirable. Freaks filled the void in the great American pastime: the search for a scapegoat. No doubt some of their values and behavior did contribute to social problems. But that topic demands a balanced monograph, not a brief chapter, and not another polemic.

The counterculture first subverted, and then with the aid of other movements, significantly altered the cold war culture. Coming out of the Great Depression, the older generation saved for the future, worked for the family, and followed the roles and the rules. The counterculture challenged that, encouraged experimentation, and provoked millions to consider, or reconsider, their lives. As one middle-aged journalist wrote about his two years visiting communes, "My route criss-crossed the country, leading me into the centers of great cities, far into the backwoods and wilderness, and up a great many mountains. It also took me—sometimes to my great surprise and distress—off the external roadmap into uncharted areas of my own consciousness, where I negotiated for the first time a bewildering tangle of fears, prejudices, and longings."

The counterculture resulted in a value system that has survived with the baby boomers. Surveys by Daniel Yankelovich Group in the early 1970s were confirmed in the late 1980s by Peter Hart Research Associates. The ethics of about 30 million people were altered in a meaningful way by the 1960s events, especially by civil rights struggle, women's liberation, and the war. Some 16 million also stated that personal changes were the result of the counterculture. Those who participated in some aspect of the movement are different from their parents. These sixties people are more skeptical about experts, leaders, politicians, and about institutions—the church, government, and military. They are more flexible, introspective, and tolerant, especially concerning race, living arrangements, and personal behavior. They are more open about their feelings, compassionate, and more liberated sexually. Women feel that they have the same right to sexual satisfaction as men, as demonstrated by a revolution of opinion about premarital sex: The double standard has been buried.[7] Even during the conservative 1980s, numbers soared of interracial marriages, gay and lesbian couples, and single men and women living together. Cohabitation and other alternative living arrangements are common. Being "normal" is no longer a mandate for behavior: Be yourself. Sixties people are more interested in self-fulfillment, defining their own lives, and they often question authority and do their own thing: Let it be.

Most of the counterculture values that since have become clichés still influence behavior. America is more casual in dress and behavior than ever before, and the daily diet includes a wide variety of health foods as corporations proclaim on their packages, "No Artificial Flavors or Preservatives." States have repealed laws prohibiting various forms of sexual behavior between consenting adults, and they have decreased penalties for personal use of drugs. Gone are the days when a court would sentence Timothy Leary to years in prison for half an ounce of marijuana, a drug that still is the most common illegal one in the nation. Youth is not necessarily defined by age, as demonstrated by a legion of middle-aged joggers, hikers, swimmers, rock stars, and others participating in behavior that in the 1950s would not have been appropriate. The result is more personal freedom than at any time in the history of the Republic—so much in fact that youth since has had little to protest, and some have become bewildered with all their options. As James Reston wrote about the graduating class of 1985, there was "nothing to confuse them but freedom." More than ever, America is the land of the free.

Most likely, the sixties will remain for some time as the benchmark for the way sixties people behave and think, just as their parents were influenced by the Great Depression and World War II. Regardless of the barrage from the press declaring that another former hippie or radical has seen the light and accepted a position on Wall Street, opinion polls and surveys have demonstrated that sixties people continue to live their life-styles. In the 1970s Michael Rossman tried to explain that to journalists who asked him what happened to radicals "when they grow up." "How can I tell them," he remarked, that "it is a process, not a state?" And in the 1990s Bernadine Dohrn added, "You can't win for losing. Either you fulfill their stereotype of being a radical 60's person or you've sold out." Most have not sold out, and evidence is supplied at college reunions. "There's no going back," stated Michigan alumna Julia Wrigley, and at the twentieth anniversary of the Columbia uprising Morris Dickstein noted that instead of describing careers in law, medicine, or banking, the former students "talked about working as labor organizers, peace activists, or campaigners for abortion rights or gay liberation." In Madison, a soci-ology professor surveyed 300 former civil rights activists and found that most of them had become teachers, lawyers, writers, and consultants: "None voted for Nixon. Two voted for Reagan." Studies have demon-strated that the protest generation remains quite distinctive in its views on civil rights, equality, politics, and lifestyle, a phenomenon *Newsweek* called "The Graying of Aquarius."[8]

Since the sixties, all of the various movements have diminished. That is natural, for the activists succeeded in bringing about a sea change, a different America. Like their predecessors during the Jacksonian period, progressive era, and 1930s, sixties activists were provoked by the inconsis-tencies between the Founding Fathers' noble ideals and the disappointing realities for many citizens. They responded by holding demonstrations that raised questions. The first wave asked about the rights of black citi-zens, the rights of students, about their obligation to fight a distant and undeclared war. They provoked the nation to look in the mirror. The second wave expanded the issues to include all minorities and women, and broadened the attack against the establishment. Since, liberation and empowerment have become threads in the nation's multicultural social and political fabric. By confronting the status quo, activists inspired a debate that since has taken place in Congress, courts, city halls, board rooms, streets, and even bedrooms. The debate involves the political and the personal, and it asks the central question of this democracy: What is the meaning of "America"? Like reformers before, provoking a re-evaluation of that question was the most significant legacy of

THE MOVEMENT and THE SIXTIES

A Note on Sources and Notes

This book, though fictional in form, is based strictly on historical fact. Everything in it is real and actually happened. And it all began just one year from today.
Edward Abbey, *The Monkey Wrench Gang*, 1975

This history is about social activism. Consequently, my research has been directed at untapped movement sources more than at official documents of the U.S. government. Researchers have done an impressive job examining presidential papers and publishing their findings, yet they have neglected movement sources. The number of those manuscripts—underground newspapers, interview transcripts, organizational papers, leaflets, and posters—dwarfs those of previous eras of social activism because the decade was the first age of offset printing, copying machines, and computers. The largest and finest collections are at the State Historical Society of Wisconsin in Madison and the Bancroft Library at Berkeley. I examined the entire Social Action Vertical File in Madison, which contains over 60 cartons of documents, and I spent months at the Bancroft. At both depositories a researcher can save time and revenue by reading underground documents and newspapers of organizations, campuses, and collectives from all over the nation.

There are many other important collections, many of which I visited briefly: the Bentley Library in Ann Arbor, Michigan; the Suzzallo Library at the University of Washington in Seattle; the University of Kansas Libraries in Lawrence; the University of Minnesota Archives in Minneapolis; the State Library in East Lansing, Michigan; the Tamiment Library at New York University; and the Chicago Historical Society Library. The Swarthmore College Peace Collection at Swarthmore, Pennsylvania, has the documents of numerous national antiwar organizations, and the Schlesinger Library at Radcliffe College holds important manuscripts concerning the women's movement. The Lyndon Baines Johnson Library in Austin possesses presidential papers, government documents, and oral histories, and the Martin Luther King, Jr. Center for Nonviolent Social Change in Atlanta has materials concerning the civil rights struggle.

Approximately 80 interviews were conducted, and they are deposited in the Vietnam Generation or Military series of the Oral History Collection at the Texas A&M University Archives: consult Terry H. Anderson, *A Guide to the Oral History Collection of Texas A&M University* (College Station, 1988, updated 1994). A few closed interviews are in my personal collection. I also used numerous video interviews conducted by Varied Directions, Inc., for the PBS six-hour series, "Making Sense of the Sixties," and they are housed at their office in Camden, Maine.

Concerning endnotes, books used once are given full citations in the notes. Books employed more frequently have abbreviated endnotes and full citations in the Select Bibliography. Some interviewees requested anonymity, so a few quoted statements are not documented.

Activists were not professional journalists and their underground publications often did not include standard information such as the date, volume, or issue. Movement sources also are replete with typographical and spelling errors, and rather than burden the reader with *sics*, spelling and minor grammatical mistakes have been corrected while maintaining the original flavor and meaning.

Although I have inspected hundreds of underground newspapers printed between 1965 and 1973, I always cite the most available source; for 1965–70 the Bell and Howell *Underground Newspaper Microfilm Collection* contains about 500 titles. Unless indicated, underground newspapers cited may be found in the Bell and Howell Microfilm Collection.

Abbreviations Used in the Notes

Bent	Bentley Library, University of Michigan, Ann Arbor
Bent UC	Bentley Library Underground Collection
LAT	*Los Angeles Times*
LBJ	Lyndon Baines Johnson Presidential Library, Austin, Texas
NYT	*New York Times*
PNC	Pacific Northwest Collection, Suzzallo Library, University of Washington, Seattle
Ross	Robert Ross Collection, University Archives, University of Minnesota, Minneapolis
SAVF	Social Action Vertical File, State Historical Society of Wisconsin, Madison
SHSW	State Historical Society of Wisconsin, Madison
SPP	Social Protest Project, Bancroft Library, University of California, Berkeley
SPP, serials	Social Protest Project, unprocessed, serials file drawers, Bancroft Library
TA	Terry Anderson, personal collection
TAMU	Texas A&M University Archives and Oral History Collection, College Station
Wil	Wilcox Collection of Contemporary Political Movements, University of Kansas Libraries, Lawrence
WP	*Washington Post*
VD	Varied Directions, Inc., interviews for and resulting episodes of "Making Sense of the Sixties," PBS series, 1991, Camden, Maine

Notes

Preface
THE MOVEMENT AND THE SIXTIES

1. *Houston Chronicle*, 24 May 1984; *Dallas Times-Herald*, 16 Sept. 1989; *NYT*, 17 April 1988 and 5 March 1989; Roszak, *Making of the Counter-culture*, 41.

2. On leaders see Select Bibliography for Lewis Feuer, Kenneth Keniston, Larry Kerpelman, James Miller, and Stanley Rothman and S. Robert Lichter; for organizations see Edward Bacciocco, Clayborne Carson, Adam Fairclough, Mitchell Hall, and Kirkpatrick Sale. Peter Clecak, Maurice Isserman and Nigel Young have emphasized ideology, and Tom Bates, David Farber, Doug Mc-Adam, and W. J. Rorabaugh have focused on one locale.

3. Evans, *Personal Politics*, 102; Leamer, *Paper Revolutionaries*, 13; Gitlin, *The Sixties*, 84; Bent UC: *Ann Arbor Argus*, 13–29 Aug. 1969.

4. TA: Michael Levy interview, 12 June 1988; *Life*, 10 Nov. 1967, p. 4; Chandler Dividson interview in *Sallyport*, Fall 1988, pp. 9–10.

5. TAMU: DuBose interview, 5 March 1989; Hoffman, *Revolution for the Hell of It*, 167–68; Rudd in Gitlin, *The Whole World Is Watching*, 234; Yankelovich, *New Morality*, 128; Mungo, *Famous Long Ago*, 30; Kaus in *Newsweek*, 5 Sept. 1988, pp. 24 and 28.

6. Vickers, *Formation of the New Left*, ix; SPP, serials: *Fatigue Press*, May 1970.

Introduction
SPAWNING GROUND: COLD WAR CULTURE

1. Mathews in *Newsweek*, 5 Sept. 1988, pp. 17–21; Kovic, *Born on the Fourth of July* (New York, 1977), 54; Thomas Bird, "Man and Boy Confront the Images of War," *NYT*, 27 May 1990.

2. Atomic fear in Paul Boyer, *By the Bomb's Early Light: American Thought*

and Culture at the Dawn of the Atomic Age (New York, 1985), 144–46, 280–81; historian is H. W. Brands, Jr., *Cold Warriors: Eisenhower's Generation and American Foreign Policy* (New York, 1988), xi, chap. 1, p. 204.

3. Stanley I. Kutler, *The American Inquisition: Justice and Injustice in the Cold War* (New York, 1982), xi, 36–38; David Caute, *The Great Fear: The Anti-Communist Purge Under Truman and Eisenhower* (New York, 1978), 49; Stone in *New York Daily Compass*, 11 July 1951.

4. Kutler, *American Inquisition*, 190; Caute, *Great Fear*, 26–45; and consult Robert Griffith, *The Politics of Fear: Joseph R. McCarthy and the Senate* (Lexington, Ky., 1970), 45–57, Richard Rovere, *Senator Joe McCarthy* (New York, 1960 ed.), 125–40, and Victor S. Navasky, *Naming Names* (New York, 1980), 24.

5. Consult Alan D. Harper, *The Politics of Loyalty* (New York, 1969), and Athan Theoharis, *Seeds of Repression* (Chicago, 1971).

6. Historian is Ellen W. Schrecker, *No Ivory Tower: McCarthyism and the Universities* (New York, 1986), 89–119, 309, 340; also see McGill, *Year of the Monkey*, 247 n. 14; Caute, *Great Fear*, 406, chap. 22.

7. Navasky, *Naming Names*, 81–87, 346; Lou Cannon, *Reagan* (New York, 1982), 83–85; and see Larry Ceplair and Steven Englund, *The Inquisition in Hollywood: Politics in the Film Community, 1930–1960* (Berkeley, 1979), chaps. 8–11; dust jacket for Herbert A. Philbrick, *I Led Three Lives* (New York, 1952).

8. For red hysteria see Douglas T. Miller and Marion Nowak, *The Fifties: The Way We Really Were* (New York, 1975), 21–22; Emerson Greenaway, "An Informed Public," *Library Journal*, July 1952, p. 1125; James Gilbert, *A Cycle of Outrage: America's Reaction to the Juvenile Delinquent in the 1950s* (New York, 1986), 75–76.

9. J. Edgar Hoover, *Masters of Deceit* (New York, 1958), foreward, chap. 22; Goldwater in Donner, *Age of Surveillance*, 11.

10. Loren Baritz, *The Good Life: The Meaning of Success for the American Middle Class* (New York, 1989), 164–65; TA: J. D. Anderson interview, 1 June 1990; and see Peter Filene, *Him/Her/Self* (New York, 1975), 169; Harry Henderson, "Rugged American Collectivism," *Harper's*, Dec. 1953, p. 81; Paul F. Lazarsfeld and Wagner Thielens, *The Academic Mind: Social Scientists in a Time of Crisis* (New York, 1958), chaps. 8 and 9.

11. Miller and Nowak, *The Fifties*, 135; Benita Eisler, *Private Lives: Men and Women of the Fifties* (New York, 1986), chap. 3; Springsteen in *Rolling Stone*, 5 Feb. 1981, p. 21; "Church and State: Religion in New York Public Schools," *For the Record*, Fall 1989, pp. 1–2; Rafferty in *Reader's Digest*, Oct. 1961, pp. 107–10.

12. Stephen J. Whitfield, *The Culture of the Cold War* (Baltimore, 1991), chap. 4 on religion; VD: Roger Wilkins interview on Michigan, 2 June 1989; Andre Schiffrin interview, 19 June 1983, in Isserman, *If I Had a Hammer*, 59; survey in Philip E. Jacob, *Changing Values in College: An Exploratory Study of the Impact of College Teaching* (New York, 1957), 1, 12; Eisler, *Private Lives*, 8, 84; Stanley Kunitz, "The Careful Young Men," *The Nation*, 9 March 1957, p. 200; Harrison Smith, "Report on a Generation," *Saturday Review*, 1 Dec. 1951, p. 22; "The 'Unsilent Generation' Breaks Silence," *Life*, 17 Feb. 1958, p. 112;

and see Filene, *Him/Her/Self*, 204–7, and Joseph Satin, ed., *The 1950s: America's "Placid" Decade* (Boston, 1960).

13. On dental school, see TA: Dick Bath interview, 15 May 1987; Kunin in *NYT*, 2 August 1993; Filene, *Him/Her/Self*, 206–7; Eisler, *Private Lives*, 9; VD: Sara Evans interview, 3 June 1989 on senior panic; for the warm hearth see Elaine Tyler May, *Homeward Bound: American Families in the Cold War Era* (New York, 1988), chap. 1, pp. 78–91.

14. Beth L. Bailey, *From Front Porch to Back Seat: Courtship in Twentieth-Century America* (Baltimore, 1989), 49–53; Miller and Nowak, *The Fifties*, chap. 6; Landon Y. Jones, *Great Expectations: America and the Baby Boom Generation* (New York, 1980), chap. 2; Boone, *'Twixt Twelve and Twenty* (Englewood Cliffs, N.J., 1959), 83–84; came of age quote in Eisler, *Private Lives*, 14.

15. Barbeque is Jones, *Great Expectations*, chap. 3; O'Brien, *Dream Time*, 38; Samuelson in *Newsweek*, 2 March 1992, p. 32; critic is Rick Mitz, *The Great TV Sitcom Book* (New York, 1980), 63–67, 107–11; TA: J. D. Anderson interview, 1 June 1990; alone is Toby Thompson, *The '60s Report*, xii.

16. *Fortune*, Aug. 1946, pp. 6–14; John P. Robinson and Phillip R. Shaver, *Measures of Social Psychological Attitudes* (Ann Arbor, 1973), 13; *Reader's Digest*, Dec. 1957, pp. 212–13; Betty Friedan, *The Feminine Mystique* (New York, 1963), 9.

17. The drive my own quote is in *Time*, 5 Nov. 1951, p. 48; smoking in Jane Alpert, *Growing Up Underground*, 35; VD: Judith Karpova interview on rape, 8 Nov. 1989; David Harris, *Dreams Die Hard*, 21.

18. Richard Kluger, *Simple Justice: The History of Brown v. Board of Education and Black America's Struggle for Equality* (New York, 1975), 9; William McCord, *Mississippi: The Long, Hot Summer* (New York, 1965), 152; TAMU: Carey Cauley interview, 29 April 1991; Wilkins, *A Man's Life*, 47, 55.

19. Davidson, *Loose Change*, 9; Choate in Cowan, *Making of an Un-American*, 4–5; Michael Harrington, *The Other America: Poverty in the United States* (New York, 1962), chap. 4.

20. Miles Wolff, *How It All Began*, 67; John Howard Griffin, *Black Like Me* (New York, 1976 ed.), 7–8; flyer in Herbert S. Parmet, *Eisenhower and the American Crusades* (New York, 1972), 442; Stephen J. Whitfield, *A Death in the Delta: The Story of Emmett Till* (New York, 1988), 51.

21. Kluger, *Simple Justice*, chap. 26; Sitkoff, *The Struggle for Black Equality*, 23–39; Morris, *The Origins of the Civil Rights Movement*, 30–35; *Houston Post*, May 18, 1954; SAVF, box 9: Citizens Councils folder.

22. SAVF, box 9: Citizens Councils folder; TA: Memorandum by W. M. Rainach, 13 March 1958; Griffin, *Black Like Me*, 75.

23. William L. O'Neill, *American High: The Years of Confidence, 1945–1960* (New York, 1986), 291; Jeffrey Hart, *When the Going Was Good! American Life in the Fifties* (New York, 1982), and to a lesser extent John Patrick Diggins, *The Proud Decades: America in War and Peace, 1941–1960* (New York, 1988).

24. Alpert, *Growing Up Underground*, 15; Hayden, *Reunion*, 14; also see Stephanie Coontz, *The Way We Never Were: American Families and the Nostalgia*

Trap (New York, 1992), chap. 2, and Wini Breines, *Young, White, and Miserable: Growing Up Female in the Fifties* (Boston, 1992).

25. TAMU: Merle Curti interview, 8 June 1990, and for the debate between professors who supported and opposed the anti-Communist crusade on campus, see Richard H. Pells, *Liberal Mind in a Conservative Age* (New York, 1989), 293 and chap. 5; seething and mystic glue quotes are Tom Findley, *Rolling Stone*, 26 Oct. 1972, p. 36; Gilbert, *A Cycle of Outrage*, 16–18.

26. TA: Allen Ginsberg interview, 4 May 1984; John Clellon Holmes, "The Philosophy of the Beat Generation," in Seymour Krim, ed., *The Beats* (Greenwich, Conn., 1960), 17, and Krim quote, 12; Kerouac, *On the Road* (New York, 1955), 105.

27. Goodman, *Growing Up Absurd* (New York, 1956), 241, x–xvi; Mills, *The Power Elite* (New York, 1956), 351–56; William Appleman Williams, *The Tragedy of American Diplomacy* (Cleveland, 1959), intro., chap. 1, p. 164; scholar is Pells, *The Liberal Mind in a Conservative Age*, ix.

28. William Atwood, "How America Feels," *Look*, 5 Jan. 1960, pp. 11–32; Newfield, *Prophetic Minority*, 28–29; Rose K. Goldsen et al., *What College Students Think* (Princeton, N.J., 1960), 97; Philip Caputo, *A Rumor of War* (New York, 1977), 7; May, *Homeward Bound*, 28.

Chapter 1
THE STRUGGLE

1. Sherrod's song in King, *Freedom Song*, 161; Hayden, *Reunion*, 31; Wolff, *How It All Began*, chap. 1, and see Carson, *In Struggle*, chap. 1; McCain interview in Raines, *My Soul Is Rested*, 75–82.

2. Morris, *The Origins of the Civil Rights Movement*, 48, chap. 9, n. 28, and for another view see Clayborne Carson, "Civil Rights Reform and the Black Freedom Struggle," in Charles W. Eagles, ed., *The Civil Rights Movement in America* (Jackson, Miss., 1986), 19–37.

3. Raleigh *News and Observer* in Chafe, *Civilities and Civil Rights*, 86, and for sit-ins as a decisive break with the past see chap. 3; Proudfoot, *Diary of a Sit-In*, 48, 93–94.

4. Sitkoff, *Struggle for Black Equality*, chap. 3; Weisbrot, *Freedom Bound*, chap. 2; activist is Jack Newfield, *A Prophetic Minority*, 43.

5. Richmond interview in Carson, *In Struggle*, 16; King interview in Raines, *My Soul Is Rested*, 84–85; activist quoted by Cowan, *Making of an Un-American*, 21; Bevel in Morris, *Origins of the Civil Rights Movement*, 206.

6. Sellers, *River of No Return*, 28–29; Chapel Hill incident in Coffin, *Memoir*, 147–48; Hayden, *Reunion*, 54; professor is Zinn, *SNCC*, 1.

7. Carson, *In Struggle*, chap. 2; interviews in Raines, *My Soul Is Rested*, 77–81, 101–2; and see Sitkoff, *Struggle for Black Equality*, 86–91.

8. James Peck, *Freedom Ride* (New York, 1962), chap. 1; Lewis interview in Cluster, *They Should Have Served That Cup of Coffee*, 4–7; and see Farmer, *Lay*

Bare the Heart, chap. 17; Carson, *In Struggle,* 34–37, chap. 3; and August Meier and Elliott Rudwick, *CORE: A Study in the Civil Rights Movement* (New York, 1973), chap. 5.

9. Zinn, *SNCC,* chap. 3; Coffin, *Memoir,* 150–52; and see Sitkoff, *Struggle for Black Equality,* 103–14, and Weisbrot, *Freedom Bound,* 55–63.

10. The buy off the movement quote is in Farmer, *Lay Bare the Heart,* 219–20; McComb in Zinn, *SNCC,* chaps. 4 and 9; Zellner interview in Morrison and Morrison, *From Camelot to Kent State,* 47–55.

11. SAVF: box 5, Ann Arbor Friends of SNCC bulletin, 30 Sept. 1962, p. 1; Casey Hayden quoted in King, *Freedom Song,* 8, 162; Richard Flacks, "Who Protests: The Social Bases of the Student Movement," and many other articles in Julian Foster and Durward Long, eds., *Protest! Student Activism in America* (New York, 1970); Hayden, *Reunion,* 76–78; Breines, *The Great Refusal,* xxv; and see Gitlin, *The Sixties,* 89, 103, 174.

12. Denitch interview by Isserman, *If I Had a Hammer,* 188–89; VD: former assistant attorney general Roger Wilkins interview, 2 June 1989; VD: Benjamin in episode 2; teenager quoted in Gottlieb, *Do You Believe in Magic?,* 34.

13. On the peace corps see Harris Wofford, *Of Kennedys and Kings: Making Sense of the Sixties* (New York, 1980), 456, chap. 8, and NYT, 2 March 1961; the quote on gentlemanly protest is in Cowen, *Making of an Un-American,* 10; Gitlin, *The Sixties,* 86–8; and see Isserman, *If I Had a Hammer,* 147–50; C. Wright Mills, *New Left Review,* Sept.–Oct. 1960, pp. 18–23.

14. Haber in Sale, *SDS,* 25–27 and 49–59; Booth interviewed by Miller, *Democracy Is in the Streets,* 107–8, chap. 6, and see the appendix for *The Port Huron Statement;* Hayden, *Reunion,* 93–102; Bacciocco, *New Left in America,* chap. 4; and Vickers, *Formation of the New Left,* chap. 4.

15. Greg Calvert and Carol Neiman, *A Disrupted History,* 10–15; Jeffrey quote in Miller, *Democracy Is in the Streets,* 106–8; Gitlin, *The Sixties,* 26–27; Nicholas Lemann's comment of Hayden's *Reunion* in NYT *Book Review,* 5 June 1988, p. 20, and for more statements see Sale, *SDS,* 89–90.

16. McAdam, *Freedom Summer,* 44–49, and see Yankelovich survey of small percentages of new left adherents, *New Morality,* 128.

17. Gitlin, *The Sixties,* 105 and chap. 5; incestuous community quote in Isserman, *If I Had a Hammer,* xviii, 168; Jeffery and Ross in Miller, *Democracy Is in the Streets,* 125; creating a movement quote in Calvert and Neiman, *A Disrupted History,* 129; and for ERAP, see Breines, *Great Refusal,* chap. 7.

18. Albany see Abernathy, *And the Walls Came Tumbling Down,* chap. 7, Powledge, *Free at Last?,* chap. 21, and Garrow, *Bearing the Cross,* chap. 4; southern town justice in Marshall, *Federalism and Civil Rights,* 42–48; for Chapel Hill incident, SPP: box 25b, *SPU News Notes* #7, n.d. [May 1964], 2.

19. Sherrod in Carson, *In Struggle,* 83–89, and see Carl M. Brauer, *John F. Kennedy and the Second Reconstruction* (New York, 1977), 167, and chap. 6; Marshall in Branch, *Parting the Waters,* 571; Kennedy quoted in Michal R. Belknap, *Federal Law and Southern Order: Racial Violence and Constitutional Conflict in the Post-Brown South* (Athens, Ga., 1987), 89, and chaps. 4–6; Kunstler, *Deep in My Heart,* 110; King, *Freedom Song,* 292–96; Forman, *Mak-*

ing of Black Revolutionaries, 265, 546; Miller, "Farewell to Liberals: A Negro View," *The Nation*, 20 Oct. 1962, pp. 235–38.

20. Miller, *Democracy Is in the Streets*, 164; Gitlin, *The Sixties*, 88–90, 100.

21. Martin Luther King, Jr., *Why We Can't Wait* (New York, 1964 ed.), 21, 54, 58; Stephen B. Oates, *Let the Trumpet Sound: The Life of Martin Luther King, Jr.* (New York, 1985 ed.), 200–205, and see Abernathy, *And the Walls Came Tumbling Down*, chap. 8.

22. Marrisett interview in Raines, *My Soul Is Rested*, 146–49; *Time*, 17 May 1963, p. 23.

23. Herbert S. Parmet, *JFK: The Presidency of John F. Kennedy* (New York, 1984 ed.), 272; King, *Freedom Song*, 293–96; Lewis in Carson, *In Struggle*, 91–95, and Garrow, *Bearing the Cross*, 281–86.

24. Mary Ward and John Lewis interviews in Morrison and Morrison, *From Camelot to Kent State*, 24, 30.

25. Woman quoted in the Associated Press, *The World in 1964: History as We Lived It* (New York, 1965), 4; Kovic, *Born on the Fourth of July*, 71; TA: J. D. Anderson interview, 15 June 1990; biographer is Parmet, *JFK*, 352–55, and for this debate see Thomas Brown, *JFK: History of an Image* (Bloomington, Ind., 1988).

26. King, *Freedom Song*, 369, and chap. 10; Carson, *In Struggle*, 112, and chap. 9; and for characteristics of volunteers see Rothschild, *A Case of Black and White*, chap. 2, and McAdam, *Freedom Summer*, 15, and chap. 2.

27. For training see Belfrage, *Freedom Summer*, chap. 1; concerning sex see Evans, *Personal Politics*, 81–83, Harris, *Dreams Die Hard*, 67, and Rothschild, *A Case of Black and White*, chap. 5; SNCC activist is Lawrence Guyot interview in Raines, *My Soul Is Rested*, 287.

28. Pathologist in E. M. Keating, *Mississippi Eyewitness* (Menlo Park, Calif., 1964), 49; Holt, *Summer That Didn't End*, 30; Seth Cagin and Philp Dray, *We Are Not Afraid: The Story of Goodman, Schwerner, and Chaney and the Civil Rights Campaign for Mississippi* (New York, 1988), chap. 9.

29. Log reproduced in Holt, *Summer That Didn't End*, 196–268, and see volunteers' letters to home in SAVF: box 29, "Mississippi Freedom Movement," and Willie Morris, *The Courting of Marcus Dupree* (New York, 1983), chap. 9; Silver, *Mississippi: The Closed Society*, x; Sellers, *River of No Return*, 74.

30. Mills, *This Little Light of Mine*, 50–51, 120–21; Lillian Smith, *Our Faces, Our Words* (New York, 1964), 61–62; Sherrod quoted in Carson *SNCC*, 127.

31. Jane Stembridge letter from Mississippi in King, *Freedom Song*, 397; Belfrage, *Freedom Summer*, xix; Holt, *Summer That Didn't End*, 143; image quotes in Gottlieb, *Do You Believe in Magic?*, 32.

32. David J. Garrow found "simply no evidence" in FBI files obtained through the Freedom of Information Act that Communism influenced the movement or Martin Luther King, Jr. See Garrow's *The FBI and Martin Luther King, Jr.* (New York, 1981), chaps. 1 and 2, and Kenneth O'Reilly, *Racial Matters: The FBI's Secret File on Black America, 1960–1972* (New York, 1989), chap. 4. For activ-

ists' views see King, *Freedom Song*, 283–89; McAdam, *Freedom Summer*, 44–53; and Rothschild, *A Case of Black and White*, 38–43. Savio interview in Bret Eynon, "Community in Motion: The Free Speech Movement, Civil Rights, and the Roots of the New Left," *Oral History Review* (Spring 1989): 51.

33. Louis Lomax, "The Unpredictable Negro," *New Leader*, 24 June 1963, pp. 3–4; Moses interview, 3 Dec. 1964, in Jack Newfield, *The Education of Jack Newfield* (New York, 1984), 166–68; David J. Garrow's "Commentary" in Eagles, ed., *Civil Rights Movement in America*, 55–64.

34. Maniacal lefty in McAdam, *Freedom Summer*, 127, and for volunteer survey results, see 131–38, chap. 4, and Rothschild, *A Case of Black and White*, chaps. 5 and 7; Eisenberg interview, NPR, "Morning Edition," 27 April 1992; Young in King, *Freedom Summer*, 469–70; personal rebellion in Cowan, *Making of an Un-American*, 37.

35. King and Casey Hayden, *Freedom Song*, 74, 7; Hayden, *Reunion*, 31–32; Zinn, *SNCC*, preface; McAdam's interview in *Freedom Summer*, 240.

Chapter 2
THE MOVEMENT AND THE SIXTIES GENERATION

1. Savio, "An End to History," *Humanity*, Dec. 1964, p. 1, and in Massimo Teodori, ed., *The New Left: A Documentary History* (Indianapolis, 1969), 159. The entire issue of *California Monthly*, Feb. 1965, was devoted to the FSM, and it includes hundreds of statements, documents, and reports from 10 Sept. to 4 Jan. 1965. Also consult Seymour Martin Lipset and Sheldon S. Wolin, eds., *The Berkeley Student Revolt: Facts and Interpretations* (Garden City, N.Y., 1965), the massive endnotes in W. J. Rorabaugh, *Berkeley at War: The 1960s* (New York, 1989), and the documentary film, "Berkeley in the '60s" (California Newsreel, 1991). FSM documents are located at the Bancroft Library and many have been copied by SHSW.

2. TA: interview with Michael Rossman, 20 May 1991, and see his *Wedding Within the War*, 30–71; for the impact of Freedom Summer on FSM and the rise of student power see McAdam, *Freedom Summer*, chap. 5, and Bret Eynon, "Community in Motion: The Free Speech Movement, Civil Rights, and the Roots of the New Left," *Oral History Review* (Spring 1989): 39–69; Sandall in Rorabaugh, *Berkeley at War*, 20; Davidson, *Loose Change*, 66.

3. Consult articles and notes in Edward E. Sampson, Harold A. Korn, et al., *Student Activism and Protest* (San Francisco, 1970); Julian Foster and Durwand Long, eds., *Protest! Student Activism in America* (New York, 1970); Christopher G. Katope and Paul G. Zolbrod, eds., *Beyond Berkeley: A Sourcebook in Student Values* (Cleveland, 1966); Ronald Lora, ed., *America in the 60's: Cultural Authorities in Transition* (New York, 1974); and see Michael W. Miles, *The Radical Probe: The Logic of Student Rebellion* (New York, 1971), and Diane Ravitch, *The Troubled Crusade: American Education, 1945–1980* (New York, 1983), chaps. 6–8.

4. Associated Press, *The World in 1964: History as We Lived It* (New York, 1965), 30–35; *Newsweek*, 11 Jan. 1965, p. 74; *Time*, 6 Jan. 1967, p. 18; beach and morals articles in *Time*, 2 April 1965, p. 61, *Newsweek*, 6 April 1964, pp. 52–59, and AP, *The World in 1964*.

5. *The Paper*, 10 Dec. 1965; AP, *The World in 1964*, 30–35; *Newsweek*, 22 March 1965, p. 43.

6. Bob Dylan, *Lyrics, 1962–1985* (New York, 1985), 53, and see Robert Shelton, *No Direction Home: The Life and Music of Bob Dylan* (New York, 1986), 173–80.

7. Baby boomer in Gottlieb, *Do You Believe in Magic?*, 304; Clark Kerr, "The Idea of a Multiversity," in his *The Uses of a University* (Cambridge, 1963), and reprinted in Christopher G. Katope and Paul G. Zolbrod, eds., *Beyond Berkeley* (Cleveland, 1966); and see Kerr's "The Frantic Race to Remain Contemporary," in Robert S. Morison, ed., *The Contemporary University* (Boston, 1966), 27; Andrew Hacker, "The College Grad Has Been Short-changed," *NYT Magazine*, 6 June 1965, p. 101.

8. *Life*, 21 June, 1963, p. 4; McGill, *Year of the Monkey*, 40; Davidson, *Loose Change*, 12; *Daily Californian*, 15 Sept. 1965; Syracuse student in Bill Ward, "Why the Students Revolt," *Nation*, 25 Jan. 1965, p. 83; TA: Rossman interview, 20 May 1991, and his unpublished manuscript.

9. Lester A. Kirkendall, "Sex on the Campus," *Nation*, 17 Feb. 1964, pp. 165–66, and see Nicholas Von Hoffman, *The Multiversity: A Personal Report on What Happens to Today's Students at American Universities* (New York, 1966), chap. 3; journalist is Bill Ward, "Why the Students Revolt," *Nation*, 25 Jan. 1965, p. 83; *Daily Texan* 16 March 1960; TA: James Bradford interview, 9 Aug. 1990, on Michigan State; Robert Hassenger, "Conflict in the Catholic Colleges," in Joseph Boskin and Robert A. Rosenstone, eds., *Seasons of Rebellion: Protests and Radicalism in Recent America* (New York, 1972), 201–2; BYU is discussed in *NYT*, 17 Dec. 1990; TA: *The Monolith* (Huntsville, Tex.) 25 Jan. and 8 Feb. 1971; Hayden, *Reunion*, 27.

10. Marc Eliot, *Death of a Rebel* (New York, 1979), 40–41; *Daily Illini*, 18 March 1960, and *NYT*, 15 June and 17 July 1960; *Newsweek*, 6 April 1964, p. 59; Ray Bayles, "Protest Sweep Nation," *Daily Utah Chronicle*, 9 Dec. 1964.

11. *Daily Texan*, 1 April 1965; *The Paper*, 10 Dec. 1965; SAVF: box 37, *New Orleans Freedom Press*, July 1966; box 39, *Freedom Forum*, 9 March 1965, and "Freedom Party Proposals for Action," winter 1966 flyer; Brandeis and Syracuse in *Newsweek*, 6 April 1964, 55, and *Nation*, 25 Jan. 1965, p. 84.

12. TA: Rossman interviewed by author, 20 May 1991, and by Mark Kitchell, 1988 transcript, 6; and see Bret Eynon, "Community in Motion: The Free Speech Movement, Civil Rights, and the Roots of the New Left," *Oral History Review* (Spring 1989): 40. With a few thousand participants in FSM, many interpretations exist of these events. For numerous statements reported that semester in the campus paper, consult "Free Speech 1964–1989," *Daily Californian*, 4 Dec. 1989, and Rorabaugh, *Berkeley at War*, chap. 1.

13. *San Francisco Examiner*, 3 Oct. 1964; Savio in Hal Draper, *Berkeley: The New Student Revolt* (New York, 1965), 98; SHSW: Free Speech Movement mss., box 1, FSM flyer, 3 Dec. 1964.

14. Bettina Aptheker, *The Academic Rebellion in the United States* (Secaucus, N.J., 1972), 22; Farmer in *California Monthly*, Feb. 1965, p. 71; and debate in *Daily Californian*, 22 and 25 Sept. 1964, and 4 Dec. 1989.

15. Norwood Russell Hanson, "Hoosier Witch Hunt," *Nation*, 25 May 1963, p. 443; SAVF: box 13, "Committee to Aid the Bloomington Students" flyers; *NYT*, 12 Oct. 1963.

16. TA: Rossman interview, 20 May 1991, and unpublished ms., "The FSM and Student Rights," 75, *New Age Blues*, 45, and *Wedding Within the War*, 92; Aptheker in Burns, *Social Movements of the 1960s*, 64.

17. Robert H. Somers, "The Mainsprings of the Rebellion," and Glenn Lyonns, "The Police Car Demonstration," in S. M. Lipset and Sheldon S. Wolin, eds., *The Berkeley Student Revolt* (New York, 1965), 530–59 and 519–30; and numerous surveys cited in Rorabaugh, *Berkeley at War*, 33–34; Sellers, *River of No Return*, 58–59.

18. Powell and many statements in *California Monthly*, Feb. 1965, p. 42; SHSW: Free Speech mss., box 1, University Students for Law and Order Newsletter, 14 Dec. 1964, and Judith Ann Faber mss., box 2, for YAF pamphlet and "The Sharon Statement," 9–11 Sept. 1960, and see SAVF: box 59, Young American for Freedom folder; *New Guard*, May 1961, Sept. 1964, Jan. and Sept. 1965; for YAF also see *NYT*, 8 March 1962, and *Time*, 10 Feb. 1961, p. 35.

19. *San Francisco Examiner*, 2 and 3 Dec. 1964; *Oakland Tribune*, 6 Dec. 1964; *U.S. News & World Report*, 14 and 21 Dec. 1964, pp. 12 and 43 respectively; Lou Cannon, *Reagan* (New York, 1982), 148; Rorabaugh, *Berkeley at War*, 26.

20. *Los Angeles Free Press*, 19 March 1965, reprinted article from *Open City Press*; *The Paper*, 10 Dec. 1965; Leamer, *The Paper Revolutionaries*, 27, and Peck, *Uncovering the Sixties*, 18–36; Davidson, *Loose Change*, 53; Irwin Silber, "Songs from Berkeley," *Sing Out!*, May 1965, p. 19; *Daily Texan*, 5 May 1967.

21. TA: James Bradford interview, 9 Aug. 1990; *Michigan State News*, 16 July 1964, and 8 and 17 Feb. and 12 April 1965; *NYT*, 26 Oct. 1951; Columbus *Dispatch*, 27 April 1962; and James S. Turner, "Ohio State: Free Speech and Student Power," and Richard E. Peterson, "The Scope of Organized Student Protest," in Foster and Long, eds. *Protest!*, 345–61 and 59–80.

22. David J. Garrow, *Protest at Selma: Martin Luther King, Jr., and the Voting Rights Act of 1965* (New Haven, Conn., 1978), chaps. 2 and 3; and see Charles E. Fager, *Selma, 1965* (New York, 1974), and SNCC paper *The Movement*, April 1965.

23. Turner and Bolden interviews in Raines, *My Soul Is Rested*, 187–96, 209–10; Sheyann Webb and Rachel West Nelson, as told to Frank Sikora, *Selma, Lord, Selma: Childhood Memories of the Civil-Rights Days* (University, Ala., 1980), 96; J. L. Chestnut, Jr., and Julia Cass, *Black in Selma: The Uncommon Life of J. L. Chestnut, Jr.* (New York, 1990), 207; Leonard, "Midnight Plane

to Alabama," *Nation*, 10 May 1965, pp. 502–5; TA: Robert Calvert interview, 11 Sept. 1990; *Daily Texan*, 26 March 1965.

24. Sellers, *River of No Return*, 111–23; Lewis, *King*, 281; and see Carson, *In Struggle*, chap. 11; Bond interview in Raines, *My Soul Is Rested*, 213–14; Webb, Nelson, Sikora, *Selma, Lord, Selma*, 115.

25. SAVF: box 28, *Midwestern Activist*, 14 March and 6 April 1965; Wynkoop, "Dissent in the Heartland," 4; *University Daily Kansan*, 10, 11, and 22 March 1965, and see Fisher, "The Turbulent Years: The University of Kansas, 1960–1975," 76–80.

26. Sharp in *Reader's Digest*, Jan. 1968, p. 102; opinions in Louis Harris, *Anguish of Change* (New York, 1973), 53–54 and chap. 4.

27. On Diem see Marilyn B. Young, *The Vietnam Wars 1945–1990* (New York, 1991), 58, 79; David Halberstam, *The Best and the Brightest* (New York, 1983 ed.), 97.

28. CIA reports in NYT edition, *The Pentagon Papers* (New York, 1971), chap. 7; Reedy in "LBJ: An American Experience," PBS video; *NYT*, 5 Aug. 1964; *WP*, 6 Aug. 1964; *Michigan State News*, 6 Aug. 1964; and see Small, *Johnson, Nixon and the Doves*, chap. 2; DeBenedetti, *An American Ordeal*, chap. 5; George Herring, *America's Longest War: The United States and Vietnam, 1950–1975* (New York, 1986), chap. 4; Larry Berman, *Planning a Tragedy: The Americanization of the War in Vietnam* (New York, 1982), chap. 3; and Brian VanDeMark, *Into the Quagmire: Lyndon Johnson and the Escalation of the Vietnam War* (New York, 1991), chaps. 5 and 6.

29. Marc Pilisuk, "The First Teach-in: An Insight into Professional Activism," along with other articles on the topic in Louis Menashe and Ronald Radosh, eds., *Teach-ins U.S.A.: Reports, Opinions, Documents* (New York, 1967), 11; SAVF: box 28, *The Midwestern Activist*, 6 April 1965 for Carleton; Easter march in Zaroulis and Sullivan, *Who Spoke Up?*, 38–42, and historian is DeBenedetti, *An American Ordeal*, 109–12.

30. *University Daily Kansan*, 22 Feb. 1965; *Michigan State News*, 12 April 1965; and see Kenneth Heineman, "A Time of War and a Time of Peace: The Anti-Vietnam War Movement at Michigan State University, 1965–1970," *Peace & Change*, (July 1989), pp. 285–323; historian is Small, *Johnson, Nixon and the Doves*, 36; VD: Christian interview, episode 4.

31. *University Daily Kansan*, 26 April 1965; Block in *Life*, 30 April 1965, p. 30; *College Press Service*, 6 Dec. 1964; Hacker, "The College Grad Has Been Short-changed," *NYT Magazine*, 6 June 1965, 25; Seymour M. Lipset, ed., *Student Politics* (New York, 1967), 200; *Newsweek*, 22 March 1965, pp. 43–63.

32. *New Guard*, Sept. 1964; *University Daily Kansan*, 14 Oct. 1967; professor in Von Hoffman, *Multiversity*, 123; *Time*, 29 Jan. 1965, p. 57; *Newsweek*, 22 March 1965, p. 44.

33. For voting rights see Oates, *Let the Trumpet Sound*, 359–60; Harris, *Dreams Die Hard*, 134; Stanford Cazier, "Student Power and In Loco Parentis," in Foster and Long, eds., *Protest!*, 506–30.

Chapter 3
DAYS OF DECISION

1. Eisenhower in *Oakland Tribune*, 17 Aug. 1965; editorials in *Oakland Tribune*, 16 Aug. 1965, and *LAT*, 20 Aug. 1965; punch in *LAT*, 15 May 1966; and see Jerry Cohen and William S. Murphy, *Burn, Baby, Burn!: The Los Angeles Race Riot August, 1965* (New York, 1966).

2. King in Oates, *Let the Trumpet Sound*, 366–68; police chief in Cohen and Murphy, *Burn, Baby, Burn!*, chap. 31; VD: Wilkins interview, 2 June 1989, and his *A Man's Life*, 170; minister quoted in Hunter S. Thompson, *Hell's Angels* (New York, 1967), 153.

3. Max interview in Maurice Isserman and Michael Kazin, "The Failure and Success of the New Radicalism," in Steve Fraser and Gary Gerstle, eds., *The Rise and Fall of the New Deal Order 1930–1980* (Princeton, 1989), 221; and see Sale, *SDS*, 158–59.

4. *Life*, 29 Oct. 1965, p. 40d; *Time*, 14 May 1965, p. 30; Caputo, *Rumor of War* (New York, 1978), 66, xiv; Kovic, *Born on the Fourth of July* (New York, 1977), 86.

5. Quotes from DeBenedetti, *An American Ordeal*, 93–102; Hersey in Zaroulis and Sullivan, *Who Spoke Up?*, 44; McAdam, *Freedom Summer*, 172–73; Moses in Carson, *In Struggle*, 184.

6. *NYT*, 4 April 1965; Hatfield, *Not Quite So Simple* (New York, 1968), 155; DeBenedetti, *An American Ordeal*, 94–95; VD: Ball interview, episode 4.

7. SAVF: box 8, "Chicago Area Draft Resisters" flyer, nd; Ferber and Lynd, *The Resistance*, chap. 2; *Life*, 20 Aug. 1965, p. 30, and see Woodstone, *Up Against the War*, chap. 2, and *Look*, 28 Dec. 1965, pp. 13–16; *Newsweek*, 1 Nov. 1965, p. 38; *NYT*, 18 Oct. 1965; George Q. Flynn, *Lewis B. Hershey: Mr. Selective Service* (Chapel Hill, 1985), 236.

8. TA: Lynd letter to author, 28 June 1992; Oates, *Let the Trumpet Sound*, 365–66; *Life*, 29 Oct. 1965, 40d; *NYT*, 19 Oct. 1965.

9. *Oakland Tribune*, 7 Aug. 1965; *Berkeley Barb*, 13 Aug. 1965; Kesey in Tom Wolfe, *The Electric Kool-Aid Acid Test* (New York, 1968), 224; Rubin, *Do It!*, 38; VD: Reagan comment, episode 4.

10. George C. Herring, "The 1st Cavalry and the Ia Drang Valley, 18 October–24 November 1965," in Charles E. Heller and William A. Stofft, eds., *America's First Battles, 1776–1965* (Lawrence, Kans., 1986), 300–326; and see "Special Report: Vietnam Story," *U.S. News & World Report* 29 Oct. 1990, pp. 32–51; polls in *WP*, 30 Oct. and 18 Nov. 1965; Rusk in *Newsweek*, 29 Nov. 1965, p. 21.

11. *NYT*, 17 and 29 Oct. 1965; *The Paper*, 20 Jan. 1966; congressmen and Nixon in *NYT*, 16 and 29 Oct. 1965; and see DeBenedetti, *An American Ordeal*, chap. 5.

12. *Life*, 29 Oct. 1965, pp. 40b and 40d; *Chicago Tribune*, 19 Oct. 1965; *Jackson Daily News*, 20 Oct. 1965; *Time*, 22 Oct. 1965, p. 25a, and 19 Nov. 1965, p. 67; and see Ted Finman and Stewart Macaulay, "Freedom to Dissent: The Vietnam Protests and the Words of Public Officials," *Wisconsin Law Review*

(Summer 1966): 632–723; *Boston Globe*, 19 Oct. 1965; *NYT*, 4, 6, 14, and 20 Nov. 1965, and 7 Jan. 1966.

13. DeBenedetti, *An American Ordeal*, 130; *New York Post*, 17 April 1965; WSHS, Staughton Lynd papers, box 19, folder 1, Vietnam Day Committee News, July–Aug. 1965; Flacks in Miller, *Democracy Is in the Streets*, 176; Kissinger in *Nation*, 21 June 1965, pp. 657–58; and see Gitlin, *The Sixties*, chap. 7.

14. White, *The Making of the President: 1968* (New York, 1969), 24; *NYT*, 15 March and 16 Oct. 1965; Jack Newfield, "The Student Left," *Nation*, 10 May 1965, pp. 491–94; Sale, *SDS*, 191–93.

15. TA: Lynd letter to author, 28 June 1992; Booth in Miller, *Democracy Is in the Streets*, 235–42; and see Sale, *SDS*, 204–11, chap. 12; Gitlin, *Whole World Is Watching*, chaps. 2–4; *NYT*, 10 Jan. 1966.

16. SAVF: box 54, Vietnam Day Committee letters, 9 and 13 Sept. 1965; *Berkeley Barb*, 13 Aug. and 24 Sept. 1965; Rubin, *Do It!*, 38.

17. Harris in *WP* 9 May, 14 June, 20 Sept. 1966; *Time*, 2 Sept. 1966, p. 12; *NYT*, 8 Jan. 1966; and see DeBenedetti, *An American Ordeal*, chap. 6.

18. *Christian Century*, 20 April 1966, p. 483; *Time*, 2 Sept. 1966, p. 12; SAVF, box 12, Committee for Nonviolent Action folder, 20 Feb. 1966 letter to Muste; *Newsweek*, 10 Oct. 1966, 72.

19. SPP: box 37b, Black Panther flyers, 12 and 26 July 1966; Carson, *In Struggle*, 191–207; Zellner in Morrison and Morrison, *From Camelot to Kent State*, 54–55.

20. *Life*, 20 March 1960, p. 40, and George Breitman, ed., *Malcolm X Speaks* (New York, 1966), 105–8; *NYT*, 22 Feb. 1965; *Los Angeles Times*, 24 and 25 Feb. 1965.

21. *NYT*, 17, 21, and 22 June 1966; Meredith and Black Power in Associated Press, *The World in 1966*, 112–16, 166–71; Sellers, *River of No Return*, 165–69; Oates, *Let the Trumpet Sound*, 388–90; Wilkins, *A Man's Life*, 144; and see Garrow, *Bearing the Cross*, chap. 9; Sitkoff, *Struggle for Black Equality*, 209–17; Carmichael and Hamilton, *Black Power*, chap. 2; and PBS video, "Eyes on the Prize II, 1964–66," Jan. 1990.

22. WSHS, Staughton Lynd papers, box 19, folder 1, "The War on Viet Nam" flyer, July 1965, and folder 3, "Prayer Meeting about Viet Nam" report, 26 March 1966; SAVF, box 1, Afro-Americans Against the War in Vietnam flyer, spring 1966, and box 6, Black United Action Front poster, April 1967; Carmichael in *National Guardian*, 22 April 1967, p. 2.

23. Baskir and Strauss, *Chance and Circumstance*, chap. 3; James Fallows, "Low-Class Conclusions," *Atlantic Monthly* (April 1993): 38–44.

24. David L. Lewis, *King: A Biography* (Urbana, Ill., 1978), 358–70; Oates, *Let the Trumpet Sound*, 412–20; Smith in VD: episode 4.

25. *NYT*, 16 Feb., 2 March, 13 May, 13 Nov., 16 Dec. 1966; *Newsweek*, 9 Jan. 1967, p. 49; TA: Dow historian, E. N. Brandt, letter to author, 24 May 1988, *The Dow Diamond*, no. 4, 1967; and Terry Anderson, "The New American Revolution: The Movement and Business," in Farber, ed., *The Sixties*, 175–205.

26. Larry Berman, *Lyndon Johnson's War: The Road to Stalemate in Vietnam*

(New York, 1989), 43–119; Henry Trewhitt, *McNamara* (New York, 1971), 235; Gelb in *NYT*, 16 June 1991; LBJ: meeting file notes, box 2, 12 Sept. 1967 meeting; Lubell, *The Hidden Crisis in American Politics* (New York, 1971), 254–60.

27. SAVF: box 46, A. J. Muste, Preliminary Mobilization Memorandum, 5 Jan. 1967, and box 42, Resistance flyers; Lynd, *We Won't Go*, 216–17; Rader in *Liberation*, July 1967.

28. *NYT*, 22 April 1967; Hall, *Because of Their Faith*, 48.

29. *Daily Texan*, 25 April and 2 May 1967; VD: interview, episode 4; SAVF: box 54, Vietnam Summer 1967 flyer.

30. SAVF, box 5, antiwar folder, and boxes 15 and 17 for flyers from Denver and Minneapolis; SPP: file drawers, CNVA, New England folder; Joan Baez, *And a Voice to Sing With: A Memoir* (New York, 1987), 120; Andy Stapp, *Up Against the Brass* (New York, 1970); and see Terry Anderson, "The GI Movement and Response from the Brass," and Amy Swerdlow, " 'Not My Son, Not Your Son, Not Their Sons: Mothers Against the Vietnam Draft," in Small and Hoover, eds., *Give Peace a Chance*, 93–115, 159–70; SAVF: box 6, Black Women Enraged flyer, 1966; Dewart letter in *Win*, 23 Nov. 1966, and see Lynd, *We Won't Go*; Beaumont letter in *Liberation News Service*, 16 Oct. 1967.

31. Hoover in LBJ: Tom Johnson notes, 24 July 1967 meeting; *Newsweek*, 7 Aug. 1967, pp. 18–26; *NYT*, *Report of the National Advisory Commission on Civil Disorders* (New York, 1968), 1–2, 143–48, 196, 206; *Newsweek*, 12 June 1967, p. 103.

32. *Time*, 7 July 1967; Perry, *Haight-Ashbury*, chaps. 4–5; Peck, *Uncovering the Sixties*, chap. 3; and see von Hoffman, *We Are the People Our Parents Warned Us Against*; Perry, *The Human Be-In*; del Renzio, *Flower Children*; and Emmett Grogan, *Ringolevio: A Life Played for Keeps* (Boston, 1972), part 3; Gruen, *The New Bohemia*, 9.

33. *Avatar*, 9–22 June 1967; *San Francisco Chronicle*, 15 March 1966, 11 Dec., 16 Jan. 1967.

34. Be-in in Ralph Gleason, *San Francisco Chronicle*, 16 Jan. 1967, p. 41; TA: Christopher interview, 29 June 1992; and see Perry, *Haight-Ashbury*, 174–75, 187, 227–31.

35. Manifesto in almost every issue of the *Black Panther*; Seale, *Seize the Time*, 77, 157, 162; *LAT*, 3 May 1967; Brown in Sellers, *River of No Return*, 199.

36. Halstead, *Out Now!*, 146; DeBenedetti, *An American Ordeal*, 186–90; *Daily Cardinal*, 19 Oct. 1967; *Wisconsin Alumnus*, Nov. 1967, pp. 4–9; SAVF: box 17, Dow Action Committee flyers, 1967.

37. Ferber and Lynd, *The Resistance*, chap. 10; SAVF, box 34, "Mobilization Report," Nov. 1967; Jezer in *Win*, 15 Nov. 1967; Dreyer and Stamberg in *Washington Free Press*, 14 Nov. 1967; Lampe in *Liberation*, Dec. 1967.

38. *Newsweek*, 30 Oct. 1967, p. 21; Garson in *Berkeley Barb*, 2 Nov., and in *New Left Notes*, 6 Nov. 1967; Nelson in *Berkeley in the '60s*, episode 2; and see Harris, *Dreams Die Hard*, 208–14.

39. Charles DeBenedetti, "A CIA Analysis of the Anti-Vietnam War Movement: October 1967," *Peace and Change*, Spring 1983, pp. 31–35; Small,

Johnson, Nixon, and the Doves, 104–13, 124–27; *U.S. News & World Report,* 4 Dec. 1967, pp. 12, 16; Herring, *America's Longest War,* 185.

40. LBJ: Tom Johnson notes, 4 Oct. and 21 Nov. 1967 meetings; Berman, *Lyndon Johnson's War,* 71, 81–84, chap. 8; *NYT,* 19 June 1967; Kopkind in *New York Review of Books,* 28 Sept. 1967, p. 3; *Newsweek,* 27 Nov. 1967, p. 68.

Chapter 4
1968: RIP TIDES

1. Hue described by Dave R. Palmer, *Summons of the Trumpet* (Presidio, Calif., 1978), 194; *Christian Century,* 21 Feb. 1968, p. 220; WP for polls, 25 March and 2 May 1968; Eisenhower in *Reader's Digest,* April 1968, p. 49; vet in Lewis Chester, Godfrey Hodgson, and Bruce Page, *An American Melodrama: The Presidential Campaign of 1968* (New York, 1969), 597; for LBJ see Herring, *America's Longest War,* chap. 6, and Berman, *Lyndon Johnson's War,* chap. 9, p. 175.

2. Stanford in Harris, *Dreams Die Hard,* 226–27; aide is Jeremy Larner, *Nobody Knows: Reflections on the McCarthy Campaign of 1968* (New York, 1970), 37; and see Eugene J. McCarthy, *The Year of the People* (New York, 1969), chap. 5.

3. Goodwin, *Remembering America,* chap. 26, pp. 493–95, 503, 513; Chester et al., *American Melodrama,* 78; and see David English et al., *Divided They Stand* (Englewood Cliffs, N.J., 1969), 89, 91, and chap. 6.

4. *NYT,* 27 Nov. 1967; Brooklyn in Caute, *Year of the Barricades,* 116; Newfield, *Robert Kennedy: A Memoir* (New York, 1988), 230.

5. LBJ: Tom Johnson notes, 26 March 1968 meeting; PBS program, "LBJ: The American Experience," 1991; and see Herring, *America's Longest War,* 206.

6. Goodwin, *Remembering America* 523; Powers, *The War at Home,* 315; O'Brien, *Dream Time,* 135.

7. Sellers, *River of No Return,* chap. 17, p. 224; AP in *NYT* 9, 10 Feb. 1968; bill of rights in Lewis, *King,* 403; Oates, *Let the Trumpet Sound,* 475–76; VD: Rodriquez interview, episode 4.

8. Gitlin, *The Sixties,* 305–6; Chavez wire in *El Grito,* Spring 1968, p. 54; William H. Grier and Price M. Cobbs, *Black Rage* (New York, 1968), 1–2.

9. Kirk and Sales in Kahn, *Battle for Morningside Heights,* 63, 109, 126, chap. 7; Rudd in Jerry A. Avorn, *Up Against the Ivy Wall: A History of the Columbia Crisis* (New York, 1969), 27; Kunen, *Strawberry Statement,* 25; *Columbia Daily Spectator,* 10 May 1968.

10. *Columbia Daily Spectator,* 24 and 29 April 1968. Kunen, *Strawberry Statement,* 25; Sue Willis, "Reflection on Communal Life," *At Issue,* 13 May 1968, p. 4; atmosphere in *NYT,* 31 April 1968, and Archibald Cox, *The Cox Commission Report: Crisis at Columbia* (New York, 1969), 138; activist in Gitlin, *Whole World Is Watching,* 193.

11. *Rat,* "Statements of Injured Students," 3–16 May 1968; *Columbia Daily Spectator,* 24 April, 2 May 1968; conservative in Unger and Unger, *Turning Point,* 271–72; SAVF: box 11, Columbia Strike Committee flyer, n.d.

12. *Columbia Daily Spectator,* 24 April, 1 and 2 May 1968; *Newsweek,* 6 May 1968, p. 40; *NYT,* 25 April 1968; *Congressional Record,* 27 May 1968, pp. E4685–87; *Barron's,* 20 May 1968, p. 1; *Fortune,* 1 June 1968, p. 73; *Rat,* 1–14 June 1968.

13. Hayden in *Ramparts,* 15 June 1968, p. 40, and see his *Reunion,* 165; Gitlin in *Motive,* Oct. and Nov. 1970, pp. 55 and 45; Rossman in Rorabaugh, *Berkeley at War,* 105.

14. For SDS-Resistance friction see Harris, *Dreams Die Hard,* 186, 190; Hayden quote in Jeremy Larner, *Harper's,* May 1969, p. 79; Coffin in Dellinger, *More Power Than We Know,* 107; Rudd in Kahn, *Battle for Morningside Heights,* 104; radical in Gitlin, *The Sixties,* 283; historian is Matusow, *Unraveling of America,* 335; SHSW: Paul Booth papers, box 2, Gitlin, "Thesis for the Radical Movement," 1967; Potter, *A Name for Ourselves,* 36; *Columbia Daily Spectator,* 2 May 1968; Hayden, *Reunion,* 164–65.

15. Kunen, *Strawberry Statement,* 36, 115–17; *Columbia Daily Spectator,* 29 April 1968; SAVF, box 11, Executive Committee of the Faculty, "To the Students of Columbia University," 17 Sept. 1968.

16. Political statements in Larner, *Nobody Knows,* and Arthur M. Schlesinger, Jr., *Robert Kennedy and His Times* (Boston, 1978), 889–94; Just in WP, 12 March 1968, and see *NYT,* 14 March 1968; Halberstam in *Harper's,* July 1968, p. 51.

17. Schlesinger, *Robert Kennedy and His Times,* 896–99, 914; Jeremy Larner, "Reflections on the McCarthy Campaign, II," *Harper's,* May 1969, p. 76; McCarthy, *Year of the People,* 168; adviser is Goodwin, *Remembering America,* 537.

18. *Newsweek,* 17 June 1968; Schlesinger, *Robert Kennedy and His Times,* 1–2; Goodwin, *Remembering America,* 534, 543; Newfield, *Robert Kennedy: A Memoir,* 303.

19. Gitlin, *The Sixties,* 310–11; Hayden in *Rolling Stone,* 26 Oct. 1972, p. 50; *Berkeley Barb,* 14–20 June 1968; Oglesby in Fraser, *1968: A Student Generation in Revolt,* 285–86; TA: Rose Eder interview, 3 Dec. 1988.

20. Bil Gilbert, "The Great World and Millersburg," *Saturday Evening Post,* 20 April 1968, 36ff; Harris, *Anguish of Change,* 67; Kunen, *Strawberry Statement,* 78.

21. Miller, *Hippies and American Values,* 10–15; Perry, *Human Be-In,* 95; *San Francisco Express Times,* 28 Jan. 1968.

22. Larner, "Nobody Knows . . . Reflections on the McCarthy Campaign: Part II," *Harper's,* May 1969, p. 79; James J. Kilpatrick, "What Makes Wallace Run," *National Review,* 18 April 1967, pp. 402–9; Alabama State Archives: Ed Ewing papers, Tom Turnipseed memo to Ewing, 15 April 1968.

23. *Houston Post,* 30 Oct. 1968; SPP serials: Youth for Wallace flyer for Rarick; many quotes in Kilpatrick, *National Review* (April 1967): 402–9, *Life* 10 Nov. 1967, p. 4, and Chester et al., *American Melodrama,* 276–94.

24. David English et al., *Divided They Stand,* chap. 15; *NYT* and *WP,* 9 Aug.

1968; guts in Stephen E. Ambrose, *Nixon: The Triumph of a Politician, 1962–1972* (New York, 1989), 170.

25. Peterson in White, *Making of the President: 1968*, 85–86; WP, 27 Aug. 1968; and see Anthony Lukas, "Dissenters Focusing on Chicago," NYT, 18 Aug. 1968.

26. Humphrey aide in White, *Making of the President: 1968*, 317; Daley and Dillinger in NYT, 18 Aug. 1968; and see Bill Gleason, *Daley of Chicago* (New York, 1970), and Chester et al., *American Melodrama*, 516; Potter, *A Name for Ourselves*, 32; Peck in *Liberation News Service*, 6 Aug. 1968.

27. Hoffman, *Soon to Be a Major Motion Picture*, 137; WP, 27 Aug. 1968; NYT, 18 Aug. 1968; *Newsweek*, 30 Oct. 1967, pp. 84–90; *Reader's Digest*, Jan. 1968, pp. 59–63; White, *Making of the President: 1968*, 335.

28. Hoffman, *Soon to Be a Major Motion Picture*, 144–47, and *Revolution For the Hell of It*, 37, chap. 5; Rubin, *Do It!*, chaps. 13, 28.

29. *Seed*, 15–30 Aug. 1968, and see Peck, *Uncovering the Sixties*, 109 and chap. 7; *Berkeley Barb*, 2–8 Aug. 1968; Farber, *Chicago '68*, chap. 2; Lowenstein in Chester et al., *American Melodrama*, 519.

30. WP, 28 Aug. 1968; NYT 27 Aug. 1968; and see Farber, *Chicago '68*, chap. 7, Thomas Whiteside, "Corridor of Mirrors," *Columbia Journalism Review* (Winter 1968–69): 35–54, and Norman Mailer, *Miami and the Siege of Chicago* (New York 1968), 151–71; activist is Kunan, *Strawberry Statement*, 117.

31. Chester et al., *American Melodrama*, 513, 582; *Rat*, 6–19 Sept. 1968; *Berkeley Barb*, 30 Aug.–5 Sept. 1968; *The Rag*, 16 Sept. 1968; Lowenstein in Harris, *Dreams Die Hard*, 255; Humphrey in White, *Making of the President: 1968*, 354; Walker in NYT, 2 Dec. 1968.

32. NYT, 30 Aug. 1968, and NYT *Magazine*, 24 Aug. 1969; Farber, *Chicago '68*, xiii, 202–7.

33. *Chicago Tribune*, 30 Aug. 1968; Daley in Chester et al., *American Melodrama*, 592–604, and see Mailer, *Miami and the Siege of Chicago*, 177; *The Rag*, 16 Sept. 1968; also see Nathan Blumberg, "The 'Orthodox' Media Under Fire: Chicago and the Press," *Montana Journalism Review* (1969): 38–60.

34. *Congressional Record*, 27 May 1968, p. E4685; Hoover in DeBenedetti, *An American Ordeal*, 231; *Seed*, 1–15 Sept. 1968; Rubin, *Do It!*, 170; Daley and Arenberg in Farber, *Chicago '68*, 254, 130.

35. NYT, 8 Sept., 10 March 1968, and see 9 Feb. 1969.

36. White, *Making of the President: 1968*, 407–8, and Chester et al., *American Melodrama*, 691.

37. Gottlieb, *Do You Believe in Magic?*, 136–37; Potter, *A Name for Ourselves*, 34; Harris, *Goliath* (New York, 1970), 49; Madison in Stickney, *Streets, Actions, Alternatives, Raps*, 84; Blumberg, "The 'Orthodox' Media," 39.

38. On LBJ see Kahn, *Battle for Morningside Heights*, 221, and Rossman, *New Age Blues*, 50; Harris, *Dreams Die Hard*, 260; Newfield, *Robert Kennedy: A Memoir*, 7, 304.

39. Wallace in Fraser et al., *1968: A Student Generation in Revolt*, 10; Staughton Lynd and George Katsiaficas, *Journal of American History* (June 1990): 375.

Chapter 5
COUNTERCULTURE

1. Kupferberg in Berke, *Counter Culture*, 85; Gardner, *Children of Prosperity*, v, 9; Lampe in *Liberation*, Dec. 1967, p. 10.

2. Genocide is Roszak, *Making of the Counterculture*, 47; Perry criticizes the categories in *Human Be-In*, 16; and see Patrick Conover, *The Alternative Culture and Contemporary Communes, Revised: A Partly Annotated Bibliography* (Monticello, Ill.: Council of Planning Librarians, 1976), exchange bibliography #952; Enroth et al., *Jesus People*, 12; Melville, *Communes in the Counter Culture*, 138; and see Fairfield, *Communes USA*, 4–5.

3. Rubin, *Do It!*, 97; *Daily Utah*, 6 Feb. 1968; Glessing, *Underground Press in America*, 59, my emphasis; and see Leamer, *Paper Revolutionaries*, 14.

4. *Other Scenes*, 28 Dec. 1968, and see Glessing, *Underground Press in America*, 53, 99; *Space City!*, 17–30 Jan. 1970; *East Village Other*, 19 Aug.–1 Sept. 1967; Sinclair in *Fifth Estate*, 28 Nov.–11 Dec. 1968; and see Miller, *Hippies and American Values*, chap. 4.

5. *Daily Californian*, 15 Sept. 1965; Farber in *Los Angeles Free Press*, 3 March 1967; examples in Michael Lydon, "The Word Gets Out," *Esquire*, Sept. 1967, pp. 106–7.

6. McDonald in *Sing Out!*, June 1968, pp. 20–21; activist is Keith Lampe, "From Dissent to Parody," *Liberation*, Dec. 1967, p. 20; Wilder in MacPherson, *Long Time Passing*, 259; Mungo, *Famous Long Ago*, 3; son in Lukas, *Don't Shoot—We Are Your Children!*, 243.

7. Thompson, *The '60s Report*, viii–ix, and see Perry, *Human Be-In*, chap. 7; activist is David Baggins, *Rat*, 6–19 Sept. 1968; PNC: People's Protest 1964–67 box, Seattle flyer, 28 April 1967.

8. Tenn. governor in *Las Vegas Free Press*, 2–8 April 1970; freak in *Rat*, 12–26 Aug. 1969.

9. Radcliffe in Goodman, *Movement Toward a New America*, 16; Kunen, *Strawberry Statement*, 79; opinion in Yankelovich, *New Morality*, 45–46, 59, 71, 120, 126; participant in Timothy Miller, "Drug Bust in Kansas," *Christian Century*, 17 March 1971, p. 332.

10. Eisler, *Private Lives* (New York, 1986), 85, 8; Mead in *Saturday Review*, 10 Jan. 1970, p. 25; Lewis, *King*, 370–71; statements in Simmons and Winograd, *It's Happening*, 76.

11. Power trips in Stickney, *Streets, Actions, Alternatives, Raps*, 30; SAVF, box 7: Canyon Collective, *Live It! Communalism*, 1; Brackman in *Esquire*, Oct. 1968, p. 127; Garson in *San Francisco Express Times*, 26 June 1968.

12. Gentle grass is Peter L. Berger and Brigitte Berger, "The Blueing of America," *New Republic*, 3 April 1971, p. 20; Chicago student in Morrison and Morrison, *From Camelot to Kent State*, 236; Anders in "Berkeley in the '60s," part 2; baby boomer is TA: Cozette McGaugh interview, 8 Dec. 1989.

13. John Sieler's poem in *Asterisk*, 8 Jan. 1969; institutions in Burke, *Counter Culture*, 3; Boyd, *Underground Church*, vii.

14. Supermarket U. in "Flowers from the Street," *San Francisco Oracle*, n.d.

(1967); free is Jerry Rubin in *Berkeley Barb*, 5–11 Jan. 1968; hippie and Gottlieb in Melville, *Communes in the Counter-culture*, 127–28; Melton in "Berkeley in the '60s," part 2.

15. Journalist is Lawrence Lipton in *Los Angeles Free Press*, 3 May 1968; love in del Renzio, *Flower Children*, 59; Romney in Lewis, *Side-saddle on the Golden Calf*, 373.

16. *Great Speckled Bird*, 6 Oct. 1969; *Other Scenes*, June 1968; Leary, *Flashbacks*, 118; Dass in *Los Angeles Free Press*, 3 Sept. 1965; *Washington Free Press*, 7 March 1968; and consult Miller, *Hippies and American Values*, chap. 2.

17. Stevens in VD: episode 3; letter in Simmons and Winograd, *It's Happening*, 85–86; Zappa in *Liberated News Service*, 2 Sept. 1970.

18. *Spokane Natural*, 8 Dec. 1967; *Seventy-nine Cent Spread*, 5 Nov. 1968; and see Miller, *Hippies and American Values*, chap. 3; SAVF: box 5, FUK flyer, n.d.

19. VD: Nash in episode 3; SAVF: box 27, Kittredge in *Madison Free Press*, 1 Dec. 1969; Kupferberg in Berke, *Counter Culture*, 85; and see Miller, *Hippies and American Values*, 112–15.

20. SPP: box 18b, *North Country News*, July 1969; change in Stevens, *Storming Heaven*, 291; Leary in David Solomon, *LSD: The Consciousness-Expanding Drug* (New York, 1966), 13; blow your minds in *The Paper*, 18 April 1967; battlefield in Berke, *Counter Culture*, 150; Sender and Laurel, *Being of the Sun*, 4; wanderlust in Gottlieb, *Do You Believe in Magic?*, 107.

21. Kunen, *Strawberry Statement*, 4; communard in Melville, *Communes in the Counter Culture*, 11–12; trashmongering in *Mother Earth News*, Nov. 1970.

22. Rip off in Jerome, *Families of Eden*, 127; SAVF: box 25, *Little Free Press*, Nov. 1971; SPP: box 15a, *Planet*, 15 June 1969; selling out in Stevens, *Storming Heaven*, 302; and for promoters see *Rat*, 12–16 Aug. 1969; *Seed*, 13 March 1970; and SPP: box 18b, *Las Vegas Free Press*, 16–22 April 1970; hip capitalist in Bent: *Goose Lake Gags*, Aug. 1970.

23. Eugene in Stickney, *Street, Actions, Alternatives, Raps*, 158; PNC: box "political campaign and handouts," file 1969–71, Seattle flyer; SAVF: box 17, ecology folder, Earth People's Park flyer.

24. SPP: box 16, *Submarine Church Press*, 2 March, Easter, 15 May 1970; Jesus flyer in *Time*, 21 June 1971, pp. 56–63; freak in *Las Vegas Free Press*, 9–15 April 1970; Love Song in Enroth, *Jesus People*, 91, and see introduction; Drane, *A New American Reformation*, chap. 6, p. 117; daughter in Melville, *Communes in the Counter Culture*, 210.

25. Communards in Melville, *Communes in the Counter Culture*, 11–13, 160; Jezer in *WIN*, 15 Feb. 1971; observer is Gardner, *Children of Prosperity*, vii, 5.

26. Diamond, *What the Trees Said*, 38–39; Houriet, *Getting Back Together*, 12; review in *Commentary* (July 1972): 62–65.

27. Frats in Stickney, *Streets, Actions, Alternatives, Raps*, 71; Mungo, *Famous Long Ago*, 2; Sinclair, *Guitar Army*, 105; Terry Anderson, "The New American Revolution: The Movement and Business," in Farber, ed., *The Sixties*, 175–205; TA: Gilbert Shelton interview, 31 July 1992.

28. *Plain Dealer,* 17–30 Sept. 1970; *The Spectator,* 4 March 1968; profits in *Business Week,* 27 Jan. 1968, p. 84.

29. Jan Hodenfield and Greil Marcus in *Rolling Stone,* 20 Sept. 1969; and see *New Yorker,* 30 Aug. 1969, p. 17; Philip Tracy, "The Birth of a Culture," *Commonweal,* 5 Sept. 1969, p. 532; *Newsweek,* 1 Sept. 1969, p. 20.

30. LNS "Woodstock" report in *Space City News,* 28 Aug.–11 Sept. 1969; *Life,* 29 Aug. 1969, p. 14b, and Aug. 1989, pp. 20–45; *NYT,* 24 Aug. 1969; Bent: Sinclair papers, box 3, Leary to Sinclair, 9 and 14 Dec. 1969, and Sinclair to Magdalene and Dave Sinclair, 14 and 15 Oct. 1969; *Berkeley Tribe,* 7–13 Nov. 1969.

31. *Newsweek,* 15 Dec. 1969, pp. 30–31; *Time,* 12 Dec. 1969, pp. 22–25; Sanders, *The Family,* 25, chap. 1; Smith and Luce, *Love Needs Care,* 255–64; Steven V. Roberts, "Charlie Manson: One Man's Family," *NYT Magazine,* 4 Jan. 1970.

32. Felton, *Mindfuckers,* 29; *LAT,* 7 Dec. 1969; freak in SPP, serials: *Overload,* April 1970; Melville, *Communes in the Counter Culture,* 189; Atcheson, *Bearded Lady,* 17.

33. Interviews in Eisen, ed., *Altamont,* 55–60, 84, 215, 234; SPP, box 15a: Horowitz and other articles in *Survival,* April 1970; and see Lewis, *Side-saddle on the Golden Calf,* 321–40, *LAT,* 7 Dec., *Berkeley Barb,* 12–18 Dec. 1969, and *Berkeley Tribe,* 12–19 Dec. 1969.

34. *Business Week,* 8 Aug. 1970, p. 21; *Christian Economics,* 27 May 1969; Anderson in *Freedom Magazine,* Summer 1971, pp. 19–20, and *Common Sense,* 1 Jan. 1970; A. Brychkov, *American Youth Today* (Moscow, 1973), 148–52; Louis Filler, *Vanguards & Followers: Youth in the American Tradition* (Chicago, 1978), 183; O'Neill, *Coming Apart,* 252–63.

35. Brats in *Reader's Digest,* June 1970, pp. 129–32; father in Drane, *A New American Reformation,* 8–9; *Second Coming,* 5–19 Oct. 1970; Mary Anne Johnson and James Olsen, *Exiles from the American Dream: First-Person Accounts of Our Disenchanted Youth* (New York, 1974), 229.

36. *Notes from the Underground,* 3–15 Jan. 1968; Atcheson, *Bearded Lady,* 20; on repression against undergrounds see Peck, *Uncovering the Sixties,* 135–38, and on the South see Stickney, *Streets, Actions, Alternatives, Raps,* 11–18, and *Newsweek,* 13 July 1970, p. 58.

37. Ad Hoc panel on Drug Abuse in David Solomon, ed., *The Marihuana Papers* (New York, 1968), 467–71; Bent: Sinclair papers, box 5, Jackie Vaughn III letter to Sinclair, 20 July 1971, and Sinclair letter in *Playboy,* 6 Oct. 1969; Sonoma in Gardner, *Children of Prosperity,* chap. 9; San Diego in *Long Beach Free Press,* 7–20 Jan. 1970; Taos in Melville, *Communes in the Counter Culture,* 142, and see *Christian Century,* 1 July 1970, p. 828; Hopper in *Atlantic Monthly* (Oct. 1969): 123.

38. Bent UC: *South End,* 18 July 1969; del Renzio, *Flower Children,* 57.

39. Sanders, *The Family,* 39–40; Fairfield, *Communes USA,* 190, and many examples in Johnson and Olsen, *Exiles from the American Dream*; Gardner, *Children of Prosperity,* 119; William H. McGlothlin, *Hippies and Early Christianity* (Los Angeles, Calif., 1967), 13.

40. Fairfield's complaints in his *Communes USA*, 186; Eisen in his *Altamont*, 12, 18–22; *Dallas Notes*, 2–15 July 1969.

41. Young in *Rolling Stone Interviews, 1967–1980* (New York, 1981), 327; Bates in Knight-Rider News Service article by Jim Ricci, 6 Sept. 1986; Sundancer, *Celery Wine*, 123; Jezer, *Abbie Hoffman*, 232–33; cold mountain in Fairfield, *Communes USA*, 43; Lonsdale in Gardner, *Children of Prosperity*, 99.

42. Dan Wakefield, "The War at Home," *Atlantic Monthly* (Oct. 1969): 119–23; Fairfield, *Communes USA*, 100, 360; Jezer in Canyon Collective, *Live It! Communalism*, 34; Rubin, *Do It!*, 99; Oglesby in Morrison and Morrison, *Camelot to Kent State*, 307; *Win*, 15 Jan. 1969; Flacks, Eugene, and hip in Stickney, *Streets, Actions, Alternatives, Raps*, 168–69, 115–16, 255.

Chapter 6
POWER AND LIBERATION

1. Ferber and Lynd, *The Resistance*, ix; TA: Rossman interview transcript, 1988, pp. 21–22; Keniston in Sampson et al., *Student Activism and Protest*, 186; Gibbs in *Minnesota Daily*, 26 Nov. 1969.

2. David Swanston, "How to Wreck a Campus," *The Nation*, 8 Jan. 1968, pp. 38–41; Hare in *Newsweek*, 10 Feb. 1969, p. 56; Carmichael and numerous statements in Karagueuzian, *Blow It Up!*, 5, 27–28, 38–39, 92–103, 120, 169; *LAT*, 7 Nov. 1968; *San Francisco Chronicle*, 3 and 4 Dec. 1968.

3. *The Daily Gater*, 4 and 6 Dec. 1968, 13 Jan. 1969, and *San Francisco Chronicle*, 3 Dec. 1968; SPP, box 20a: special announcement, 29 Jan. 1969, and board of trustees to faculty members, 20 Feb. 1969; Karagueuzian, *Blow It Up!*, 170–94.

4. McCormick, *Black Student Protest Movement at Rutgers*, chap. 4; *NYT*, 21 and 22 April 1969 for Cornell, and 13 March and 29 April 1969 for militant unions; Forman, *Making of Black Revolutionaries*, 547; and see Van Deburg, *New Day in Babylon*, chap. 3.

5. Uyematsu in *GIDRA*, Oct. 1969, and in Tachiki, *Roots*, 9–13, and see Wei, *Asian American Movement*, chap. 1; *The Nation*, 3 March 1969, pp. 271–74; *NYT*, 13 Dec. 1968; and see Robert Coles and Harry Huge, "Thornes on the Yellow Rose of Texas," *New Republic*, 19 April 1969, pp. 13–17.

6. Martinez in *El Grito*, Summer 1969, pp. 3–13; Rendon, *Chicano Manifesto*, 47–57; on education see Steiner, *La Raza*, 208–15; on justice see Acuna, *Occupied America*, 372–79, and Morales, *Ando Sangrando*, chaps. 3 and 4.

7. Journalist is Andrew Kopkind in *New Republic*, 29 Jan. 1966, pp. 12–15; and see Levy, *Cesar Chavez*, chap. 6; Acuna, *Occupied America*, 351.

8. Journalist is *LAT*, 17 March 1968; *NYT*, 11 March 1968, 19 and 29 June 1969; Matthiessen, *Sal Si Puedes*, 73, 109, 312–15.

9. Militant and Alurista in Rendon, *Chicano Manifesto*, 192–97, 205, 336–37; Guzman in *LAT West Magazine*, 26 Jan. 1969, pp. 9–14; Varela in Steiner, *La Raza*, 389; Coronela in *Chicano Student Movement*, Aug. 1969; and see

Bongartz, "The Chicano Rebellion," *The Nation*, 3 March 1969, pp. 271–74; Castro, *Chicano Power*, chap. 8, and Munoz, *Youth, Identity, Power*, chaps. 2 and 3.

10. Chicano Selma in Rendon, *Chicano Manifesto*, 200–203, 332–36, and *San Antonio Express*, 30 March 1969; Tijerina in Steiner, *La Raza*, 89–91, *Saturday Evening Post*, 20 April 1968, p. 22, and *LAT*, 17 March 1968; *Newsweek*, 25 March 1968, p. 37; Guzman in *LAT West Magazine*, 26 Jan. 1969, pp. 9–14.

11. Vasquez in Rendon, *Chicano Manifesto*, 186; Holtzman in *NYT*, 7 June 1992; Miller and many such comments in *Esquire*, July 1973, pp. 122–26; *Life*, 24 Dec. 1956, pp. 109–18.

12. NOW in Hole and Levine, *Rebirth of Feminism*, chap. 1, and Friedan, *It Changed My Life*, 75–91; coed in *The Carletonian* (Carleton College, Minn.), 10 Oct. 1968, reprinted in Goodman, *Movement Toward a New America*, 39.

13. King, *Freedom Song*, 450–59, 567–74, 471; Evans, *Personal Politics*, 154–60, 177, 235; Piercy in Morgan, *Sisterhood Is Powerful*, 483; Sale, *SDS*, 357; Amatniek (later Sarachild), in Hole and Levine, *Rebirth of Feminism*, 114–19.

14. Willis in *Guardian*, 15 Feb. 1969; and see Gitlin, *The Sixties*, chap. 16; Echols, *Daring to Be Bad*, prologue; and Evans, *Personal Politics*, chaps. 8 and 9; Biberman in *At Issue*, 13 May 1968.

15. Communard in Canyon Collective, *Live It! Communalism*, 16, 25, 41; rock in *NYT*, 14 March 1971; Morgan, *Going Too Far*, 64; "jokes" in *Reader's Digest*, Jan. 1968, p. 112, and July 1968, p. 80; Heinemann's in *Milwaukee*, Sept. 1988, pp. 30–39; SAVF: box 58, Women's Liberation, San Francisco flyer; *Ann Arbor Argus*, 28 March 1969; Wildflower in Potter, *A Name for Ourselves*, xv–xvi; Morgan in *RAT*, 12–26 Aug. 1969.

16. *NYT*, 29 and 30 June 1969, and see *Village Voice*, 3 July 1969; psychologists in Katz, *Gay American History* (New York, 1985), 1–2, 181–207; *Rat*, 12–26 Aug. 1969.

17. SAVF, box 3: Fred Halstead pamphlet, "Antiwar GIs Speak Out: Interviews with Ft. Jackson GIs United Against the War," Nov. 1969; *NYT*, 2 April 1969; TAMU: author's interview with James Hollingsworth, 16 June 1986; *NYT Magazine*, 18 May 1969, pp. 25–27; and see Terry Anderson, "The GI Movement and the Response from the Brass," in Small and Hoover, eds., *Give Peace a Chance*, 99–101.

18. SPP, serials: *GI Press Service*, 26 June 1969, and see Robert Heinl, "Collapse of the Armed Forces," *Armed Forces Journal*, 7 June 1971, p. 31; *Newsweek*, 2 Feb. 1970, p. 24, and 25 May 1970, p. 45; Reston in *NYT*, 27 Aug. 1969.

19. Number of exiles in MacPherson, *Long Time Passing*, 354, and for evaders see Baskir and Strauss, *Chance and Circumstance*, chap. 1; Jezer, *Abbie Hoffman*, 185–87, chap. 9; Theoharis, *Spying on Americans*, 16, and chap. 1; Martinez in Donner, *Age of Surveillance*, 248–52, 347, and chap. 6.

20. *U.S. News & World Report*, 16 June 1969, p. 11; *LAT*, 31 Jan. 1969;

NYT, 3 Nov. 1969; Kilpatrick in *Human Events*, 8 March 1969, p. 152; *Time*, 9 May 1969, p. 22, and 27 June 1969, pp. 16–17.

21. Alan Copeland, ed., *People's Park* (New York, 1969), 109; "Berkeley in the '60s," part 3; *Daily Californian*, 16 Feb. 1989 special issue; Reagan in Gitlin, *The Sixties*, 414.

22. *NYT*, 10 and 17 Dec. 1969; and see Donner, *Age of Surveillance*, 221–37.

23. Sale, *SDS*, 562, 590, 606, 614–15; Ono in Jacobs, eds., *Weathermen*, 354–56; Stern, *With the Weathermen*, 118, 133–35; Gallup in *NYT*, 25 May 1969; Jezer, *Abbie Hoffman*, 182.

24. Small, *Johnson, Nixon, and the Doves*, 183, 179–92; and see DeBenedetti, *An American Ordeal*, chap. 9; father in *WP*, 14 Nov. 1969; G.I.s in Bent: *Broken Arrow*, 1 Dec. 1969; and see Zaroulis and Sullivan, *Who Spoke Up?*, 263–73.

25. Shockley, *Chicano Revolt in a Texas Town*, chap. 5; Garcia, *United We Win*, 37–50.

26. *Look*, 2 June 1970, p. 45; *NYT*, 10 Dec. 1969; *Newsweek*, 8 Dec. 1969, p. 52; and see *Ramparts*, Feb. 1970, pp. 31–32.

27. *Newsweek*, 6 July 1970, p. 38; *Time*, 9 Feb. 1970, p. 14; *New Republic*, 17 Jan. 1970, pp. 10–11; SPP, serials: Native American folder, *The Warpath*, Spring 1970; Kennedy in *Look*, 2 June 1970, pp. 36–38.

28. Allen, *Free Space*, 6, and see SHSW: Pamela Allen Papers, box 1, and Carden, *New Feminist Movement*, 33–37.

29. Feminists disagree on the impact of sexual harassment on the rise of women's liberation. See King, *Freedom Song*, 459–66, and Belfrage, *Freedom Summer*, xvii, who basically disagree with Evans, *Personal Politics*. On discrimination see Scott and Komisar, *And Justice for All*, 5–16, and most of Komisar, *New Feminism*, and Deckard, *Woman's Movement*.

30. For employment see Marilyn Mercer in *Saturday Evening Post*, 27 July 1968, pp. 17–21; for education see Pamela Roby in Freeman, ed., *Women: A Feminist Perspective*, 171–93; Young in Ruddick and Daniels, *Working It Out*, 223; Ginsburg in *NYT*, 25 June 1993; Griffiths in Komisar, *New Feminism*, 127.

31. *Time*, 21 Nov. 1969, pp. 53–56; Rendon, *Chicano Manifesto*, 186–87; Murray in Freeman, ed., *Women: A Feminist Perspective*, 351–63; Davis, *If They Come in the Morning*, 197, and see Bambara, ed., *The Black Woman*, 111–18.

32. Webb in *Win*, 1 Jan. 1970; Willis in *Guardian*, 15 Feb. 1969; Kreps in Koedt et al., *Radical Feminism*, 239; Amatniek in *NYT*, 14 Feb. 1969; Morgan, *Going Too Far*, 4, 121–30; Friedan, *It Changed My Life*, 109, and *NYT*, 23 March 1970.

33. Philadelphia in *Architectural Forum*, Oct. 1971, pp. 38–45; Derek Shearer in *Ramparts*, Oct. 1973, pp. 12–16, and see Boyte, *Backyard Revolution*, 57–59, and Sanford Horwitt, *Let Them Call Me Rebel: Saul Alinsky—His Life and Legacy* (New York, 1992), 531–32.

34. Nadar in *Time*, 12 Dec. 1969, pp. 89–98; *Liberated News Service*, 19 Nov. 1970; SPP: 19a, *The Common Woman*, 18 March 1971; *Forbes*, 15 Sept. 1970, p. 46, and 15 May 1970, p. 60; *Business Week*, 7 March 1970, p. 106; and see Terry Anderson, "The New American Revolution: The Movement and Business," in Farber, ed., *The Sixties*, 175–205.

35. *LAT*, 31 Jan. and 2 Feb. 1969; *Newsweek*, 16 June 1969, p. 60; Lake Erie in *Saturday Review*, 20 Sept. 1969, pp. 19–21; *NYT*, 1 April 1970; *Newsweek*, 26 Jan. 1970, p. 35; students in *Business Week*, 7 Feb. 1970, and see *NYT*, 30 Nov. 1969.

36. SAVF: box 52, U.W. activities, chronological file folder, president's Declaration of Suspension of Classes, 8 May 1970; *Minnesota Daily*, 11 May 1970; Rossman, *New Age Blues*, 47.

Chapter 7
THE MOVEMENT TOWARD A NEW AMERICA

1. SHSW: Paul Booth papers, box 1, "A New Left Manifesto," 28 Jan. 1968, p. 1; Sykes, *The Nation*, 19 April 1971, p. 490; Hughes, *NYT Magazine*, 4 April 1971, p. 24; *Time*, 17 Aug. 1970, p. 35; *Saturday Review*, 24 July 1971, p. 32.

2. Bent: *The Second Coming*, April 1971; Associated Press, *The World in 1971*, 123; and see Case and Taylor, *Co-ops, Communes & Collectives*, 4, 20, 67, 91.

3. TA: R. J. Q. Adams comments, 17 Oct. 1987; observer is Sonya Rudikoff in *Commentary* (July 1972): 62.

4. *NYT*, 23 March, 9 and 27 Aug. 1970; *WP*, 27 Aug. 1970; *Newsweek*, 24 Aug. 1970, p. 15; ten feet tall in Friedan, *It Changed My Life*, 146–51; response is *NYT*, 26 and 27 Aug., 28 Sept. 1970, and *Time*, 31 Aug. 1970, pp. 20–21.

5. Kaplow in Koedt, ed., *Radical Feminism*, 36–41; Mungo, *Famous Long Ago*, 58; Potter, *A Name for Ourselves*, 171; *Minnesota Daily*, 14 April 1970; SAVF: box 53, Madison Defense League people's release, Nov. 1971.

6. *LAT* survey by Monica B. Morris in *Sociology and Social Research* (July 1975): 526–43; SAVF: box 57, Women for the Inclusion of Sexual Expression flyer; historian is Wandersee, *On the Move*, 42.

7. Union see *NYT*, 15 July 1971; Ross: New American Movement flyer on Ma Bell; flesh quote in Luker, *Abortion and the Politics of Motherhood*, 97, and see Komisar, *New Feminism*, chap. 17.

8. *U.S. News & World Report*, 13 Dec. 1971, pp. 79–81; *Newsweek*, 26 April 1971, pp. 61–62, and 17 May 1971, pp. 99–102; Gornick, *Essays in Feminism* (New York, 1978), 71.

9. *LAT*, 30 Aug., 16 and 22 Oct. 1970, and see Edward J. Escobar, "The Dialectics of Repression: The Los Angeles Police Department and the Chicano Movement, 1968–1971," *Journal of American History* (March 1993): 1483–1514, and Morales, *Ando Sangrando*, chaps. 7 and 8; Munoz and other letters in *LAT*, 23 Jan. 1971; Martinez in Castro, *Chicano Power*, 138–41.

10. Steiner, *La Raza*, 200; *Houston Chronicle*, 2 May 1971; Rendon, *Chicano Manifesto*, 3; Guzman in *Time*, 4 July 1969, p. 21.

11. Violence in *U.S. News & World Report*, 9 Nov. 1970, p. 52, *NYT*, 17 Aug. and 15 Oct. 1970; Armstrong see *Milwaukee Journal*, 18 and 25 May 1986,

and Bates, *Rads*, 153–306; opinion in *NYT*, 14 Dec. 1970, and *Saturday Review*, 20 Feb. 1971, p. 22.

12. *NYT*, 18 Jan., 8, 10, and 25 March, 2, 6, 7, and 9 April 1971.

13. Balboni in *New Republic*, 19 Dec. 1970, pp. 13–15; transcript of Winter Soldier hearings are in *Congressional Record*, 6–7 April 1971, and veteran's statements are in Kerry, *New Soldier*, WP, 24 April 1971, and VVAW, *The Winter Soldier Investigations: An Inquiry into American War Crimes* (Boston, 1972). Also see film by VVAW and Winterfilm, "Winter Soldier" (1972), and Elliott L. Meyrowitz and Kenneth J. Campbell, "Vietnam Veteran and War Crimes Hearings," and William F. Crandell, "They Moved the Town: Organizing Vietnam Veterans Against the War," in Small and Hoover, eds., *Give Peace a Chance*, 129–54.

14. *Life*, 17 July 1970, pp. 26–29; *Newsweek*, 22 Mar. 1971, p. 26; *Time*, 8 Mar. 1971, p. 19; *U.S. News & World Report*, 7 June 1971, p. 16; *NYT*, 21 April 1971.

15. Nixon in Colson, *Born Again* (Old Tappan, N.J., 1976), 45; *NYT*, 4, 11, and 14 May, 11 June 1971; and see DeBenedetti, *An American Ordeal*, 298–311, and Zaroulis and Sullivan, *Who Spoke Up?*, 343–67.

16. SPP, serials: *Navy Times Are Changin'*, June 1971; *Fat Albert's Death Ship Times*, 30 Nov. 1972; general in *The Observer* (London), 18 April 1971; Heinl in *Armed Forces Journal*, 7 June 1971, pp. 30–31; Seay in *Marine Corps Gazette*, Sept. 1971, pp. 27–32; and see *Newsweek*, 24 May 1971, pp. 21–23, Terry Anderson, "The GI Movement and the Response from the Brass," and David Cortright, "GI Resistance During the Vietnam War," in Small and Hoover, eds., *Give Peace a Chance*, 93–128.

17. *NYT*, 8 April 1971; Scott in *Newsweek*, 19 April 1971, p. 27; Hoppe in *San Francisco Chronicle* and DeBenedetti, *An American Ordeal*, 299.

18. Kissinger, *White House Years* (Boston, 1979), 976, 984, and see Small, *Johnson, Nixon and the Doves*, 210–24; survey and students in *NYT*, 22 April 1971; Columbia is in McGill, *Year of the Monkey*, 200–201; scaling down in *NYT*, 20 Oct. 1971.

19. *Time*, 21 June 1971, pp. 56–63; see James A. Sleeper and Alan Mintz, eds., *The New Jews* (New York, 1971), 24–33, and Porter and Dreier, *Jewish Radicalism*, 149–67; Catholic charismatic in Glock and Bellah, *New Religious Consciousness*, chap. 8.

20. Lecturer in *Harvard Business Review* (Jan.–Feb. 1970): 49–61; *Fortune*, March 1971, pp. 100–104; Yankelovich, *New Morality*, 68, 128.

21. Ross: Honeywell Project papers, flyers; SPP, serials: *Stranded Oiler*, Sept. and Oct. 1971; *The Nation*, 13 Sept. 1971, pp. 206–212; and see Ralph Nader et al., eds., *Whistle Blowing: The Report of the Conference on Professional Responsibility* (New York, 1972), *The Consumer and Corporate Accountability* (New York, 1973), and Terry Anderson, "The New American Revolution: The Movement and Business," in Farber, ed., *The Sixties*, 175–205.

22. CAP in *Ramparts*, Oct. 1973, p. 15, and see Boyte, *Backyard Rebellion*, 80–92; David Vogel, *Fluctuating Fortunes: The Political Power of Business in America* (New York, 1989), 53–58; Rockefeller in *LAT*, 3 Jan. 1971.

23. Thompson in Boyte, *Backyard Revolution*, 33–34; Magaziner in *NYT*, 26 Feb. 1993; DeLeeuw in Delgado, *Organizing the Movement*, 13, and see chap. 2; ACORN in *Working Papers for a New Society*, Summer 1975, pp. 13–20.

24. Consult Robert Fisher, *Let the People Decide: Neighborhood Organizing in America* (Boston, 1984), chap. 5; century in *LAT*, 10 Oct. 1993; VD: Joyce Zick in episode 5; Mikulski in *America*, 26 Dec. 1970, pp. 558–63; Chicago, Baltimore, and historic preservation in Steward Dill McBride, "A Nation of Neighborhoods" series, *Christian Science Monitor*, 9 Sept., 14 Oct., 4 Nov. 1977.

25. *Newsweek*, 12 Oct. 1970, p. 101; Kuhn in *Retirement Living*, Dec. 1972, pp. 32–37; *NYT*, 18 Jan. 1971; for results see *Aging*, Nov.–Dec. 1971, pp. 10–11, and *NYT*, 24 Oct. 1977.

26. Barnyard radicals in *Minneapolis Tribune*, 23 Nov. 1977; *Life*, 5 March 1971, pp. 30–34; *Forbes*, 15 June 1971, pp. 22–30; journalist McBride in *Christian Science Monitor*, 18 Nov. 1977.

27. Cincotta in Boyte, *Backyard Revolution*, 33, and see chap. 1; McBride's 12-part retrospective in *Christian Science Monitor*, 9 Sept.–Dec. 1977, and see Schlesinger, *New Reformers*, xi. Also see *NYT* articles on gray power Oct. and Nov. 1977; *Mother Jones*, Feb.–March 1976, pp. 18–28; Robert Cassidy, *Livable Cities* (New York, 1980), chap. 1, and Fred R. Harris, *Now Is the Time* (New York, 1971), chap. 1.

28. White, *The Making of the President: 1972* (New York, 1973); 44–47, 101, chaps. 2 and 5; Byron E. Shafer, *Quiet Revolution: The Struggle for the Democratic Party and the Shaping of Post-Reform Politics* (New York, 1983), 4, and see conclusion; Thompson, *Fear and Loathing*, 278–79, 382; Norman Mailer, *St. George and the Godfather* (New York, 1972), 62–70, 130–31, 168–83, 211–17; McGovern, *Grassroots: The Autobiography of George McGovern* (New York, 1977), 128–249, 174 (italics added); and see Jonathan Schell, *The Time of Illusion* (New York, 1975), chaps. 4 and 5.

29. Kissinger, *White House Years* (Boston, 1979), 1179; Nixon, *RN: The Memoirs of Richard Nixon* (New York, 1978), 586–95, 602–3; Seymour Hersh, *The Price of Power: Kissinger in the Nixon White House* (New York, 1983), 568; and see Stephen Ambrose, *Nixon: The Triumph of a Politician, 1962–1972* (New York, 1989), 538, 592, and chap. 23.

30. SAVF: box 60, Youth International Party folder, Zippie flyers; Thompson, *Fear and Loathing*, 385–92; Kovic, *Born on the Fourth of July*, 170–84; and see *Harper's*, Nov. 1972, pp. 60–68; *U.S. News & World Report*, 4 Sept. 1972, pp. 21–22; *NYT*, 22–25 Aug. 1972.

31. Nixon on Watergate in *Newsweek*, 31 May 1993, p. 17; McGovern, *Grassroots*, 191; Wallace in Fred R. Harris, *Now Is the Time*, 25; promises to South Vietnam in Nguyen Tien Hung and Jerrold L. Schecter, *The Palace File* (New York, 1986), and Bruce Oudes, ed., *From: The President Richard Nixon's Secret Files* (New York, 1989).

32. Calvert and Neiman, *A Disrupted History*, x; Burlingham in *Mother Jones*, Feb.–March 1976, p. 28; Clayborn Carson in Charles W. Eagles, ed., *The Civil Rights Movement in America* (Jackson, Miss., 1986), 19.

33. *Newsweek*, 12 June 1972, pp. 46–55; *Business Week*, 26 Feb. 1972; p. 86; Rosen in "Berkeley in the 60s," episode 3; elderly in *NYT*, 28 Nov. 1977; Hayden and ROAR in Fisher, *Let the People Decide*, 126, 141–43.

34. SAVF: box 59, Wounded Knee flyers and communiques; *WP*, 1 Mar. 1973; *Time*, 12 Mar. 1973, p. 21; *Newsweek*, 9 April and 21 May 1973, pp. 38, 31–32; and see *The Nation*, 25 June 1973, pp. 806–9.

35. Opinion in Yankelovich, *New Morality*, 74, and *NYT*, 18 Feb. 1973; Oberlin president in *NYT*, 24 Oct. 1971; sociologist is Stephen A. Kent, "Slogan Chanters to Mantra Chanters," *Sociological Analysis*, 49 (1988): 104–118; for human potential movement see Glock and Bellah, *New Religious Consciousness*, 93–115; Hayden in Stickney, *Streets, Actions, Alternatives, Raps*, 36.

36. Mixner and movement's demise in *NYT*, 18 Feb. 1973, and see Peter F. Drucker in *Harper's*, July 1971, pp. 35–39; Weinberg in "Berkeley in the '60s," episode 3.

Legacies
THE SEA CHANGE

1. Kornbluth, *Notes from the New Underground*, xv; Will in *Newsweek*, 25 March 1991, pp. 65–66; Gitlin, *The Sixties*, 7; VD: Wilkins interview, 2 June 1989. For other opinions on the legacies see Maurice Isserman and Michael Kazin in Steve Fraser and Gary Gerstle, eds., *The Rise and Fall of the New Deal Order, 1930–1980* (Princeton, N.J., 1989), chap. 8, and Morgan, *The 60s Experience*, chap. 7.

2. See Isserman and Kazin in Fraser and Gerstle, *Rise and Fall of the New Deal Order*, chap. 8, and Louis Harris, *Inside America* (New York, 1987) for opinion in the 1980s.

3. Mathis in *NYT*, 3 Jan. 1994; opinion in *NYT*, 4 April 1993, and see Andrew Hacker, *Two Nations: Black and White, Separate, Hostile, Unequal* (New York, 1992), 67–106, and Burns, *Social Movements of the 1960s*, chap. 4; *Newsweek*, 11 May 1992, p. 54; Jackson in Sitkoff, *Struggle for Black Equality*, 210, 225; Ashe in *People*, 8 June 1992, p. 44.

4. Van Camp in *National Observer*, 20 Jan. 1969, p. 4; Bloom, *The Closing of the American Mind* (New York, 1987), 320.

5. Nixon, *No More Vietnams* (New York, 1985), 97; see Jeffrey P. Kimball, "The Stab-in-the-Back Legend and the Vietnam War," *Armed Forces and Society*, Spring 1988, pp. 433–57; "Schwartzkopf in Vietnam," CBS program, 30 June 1993; Rubin, *Do It!*, 139; Small, *Johnson, Nixon, and the Doves*, conclusion; TA: Herring speech, 4 May 1990.

6. *Business and Society Review* (Winter 1975–76): 5–10; *Ladies' Home Journal*, Aug. 1970, p. 63; Harris, *Inside America*, 87, 94, 96–100; Ginsburg in *NYT*, 27 June 1993; and see Susan Faludi, *Backlash: The Undeclared War Against American Women* (New York, 1991).

7. Atcheson, *Bearded Lady*, 4; Yankelovich, *New Morality*, chap. 2, and VD:

Madelyn Hochstein interview, 2 June 1989; Peter Hart in *Rolling Stone*, 7 April and 5 May 1988, and see VD: episode 6; on tolerance see James A. Davis in *American Journal of Sociology* (Nov. 1975): 491–513, and Morton M. Hunt, *Sexual Behavior in the 1970s* (Chicago, 1974).

8. Rossman, *On Learning and Social Change*, 26; Dohrn in *NYT*, 18 Nov. 1993; Michigan in *The Nation*, 31 Oct. 1987, pp. 480–81; Dickstein in *NYT Magazine*, 15 May 1988, p. 32; sociologist Gerald Marwell in *On Wisconsin*, Nov.–Dec. 1993, p. 19; and see M. Kent Jennings, "Residues of a Movement: The Aging of the American Protest Generation," *American Political Science Review* (June 1987): 367–81, and Whalen and Flacks, *Beyond the Barricades*; *Newsweek*, 30 March 1987, pp. 56–58.

Select Bibliography

Enough to fill a library has been written on the era from the 1950s to the 1970s. Just on the Vietnam War, Richard Dean Burns and Milton Leitenberg's 1984 bibliographic guide, *The Wars in Vietnam, Cambodia, and Laos, 1945–1982,* is 300 pages. Historians have produced superb books on various aspects of social activism, while activists have written dissertations, memoirs, participant histories, or have submitted to interviews, which have been published in numerous anthologies. A *complete* bibliography would greatly enlarge this volume, tax the kindest editor and wealthiest publisher, and so what follows is a selective listing of books on the movement. Additional sources are cited in the notes.

Abbott, Sidney, and Barbara Love. *Sappho Was a Right-On Woman.* New York: Stein and Day, 1973.

Abernathy, Ralph David. *And the Walls Came Tumbling Down: An Autobiography.* New York: HarperPerennial, 1990.

Acuna, Rodolfo. *Occupied America: A History of Chicanos.* New York: Harper & Row, 1981.

Adam, Barry D. *The Rise of a Gay and Lesbian Movement.* Boston: Twayne, 1987.

Adelson, Adam M. *SDS.* New York: Scribners, 1972.

Albert, Judith Clavir, and Edward Albert Stewart. *The Sixty Papers: Documents of a Rebellious Decade.* New York: Praeger, 1984.

Alinsky, Saul D. *Rules for Radicals.* New York: Random House, 1971.

Allen, Pamela. *Free Space: A Perspective on the Small Group in Women's Liberation.* New York: Times Change Press, 1970.

Alpert, Jane. *Growing Up Underground.* New York: Morrow, 1981.

Anders, Jentri. *Beyond Counterculture: The Community of Manteel.* Pullman: Washington State Univ. Press, 1990.

Atcheson, Richard. *The Bearded Lady: Going on the Commune Trip and Beyond.* New York: John Day, 1971.

Bacciocca, Edward Jr. *The New Left in America: Reform to Revolution, 1956 to 1970.* Stanford, Calif.: Hoover Institution, 1974.

Bambara, Toni Cade. *The Black Woman: An Anthology.* New York: Mentor, 1970.

Baskir, Lawrence M. and Willaim A. Strauss. *Chance and Circumstance: The Draft, the War, and the Vietnam Generation.* New York: Knopf, 1978.

Bates, Tom. *RADS: The 1970 Bombing of the Army Math Research Center at the University of Wisconsin and Its Aftermath.* New York: HarperCollins, 1992.

Belfrage, Sally. *Freedom Summer.* Charlottesville: Univ. of Virginia Press, 1990 ed.

Berke, Joseph, ed. *Counter Culture.* London: Peter Owen, 1969.

Berrigan, Daniel. *The Dark Night of Resistance.* Garden City, N.Y.: Doubleday, 1971.

Birmingham, John, ed. *Our Time Is Now: Notes from the High School Underground.* New York: Praeger, 1970.

Blum, John Morton. *Years of Discord: American Politics and Society, 1961–1974.* New York: Norton, 1991.

Bond, Julian. *A Time to Speak, a Time to Act: The Movement in Politics.* New York: Simon & Schuster, 1972.

Boskin, Joseph, and Robert A. Rosenstone, eds. *Seasons of Rebellion: Protest and Radicalism in Recent America.* New York: Holt, Rinehart, and Winston, 1972.

Boyd, Malcolm, ed. *The Underground Church.* New York: Penguin, 1969.

Boyte, Harry C. *The Backyard Revolution.* Philadelphia: Temple Univ. Press, 1980.

————, and Frank Riessman, eds. *The New Populism: The Politics of Empowerment.* Philadelphia: Temple Univ. Press, 1986.

Branch, Taylor. *Parting the Waters: America in the King Years, 1954–63.* New York: Simon & Schuster, 1988.

Breines, Wini. *Community and Organization in the New Left, 1962–1968: The Great Refusal.* New Brunswick, N.J.: Rutgers Univ. Press, 1989.

Brown, Elaine. *A Taste of Power: A Black Woman's Story.* New York: Pantheon, 1992.

Brown, H. Rap. *Die Nigger Die!.* New York: Dial Press, 1969.

Buhle, Paul, ed. *History and the New Left: Madison, Wisconsin, 1950–1970.* Philadelphia: Temple Univ. Press, 1990.

Bunzel, John, ed. *Political Passages: Jouneys of Change Through Two Decades 1968–1988.* New York: Free Press, 1988.

Burns, Stewart. *Social Movements of the 1960s: Searching for Democracy.* Boston: Twayne, 1990.

Cahn, Edgar, S., ed. *Our Brother's Keeper: The Indian in White America.* New York: New Community/World Publishing, 1969.

California Newsreel. "Berkeley in the '60s." 1991, video.

Calvert, Greg, and Carol Neiman. *A Disrupted History: The New Left and the New Capitalism.* New York: Random House, 1971.

Canyon Collective. *Live It! Communalism.* Canyon, Calif.: Canyon Collective, 1971.

Carawan, Guy and Candie. *Sing for Freedom: The Story of the Civil Rights Movement Through Its Songs.* Bethlehem, Pa.: Sing Out, 1990.

Carden, Maren Lockwood. *The New Feminist Movement.* New York: Russell Sage Foundation, 1974.

Carmichael, Stokely, and Charles V. Hamilton. *Black Power: The Politics of Liberation in America.* New York: Vintage, 1967.

Carroll, Peter N. *It Seemed like Nothing Happened: The Tragedy and Promise of America in the 1970s.* New York: Holt, Rinehart, and Winston, 1982.

Carson, Clayborne. *In Struggle: SNCC and the Black Awakening of the 1960s.* Cambridge: Harvard Univ. Press, 1981.

Case, John, and Rosemary C. R. Taylor, eds. *Co-ops, Communes & Collectives: Experiments in Social Change in the 1960s and 1970s.* New York: Pantheon, 1979.

Castro, Tony. *Chicano Power: The Emergence of Mexican America.* New York: Dutton, 1974.

Caute, David. *The Year of the Barricades: A Journey Through 1968.* New York: Harper & Row, 1988.

Chafe, William H. *Never Stop Running: Allard Lowenstein and the Struggle to Save American Liberalism.* New York: Basic Books, 1993.

Chalmers, David. *And the Crooked Places Made Straight: The Struggle for Social Change in the 1960s.* Baltimore: Johns Hopkins Univ. Press, 1991.

Chappell, David L. *Inside Agitators: White Southerners in the Civil Rights Movement.* Baltimore: Johns Hopkins Univ. Press, 1994.

Chestnut, J. L. Jr., and Julia Cass. *Black in Selma: The Uncommon Life of J. L. Chestnut, Jr.* New York: Farrar, Straus and Giroux, 1990.

Clecak, Peter. *America's Quest for the Ideal Self: Dissent and Fulfillment in the 60s and 70s.* New York: Oxford Univ. Press, 1983.

———. *Radical Paradoxes.* New York: Harper & Row, 1973.

Cluster, Dick, ed. *They Should Have Served That Cup of Coffee.* Boston: South End Press, 1979.

Coffin, William Sloane Jr. *Once to Every Man, a Memoir.* New York: Atheneum, 1977.

Collier, Peter, and David Horowitz. *Destructive Generation: Second Thoughts About the 60's.* New York: Summit Books, 1989.

———, eds. *Second Thoughts: Former Radicals Look Back at the 60's.* Lanham, Md.: Madison Books, 1989.

Commager, Henry Steele. *The Defeat of America: Presidential Power and the National Character.* New York: Simon and Schuster, 1974.

Cortright, David. *Soldiers in Revolt: The American Military Today.* New York: Anchor/Doubleday, 1975.

Couto, Richard A. *Ain't Gonna Let Nobody Turn Me Round: The Pursuit of Racial Justice in the Rural South.* Philadelphia: Temple Univ. Press, 1991.

Cowan, Paul. *The Making of an Un-American.* New York: Delta/Dell, 1970.

Cudlipp, Edythe. *Understanding Women's Liberation.* New York: Paperback Library, 1971.

Daniels, Robert V. *Year of the Heroic Guerrilla: World Revolution and Counter-revolution in 1968.* New York: Basic Books, 1989.

Davidson, Sara. *Loose Change: Three Women of the Sixties.* New York: Pocket Books, 1977.

Davis, Angela Y. *Angela Davis—An Autobiography.* New York: Random House, 1974.

———, et al. *If They Come in the Morning: Voices of Resistance.* New York: Signet, 1971.

De Leon, David. *Everything Is Changing: Contemporary U.S. Movements in Historical Perspective.* New York: Praeger, 1988.

DeBenedetti, Charles. *The Peace Reform in American History.* Bloomington: Indiana Univ. Press, 1980.

———, and Charles Chatfield, assisting author. *An American Ordeal: The Antiwar Movement of the Vietnam War.* Syracuse, N.Y.: Syracuse Univ. Press, 1990.

Deckard, Barbara Sinclair. *The Women's Movement: Political, Socioeconomic, and Psychological Issues.* New York: Harper & Row, 1983.

Dees, Morris, with Steve Fiffer. *A Season for Justice.* New York: Scribner's, 1991.

del Renzio, Toni. *The Flower Children.* London: Solstice, 1969.

Delgado, Gary. *Organizing the Movement: The Roots and Growth of ACORN.* Philadelphia: Temple Univ. Press, 1986.

Deloria, Vine Jr. *Custer Died for Your Sins: An Indian Manifesto.* New York: Macmillan, 1969.

Dellinger, Dave. *From Yale to Jail: The Life Story of a Moral Dissenter.* New York: Random House, 1993.

———. *More Power Than We Know: The People's Movement Toward Democracy.* Garden City, N.Y.: Anchor/Doubleday, 1975.

Diamond, Stephen. *What the Trees Said: Life on a New Age Farm.* New York: Dell, 1971.

Dickstein, Morris. *Gates of Eden: American Culture in the Sixties.* New York: Basic Books, 1977.

Donner, Frank J. *The Age of Surveillance: The Aims and Methods of America's Political Intelligence System.* New York: Knopf, 1980.

———. *Protectors of Privilege: Red Squads and Police Repression in Urban America.* Berkeley: Univ. of California Press, 1990.

Drane, James. *A New American Reformation: A Study of Youth Culture and Religion.* New York: Philosophical Library, 1973.

Duberman, Martin. *Stonewall.* New York: Dutton, 1993.

Echols, Alice. *Daring to Be Bad: Radical Feminism in America, 1967–1975.* Minneapolis: Univ. of Minnesota Press, 1989.

Eisen, Jonathan, ed. *Altamont: Death of Innocence in the Woodstock Nation.* New York: Avon, 1970.

Ellison, Harlan. *The Glass Teat.* New York: Ace, 1983.

———. *The Other Glass Teat.* New York: Ace, 1983.

Enroth, Ronald M., Edward E. Ericson, Jr., and C. Breckinridge Peters. *The*

Jesus People: Old-Time Religion in the Age of Aquarius. Grand Rapids, Mich.: William B. Eerdmans, 1972.

Epstein, Barbara. *Political Protest and Cultural Revolution: Nonviolent Direct Action in the 1970s and 1980s.* Berkeley: Univ. of California Press, 1991.

Evans, Sara. *Personal Politics: The Roots of Women's Liberation in the Civil Rights Movement and the New Left.* New York: Vintage, 1980.

Fairclough, Adam. *The Southern Christian Leadership Conference and Martin Luther King, Jr.* Athens: Univ. of Georgia Press, 1987.

Fairfield, Richard. *Communes U.S.A.: A Personal Tour.* New York: Penguin, 1972.

Farber, David. *Chicago '68.* Chicago: Univ. of Chicago Press, 1988.

————, ed. *The Sixties: From Memory to History.* Chapel Hill: Univ. of North Carolina Press, 1994.

Farmer, James. *Lay Bare the Heart: An Autobiography of the Civil Rights Movement.* New York: New American Library, 1985.

Farrell, Warren. *The Liberated Man.* New York: Random House, 1975.

Felton, David, ed. *Mindfuckers.* San Francisco: Straight Arrow, 1972.

Ferber, Michael, and Staughton Lynd. *The Resistance.* Boston: Beacon, 1971.

Feuer, Lewis S. *The Conflict of Generations: The Character and Significance of Student Movements.* New York: Basic Books, 1969.

Finks, P. David. *The Radical Vision of Saul Alinsky.* New York: Paulist Press, 1984.

Firestone, Shulamith. *The Dialectic of Sex: The Case for Feminist Revolution.* New York: William Morrow, 1970.

————, and Anne Koedt, eds. *Notes from the Second Year: Women's Liberation.* New York: Radical Feminists, 1970.

Fish, John Hall. *Black Power/ White Control: The Struggle of the Woodlawn Organization.* Princeton, N.J.: Princeton Univ. Press, 1973.

Fisher, Michael P. "The Turbulent Years: The University of Kansas, 1960–1975." Ph.D. dissertation, Univ. of Kansas, 1979.

Flacks, Richard. *Making History: The American Left and the American Mind.* New York: Columbia Univ. Press, 1988.

Forman, James. *The Making of Black Revolutionaries.* New York: Macmillan, 1972.

Foss, Daniel. *Freak Culture: Life-style and Politics.* New York: Dutton, 1972.

Foster, Julian, and Durward Long, eds. *Protest! Student Activism in America.* New York: Morrow, 1970.

Fraser, Ronald, et al., eds. *1968: A Student Generation in Revolt.* New York: Pantheon, 1988.

Freeman, Jo. *The Politics of Women's Liberation.* New York: Longman, 1975.

————, ed. *Social Movements of the Sixties and Seventies.* New York: Longman, 1983.

————, ed. *Women: A Feminist Perspective.* Palo Alto, Calif.: Mayfield, 1975.

Friedan, Betty. *The Feminine Mystique.* New York: Norton, 1963.

————. *It Changed My Life: Writings on the Women's Movement.* New York: Random House, 1976.

Garcia, F. Chris, ed. *Chicano Politics: Readings.* New York: MSS Information, 1973.

Garcia, Ignacio M. *United We Win: The Rise and Fall of La Raza Unida Party.* Tucson: Univ. of Arizona Press, 1989.

Gardner, Hugh. *The Children of Prosperity: Thirteen Modern American Communes.* New York: St. Martin's, 1978.

Garrow, David J. *Bearing the Cross: Martin Luther King, Jr., and the Southern Christian Leadership Conference.* New York: Vintage, 1988.

———. *Protest at Selma: Martin Luther King, Jr., and the Voting Rights Act of 1965.* New Haven: Yale Univ. Press, 1978.

Gaskin, Stephen. *Haight Ashbury Flashbacks.* Berkeley, Calif.: Ronin, 1990.

Gioglio, Gerald R. *Days of Decision: An Oral History of Conscientious Objectors in the Military During the Vietnam War.* Trenton, N.J.: Broken Rifle Press, 1989.

Gitlin, Todd. *The Sixties: Years of Hope, Days of Rage.* New York: Bantam, 1987.

———. *The Whole World Is Watching: Mass Media in the Making & Unmaking of the New Left.* Berkeley: Univ. of California Press, 1980.

Glessing, Robert J. *The Underground Press in America.* Bloomington: Indiana Univ. Press, 1970.

Glock, Charles Y., and Robert N. Bellah, eds. *The New Religious Consciousness.* Berkeley: Univ. of California Press, 1976.

Goldman, Albert. *Freakshow: The Rocksoulbluesjazzsickjewblackhumorsexpoppsych Gig and Other Scenes from the Counter-culture.* New York: Atheneum, 1971.

Goldstein, Richard. *Reporting the Counterculture.* Boston: Unwin Hyman, 1989.

Gomez-Quinones, Juan. *Mexican Students Por La Raza: The Chicano Student Movement in Southern California, 1967–1977.* Santa Barbara, Calif.: Editorial La Causa, 1978.

Goodman, Mitchell, ed. *The Movement Toward a New America: The Beginnings of a Long Revolution.* Philadelphia: Pilgrim Press, 1970.

Goodwin, Richard N. *Remembering America: A Voice from the Sixties.* New York: Harper & Row, 1988.

Gosse, Van. *Where the Boys Are: Cuba, Cold War America and the Making of a New Left.* London: Verso, 1993.

Gottlieb, Annie. *Do You Believe in Magic? Bringing the Sixties Back Home.* New York: Simon & Schuster, 1987.

Graham, Hugh Davis. *The Civil Rights Ear: Origins and Development of National Policy, 1960–1972.* New York: Oxford Univ. Press, 1990.

Grele, Ronald J., and Ronald Fraser, et al. *1968: A Student Generation in Revolt.* New York: Pantheon, 1988.

Gruen, John. *The New Bohemia: The Combine Generation.* New York: Shorecrest, 1966.

Hall, Mitchell K. *Because of Their Faith: CALCAV and Religious Opposition to the Vietnam War.* New York: Columbia Univ. Press, 1990.

Halstead, Fred. *Out Now! A Participant's Account of the American Movement Against the Vietnam War.* New York: Monad Press, 1978.

Hampton, Henry, and Steve Fayer. *Voices of Freedom: An Oral History of the Civil Rights Movement from the 1950s through the 1980s*. New York: Bantam, 1990.

Harris, David. *Dreams Die Hard*. New York: St. Martin's, 1982.

———. *Goliath*. New York: Sidereal Press, 1970.

Harrison, Cynthia. *On Account of Sex: The Politics of Women's Issues, 1945–1968*. Berkeley: Univ. of California Press, 1988.

Hartmann, Susan M. *From Margin to Mainstream: American Women and Politics Since 1960*. New York: Knopf, 1989.

Hatfield, Mark O. *Not Quite So Simple*. New York: Harper & Row, 1968.

Hayden, Tom. *Reunion: A Memoir*. New York: Random House, 1988.

Hayes, Harold, ed. *Smiling Through the Apocalypse*. New York: McCall Publishing, 1969.

Heath, G. Louis, ed. *Mutiny Does Not Happen Lightly: The Literature of the American Resistance to the Vietnam War*. Metuchen, N.J.: Scarecrow Press, 1976.

Heineman, Kenneth J. *Campus Wars: The Peace Movement at American State Universities in the Vietnam Era*. New York: New York Univ. Press, 1993.

Hoffman, Abbie (Free). *Revolution for the Hell of It*. New York: Dial Press, 1968.

———. *Soon to Be a Major Motion Picture*. New York: Putnam, 1980.

———. *Steal This Book*, Worcester, Mass.: Jack Hoffman Presents, n.d.

———. *Woodstock Nation: A Talk-Rock Album*. New York: Vintage, 1969.

Hole, Judith, and Ellen Levine. *Rebirth of Feminism*. New York: Quadrangle, 1971.

Hopkins, Jerry, ed. *The Hippie Papers: Notes from the Underground Press*. New York: Signet, 1968.

Houriet, Robert. *Getting Back Together*. New York: Coward, McCann & Geoghegan, 1971.

Isserman, Maurice. *If I Had a Hammer . . . The Death of the Old Left and the Birth of the New Left*. New York: Basic Books, 1987.

Jacobs, Harold, ed. *Weatherman*. New York: Ramparts, 1970.

Jacobs, Paul, and Saul Landau. *The New Radicals: A Report with Documents*. New York: Vintage, 1966.

Jay, Karla, and Allen Young, eds. *Out of the Closets: Voices of Gay Liberation*. New York: Pyramid, 1974 ed.

Jenkins, J. Craig. *The Politics of Insurgency: The Farm Worker Movement in the 1960s*. New York: Columbia Univ. Press, 1985.

Jerome, Judson. *Families of Eden: Communes and the New Anarchism*. New York: Seabury, 1974.

Jezer, Marty. *Abbie Hoffman: American Rebel*. New Brunswick, N.J.: Rutgers Univ. Press, 1992.

Joseph, Peter. *Good Times: An Oral History of America in the Nineteen Sixties*. New York: Charterhouse, 1973.

Kahn, Roger. *The Battle for Morningside Heights: Why Students Rebel*. New York: William Morrow, 1970.

Karagueuzian, Dikran. *Blow It Up! The Black Student Revolt at San Francisco State College and the Emergence of Dr. Hayakawa.* Boston: Gambit, 1971.

Katsiaficas, George. *The Imagination of the New Left: A Global Analysis of 1968.* Boston: South End Press, 1987.

Katz, Elia. *Armed Love.* New York: Holt, Rinehart and Winston, 1971.

Keniston, Kenneth. *Radicals and Militants: An Annotated Bibliography of Empirical Research on Campus Unrest,* Lexington, Ma.: Heath, 1973.

———. *The Uncommitted: Alienated Youth in American Society.* New York: Harcourt, Brace and World, 1965.

———. *Young Radicals: Notes on Committed Youth.* New York: Harcourt, Brace and World, 1968.

Kerpelman, Larry C. *Activists and Nonactivists: A Psychological Study of American College Students.* New York: Behavioral Pubs., 1972.

Kerry, John, and the Vietnam Veterans Against the War. *The New Soldier.* New York: Collier Books, 1971.

Kessler, Lauren. *After All These Years: Sixties Ideals in a Different World.* New York: Thunder's Mouth Press, 1990.

King, Mary. *Freedom Song: A Personal Story of the 1960s Civil Rights Movement.* New York: Morrow, 1987.

Koedt, Anne, Ellen Levine, Anita Rapone, eds. *Radical Feminism.* New York: Quadrangle, 1973.

Kolkey, Jonathan M. *The New Right, 1960–1968: With Epilogue, 1969–1980.* Washington, D.C.: Univ. Press of America, 1983.

Komisar, Lucy. *The New Feminism.* New York: Franklin Watts, 1971.

———, and Ann Scott. *And Justice for All.* Chicago: National Organization for Women, 1971.

Kornbluth, Jesse, ed. *Notes from the New Underground.* New York: Viking, 1968.

Kriyananda, Swami. *Cooperative Communities: How to Start Them, and Why,* Nevada City, Calif.: Ananda, 1971.

Kuhn, Maggie, Christina Long, and Laura Quinn. *No Stone Unturned: The Life and Times of Maggie Kuhn.* New York: Ballantine, 1991.

Kunen, James Simon. *The Strawberry Statement—Notes of a College Revolutionary.* New York: Random House, 1969.

Kunstler, William. *Deep in My Heart.* New York: William Morrow, 1966.

Lader, Lawrence. *Power on the Left: American Radical Movements Since 1946.* New York: Norton, 1979.

Leamer, Laurence. *The Paper Revolutionaries: The Rise of the Underground Press.* New York: Simon and Schuster, 1972.

Leary, Timothy. *Flashbacks: An Autobiography.* Los Angeles: J. P. Tarcher, 1983.

———. *The Politics of Ecstasy.* New York: Putnam, 1968.

Lee, Martin A., and Bruce Shlain. *Acid Dreams: The CIA, LSD and the Sixties Rebellion.* New York: Grove Press, 1985.

Lester, Julius. *Look Out Whitey! Black Power's Gon' Get Your Mama!.* New York: Grove Press, 1968.

Levy, Jacques E. *Cesar Chavez: Autobiography of La Causa.* New York: Norton, 1975.

Lewis, David L. *King: A Biography.* Urbana: Univ. of Illinois Press, 1978.

Lewis, George H., ed. *Side-saddle on the Golden Calf: Social Structure and Popular Culture in America.* Pacific Palisades, Calif.: Goodyear, 1972.

Lewis, Roger. *Outlaws of America: The Underground Press and Its Context.* London: Penguin, 1972.

Linden-Ward, Blanche, and Carol Hurd Green. *American Women in the 1960s: Changing the Future.* New York: Twayne, 1993.

Lora, Ronald, ed. *America in the 60's: Cultural Authorities in Transition.* New York: John Wiley & Sons, 1974.

Lukas, J. Anthony. *Don't Shoot—We Are Your Children!.* New York: Random House, 1968.

Luker, Kristin. *Abortion and the Politics of Motherhood.* Berkeley: Univ. of California Press, 1984.

Lynd, Alice, ed. *We Won't Go: Personal Accounts of War Objectors.* Boston: Beacon, 1968.

Lyon, Danny. *Memories of the Southern Civil Rights Movement.* Chapel Hill: Univ. of North Carolina Press, 1992.

Lyttle, Bradford. *The Chicago Anti-Vietnam War Movement.* Chicago: Midwest Pacifist Center, 1988.

McAdam, Doug. *Freedom Summer.* New York: Oxford Univ. Press, 1988.

McCarthy, Eugene J. *The Year of the People.* Garden City, N.Y.: Doubleday, 1969.

McClellan, Grant S., ed. *American Youth in a Changing Culture.* New York: H. W. Wilson, 1972.

McCormick, Richard P. *The Black Student Protest Movement at Rutgers.* New Brunswick, N.J.: Rutgers Univ. Press, 1990.

McCourt, Kathleen. *Working-Class Women and Grass-Roots Politics.* Bloomington: Indiana Univ. Press, 1977.

McGill, William J. *The Year of the Monkey: Revolt on Campus 1968–69.* New York: McGraw-Hill, 1982.

McLaughlin, Corinne, and Gordon Davidson. *Builders of the Dawn: Community Lifestyles in a Changing World,* Walpole, N.H.: Stillpoint, 1985.

McNeill, Don, *Moving Through Here.* New York: Knopf, 1970.

MacPherson, Myra. *Long Time Passing: Vietnam and the Haunted Generation.* Garden City, N.Y.: Doubleday, 1984.

McQuaid, Kim. *The Anxious Years: America in the Vietnam-Watergate Era.* New York: Basic, 1989.

Mailer, Norman. *The Armies of the Night: History as a Novel the Novel as History.* New York: Signet, 1968.

———. *Some Honorable Men: Political Conventions 1960–1972.* Boston: Little, Brown, 1976.

Makower, Joel. *Boom! Talkin' About Our Generation.* Chicago: Tilden, 1985.

Malcolm, Henry. *Generation of Narcissus.* Boston: Little, Brown, 1971.

Marshall, Burke. *Federalism and Civil Rights*. New York: Columbia Univ. Press, 1964.

Matthiessen, Peter. *Sal Si Puedes: Cesar Chavez and the New American Revolution*. New York: Delta, 1969.

Matusow, Allen J. *The Unraveling of America: A History of Liberalism in the 1960s*. New York: Harper & Row, 1984.

Mehnert, Klaus. *Twilight of the Young: The Radical Movements of the 1960s and Their Legacy*. New York: Holt, Rinehart, Winston, 1976.

Melville, Keith. *Communes in the Counter Culture: Origins, Theories, Styles of Life*. New York: William Morrow, 1972.

Menashe, Louis, and Ronald Radosh. *Teach-ins: USA Reports, Opinions, Documents*. New York: Praeger, 1967.

Miles, Michael W. *The Radical Probe: The Logic of Student Rebellion*. New York: Atheneum, 1971.

Miller, James. *"Democracy Is in the Streets": From Port Huron to the Siege of Chicago*. New York: Simon and Schuster, 1987.

Miller, Timothy. *The Hippies and American Values*. Knoxville: Univ. of Tennessee Press, 1991.

Millett, Kate. *Sexual Politics*. Garden City, N.Y.: Doubleday, 1970.

Mills, Kay. *This Little Light of Mine: The Life of Fannie Lou Hamer*. New York: Dutton, 1993.

Mills, Nicolaus. *Like a Holy Crusade: Mississippi 1964—The Turning of the Civil Rights Movement in America*. Chicago: Ivan Dee, 1992.

Morales, Armando. *Ando Sangrando: A Study of Mexican American—Police Conflict*. La Puente, Calif.: Perspectiva Publications, 1972.

Morgan, Edward P. *The 60s Experience: Hard Lessons About Modern America*. Philadelphia: Temple Univ. Press, 1991.

Morgan, Robin. *Going Too Far: The Personal Chronicle of a Feminist*. New York: Random House, 1977.

———, ed. *Sisterhood Is Powerful: An Anthology of Writings from the Women's Liberation Movement*. New York: Vintage, 1970.

Morris, Aldon D. *The Origins of the Civil Rights Movement: Black Communities Organizing for Change*. New York: Free Press, 1984.

Morrison, Joan, and Robert K. Morrison. *From Camelot to Kent State: The Sixties Experience in the Words of Those Who Lived It*. New York: Times Books, 1987.

Mungo, Raymond. *Famous Long Ago: My Life and Hard Times with Liberation News Service*. Boston: Beacon, 1970.

———. *Total Loss Farm: A Year in the Life*. New York: Dutton, 1970.

Munoz, Carlos, Jr. *Youth, Identity, Power: The Chicano Movement*. New York: Verso, 1989.

Myerson, Michael. *These Are the Good Old Days: Coming of Age as a Radical in America's Late, Late Years*. New York: Grossman, 1970.

Newfield, Jack. *A Prophetic Minority*. New York: Signet, 1966.

Oates, Stephen. *Let the Trumpet Sound: The Life of Martin Luther King, Jr.* New York: New American Library, 1985.

Obst, Lynda Rosen, ed. *The Sixties: The Decade Remembered Now by the People Who Lived Them*. New York: Random House, 1977.

O'Neill, William L. *Coming Apart: An Informal History of America in the 1960's*. New York: Quadrangle, 1971.

O'Reilly, Kenneth. *"Racial Matters": The FBI's Secret File on Black America, 1960–1972*. New York: Free Press, 1989.

Peck, Abe. *Uncovering the Sixties: The Life and Times of the Underground Press*. New York: Pantheon, 1985.

Perrow, Charles. *The Radical Attack on Business*. New York: Harcourt, Brace, Jovanovich, 1972.

Perry, Helen Swick. *The Human Be-In*. New York: Basic Books, 1970.

Perry, Charles. *The Haight-Ashbury: A History*. New York: Random House, 1984.

Piven, Frances Fox, and Richard A. Cloward. *Poor People's Movements*. New York: Pantheon, 1977.

Pettitt, George A. *Prisoners of Culture*. New York: Scribner's Sons, 1970.

Porter, Jack Nusan, and Peter Dreier, eds. *Jewish Radicalism: A Selected Anthology*. New York: Grove Press, 1973.

Potter, Paul. *A Name for Ourselves*. Boston: Little, Brown, 1971.

Powers, Thomas. *Vietnam: The War at Home*. Boston: G. K. Hall, 1984.

Powledge, Fred. *Free at Last? The Civil Rights Movement and the People Who Made It*. New York: HarperPerennial, 1992.

Proudfoot, Merrill. *Diary of a Sit-In*. Urbana: Univ. of Illinois Press, 1990.

Rader, Dotson. *Blood Dues*. New York: Knopf, 1973.

Raines, Howell. *My Soul Is Rested: Movement Days in the Deep South Remembered*. New York: Penguin, 1983.

Reagon, Bernice Johnson. "Songs of the Civil Rights Movement 1955–1965: A Study in Culture History." Ph.D. dissertation, Howard University, 1975.

Reich, Charles A. *The Greening of America*. New York: Random House, 1970.

Rendon, Armando B. *Chicano Manifesto*. New York: Collier-Macmillan, 1972.

Revel, Jean-François. *Without Marx or Jesus*. Garden City, N.Y.: Doubleday, 1971.

Rips, Geoffrey, et al. *The Campaign Against the Underground Press*. San Francisco: City Lights, 1981.

Roberts, Ron E. *The New Communes: Coming Together in America*. Englewood Cliffs, N.J.: Prentice-Hall, 1971.

Rodnitzky, Jerome L. *Minstrels of the Dawn: The Folk-Protest Singer as a Cultural Hero*. Chicago: Nelson-Hall, 1976.

Romm, Ethel Grodzins. *The Open Conspiracy: What America's Angry Generation Is Saying*. Harrisburg, Pa.: Stackpole Books, 1970.

Rorabaugh, W. J. *Berkeley at War: The 1960s*. New York: Oxford Univ. Press, 1989.

Rossman, Michael. *New Age Blues: On the Politics of Consciousness*. New York: E. P. Dutton, 1979.

———. *The Wedding Within the War*. Garden City, N.Y.: Doubleday, 1971.

Roszak, Theodore. *The Making of the Counter-culture: Reflections on the Techno-*

cratic Society and Its Youthful Opposition. Garden City, N.Y.: Doubleday, 1969.

Rothman, Stanley, and S. Robert Lichter. *Roots of Radicalism: Jews, Christians, and the New Left.* New York: Oxford Univ. Press, 1982.

Rothschild, Mary Aickin. *A Case of Black and White: Northern Volunteers and the Southern Freedom Summers, 1964–1965.* Westport, Conn.: Greenwood, 1982.

Rubin, Jerry. *Do It! Scenarios of the Revolution.* New York: Simon & Schuster, 1970.

———. *Growing (Up) at Thirty-seven.* New York: M. Evans, 1976.

Ruddick, Sara, and Pamela Daniels, eds. *Working It Out: 23 Women Writers, Artists, Scientists, and Scholars Talk About Their Lives and Work.* New York: Pantheon, 1977.

Sale, Kirkpatick. *SDS.* New York: Random House, 1973.

Sampson, Edward E., et al. *Student Activism and Protest.* San Francisco: Jossey-Bass, 1970.

Sanders, Ed. *The Family: The Story of Charles Manson's Dune Buggy Attack Battalion.* New York: E. P. Dutton, 1971.

Santelli, Robert. *Aquarius Rising: The Rock Festival Years.* New York: Dell, 1980.

Sayres, Sohnya, Anders Stephanson, Stanley Aronowitz, and Fredric Jameson, eds. *The 60s Without Apology.* Minneapolis: Univ. of Minnesota Press, 1984.

Schlesinger, Arthur M. Jr. *Robert Kennedy and His Times.* New York: Houghton Mifflin, 1978.

Schlesinger, Stephen. *The New Reformers: Forces for Change in American Politics.* New York: Houghton Mifflin, 1975.

Schultz, Bud, and Ruth Schultz. *It Did Happen Here: Recollections of Political Repression in America.* Berkeley: Univ. of California Press, 1989.

Scott, Ann, and Lucy Komisar. *And Justice for All: Federal Equal Opportunity Enforcement Effort Against Sex Discrimination.* Chicago: NOW, 1971.

Seale, Bobby. *Seize the Time: The Story of the Black Panther Party and Huey P. Newton.* New York: Random House, 1970.

Sellers, Cleveland, with Robert Terrell. *The River of No Return: The Autobiography of a Black Militant and the Life and Death of SNCC.* New York: William Morrow, 1973.

Sender, Ramon, and Alicia Bay Laurel. *Being of the Sun.* New York: Harper & Row, 1973.

Shockley, John S. *Chicano Revolt in a Texas Town.* South Bend, Ind.: Univ. of Notre Dame Press, 1974.

Simmons, J. L., and Barry Winograd. *It's Happening: A Portrait of the Scene Today.* Santa Barbara, Calif.: McNally & Loftin, 1966.

Simons, Donald L. *I Refuse: Memories of a Vietnam War Objector.* Trenton, N.J.: Broken Rifle Press, 1992.

Sinclair, John. *Guitar Army.* New York: Douglas Books, 1972.

Sitkoff, Harvard. *The Struggle for Black Equality, 1954–1980.* New York Hill & Wang, 1981.

Slater, Philip. *The Pursuit of Loneliness: American Culture at the Breaking Point.* Boston: Beacon, 1970.

Small, Melvin. *Johnson, Nixon, and the Doves.* New Brunswick, N.J.: Rutgers Univ. Press, 1988.

————, and William D. Hoover, eds. *Give Peace a Chance: Exploring the Vietnam Antiwar Movement.* Syracuse, N.Y.: Syracuse Univ. Press, 1992.

Smith, Curt. *Long Time Gone: The Years of Turmoil Remembered.* South Bend, Ind.: Icarus, 1982.

Smith, David, and John Luce. *Love Needs Care: A History of San Francisco's Haight-Ashbury Free Medical Clinic and Its Pioneer Role in Treating Drug-Abuse Problems.* Boston: Little, Brown, 1971.

Staggenborg, Suzanne. *The Pro-Choice Movement: Organization and Activism in the Abortion Conflict.* New York: Oxford Univ. Press, 1991.

Steiner, Stan. *La Raza: The Mexican Americans.* New York: Harper Colophon, 1970.

Stern, Susan. *With the Weathermen: The Personal Journal of a Revolutionary Woman.* Garden City, N.Y.: Doubleday, 1975.

Stevens, Jay. *Storming Heaven: LSD and the American Dream.* New York: Harper & Row, 1987.

Stickney, John. *Streets, Actions, Alternatives, Raps.* New York: Putnam, 1971.

Sundancer, Elaine. *Celery Wine: The Story of a Country Commune.* Yellow Springs, Ohio: Community Publications Cooperative, 1973.

Tachiki, Amy, Eddie Wong, and Franklin Odo, eds. *Roots: An Asian American Reader.* Los Angeles: UCLA Asian American Studies Center, 1971.

Taylor, Harold. *How to Change Colleges: Notes on Radical Reform.* New York: Holt, Rinehart and Winston, 1971.

————. *Students Without Teachers: The Crisis in the University.* New York: McGraw-Hill, 1969.

Theoharis, Athan. *Spying on Americans: Political Surveillance from Hoover to the Huston Plan.* Philadelphia: Temple Univ. Press, 1978.

Thompson, Hunter S. *Fear and Loathing: On the Campaign Trail, '72.* New York: Fawcett, 1973.

————. *The Great Shark Hunt: Strange Tales from a Strange Time.* New York: Fawcett, 1979.

Thompson, Mary Lou, ed. *Voices of the New Feminism.* Boston: Beacon, 1970.

Thompson, Toby. *The '60s Report.* New York: Rawson, Wade, 1979.

Tipton, Steven M. *Getting Saved from the Sixties: Moral Meaning in Conversion and Cultural Change.* Berkeley: Univ. of California Press, 1982.

Tischler, Barbara L., ed. *Sights on the Sixties.* New Brunswick, N.J.: Rutgers Univ. Press, 1992.

Unger, Irwin. *The Movement: A History of the American New Left, 1959–1972.* New York: Harper & Row, 1974.

————, and Debi Unger. *Turning Point: 1968.* New York: Scribner's, 1988.

Urban Research Corporation. *Harvard's Student Strike: The Politics of Mass Mobilization.* Chicago: Urban Research Corporation, 1970.

————. *Student Protests 1969.* Chicago: Urban Research Corporation, 1970.

Van Deberg, William L. *New Day in Babylon: The Black Power Movement and American Culture, 1965–1975*. Chicago: Univ. of Chicago Press, 1992.

Vickers, George R. *The Formation of the New Left*. Lexington, Mass.: Heath, 1975.

Vietnam Veterans Against the War and Winterfilm Collective. *Winter Soldier*. Trenton, N.J.: Broken Rifle Press, 1972 video.

Vigil, Maurilio. *Chicano Politics*. Washington, D.C.: Univ. Press of America, 1978.

Viorst, Milton. *Fire in the Streets*. New York: Simon & Schuster, 1980.

von Hoffman, Nicholas. *We Are the People Our Parents Warned Us Against*. Chicago: Ivan R. Dee, 1989.

Wakefield, Dan. *Supernation at Peace and War*. Boston: Little, Brown, 1968.

Wandersee, Winifred D. *On the Move: American Women in the 1970s*. Boston: Twayne, 1988.

Wei, William. *The Asian American Movement*. Philadelphia: Temple Univ. Press, 1993.

Weiner, Rex, and Deanne Stillman. *Woodstock Census: The Nationwide Survey of the Sixties Generation*. New York: Viking, 1979.

Weisbrot, Robert. *Freedom Bound: A History of America's Civil Rights Movement*. New York: Plume, 1991.

Weiss, Walter F. *America's Wandering Youth: A Sociological Study of Young Hitchhikers in the United States*. Jericho, N.Y.: Exposition Press, 1974.

Wells, Tom. *The War Within: America's Battle over Vietnam*. Berkeley: Univ. of California Press, 1994.

Wellstone, Paul David. *How the Rural Poor Got Power: Narrative of a Grassroots Organizer*. Amherst: Univ. of Massachusetts Press, 1978.

West, Guida. *The National Welfare Rights Movement: The Social Protest of Poor Women*. New York: Praeger, 1981.

Westin, Alan F., ed. *Freedom Now! The Civil-Rights Struggle in America*. New York: Basic, 1964.

Whalen, Jack, and Richard Flacks. *Beyond the Barricades: The Sixties Generation Grows Up*. Philadelphia: Temple Univ. Press, 1989.

Wilkins, Roger. *A Man's Life: An Autobiography*. New York: Simon & Schuster, 1982.

Wofford, Harris. *Of Kennedys and Kings: Making Sense of the Sixties*. New York: Farrar, Straus, Giroux, 1980.

Wolf, Deborah Goleman. *The Lesbian Community*. Berkeley: Univ. of California Press, 1979.

Wolfe, Burton H. *The Hippies*. New York: Signet, 1968.

Wolff, Miles. *How It All Began: The Greensboro Sit-Ins*. New York: Stein and Day, 1971.

Woodstone, Norma Sue. *Up Against the War*. New York: Tower, 1970.

Wynkoop, Mary Ann. "Dissent in the Heartland: The Student Protest Movement at Indiana University, Bloomington, Indiana, 1965–1970." Ph.D. dissertation, Indiana University, 1992.

Yablonsky, Lewis. *The Hippie Trip*. New York: Pegasus, 1968.

Yankelovich, Daniel. *The New Morality: A Profile of American Youth in the 70s.* New York: McGraw Hill, 1974.

Yates, Gayle Graham. *What Women Want: The Ideas of the Movement.* Cambridge: Harvard Univ. Press, 1975.

Yinger, J. Milton. *Countercultures: The Promise and the Peril of a World Turned Upside Down.* New York: Free Press, 1982.

Young, Nigel. *An Infantile Disorder? The Crisis and Decline of the New Left.* Boulder, Colo.: Westview, 1977.

Zaroulis, Nancy, and Gerald Sullivan. *Who Spoke Up? American Protest Against the War in Vietnam 1963–1975.* Garden City, N.Y.: Doubleday, 1984.

Zinn, Howard. *SNCC: The New Abolitionists.* Boston: Beacon, 1965.

Index

Abernathy, Ralph, 44–45, 53, 66
Abortion, 25, 312, 342, 361, 362, 363, 400–401, 402, 405, 440
Abzug, Bella, 369, 397, 405
Activists: alienation of, 84–85, 353; alternatives for, 353; attitudes about, 331–32; and the cold war culture, 39; dossiers on, 369–70; as a legitimate part of democracy, 84; as a minority, 107–8, 237; and the political spectrum, 109–10; political style of, 107; profile of, 57–58, 107; and reasons for rebellion, 89; and the sixties generation, 89, 107–10, 127–28. *See also* Cultural activists; *specific movement, organization, or demonstration*
Ad Hoc Panel on Drug Abuse, 284
Adelphi College, 148
Affirmative action, 308, 337–38, 415, 420
African American studies, 295, 298–99
Afro-Americans Against the War in Vietnam, 158
Agent Orange, 357
Agnew, Spiro, 214, 232, 331, 368–69
Agribusiness Accountability Project, 389
Alabama: and the Freedom Rides, 51–53. *See also* University of Alabama; *specific city*
Albany, Ga., 66
Albert, Stew, 226
Alcatraz Island, 333–36
Ali, Muhammad, 294
Alianza movement, 305
Alinsky, Saul, 295, 344, 383
Allen, Pamela, 337
Allen, Richard, 109
Alpert, Jane, 32
Altamont rock festival, 280–82
Amatniek, Kathie. *See* Sarachild, Kathie

American Dream, 39–40, 129
American Friends Service Committee, 124, 146
American Independent party, 211
American Indian Movement, 336, 407–8
American Servicemen's Union, 167
Americans for Democratic Action, 124, 146, 234
Americus, Ga., 66
Anders, Jentri, 250
Antioch College, 148
Antiwar movement: and the 1968 Democratic convention, 214, 215, 216–17, 221, 222, 223; aims/tactics of the, 149–50, 151–52, 203–4; and blacks, 158–59, 351; and Cambodia, 349–52; and civil rights, 138, 140–41, 158–60, 164; and communism, 141, 144, 145, 150, 180, 181; and the counterculture, 126, 171, 178; culture of the, 142; decline of the, 380–81, 399; divisiveness within the, 146–50; and drugs, 142, 398; early reaction to, 143–45; and the elections of 1968, 185, 186–91, 204, 206, 211, 214, 215, 216–17, 221, 222, 223, 233, 234; and the elections of 1970, 369; and the elections of 1972, 396, 398–400; emergence of the, 124–25; expansion of the, 125–27, 140, 147–48, 166; and generational issues, 165–66; and the Hispanic American movement, 364–65; and individual actions, 167–68; and the last major national demonstration, 380; leadership of the, 145–46, 148–49; and the legacies of the Movement, 417, 418; and the liberals, 145–47, 149–50, 166; as mainstream, 396; as the major issue for the sixties generation, 129–30, 135–36;

March on the Pentagon, 178–79, 180, 202
Marches on Washington: in 1963, 73–74, 164; in 1968, 191–92
Marcuse, Herbert, 37–38, 58, 245, 299
Marijuana: and the counterculture, 243, 259–60, 261, 264, 276, 284, 285; and the legacies of the Movement, 422; and the New America, 356. *See also* Drugs; Drugs—and the counterculture
Marion, Ala., 114
Marist College, 125
Marriage: age at, 21; and the cold war culture, 15–23; and the counterculture, 251, 271; and homosexuals, 318; and the women's movement, 315. *See also* "Happy family"
Marshall, Burke, 67, 71
Massachusetts Institute of Technology (MIT), 11, 159, 347
Masters, William, 312–13
Materialism. *See* Consumption/materialism
Max, Steve, 135, 149, 385
MAYO (Mexican American Youth Organization), 306, 307, 308, 324
Me Decade, 408–9
Means, Russell, 407
Media: Agnew's attack on the, 331; and the antiwar movement, 128, 136, 140, 143, 144–45, 146, 151, 160, 163, 166, 380, 399; and the Birmingham demonstrations, 71; and the Cambodia demonstrations, 350; and civil rights, 82, 191; and the Columbia demonstrations, 194, 197, 199, 200; and communism, 13–14; and the consumer movement, 345, 404; and the counterculture, 171–72, 174, 176, 218, 241, 279, 280; and the death of the sixties decade, 391–92; decline in coverage of the Movement by the, 294; and dissent within the military, 320; and draft resistance, 139, 140, 141; and the elections of 1968, 221, 222, 223, 224, 226, 233; and the elections of 1972, 394–95; and the environmental movement, 345, 347, 348, 391, 404; exaggerations by the, 128; and the FBI dossiers on activists, 369–70; and the Free Speech Movement, 102–3, 110; and the Freedom Rides, 52, 54; and the frustration of the nation, 182; and the Hispanic American movement, 305, 306, 309, 310, 365; and homosexuality, 319; importance of the, 82; and King, 158; and leadership of the Movement, 202; and Malcolm X, 153–54; and the Manson murders, 279, 280; and the

Moratorium, 330–31; and the Native American movement, 334, 335, 407–8; and the New America, 356; and the Olympics, 231; and polarization in the U.S., 235; and religion, 381–82; and repression of the Movement, 327, 369–70; and revolution, 202; and the San Francisco State College demonstrations, 296–97; and sexual issues, 280; and the sixties generation, 92; and Vietnam issues, 184, 185, 190, 378–79; and violence, 309, 325, 329; and the women's movement, 229, 337, 343, 359, 361, 440; and the Yippies, 221. *See also* Newspapers; Television
Melton, Barry, 239, 257
Memphis, Tenn.: and King's assassination, 191–92
Men for Women's Rights, 359
Men's liberation, 419
Meredith, James, 151–52. *See also* March Against Fear
Mexican American studies, 306
Mexican American Youth Organization. *See* MAYO
Mexican Americans, 193. *See also* Hispanic American movement
Michigan State University, 25, 99, 101, 111, 112, 123, 125, 126, 144, 145
Mikulski, Barbara, 388, 404
Military: and the antiwar movement, 376–78, 417; blacks in the, 376; and "combat refusal," 321–22; desertions from the, 322, 377; discharges from the, 377; discrimination in the, 27, 159–60, 230; dissent/rebellion within the, 166–67, 229–30, 319–22, 332, 376–77, 418; dress in the, 376; and drugs, 376, 377, 378; enlistments in the, 137, 139; and the Fort Jackson affair, 319–20; and G.I. rights, 319–22; and the Hamburger Hill incident, 320–21, 351; hippies in the, 376, 377; and homosexuals, 318; and intelligence activities about U.S. civilians, 369; and the legacies of the Movement, 417, 418; morale/discipline in the, 376–78; and the Moratorium, 330; and underground publications, 229–30, 376; volunteer, 418; and the women's movement, 339, 362
Military-industrial complex, 39, 252, 412–13
Millersburg, Pa., 208–9
Millett, Kate, 359, 363
Mills, C. Wright, 36, 37, 38, 57–58, 60, 62, 245

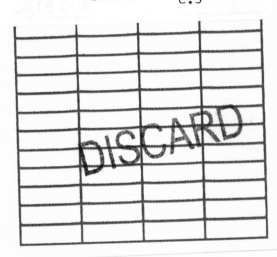